DIALOGUE ON WRITING

Rethinking ESL, Basic Writing, and First-Year Composition

D1605683

DIALOGUE ON WRITING

Rethinking ESL, Basic Writing, and First-Year Composition

Edited by

Geraldine DeLuca
Len Fox
Mark-Ameen Johnson
Brooklyn College, CUNY

Myra Kogen
Brooklyn College Learning Center, New York

2002

LAWRENCE ERLBAUM ASSOCIATES, PUBLISHERS
Mahwah, New Jersey   London

Senior Acquisitions Editor: Naomi Silverman
Textbook Marketing Manager: Marisol Kozlovski
Assistant Editor: Lori Hawver
Cover Design: Kathryn Houghtaling Lacey
Textbook Production Manager: Paul Smolenski
Full-Service & Composition: Black Dot Group/An AGT Company
Text and Cover Printer: Hamilton Printing Company

This book was typeset in 10/12 pt. New Baskerville, Bold, and Italic.
The heads were typeset in New Baskerville Bold.

Lawrence Erlbaum Associates, Inc., Publishers
10 Industrial Avenue
Mahwah, New Jersey 07430

Library of Congress Cataloging-in-Publication Data

Dialogue on writing : rethinking ESL, basic writing, and first-year
    composition / edited by Geraldine DeLuca ... [et al.].
       p.   cm.
    Includes bibliographical references and index.
    ISBN 0-8058-3861-9
    1. English language—Rhetoric—Study and teaching. 2. English language—
Study and teaching—Foreign speakers. 3. Report writing—Study and teaching
(Higher). 4. Basic writing (Remedial education) I. DeLuca, Geraldine.
PE1404.D44 2001
808'.042'071—dc21   2001054453

Printed in the United States of America
10   9   8   7   6   5   4   3   2   1

To my children, Katharine and Jeffrey, for my mother, Rose, and for Don
—Geri

To some of my best communication teachers: my wife Ginny, my friends
Elaine and Geri, and my students
—Len

To Mona Gebara Johnson and Andrew Johnson, precious cornerstones.
To my beautiful sister, Lisa Emily Johnson, my foundation's second tier.
To George Versakos, friend when I had none, Dawn, who shines forth,
and their son, Christopher, from "Uncle Mark." And, finally, to Thomas
DeGeorges, of course, lighthouse in every storm.
—Mark

To David, he knows why.

—Myra

Contents

Preface xi

About the Editors xv

I   Teaching Writing 1

Introduction

1   Reclaiming the Classroom 9
    Mike Rose

2   Teaching Basic Writing: An Alternative to Basic Skills 29
    David Bartholomae

3   The First Day of Class: Passing the Test 53
    Ira Shor

4   Collaboration, Conversation, and Reacculturation 63
    Kenneth Bruffee

5   From "Let's Flip the Script: An African American Discourse on
    Language, Literature, and Learning" 83
    Keith Gilyard

6   Pedagogy of the Distressed 105
    Jane Tompkins

7   Pomo Blues: Stories From First Year Composition 115
    Lee Ann Carroll

II **Becoming a Writer**   135

   Introduction

   8 The Process of Writing—Growing   141
          Peter Elbow

   9 Translating Self and Difference Through Literacy
          Narratives   157
          Mary Soliday

   10 From Silence to Words: Writing as Struggle   173
          Min-Zhan Lu

   11 Listening for Difference   187
          Roni Natov

   12 ESL Tutors: Islands of Calm in the Multicultural Storm   199
          Mark-Ameen Johnson

   13 Writing Alive   213
          Ellie Friedland

   14 Toward a Post-Process Composition: Abandoning the
          Rhetoric of Assertion   233
          Gary A. Olson

III **Responding to Writing**   243

   Introduction

   15 Responding to Texts: Facilitating Revision
          in the Writing Workshop   251
          C. H. Knoblauch and Lil Brannon

   16 The Listening Eye: Reflections on the Writing Conference   271
          Donald M. Murray

   17 Errors: Windows Into the Mind   279
          Ann Raimes

   18 High Stakes and Low Stakes in Assigning and
          Responding to Writing   289
          Peter Elbow

19 The Myths of Assessment
Pat Belanoff

299

20 Evaluating ESL Writing
Elaine Brooks

311

21 Fault Lines in the Contact Zone
Richard E. Miller

323

IV Beyond the Writing Classroom

339

Introduction

22 The Argument for Writing Across the Curriculum
Toby Fulwiler

345

23 Strangers in Academia: The Experiences of Faculty and ESL Students Across the Curriculum
Vivian Zamel

359

24 Opinion: The Wyoming Conference Resolution Opposing Unfair Salaries and Working Conditions for Post-Secondary Teachers of Writing
Linda R. Robertson, Sharon Crowley, and Frank Lentricchia

377

25 Distant Voices: Teaching and Writing in a Culture of Technology
Chris M. Anson

387

26 Basic Writing: Curricular Interactions With New Technology
Susan Stan and Terence G. Collins

409

27 Community Service and Critical Teaching
Bruce Herzberg

433

28 Places to Stand: The Reflective Writer-Teacher-Writer in Composition
Wendy Bishop

447

Credits

471

Index

475

Preface

This anthology grew out a series of discussions by four colleagues who teach composition at Brooklyn College, a branch of the City University of New York. Though we were all working hard to help our students improve their writing, we realized that we were doing the same job from somewhat different perspectives. Geri DeLuca was director of freshman writing and is now coordinator of writing across the curriculum; Len Fox is Professor of English and past director of the ESL program; Myra Kogen directs the college Learning Center, a large-scale peer-tutoring operation; and Mark-Ameen Johnson teaches in ESL and immersion programs and supervises English as a second language (ESL) tutoring. As our conversations continued month after month, we realized that we each had received different training, attended different professional conferences, and made use of certain theories and practices unknown to the others.

We believe *Dialogue on Writing: Rethinking ESL, Basic Writing, and First-Year Composition* to be the first work that treats these various approaches under one cover. Also, although all four of us teach at Brooklyn College and roughly a quarter of the articles we selected highlight CUNY concerns, readers will find that most of the issues CUNY faculty raise mirror those in academia at large. In addition, our anthology showcases not only the voices of instructors in large universities, but the voices of academics in rural, small-campus colleges and teachers in nonacademic settings as well.

The basis for our selection of articles lies in our collective experience in training writing teachers and tutors. Brooklyn has long required that its part-time instructors take a graduate course in the teaching of freshman composition and that peer tutors attend ongoing workshops that prepare them to help students with writing assignments from across the curriculum. In addition, there are meetings in which writing faculty discuss issues of concern and yearly training sessions on scoring the CUNY writing assessment tests. Another strength of the selections in this anthology is that they reflect the editors' different positions within the academy—DeLuca and Fox are full professors in the Department of English, Kogen is an administrator in the Office of Undergraduate Studies, and Johnson is an adjunct in the English Department.

Reflecting these different perspectives, the final selection of articles in the book is the result of a careful, not always harmonious, process of give and take. Fox proposed a table of contents and produced a stack of photocopies much larger than those that eventually became *Dialogue on Writing*. Kogen, DeLuca, and Johnson made changes, omissions, additions, and clarifications to produce new aims and new lines of thought. Fox contributed a respect for concrete ideas and straightforwardness, Kogen for theoretical writing and complexity. DeLuca championed voices that were alternative, occasionally New Age, and sometimes silenced. Johnson argued for the inclusion of adjuncts' perspectives and concerns, which are often dismissed by tenured faculty. In short, we were eager to grow and be mutually supportive but were equally stubborn in arguing our individual points.

Thus our four-way dialogue played out. Our own diversity and academic peccadilloes proved to be our team's strength. After 3 years, 300 plus articles, and more letters and e-mail than any of us could keep track of, we selected 28 articles organized into 4 basic sections. We decided that readers would appreciate overviews and DeLuca wrote four separate introductory essays explaining the relationship among the articles in each section. The articles we selected and the questions that follow them are suggestions for pedagogy and invitations for exploration. We hope that both the articles and the questions will spark both animated group dialogue and private inner dialogue. We strongly encourage readers to be Socratic and challenge everything they read—but also to remember that the experienced teacher–theorists represented here have learned a thing or two in the trenches.

Although we did our best to present both key ideas and alternative views, our biases may manifest themselves from time to time. In a perfect anthology, that might not happen. But as DeLuca has often reminded the rest of us: "There is no perfect anthology. This is the good enough anthology." We, your *good enough* editors, have selected the articles we thought "best," but we do not claim that either we or our selected writers have a monopoly on **truth.** We invite you to look for instances where truths are hidden, disguised, distorted, half-baked, or fully cooked and burned. But remember also the point that James Berlin makes in *Rhetoric and Reality,* that rhetoric for most English instructors has often meant one theory and one theory only, whereas many useful alternative models have gone largely unnoticed.

Acknowledgments

We would like to thank Naomi Silverman, Editor at Lawrence Erlbaum, for taking on this project, for believing in it, and for offering us her astute advice as we compiled this collection. Many thanks also to Lori Hawver, her assistant, for carefully attending to endless details, and our gratitude to Sandy Reinhard and the Black Dot Group for meticulously editing the proofs. Thanks to Susan Barker, Promotion Coordinator, and to Paul Smolenski for his beautiful cover design. And finally, thank you to the following reviewers of the first draft of this manuscript for their time and valuable suggestions for revision: Linda Harklau, University of Georgia; Judith Rodby, California State University; and Chico Carl Whithaus, Stevens Institute of Technology.

About the Editors

Geraldine DeLuca is Professor of English at Brooklyn College, CUNY. She directed the Freshman Writing program at Brooklyn College for 12 years and is now coordinator of the program in Writing Across the Curriculum. With Roni Natov, she founded and for 15 years coedited *The Lion and the Unicorn: A Critical Journal of Children's Literature,* now published by The Johns Hopkins University Press. She has published many articles on children's literature, some stories, poems, and personal essays and is now working on a memoir about growing up Italian-American.

Len Fox, Professor of English and ESL at Brooklyn College, CUNY, has been teaching ESL at the college since 1977. He has trained ESL teachers and has made many presentations at city, state, and national conferences. He has written five textbooks for teaching ESL: *Perspectives, Passages,* and *Gateway,* all of Harcourt Brace Jovanovich; *Focus on Editing,* Longman; and *Making Peace,* coedited with Elaine Brooks, St. Martin's.

Mark-Ameen Johnson has directed Brooklyn College's Starr ESL Learning Center and taught CUNY students since 1994. He has also served as the Pace University Liberaty and Stay-in-School Partnerships Program Manager, a Brooklyn Public Library literacy consultant and tutor trainer, and a New York City Board of Education teacher. He first began teaching when he was in grammar school; his younger sister was his first student. While enrolled in junior high school, he carried out volunteer work with mentally retarded children. These first experiences hooked him, and he has been teaching in one form or another ever since. He is also a freelance writer specializing in travel and popular culture.

Myra Kogen is Director of the Brooklyn College Learning Center, which provides peer tutoring for students in courses across the curriculum. She has taught composition, technical writing, and literature and has edited a collection of articles, *Writing in the Business Professions,* published by NCTE. Her articles have appeared in the *Journal of Basic Writing, Technical Writing,* and *American Literary Realism.* Kogen has done extensive faculty training on the use of collaborative learning and writing in courses across the disciplines. In the past few years, she has devoted considerable time to writing proposals for projects funded by NEH, NSF, FIPSE, and the U.S. Department of Education Title III program.

Teaching Writing

Who are our students? When they enter our classrooms, what do they need from us? When we read the newspapers on the state of education in the United States today, we often get a sense of disaster. The gap between the rich and poor is widening. The college students of the affluent come from private schools or well-funded suburban public systems, and they are receiving ever more elaborately enriched educations. At the same time, the poor and working class barely get by, often holding jobs for many hours per week and trying to squeeze their classes and their studies into the few precious hours left. Conservative commentators say these students are not ready to be in the university. But if the public schools and their communities have failed them, or if they are members of a different culture, speakers of a different language, and we bar the doors, then what happens? Our politicians declare that every young person should have the chance to go to college. If this is something we really believe, then how do we go about making it happen? And once they are there, what do we teach them?

As Mike Rose demonstrates in his introduction to *Lives on the Boundary,* our sense of disaster may rest on flawed memories of a better age—an age that never dreamed of educating so many people on such a large scale.

In 1890, 6.7 percent of America's fourteen- to seventeen-year-olds were attending high school; by 1978, that number had risen to 94.1 percent.... In the 1930s "functional illiteracy" was defined by the Civilian Conservation Corps as a state of having three or more years of schooling; ... by 1960 the Office of Education was setting the eighth grade as a benchmark.... In the United States [in 1989] just over 75 percent of our young people complete high school; in Sweden 45 to 50 percent complete the gymnasium (grades 11 to 12); in the [former] Federal Republic of Germany about 15 percent are enrolled in the *Oberprima* (grade 13). In 1900 about 4 percent of American eighteen- to twenty-two-year-olds attended college; by the late 1960s, 50 percent of eighteen-to-nineteen-year-olds were entering some form of postsecondary education. Is

1

this an educational system on the decline, or is it a system attempting to honor—through wrenching change—the many demands of a pluralistic democracy?

It would be an act of hollow and evil optimism to downplay the problems of American schools. . . . But what a curious thing it is that when we do criticize our schools, we tend to frame our indictments in terms of decline.[1]

Even when higher education was restricted to the sons of the elite, their teachers complained about their inadequacies. How do we meet our new students where they are and help them grow intellectually? What assumptions do we make when we assess their competence? What do we make of what we see on the page? What are our goals?

Part I of this book offers perspectives and models for courses that have worked for other teachers–researchers. The commonsense approach of moving from the simplest to the most complex forms of writing—from parts of speech to sentence structure to paragraphs to full essays—may seem like an obvious, sensible strategy to a well-meaning teacher assessing students' writing problems. And in fact it holds great sway in the university. Entering students are tested for their ability to write fluent standard English. The low scorers are then separated into remedial classes based on their tests scores, and there they are taught the "simple logic" of grammar, sentence structure, and paragraphing. Then they are tested again.

But as the selections by Mike Rose, David Bartholomae, and Ira Shor demonstrate, these assumptions and divisions create problems of their own. First, as Rose says in "Reclaiming the Classroom," teachers sometimes work on the assumption that because students speak a dialect other than standard English, or because they are inexperienced writers, they are therefore incapable of complex thought. By thus "scaling down our expectations—as so many remedial programs do," teachers restrict students and make writing a joyless and mechanical chore—one that is mostly about rules and developing strategies for not breaking them.

Rose and Bartholomae each describe a course of study for basic writers that demands serious thinking and that creates a structure in which it may occur. Rose's course grew out of his own experience as a student who was almost forsaken by an educational system with many damning labels for its children. In *Lives on the Boundary*, he chronicles his boyhood in East Los Angeles. Though his parents were loving and concerned, they were troubled by economic and physical problems and by an overriding sense of hopelessness that prevented them from questioning the way the schools were evaluating their son. About midway through high school, where he had, through a clerical error, been placed in a vocational program, Rose

---

[1]Mike Rose, *Lives on the Boundary: A Moving Account of the Struggles and Achievements of America's Educationally Underprepared* (New York: Penguin, 1989) 6–7.

found a teacher who recognized his intelligence and began the process of teaching him how to think, opening to him a world of intellect and spirit beyond his bleak neighborhood.

In "Reclaiming the Classroom," an excerpt from Rose's book, he draws on that experience to give a group of veterans the kind of training in thinking that helped him. His curriculum runs right down the center of the academic world. He teaches his students to summarize, classify, compare, and analyze, helping them to form the habits of mind that are the hallmark of academic writing. In a practical sense he is training them to play by the rules of the university. But he also knows that by laboring through difficult material, they will discover the world of the mind. They will deepen, as he deepened, and grow as he grew.

David Bartholomae's two courses are based on similar convictions: that students have lived in complex, if unexamined, situations their whole lives, and that they need to engage complexity in the writing classroom as well. His course helps students to see themselves differently by helping them understand that their writing is not just "what they said," that is, what happens to roll onto the page when they pick up a pen, but "deliberate, strategic, and systematic behavior" that is capable of being reflected on, changed, contracted, or expanded. To be writers, students need to imagine themselves as writers. They need to be aware that writing is a process they engage in, that a sense of chaos often accompanies first drafts, that one can gain control over successive drafts, that sometimes it feels easy and sometimes it feels hard. Bartholomae is particularly concerned with preparing students for their college courses by giving them an idea of how the academy uses language, helping them "to imagine the kind of relation between themselves and their world that allows them to turn their experience into 'subject matter' and to define a relationship with that subject that makes creative thinking possible." Students write and share autobiographical essays to discover common themes, to discover differences, and to become attuned to the ambiguity and contradiction often built into complicated material.

The second course Bartholomae describes here includes reading. As in his writing course, his goal is to heighten students' sense of themselves as people functioning in a university, whose job it is not only to summarize and analyze a text, but also to "take a stance in relation to it." This course led to the curriculum outlined in Bartholomae's and Anthony Petrosky's *Facts, Artifacts, and Counterfacts*[2] as well as to their widely used and challenging anthology, *Ways of Reading*.[3]

---

[2]David Bartholomae and Anthony Petrosky, *Facts, Artifacts and Counterfacts: Theory and Method for a Reading and Writing Course* (Portsmouth, NH: Boynton/Cook, 1986).

[3]David Bartholomae and Anthony Petrosky, eds., *Ways of Reading: An Anthology for Writers*. 5th Ed. (Boston: Bedford Books of St. Martin's, 1998).

"The First Day of Class: Passing the Test" is Ira Shor's introduction to his book, *Empowering Education,* which is based on the critical pedagogy of Paulo Freire. Freire was a radical Brazilian educator who spent his early years teaching peasants to read, write, and "think critically" about the condition of their lives. In *Pedagogy of the Oppressed,*[4] Freire argues that the traditional "banking concept of education," in which the teacher/authority deposits knowledge in the minds of passive students, must be replaced by a "problem-posing"method of education that allows the teacher and the students to learn from one another. Together they create a curriculum in which students work outward from the language of their daily lives to develop a "critical consciousness"and to work from that consciousness toward change—so that ultimately education becomes the "practice of freedom."

Shor's essay describes a basic writing class in which his students are angry at the test that has placed them there and that they perceive to be unfair. He describes in some detail how he moved the students toward a conception of what a fairer test would be and then to a reading and writing curriculum that evolved out of their needs and interests and that enabled most of them to pass the test at the end of the term. This was not, of course, the solution to all their problems, but Shor's essay demonstrates how one can begin with students' resistance and with the conditions of their lives to help them become critical thinkers in the university.

Kenneth Bruffee's "Collaboration, Conversation, and Reacculturation" is a story of how he responded to the beginning of an open admissions policy at the City University of New York. In this opening essay to his book *Collaborative Learning: Higher Education, Interdependence, and the Authority of Knowledge,* he recounts his own experience as a new director of freshman English who found himself in a "contact zone"—Mary Louise Pratt's often-quoted phrase for a place "where cultures meet, clash, and grapple with each other, often in contexts of highly assymetrical relations of power."[5] In 1970, when Open Admissions began at CUNY, thousands of underprepared students suddenly entered the university. Bewildered about how to work with these students, Bruffee turned to the writing directors at the other CUNY colleges, and together they came to recognize that what they were dealing with was not just "error" but culture. The students "arrived in our classes already deeply acculturated, already full-fledged, competent members (as we were, too) of some community or other. In fact, they were already members of several interrelated communities (as we were too)."

[4]Paulo Freire, *Pedagogy of the Oppressed* (New York: Continuum, 1969).

[5]"Arts of the Contact Zone," *Profession* 91, 1991. Reprinted in Vivian Zamel and Ruth Spack, eds., *Negotiating Academic Literacies: Teaching and Learning Across Languages and Cultures* (Mahwah, NJ: Lawrence Erlbaum, 1998) 173.

Now they were all meeting in the university, and if Bruffee and his colleagues were going to help these students become members of the academic community, they had to work together to find out who their students (and they themselves) were, how the students learned, what would help them, what stood in their way. And they had to try to imagine what new community would evolve out of that contact. They read Freire, they studied group dynamics, they took cues from newly forming feminist consciousness-raising groups. To help his students enter the culture of the university, Bruffee realized, he had to help his class "constitute itself as a community with is own particular mores, goals, linguistic history, and language." Students together, with the teacher as a Freirian problem poser, had to grapple with knowledge—how it is constituted, on whose authority, and how together they could create it in the classroom.

Bruffee has been a pioneering researcher into the value and structures of peer tutoring and collaborative learning, and his work has radically changed the way many teachers run their classes. His argument that students learn best by working together has forced many of us to acknowledge that the lecture format, even at its most eloquent, is a "banking" strategy, that the teacher in the act of composing the lecture is the one doing all the learning, and learning perhaps of a particularly safe kind, in order to make the presentation. But for at least part of the time, students need to take on the authority of working through difficult material themselves, in the context of their own lives, their own past education, and the experiences of others in the classroom.

The next selection is by Keith Gilyard, the director of freshman writing at Syracuse University and a person who speaks from painful personal experience about the clashing of cultures in the classroom. Having grown up in New York City, he describes in his autobiography, *Voices of the Self,*[6] the high price that African-American children pay for being taught that the dialect of their community is "broken English." As a child, Gilyard constructed two identities—Keith for home and Raymond for school. He was bright and successful to a point, but the contradictions and mixed allegiances and anger of his young life pushed him toward drugs and theft. When he came back, he did so with a vivid sense of what young people like the boy he was need in order to overcome the odds against them.

The two chapters reprinted here are from *Let's Flip the Script: An African-American Discourse on Language, Literature and Learning.* The first piece is a clear summary of the features of Atlantic Creole, a dialect of English (minus some regional variations) spoken by many African-American and

---

[6]Keith Gilyard, *Voices of the Self: A Study of Language Competence* (Detroit: Wayne State University Press, 1991).

Caribbean students at least some of the time. Gilyard notes that, like other dialects, "these language varieties are rule-governed systems that have developed as a result of conflict, conquest, and cultural mixing. They are equal in a linguistic sense to any other varieties of English and are not a major obstacle to literacy."

The controversy over the place of students' dialects in the classroom gave rise in the 1970s to the National Council of Teachers of English (NCTE) statement of "Students' Right to their Own Language." It again received national attention in the 1990s as the Ebonics debate that took place in California. Both the NCTE and the California teachers supported a pluralist position advocated here by Gilyard, in the hope that "language variation [would not] play out so negatively in the classroom." Pluralists do not ignore the importance of learning standard English, but they accord respect and space in the classroom for students to express themselves in dialect, not to be condescended to and not to be ridiculed. Standard English should be taught in the context of a conversation that acknowledges the child's own dialect, that makes language use the center of discussion, that respects it in all its various forms. We cannot ignore the "social relations and student perceptions" that underlie writing instruction in the schools, Gilyard says. If we do, we continue to lose "many of those of African descent, who feel reasons not to melt on into the program."

In his second essay, Gilyard explains that his work is based on the goal of achieving "true democracy," and he begins by defining that phrase in terms of ideals articulated by Thomas Jefferson, John Dewey, and Paulo Freire. He moves in his teaching from "covering the material" to "uncovering" the material, from narration to dialogue. This essay was first delivered as a speech to teachers of adult education, and he begins with the recognition that returning students are often those who were lost to the system, who refused to participate, who found it irrelevant, or who simply could not locate themselves there. Such students often return with a readiness to learn standard grammar and write formulaic essays. They are often suffering from what Freire calls "narration sickness," engendered by the teacher's and their own belief that the teacher knows what they need and their job is to write it down. Such students, Gilyard says, are often intimidated by literature. They have not experienced it as being about them, and they are afraid of their own reactions to it. Gilyard argues that, in his own experience, "Literature has always been a powerful way of reminding me that I am not just in the world but of it." Thus, he argues, students should be required to read literature—literature that is of necessity multicultural—that they should be encouraged to honor their own responses, and that in such an environment, they will grow as critical thinkers, expressive writers, debaters, and finally, people who can be heard in a true democracy.

Gilyard's course includes the history of the English language; it includes literature of many cultures; it includes debate; it includes the sharing of writing and the development of "conventional usage." He reminds us that it has never been the practice in America to educate everyone equally. "Numerous scholars have argued convincingly that American education has generally focused on producing a highly literate elite and a minimally literate general populace." But at this point in history, minimal literacy no longer suffices. We have to do a better job of educating all our students if we want a democracy where all have voices, and all vote "if our society is genuinely to become more inclusive and approach its full potential for humanism."

Jane Tompkins was one of those "highly literate elite" that Gilyard mentions. And in *A Life in School,* she chronicles the hazards of privilege.[7] In "Pedagogy of the Distressed," Tompkins too steps off from Freire by describing the pressures of the "narrator," the one who is supposed to know what everybody else needs to hear. We may have gone beyond the "banking concept" in its pure form, she says, but we are still living with the "performance model" of teaching, whereby the teacher shows in class how smart, knowledgeable, and well prepared she is, so that whether students learn or not, they will leave the class with a good opinion of the teacher, and if and when their turn at the front of the room comes, they will adopt that model for themselves. We perform out of fear, she says, fear of being exposed as inadequate, as not having the right knowledge, the right delivery, maybe a kind of urbane cleverness that covers up whatever doubts may be rising to the surface inside us. The fear is usually developed early, as we learn from parents and teachers that to please them we must be smart and perform well. And we are fearful of talking about what we do in class because of what we may reveal about ourselves. Even an interest in pedagogy is suspect. In the hierarchy of values that define the university, what is most celebrated and rewarded is not teaching but publication.

Tompkins's recent work has been to shake off that unsatisfying model and, along with her students, to find a better one. Teaching is not about impressing students but about paying attention to what they need on a given day. The classroom is a place where we "practice whatever ideals we may cherish," where we allow students to work together not just to learn a body of material, but to construct that material and to be with each other as it shapes itself in the room. The purpose of the classroom is not to suffer, not to overwork, not to prove ourselves the smartest, not to be sleep deprived and worried, but to be whole people, teacher and student both, thought and emotion connected.

---

[7]Jane Tompkins, *A Life in School: What the Teacher Learned* (Reading, MA: Addison-Wesley, 1996).

The final essay in this section shifts to a postmodern perspective. In "Pomo Blues: Stories from First-Year Composition," Lee Ann Carroll struggles with the question of what students are doing when they write. Do we see their writings as "authentic reflections of autonomous individuals" or as "verbal artifacts heavily structured by the cultural and institutional contexts in which they are produced"? Her essay sets forth the basic assumptions of postmodernist thought—all of which challenge the notion of a unified "truth," a unified "self." Like David Bartholomae, she challenges the "master narratives" of students' lives, asking them to see their arguments another way, to understand the cultural contexts that underpin not just their initial assumptions of reality but their second takes as well. The article raises many questions: Is there a way out of a condition where all ideas are "written" before we write them, where we see what we are taught to see? Do the unarticulated personal narratives that support our beliefs need to be articulated? If we articulate them, do they limit our perception of the "larger" reality? Is all knowledge partial, local, and provisional? In such an atmosphere, how do we ever find the courage to write anything at all? How do we find positions that seem to us ethically and aesthetically convincing, that allow us to act in the world? Do we allow ourselves to be paralyzed or do we take the relativity of all our positions as a way to free ourselves from someone else's judgment?

Carroll's course in Freshman Writing presents students with a series of assignments that ask them to keep shifting perspectives, to keep interrogating and complicating their last assumption, to write from different genres: to argue, narrate, dramatize, to find aesthetic forms that allow a complicated and perhaps submerged position to express itself. She considers also the needs of students to perform for us in order to complete the semester and get good grades. Is part of their truth finding out what the teacher wants and figuring out how to write it?

Carroll's essay offers no answers—as its point is that such answers are all provisional. Instead there are several possible ways out. If her students work hard, if they become aware of other voices, other cultures, other genres, if they develop a postmodern consciousness and then tweak that too, then she considers the job well-enough done. "IT'S ALL TRUE", says one student, "and therefore I deserve an A." Carroll does not presume to change students' lives—an outmoded thought in such a context. She is only "improvising a postmodern tune," giving them a point of view with which they may think about points of view, in the hope that somehow, as they continue to improvise, they will do so with a consciousness of other notes they might have played.

Geraldine DeLuca

Chapter 1

Reclaiming the Classroom

Mike Rose

Mike Rose is a professor at the UCLA Graduate School of Education and Information Studies and a nationally recognized expert on language and literacy. He is the author of *Possible Lives: The Promise of Education in America* and, with M. Kiniry, *Critical Strategies for Academic Thinking and Writing.* The son of immigrants, Rose was raised in South Central Los Angeles, attended both parochial and public schools and colleges, and has taught at all levels of the nation's public school system. The following selection is from *Lives on the Boundary: The Struggles and Achievements of America's Underprepared,* an award-winning investigation of remedial education (The Free Press, a division of Simon and Schuster, 1989).

There was not much space in Room 316, the third-floor office of the Veteran's Program, but the staff managed to fit a desk and two chairs into a storeroom, just inside the door. That was where I tutored. There were stacks of mimeograph paper and old files and textbooks behind me. A portable blackboard rocked noisily on wobbly casters. The Veteran's Program had been fashioned by an educational psychologist named Chip Anderson and was, in effect, a masterful crash course in the three Rs of higher education. It was housed in the old UCLA Extension Building in downtown Los Angeles. Students were enrolled right out of the service— the Marine Corps particularly—or through veteran's centers in Southern California. Virtually all who signed up were men. They took classes in English, speech, and mathematics, and participated in workshops to improve their reading and study skills. They were also enrolled in The Psychology of Human Relations. This introduced them to the mysteries of the college lecture course and had the additional benefit of dealing with communication and social interaction for a group returning to a culture that must have seemed pretty strange. All students received tutoring and academic and personal counseling. The curriculum was comprehensive and sensible; it provided an opportunity to develop the speaking, reading, writing, and mathematical abilities needed for college. The men I worked with called it academic boot camp.

I tutored three afternoons a week, and saw about five or six students a day. Our discussions ranged from subject-verb agreement to the taking of timed essay exams, and, fairly often, ranged outward to the NFL draft, music, wives, lovers, anger about the past, and confusion about the future. On the average the men were in their mid-twenties, some were younger, a few were lifers: gunnery sergeants or petty officers who, in their forties, were trying to change radically the direction of their next twenty years. Most of the students had been in the military from four to six years and had been, to use their term, the grunts—the privates and corporals who, in the years just after the prom, found themselves in marshland and firestorms. Some of these men started the program during their last few months of service, and others had been out for anywhere from weeks to years. Hair length became the dating gauge. If a student hadn't been to Vietnam, he came to the program with a legacy of boredom and a handful of firm resolves; some of those who were in Vietnam brought other things. They came directly from hospitals or drug and alcohol rehabilitation centers and, in a few cases, from prison. And some of them were continuing treatment as outpatients for particularly destructive physical injuries or for flitting horrors that could not be stitched or trussed.

I got to talk pretty intimately with men who saw the world very differently from the way I did and who had been through things I could barely imagine. The politics of the group ranged from reactionary to radical, white supremacist to black nationalist, with most mixing hawkish foreign policy with fairly liberal social mores. Some had dropped out of high school, were functionally literate, and were coming to the Veteran's Program to gain their high school equivalency; others were readers and theory builders and street poets. From what they told me, it was clear that most of them had academic histories like the kids in El Monte and the guys in Voc. Ed. Their school memories were dreary; I was seeing people at the other end of a frustrated educational journey. They were mustering their resources, though, for one last go at it. About a third of our students were wild boys with few responsibilities, while others were somber men with families and debts. Some had been shot while others spent their time in a sleepy town. I started noticing the scars. David had lost most of his right thumb—he held his pen in place with a nub—and had a scar that ran up beyond his wrist. Richard was missing the tops of two fingers, and the nails on Clayton's hands were replaced by fungus. The underside of Bill's arm, the place where the radial muscles flex to a rounded fullness, was gouged—a layer of slick, brownish skin stretched into place like wet and wrinkled paper.

The ethnic and geographic mix was rich: whites, Chicanos, blacks, a few Asians, fewer American Indians; New Yorkers and Oregonians, men from the Motor City and men from Southern farms. They drove in from El Toro or Camp Pendleton seventy miles to the south, from apartments scattered from Orange County to the far end of the San Fernando Valley, or from homes in East L.A., Lynwood, or Compton. A few lived in awful places close to the program, like the Morrison, a musty hotel that gained a flicker of notoriety when it was photographed for the cover of a mediocre Doors album. And some bused in from the Veteran's Hospital in West Los Angeles. Their needs were profound and, at times, overwhelming to someone as young as I was. They came for education, for counseling, for friendship, for decompression. They came to get themselves back into the stream of things.

The Extension Building is on South Grand Avenue, five or six blocks this side of the rich hub of downtown Los Angeles: CitiCorp, the Bonaventure, the Arco Towers. It is one block east of Hope. It is a dirty beige stone building, four stories high. A fire escape crisscrosses all but the first floor of the south side. The windows are opaque, and the curtains you can see on the second floor are light gray. One is torn from its rung and tied back. Next door is a sandstone-colored hotel with bars on the ground-floor windows and 1120 crudely painted on a stucco post by the front stairs. It has no name. In the immediate vicinity are two parking lots and some small, depressed industries: sewing machines, garment hangers, baby furniture, Boston Shoe, ADM Button and Belt. Jo's Liquor and the Morris Cafe are a few blocks to the south. Beer and wine and pool.

Every quarter, fifteen or so teachers and tutors and a couple of hundred students moved in and out of the hallways of the Extension Building, moving through the elevators, the lobby, the lunchroom in the basement. And during breaks between classes, Grand Avenue would intermittently feel the tingling scrape of peripatetic chatter and the heat of a quick smoke. The main meeting place was the lunchroom, presided over by Al Petrillo, a vendor of sandwiches, a player of ponies, and an indefatigable dispenser of jokes with punchlines like "Jeez, Doc, I hope they don't amputate around here, 'cause I'm only in for prickly heat!" Al was a short man with sleepy eyes who would cradle his forehead in his left hand and slowly look up at you as he made change and insulted your choice of sandwiches or your looks. And behind him, a hundred people lamented and laughed and made bets and dreamed.

I had been tutoring for about two months when Dr. Anderson called me into his office and offered me a full-time job. He said he had been talking to the men and decided he wanted me to teach English and reading and maybe do a little counseling. I would be taking my master's orals at UCLA in December, so I'd be set to go by January, the start of a new quarter. How about it? I liked working with the veterans very much, felt at ease, for so many of them had grown up in neighborhoods like mine. I accepted on the spot. It was after I left Anderson's office that I started having second thoughts.

In the Teacher Corps I worked informally with small groups of children and had ongoing connection with a team. And tutoring in the Veteran's

Program seemed a lot safer than teaching. Someone else created the curriculum, set the assignments, and gave the grades. I was a coach, a compatriot, helping the men as they struggled with their test taking and their writing. If they thought an assignment was stupid or a grade unfair, I could just nod sympathetically and get on with the paper before us. Now I would have to fashion my own curriculum, give the grades, and take the heat for it.

I worried most about the curriculum. One of the English teachers in the Veteran's Program had fashioned a wildly inventive set of assignments that had the students comparing two apples one week and writing a poem the next. It was a maverick curriculum, and I admired its ambition, but a lot of the men I tutored were simply perplexed by it. The other teachers relied on more traditional curricula: a handbook of rules of grammar, lectures on subordination and parallelism, papers requiring students to narrate and describe. I went to the UCLA bookstore and browsed through the various texts in use on the campus: more grammar handbooks. This all seemed cheerless. And the old standby, the writing of essays on unforgettable grandparents and My First Job, seemed as appropriate for the veterans as a hymn at a crapshoot. I had a month, so I started looking around for a base on which to build my course.

The first possibility that offered itself was, of course, Vietnam. It would seem natural to draw on the veterans' experience, present and vibrant as it was. Such a curriculum would be relevant at a time when relevance was dearly sought. But when I imagined teaching a course on the war, it didn't feel right—felt presumptuous, intrusive. After spending two months with the veterans, I could see that each man was on his own psychic timetable: Some were fairly comfortable talking about Vietnam; others couldn't bear to do it, at least not publicly. And in either case, they were looking forward to an education that would create a future, not one that would force them back through a past of shrapnel and deadly surprise.

It was when I started thinking about why the men had come to the program that I found an answer, one that lay at the intersection of the veterans' lives and mine. The men wanted to change their lives, and for all their earlier failures, they still held onto an American dream: Education held the power to equalize things. After Vietnam, they had little doubt about what their next step had to be: up and out of the pool of men society could call on so easily to shoot and be shot at. From what they told me, it was clear that a number of the veterans were a high school teacher's bad dream: detached or lippy or assaultive. They were my Voc. Ed. comrades reincarnated. But here they were now: "I'm givin' it a hundred percent this time." There's probably little any teacher can do with some kids in some high schools: the poverty and violence of the neighborhoods, the dynamics of particular families, the ways children develop identities in the midst of economic blight. You rely on goodwill and an occasional silent prayer to keep your class from exploding, hope that some wild boy doesn't slug another, pray that your authority isn't embarrassed. But here those students were, five or ten years down the line: different life experiences, different perspectives on learning. It makes you think about those sullen high schoolers in a different light, see their lives along a time line. Maybe no one could have gotten to some of the veterans when they were sixteen, but they were ready now. They were bringing with them an almost magical vision of what learning could do for them, and regardless of what I had come to know about the realities of higher education, I could sure understand the desire to be transfigured by books.

The veterans' encounter with college led me to reflect on my education in a way I hadn't done before. More than I realized, I had learned a lot in El Monte about developing a curriculum: I approached learning carefully, step by step, systematically. I found that I knew what questions to ask. What had I really learned from studying history and psychology and literature? I thought a lot about my best teachers, about Jack MacFarland at Mercy High, about Dr. Carothers and Ted Erlandson and the others at Loyola. I browsed through the books that had mattered and thought about those courses that had opened up ways of considering the world. What intellectual orientations persisted? I went back to UCLA and sat in on a few lectures in the humanities and the social sciences, listening, this time, with a different ear. I talked with other teachers. And this is how I started to think about the curriculum I would fashion.

Given the nature of these men's needs and given the limited time I would have with them, could I perhaps orient them to some of the kinds of reading and writing and ways of thinking that seem essential to a liberal course of study, some of the habits of mind that Jack MacFarland and the many that followed him had helped me develop? If I could do this in some systematic and manageable way, then I would be enhancing the veterans' chances of participating in the institutions they would soon be entering. And while I wanted to be pragmatic—college preparation was the name of this game—I also wanted to go beyond utility. I was looking for a methodical way to get my students to think about thinking. Thinking. Not a fussbudget course, but a course about thought. I finally decided to build a writing curriculum on four of the intellectual strategies my education had helped me develop—some of which, I would later discover, were as old as Aristotle—strategies that kept emerging as I reflected on the life of the undergraduate: summarizing, classifying, comparing, and analyzing.

Liberal studies had really sharpened my ability to find the central notion in an argument or the core of a piece of fiction. Thinking back on it, I couldn't imagine a more crucial skill than summarizing; we can't manage information, make crisp connections, or rebut arguments without it. The great syntheses and refutations are built on it. The veterans would have to have practice summarizing various kinds of academic materials. It would give them a nice sense of mastery if they could determine and express the gist of readings that might, at first glance, seem opaque as medieval texts.

Classifying. You could almost define the undergraduate's life as the acquisition of the ways Western scholars have classified their knowledge. The very departments in which I took my classes represented one way to classify inquiry, and I encountered classification schemes in every course I took: taxonomies in biology, genres and periods in literature and the arts, the catalogs of motive and behavior in psychology and sociology. I wanted the veterans to become familiar with academic classification schemes, to sharpen their own abilities to systematize what they study, and to develop a critical awareness of the limitations of the classification schemes that will surround them. I thought up some simple exercises: Bring to class twenty copies of paintings of the human body. Have the paintings represent a wide range of styles, from Florentine humanism to cubist geometrics, but have all information on artist and period removed. It would be the students' job to classify this collection of paintings by any system they could develop. They would probably begin with a simple binary scheme: some of the paintings look like people and some don't. But through my questions as well as through the observations rising from their interaction, they would be encouraged to elaborate and revise until they'd agreed that they could go no further. I would then ask them to discuss what they felt was gained and what was lost as they classified paintings and moved from one scheme to another.

Another thing that became clear to me was how much knowledge in the arts and sciences is gained by methodically examining one object or event or theory in relation to another. What comes into focus when a student places *A Farewell to Arms* alongside a piece of journalism? What understanding is gained by listing the features of French schooling next to a description of American education? Entire disciplines—comparative politics to comparative anatomy—are built on this intellectual strategy. Simply by virtue of their humanity, the men in the Veteran's Program continually made comparisons, but I wanted to give them the chance to develop confidence and facility in comparing points of view and explanations and works of art.

The further along I got in college, the more I was asked to "analyze" an artistic product, a physical phenomenon, a social event, *to analyze* meaning to break something down to its constituent elements so as to better understand its nature. But that wasn't the whole story. There was a kind of implied directive to the request to analyze, and it took me quite a while before I realized it. Students are not usually told that such analytic investigation is always carried out with a set of assumptions, and these assumptions are crucial determinants of how you proceed in your examination, what you find, and how you explain your discovery to others. I figured that developing the ability to probe the assumptions beneath an analysis or explanation would be exciting and empowering for the veterans, a little insight into how to pick the academic lock. They would be able to read with a critical eye and thus speak and write with more authority. While I could probably develop this critical awareness by modeling it for the class and by questioning them on their reading, I thought they might also benefit by engaging in a kind of intellectual roleplaying that would highlight the assumptive base of analysis. I could, for example, present them with a newspaper story about a man who commits an apparently senseless murder. Next would come an account of how Freud would explain violent behavior. It would be the students' job to slip into that perspective and discuss the story as though they were psychoanalysts. This passage would be followed by one written by a more existentially oriented social critic. The class would then discuss the crime with that perspective, discussing as well what happens to their analysis as they shift assumptions about human nature. How did the frameworks they used affect what they saw?

Most of the veterans were considered to be "remedial level" students. Even those who came to the program as pretty capable writers were hesitant and wrote prose that displayed the signs of an inadequate education: misspellings, verbs that didn't agree with subjects, sentences that strangled in their own convolutions. As for the less capable students—the kinds of writers I saw struggling as children in El Monte—composing was a source of embarrassment, a halting, self-conscious duty that resulted in stunted, error-ridden prose. It has been customary for remedial writing programs to focus attention on the kinds of grammatical problems that were found in the pages these men wrote. The programs instruct students in principles of grammar and usage ("Use a comma between coordinate adjectives not joined by 'and' "), distribute workbook exercises that require students to select correct forms ("Write in 'who' or 'whom' in the following sentences"), and assign short, undemanding bits of writing. The assumption is that error can be eradicated by zeroing in on the particulars of language. And that assumption seems to rest on a further assumption that grammatical error signals some fundamental mental barrier to engaging in higher-level cognitive pursuits: until error is isolated and cleaned up, it will not be possible for students to read and write critically, study literature, or toy with style.

It would not be until later in my career that I could methodically challenge these assumptions; at this early stage in my development as a writing teacher I had to rely more on the feel of things. It just didn't make sense that not knowing the delicacies of usage or misplacing commas or blundering pronouns and verb forms or composing a twisted sentence indicated arrest at some cognitive linguistic stage of development, a stage that had to be traversed before you could engage in critical reading and writing. Such thinking smacked of the reductionism I had seen while studying psychology at UCLA. Besides, I had never gotten some of this stuff straight, and I turned out okay. It seemed that, if anything, concentrating on the particulars of language—schoolbook grammar, mechanics, usage—would tremendously restrict the scope of what language use was all about Such approaches would rob writing of its joy, and would, to boot, drag the veterans back through their dismal history of red-pencilled failure. Furthermore, we would be aiming low, would be scaling down our expectations—as so many remedial programs do—training to do the minimum, the minimum here being a simple workbook sentence free of error. The men had bigger dreams, and I wanted to tap them.

My students needed to be immersed in talking, reading, and writing, they needed to further develop their ability to think critically, and they needed to gain confidence in themselves as systematic inquirers. They had to be let into the academic club. The fact that they misspelled words or wrote fragments or dropped verb endings would not erect insurmountable barriers to the benefits they would gain from such immersion. A traveler in a foreign land best learns names of people and places, how to express ideas, ways to carry on a conversation by moving around in the culture, participating as fully as he can, making mistakes, saying things half right, blushing, then being encouraged by a friendly native speaker to try again. He'll pick up the details of grammar and usage as he goes along. What he must *not* do is hold back from the teeming flow of life, must not sit in his hotel room and drill himself on all possible gaffes before entering the streets. He'd never leave the room.

My students, too, were strangers in a strange land, and I wanted to create a safe section of the city and give them an opportunity to acquire the language. We would cover some common errors together during the first few days of class, but, for the most part, I and the tutors I now had would work with students individually through the quarter as particular problems came up on particular papers. This would be a more sensible way to deal with grammatical error and would, as well, give students the sense that grammatical correctness is only one of the concerns of a writer, not the only one, and certainly not the force that brings pen to paper.

Aiming high, however, brought with it a real risk: the possibility that I would overwhelm the men, defeat them once again by asking them to do things that were beyond their reach, mystify them with impenetrable language. The only article of faith I had came from a little book by Jerome Bruner called *The Process* of *Education*. Bruner begins one of his chapters with this remarkable dictum: "Any subject can be taught effectively in some intellectually honest form to any child at any stage of development." I transposed the promise and challenge of that sentence to adults. It seemed that I could honor the challenge if I used accessible materials and if I had the students work with them in ways that built from the simple to the complex.

I paged through newspapers, magazines, and political pamphlets. I copied out song lyrics. I rifled the books I had been collecting since my days with Jack MacFarland. I excerpted, deleted, Xeroxed, cut, pasted, and rewrote. To give students a sense of how social criticism reads, I used an Erich Fromm essay from *McCall's* rather than assign a section out of *Escape from Freedom* or *Socialist Humanism*. To provide illustrations of psychological states for our analysis assignments, I relied on song lyrics like John Prine's "Donald and Lydia." To raise liberal studies themes like Appearance and Reality, I lifted a few pages from *Invisible Man.* And so on.

Each quarter, I began by having the students summarize short, simple readings, and then moved them slowly through classifying and comparing to analyzing, which became the capstone of the curriculum. I didn't do enough of this careful sequencing in El Monte, and my curriculum there suffered for it. I explained and modeled, used accessible readings, tried to incorporate what the veterans learned from one assignment into the next, slowly increased difficulty, and provided a lot of time for the men to talk and write. So, for example, I introduced them to the strategy of comparing with this pair of sentences:

> In the whole world no poor devil is lynched, no wretch is tortured, in whom I too am not degraded and murdered.
>
> —AIMÉ CÉSAIRE

> There exists among men, because they are men, a solidarity through which each shares responsibility for every injustice and every wrong committed in the world.
>
> —KARL JASPERS

I asked them to talk about the message each sentence contains and to talk, as well, about the way each is written: the academic sound of one, the emotional quality of the other. Did the sound affect the message? I would tell them a little about Césaire, the African poet and statesman, and about Jaspers, the German philosopher. Did that information about time and place affect their reading? They would go through many such pairs—finger exercises, as a friend of mine would later call them—doing them orally, writing on them in class as a tutor and I provided advice on wording and direction, and then, finally, going it alone at home. Within three or four weeks, they were working with more difficult passages, like these two cosmogonies—one an Australian aboriginal myth, the other from an astronomy textbook:

I

In the very beginning everything was resting in perpetual darkness: night oppressed all the earth like an impenetrable thicket.

(And) Karora was lying asleep, in everlasting night, at the very bottom of the soak of Ilbalintja: as yet there was not water in it, but all was dry ground.

Over him the soil was red with flower & overgrown with many grasses & a great pole was swaying above him.

. . . And Karora's head lay at the root of the great pole; he had rested thus ever from the beginning.

And Karora was thinking, & wishes & desires flashed through his mind. Bandicoots began to come out from his navel & from his arm-pits. They burst through the sod above & sprang into life.

And now dawn was beginning to break.

From all quarters men saw a new light appearing: the sun itself began to rise at Ilbalintja, & flooded everything with its light.

Then the gurra ancestor was minded to rise, now that the sun was mounting higher.

He burst through the crust that had covered him: & the gaping hole that he had left behind became the Ilbalintja Soak, filled with the sweet dark juice of honeysuckle buds.

II

Theoreticians have calculated a "standard" model of what the big bang may have been like. In the beginning we imagine a great primeval fireball of matter and radiation. We do not have to imagine any particular mass, or even a finite mass, for the fireball. Its density was very high and it was at a temperature of perhaps 10^{10}K.

At first the matter consisted only of protons, neutrons, electrons, positrons, and neutrinos, all independent particles. After about 100 seconds, however, the temperature had dropped to 10^9K, and the particles began to combine to form some heavier nuclei. This nucleogenesis continued, according to the model, for a few hours until the temperature dropped to about 10^8K. During this time, about 20 percent of the mass of the material formed into helium. Some deuterium also formed (deuterium is an isotope of hydrogen with a nucleus containing one proton and one neutron) but only a small amount—probably less than one part in a thousand. The actual amount of deuterium formed depends critically on the density of the fireball; if it was fairly high, most of the deuterium would have been built up into helium. Scarcely any nuclei heavier than those of helium are expected to have survived. So the composition of the fireball when nuclear building ceased is thought to have been mostly hydrogen, about 20 percent helium, and a trace of deuterium.

For the next million years the fireball was like a stellar interior—hot and opaque, with radiation passing from atom to atom. During the time, the temperature gradually dropped to about 3000K, and the density to about 1000 atoms/cm^3. At this point the fireball became transparent. The radiation was no longer absorbed and was able to pass freely throughout the universe. After about 1000 million years, the model predicts that the matter should have condensed into galaxies and stars.

We emphasize again that the fireball must not be thought of as a localized explosion—like an exploding superstar. There were no boundaries and no site of the explosion. It was everywhere. The fireball is still existing in a sense. It has expanded greatly, but the original matter and radiation are still present and accounted for. The atoms of our bodies came from material in the fireball. We were and are still in the midst of it, it is all around us,

I knew from my own early struggles that students who have not had a privileged education often freeze up when they see readings like these, particularly the big bang discussion with its superscripted numbers, the vocabulary of its first two paragraphs, and the heady notions in the last. And they don't have the background knowledge or the conceptual grab bag of received phrases to make connections between scientific theorizing and mythic explanation. But give them time. Provide some context, break them into groups or work with the whole class, involving everyone. Let them see what, collectively, they do know, and students will, together, begin to generate meaning and make connections. One person once read something else about big bang, and his knowledge helps a second person understand the nuclear processes in paragraph two, and that second person then asks a question that remained ill-formed in the mind of a third. And the teacher darts in and out of the conversation, clarifying, questioning, repeating, looping back to link one student's observation to another's. And so it is that the students, labeled "remedial," read and talk and write their way toward understanding.

* * * * * * * *

The Teacher Corps introduced me to the risk and reward of education, but it was the Veteran's Program that really enabled me to come into my own as a teacher, to publicly define myself as someone engaged with the language of others. It was a good place to grow up. The work, successful or failed, had unusual power. The students possessed long and complex life histories, and they were trying to reclaim a place in the classroom they once lost or never really had. Here are a few of those students and a few of the pieces of their history.

It was the third or fourth day of my second quarter in the Veteran's Program, and I was, by now, very much aware of a bald man staring at me from a rear seat along the west wall of the room. His skin was dark, dark brown, his head perfectly slick, his ear pierced by a tiny gold ring. He wore a leather pilot's jacket and kept his arms folded tightly across his chest. I noticed the arms. Pilot's jackets are big, loose things, and this man's upper arms filled out the sleeves, the leather stretching firmly over his shoulders and biceps. As I moved around day after day talking about writing, and memorizing names, and tapping people on shoulders, and getting one man to address another, this man, Willie Oates, sat back and said nothing. He seemed all forearms and pectorals and husky silence.

At the end of the fourth class, he walked slowly up to the podium, waiting his turn behind the three or four men who were asking about their assignment. I kept talking, half hoping they wouldn't leave. But they did. Then Willie took a step forward and began speaking, pounding his fist on the podium in slow pace with each deliberate word: "You," he said. "You—are—" and here he looked up from his fist and into my eyes. "You—are—teaching—the—fuck—outta—me!"

Willie had just spent two years in federal penitentiary. His muscles were the muscles you get from lifting weights two and three hours a day to cleanse your respect in spasms of rushing blood. During this time, Willie started reading. He read all the literature in the prison library, and while some of that was Hemingway, some of it was also Jane Austen. As he read, he wrote in a journal, and he began to develop a style that was ornate as a drawing room.

Willie Oates and I spent a lot of time in the lunchroom. Al Petrillo would be holding court at the cash register, and we'd be in a far corner, Willie's papers and Cokes and open bags of potato chips spread before us. Willie had all sorts of stylistic moves; it was my job to get him to weigh their merits. I would go over an essay sentence by sentence, showing him where he'd kill an effect with excess, or get himself into a hopeless tangle with his eighteenth-century syntax, or use a word that sounded pretentious to the twentieth-century ear. The assessing gaze that Willie had fixed on me was gone. Now there was a gentler look, one full of need—an unprotected intensity of mind. He slid into schooling like an athlete lowering himself into a whirlpool, feeling the heat deep in his tissue. He read Chinese poetry and stories by Pirandello. He wrote a paper using the British social historian J. H. Plumb to analyze American counterculture. He talked about Malcolm X and Eldridge Cleaver, two other black men who had transformed themselves in a prison library.

When Willie was released from the service years before, he returned to a neighborhood that was poor and burned out. He was an aching, dreamy man who couldn't dull himself and who, eventually, stole some money and a car to try to rip away from the projects and pool halls and indolent streets. He was caught within a week. And now, two or three years later, he saw his chance again. He wanted to know everything, was as hungry as anyone I'd seen. One day he showed me the journal he kept in prison—it was a thick National copybook with a cardboard cover pressed to look like leather. As I paged through it, I saw black, working-class experience fused with the language of teapots and Victorian gardens: whole pages of *Sense and Sensibility* and *The Mill on the Floss* copied down, strained and awkward imitations, beginnings of short stories, reflections on prison that seemed forced but that contained elegant moments. It was a remarkable book, the record of a clash of cultures and a testament to the power of Willie's desire.

He kept a journal now, one filled with assignments from Speech and Psychology and Math and various rough drafts for me. He continued to write down quotations that caught his ear, these from the lectures and books that presently surrounded him. One from my class that I remember seeing there came from Niels Bohr: "Your theory is crazy—but not crazy enough to be true."

Willie was finding a way to direct his yearning. I would pass on to him books I was just discovering—*The Other America; Black Skin, White Masks*—and we would talk about the anger that used to knot him up, the hopelessness that landed him in prison. We talked about education and the use of it to direct the anger outward—dissent rather than involuted despair. Willie developed into a truly individual writer and, as well, learned to handle the academy. He received A's in psychology, English, speech, and mathematics. He went on to major in English at a local state university. He continued to write in his journal. Writing, now, in the university, writing to try out new ideas, writing to redefine himself. Writing and writing and writing.

Sergeant Gonzalez was a twenty-year man, a Marine who, at forty, was near retirement. He was tall and square-shouldered as a recruiting poster. He spoke his mind and he rarely smiled, and he was getting, at best, a C from me. He tried and tried but his writing remained too stunted, too abbreviated and superficial. He tended toward literal interpretations and preferred unambiguous answers. He had worked hard all his life, and hard work always gave him tangible results. So here he was, dropping his head and going over tackle again, and yet again, but with the same step, no little juke, no variation. I knew that he would never give up but that he was close to despair.

I set aside an hour after class and dug up something that I thought might help, a poem from Edgar Lee Masters's *Spoon River Anthology:*

BUTCH WELDY

After I got religion and steadied down
They gave me a job in the canning works,
And every morning I had to fill
The tank in the yard with gasoline,
That fed the blow-fires in the sheds
To heat the soldering irons.
And I mounted a rickety ladder to do it,
Carrying buckets full of the stuff.
One morning, as I stood there pouring,

The air grew still and seemed to heave,
And I shot up as the tank exploded,
And down I came with both legs broken,
And my eyes burned crisp as a couple of eggs.
For someone left a blow-fire going,
And something sucked the flame in the tank.
The Circuit Judge said whoever did it
Was a fellow-servant of mine, and so
Old Rhodes' son didn't have to pay me.
And I sat on the witness stand as blind
As Jack the Fiddler, saying over and over
"I didn't know him at all."

David could follow Butch Weldy's story. The poem depicted a real-life situation and did so along a straight narrative line. It nicely fit David's own interpretive predilections.

"So why," I asked him, "does Masters have Butch say 'someone' left a fire going, and 'something' caused an explosion? 'Someone' and 'something' sound pretty vague to me. Is Butch a little slow?"

"No, he's not slow. He just don't know who did it."

"David, who is Old Rhodes' son?"

"I'm not sure."

"If he's someone who has the ability to pay money to Butch, what position would he hold?"

"The boss? No. The owner. He owns the place."

"The judge said that whoever caused the accident to happen was a worker like Butch, and so, therefore, the owner wouldn't have to pay Butch. Pay for what?"

"The accident."

"What would we call it now if someone paid for the accident?"

"Workman's comp."

"Okay, David, now here's an interesting question for you. You're the head of a motor pool, right?"

"Right."

"If one of your soldiers stumbled and released the trip on a jack, and a car fell on a mechanic and injured him, whose fault would it be? The Marine Corps'?"

"Well, no."

"Could you think of any situation where it might be the Marine Corps' fault?"

We went on like this for a little while longer, and then I asked David to list all the information we had gleaned about Butch and his situation: He was seriously injured at work, is now blind, won't receive compensation, is being shuttled through the legal system, and so on. After making our list, I picked up the questioning again, this time about Butch Weldy's past ("What does the first line—'*After* I got religion and steadied down'—tell us about Butch before he got this job?") and about the degree of control he seems to have over his life. This last issue was an interesting one to pose to David, for he was clearly a man who prided himself on being at the center of his actions.

"David, could you picture yourself in Butch's situation?"

"Well, yes and no. I mean I could imagine getting hurt, but—"

"But? But you would have been more careful?"

"Yeh. Yeh, I'd have been more careful."

"How does Masters describe the ladder Butch was climbing?"

"Rickety."

"Yep."

And so it went. Within a half hour, we had a long, rich list of detail about Butch Weldy. It was then that I started turning the key.

"Okay, David, look at the wealth of information we got from this little poem. Could we really understand the mess Butch Weldy is in without all this detail?"

"Um, no, no we couldn't, not really."

"That's right. The detail makes the whole thing come alive to us."

This continued for a few minutes, then: "Now, look, you are a powerful guy, and you take charge of things, and you like to have answers, and you can answer for yourself short and sweet . . . but, man, not everyone is like that. Butch is in a hell of a mess, and to tell somebody about it, we'd have to give a little history, and spell out what we know about the accident, and explain what kind of person Butch seems to be and how he feels. . . . Now, what sorts of things are we sure of; what can we say straight out?"

"Well, we could say what happened in the accident, I mean the ladder . . . the gasoline . . . the explosion . . . all that stuff. And we could say he's blind now and he's going to get screwed by the law."

"Right. Good. Now, what will we have to hedge our bets on? What will we have to say we're unsure about?"

"Hm. Well, we don't know who left the fires going, and we don't know exactly how the explosion happened."

"Okay. And, again, what are the words Masters uses?"

"Um . . . 'someone' and 'something.' "

"Now, what about Butch's character? What kind of guy is he?"

"It's hard to say, but he don't seem to have a grip on things, and maybe he never did. He sure as hell is lost."

"Good. And remember, you started what you just said with 'It's hard to say,' and that's a perfectly acceptable way to talk about some of the things going on in this little snapshot of a man's life."

I won't tell you that this session made David a dramatically better writer; only in Hollywood pedagogy does such change happen overnight. But the paper he wrote on "Butch Weldy" was richer in detail than was his previous work, and it displayed attempts to deal with the uncertain. David's writing started getting a little more ambitious and a little more specific. He was learning some new moves, a few ways to take chances in his writing. That created another set of problems, of course. Saying complex things forces you away from the protected syntax of simple sentences. But error that crops up because a student is trying new things is a valuable kind of error, a sign of growth.

Jerry Williams was thin and walked with a slight sideways bend at the waist; he wore wire-rim glasses that were deeply tinted. Jerry was quiet and solitary and tended to be irritable and rude with the other veterans. No one was close to him. He was a poor writer ("I think that the state of blacks in the U.S. is a easly debated subject. I think this becaus their is evidence if you want to look at it . . . "), and he'd miss class often. The tutors and I kept trying to catch him up, but then he'd miss school again, and we'd try again, and he'd slip further and further behind. He was a Seconal junkie, "reds," and the other men called him "Redhead." He was loaded most of the time I worked with him. I would guide him as he wrote a slow paragraph or talk ineffectually with him about an essay he'd forgotten to read. He'd look at me, eyes half-closed behind amber lenses, and respond to my suggestions with hip monosyllables: "dig it" and "right on" and like that. I hoped something was sinking in, though I didn't think much was. He stopped showing up at all during the last two weeks of school.

On the last day of that quarter, while the men were writing their final in-class papers, the door to my room slammed open and Jerry stumbled through. I had never seen him anywhere near that stoned. He made his way down the right aisle, steadying himself against the wall, and walked slowly to my desk. The class had stopped writing and was watching us. "I want to take the exam," he said. I told him I didn't think that was a good idea, that he was way too loaded to write anything. "Motherfucker," he yelled, "don't tell me that!" He slammed his hand on the desk and, in a quick tipsy glide, slid behind me. I wheeled around and grabbed his arms. Two or three guys in the front were out of their seats. But it was a burst of rage, and it faded quickly. Jerry put his hands back on the chalk tray and slumped into the blackboard. "Just let me take the exam," he slurred. Beneath the fuzz of the Seconal was some quavering desire to be schooled. He looked back up, not at me, but at the men in the first few rows: "I got a right to take the exam."

The veterans and I spent a lot of time talking about language. Sometimes a major part of a class would be taken up with a poem or song lyric, other times I would sneak a quick opportunity for word play into a lesson: "Try writing a sentence like this one from *Native Son*," or "Give me a phrase someone said or a song you heard that caught your ear today." That would go on the board and spark discussion. A lot of the men took to language. For some, linguistic play was part of their culture; for others, it seemed okay to fool around with words if the teacher was getting all worked up about them, was—for God's sake—walking backward into the podium because of a turned phrase.

Jack Cheney was a special kind of student. Every quarter we would get two or three men who had read a lot and were skilled writers. These were the guys who were bored to tears by high school—didn't fit in, were out of step, quit going. But unlike some gifted dropouts, they weren't from families who could afford to send them to special schools, so they were scooped up by the military with all the other uncovered eighteen-year-olds.

Jack could do the program's work easily and started asking for books to read on his own. I had a copy of *The Great Gatsby* in my desk, so I gave it to him. A week or so later, he stopped by the office to tell me about a line of Fitzgerald's: He describes the sound of a phonebook hitting the floor as a *splash*. The metaphor stirred Jack's curiosity. "So I picked up our phonebook," he said, all enthused, "and dropped it. It hit on the spine and went thud. Then I tried it again, and the pages hit, and—check it out, Mike—it splashed! How about that?"

Jon Davis wasn't as well-read as Jack, and, in fact, never saw himself as an intellectual, didn't care much for school. He entered the Veteran's Program just to gain a few months reprieve from a Marine Corps life that had become intolerable to him. But during his twelve weeks with us, his deep need to be free of military codes and restrictions fused powerfully with his growing facility with written language. Halfway through the program, he made me promise not to laugh and then told me that he thought he might want to be a writer.

Jon still wasn't sure about college. The military had seeped so thoroughly into his being that his response to any institution—church, school, state—was harsh and physical, an existential gag reflex. So when he finished the program, he headed north, away from L.A.'s industrial terrain, toward that magical, rootless garden so many young Americans were seeking. And the era met him, of course, with its Zen farmers and hippie craftsmen, with Kesey and Brautigan and Gary Snyder. Several months after he left, I received a long letter telling me he'd settled, finally, in a small town in Alaska. The stores weren't crowded, he said, and he worked in the forests, and he lived in a fine old house:

> I was sitting here smoking cigarettes . . . half-listening to some A.M. disc-jockey . . . letting thoughts come and pass and thinking maybe one will take

hold. . . . Alaska affords a fellow a good atmosphere in which to think and write: there's a lot of air and ground, trees and tundra; wide open meadows where you can spy moose if you're quiet and in a pious mood at early dawn. . . .

No one could doubt the veterans' motivation; some were nearly feverish. But over my time with them, I had come to see how desire was only part of the equation. A number of the men—like me during my early schooling—had skated along the surface of true education, had read too little, were propelling themselves forward on the jet streams of fleeting dreams. So they did all the things that learners, working class to upper crust, do when they lose focus or get scared or give up: They withdrew or faked it or cheated or got stoned or stayed home or blew up.

I and the other English teachers had three tutors to assist us—Tony, Patrick, and Kevin—and once we began to understand the fear of failure at the origin of the veterans' troubling behavior, we refused to give in to it. The more we worked together, the more we pepped each other into trying almost anything to reach the men we taught. We would flatter and plead and use the phone and yell and breathe deep and, more than once, walk down to the Morrison Hotel to pound on a door. Sometimes we pushed too far and found ourselves in situations we were too inexperienced to handle—like the time I sat in a shabby apartment with a blue-eyed addict and looked at the needles and saw open up before me a hopelessness and screaming rejection that I could not begin to address. But we also succeeded, and our successes fueled us. Kevin once said about one of our students: "If I have to, I'll kiss his ass to make him learn." If any of us could have translated that into Latin, it would have become our motto.

Morgan was a Marine scout who had been sent back to the states with two Purple Hearts and bits of shrapnel alongside his knee. He was a quiet man and his childhood couldn't have been more different from mine. He boxed, wrestled, and played up on the line and graduated to racing motorcycles and hunting wild boar with a handgun. At first glance, Morgan did not look all that imposing—five feet nine maybe—sloping shoulders, a slightly large rump. But then you think about it, about the guys you've seen with that certain angle to their trapezius muscles and with that wide beam and those thick thighs, and then you know: This man carries a tremendous centered power.

Morgan had meant grief for teachers since the day he got off his kindergarten mat. He had shined on innumerable lessons, sneered at too many ideas, turned thumbs-down on the mind. He had driven his parents nuts, wildly, almost suicidally trying to forge an identity. But he had something, and though his tolerance for diversity rivaled the Emperor Nero's, you wanted the guy to like you. I used to require students to see me after I'd returned their essays. One of the first times I was scheduled to meet with Morgan, he appeared in my doorway with his essay crumpled and proceeded, in a remarkable act of frustration, to bite off the corner of the paper. His grade wasn't so hot, and, to make matters worse, he found out that another student he couldn't stand had received a higher mark. He walked around the room and ranted and waved the paper and, finally, sat down begrudgingly and smoothed it out so we could work on it. We went at the essay point by point, and I remember how happy I was, thinking, "I got him now. I've really got him."

QUESTIONS FOR REFLECTION, JOURNAL WRITING, AND DISCUSSION

1. Rose decided not to base his curriculum for the veterans on Vietnam because it would have seemed to him "presumptuous" and "intrusive." What do you think of his decision?

2. Mike Rose's students were novice writers with powerful life experiences. In teaching them, he decided to have them write about complex material. Would his students have been better off starting with more basic tasks?

3. How much attention did your teachers pay to "schoolbook grammar, mechanics, and usage"? Did it help you?

4. Rose found much in his personal and intellectual background that helped him form a common ground with his students. What might you draw on in your background in teaching disempowered students?

Chapter 2

Teaching Basic Writing:
An Alternative to Basic Skills

David Bartholomae

David Bartholomae is Professor of English and Chair of the English Department at the University of Pittsburgh. He is currently on the Executive Council of the MLA and he is coeditor (with Jean Ferguson Carr) of the University of Pittsburgh Press Series, *Composition, Literacy and Culture*. He has written widely on composition and pedagogy, including *Facts, Artifacts, Counterfacts* and the textbook, *Ways of Reading*. The following article appeared in the *Journal of Basic Writing*, 2, 2, 1979.

At the University of Pittsburgh, we teach Basic Writing to around 1,200 students each year. The instruction is offered through two different courses—Basic Writing (3 hours, 3 credits) and Basic Reading and Writing (6 hours, 6 credits). We also have a Writing Workshop, and basic writers frequently attend, but their attendance is voluntary, and the workshop is not specifically for writers with basic problems.

The courses are not conventional remedial courses: they carry full graduation credit and there is little in the activity the courses prescribe to distinguish them from any general or advanced composition course. In fact, because of the nature of the assignments, the courses would be appropriate for students at any level. This is certainly not to say that there is no difference between a basic writer and any other student writer. There are significant points of difference. But it is a way of saying that writing should be offered as writing—not as sentence practice or paragraph practice—if the goal of a program is to produce writers. The assignments, about 20 in a 15-week term, typically ask students to consider and, from various perspectives, reconsider a single issue, like "Identity and Change" or "Work and Play."[1] In the most general terms, the sequence of assignments presents writing as a

---

[1]For an example of such a sequence of assignments, and for discussion of sequence as a concept, see: William E. Coles, Jr., *Teaching Composing* (Rochelle Park, New Jersey: Hayden Book Company, 1974) and William E. Coles, Jr., *The Plural I* (New York: Holt, Rinehart and Winston, 1978). My debt to Bill Coles will be evident everywhere in the paper.

process of systematic inquiry, where the movement from week to week defines stages of understanding as, week by week, students gather new information, attempt new perspectives, re-formulate, re-see, and, in general, develop a command of a subject.

The instruction in writing, which is basically achieved through discussion of mimeographed copies of student papers, directs students in a systematic investigation of how they as individuals write, and of what they and their fellow students have written. The assumption behind such a pedagogy is that growth in writing ability is individual; that is, it will follow its own developmental logic, one that derives from a syllabus "built into" the learner, and such growth takes place not through the acquisition of general rules but through the writer's learning to see his language in relation to the languages around him, and through such perception, to test and experiment with that language. Such a process begins not with the study of Writing in the abstract, but only when a student develops a way of seeing his own writing, and a way of seeing that his writing has meaning beyond its paraphrasable context, that it is evidence of a language and a style.

We set out, then, to construct a pedagogy to develop that analytical reflex that would enable students to see their writing as not only "what they said," but as real and symbolic action: real, as deliberate, strategic, and systematic behavior, not random or outside the realm of choice and decision; and symbolic, as dramatically represented through such terms as "voice" or "writer," "audience," "approach," and "world view."[2] For the basic writer, this might mean the recognition that the errors in his writing fall into patterns, that those patterns have meaning in the context of his own individual struggle with composing, and that they are not, therefore, evidence of confusion or a general lack of competence.[3] This perspective might mean the recognition that one's writing defines a stance in relation to an imagined audience or an imagined subject and that any general improvement would include improved control over that kind of imagining. Or this perspective might bring about the recognition that writing is deliberate and strategic, not random, not something that just happens to a writer. When students are able to see that they have been making decisions and exercising options, other decisions and other options become possible.

---

[2]I am making a distinction here very similar to that in Richard Ohmann, "In Lieu of a New Rhetoric," *College English*, 26 (October, 1964), 17–22.

[3]I am, of course, summarizing one of the key findings of Mina Shaughnessy, *Errors and Expectations* (New York: Oxford University Press, 1977). This paper draws heavily on Shaughnessy's work.

The nominal subject of the course, then, is defined by an issue like "Work and Play," but the real subject is writing, as writing is defined by students in their own terms through a systematic inquiry into their behavior as writers. Behind this pedagogy is the assumption that students must be actively writing and simultaneously engaged in a study of their own writing as evidence of a language and a style, as evidence of real and symbolic action.

Most basic writing programs I observe, and most basic writing texts, are developed as though this were not possible. They begin with the assumption that the writing of basic writers is a "simpler" version of a universal writing process, or that it is evidence of unformed or partially developed language behavior, that the performance of basic writers is random, incoherent, as if basic writers were not deliberately composing utterances but responding, as the dominant metaphor would have it, mechanically and doing so with unreliable machinery. The end product of this reasoning is that basic writers need, finally, to learn basic or constituent skills, skills that somehow come prior to writing itself. Before students can be let loose to write, the argument goes, they need a semester to "work on" sentences or paragraphs, as if writing a sentence in a workbook or paragraph in isolation were somehow equivalent to producing those units in the midst of some extended act of writing, or as if the difficulties of writing sentences or paragraphs are concepts rather than intrinsic to the writer and his struggle to juggle the demands of a language, a rhetoric, and a task. These basic skills are defined in terms of sequences—"words, sentences, paragraphs, essays" or "description, narration, exposition, persuasion"—that, in turn, stand for a pedagogy.

Such a pedagogy meets the immediate needs of teachers who are frustrated by an almost complete inability to understand what could be happening in the heads of students whose writing seems to be so radically different from their own, or from the writing they've learned to read. And it is the convenience of this pedagogy, which frees all parties, teachers and students, from ever having to talk about writing, that leads teachers to hang on to it in the face of evidence that it produces limited returns. The skills curriculum is not founded on any investigation of the language that students produce, nor any systematic investigation into how writing skills are acquired. If there is a syllabus common to such skills courses, it derives its logic and its sequence from the traditional study of the sentence and the paragraph, units the learner is seen as incompetent to produce, rather than from any attempt to imagine a sequence of instruction drawing on the syllabus built into the learner, corresponding to his particular competence and the stage of his development in the acquisition of the formal, written dialect.

The distinction that needs to be made, I think, is the distinction between competence and fluency.[4] Mina Shaughnessy's brilliant study of the writing of basic writers in *Errors and Expectations* shows the fallacy behind the thinking that equates signs with causes, that necessarily assumes a student misspells because he can't spell, leaves endings off verbs because he doesn't know how tenses are formed, or writes a sentence fragment because he doesn't understand the concept of a sentence. Her work defines both the theory and the method of analysis that can enable us to see student error as other than an accident of composing or a failure to learn. In fact, she argues that the predictable patterns of error are, themselves, evidence of students' basic competence, since they show evidence that these writers are generating rules and forming hypotheses in order to make language predictable and manageable.[5] Errors, then, can often be seen as evidence of competence, since they are evidence of deliberate, coherent action. Error can best be understood as marking a stage of growth or as evidence of a lack of fluency with the immensely complicated process of writing, where fluency can be as much a matter of manipulating a pen as it can be of manipulating constituents of syntax.

A pedagogy built upon the concept of fluency allows distinctions analogous to those Frank Smith makes in his analysis of the reading process. A fluent reader, according to Smith, is one who can immediately process large chunks of information, as compared to the reader for whom the process is mediated by mental operations that are inefficient, inappropriate or a stage in some necessary developmental sequence.[6] Basic skills, then, are basic to the individual's ability to process information and can be developed only through practice. The natural process of development can be assisted by pedagogies that complement an individual developmental sequence, and by those that remove barriers, false assumptions, like the assumption that readers read each word, or read sounds, or understand everything at every moment.

BASIC WRITING

Our program begins, then, with the recognition that students, with the exception of a few who are learning disabled or who have literally never been taught to form words, possess the skills that are truly basic to writing.

---

[4]For a discussion of this distinction between fluency and competence, see David Bartholomae, "The Study of Error," *Linguistics, Stylistics and the Teaching of Composition,* Donald McQuade, ed. (Akron, Ohio: Akron University Press, scheduled for publication in November, 1978).

[5]Shaughnessy, *Errors and Expectations,* 104–5, 117–18.

[6]Frank Smith, *Understanding Reading* (New York: Holt, Rinehart and Winston, Inc., 1971).

They have the ability to transcribe speech into writing, and the writing they produce is evidence of the ability to act deliberately in the production of units of discourse to some degree beyond the single sentence. We separate out, as secondary, what can justifiably be called mechanical skills, skills that can be taught as opposed to those that can only be developed.[7] D'Angelo has defined these skills as handwriting, capitalization, punctuation and spelling.[8] Since a knowledge about these is of a different order than linguistic or rhetorical knowledge, they are not the immediate subject of a course in composition. Since, however, errors of capitalization, punctuation, or spelling are not necessarily due to a simple lack of information about capitalization, punctuation, or spelling but must be seen in the context of an individual's confrontation with the process of composing through written language, this is not to say that a concern for those errors is secondary.

A responsible pedagogy, I've been arguing, begins by making the soundest possible speculation about the syllabus built into the learner, rather than imposing upon a learner a sequence serving the convenience of teachers or administrators. We have decided that the key to such a sequence lies in what we might call a characteristic failure of rhetorical imagining, a failure, on the part of basic writers, to imagine themselves as writers writing. Or, to phrase it another way, the key to an effective pedagogy is a sequence of instruction that allows students to experience the possibilities for contextualizing a given writing situation in their own terms, terms that would allow them to initiate and participate in the process by which they and their subject are transformed. This, I take it, is the goal of Friere's pedagogy for non-literate Brazilians, a "problem-posing" education that enables the individual to turn his experience into subject matter and himself into the one who names and, thereby, possesses that subject."[9]

The goal of instruction in basic writing at the University of Pittsburgh is to enable students to locate ways of perceiving and describing themselves as writers. We've chosen to do this by involving them, through class discussion of student papers, in the regular, systematic analysis of what they have written and how they went about writing it. The only text for the course, then, is the students' own writing and if there is a theory of instruction, it is embodied in the kinds of conversations we have in class about that writing.

---

[7] John Warnock, "New Rhetoric and the Grammar of Pedagogy," *Freshman English News*, 5 (Fall, 1976), 12.

[8] Frank J. D'Angelo, "The Search for Intelligible Structure in the Teaching of Composition," *College Composition and Communication*, 27 (May, 1976), 142–147.

[9] Paulo Freire, *Pedagogy of the Oppressed* (New York: The Seabury Press, 1968). See chapter two.

The classes are designed to enable students to develop, for themselves and in their own terms, a vocabulary that will allow them to name and manipulate their own idiosyncratic behavior as writers. The conversations in class, as the class evolves over the term, approach writing in four ways. The approaches, of course, overlap and at times seem identical rather than different, but for convenience's sake let me describe four perspectives we want students to develop on their performance as writers.

The first of these "approaches" asks students to consider writing as an experience by asking them to analyze and describe their experience with our assignments over the course of the semester. If they do nothing else, discussions about how an assignment was done, what it was like and how it felt can enable students to see the ways in which writing is a human activity, one that can be defined in personal terms. For students who see writing as a mystery, or as a privilege of caste, it is liberating to hear others, including instructors, talk about how sloppy the process is, or about ways others have dealt with the anxiety and chaos that so often accompany writing. It's liberating to hear of the habits and rituals of other writers. It's liberating to find out that ideas often start out as intuitions, as a sense of a connection it would be nice to make, and that the ideas only become reasoned and reasonable after repeated acts of writing. It's helpful to discover that other writers get stuck or have trouble starting at all, just as it is helpful to hear about ways others have found of getting past such blocks. And finally, it is always liberating for students to hear that successful and experienced writers produce good sentences and paragraphs only after writing and throwing away a number of lousy sentences and paragraphs. This is not how writing is described in our textbooks, and students, even if they know how to talk about "topic sentences," "development," or "transitions," don't know how to talk about writing in ways that make sense given their own felt experience with the process.

Writing is a solitary activity and writers are limited by the assumptions they carry with them to the act of writing. They are limited, that is, by the limits of their ability to imagine what writing is and how writers behave. The basic writers we see characteristically begin with the assumption that good writers sit down, decide what they want to say and then write straight through from an Introduction to a Conclusion without making any mistakes along the way. So if it is liberating to hear about the struggles and rituals of other writers, the power of such liberation extends beyond the comfort that one is not alone, since the process of identifying a style of composing, and seeing that style in relation to other styles, is the necessary prelude to any testing and experimenting with the process of writing.

In addition, the activity of collecting information from the reports of other students, generalizing from that information, and defining a position in relation to that general statement recapitulates the basic intellectual activity of the course. It is exactly what students are doing as they write papers on "Work and Play."

One way of approaching student writing, then, is to have students, once they have finished an assignment, gather specific information on what was easy and what was hard, what was frustrating and what was satisfying, where they got stuck, what they did to get going again, and so on.

Another way of approaching writing is to have students analyze their performance as a task or a problem-solving procedure.[10] Since writing is, by its nature, a strategic activity, any discussion of strategy in general ought to begin with students' analyses and descriptions of the strategies underlying and perhaps inhibiting their own performance as writers. The point of such discussion is not to give students rules and procedures to follow, recipes for putting a paper together, but to put them in a position to see their own writing as deliberate, strategic activity and to put them in a position to find labels for that phenomenon.

There are any number of ways of initiating such an inquiry. We ask students, once they've finished a series of papers, to go back and find what they see to be their best piece of writing in order to draw some conclusions about where those ideas or where that writing came from. We also ask students to conduct a general survey of how people write. Each student is asked to describe the preparation of a specific assignment as evidence of distinct "stages" in the writing process, and each class develops its own model of the composing process by pulling together the information from the individual accounts and defining categories, or general definitions of stages. This model, and the labels students invent to define it, serves as a point of reference throughout the term. Students may return at a later date to consider their activity in a single stage, like revision or pre-writing, through the same process of analysis. Again, students are gathering information, generalizing and locating themselves in relation to general truths.

Clearly one of the lessons that emerges from this inquiry is that there is no one way of describing writing, since individual composing styles will define points that can't be brought together by a generalization. So if it is true that a writer's performance is limited by his ability to imagine how writers behave, then the process of objectifying a composing style and measuring it against the styles of other writers, and against models for the composing process offered by the instructor, is one way of improving that performance.

---

[10]For a "task analysis" approach to writing see: Susan Miller, *Writing: Process and Product* (Cambridge, Massachusetts: Winthrop Publishers, Inc., 1976). For writing as problem-solving see: Linda Flowers and John R. Hayes, "Problem-Solving Strategies and the Writing Process," *College English*, 39 (December, 1977), 449–462.

There are two occasions when the instructors step in and impose terms on the general inquiry. Early on, if students' own responses don't lead us to it, we make a distinction between generating and editing, since we are anxious to involve students with two different "modes" of writing—one self centered or subject centered and the other audience centered. Writing in the first mode, which can be tentative, exploratory and risk-free, a way of talking to oneself, doesn't ever emerge without extensive prompting.

We also direct students, after the first few weeks, to both write and re-write. And re-writing is defined as separate from editing, which is presented as clean-up work. Re-writing is defined as the opportunity for the discovery of new information and new connections, where the first draft serves as a kind of heuristic. It is also the occasion for consolidating and reshaping the information in the first draft, where the first draft is a rough draft. Every assignment, in fact, falls into a sequence in which papers are re-written at least once. The re-writing is done with very specific directions and the resulting papers are reproduced and considered in the next class discussion. The emphasis on rewriting reflects our own bias about how successful writers write, and about the importance of enabling non-fluent writers to separate the various demands, like generating and editing, that writing makes upon them in order to postpone concentrating on some while focusing on others. In conjunction with this, there is an assignment that asks students to consider successive drafts, both their own and others', in order to draw conclusions about what they see happening, and to come up with advice they could offer to other writers.

The third focus for conversation is the students' writing as evidence of intellectual activity, as a way of knowing. Each focus could be represented by a basic question. The questions for the first two might be something like, "What was writing like?" and "How did you do it?" The question representing this third area of focus would demand a much higher degree of reflexiveness, since it asks students now to see their writing as symbolic action. The appropriate question would be something like, "Who do you become by writing that?" or "What sort of person notices such things and talks about them in just such a way?" Or perhaps the question would be, "Who do I have to become to take this seriously, to see reading this as the occasion for learning and discovery?" The aim of such questions is to enable students to imagine a rhetorical context, another way of seeing "meaning" in their language beyond its paraphrasable content. If writing is a way of knowing, each act of knowing can be represented by dramatizing the relation between writer, subject, and audience. A student's uncertainty about how one establishes authority in a paper, or about what constitutes intelligent observation, can be represented for that student in dramatic terms when, for example, the discussion in class leads to a description of the writer as a parent pounding on the dinner table and giving Lessons on Life to a wayward child.

It's been noted in several contexts that when basic writers move from report to generalization they characteristically turn to formulary expressions, Lessons on Life.[11] In response to students' difficulty in producing meaningful generalizations, much attention is being paid to research in cognitive psychology, presumably in hopes of finding a key to the mechanism that triggers generalization. A response more in keeping with our own training, however, is to acknowledge the motive in such an utterance and to redirect the writer by asking him to re-imagine both his audience and his reason for writing. While it is initially funny for students to realize the role they have cast for me and for themselves in such writing, discovering an alternative is a problem they will wrestle with all semester, since it requires more than just getting things "right" the next time. It means finding a new way of talking that is, at the same time, a new way of representing themselves and the world.

This approach to the relation between the student's language and the conventions of academic discourse is more likely to engage a student's own sense of his knowledge, of the ways in which he can become an intelligent observer and recorder, than any set of lessons on the structure of academic prose, since it is based in a student's own writing and represents that writing as a dramatic act of verbal placement rather than as the mechanical yoking of something called "ideas," on the one hand, and "form," on the other.

There are also more specific ways to account for the difficulty these students have participating in the world of ideas. Surely part of the problem can be seen as external to a student's innate competence as a concept maker, since one universal of basic writing is the students' conviction that while other people's lives provide the stuff out of which concepts are made, this is certainly not true of their own. Basic writers' relations to the world of verbal culture are often defined in such a way as to lead them to conclude that no relation is possible. To use a metaphor offered by one student of mine, ideas may be "stolen" from books or from teachers. It is foolish, then, to assume that they can be "offered" or "shared."

The responsibility of a pedagogy is to enable students to imagine the kind of relation between themselves and their world that allows them to turn their experience into "subject matter" and to define a relationship with that subject that makes creative thinking possible. This is not just a matter of a lesson in class or a pep talk, since whatever we say in class will be understood only in relation to our actual assignments, where we are, in effect, establishing the conditions of such a relationship. Let me describe

---

[11]See, for example: Thomas J. Farrell, "Literacy, the Basics, and all that Jazz," *College English*, 38 (January, 1977), 446–447, and Shaughnessy, *Errors and Expectations*, 230–233.

one response to this problem by describing a sequence of assignments taken from our Basic Reading and Writing course.

The students write a series of papers that describe a change that has occurred in their lives in the last two or three years in order to draw conclusions about how change occurs in adolescence. These papers lead up to a longer autobiographical essay that asks them to draw some conclusions about change in general. At the same time, they are reading autobiographical accounts of children and young adults caught up in change— Margaret Mead in *Blackberry Winter,* Maya Angelou in *I Know Why the Caged Bird Sings,* Holden Caulfield in *Catcher in the Rye* and Huck in *Huckleberry Finn.*[12] The autobiographical essays are reproduced, bound together, and offered to the class as the next text in the series of assigned readings. Students read the autobiographies in order to report, in writing, on what they see to be the significant patterns—common themes and experiences or contradictory themes and experiences—and to provide names or labels for those patterns. They do this in order to go on to speculate, in general, on the ways adolescents change and the kinds of changes that occur. The next set of assignments directs them to the first half of Gail Sheehy's *Passages,* where they see her involved in an identical process of inquiry, report, labeling and speculation. As writers, they are asked to go back to reconsider the autobiographies, this time using Sheehy's labels as well as their own. The last two books for the course are Edgar Friedenberg's *The Vanishing Adolescent* and Margaret Mead's *Coming of Age in Samoa.*

The point of the sequence is to allow students to reconsider the positions they have achieved in their own study of adolescence by defining new positions in relation to the more formal representations of psychologists and anthropologists. But their own attempts to categorize and label provide the source of their understanding of Sheehy, Friedenberg, and Mead. The labels and categories of academic culture are not given prior to the students' attempts to make sense out of the subject in their own terms. As a consequence, the students are allowed not only an aggressive stance in relation to these ideas, but also, and this is the most important point, in relation to the intellectual activity which these ideas represent. Theories, in other words, are seen as things real people make in order to try and make sense out of the world, not as gifts from heaven. These assignments also provide occasion for students to consider the methods they used for going back to a book and rereading in preparation for writing, and to confront, through

---

[12]Our sequence of reading and writing assignments grew out of our reading of James Moffett, *Teaching the Universe of Discourse* (Boston: Houghton Mifflin Company, 1968), especially chapter four.

a consideration of their own papers, the question of presenting information through quotation and paraphrase.

Earlier in this paper I argued that basic writers are limited by the ways they imagine writers behave. It is also true, however, that they are limited by their assumptions about how thinkers behave. When we chart in class, whether through a student paper or some problem-solving exercise, the *ad hoc* heuristics that underlie a student's thinking, the most common heuristic is the heuristic of simplification. Basic writers, because they equate thought with order, profundity with maxims, often look for the means of reducing a subject to its simplest or most obvious terms. Ambiguity, contradiction, uncertainty—those qualities that are most attractive to academics— are simply "wrong" in the minds of students whose primary goal is to produce controlled and safe essays.

As long as writing teachers' instruction represents thinking in terms of structures, and not process, the attitude that courts uncertainty or contradiction is unlikely to develop. Consider, for example, what one formula for paragraphing invites students to do. We tell them to begin by stating an idea, which means they will put down the first thing to come to mind, which, for any of us, is most likely to be a commonplace. Then we tell them to "restrict" that idea and to "support" it with some examples, so that writing "about" the idea precludes any chance to test or probe that idea. If a piece of contradictory evidence worms its way in, or if a student changes his mind half way through, he has, as my students never fail to remind each other, made a "mistake," since the contradictory movement—the one place where something might be said to happen—destroys the "unity" and "coherence" of the paragraph. This image of coherence invites students to be stupid, and that invitation is confirmed whenever we praise an empty paragraph for being well developed.

At the University of Pittsburgh, courses are designed, then, to enable students to see their own writing from various perspectives: as an experience, as a task, as a way of knowing. The last perspective we need to provide for basic writers is a way of analyzing their writing for error. Since our courses are designed to invite students to take risks, to try to do and say things they cannot immediately do and say, we are inviting them to make mistakes. To cover their papers with red circles would be a betrayal of this trust, and yet it would be irresponsible to act as though error didn't matter. Since each set of assignments makes a distinction between first drafts, revisions, and editing, we have the opportunity to provide a context where focus on error can be meaningful, where it can be seen in relation to other ways of talking about writing.

We make no reference to error or to editing at all for the first third of the term. We've found that certain errors will disappear and others will become less frequent as students simply practice writing and become more limber and fluent. In addition, we want to establish firmly a way of talking about and valuing writing as something other than the production of correct sentences, since a recognition of what writing can be and the ways one can be serious about writing can provide the incentive to spend the time it takes to make writing correct.

We introduce editing by tacking a third stage onto writing and re-writing, a time set aside to re-read final drafts in order to circle mistakes and then, if possible, make corrections. We have found, from this, that one of the most difficult tasks we face is teaching students to spot errors in their writing, and this difficulty is not necessarily due to an inability to distinguish between "correct" and "incorrect" forms.[13] Consider, for example, the student who wrote the following:

> This insight explain why adulthood mean that much as it dose to me because I think it alway influence me to change and my outlook on certain thing like my point-of-view I have one day and it might change the next week on the same issue. My exprience took place in my high school and the reason was out side of the school but I will show you the connection. Let me tell you about the situation first of all what happen was that I got suspense from school. For thing that I fell was out of my control sometime but it taught me alot about respondability of a growing man. The school suspense me for being late ten time. I had accumate ten dementic and had to bring my mother to school to talk to a conselor.

When this student read the passage out loud, he automatically filled in the missing words, corrected every incorrect verb by speaking the correct form, and added S's where they were missing from plurals. He also gave the correct phonetic representation of "accumate" (accumulate) and "dementic" (demerit). And he made all these corrections as a reader even though in most cases he could not, at least without a great deal of coaching, see the discrepancy between the words he read and the actual black and white marks on the page. The issue with this student is not so much one of competence but of fluency with the extremely complicated process of transcription.

The fact, then, that students overlook errors while editing is not, necessarily due to carelessness or a lack of understanding of standard forms. In most cases, we've found the difficulty lies in the trouble basic writers have objectifying their language and seeing it as marks on a page rather than perceiving it as the sound of a voice or a train of ideas. Students "see" correct forms when they proofread because they read in terms of their own

---

[13]For a full discussion of this problem and some suggested exercises see: Patricia Laurence, "Error's Endless Train: Why Students Don't Perceive Errors," *Journal of Basic Writing*, 1 (Spring, 1975), 23–43.

grammatical competence. Clearly there is a class of error, most often errors
of syntax, that some students cannot see because they lack some basic conceptual understanding, such as an understanding of the boundaries of the
sentence. But there is another class of error that students have great trouble spotting which makes it impossible to generalize that basic writers fail
to see errors because the errors represent ignorance in the first place.

We teach editing by having students edit their own papers and those of
their colleagues. We also do sentence by sentence editing of papers as a
group, where the students are directed to both look for patterns of error, in
order to draw conclusions about the kinds of errors and sources of errors,
and to speculate in general on editing as a strategy. This allows instructors
the occasion to offer the standard advice about reading out loud and reading from bottom to top. Students do all their editing in red, with errors both
circled and corrected on a separate sheet, so that the instructors can work
with individual students to chart and document the patterns that emerge.
This allows the instructors to identify the students who can manage editing
on their own, or with only a minimum of coaching, and those who will
require close individual supervision in order to cope with both the errors
that they have the resources to correct but cannot find, and those errors
that they cannot find and cannot correct. We have found that no matter
how similar the kinds of errors students make, a diagnosis of those errors
leads us to sources so bound to individual problems and individual styles as
to make general instruction virtually impossible, with the exception of
instruction in a generally unknown piece of punctuation like the semicolon.

By giving students typed copies of their papers to work with, by highlighting groups of three lines and indicating the number of errors these
lines contain, by reading passages out loud and having students read their
writing out loud, we can determine which errors lie beyond a student's
immediate competence, and we have found that we can both increase a student's ability to spot errors and develop those reflexes that allow him to
make decisions about correct forms. It has become commonplace to note
that such decisions can be made independently of "knowledge about" language, without, that is, knowledge of school book grammar. Once students
learn to spot errors on the page, which is a matter of learning to see their
language as a language, a significant percentage of students we work with
have the resources to correct a significant percentage of the errors themselves.[14] We encourage students to trust their own "sense" of correctness
and to test that "sense" against the editing we do as a group. We want to
assist, then, the natural process of testing and rule formation. In individual
sessions with students, we remain as silent as possible, serving primarily to

---

[14]This is an impression. I have no data on this at this time although we have begun
research in this area.

focus their attention on the page. Students chart their own errors looking for patterns and speculating on what the patterns mean in terms of their own specific activity as writers. We insist, however, that students provide their own names for the errors they observe, since it makes no pedagogical sense for them to work from our labels through to the phenomena they observe in their own writing, particularly if the goal of the instruction is to allow students to develop their own resources for correcting.

Finally, however, we are left with a core of students who make a set of errors that they cannot find and do not have the resources to correct. The difficulty here is finding a way to talk with students about their writing, since such talk will inevitably need to revert to grammatical terms and concepts. Here we have reached the point where there is information, "knowing about," students must have. Shaughnessy isolates four key grammatical concepts that teachers and students will need to share for such conversations to be possible: the concept of the sentence, of inflection, of tense, and of agreement.[15] In our Basic Reading and Writing course, the course where problems are such that this kind of instruction is often required, we use a series of sentence-combining exercises that run throughout the semester, so that we have an additional resource for talking to students about constituents of syntax. Our instruction at this level, however, is based almost entirely on the sample exercises in *Errors and Expectations*.

BASIC READING AND WRITING

This 6-hour course was developed in response to a need to provide another mode of instruction for students with skills equivalent to the third, or bottom level of proficiency described by Shaughnessy in *Errors and Expectations*.[16] Students are identified for the course on the basis of a writing sample and the Nelson-Denny Reading Test. Of the group identified for the course, approximately the bottom 5% of the freshman class, the mean vocabulary score on the Nelson-Denny Reading Test was 24.1 (the 8th percentile for grade 13) and the mean comprehension score was 18 (the 35th percentile), with the mean total score failing at the 29th percentile. No one scored above 40 on the vocabulary test or 27 on the test of comprehension, and scores went as low as 10 in vocabulary (with 10% at or below 15 and 24% at or below 20) and as low as 9 in comprehension (with 24% at or below 15).

---

[15]Shaughnessy, *Errors and Expectations*, 128–159. Shaughnessy also makes a basic distinction between grammatically based errors and performance based errors.

[16]Shaughnessy, *Errors and Expectations*, 2. This course was designed with the assistance of Professor Anthony Petrosky, University of Pittsburgh School of Education, and tested in a pilot study in fall term, 1977.

These are students whom we found could read through an essay like those found in freshman readers but who seemed powerless to make any response to the reading. When they were done reading, they literally had nothing to say, and we came to define comprehension for our own purposes as the ability to follow an act of reading with a written response that was pertinent and coherent. We learned from a survey that they were also students, who had, by and large, never read a book. They had crammed for tests from textbooks, and had learned to strip-mine books for term papers, but most of them had never had the experience of working from cover to cover through books of their own choosing, of deciding what to read and paying consistent deliberate attention to a text.

In designing a course, we were seeking, then, to provide for students who were not being served by the existing Basic Writing courses. We decided that these needs would not be best served by an additional semester of writing instruction, since the additional time for writing offered by an extra 15 weeks is really no time at all given the extremely slow growth of writing abilities and the diminishing returns of back to back writing courses, where students are actually denied the opportunity to test new behavior against "real" writing situations or to allow these newly found skills to follow their own developmental sequence. We decided, rather, to argue for more concentrated instruction at the outset, where we could double the amount of writing and the time spent analyzing the activity of writing, and where we could include experience with, and analysis of, acts of reading.

The design of the course, in part, was motivated by my frustration with the existing reading instruction on campus. I had done some work with reading specialists and had grave reservations about the model of reading presented through instruction in reading skills. Such instruction relies primarily on exercises that take the paragraph as the basic unit of a reader's comprehension. In a reading "lab," students read paragraphs in order to answer questions on main ideas, vocabulary and inferences. Whether or not the paragraph is the key unit in reading comprehension, and I doubt it is, comprehending a paragraph isolated in a workbook is so very different from comprehending a paragraph embedded in a whole text, and so very different from comprehending a whole text, as to make it virtually impossible for one to stand for the other. With the workbook approach, students can take a semester of reading instruction without, in effect, ever doing any reading, at least as reading means reading whole texts. And the overriding problem with the concept of a single, identifiable "main idea" that all readers will agree upon is that it denies readers their own transaction with a text, and it denies them the perception that reading is such a transaction, not a series of attempts to guess at meanings that belong to someone else. It does not involve a student in an active process of meaning-making, where meaning is determined by the individual reader, his purpose for reading and prior understanding of the subject. In fact, the exercises used in reading skills instruction are set up as if these variables didn't exist, or as if they were just static, mere annoyances.

We also decided not to model our curriculum· on the study skills approach to reading, which is, more or less, instruction in how to read a text book, and which becomes, given the ethos of such survival courses, instruction in how to avoid reading by learning to read only topic sentences or tables of contents. Our goal was to offer reading as a basic intellectual activity, a way of collecting and shaping information. As such, we were offering reading as an activity similar, if not identical, to writing. The skills we were seeking to develop were not skills intrinsic to "encoding" or "decoding"; that is, they were not basic or constituent skills, like word attack skills, vocabulary skills or the ability to recognize paragraph patterns.

We wanted to design a pedagogy to replace those that define reading as the accurate reception of information fixed in a text, and fixed at the level of the sentence or the paragraph, since that representation of reading reflects our students' mistaken sense of what it means to read. They see the inevitable confusion that comes with working through a whole text, at least one worth reading, as evidence that they have "gotten lost" or "missed something." They are primarily concerned that they can't remember everything they read. This, they feel, is what separates them from "good" readers. In place of this misrepresentation, this inability to imagine themselves as readers reading (for what reader doesn't forget?), we wanted to offer a model that allowed them to postpone their immediate need for certainty in order to read for the larger context that makes individual bits of information meaningful, or worth remembering. We wanted to offer a model of comprehension that allowed students to work with whole texts and to see the ways in which reading requires that they re-assemble a text in their own terms by discovering patterns of significance that are as much statements about themselves as readers as they are statements about a text. This interaction between reader and text is the source of those meanings that transform the paraphrasable content of the text into some other form of meaning.

We were not concerned, then, with decoding, with questions about what a text said, but with what one could say about a text and with what could be said about any individual act of saying. Extended written responses were the only way of representing the kind of comprehension we were interested in teaching, and such written records were the only source of inquiry into the acts of comprehension our students could, at any moment, perform.

We reviewed the recent work in psycholinguistics and reading, work which defines comprehension in terms of the processing of syntax, where general fluency and comprehension can be developed through activities like sentence-combining. Some of the work in this area, like the work by

Stotsky[17] and Sternglass,[18] is quite compelling and may be appropriate for students with problems different in kind from those we confronted in our students. We felt, in designing the course, that our concern should be with acts of comprehension beyond the sentence or the paragraph, and our bias towards larger units of discourse was justified by later findings from the research we did on the course. We administered a series of Cloze tests, which are tests of literal comprehension, of the ability to process syntax and predict meaning, and we found that all of our students, even with the tests at the beginning of the term, scored above the level that indicates adequate literal comprehension of texts whose readability was scaled at grade 13. We concluded that students' low reading speeds, their general failure to comprehend or give adequate response and the general difficulty they had with academic reading tasks must be attributed to something other than difficulty processing syntax.

The writing assignments in the course were developed on the same principles as those for the Basic Writing course described earlier. There were two types of reading assignments, each defining a different context for reading. Students read regularly in class from books of their own choosing.[19] If, as is certainly the case, students learn to read complete texts by reading complete texts, and if our students have little or no experience with this, then a reading class ought to be a place where people read. And ours was—twice a week, for 30 and then 45 minutes we all, students and teachers, sat and read. Our primary goal was to help students develop the discipline and attention it takes to sit down and pay consistent, careful attention to a book. Many of the students in the classes I taught confessed that this experience was entirely new to them. By the amount of reading in these books that went on outside of class, and on the basis of conversations I've had with students since the course, there is reason to believe that some students discovered the habit of reading.

For this in-class reading, students declared an area to read in, something they had always wanted to have the time to pursue, and they went to the library or bookstore and prepared a list of books to read. After each reading session, students wrote in a journal they kept as a record of their

[17]Sandra L. Stotsky, "Sentence-Combining as a Curricular Activity: Its Effect on Written Language Development and Reading Comprehension," *Research in the Teaching of English*, 9 (Spring, 1975), 30–71.

[18]Marilyn S. Sternglass, "Composition Teacher as Reading Teacher," *College Composition and Communication*, 27 (December, 1976). See also, Marilyn S. Sternglass, "Developing Syntactic Fluency in the Reading Process," ERIC.

[19]For a description of "sustained silent reading" see: Charles Cooper and Tony Petrosky, "A Psycholinguistic View of the Fluent Reading Process," *Journal of Reading* (December, 1976).

reading. At first these entries were open. Students were asked to record whatever struck them as important in what they read. As the course developed, we asked for more formal representations of what they had read—summaries, comparisons with earlier reading, or speculation about where the book was going, and so on. We reviewed the journals each week and used them as the basis for conferences on individual problems.

There was also a core of seven assigned texts, all relating to the theme of "Identity and Change" which provided the subject for the course. The books represented a variety of modes—fiction, autobiography and analytical works written for a general academic audience.

We approached the reading in three ways. Initially we asked students to talk about their experience with a particular text and, in response to these discussions, to look for patterns in the experience that their colleagues reported. The primary goal was to define reading as a human activity, one that can be understood in intimate, personal terms rather than in terms of mystery or maxims. By talking about where people got stuck and what they did, about the anxiety and frustration they felt, about what one can expect to remember and what any reader is sure to forget, we could also make specific points about successful reading—about dealing with unfamiliar words, for example, or dealing with the confusion that always comes with the beginning of a book. We were allowing students a way of imagining what reading is like in order to imagine themselves as readers.

We also asked students to analyze reading as a task, as something necessarily embodying a strategy, in order to have them draw conclusions about the strategies underlying and perhaps inhibiting their own behavior as readers, behavior they are quick to believe lies totally outside their control. We approach the analysis of reading strategy in two ways. Strategy is seen as the deliberate approach to a specific text and purpose for reading, so that a student could be prepared to talk, for example, about the best strategy for reading a textbook. But students' reading is also analyzed to reveal those predictable individual responses, strategic but not at the level of deliberate strategy, that characterize an individual's reading style. By enabling students to perceive the decisions they make while reading, we make other decisions possible. This kind of discussion of reading also provides the occasion for instructors to make specific points about pre-reading, re-reading, underlining and so on.

The bulk of the instruction in reading, however, comes with the writing that is assigned in response to the reading, and with the work students do during class in groups to prepare reports on what they've read. With few exceptions, the assignments require students to write about the books before there is any discussion in class. The students use writing, then, to locate a stance in relation to a book and to locate something to say. The discussion in class begins with these individual positions and considers them in relation to the text, to each other, and to the specific task set by the assignment.

The assignments, and they are all variations on a single assignment, define a heuristic for the reading process, a model of how a thoughtful reader responds to a book. We assume that a text becomes meaningful and acquires a structure, or a set of intentions, through a reader's own immediate needs (which includes his imagined purpose for reading) and prior experience with the subject (or what he defines as a "subject"), both of which determine patterns of significance in a text. The process of assigning significance is central to the version of reading we were teaching in our classes, since it is a way of demonstrating how one connects with a book, how a book becomes meaningful through a personal rather than formulaic transaction.

If, after locating patterns of significance, students were to record what they "know" about a book, they would record summaries of sections that stand out for them as somehow important. They would, to use the jargon of tagmemics, have segmented the phenomena into manageable units (and, in analyzing their responses, we found that our students tended to see "particles" and "waves" rather than "fields"), but the representation would still be at the level of narrative. Our goal was to move students from narrative to some position from which they could conceptualize, from which they could see the information or patterns of information they have located as representative, as having meaning beyond any summary or report. In teaching reading, then, we are finally teaching that process of naming, of locating conceptual analogs, of discovering a language that can move the information in the book to the level of dialectic. Teaching reading, then, is teaching invention, that skill we defined as most "basic" to the development of these students as writers.

Because I did research on this part of the curriculum, I have evidence that it was successful, beyond my own and my students' enthusiasm for a course that allows people to read and write rather than be condemned to the drudgery of workbooks or textbooks. The pre- and post-tests of reading comprehension (the Nelson-Denny Reading Test) showed little change. This, however, ran counter to the instructor's impression of what happened to these students as readers. The reason for the lack of statistical evidence of change, we feel, is due to the nature of the available reading tests, tests that ask students to read paragraphs and identify main ideas. It can be argued that tests like these monitor students' ability to take such tests, not their ability as readers, since they don't pose real reading situations and since they are based on such a limited notion of comprehension itself.[20]

---

[20]James Moffett and Betty Jane Wagner, *Student-Centered Language Arts and Reading, K-13* (Boston: Houghton Mifflin, 1976), 123–124.

The pre- and post-tests of writing ability, however, showed very different results. Students taking the six hour course showed significant improvement on a standardized test of writing ability *(STEP)*, a holistic assessment, and the Daly-Miller measure of writing anxiety. In every case, the Basic Reading and Writing students began the semester well behind students in the regular Basic Writing course, and in every case they ended the 15 weeks on almost an exact par with those students at the end of their 15 week course. So if the purpose of the concentrated course was to bring this special group to the level of the general population in a single term, that purpose was achieved.

DIAGNOSIS AND EVALUATION

It's hard to know how to describe the students who take our basic writing courses beyond saying that they are the students who take our courses. Students are screened for basic writing during summer orientation. They write an essay which is holistically scored and take the Nelson-Denny Reading Test (Forms C and D). The mean SAT verbal score for those taking Basic Writing last fall was 429, with scores ranging from 240 to 580. The mean SAT verbal score for those taking Basic Reading and Writing was 362, with scores ranging from 200 to 480.

Those of us working with basic writing programs ought to be concerned about our general inability to talk about basic writing beyond our own institutions, at least as basic writing is a phenomenon rather than a source. We know that we give tests and teach courses and we know that this is done at other schools, but we know little else since there is no generally accepted index for identifying basic writing. Perhaps the only way to compare one's students with those elsewhere, since there is a good reason to be suspicious of SAT scores or error counts or objective tests, is by sharing something like the essays that are used as models to prepare readers for holistic readings. I can briefly describe the writing that characterizes our "range-finders" by pointing to three features we have isolated in a study of orientation essays written by students whose instructors felt they were correctly advised into Basic Writing. The first feature is the type and frequency of error. Since our analysis was based on Mina Shaughnessy's taxonomy of error in *Errors and Expectations*, there is no need to provide any explanation of "type" except to say that it is possible to distinguish between "deep" errors and those that are characteristic of the writing of more fluent students.

The second feature we identified was coherence, coherence as evidence of relatedness between sentences and larger units of discourse, but coherence also as evidence of the ability to define a subject as a problem that can be addressed systematically. While reading the essays, we look for evidence that the writer imagines the act of writing as doing something, no matter how conventional that "something" might be. We identify those students whose papers lack either type of coherence as basic writers.

The third characteristic feature presents the biggest problem to our readers since, at one remove, it seems to be a universal characteristic of student writing. We found, in our analysis of the writing of basic writers, that even when presented with an assignment that specifically called for it, these students were unable to draw general conclusions. If asked to describe a time when they made a decision and to draw some conclusions about decision-making, most writers could report an experience, but few could offer more in the way of a generalization than a single sentence ("Therefore decision making is difficult.") or a collection of maxims ("Experience is the best teacher." "Follow your conscience.").

When we contrasted these essays with those written by writers with higher holistic ratings, we found the successful writers were, in fact, often able to represent themselves as decision-makers as well as someone making a simple decision. They were able to see their experience as representative experience, and to extend the general discussion dialectically, so that they began to manipulate the terms they had used to re-name their experience (terms like "peer pressure," "responsibility," "deduction") in order to represent that experience as something other than what it was for them when they began writing. Where their papers never went beyond narrative, the narrative was shaped so that, in itself, it was clearly making some point that remained unarticulated. The basic writers, on the other hand, produced undifferentiated accounts of experience, in which the representation of the experience could be described as a random recollection of what happened ordered, at best, by chronology. We have many students taking Basic Writing, then, who are not "bound by error," as that phrase is illustrated by the writing of the students Shaughnessy studied.

One of the most difficult questions a program director faces is the question of what, exactly, a passing grade in a writing course represents. The university operates with an Algebra I/Algebra II paradigm—fifteen weeks of Algebra I and a test determine who goes on to Algebra II. Given the very real difficulty of measuring, or even defining, proficiency in writing, and given the irregular pace and nature of growth in writing for any group of students, there is no such thing as knowing exactly what any grade "means" in terms of actual writing ability. At the same time, however, because enrollment in basic writing represents an institution's judgment that the student lacks skills necessary for full participation in the college curriculum, a passing grade in basic writing is expected to stand as certification that such skills have been acquired. The question we faced was how to reasonably determine that a passing grade in Basic Writing did indicate a specified level of proficiency without misrepresenting the limits of our ability to make judgments about writing ability. We finally settled on an end of term review for all Basic Writing students.

At the end of each semester, students in all Basic Writing sections are given two hours to write an in-class essay. The two hours are meant to provide ample time for preparing, revising and editing. Each essay is then evaluated by members of the complete composition staff who make only a pass/fail distinction. A "pass" on the exam means that a student has demonstrated the proficiency assumed of students in the opening weeks of our general composition courses. The models, or "range-finders," we use to prepare readers for the reading were chosen by the staff after considering hundreds of student papers written during a trial examination program.

We also provide both students and instructors, however, with a general set of criteria that are the result of our attempt to summarize features that have distinguished passing from failing essays. In order to pass, students must be able to write a paper that

> —is reasonably error free—"reasonableness" makes allowances for commonly misspelled words, errors with fine points of punctuation or unobtrusive errors of punctuation, errors with "who" and "whom"; "reasonableness," that is, makes allowances for the kinds of errors most of us make and those instructors are generally willing to tolerate in freshman writing,

> —is coherent—which means that what is said can be understood and understood as an attempt to address the assigned problem systematically,

> —shows the ability to state general principles on the basis of specific evidence, and to develop a general discussion beyond a single sentence.

A failing score on the essay does *not* mean that a student fails the course. Holistic scoring, particularly of essays written under such artificial conditions, is simply not reliable enough to allow us to make that kind of decision. When a student fails the essay review, a folder containing all his work for the term is reviewed by a committee of three staff members. If the work done in the last quarter of the term confirms the judgment made by the readers, the student is not given credit for the course. At the end of a semester of Basic Reading and Writing, on the other hand, students are either passed on to Basic Writing or passed into the general curriculum without restriction.

QUESTIONS FOR REFLECTION, JOURNAL WRITING, AND DISCUSSION

1. Bartholomae says that a student's inability to write is sometimes a "failure to imagine" oneself as a writer. In what ways have you felt that your own difficulties with writing have been a "failure of imagination"? Was there a case where you overcame that failure?

2. Do you agree with Bartholomae that "growth in writing is individual" and that it "derives from a syllabus 'built into' the learner"? What are the implications of this for teaching?

3. Bartholomae says "ambiguity, contradiction, uncertainty—those qualities that are most attractive to academics—are simply 'wrong' in the minds of students whose primary goal is to produce controlled and safe essays." Why might students prefer to produce "controlled and safe essays"? Would Bartholomae's pedagogy help students or lead them astray?

4. Bartholomae claims that "comprehending a paragraph isolated in a workbook is very different from comprehending a whole text, as to make it virtually impossible for one to stand for the other." Yet many teachers use a "workbook" approach to teaching writing or reading skills. Did you ever use workbooks? What do you think of a "workbook" approach to teaching reading or writing skills?

5. Compare how Rose and Bartholomae structure their courses. Which way would you prefer?

Chapter 3

The First Day of Class: Passing the Test

Ira Shor

Ira Shor is a professor in the City University of New York's Graduate School, where he originated the doctorate in composition/rhetoric in 1993. He also serves on the English faculty at the College of Staten Island, CUNY. His nine books include a recent three-volume set in honor of the late Paulo Freire, the noted Brazilian educator who was his friend and mentor, *Critical Literacy in Action* (for college language arts) and *Education Is Politics* (Vol. 1, K–12, and Vol. 2, Postsecondary Education Across the Curriculum). Shor also authored *Empowering Education* (1992) and *When Students Have Power* (1996), two foundational texts in critical teaching. Shor came out of the public schools of New York City, where he grew up in the Jewish working class neighborhood of the South Bronx, went to the Bronx High School of Science, and then to the University of Michigan and University of Wisconsin. The following selection is from *Empowering Education: Critical Teaching for Social Change* (University of Chicago Press, 1992).

Like many kids, I loved learning but not schooling. I especially dreaded the first day of class. I would wake up early, jump nervously out of bed, and run to open the window. From my fifth-floor apartment in the South Bronx, where I grew up, I would lean out and see my old public school across Bruckner Boulevard, a street busy with a stream of traffic on the way to Manhattan. Sometimes, if I was lucky, a big gray fog bank rolled in from the Long Island Sound, covered the weedy flats behind the school where Gypsies camped and veterans once lived in Quonset huts, and swallowed P.S. 93. My dreams were answered. Miraculously, the school had disappeared.

Years later, as a college teacher, I was walking to the first day of my basic writing class. I had a black book bag on my shoulder, a lesson plan in hand, and butterflies in my stomach.

I entered B building on our concrete campus and climbed the stairs, passing students smoking and talking loudly to each other. My writing class was in room 321, a place I knew well, with its gray tile floor, cinder-block walls, dirty venetian blinds, fiber glass chairs and cold fluorescent lights. Since I began teaching English at this low-budget public college in New York City in 1971, I had spent a few semesters in the long, narrow rooms of B building.

On this first day, I wondered what would happen in class. I always bring a plan and know what I want to do, but what would the students do? I had been experimenting for some time with "student-centered teaching," hoping to engage students in critical learning and to include them in making the syllabus. But they came to class wary and uninspired, expecting the teacher to tell them what to do and to lecture them on what things mean. I knew their intelligence was strong, but could I convince them to use their brains in school?

My confidence was shaken a little that first day when I reached the open door of B-321 and heard not a sound. Was this the right classroom? Had my room been changed at the last minute?

I took a step forward, peeked in the doorway, and saw twenty-four students sitting dead silent in two long rows of fiberglass chairs. They were staring straight ahead at the front desk. They were waiting for the teacher to arrive and do education to them, I thought to myself—one more talking head who would shellack them with grammar and knowledge.

Just then, as I stood in the doorway, all eyes turned in my direction. There were many eyes, but no smiles. New York, my home town, is famous for its tough faces, but these were some of the toughest I had ever seen on students. The class was made up mostly of young white men from Brooklyn, with some women and a few minority students. I looked away from their eyes, quietly took a breath, and strode to the desk, where I put down my shoulder bag and said, "Hello! Welcome to English One. My name is Ira Shor. Why don't we put the chairs in a discussion circle, to make it easier to talk to each other?"

No one moved. I wondered if I should give up on the circle. But maybe it was too soon to retreat. So I stepped forward and asked them once more to form a circle, but deep in my heart I asked myself if it was time to change careers. Should I go sell computers in the suburbs?

The students waited for me to make my move. I reached for one empty chair and turned it around, to confirm my resolve. Then I stood close to some students in the front row and gestured to help them turn their seats. Grudgingly, one, and then another, inched their chairs around into a loose circle, actually more like a wandering amoeba than a circle. The sound of the chairs banging and scraping was a relief from the silence.

I sat down in the circle. I said hello again and asked them to spend a few minutes interviewing each other and then to tell us something about their partners, so that we could get to know who was in the room. This was supposed to be an icebreaker. But some ice can survive August in New York. Their aggressive silence once again greeted my request, so I began pointing out partners for people to work with and nudged them to begin. A few did start talking in pairs, and then a few more, but their conversations crawled, then died.

I was getting impatient, which felt better than anxiety, and I decided to run at the problem instead of away from it. I followed an intuition to make their resistance itself the theme we talked about. I had been developing "critical teaching" and "dialogic pedagogy" that posed problems from student experience for class inquiry. I thought to pose the problem of their silence. Why not have a dialogue about the absence of dialogue? Would they be willing to communicate with me about why they weren't communicating? Who knew? Anyway, I was getting nowhere fast. Confronting their resistance to dialogue might warm up a discussion about our icy situation.

I took a small risk and asked them about their silence, saying something like this: "What's going on here? I walk in and nobody wants to move a chair or talk or relate to me. What's the story? You don't even know me. At least get to know me before you decide you don't want to talk. Maybe I'll do a lot of things to make you angry, maybe I won't. Now, who'll tell me why you're sitting so silent?"

After a moment that felt like an hour, one of the bigger guys in class suddenly spoke. His voice was loud and direct. I was so startled to hear even a word that I didn't catch what he said. "What was that?" I asked. He replied, simply, "We hate that test."

"What test?" I asked.

"That writing test," he answered.

"The one you took for the college?"

"Yeah."

"What's wrong with the test?" I asked him.

He looked me dead in the eye and answered, "It ain't fair." I glanced away and saw a few heads nodding in agreement, so I put the question to the class, "Is anyone else angry about the writing test?" Hands shot up around the room.

I should say here that soon after tuition was forced on the City University of New York for the first time in 129 years, in the fiscal crisis of 1976, standardized examinations in writing, reading and math were also imposed. Since then, these examinations have been given to entering freshmen, producing an enormous amount of failure and frustration as well as a record-keeping nightmare and an expanding empire of remedial classes. More students have had to spend more time and tuition dollars in low-credit remediation, which delays their accumulation of course credits toward a degree. In a few years, the single remedial course in my English department of 1971 had grown to ten separate courses and a college testing program.

After a number of hands shot up in class when I asked if anyone else was angry at the writing test that had landed them in this basic writing course, I asked, "What's wrong with the test? Why is it unfair?"

To my amazement, this silent group began an avalanche of remarks. The students found their voices, enough to carry us through a ferocious hour, once I found a "generative" theme, an issue generated from the problems of their own experience. When I first said hello to them, no one wanted to speak. Now they all wanted to speak it once. My teaching problem shifted from no participation to wrestling with a runaway discussion. They began complaining in outbursts that confirmed each other's feelings. They interrupted each other. They spontaneously broke off into small groups that talked to themselves. It was dizzying until I managed to assert some order. What emerged was a collective sense that the imposed writing exam and this remedial class were unfair punishments.

To give some structure and depth to this perception, I asked them to write for a while, explaining why they thought the requirement was unfair and what should be done about it. I said something like this: "I agree with you that the exam is unfair. I also oppose it. But it's not enough to yell and complain. You have to take your ideas seriously, explain how you see the situation, and come up with an alternative you think makes more sense." I suggested they each write two pages or so about the writing exam. To my great relief, they agreed. For the next twenty minutes, the room was quiet and busy.

When they had finished rough drafts, I asked them to practice writing exercises I'd be asking them to do during the term, exercises which I will explain in a later chapter on the structure of "problem-posing dialogue." Basically, I said that they had powerful voices, as anyone could tell from the talk that had raged around the room a few minutes earlier. They had much to say, displayed broad vocabularies, and spoke fairly grammatically. I encouraged them to use the already existing good grammar in their speaking voices to help improve their less-developed writing hands. In this "voicing" exercise they read aloud their compositions singly or in pairs. By reading aloud slowly and carefully, they can become better editors of their written work, noticing and correcting the small errors usually left for the teacher to find. After voicing, I asked them to read their drafts in groups of three, to discuss the ideas, compare their criticisms, and choose one essay to read to the whole class for discussion. When they chose the material for class discussion, they were codeveloping the curriculum with me, a key idea for critical and democratic teaching, which I will be focusing on in this book. Students formed small groups and spent some time discussing their positions. The first session ended about then, and we picked up the project the next time the class met.

In the ensuing classes, I took notes as the students read their selected essays. Using my notes, I re-presented to them some of the key issues, so that they could reflect on their thoughts, which is one way to develop a critical habit of mind. As it turned out, that basic class evolved an alternative policy for the writing exam which they thought was more sensible and equitable. First, they disagreed with the fifty-minute time limit. They said that students should have as long as they needed to write the best essay they could. This sounded reasonable to me. The fifty-minute limit is a bureaucratic convenience to control costs by fitting the test into a single class hour. If the time was open-ended, special proctors would have to be hired to monitor the students. The time limit, then, benefits the institution, not the students. A developmental writing process requires time to think over the issues, discuss them with other people, write notes and rough drafts, share them with peers, get feedback, do relevant reading, and make revisions. The administrative time limit blocks this process. Further, the students thought that they should not have required topics. In their opinion, they wrote at their best not only when they had as much time as they needed but also when they wrote about what they knew and liked. Sitting down to write about themes out of the blue, like "Does TV make children violent?" may make it harder for them to write at their best. They proposed that the two prompts on the writing exam should be kept for those students who wanted to use them, but the others should be free to pick their own themes. Put simply, the prompt questions on the exam are often experienced by them as issues without a context. Lastly, they wanted the exam given at a different point in their academic lives. Many had taken it in the spring or summer of their senior year in high school when "senioritis" had set in, jeopardizing the seriousness with which they do academic work. They thought the exam should be given in the fall of their senior year, while they were still focused on their school work.

Their policy proposals for the writing exam made sense to me. This basic skills class of twenty-four students had been unable to pass an apparently simple writing exam, but they were able in a student-centered classroom to critique the policy and come up with alternatives. The exercise was not only centered in their thoughts, language, and conditions, but it also focused their critical intelligence on an issue they had not thought about in depth before. Though they had bad feelings about the test and the remedial class, they had not reflected on the situation. They had simply acted out their bad feelings by refusing to participate in class. By reflecting critically on the problem, they went beyond mere opinions or bad feelings.

But some things did not work out well. For one thing, in this class, student-centered teaching sometimes left me overtaken by events, trying to catch up with student expression. When students codevelop themes for study and share in the making of the syllabus, the class dialogue sometimes moves faster than I can understand it or organize it for academic study. Finding a generative theme, that is, a theme generated from student conditions which is problematic enough to inspire students to do intellectual work, can produce a wealth of student expression. I listen carefully in class to students so that I can develop critical study based in their thoughts, but I often need to go home to mull over what they said and to figure out what to do next. For example, in the exercise over the required writing examination, I would have liked a slower pace to give me time to find material on its history and to bring in articles and documents for the students to discuss. This would add outside texts to the critical dialogue in class, so that the students' essays would not be the only reading matter we examined. When projects emerge in-progress from student themes, the opportunity to deepen academic inquiry about them is often limited by the pace of student-centered dialogue. I kept this in mind for the next round of projects we undertook in this class, to make sure that reading matter would be built into the work.

A second problem was the small participation of the few minority students in class. I encouraged them to speak, met with them after class, and kept in touch with their work. They did their assignments but were reluctant to speak in class. As I will discuss later, this reluctance is understandable on a campus and in classes that are predominantly white and in an area where race relations are tense.

A third problem emerging from this project on the writing examination is that understanding reality is not the same thing as changing it. Knowledge is not exactly power. Knowledge is the power to know, to understand, but not necessarily the power to do or to change. The learning process we shared helped reduce the students' alienation from intellectual work. They gained an empowering relationship to the teacher, to writing, and to the act of studying. But while their writing and thinking developed, the testing policy remained the same. Literacy and awareness by themselves do not change oppressive conditions in school and society. Knowledge is power only for those who can use it to change their conditions,

To face this problem, I invited the class to consider acting on their new knowledge, perhaps to change their oppressive reality while also developing their thinking and writing. If they thought their policy proposals made more sense than the existing ones, why not publish them in the school newspaper, take them to the student government for support, and campaign for them among faculty and other students who might agree with them? I suggested that there were outside arenas where their proposals might have an impact.

A few mulled over my suggestion, but the group as a whole was unenthusiastic about becoming activist. They had never done anything like that before and were not yet ready to try it. In my heart and thoughts, I was a little disappointed but not surprised, given the conservative climate in the country, on our campus, and in their community. So I dropped my proposal, but I did mention that I would talk about their policies whenever I could in faculty meetings, because they were good ones.

For the rest of the term, that class took on ambitious projects. They formed project groups on such self-selected issues as abortion, child abuse, unemployment, education, women's equality, and drugs. Students chose which committee to join. I asked each group to do research and bring to class something for us to read on their theme, to make sure that this next round of projects would integrate outside texts into the discussion. I also brought in reading matter relevant to each of the themes. The groups did research, organized their work during class time and also outside, and then took over a class session. I had wanted them to chair the sessions, to develop their authority and leadership skills, but they were shy and inexperienced in running the class, so I had to sit with each committee and act as chair. During their sessions, the committees offered their readings for discussion, then posed a problem for the whole class to write on for twenty minutes, after which we did some literacy exercises and then had discussion. The committees took home the student papers after class, to read, respond to, and return next time. This way, they became readers and evaluators of each other's work. I read their papers as well, asked for some to be revised at home, and offered exercises when I noticed recurring writing problems in their essays.

I also led discussions on themes and readings of my own choosing. One topic was particularly challenging. I wondered if this basic writing class would participate in the nuclear arms debate then under way in many places but not visible at my college or in their communities. Around the world, many people were alarmed at the spread of nuclear weapons and at the vast sums spent on militarism. To raise this social concern with my students, I read with them various materials, including an excerpt from Thompson and Smith's *Protest and Survive* (1981), about the "destructivist" consciousness spreading as nuclear weapons became a way of life. They struggled with the conceptual frameworks, evaluating their own positions in terms of being destructivist or activist. In general, I was gratified by the seriousness with which they took on this difficult issue. My suggesting an outside social theme like the arms race did not silence the students. I did not lecture them on my point of view but followed the discussion format of their own project groups. During these weeks, one young veteran in class decided to write a critical narrative of his military service, which he had not examined before. He shared a strong essay with the class, which I later published in a professional volume of student writing.

Overall, the class developed an emotional tone which made it attractive. We laughed. We spoke about our differences. The students got down to work in class and organized trips to the beach after class. Attendance was high. I brought a colleague or two to sit in and enjoyed seeing the students emerge as distinct personalities as well as writers and thinkers. There were some memorable moments, too. When the women's group led class, several of the men said that women couldn't do men's work. One tall, muscular guy was especially angry at the city for lowering the physical strength standards for firefighters so that females could qualify. Some male students made the case that women were too weak and unmechanical to do the work of real men, like construction, truck driving, and so on. At that point, Marie, about twenty-two, turned to the men and announced that she was an auto mechanic. For weeks she had kept this to herself. She did not look like the men's idea of a mechanic, but she spoke with confidence when she said that she could tune a car better than any of the guys in the room and was ready to prove it. We looked at her in awed silence. None of the men took up her challenge. Marie's intervention was a real-life rebuttal to the men's sexist prejudice, coming at just the right time. It reminded me that the students are complicated people whose authentic personalities can emerge in the context of meaningful work.

Later on, Marie's authenticity left me in awed silence again. During the abortion committee session, one question was "What would you do if your teenage daughter came home one day and announced she was pregnant?" Students debated various answers. When I turned to a silent Marie and asked her opinion, she said without hesitation, "I'd break both her legs." The class roared with laughter at her matter-of-fact response. I was left speechless by her casual brutality, because I thought of her as a natural feminist who would have an enlightened opinion on teenage pregnancy. Instead, she stood by her position that her daughter would have two broken legs to go along with being pregnant. This reminded me again not to take students for granted. I learn a lot about them, but they are always capable of surprising me with something new. I was stumped by Marie's answer. Not knowing how to respond, I re-presented it to the class and was relieved that few people agreed with this mechanic's solution.

By the end of the term, six of the original twenty-four had dropped out of the class, and I was sorry to see them go. I had a chance to consult with some of them and got a feel for why they left. One student had no front teeth and was ashamed to talk in class. I told him he didn't have to, that he could talk to me in private until he felt ready to speak publicly. But then I discovered that he didn't want to write in class or out, because he was a poor writer. I worked tutorially with him, but he missed appointments and didn't hand in assignments. Apparently he had gotten through high school with very little expected of him, and now was unable to face a serious class. A couple of other students also dropped out when I expected them to rewrite poorly written work.

Eventually, sixteen of the eighteen remaining students passed the writing exam when they took it again at the end of the term. The two who failed made another try a week later. One was Tommy, a bright young guy who handed in work late all term. He was behind in his assignments but produced passing material when I pushed him to get the writing done. On the writing exam in class, he froze and handed in a blank booklet, something I had never expected. Afterwards, to prepare for the exam again, I counseled him on ways to get started when he felt a block. But he failed the test once more, didn't hand in all his missing course work, got an *F* for my class, and took a second-term basic skills class. After that, he finally passed the writing exam and went on to get a *B* in freshman composition.

The other student who failed the exam at the end of my course was Marie, the mechanic. I tutored her, too, before her next try at it. When we finished discussing her failed text paper, she stood up, shook my hand, and said, "Mr. Shor, I ain't gonna write no more comma splices." She then took the exam once more and failed yet again. Apparently resourceful, Marie managed to bypass the exam and another term of basic skills. Instead of prolonged life in the remedial empire, she found her way directly into freshman composition and got an *A*. The next term she took creative writing and got a *B*, all without having passed the entry exam in writing. Good for her. But I still wonder if she will break her future daughter's legs and if she was influenced by our discussion of militarism.

Because most students got through an exam that frustrated their progress in college, the overall results were acceptable to me, but I think many of them could have passed the first time if the text had been structured the way they wanted and if their education had helped them perform at their peak abilities. They also could have gone directly on to freshman composition and, like Marie, passed without the obstacle of remediation. Something is very wrong with their education when it suppresses instead of develops their skills and intellectual interests. They need a different kind of learning, critical and democratic, the kind that will be discussed in this book.

Some classes turn out well enough, like the basic writing group I've discussed here. Others don't. Some groups of students resist all term. They remain too unhappy with education or too distracted by jobs, commuting, other courses, money problems, family life, or relationships to focus on learning.

Over the years, the classes that resist and those that open up have kept me asking what kind of learning process can empower students to perform at their best. Many teachers want a learning community in class that inspires students whose creative and critical powers are largely untouched. A democratic society needs the creativity and intelligence of its people. The students need a challenging education of high quality that empowers them as thinkers, communicators, and citizens. Conditions in school and society now limit their development. Why? How can that be changed? What helps students become critical thinkers and strong users of language? What education can develop them as active students and as citizens concerned with public life? How can I promote critical and democratic development among students who have learned to expect little from intellectual work and from politics? These are the questions underlying this book.

QUESTIONS FOR REFLECTION,
JOURNAL WRITING, AND DISCUSSION

1. Shor begins his essay, "Like many kids, I loved learning but not schooling." Is this how you felt as a kid?

2. Define "student-centered" and "teacher-centered" pedagogies as you know them. What are advantages and disadvantages of each approach?

3. Do students usually wait for teachers to "do education to them"? Why would they do this?

4. Why did Shor's students hate the writing test? Do you agree with their complaints and suggestions for improvement? How do your students feel about the tests that they have to take?

5. How did Shor's student Marie manage to get an *A* in freshman composition and a *B* in creative writing without passing the remedial English test? What does this suggest about the test?

Chapter 4

Collaboration, Conversation, and Reacculturation

Ken Bruffee

Kenneth A. Bruffee is Professor of English and Director of the Scholars Program and the Honors Academy at Brooklyn College, City University of New York. He has been a member of the editorial advisory board of *Liberal Education,* and he was the first Chair of the Modern Language Association Teaching of Writing Division and the founding editor of *WPA, the Journal of the National Council of Writing Program Administrators.* His publications include *Collaborative Learning: Higher Education, Interdependence and the Authority of Knowledge* (The Johns Hopkins University Press, 2nd ed. 1999); *A Short Course in Writing* (Longman, 4th ed., 1992); *Elegiac Romance: Cultural Change and Loss of the Hero in Modern Fiction* (Cornell University Press, 1983); and a series of articles in *Liberal Education, College English,* and *Change* on collaborative learning, liberal education, and the authority of knowledge. The following selection is from *Collaborative Learning.*

Once upon a time, many years ago, a time when the youngest faculty member at most colleges and universities today had not yet entered puberty, a young assistant professor at one of those colleges was assigned a task that was in those days de rigueur for low level English Department types. He was asked to become Director of Freshman English. Feeling flattered, having a modicum of interest in teaching writing, but lacking even the most rudimentary sense of caution, and in any case not having a great deal of choice in the matter, he agreed. The year was 1971. The college was Brooklyn College. The young assistant professor was me. And at the City University of New York, of which Brooklyn College is a constituent campus, 1970 turned out to be the first year of open admissions.

In open admissions, some 20,000 new students, many of them lacking the basic skills of reading, writing and mathematics needed for college work, entered the City University of New York. These new students challenged the university's faculty in ways that often far exceeded the experience, training, and expectations of scholars and scientists bred in the quiet intensity of library carrels and research labs. To most of us it felt like a rout.

My job as the new Freshman Comp Director was to organize, more or less from scratch, a program of courses in writing at all levels, remedial to advanced, that would meet the needs of those new students, teach freshman composition and a literature survey course, teach my English Department colleagues how to teach remedial writing and freshman composition to the college's new unprepared students, and manage upwards of 108 composition instructors teaching some 160-odd sections each term.

I don't mind admitting I was soon desperate. I thought wistfully about that manuscript sitting half-finished on a shelf in my study, a truly splendid book of literary criticism about the great monuments of modern fiction, and my pellucid lecture notes on Wordsworth and the English Romantics yellowing away in a drawer, unthumbed, unreferred to, unapplauded.

In my state of confusion and despair, it occurred to me that there must be other people in my shoes on other City University campuses—CCNY, Hunter, Queens, somewhere. Surely they must be coping better than I. I had never heard of any of them, and they had never heard of me. But surely someone in this anonymous crowd would help me understand and accomplish the seemingly impossible task I had committed myself to. I called them up. They all claimed that they too were desperate. Warily, we agreed to get together for a beer.

They did help me, as it turned out, but not quite the way I had expected. I thought I would ask some questions and they would provide the answers. But it wasn't long before we were all startled to discover not just that none of us had any answers, but that none of us even knew the right questions.

It bears witness to our collective state of mind that we found this appalling discovery refreshing and provocative. The tedium of petty college and university administration had unaccountably coughed up an intellectual challenge. We decided to meet again and talk some more. We began converging Saturday mornings on a mutually convenient Manhattan coffee shop. We also met several times at a wonderful soup shop that had just opened on Fifth Avenue called La Potagerie. We had a pretty good time. To focus our discussions in the midst of all this medium-high living, we decided to give ourselves some reading assignments. We chose several books and articles that one or another of us had run across in some context or other and that seemed to offer some help in looking at the needs of our students, if possible in a larger than merely academic context.

Working together in this way, we gradually began to make some striking discoveries about our students, ourselves, and our profession. In fact, what we found out about our students was not unlike what we found out about ourselves and our profession.

One of the first things we read together was Sennett and Cobb's *The Hidden Injuries of Class,* a book that talks about families of blue-collar workers living in and around Boston. These families had a lot in common with the family I had grown up in and, as we eventually learned from one another, with the family life many of us in the group had experienced. They also had a good deal in common with the families of the students we were now teaching. One of the first and most important things that Sennett and Cobb suggested to us was that teaching writing to open admissions students might raise issues that were more profound than simply how to "correct errors." Teaching writing might in fact involve an issue that seemed altogether beyond our professional training and expertise to understand: acculturation.

It began to dawn on us, in short, as we read and talked about what we read, that our students, however poorly prepared academically, did not come to us as blank slates. They arrived in our classes already deeply acculturated, already full-fledged, competent members (as we were, too) of some community or other. In fact, they were already members of several interrelated communities (as we were, too).

If that was the case, we concluded, then in the first instance the way our students talked and wrote, and even the way they behaved in class, did not involve "errors" at all. They talked, wrote, and behaved in a manner that was perfectly correct and acceptable within the community they were currently members of. The way they talked, wrote, and behaved was "incorrect" and unacceptable, we found ourselves saying, only in a community that they were not—or were not yet—members of. The community that the students were not yet members of and were asking to join by virtue of committing themselves to attend college was of course the (to them) alien community of the "literate" and the "college educated." In a word, us.

Beginning to describe our students in this new way, we also began to talk about our job as their teachers in a new way, a way that differed strikingly from the way we were in the habit of talking about college and university teaching. If how our students talked, wrote, and behaved was not in the first instance a matter of "error," we began to say, then perhaps our job as teachers was not in the first instance to "correct" them. We recognized, of course, that what the community of the "literate" and the "liberally educated" regarded as correct and incorrect talk, writing, and behavior remained an issue. But what we were now saying was that in the first instance our job as teachers was to find ways to begin and to sustain a much more difficult, painful, and problematical process than "correcting errors" in our students' talk, writing, and behavior. Our job as teachers, we were saying, was to find out how, in some way and in some measure, to reacculturate the students who had placed themselves in our charge.

The way my colleagues and I were beginning to talk about college and university education was not only new to us, it was entirely different from the way our disciplinary colleagues on our home campuses still talked about it. Increasingly, we found, they failed to understand what we were saying. As a result, we felt less and less comfortable with those at home and abroad to whose professional company, values, and goals we had committed ourselves as graduate students. It seemed like a pretty risky situation to most of us, and would have seemed even riskier except for our realization that we were feeling more and more comfortable with one another. In short, we began to be aware that the change in the way we talked about what we were doing signaled a cultural change in ourselves, about which we were deeply ambivalent.

In fact, I would say now, the change in the way we talked about college and university education was more than a signal of change. Change in the way we talked was the cultural change itself that we were undergoing. The language we had begun to use literally constituted the small transition community of which we were now increasingly devoted members. Learning, as we were experiencing it, was not just inextricably related to that new social relationship among us. It was identical with it and inseparable from it. To paraphrase Richard Rorty's account of learning, it was not a shift inside us that now suited us to enter new relationships with reality and with other people. Learning *was* that shift in our language-constituted relations with others.

To further this process of cultural change we were experiencing, another text we assigned ourselves was Paulo Freire's *Pedagogy of the Oppressed*. This book is about teaching reading and writing to the illiterate poor in Brazil, and it has an unmistakably Marxist slant. Now, I don't think anyone in our group would have called us Marxists. Observing us lunching on parmentier and Perrier water at La Potagerie, no outsider would be ineluctably driven to this conclusion. For the most part we shared a bias that was fairly typical of the early-nineteen seventies academics that we were: a bias that was mostly white, mostly male, and solidly American middle-class.

Despite that bias, however, we were fully aware that there was a sense in which many of our students were forced to pursue postsecondary education, largely through economic pressure, by a society that paid workers better who were literate in the standard dialect of English than those who were not literate in it. A job at the telephone company turned up as a point of reference, and a high proportion of those who even today fail the New York Telephone Company employee entrance exams suggests that that was not a wholly unrealistic criterion. And one thing we learned from Freire was that our middle-class American goal of establishing literacy in the standard dialect was shared by at least one person whose basic political assumptions differed quite a bit from our own.

Stirred by these concerns, our discussion of Freire began by addressing the troubling key word in his title, the term "oppressed." I think we all found it somewhat melodramatic as applied to open-admissions students. But we had to admit also, without casting aspersions as to the source of that condition, that to say that our students existed in a state of "oppression" was not entirely inappropriate. Sennett and Cobb had taught us that our students had been acculturated to talk to and deal effectively only with people in their own crowd, their own neighborhood, perhaps only in their own family or ethnic group.

Their worlds were closed by walls of words. To be acculturated to those perfectly valid and coherent but entirely local communities alone had severely limited their freedom. It had prepared them for social, political, and economic relations of only the narrowest sort. It had closed them out of relations with other communities, including the broader, highly diverse, integrated American (or for that matter, international) community at large represented in a perhaps minor but (from their point of view) not insignificant way by a job at the New York Telephone Company.

One result of this exclusively local acculturation appeared to be that many of our students could not discover their own buried potential and could not achieve the more economically viable and vocationally satisfying lives they aspired to. We suspected (given our middle-class, professional, liberal-humanistic bias) that our students' acculturation also prevented them from living lives that were intellectually, emotionally, and aesthetically fulfilling. We realized furthermore that this was not exclusively an "open admissions" problem. Parochialism of undergraduate experience and thought is a problem that, on William Perry's testimony, is not unknown even among undergraduates at Harvard College.

So, although we knew that what Freire meant by the key word in his title, "oppressed," was not exactly what we meant by it, to the extent that our more liberal sense of the word did correspond with Freire's intent, it led us in a useful direction. In order to make any positive impression at all on the students we were encountering in our classes, it was clear that we too needed a pedagogy of the "oppressed," even in our more pallid sense of it.

The pedagogy that Freire offered turned out, furthermore, to be something we had come across before in our reading and would come across again, used to accomplish a similar end. The feminist movement of the sixties and seventies, for example, had used this pedagogy to help women change their attitudes toward themselves and to reconstruct their role in society. Kurt Lewin had used it to help people accept dietary changes caused by food scarcities during World War II and to liberate children and adolescents who had been raised as Hitler Youth. A pedagogy that could relieve or overcome "oppression" in many relevant senses, we began to see, would inevitably be a pedagogy of reacculturation: a pedagogy of cultural change.

Freire, in fact, went well beyond leading us toward considering the possibility that a pedagogy of reacculturation could meet our needs. He and others also told us something about what a pedagogy of reacculturation might be, and how it might work. We learned first that reacculturation is at best extremely difficult to accomplish. It is probably next to impossible to accomplish individually, reacculturation fantasies such as *The Taming of the Shrew* and *Pygmalion* notwithstanding.

What does seem just possible to accomplish is for people to reacculturate themselves by working together. That is, there does exist a way in which we seem able to sever, weaken, or renegotiate our ties to one or more of the communities we belong to and at the same time gain membership in another community. We can do that if, and it seems in most cases only if, we work collaboratively. What we have to do, it appears, is to organize or join a temporary transition or support group on the way to our goal, as we undergo the trials of changing allegiance from one community to another.

The agenda of this transition group is to provide an arena for conversation and to sustain us while we learn the language, mores, and values of the community we are trying to join. Transition groups provide us with understanding peers whom we can rely on as we go through the risky process of becoming new members of the knowledge communities we are trying to join. Students can achieve together in transition communities what John Dewey calls the ideal aim of education: the "power of self-control" as they develop the ability and confidence to exercise the craft of interdependence.[1]

First, students learn to vest authority and trust, tentatively and for short periods of time, in other members of their transition group. Then, with more confidence, they learn to vest authority and trust in the larger community that constitutes the class as a whole, in which their transition group is nested. Finally, students learn to vest authority and trust in themselves, as individuals who have internalized the language, values, and mores of the still larger community, the disciplinary community of knowledgeable peers that they have been striving to join. They gain that larger authority because the teacher is the disciplinary knowledge community's representative in the classroom. By virtue of that representation, the knowledge community of the class as a whole, with its constituent small groups nested within it, is to one degree or another nested in the discipline.

In short, this pedagogy of reacculturation had been right under our noses all along. What we had been doing ourselves was exactly that. We ourselves were engaged in the complex, tortuous, wearing, collaborative process of reacculturation. Faced with a situation that seemed alien to us and which our training as conventional academic humanists, library mice, and English-teacher types did not prepare us to cope with, we had in self-defense recognized the degree of affinity that existed among us, on that basis formed a transition group, and assigned ourselves tasks to do collaboratively. We read. We met regularly. We treated ourselves well and had a good time. We got to know one another. We talked. We wrote, and we read one another's writing. We even managed to get some of it into print.

---

[1]Dewey, *Experience* 64.

We learned a lot from reading, of course. That was because reading is one way to join new communities, the ones represented by the authors of the texts we read. By reading, we acquire fluency in the language of the text and make it our own. Library stacks from this perspective are not a repository; they are a crowd. Conversely, we make the authors we have read members of our own community. Our little discussion group had, in effect, adopted Sennett and Cobb and Freire into membership.

But although we learned a lot from what we read, we learned a lot more from what we said to one another about what we read. Each of us began to change, and we discovered that the most powerful force changing us was our influence on one another. In the process we became a new community. It was a knowledge community in which its members talked about college and university education as quintessentially reacculturative and talked about reacculturation as quintessentially collaborative.

Not everyone has gone through an experience of boundary conversation and collaborative reacculturation quite as extensive and long-lived as the one in the tale I have just told. But the essence of it will be familiar to anyone who has been in a mutual-aid self-help support group devoted to a special interest or disability. Groups of this sort concentrate on solving or dealing with a formidable problem. They constitute in many cases a transition community between small, isolated communities of despair (such as alcoholics or families of alcoholics, those who take care of cancer victims or victims of Alzheimer's disease, battered women, and so on) and a larger community of more confident, more knowledgeable, more competent, and a good deal less lonely people who can cope. Group members distribute knowledge and authority among themselves, taking it upon themselves to help each other in times of threat and calamity to find the will and the way.

The essence of collaboration will even be familiar to those who have worked with an intelligent, compatible committee or task force on an interesting, demanding project. People in groups of this sort assume one another's will to do the job. They concentrate instead on a way to get the job done. One person gets an idea, stumbles around with it a bit, and then sketches it out. Another says, wait a minute—that makes me think of . . . A third says, but look, if we change this or add that . . . People who take part in a collaborative enterprise such as this exceed, with a little help from their friends, what any of them alone could have learned, accomplished, or endured.

Collaboration will be familiar, too, to lawyers, journalists, accountants, science and technical writers, and others who have ever asked colleagues to read a manuscript of theirs or who have ever "done an edit" (as my wife the lawyer puts it) on something a colleague has written. Constructive readers of that sort read a draft, scribble some notes in the margins, maybe write a page or two of comments congratulating the writer on a good start, suggest a few changes, and mention one or two issues to be thought through a bit further. Then the two of them, reader and writer, sit down together and talk the draft over before the writer goes back to work on it.

If I am right that experiences of this kind are familiar to many people, then few are likely to be strangers to reacculturation by means of collaboration. When shopkeeper A asks shopkeeper B to take a look at the way she has rearranged the floor of her shop, and A agrees to do it, they become an autonomous collaborative group of two with the task of revising and developing the product of one of its members. The collaboration is worthwhile for both of them for two reasons. As members of the same, concentric, or overlapping communities of interest and expertise, they speak much the same language. And as members of communities or subgroups, they look in upon each other's communities with the uncommitted eyes of outsiders. Both know in general what it takes to display wares in an attractive way, but shopkeeper B doesn't know much about handling the particular line of goods that A is selling. B will understand and agree with some of what A has done with her store but will raise questions about other things. Challenged, A will translate unfamiliar terms and ideas into language that B can more or less understand and accept. They will come to terms, reach a consensus.

The same sort of thing happens when anyone, even a college or university student, works collaboratively. With material his students generated in a course he taught collaboratively some years ago, John Trimbur, of Worcester Polytechnic Institute, shows what happens in such a collaborative group.[2] The assignment was to read a Studs Terkel interview with a former Ku Klux Klan leader who had reversed his position, coming in the end to agree with Martin Luther King. While the students were reading, thinking, and discussing, they were to keep a personal log. Trimbur first asked them to discuss the piece in small, task-oriented groups. Then he asked them to go home and write an essay explaining that change, all the while keeping track of their thinking and their class discussion in their logs. He tells the rest of the story this way.

> One woman wrote in her log that at first she couldn't think of anything to say [about the Terkel interview]. She found the assignment difficult because she did not want to "judge" the guy. She went on quite a while in this entry to say how in her family she had been brought up not to "judge" other people.

Notice that the student herself (I'll call her Mary) attributes her difficulty in discussing the subject to the way she had been acculturated in the first place: the way "in her family she had been brought up." Mary's teacher was asking her to talk about something beyond the boundaries of the knowledge community she belonged to. Trimbur continues:

---

[2]I have adapted Trimbur's story from the introduction to my *Short Course in Writing*, 3d ed., 7–8.

Then, in a log entry written a few days later, she wrote again about the class hour when we discussed the Terkel piece and the writing assignment. What she remembered now was something that another woman in the class had said about "conversion." She found herself "talking it over" with that woman in her mind, and as she talked it over she began to connect the idea of conversion with the story of Saint Paul in the Bible. Making this connection was a dramatic event for her, as the entry describes it. "Dramatic" is not too strong a word for the experience, because it actively involved an imagined conversation with a classmate. Once that event occurred she felt ready to write and interested in what she had to say.

One thing this passage tells us is that change—reacculturation, learning—began for Mary when she engaged in conversation with a peer at the boundary between the community she was brought up in and the community her classmate was brought up in. Her classmate shared part of her cultural background, the religious part, but did not share another part of it, the antijudgmental part. In this conversation, Mary's peer provided the new word that allowed her to talk about the topic she had been assigned. She interposed, helping her to "translate" a word she was familiar with (*conversion*) from a strictly religious context to a secular one. Then she internalized this boundary conversation with her peer and continued it on her own, in her imagination, as thought.

After direct conversation ended for Mary, collaboration continued indirectly, because direct conversation had provided the language she needed in order to "talk to herself"—that is, think—productively in a new way. As it had for my colleagues and me, boundary conversation had given Mary the means for crossing that boundary. It gave her the terms with which to renegotiate her relationship with two communities, the one she was brought up in and the one she was entering by virtue of her college education.

Another thing the passage tells us is that at the same time that conversation, external and internalized, changed Mary's opinion, it also changed her feelings about the topic, about the conversation, and about herself. It made her feel "ready to write and interested in what she had to say." Her early acculturation into one community (being "brought up not to 'judge' people") made her reject the whole idea being presented in the Terkel interview. Conversation changed this attitude to a willingness to entertain the idea. It also let her formulate a new opinion and want to write about it.

In recording that change and its educational consequences, this student has recorded the crucial step in educational collaboration, the first step we take whenever we set out to join a larger, more inclusive community of knowledgeable peers. That step is to overcome resistance to change that evidences itself as ambivalence about engaging in conversation at the boundaries of the knowledge communities that we already belong to. As Roberto Unger tells us, we are drawn to one another and distrust one another at the same time. We want to get to know one another, but we are disinclined to talk with strangers. We continue to resist and feel uncomfortable with one another, until we find terms that we feel are translatable, terms that we know are appropriate and acceptable in the community we currently belong to and that we can also displace in acceptable and appropriate ways into the community we are tempted to join. In Mary's case, the term that served this purpose was "conversion." In the case of my City University colleagues and me, the same purpose was served by terms such as "culture," "reacculturate," and "oppressed."

This transitional process of translation, this willingness to learn the elements of new languages and gain new expertise, is the most important skill in the craft of interdependence. It is a willingness to become members of communities we have not belonged to before, by engaging in constructive conversation with others whose background and needs are similar to our own but also different. Reacculturative conversation of the sort exemplified in the tale that begins this chapter combines the power of mutual-aid self-help groups with the power of successfully collaborative intellectual work. It integrates the will and the way. In this process of arriving at consensus, dissent may also play an important, sometimes even decisive, role.

To be able to engage in constructive, reacculturative conversation, however, requires willingness to grant authority to peers, courage to accept the authority granted to one by peers, and skill in the craft of interdependence. This book takes the position that a good college or university education fosters that willingness, courage, and skill, but that many college and university educations today, widely regarded as very good indeed, do not in fact foster them.

Understanding the importance of conversation to college and university education began in the late 1950s with M.L.J. Abercrombie's research on educating medical students at University Hospital, University of London. Abercrombie showed that her medical students learned the key element in successful medical practice, diagnosis—that is, medical judgment—more quickly and accurately when they worked collaboratively in small groups than when they worked alone.

A close look at Abercrombie's results in light of Mary's experience is revealing. Abercrombie began her work by observing the scene that most of us think is typical of medical education: the group of medical students with a teaching physician on "rounds," hovering over a ward bed to diagnose a patient. She changed that scene by making a slight but crucial difference in the way it is usually played out. Instead of asking each individual member of the group of medical students to diagnose the patient on his or her own, Abercrombie asked the whole group to examine the patient together, discuss the case as a group, and arrive at a consensus: a single diagnosis that they could all agree on.

The result, that students who learned diagnosis collaboratively acquired better medical judgment faster than individual students who worked alone, showed that learning diagnostic judgment is not an individual process but a social, interdependent one. It occurs on an axis drawn not between individuals and things but among people. Students learn judgment best in groups, Abercrombie inferred, because they tend to talk each other out of their unshared biases and presuppositions. That is, the differences among them push them into socially justifying their beliefs or, failing that, into acknowledging that their beliefs are socially unjustifiable and abandoning them.[3]

This is also the message of Uri Treisman's work at the Berkeley campus of the University of California, for which he has won the Dana prize and a MacArthur Fellowship. On that polyglot, multiethnic campus, Treisman, who is a mathematician, was puzzled by the fact that students in some ethnic groups did significantly better at math and science than students in other ethnic groups. In particular, Asian-American students at Berkeley tended to excel, whereas African-American and Hispanic students tended not to.

To find out why, Treisman devised an elegantly simple experiment. He followed the Asian-American students around campus to see how they did it. What he discovered was that they were continually engaged in conversation about their work. They moved in packs, ate together, studied together, went to classes together. In contrast, the African-American and Hispanic students Treisman watched were largely isolated from one another. They seldom studied or talked together about their work.

Treisman surmised that this was the crucial difference between the academic success level of these two groups of students. So he set out to change

---

[3]Some of the principles developed in Abercrombie's research seem to have been applied in a justly celebrated, closely watched, and increasingly imitated program in postgraduate education: the New Pathways program at Harvard Medical School. What makes the program collaborative is the way it organizes students to work together and the kind of tasks it asks them to work together on. New Pathways excuses a portion of each entering class from the traditional first year curriculum—upwards of eight hours of lecture a day, five days a week. Instead, the program subdivides them into consensus groups of six to eight, gives them a diagnostic problem with clinical and scientific ramifications, and allows them six weeks to come up with a solution. Each group has a faculty mentor and access to all of Harvard Medical School's extraordinary resources. But the problem is theirs alone to solve—collaboratively. New Pathways does not foster cooperation among students to help them jump through hoops of well-defined subject matter using well-defined methods. It is not another way to produce physicians who are good at answering exam questions. Harvard's traditional medical curriculum does that superlatively well. New Pathways responds to the general public's perception that our hospitals and clinics are staffed by physicians who must have been wonderfully adept at taking exams, but who can't "doctor." And this perception is seconded by many in the medical profession itself, who argue that although traditional medical education stuffs young physicians full of facts, it leaves their diagnostic judgment rudimentary and does not develop their ability to interact socially, with either colleagues or patients, in addressing complex, demanding, perhaps life-and-death issues (Oliver Wendell Holmes Society).

the way in which Berkeley's remedial math and science program was organized. He brought the African-American and Hispanic students together, gave them a place to study collaboratively, showed them how to work together effectively, and insisted that they work collaboratively on a regular basis. Lo and behold, many of Treisman's remedial students soon became B and A students. Conversation, Treisman discovered, is of such vital importance to learning that, with it, any of us has a shot at doing whatever we want to do. Without it, none of us stands a chance.

Institutionalized educational collaboration in whatever form, however, is never unproblematical. It almost always involves an attempt on the teacher's part to reacculturate students at several levels. Reacculturation extends beyond initiation into a disciplinary community of mathematicians, sociologists, or classicists to initiation into a community of willingly collaborative peers. A class must somehow manage to constitute itself as a community with its own particular mores, goals, linguistic history, and language.

This process is not always easy, because students do not always work effectively as collaborative peers, especially at first. There are several reasons for this. First, given most students' almost exclusive experience of traditional classroom authority, many have to learn, sometimes against considerable resistance, to grant authority not to the teacher alone but to a peer ("What right has he got . . . ?") instead of the teacher. They also have to learn, sometimes against considerable resistance, to accept the authority given them by a peer ("What right have I got . . . ?") and to exercise that authority judiciously and helpfully in the interest of a peer.

In most cases this resistance is not intractable, although overcoming it may generate a good deal of stress in some students. David L. Rubin tells a story about a student in his University of Virginia French literature class that is a classic case study of resistance to collaborative learning, the potential for overcoming that resistance, and the stress that may nevertheless be involved in overcoming it.[4]

> In the first week of class this term, I asked my students to write a short paper. On the day the paper was due, I organized them into small study groups and asked the students in each group to trade papers with students in another group. They were to read the papers written by the students in the

---

[4]David Rubin and I wrote this tale together by e-mail (code word: Zeldiad) based on Rubin's classroom experience as it transpired during the 1997 fall semester. I am grateful to him for lending his acute observation and interpretive expertise to this enterprise. I am also grateful to the student in question (whose name is of course not Zelda). At the beginning of the semester, Rubin obtained her permission to record her experience anonymously in the form of this interpretive account. She has made an important contribution to our understanding of the pressures and tensions of educational reacculturative change.

other group and develop lines of questioning about them. Then they were to negotiate with one another about incisive ways to discuss the other study group's papers when the class met Monday morning.

On Sunday evening, one of my students, I'll call her Zelda, phoned me after reading the set of papers her classmates had written. She was irked. The papers were terrible. And she really didn't want to waste any more time thinking about them and talking about them with the other members of her group. Couldn't I just lecture instead or let her drop the course and give her a tutorial about Greek myths in French classical theater? Throughout the conversation she repeated emphatically that she did *not* think she was smarter than everyone else in the class.

I turned down her requests and told her we could talk after class on Monday. Come Monday noon when the class ended, Zelda was mortified with embarrassment. She found that the members of her group not only had come up with better questions than she had, but that their lines of inquiry added up to something unexpectedly solid and penetrating. The negotiated product, she said, would spark great discussion in three class meetings to come, for which she couldn't wait. She wouldn't speak for the students who had written those papers, but her group was ready to take them on.

Still, Zelda continued to profess herself skeptical about the way I was running the class. Didn't I think it was a cop-out for a professor to make students do all the work while not giving out any right answers? I judged that Zelda was intrigued but still had a ways to go.

On Wednesday, she did beautifully. She proved to be an assertive yet fair and reasonable questioner of her peers, skillfully linking her queries to previous answers and engaging authors in exploratory dialogue. After class she declared herself pleased with her performance.

So far, Rubin narrates a crucial moment in students' understanding of collaborative learning and their consent to take part in it. His story is about accepting and granting authority among peers. When Zelda called her professor on Sunday night, she didn't understand collaborative learning and wasn't having any of it. She could accept only what she did understand, was familiar with, and wasn't threatened by. She insisted that her professor was the only person in the class with authority and that he ought to be exercising it as she had always known teachers to do. In pleading with her professor to teach traditionally and provide "right answers," she was revealing a dependence on centralized classroom authority that is common among students and difficult to give up, however much they may protest against it.

During the phone call, by repeatedly insisting that the reason she was impatient with the other students' papers was not that she thought she was smarter than everyone else in the class, she assured her teacher and reassured herself that she felt a genuine sense of peership with her classmates that she did not want to put at risk. But her relationship with the other students in the class was in fact somewhat insecure. Not yet quite aware of the consequences of doing so, she had taken an important step by granting her peers the authority to read her paper and comment on it. Granting authority to her peers was not yet therefore what was distressing her. What distressed Zelda at this point, and prompted her phone call, was being granted authority *by* her peers to read *their* papers. Being faced with having to accept that authority and act on it drove her to the contradictory and somewhat embarrassing act of asking her professor's permission to reject the authority her peers had granted her.

Her eagerness to affirm that she did not think she was smarter than everyone else in the class told her professor that Zelda did not want, as she saw it, to set herself above and apart from her peers. This way of affirming peership with her classmates tipped her professor off to the appropriate response. Despite her gesture of despair—asking to drop the course and be tutored—Zelda really did want to remain engaged with the class. By refusing to release her from that engagement, her professor told her something that was not likely to have occurred to her before, that maintaining—indeed, reconstructing and strengthening—her relationship with her peers was as important to him as it was to her.

At this point in the story, as Rubin puts it, Zelda had yet to "face the music." Two weeks into the course, she had not yet been "under peer pressure to clarify, justify, and show the significance of her own evidence and reasoning." Having granted authority to her peers by giving her paper to a group of them to read and comment on, she now had to face the consequences of granting that authority. How would she respond to the examination of her paper by her classmates, whose papers she had so effectively examined? Of the two, accepting authority and granting it, granting authority is often the more painful, as Zelda's experience reveals.

Rubin's tale continues:

> When it became Zelda's turn to have her paper examined by students who had read it, she was delighted with their questions, and she engaged in real dialogue with them. Her discussion of her classmates' papers exceeded my requirements by a mile. The conversation among them was thoughtful, mutually respectful, responsible, heartfelt, focused, and tactful.
>
> Especially, as it turned out, tactful. Zelda's classmates talked about every aspect of the paper but one. Nobody said a word about the introduction. Zelda was miffed. But (to my astonishment) she waded into the silence and asked expressly for the class's reaction to the introduction. Forced into the open, they admitted that their reaction was largely negative. The introduction, they suggested, was a purple patch about the history of France at the time the play the class is reading was first performed. Zelda's introduction was, they said, irrelevant to the rest of the paper.
>
> After class, Zelda asked me what I thought. I turned the question back to her. What did she think after hearing her classmates' critique? She seemed

chastened. She allowed as how she might revise. It began to seem that Zelda had taken a second important step. On her own, she had explicitly confirmed her peers' authority to say whatever they felt they had to say about her work. Equally important, on her own she accepted my refusal to arbitrate and arrived at the necessary conclusion that she had to revise.

But here Zelda hit a snag. Rubin observed that Zelda's discussion of her classmates' papers exceeded his requirements "by a mile." The reason was that she was expending most of her energy in exercising the authority her peers had granted her. She was not yet balancing that effort with a constructive response to their exercise of authority relative to herself. About her experience at this stage she wrote, "I'm still in the process of being convinced that the [class's collaborative] format is the most beneficial way to spend my time. I feel I waste a lot of time filling out protocols and critiquing other people's essays when I would like to spend more time on critiquing my own."

Rubin observes, therefore, that Zelda's "unwillingness to rethink and rewrite"—her refusal to make changes that she had acknowledged were necessary—"indicates a limit to her involvement with the process." In response to her peers' constructive criticism in class discussion (the paper did not meet its own goal, it made several irrelevant and logically incoherent interpretations, it partially garbled the historical backgrounds brought in to make its case, and it chose poor secondary sources and did not critique them adequately) Zelda made "only superficial changes." Her professor gave her a C- on the paper, a B- for quality of written French, and an A for participation. Although with the help of her peers Zelda could analyze her own work accurately, she could not yet see her way clear to improving it on the basis of that analysis. She understood what she should do, and she wanted to do it. She could not face the possibility that she was not yet doing it well.

Abercrombie's observations help us understand what Zelda was facing at this stage of resistance, and they suggest what has to happen next. Students tend to begin their work together with their own distinctive preconceptions firmly in place and a profound feeling that those preconceptions are right. Conversation toward consensus requires them to confront and come to terms with the difference between their own fixed beliefs and the contradicting fixed beliefs of their peers. Collaborative learning places students in a position, that is, in which they must reconcile their preconceptions in conversation with one another.

That conversation alone, Abercrombie's research demonstrated, has the power to move students both toward consensus and toward a better understanding of the issue at hand. Students have to learn to trust the power of conversation. That means learning to trust the authority they have granted to one another as well as understanding its limits. It also means coming to terms with the dependence implied in the traditional classroom relation-ship between students and professor.

Coming to terms with differences between firmly held beliefs and modify-ing them may be stressful for many students, and for some, such as Zelda, especially so. One of Rubin's students who had gone through the process and come out the other side— "a member of [his] first full-scale collabora-tive learning class, some five or six years ago"—told him she was "appalled" at what she called Zelda's "discourtesy in accusing [him] in front of other stu-dents of 'copping out' by making the students do all the work." At the same time, this former student granted with eloquent understatement that, on the basis of her own experience, "professors trying to make students accountable to critical peers for the quality of their work are bound to set some students' teeth on edge." That collaborative learning can occasionally drive even a well-brought-up young woman such as Zelda to express her distress forceful-ly reveals both the depth and complexity of the process—and its necessity.

Since Zelda had accepted the authority that her peers had granted her to read their papers, what had to happen next in Zelda's experience of col-laborative learning was for her to accept the consequences. She now had to grant to her peers the authority to read her papers. The first signs that she had begun to turn around in this respect, Rubin reports, appeared in her collaborative work on the second paper he assigned the class. That one, he says, "went much better." During the second month of the course, Zelda

> continued to do very good peer editing, and she engaged other students in incisive, pertinent, open-ended dialogue, both when she questioned and when she was questioned. But this time, she took other students' strictures on her prefinal draft seriously. She rethought, and she rewrote radically. The final product was excellent: clear and fully justified, with as much breadth and depth as is possible in about 1500 words.
>
> What seems to have happened is that she broke the umbilical cord to sec-ondary sources. That is, working collaboratively helped her develop greater confidence in her own ability to read and interpret on her own, and greater confidence in her peers' ability to support and guide her in that. When she came by my office to pick up her spring registration card, I questioned her about her current attitude to the course. Her replies amazed me. She still found reading other students' papers a burden ("some of them don't repay the effort"), but she admitted that reading them exposed her to viewpoints, approaches, and principles that had not occurred to her. She also said she found the plenary sessions a bit boring. I suspect this happens when she is not herself directly involved.
>
> At the same time, however, she admitted that she had been "floored" by the quality of questioning her paper elicited from her classmates and the opportunity the experience afforded her to reconsider her position and make her paper better. Those responses seem to mark a clear advance over the opening weeks of the course.

Three weeks later, Zelda confirmed Rubin's surmise. By that time, he reports:

> Zelda seemed to have fully accepted the format. Her papers were very good, thanks in part to striking a balance between independence from secondary sources and open yet critical engagement with other students' reactions to her work. Her interim evaluations of the course and her own work in it indicated that she had begun to consider the course a valuable experience, even though she may not have become a triple-dyed true believer. The real test, however, is the result: a young woman whose constructive conversation with her peers demonstrably improved her work.

Any professor who asks students to criticize one another's work will encounter this resistance at first, and most are gratified by students' ability to come to terms with the challenge as Zelda did. Students' first reaction to being asked to comment on another student's work may be to interpret it as an invitation to rat on a friend: mutual criticism as a form of treason. If the teacher does manage somehow to break through this refusal to comment on another student's work except in the blandest terms, the alternative reaction may be to go to the opposite extreme: almost vile excoriation. At first students refuse to admit that they see anything wrong with a fellow student's work. Then they refuse to admit that there is anything of value in it at all. They become, as a student once put it to me, either teddy bears or sharks. Both responses are typical of group solidarity, which tends to enforce loyalty and mutual defense and to scapegoat some members of the group, ejecting them and closing ranks against them. Needless to say, neither response is likely to develop the craft of interdependence and lead to mature judgment.

These typically solidarian responses show that most college and university students have thoroughly internalized long-prevailing academic prohibitions against collaboration. Traditionally, after all, collaboration skates dangerously close to the supreme academic sin, plagiarism. Furthermore, most college and university students are confirmed in the habit of identifying the authority of knowledge in a classroom exclusively with the teacher's authority. As a result, they often do not believe that a request to collaborate is genuine, and they do not always know what might be in it for them if they do collaborate.

Of course, even in a collaborative classroom, authority does begin in most cases (as it should) with the institutional representative or agent, the professor. Mary and her classmates did not read and discuss Studs Terkel on their own initiative. Their teacher asked them to do it. Furthermore, most students start most semesters in most classrooms as strangers. They do not begin, as shopkeepers A and B did, as trusted neighbors, colleagues, or friends. They begin with the wariness of one another that my City University colleagues and I began with. And, semesters being short, students do not have the kind of time that we had to get to know and trust one another. It is therefore not surprising that some students may not be overly eager at first to collaborate, and that a few may remain skeptical.

But the experience of skillfully managed classroom collaboration can help move students toward incorporating into their intellectual work much of what they have learned about working interdependently in their many collaborative experiences outside class. For students who are inexperienced in collaboration, a series of modestly challenging tasks can, over time, give them a chance to discover the value, interest, and often in fact the excitement that they can derive from interpreting tasks on their own and inventing or adapting a language with which to negotiate the consensus that they need in order to get the work done. With the professor for the moment out of the way and the chain of hierarchical institutional authority for the moment broken, most students enjoy the freedom to reinvent in class the collaborative peership that most of them are quite familiar with in their everyday lives.

REFERENCES

Abercrombie, M. L. J. *The Anatomy of Judgement*. Harmondsworth, England: Penguin, 1939; New York: Basic Books, 1960.
Bruffee, Kenneth A. *A Short Course in Writing*. 3rd edition. Boston: Little Brown, 1985. 4th ed. New York: Addison Wesley Longman, 1992.
Dewey, John. *Experience and Education*. New York: Collier, 1963; first published in 1938.
Freire, Paulo. *Pedagogy of the Oppressed*. Trans. Myra Bergman Ramos. New York: Herder, 1972.
Lewin, Kurt, and Paul Grabbe. "Conduct, Knowledge, and the Acceptance of New Values." Reprinted from *Journal of Social Issues* 1 (1945): 53–64.
Perry, William G., Jr. "Examsmanship and the Liberal Arts: A Study in Educational Epistemology." *Examining in Harvard College: A Collection of Essays by Members of the Harvard Faculty*. Cambridge: Harvard UP, 1963.
———. *Forms of Intellectual and Ethical Development in the College Years: A Scheme*. New York: Holt, 1968.
Rorty, Richard. *Contingency, Irony, and Solidarity*. Cambridge: Cambridge UP, 1989.
———. *Philosophy and the Mirror of Nature*. Princeton: Princeton UP, 1989.
Sennett, Richard, and Jonathan Cobb. *The Hidden Injuries of Class*. New York: Knopf, 1973.
Unger, Roberto Mangabeira. *Passion: An Essay on Personality*. New York: Free Press, 1984.

QUESTIONS FOR REFLECTION, JOURNAL WRITING, AND DISCUSSION

1. Bruffee describes his sense of disorientation in trying to reconcile his conventional academic expectations with the level of preparedness of the new students coming into his classes and the process he

went through as a kind of "reacculturation." Have you ever had a similar experience?

2. Bruffee points out that an "error" in language use is not the same thing as an error in mathematics. Students speak the way they have learned to speak in their communities. How might this perception affect the way you approach "correction" in your work with students?

3. Do your students work as a community of "collaborative peers"? Would it be good to try to get them to do this? How could that be done?

4. Do you think students may have reservations about their professor engaging them in a "constructive, reacculturative conversation"?

Chapter 5

From "Let's Flip the Script: An African American Discourse on Language, Literature, and Learning"

Keith Gilyard

Keith Gilyard is Professor of English at Pennsylvania State University and former head of the Conference on College Composition and Communication. His books include the educational memoir, *Voices of the Self*, for which he received an American Book Award. He has also published in such journals as *College English, College Composition and Communication,* and the *Journal of Basic Writing*. The following article is from *Let's Flip the Script: An African American Discourse on Language, Literature, and Learning,* Wayne State University Press, 1996.

ONE MORE TIME FOR PROFESSOR NURUDDIN

Yusuf Nuruddin, MY BROTHER. Surely the best arrangement is for me to be there at Medgar Evers College to visit your Black Studies courses. But now that I live two hundred fifty miles from Brooklyn, that option is no longer convenient. So, as per your request, I have sent what you need to do justice to the language unit in your classes. I hope you'll appreciate that I treat African American and Caribbean varieties of English together. You may catch some flak for this. As you know, you teach at the college with the largest concentration in the country of Caribbean students with African bloodlines, many of whom insist upon a cultural distinction in every detail between themselves and African Americans. On the other hand, as you are also well aware, African American students on campus haven't always welcomed their Caribbean schoolmates warmly. So expect some tension. But hold your ground, for this is the way to go. And perhaps this current crop is much hipper anyway, past all that jingoism.

My examples of linguistic features are purposely restricted to the sentence level. I feel you can talk well enough about discourse features such as call-response, talking sweet, toastin', and so on. If not, we can consult some more sources. That analysis is never as complicated as the syntactic stuff, and I imagine it would be more interesting for you to read.

You may get to repay this favor, as I may need a good sociological and historical analysis for an English class soon, you know, with new historicism and all. I'll call.

Overview

Certain language varieties spoken by African Americans and Afro-Caribbeans have often been termed "Broken English" by teachers, students, and the general public. The underlying assumptions are that the language varieties in question are unsystematic, inferior, and the direct cause of poor reading and writing. Nothing could be more inaccurate. These language varieties are rule-governed systems that have developed as a result of conflict, conquest, and cultural mixing. They are equal in a linguistic sense to any other varieties of English and are not a major obstacle to literacy.

Origin and Development

Just as English grew and changed because of the Anglo-Saxon invasions, the Danish raids, the Norman conquest, and class divisions within Great Britain, the language changed again when it was exported overseas. Because of British colonizing activity in the New World accompanied by the mass importation of African slaves, the dialects, to use the most familiar label, spoken by most African Americans and Anglophone Caribbeans represent a merging of some aspects and practices of English and several languages of Africa. Although it was standard procedure to mix slaves from different groups together in an attempt to stifle their verbal interaction, some degree of verbal communication among them was necessary for plantations to operate effectively. In addition, masters and overseers needed to be able to address and receive reports from their workers. To accomplish these ends, new language varieties were created by combining what appeared to be the simplest (which usually meant least redundant) elements of two or more existing languages. Such newly created language systems are called *pidgins*.

In time, children are born who acquire a pidgin as their first language. The language combination is then said to have *creolized* and is referred to as a *creole*. People from the Caribbean sometimes say they speak Creole, which is true, but they are really talking about a particular creole, as *creole* also functions as a generic term. Jamaican Creole, for instance, also known as *patois*, is indeed a creole. But so are the range of dialects we generally call Black English.

The language varieties being considered can all be classified, following the lead of John Holm, under the heading *Atlantic Creole, AC* for short.* Creoles basically contain the syntax of the language of less or least prestige and the lexicon of the privileged tongue. AC, then, is an amalgam of English and structures from several African languages. But proportions are not absolute. Some brands of AC are closer to Standard English syntax than others, and African lexical items have been incorporated into Standard English. Words borrowed from Africa include *yam, tote, gumbo, gorilla, elephant, okra, jazz, oasis, sorcery, cola, banana,* and *banjo*.

The above view of language formation is known as the *creole hypothesis* and is the explanation for AC given the most credence by contemporary linguists. Competing claims that AC symbolizes cognitive deficiency, or attests to physiological differences, or derives from white regional speech, or mostly signifies an evolution of Portuguese trade pidgin lack compulsion.

Creoles change over time, as all varieties do, usually moving closer to the dominant language. This is *decreolization*. Language varieties can also *recreolize*, that is, move in the opposite direction. It all depends upon social activities at large. That African Americans have been a numerical minority in the United States accounts for the great degree of decreolization in this country. Differences between AC in Jamaica and Barbados result largely from different histories of colonization and economic organization. Jamaica, for example, was ruled by Spain, then Britain, and housed large sugar plantations with relatively high slave-to-master ratios, while Barbados, "Little England," was never colonized by anyone but Big England and featured mainly small farms and low slave-to-master ratios.

Geography also accounts for differences. Jamaica, after all, is one thousand miles from Barbados, roughly the distance from New York to St. Louis. Usage is also influenced by gender, class, education, attitude, age, degrees of assimilation, contact with languages other than English, and so on. AC will vary slightly, therefore, from nation to nation and within nations, similar to how Standard English varies from Australia to New Zealand and from New England to Texas. What must be stressed, however, is AC's essential character. Despite differences among varieties, their similarities are far greater. They don't vary as much from one another as they do from Standard English. As J. L. Dillard points out, "the English of most American Blacks retains some features which are common to both Caribbean and West African varieties of English" (6).

---

*Atlantic Creoles also include those based on other dominant languages like Dutch, French, and Spanish. For convenience I limit the term's use to English-based creoles.

Language Features

The following examples come from speech samples or student essays. The country where each subject spent his or her formative years is noted in parentheses. Although I approach them from the angle of inflections and spelling, there are other classification schemes for discussing syntax and phonology issues. I am not attempting an exhaustive or theoretically sophisticated review. I wish to keep this both condensed and useful.

Inflections

Inflections are changes in word form that indicate how a particular word is being used. For example, in the statement "We are interested in Malcolm's ideas," the 's is a suffix that completes the possessive construction. Generally, inflections proliferate when word order is relatively unimportant. That is why English, centuries ago, deriving mainly from German, had many noun and verb inflections. Word order wasn't an overriding feature of the language then. It since has become so. Subject, object, and possession can all be demonstrated by word order, and inflections are not needed to convey meaning—the reason, in fact, many have become obsolete. Even the distinction between *who* and *whom* is weakening and perhaps disappearing.

Inflections were not a feature of West African languages, and in the merger of those languages with English, inflections, being unnecessary to making meaning, did not become a significant feature of the creoles. Speakers of AC systematically eliminate certain redundancies relative to nouns, pronouns, and verbs. Instances commonly described as subject-verb (dis)agreement, tense, pronoun, or possessive errors are directly tied, as illustrated below, to this practice.

1. *She have* a Benz that she and Carl call the Status Symbol. (Guyana)
2. When *a young child have* a baby she is not ready for, problems come. (Guyana)
3. *A student do* have some say in the matter. (Jamaica)
4. *He need* to get with the program. (U.S.A.)
5. *Blacks* in South Africa *is refused* decent health care. (Barbados)
6. *He play* four instruments. (Trinidad).

No doubt, these types of constructions irk more than a few speech and English teachers, many of whom would be quick to assert that the speakers or writers don't know grammar or, even worse, that the sentences make no sense. But these configurations result from the application of a specifiable rule, in this case that only one form of a verb be used with all subjects. In an absolute sense, these constructions are no less meaningful or more ambiguous than their Standard English translations:

7. *She has* a Benz that she and Carl call the Status Symbol.
8. When *a young child has* a baby she is not ready for, problems come.
9. *A student does* have some say in the matter.
10. *He needs* to get with the program.
11. Blacks in South Africa *are refused* decent health care.
12. *He plays* four instruments.

The substitutions of *has* for *have*, *does* for *do*, *needs* for *need*, and *plays* for *play* don't clarify the statements. That the latter forms indicate singularity is true, but they don't create it. A *student* and *a young child* would not be confused with plural forms by any native speaker of English. To inflect a verb to show singularity, plurality, or person is redundant because the subject alone denotes these attributes.

AC speakers will sometimes produce forms like *they does* because they are struggling with conflicting rule systems. This is called *hypercorrection*. Hypercorrect forms are actually incorrect in all varieties of English. It is the same type of overgeneralization committed when a speaker learns how to indicate past tense but says *he goed* instead of *he went*. An additional example:

13. Sometimes in life we experience certain *things that tells* us we have to make a decision. (Guyana)

As stated previously, speakers of AC often do not mark for tense:

14. I was on my own.
15. It was very hard because I *have* to work day and night. (Jamaica).
16. Back when I was fourteen, I *drop* out of school. (Antigua)
17. Most of the factors *mention* about teenagers in my paragraphs are trends followed by most teenagers today. (Grenada)
18. I finally got away from my family.
19. Then I *start* having children right after I got married. (U.S.A.)

One would be justified in saying, to the horror of many language guardians, that AC represents an advanced variety of English, historically speaking, particularly with respect to verb usage. As Frederic Cassidy explains:

Those of us who were brought up on Latin Grammar sometimes do not realize that the Standard English verb today has only three living inflectional suffixes: *(e)s* of the third person singular (*goes, sings*), *(e)d* (or *t*) of the weak past (tast*ed*, swep*t*) and *ing* of the present participle (com*ing*). One cannot even include the *(e)n* of such verbs as brok*en*, since it is never added to new verbs, and survives in a decreasing number of old ones. In the course of its history the English verb has been discarding inflection more and more. (57–58)

AC varieties of English assign a fixed form to nouns, usually the Standard English singular. Thus, we obtain the following:

20. Teenagers especially in America have the attitude of separating most *adult* from them. (Grenada)
21. Especially in those high technology *continent* such as America and Europe. (Grenada)
22. The hard facts hit us about a few *week* later when we had to start finding jobs to support ourselves. (Jamaica)

Hypercorrect utterances include:

23. I did not think *an adults* could say much.

One form of a pronoun is generally chosen or repeated. The subject pronoun may serve as the possessive pronoun also:

24. They still don't think that we are *they* equal. (Barbados)
25. They better bring *they* best! (U.S.A.)

Sometimes the Standard English subject pronoun becomes the object pronoun. Instead of *her* and *they*, we get:

26. Look at *she!* (Trinidad)
27. There are too many young people having babies and *them* themselves are still babies. (Guyana)

Along with possessive pronouns and "apostrophe *s*" (*town's people*), possession is indicated in Standard English by preposition (*people of the town*) or by juxtaposition (*townspeople*). Speakers of AC rely almost exclusively on juxtaposition:

28. *My parents business* was about to collapse. (Jamaica)

The convergence of AC pronunciation and the redundant aspect of all inflections determine the nature of auxiliary constructions:

29. This *has strengthen* me to be an example for my peers. (Trinidad)
30. But where his kids *were concern*, nothing was too strenuous for my dad. (Trinidad)

Hypercorrect forms produced include:

31. But he *did not succeeded* in doing so. (Jamaica)
32. This *could indicated* that this area was new to her. (Guyana)

Spelling

Anyone can have trouble with words that sound alike. Speakers of various English varieties confuse your/you're, no/know, to/too (and even two), and there/their. One can, of course, add other examples. Speakers of AC share the potential for these problems, and, because of pronunciation rules of AC, they have additional sets of homophones. Influenced heavily by the phonology of West African languages, speakers of AC soften consonant clusters at the beginning and end of many words. The initial *th* sound, for example, becomes *d* or *t*. So, where *taught* and *thought* are not homophones to speakers of Standard English (in this case, not for speakers of the U.S. creole either), they are to many speakers of AC. Sentences like these are written frequently:

33. Fred wrote an essay he *taught* was excellent. (Grenada)
34. One must be *thought* responsibility. (Trinidad)
35. The kids who were being *thought* by Miss Moore didn't have much pride because of their environment. (Trinidad)

Although the softening of the initial *th* is only one of many AC phonological rules, it receives a lot of attention because initial *th* is a feature of many of the most commonly used words in English.

The softening of final consonant clusters also creates homophones specific to AC. For example: *mine/mind, fine/find:*

36. I really wouldn't *mine* having an Acura Legend. (U.S.A.)
37. In the 1980s you will *fine* more people having sex than in the 1960s. (Guyana)

Among AC speakers, Jamaicans possess a distinct feature:

. . . *h* behaves in a non-Standard way. It is, as often as not, prefixed to stressed vowels or diphthongs, as in *heggs* and *hice,* and dropped irregularly from other words — *'ow 'igh, 'ouse.* This is very much like Cockney usage—indeed, some historical connection is not at all impossible; yet the Jamaican and Cockney confusions with *h* may merely result from the same conditions: loss of the sound, followed by an attempt to replace it that goes awry and puts it in the un-Standard places. (Cassidy 36–37)

Educational Implications

I promise not to take you too far afield here, but I think it's important to indicate the major camps in terms of dialect and education issues. I term them *eradicationists, bidialectalists,* and *pluralists.*

The eradicationists would argue that schools should attempt to eradicate AC because it represents deficient speech and interferes with the acquisition of Standard English. But while linguistic variation can contribute to minor problems of reading and writing, it is not the major cause of reading and writing problems. (Remember, dialects of English are far more alike than they are unalike.) Grapholects (writing systems) bridge dialects, which is why people from various English-speaking regions can read common texts in Standard English, or even in dialects such as AC. People don't read solely the way they speak. Nor do they write the way they speak unless they draw only upon native oral resources. To develop a Standard English "writing voice" is the key, and that comes through continual and plentiful practice by motivated students, not through drills aimed at eliminating the vernacular. To spend time on eradicationist attempts, given the badge of identity that language is, invites cultural resistance that hampers, perhaps even dooms, instructional efforts. This is not to argue that teaching Standard English, the language of wider communication, is never a legitimate school goal, only that it is not likely to happen through a policy of eradicationism.

Pluralists would maintain that most of the educational problems encountered by speakers of AC stem from who they are, not which language variety they utter. They understand that AC and Standard English are linguistically equal and know that the fact that they are not equal in society is a matter of society, not linguistics. The crucial work for pluralists is expressly political: shake up school and society so language variation doesn't play out so negatively in classrooms. Get AC some real respect, some acceptance. Pluralists wouldn't ignore Standard English, but they do feel that in a more equitable societal arrangement and school situation, students generally would want to expand their use of Standard English and, in fact, do so very well.

Bidialectalists know what pluralists know, namely that AC is not inferior to Standard English in a linguistic sense. However, they would make the seemingly pragmatic argument that AC speakers will need Standard English to succeed in the mainstream. Theirs is all accommodationist strategy: they don't want to make much of a fuss.

I'm down with the pluralists. Educational initiatives that fail explicitly to consider or address social relations and student perceptions are impoverished in my view and are geared to fail students, like many of those of African descent, who feel reasons not to melt on into the program.

I'll stop for now. You easily have one whole class period covered. Maybe two. And you call assign field work.

References

Cassidy, Frederic G. *Jamaica Talk: Three Hundred Years of the English Language in Jamaica* (1961). London: McMillan Education, 1982.

Dillard, J. L. *Black English: Its History and Usage in the United States* 1972. New York: Vintage, 1973.

Holm, John A. *Pidgins and Creoles: Reference Survey*. Cambridge: Cambridge UP, 1989.

————. *Pidgins and Creoles: Theory and Structure*. Cambridge: Cambridge UP, 1988.

Smitherman, Geneva. *Talkin and Testifyin: The Language of Black America* (1977). Detroit: Wayne State UP, 1986.

LANGUAGE LEARNING AND DEMOCRATIC DEVELOPMENT*

I have sought to avoid hopping from one bandwagon to another, a behavior characteristic of American educators. My decisions to embrace or reject phonics or teaching grammar or back-to-basics or process writing instruction or critical thinking courses have not been based upon the shrillness or popularity of rhetoric but upon cautious consideration of practice and theory. As I have argued, often in a winding and inductive way, in favor of pluralistic educational initiatives, against monocultural ideals, in favor of emphasizing literature in basic writing courses, I have been approaching, sometimes unwittingly, a deductive vantage point from which I can efficiently analyze educational proposals. This viewpoint mainly entails a concern with democratic schooling and affords an extremely useful typology: either educational proposals promote democracy and thus are to be favored, or they do not. This is how I am viewing language arts learning proposals for all levels, including adult education programs.

Let me confess at this point, while I'm being purposely political, that a small part of me leans toward benevolent dictatorship as the superior form of government. I believe it was Sartre who asserted that when one chooses, one chooses for all, and I take those words too literally at times, as I'm sure Sartre would discourage. At any rate, since I would never trust any dictator to be totally beneficent other than myself, the greater part of me sees true democracy as our nation's best hope. If we're not struggling toward that as educators, we're not struggling toward anything worthwhile.

---

*Presented December 9, 1992, at the Graduate School and University Center of the City University of New York, as part of the Distinguished Speakers Series in Adult Learning sponsored by the CUNY Office of Academic Affairs.

Our work as teachers is political—whether we construe it that way or not—and our obligation, which we sometimes shun, is to provide clarity of political vision regarding our teaching endeavors. My vision yields the following mission statement: literacy educators further the development of authentic democracy—enlightened citizenry and all that—by helping to create informed, critical, powerful, independent, and culturally sensitive student voices.

Of course I'm not pretending to be original. Thomas Jefferson knew the value of heightened dialogue and asserted more than two hundred years ago that given a preference, he would choose newspapers without government rather than government without newspapers, although Jefferson may have softened that stance somewhat had he been around to watch newspapers beat up Gary Hart and Bill Clinton or to discover how susceptible to propaganda, especially in the television age, many Americans have become. There can be no democracy in the full sense he envisioned without universal, critical literacy. This condition does not exist in our society and is why I have been qualifying the term *democracy* with descriptors like *true* and *authentic*. Because Jefferson was a slaveholder, he was more than a little bit hypocritical, but his better notions, like his understanding that governance by internal authority requires widespread informed debate, are yet worthwhile.

John Dewey took this conception a step further. In *Democracy and Education,* which appeared more than eighty years ago, he wrote:

A democracy is more than a form of government; it is primarily a mode of associated living, of conjoint communicated experience. The extension in space of the number of individuals who participate in an interest so that each has to refer his own action to that of others, and to consider the action of others to give point and direction to his own, is equivalent to the breaking down of those barriers of class, race, and national territory which kept men from perceiving the full import of their activity. These more numerous and more varied points of contact denote a greater diversity of stimuli to which an individual has to respond; they consequently put a premium on variation in his action. They secure a liberation of powers which remain suppressed as long as the incitations to action are partial, as they must be in a group which in its exclusiveness shuts out many interests. (87)

Paulo Freire also develops this idea of culturally diverse stimulation, while examining more directly the relative positions of students and teachers. In *Pedagogy of the Oppressed,* which appeared more than twenty-five years ago, he asserts:

A careful analysis of the teacher-student relationship at any level, inside or outside the school, reveals its fundamentally narrative character. This relationship involves a narrating subject (the teacher) and patient, listening objects (the students). The contents, whether values or empirical dimensions of reality, tend in the process of being narrated to become lifeless and petrified. Education is suffering from narration sickness. (57)

There was enough of a Jeffersonian-Deweyan-Freirean strain kept alive among language arts professionals to bring about the English Coalition Conference of 1987, convened in a nation probably more diverse and booming with more narration than could have been predicted by these intellectual antecedents of the conference participants. At the gathering, the theme of which was "Democracy through Language," old ideas were reworked and invigorated. An excerpt from the conference report reads.

The increased heterogeneity of our society also gives new urgency to enhancing students' ability to appreciate cultural diversity and multiple ways of reading and writing. The information explosion makes learning how to read and write absolutely vital for living, because without these abilities students will not be able to assimilate, evaluate, and control the immense amount of knowledge and the great number of messages which are produced every day. The development of new media similarly requires of citizens an enhanced ability to use different ways of reading and writing, and language arts instruction has an important role to play here. (86)

Perhaps no students have been more shut out, objectified, and bewildered than those who eventually enroll in adult education programs or those who enter so-called remedial programs in open-admissions colleges. These two groups can reasonably be viewed as one in some respects. I have, in fact, seen students proceed from adult education programs into colleges as discretionary admits, meaning without high school diplomas, and subsequently be referred back to adult education programs. The important matter is that most of these students have not prospered in our system of public education.

Many adult education students are members of ethnic minority or immigrant groups, of a people whose numbers on these shores are tied directly either to bloodshed or to dreams. When we meet them, they have not given up hope of securing credentials that will, they feel, enable them to succeed. Unfortunately, however, a large percentage of these students (like too many students overall) will be subjected to instructional practices that will not help them toward their goal. They are eager yet passive, maybe the worst disposition, in the long run, any group of students can possess. They search for saviors, instead of guides, in teachers, many of whom all too willingly accept the role. These students search for magic in methods; they settle for getting taught at while they fail to see themselves as largely responsible for their own learning. And what is especially ironic and painful to realize, as a spectator to some of this educational parade, is that these students' lives in many instances are the very case studies that indicate the ineffectiveness, from the standpoint of their own benefit, of dictatorial teaching. They indeed suffer—they, not education—personally, not abstractly—from narration sickness. And we lose them again.

I always hope to get in my class students who have been rather rebellious in previous schools and who prove to be somewhat contentious in general. I want to work with these spunky souls, who often not only know where they want to go (which most students know at least vaguely) but may have some strong and sensible ideas about how they want to get there. But, alas, I don't start out with these nervy types very frequently. I see instead remedial students doing the good old remedial thing, waiting on the remedy. They are expecting isolated, prepackaged grammar lessons. They are waiting on presentation of written format divorced from ongoing reading. I have had basic writing students ask me why I put so many reading assignments on the syllabus. After all, they reason, ever mindful of their convoluted prose, they have taken the course to learn how to write. And they are almost hopelessly intimidated by literary texts. I'll stretch this last point out a bit further, for I think that attempting to resolve the problem indicated here is perhaps the most important work I have done in class.

Several years ago, when reading essays students had submitted after reading a William Faulkner short story, "Dry September," I encountered a startling beginning: "This story was written in 1931 on a hot dry day in the month of September."

I was taken aback because a hot dry September day is simply the backdrop *in* the tale, and 1931 is the publication date indicated on the opening page of the story as it appeared in the anthology. The student demonstrated no understanding of a writer's ability to use language to create a world. In her mind Faulkner was doing the work of a stringer, and she was content to summarize what she perceived to be his impartial recording of events.

When I shared my own reading of "Dry September," a story on one level about a rumor of rape, I started explaining how it spoke to me about a certain psychosexual sickness that lies just below the surface of Southern life easily exposed by even the slightest suggestion of black-on-white rape and how the description of aridity illustrates that sickness. This same student interrupted me. Peevishly she inquired, "Where did you get that from?" She wasn't challenging my originality; she didn't understand my symbol making. Prepared to scour the text for literal evidence, for some words she had missed, she failed to see that an examination of my belief system was more appropriate if she wished to know the total sources from which I derived meaning. Despite my subsequent request for interpretive papers, she penned one of the most detached efforts ever given to me in an English class. Indeed, she was far more concerned with her usage—which, no surprise to me, was poor—than with interpretation. This was a Freshman English class, not a basic writing course, mind you. She had passed one of those already.

Although the most memorable case of what I call low literary self-esteem, this student's plight is not uncommon. A number of students have, like her, staggered through watered-down basic skills or adult education courses only to be left with little or no conception about how to proceed successfully in, say, College English I. This episode helped to convince me that work in literary response should be a mainstay of all reading and writing courses I teach, basic and developmental classes as well as those designated Freshman English. But I still didn't have a broad view, not anything like a theory of democratic schooling. I saw myself as simply making a reasonable response to an immediate problem. As a practical matter, I figured, if students could write critical papers on literature, they could fulfill their English course requirements. The sooner they started working toward that goal, the better. Addressing the question of teaching literature, Peter Roberts writes:

> One answer to this argument is that in the teaching of Appropriate and Effective English, because people have always drawn on the techniques of persuasion inherent in the language of written literature, the study of written literature is the most fertile ground for understanding language use. In other words, the traditional categories of literature study—theme, structure/plot, style, content, purpose—are the very same factors that govern Effective English. Therefore, where once literature was an objective in itself, whose appreciation was aided by knowledge of its constituent factors, it can now be treated as general exemplification of factors which are used in specialized forms of persuasion (i.e. in advertising, labels, newspaper articles, etc.). (*West Indians and Their Language*, 201)

Influenced by the work of James Britton, through his book, *Language and Learning* and such essays as "The Role of Fantasy" and "English Teaching: Retrospect and Prospect," I became acutely aware of the possibilities of using literature as a way to expand students' conceptual powers and to foster expressive ability. Naturally, I held a vague notion that it had worked that way for me. Literature has always been a powerful way of reminding me that I am not just in the world but of it. Writing about literature or attempting to compose some myself makes up the bulk of the scribing I have managed. Through the realm of literature, it can be argued, runs the clearest path to proficiency in both reading and writing. In the wider world, stories engage people much more deeply than drills or restricted assignments, a relationship that should also hold in educational circles provided students are given a proper forum.

I came to recognize that the problem with students like the one who summarized the Faulkner story is not that they are totally devoid of critical ability. However, because they have learned to be intimidated, they usually don't bring what are at times substantial evaluative talents into the arena of formal education. They don't cope well with the surprising experience of being asked to pass judgment on texts already certified as great works, or so it appears, signified by their presence in an anthology or on a teacher's syllabus. Teachers themselves, sometimes merely by the sureness and forcefulness with which they speak about a piece of literature, frequently dominate class discussion and give the impression that their opinion is really the only important one, even as they push transactional or reader-response theory. I know I have quoted Louise Rosenblatt on the one hand, trying to persuade students that the primary subject matter of their papers had to be "the web of sensations and ideas that they spun between themselves and the text" (*The Reader, the Text, the Poem* 137), while on the other hand becoming too directive of their spinning. Such intrusion short-circuits the interpretive endeavor and fails to lend strength to student voices. Rather than look to deficit and skills models to explain student withdrawal from classroom literary encounters, teachers would do well to examine their own roles during such activities. There certainly are specific strategies that readers at every level can learn to employ to make better sense of texts, but these strategies are not the discrete "skills" about which many reading teachers are concerned. We could introduce teachers themselves to deconstruction, for example, as a critical tool without assuming a skills or decoding deficiency on their part. If we did assume deficiency of this sort, they would be right to feel insulted.

As my outlook broadened, with graduate study and the like, as well as finally and consciously linking political ideas I had held more explicitly to my work, I was able to articulate more substantial reasons for using literature in all language arts classes. I understood that along with passing courses and becoming more literate, it is fundamental that students begin practice in developing beliefs that are to be defended, amended, or discarded as they participate in the discourse of academic and wider formal settings, since informed and powerful voices existing in dialogic and critical relationships is the form of discourse this society supposedly privileges. Other voices, less informed, less powerful, generally are excluded from the dominant societal conversation. I wrote a few years back that surrounding a text in class, being united by it, being at odds with others because of it, approving and/or disapproving it, discussing it confidently, feeling passionate enough to write about it and want to share that writing (which then means attention to conventional usage), seeking new texts, and searching out new talk are some of the most important activities students can undertake—not because they are good ideas in and of themselves, I see now, but because they support democratic development and are on that basis to be favored.

By 1987, I was ready for the English Coalition Conference—if only I had been called. I'm not sure I would have gone anyway. It was held on an old plantation in Maryland, and that's a spooky kind of thing to me. Nonetheless, in my painstaking manner, I had moved very close in spirit to those who participated. To cite another section of their report:

> Teaching students how and why different ways of reading can find different meanings in the same text can provide important experience in understanding and appreciating opposing perspectives. Learning about the many different kinds of writing and ways of thinking which are the subject matter of the language arts curriculum can expand the capacity of students to imagine and value worlds other than their own. The ability to communicate their views in oral and written form and to listen with comprehension to the views of others is also indispensable to citizens in a democracy, and enhancing this ability is a major aim of language arts education. (86)

So neither I nor the folks at the conference would support narrowly defined skills curriculums in adult literacy programs or in any other programs. Interpretive work should characterize the academic lives of students. Reader-response theory, though a step in the right direction, is no miracle cure for all that has gone wrong. And there were no miracles in the class I alluded to earlier. Some students showed marked improvement as critics, while others, including the woman who struggled with the Faulkner story, did not. And even the students who did progress significantly were not as ready for College English II as I would have liked. They were still too afraid of "literature" and not trusting enough of themselves. They didn't display enough of the arrogance that is part of the temperament of all good readers and writers—and viewers, too, I might add, having observed the critical activity surrounding the movie *Malcolm X*.

Some moviegoers pointed out the historical inaccuracies of the film, legitimately so, given that many less informed viewers were ready to accept the film as historically accurate in every detail. Director Spike Lee, equally correct, insisted the film was a dramatic representation of Malcolm's life, not a documentary. As a result, Lee felt justified in taking artistic license. I had no quarrel with any party on this score. In fact, I found this particular debate relatively boring. A more interesting activity for language arts classes is for students and instructors to question how valid the division is that Lee made between dramatic and documentary. Could any film, even a documentary, be completely objective? Or consider *The Autobiography of Malcolm X*, a text regarded as a virtually indisputable source of authority by Lee and many others. Does autobiography have an absolute claim on truth or just a particular one—a subject requesting that we believe the one story of his or her life that only he or she can narrate in first person? I'm not anywhere near commending Bruce Perry's misguided psycho-babble about Malcolm, and I'm certainly not disparaging autobiography as a genre. I wrote one myself. I raise these questions to suggest more ways of talking and getting students to talk about textual authority, maybe to change relations of power between students and texts, to get students to see that they can act powerfully on stories, that stories don't just act on them.

Oprah Winfrey, at least three times on her television talk show discussing Lee's film, implored people not to worry about *Malcolm X*'s length, 201 minutes, but to go see it anyway. I would have liked to hear students talk about why Winfrey felt such exhortation was necessary. To whom did they think Oprah was specifically addressing her remarks? Did they think that a comment was being made about their interests and abilities? If so, what was their response? And what I'd be most interested in regarding any venture involving Malcolm X is what do students, especially adult education students (of whom Malcolm was one), think is the crucial lesson to be learned from his life? Do they accept the weak, tepid line that the central import of his life is that he overcame obstacles and had a tremendous capacity for reinventing himself? I know I don't accept it. You can run to your nearest politician to find a master of hurdling and reinvention. Malcolm stood straight up and aimed a fiery verbal assault directly against white supremacy and economic exploitation. That is what thrilled me on the verge of adolescence. I didn't care that he liked jazz and danced the Jitterbug. I liked Motown and did the Brooklyn Hustle. I didn't care what hard times he had gone through to get to that stance. I had my own hard times to go through. No, what was essential was that he was on the scene by whatever circumstances, tall, majestic, being defiant, and mostly being right. While I am witness to the commodification of X, I'm looking for some X-ification, if you will, some basic decency and far less greed in our structures of commodity. I'm seeking some X-ification, some gentle equalities and student empowerment in our establishments of education. This is how I am reading X as text.

I may seem far afield from my basic argument, but actually I have merely stepped inside it for a moment, personifying critical reading ability, conceived broadly, though, of course, I don't imagine that everyone shares my views or endorses my explication.

Before I begin to wind down, and point out some specific contrasts between authoritarian and democratic practices, I want to be as clear as possible about some of my previous remarks concerning students. I don't mean to imply that all adult education students are so easily victimized or that all programs are set up in such a way as to achieve victimization. Neither do I mean to underplay psychological strategies that account for student behavior, a passive rejection of certain kinds of formal instruction, for example. Nor do I ignore external social factors that undermine success. I simply wish to emphasize what I feel most familiar with, a seemingly enabling eagerness and availability to learn rendered nearly useless in school by a learned passivity about how schooling should proceed.

A view of knowledge as lore, then, as accumulated information, is an authoritarian view. A teacher holding this view would consequently conduct classes in all authoritarian manner, assuming his or her rightful function to be that of distributing knowledge to his or her charges. This promotes the student passivity I have been describing. On the other hand, from a democratic view, knowledge is a process that is only successful in schools with active student participation, which is proper preparation for the active participatory lifestyles envisioned by some of the scholars mentioned earlier.

The construct that admirable progress is being made as teachers "cover the material" is an authoritarian construct. That more meaningful activity occurs when students "uncover material" is a democratic construct.

To focus exclusively on teachers' purposes is authoritarian. Cointentional education, as Freire puts it, is preferable—not because it has a nice ring to it, but because it is democratic.

A deficit model of language differences is also authoritarian. Deviations from standard or target usage are treated as deficiencies. Black English is "Broken English" and has to be repaired. Jamaican Creole is "Broken English" and has to operated upon. There is a line on the back of the City University of New York Writing Assessment Test booklet on which students are to indicate their native language. Many students from the Caribbean indeed write "Broken English" on this line. The first few times I saw this, I thought the students were being facetious. But I soon changed my mind. The rate at which they were failing the exam was no joke. Students, not dialects, have been broken, and negative responses to language differences have been much of their problem. An equality model of language variation, the only one supported by modern sociolinguistic scholarship, does not support repair-model instruction. Understanding, as George Bernard Shaw did, that "a language is a dialect with an army behind it," democratic educators focus upon repertoire expansion. They accept the legitimacy of various types of English and study them so as contribute to an enlightened discussion of learning and teaching with respect to the various speaking populations to be served.

I think the history of English, if only in a rudimentary way, is an important topic for language arts classrooms. We could all stand to know how closely the earlier evolution of English was tied to politics and warfare. We could start with the collapse of the Roman Empire in the fifth century, talk some about clashes among Jutes, Celts, Angles, and Saxons, and how this activity led to the development of certain Englishes, as did conflict with the

Norse, from whom were borrowed such essential items as the pronouns *they*, *them*, and *their*. We could talk about Duke William and his posse of Normans, their (remember a word from the Norse) conquest causing a considerable "Frenchifying" of English. *Government*, a word central to this presentation, is a French word. Then we have to notice the Anglo-Saxons, back in charge and growing strong enough to export English around the world to become the tongue upon which the sun never set. During this period dictionaries and prescriptive grammar books were produced. Standards of usage were established.

Writing instruction in schools has much to do with standards set by powerful groups. Being able to produce texts that meet that standard may be valuable ability. However, a focus on the standard to be reached, accompanied by disregard for different ways students may try to get there, is authoritarian and disabling. An approach in which the prevailing spirit is to take advantage of varying talents, strengths, and interests of students is more enabling, more democratic.

The final area I want to talk about is *multiculturalism*. I find it a term that obscures more than it illumines when forwarded as an educational concept; at least, that's what my conversations with people have led me to conclude. It is easy enough to argue against a monocultural ideal. To privilege one culture amid the wealth of diversity in this nation is certainly to be authoritarian. To celebrate cultural diversity is sensible. But of what is the celebration to consist? I often hear discourse on multiculturalism reduced to the level of cuisine, a chicken chow mein, chicken fettucini, Southern fried chicken, arroz con pollo kind of multiculturalism. I hear leaders say our nation's strength lies in its diversity, though I don't often hear them articulate why, that the real virtue of multiculturalism or ethnic diversity is that it supremely tests the nation's resolve to live up to the rhetoric contained in its most cherished documents. Will we comprehend the teasing oxymoron near the end of Ellison's *Invisible Man*? To quote:

> It's "winner take nothing" that is the great truth of our country or any country. Life is to be lived, not controlled; and humanity is won by continuing to play in the face of certain defeat. Our fate is to become one, and yet many— This is not prophecy, but description. (564)

Ira Shor, who is on the faculty at CUNY's Graduate Center, posed to me a question: what would college language arts classes look like if we took multiculturalism seriously? The obvious answer is that the content of curriculums would change. It would become more diversified. More and more literature by authors from so-called minority groups would be incorporated, and so on. Again, that's the easy answer. I contend, however, that three other results, usually overlooked, of taking multiculturalism seriously are ultimately more important than mere diversification of the canon.

The first result I'm thinking about is that whole departments would be more serious about multiculturalism. This may seem an odd point to make, since I have already mentioned a diversified canon. But such progressive activity is often confined to only a few members in a department. It becomes someone's specialty. We create a cadre of experts on multiculturalism when, in fact, we should all be striving for expertise. Some usually well-intentioned colleagues are still asking me to, quote, "give them something on multiculturalism," like my name is Mr. Multicultural or something like that, like I'm not just one African American man. I see the term on numerous job announcements these days: "Candidate must have demonstrated commitment to multicultural education." I surmise that the insistence on this quality in applicants is because the employers possess so little of it themselves.

The second result I foresee is that the ethnic composition of classrooms would change, especially in upper-level literature courses. A higher concentration of students from so-called minorities might even become language arts professionals. I'm not sure what the exact effect would be on adult education programs, but it would ultimately be positive.

The third result, most important, of taking multiculturalism seriously is that it would disappear, that is, as a distinct educational concept, at least in the sense it now exists. At present, it is an *ism* that circumscribes the failure to take full advantage of the diversity that has always surrounded us. The United States has been a polylingual, multicultural nation since its inception, and if the educational system had reflected this reality all along, there would never have been a need to propose this particular *ism* as a panacea for educational ills. If a multicultural ideal were ever present, it would not have become a special movement. In fact, it may be time for another movement, one that stresses not just recognition of diversity but diverse interaction. This new movement, really an eve-of-the-twenty-first-century update of an intellectual tradition I sketched earlier, would emphasize not just multicultural existence but transcultural dialogue.

One evening in a restaurant, I remarked to my friend and colleague Nancy Lester that with all the new experts on multiculturalism running around, it was a clear signal to stop using the term to explain anything. It was time to light out, as Huck Finn might put it, for other rhetorical territory. I was amazed by the numbers. As I reexamined the program for the annual convention of the National Council of Teachers of English in 1981, the first year I attended, I hardly noticed any reference to multiculturalism, though by then I had heard the term used among literary artists for at least a decade. Of approximately two hundred panels and workshops at the six-day conference, only three were billed as multicultural or multiethnic in perspective, and one of those panels was composed entirely of presenters from Canada. The conference theme was "Sustaining the Essentials." For the 1989 NCTE annual convention, the theme was "Celebrating Diversity." Did I hear someone say bandwagon, that it won't last? We'll see.

Insofar as *multi* means diverse fluidity, it sounds good to me. But where *multi* means distinct, as the fixed tile in a mosaic, I think we have problems. This is one reason I enjoyed Toni Morrison's book *Playing in the Dark*. Her ideas about American Africanism—Morrison's phrase to describe how the African presence in the United States profoundly affected the work of writers such as Willa Cather, Ernest Hemingway, and Mark Twain—make for good cross-cultural conversation.

It is all before us now. There is a past to draw upon but not to duplicate. What about the golden age of American education when all was fine? Forget it. It never happened. Numerous scholars have argued convincingly that American education has generally focused on producing a highly literate elite and a minimally literate general populace. Never was it the most widely held view among administrators to provide high level literacy for everyone, what business leaders are calling for urgently. It is indeed a new literacy challenge we and our students face, a task we must be equal to if we are to have the most favorable participation in civic and business affairs, if our society is genuinely to become more inclusive and approach its full potential for humanism.

References

Britton, James. "English Teaching: Retrospect and Prospect." In Gordon M. Pradl, ed., *Prospect and Retrospect: Selected Essays of James Britton*. Montclair, NJ: Boynton/Cook, 1982. 210–15.

———. *Language and Learning* (1970). Harmondsworth: Penguin, 1972.

———. "The Role of Fantasy." In Gordon M. Pradl, ed., *Prospect and Retrospect: Selected Essays of James Britton*. Montclair, NJ: Boynton/Cook, 1982. 38–45.

Dewey, John. *Democracy and Education* (1916). New York: Free Press, 1966.

Ellison, Ralph. *Invisible Man* (1952). New York: Vintage, 1972.

Freire, Paulo. *Pedagogy of the Oppressed*. New York: Continuum, 1970.

Lloyd-Jones, Richard, and Andrea Lunsford, eds. *The English Coalition Conference: Democracy through Language*. Urbana, IL: NCTE, 1989.

Morrison, Toni. *Playing in the Dark: Whiteness and the Literary Imagination*. Cambridge, MA: Harvard UP, 1992.

Perry, Bruce. *Malcolm X: The Life of a Man Who Changed Black America*. Barrytown, NY: Station Hill Press, 1991.

Roberts, Peter. *West Indians and Their Language*. Cambridge: Cambridge UP, 1988.

Rosenblatt, Louise. *The Reader, The Text, The Poem: The Transactional Theory of the Literary Work*. Carbondale, IL: Southern Illinois UP, 1978.

QUESTIONS FOR REFLECTION, JOURNAL WRITING, AND DISCUSSION

1. According to Gilyard, what is wrong with the kind of education often given to remedial students? Do you agree?

2. Would you define yourself as an eradicationist, bidialectalist, or pluralist, in regard to Black dialects? How would you defend this position to a colleague with a different point of view?

3. Why is Gilyard happy to find rebellious students in his class? How would you feel about finding such students in yours?

4. Gilyard says that many scholars believe that "American education has generally focused on producing a highly literate elite and a minimally literate general populace." Do you agree?

5. Gilyard says, "Our work as teachers is political—whether we construe it that way or not—and our obligation, which we sometimes shun, is to provide clarity of political vision regarding our teaching endeavors." Do you agree?

Chapter 6

Pedagogy of the Distressed

Jane Tompkins

Jane Tompkins was, until recently, Professor of English at Duke University and is now Professor of Curriculum and Instruction in the College of Education at the University of Illinois at Chicago. She edited *Reader-Response Criticism: From Formalism to Poststructuralism* (1980) and is the author of *Sensational Designs: The Cultural Work of American Fiction, 1790–1870* (1985); *West of Everything: The Inner Life of Westerns* (1992); and her memoir of teaching and learning, *A Life in School: What the Teacher Learned* (1996). *A Life in School* won the 1998 Frederick W. Ness Award for a book on liberal education, granted by the American Association of Colleges and Universities. She currently gives lectures and workshops around the country on making the classroom a more humane environment. The following article is from *College English*, 52, October 1990.

> *Fear is what prevents the flowering of the mind.*
> —J. Krishnamurti, *On Education*

I

As professors of English we are always one way or another talking about what we think is wrong with the world and to a lesser extent about what we'd like to see changed. Whether we seek gender equality, or economic justice, or simply believe in the power and beauty of great literature, we preach some gospel or other. We do this indirectly, but always. What I have to say is very simple and comes directly off this point: our practice in the classroom doesn't often come very close to instantiating the values we preach.

I was led to think about the distance between what we do as teachers and what we say we believe in by Paulo Freire's *Pedagogy of the Oppressed*, whose great theme is that you cannot have a revolution unless education becomes a practice of freedom. That is, to the extent that the teaching situation reflects the power relations currently in force, which are assumed to be oppressive and authoritarian, to that extent will the students themselves, when they come to power, reproduce that situation in another form. He argues that if political revolution is to succeed, pedagogy must first enact that very unalienated condition which the revolution presumably exists to usher in. Now the situation that currently pertains in the classroom, according to Freire, can best be understood through the analogy of banking. "In the banking concept of education," he writes, "knowledge is a gift bestowed by those who consider themselves knowledgeable upon those whom they consider to know nothing. . . . Education thus becomes an act of depositing, in which the students are the depositories and the teacher is the depositor. Instead of communicating, the teacher issues communiques and makes deposits which the students patiently receive, memorize, and repeat" (58).

I don't think that this is the model we have to contend with in the United States today, at least not in higher education, at least not for the most part. We have class discussion, we have oral reports, we have student participation of various kinds—students often choose their own paper topics, suggest additional readings, propose issues for discussion. As far as most of us are concerned, the banking model is obsolete. But what we do have is something no less coercive, no less destructive of creativity and self-motivated learning, and that is something I'll call the performance model.

I became aware of this phenomenon some four or five years ago when I was teaching a combined graduate-undergraduate course at Columbia University. Why the realization came to me then I cannot explain. I remember walking down the empty hall to class (always a little bit late) and thinking to myself, "I have to remember to find out what they want, what they need, and not worry about whether what I've prepared is good enough or ever gets said at all." Whereas, for my entire teaching life, I had always thought that what I was doing was helping my students to understand the material we were studying—Melville or deconstruction or whatever—I had finally realized that what I was actually concerned with and focused on most of the time were three things: a) to show the students how smart I was, b) to show them how knowledgeable I was, and c) to show them how well-prepared I was for class. I had been putting on a performance whose true goal was not to help the students learn but to perform before them in such a way that they would have a good opinion of me. I think that this essentially, and more than anything else, is what we teach our students: how to perform within an institutional academic setting in such a way that they will be thought highly of by their colleagues and instructors.

What is behind this model? How did it come to be that our main goal as academicians turned out to be performance? I think the answer to the question is fairly complicated, but here is one way to go. Each person comes into a professional situation dragging along behind her a long bag full of desires, fears, expectations, needs, resentments—the list goes on.

But the main component is fear. Fear is the driving force behind the performance model. Fear of being shown up for what you are: a fraud, stupid, ignorant, a clod, a dolt, a sap, a weakling, someone who can't cut the mustard. In graduate school, especially, fear is prevalent. Thinking about these things, I became aware recently that my own fear of being shown up for what I really am must transmit itself to my students, and insofar as I was afraid to be exposed, they too would be afraid.

Such fear is no doubt fostered by the way our institution is organized, but it is rooted in childhood. Many, perhaps most people, who go into academic life are people who as children were good performers at home and in school. That meant that as children they/we successfully imitated the behavior of adults before we were in fact ready to do so. Having covered over our true childish selves, we have ever since been afraid of being revealed as the unruly beings we actually are. Fear of exposure, of being found out, does not have its basis in any real inadequacies either of knowledge or intelligence on our part, but rather in the performance model itself which, in separating our behavior from what we really felt, created a kind of false self. (This notion of the false self comes from Alice Miller's *The Drama of the Gifted Child*). We became so good at imitating the behavior of our elders, such expert practitioners at imitating whatever style, stance, or attitude seemed most likely to succeed in the adult world from which we so desperately sought approval that we came to be split into two parts: the real backstage self who didn't know anything and the performing self who got others to believe in its expertise and accomplishments. This pattern of seeking approval has extended itself into our practice as teachers. Still seeking approval from our peers and from our students, we exemplify a model of performance which our students succeed in emulating, thus passing the model down to future generations. Ironically, as teachers we are still performing for the teachers who taught us.

There is one other kind of fear that I want to mention here, institutional in its origin, and that is the fear of pedagogy itself as a focus of our attention. We have been indoctrinated from the very start, at least I was, to look down on pedagogy as a subject matter and to deride colleges of education. I was taught to see them as a sort of natural repository for the unsmart, the people who scored in the 50th percentile on their tests and couldn't make it into the higher realms to which I had so fortunately been admitted.

I remember quite vividly my introduction to this point of view. It was in an anteroom at Swarthmore College while waiting to be interviewed by a committee representing the Woodrow Wilson Foundation. While I sat there in a state of abject terror, I overheard a conversation between two young men also hoping to convince the committee's greybeards to find them worthy of a fellowship. One of them said to the other—I no longer remember his exact words—that thinking about teaching was the lowest of the low and that anyone who occupied himself with it was hopelessly beyond the pale and just didn't belong in higher education. I'll never forget my surprise and dismay at hearing this opinion which had never occurred to me before, for I had previously thought (coming from a family of teachers) that teaching was an important part of what any college professor would do. As things turned out, I subsequently embraced the view I overheard and held it as my own for some thirty years; or rather, this view embraced me, for my antipedagogical indoctrination went on pretty steadily throughout graduate school.

Now obviously, despite all this, I must have given some thought over the years to what went on in my classroom. One cannot be a total somnambulist and still survive, though I think a lot of people, myself included, have come pretty close. But I paid attention only when forced to because things weren't going well, and even then I felt I was doing something vaguely illegitimate. I used to wonder by what mysterious process others managed their classes, since no one I knew had been trained to do it and no one ever talked, really talked, about what they did. Oh, there were plenty of success stories and the predictable remarks about a discussion that had been like pulling teeth but never anything about how it really felt to be up there day after day.

In this respect teaching was exactly like sex for me—something you weren't supposed to talk about or focus on in any way but that you were supposed to be able to do properly when the time came. And the analogy doesn't end there. Teaching, like sex, is something you do alone, although you're always with another person/other people when you do it; it's hard to talk about to the other while you're doing it, especially if you've been taught not to think about it from an early age. And people rarely talk about what the experience is really like for them, partly because, in whatever subculture it is I belong to, there's no vocabulary for articulating the experience and no institutionalized format for doing so.

But there is one thing people do sometimes talk about in relation to teaching, and they do this now more frequently than in the past. They talk about using teaching as a vehicle for social change. We tell ourselves that we need to teach our students to think critically so that they can detect the manipulations of advertising, analyze the fallacious rhetoric of politicians, expose the ideology of popular TV shows, resist the stereotypes of class, race, and gender; or, depending on where you're coming from, hold the line against secular humanism and stop canon-busting before it goes too far.

But I have come to think more and more that what really matters as far as our own beliefs and projects for change are concerned is not so much what we talk about in class as what we do. I have come to think that teaching and learning are not a preparation for anything but are the thing itself. There is a catch-22 in the assumption that what you say in class or what you write for publication is the real vehicle for change. For if you speak and write only so that other people will hear and read and repeat your ideas to other people who will repeat them, maybe, to other people, but not so that they will do something, then what good are your words?

I've come to realize that the classroom is a microcosm of the world; it is the chance we have to practice whatever ideals we may cherish. The kind of classroom situation one creates is the acid test of what it is one really stands for. And I wonder, in the case of college professors, if performing their competence in front of other people is all that that amounts to in the end.

II

I've now made an awkward lunge in the direction of creating a different world in the classes I teach. It wasn't virtue or principle that led me to this but brute necessity caused by lack of planning. A year ago last fall, because I knew I wouldn't have time to prepare my classes in the usual way, I borrowed a new teaching method from a colleague and discovered, almost by accident, a way to make teaching more enjoyable and less anxiety-producing.

More enjoyment and less anxiety do not sound like very high-minded goals. In fact, they are self-centered. My upbringing taught me never to declare that anything I did was self-centered, especially not if it had to do with an activity like teaching, which is supposed to be altruistic. But I had discovered that under the guise of serving students, I was being self-centered anyway, always worrying about what people thought of me. So I tried something else for a change.

What the method boils down to is this: the students are responsible for presenting the material to the class for most of the semester. I make up the syllabus in advance, explain it in detail at the beginning of the course, and try to give most of my major ideas away. (This is hard; holding on to one's ideas in case one should need them to fill some gap later on is bred in the bone after twenty-odd years in the classroom). The students sign up for two topics that interest them, and they work with whoever else has signed up for their topic: anywhere from two to four people will be in charge on any given day. On the first round of reports the groups meet with me outside of class to discuss their ideas and strategies of presentation. I give plenty of feedback in written form, but no grades.

I find that my classes are better. The students have more to say in every class, more students take part in the discussions, students talk more to each other and less to me, and the intensity and quality of their engagement with the course materials is higher than usual. Because I don't have the burden of responsibility for how things are going to go every time, I can contribute when I feel I really have something to say. I concentrate better on what is being said, on who is talking, and on how the class is going—how things feel in the class.

The upshot is I do less work and enjoy class more. But I feel guilty about this. Partly because somewhere along the way I got the idea that only back-breaking work should produce good results. I struggle not to feel guilty at teaching in a way that is pleasurable to me and free from fear because part of what I now try to do as a teacher conveys a sense of the way I think life ought to be. This means, among other things, offering a course that is not a rat race, either for me or for the students. I no longer believe that piling on the work is a good in itself or that it proves seriousness and dedication. The point is not to make people suffer. The trial-by-fire model that graduate school sets is a bad one for the classroom. Education is not a preparation for war; the university is not a boot camp.

Still, there is the question of whether, in shifting the burden of performance onto the students, I'm not making them do work I'm too lazy to do myself, sending them off on a journey with inadequate supplies, telling them to go fishing without a rod or bait, demanding that they play the Kreutzer Sonata before they can do a scale. It's true that in some cases the students don't deal with the material as well as I could, but that is exactly why they need to do it. It's not important for me to polish my skills, but they do need to develop theirs and to find a voice.

When the same person is doing the presenting all the time, inevitably one line of approach to the materials is going to dominate. But when it's not the teacher who is always calling the shots, the interests of the individual students have a chance to emerge. You find out what they want to focus on, think is important, believe in. Several points of view get to be enunciated from the position of designated speaker: students get practice in presenting material in a way that is interesting and intelligible to other people; the variety keeps the class entertained and passes responsibility around so that even the quietest students have to contribute and end up feeling better about themselves.

Almost every class I've conducted in this way has had its own intellectual center of gravity. A cluster of issues, or sometimes a single problem, keeps on coming up; the students develop a vocabulary and a common set of references for discussing it. This gives the class a sense of identity, a coherence as much social as intellectual.

But I want not so much to make a pitch for this method, which, after all, is not that new, as to relay what I have learned from these experiences.

Last spring I taught a course on a subject I had been wanting to explore but knew little about: the subject was emotion. The course was offered under the rubric Feminist Theory in the Humanities, one of three core courses in a women's studies graduate certificate program newly launched at my university. I'd gotten the idea for this course from a brilliant lecture

Alison Jaggar had given entitled "Love and Knowledge." Jaggar argued that since reason, in Western epistemology, had traditionally been stipulated as the faculty by which we know what we know, and since women, in Western culture, are required to be the bearers of emotion, women were automatically delegitimized as sources of knowledge, their epistemic authority cut off from the start.

Using this idea as my inspiration, I decided we would look at the way emotion had been dealt with in the West—in philosophy, psychology, anthropology, literature and literary criticism, and religious studies (this was an interdisciplinary course both in subject matter and in enrollment). We ended by looking at examples of feminist writing that integrated emotion and ideation both in substance and in form.

This was the most amazing course I've ever taught, or rather the most amazing course I've never taught, because each class was taught by the students. Since I had no expertise in any of the areas we were dealing with except the literary, there was no way I could be responsible for presenting the material every time. So, having put together a syllabus by hook or by crook, I distributed responsibility for class presentations in the way I've just outlined. I encouraged the students to be creative in their modes of presentation, and, since this was a course in emotion, encouraged people to be free in expressing their feelings and to talk about their own experiences whenever they seemed relevant. One of the points of the course was, in practice, to break down the barrier between public discourse and private feeling, between knowledge and experience.

You see, I wanted to be iconoclastic. I wanted to change the way it was legitimate to behave inside academic institutions. I wanted to make it OK to get shrill now and then, to wave your hands around, to cry in class, to do things in relation to the subject at hand other than just talking in an expository or adversarial way about it. I wanted never to lose sight of the fleshly, desiring selves who were engaged in discussing hegemony or ideology or whatever it happened to be; I wanted to get the ideas that were "out there," the knowledge that was piled up impersonally on shelves, into relation with the people who were producing and consuming it. I wanted to get "out there" and "in here" together. To forge a connection between whatever we were talking about in class and what went on in the lives of the individual members. This was a graduate course, and the main point, for me, was for the students, as a result of the course, to feel some deeper connection between what they were working on professionally and who they were, the real concerns of their lives.

This may sound utopian. Or it may sound child-like. But I did and do believe that unless there is some such connection, the work is an empty labor which will end by killing the organism that engages in it.

The course was in some respects a nightmare. There were days when people went at each other so destructively that students cried after class or got migraine headaches (I started getting migraines after every class before long). There were huge misunderstandings, factions, discussions at cross purposes, floundering, a sense of incoherence, everything that one might have feared. There were days when I decided I had literally opened Pandora's box and that we would all have been better off conducting business as usual. One day I myself was on the verge of tears as I spoke.

But this was also the most exciting class I've ever been in. I never knew what was going to happen. Apart from a series of stunning self-revelations, wonderful readings added to the reading list by the students, and reports whose trajectory came as a total surprise, we were led, as a class, by various reporting groups into role-playing, picture drawing, and even on one occasion into participating in a religious ceremony.

I learned from this class that every student in every class one "teaches" is a live volcano, or, as James Taylor puts it in his song, "a churnin' urn o' burnin' funk." There is no one thing that follows from this discovery, but for me it has meant that I can never teach in the old way again. By which I mean that I can never fool myself into believing that what I have to say is ultimately more important to the students than what they think and feel. I know now that each student is a walking field of energy teeming with agendas. Knowing this I can conduct my classes so as to tap into that energy field and elicit some of the agendas.

Which brings me, in conclusion, to my current rules of thumb reminders of what I've learned that keep me pointed in the right direction.

— Trust the students. Years of habit get in the way, years of taking all the responsibility for the class on yourself. You have to believe that the students will come through and not be constantly stepping into the breach. The point is for the students to become engaged, take responsibility, feel their own power and ability, not for you, one more time, to prove you've got the right stuff.

— Talk to the class about the class. For mnemonic purposes, we might call this the "good sex directive." Do this at the beginning of the course to get yourself and the students used to it. Make it no big deal, just a normal part of day-to-day business, and keep it up, so that anything that's making you or other people unhappy can be addressed before it gets too big or too late to deal with.

— Less is more. It's better to underassign than to overassign. Resist the temptation to pile on work. Work is not a virtue in and of itself. Quality of attention is what you're aiming at, not burn-out.

— Offer what you have. Don't waste time worrying that your thoughts aren't good enough. A structure for people to use in organizing their thoughts, to oppose, to get their teeth into is what is needed. Not *War and Peace.*

— Don't be afraid to try new things. This is a hard one for me. I'm always afraid a new idea will flop. So it flops. At least it provides variety and keeps things moving. I call this the Shirley MacLaine Principle: if you want to get the fruit from the tree, you have to go out on a limb.

— Let go. Don't hang on to what's just happened, good or bad. In some situations you probably can't tell which is which anyway, so let things happen and go on from there. Don't cling to the course, to the students, to your own ideas. There's more where they all came from. (A corollary to this rule is: you can't do it all. The whole point of this approach is that the teacher doesn't do everything.)

Gay Hendricks writes in *The Centered Teacher:*

> It is easy, if we view teaching as a one-way street, to fall into the trap of doing more than 50% of the work in the classroom. If we see teachers as having the answers and the students as having the questions we invite an imbalance in the relationship which can only cause a drain on teachers' energy. It is important to have a relationship with students which generates energy for all concerned rather than drains it. (27)

Teaching is a service occupation, but it can only work if you discover, at a certain point, how to make teaching serve you. Staying alive in the classroom and avoiding burn-out means finding out what you need from teaching at any particular time. I went from teaching as performance to teaching as a maternal or coaching activity because I wanted to remove myself from center stage and get out of the students' way, to pay more attention to them and less to myself. On an ideological plane, then, you might say I made the move in order to democratize the classroom. But on a practical plane I did it because I was tired. Sometimes, I used to think of my teaching self as the character played by Jane Fonda in a movie about a couple who had entered a dance marathon to earn money during the Depression; it was called *They Shoot Horses, Don't They?* In moving from the performance to the coaching model, I was seeking rest.

I'm not suggesting that other teachers should adopt this particular method. There are a million ways to teach. (Nor do I think the method is suitable only for graduate students or students in elite institutions: Freire worked with illiterate peasants). What I'm suggesting are two things. First, what we do in the classroom is our politics. No matter what we may say about Third World this or feminist that, our actions and our interactions with our students week in week out prove what we are for and what we are against in the long run. There is no substitute for practice. Second, the politics of the classroom begins with the teacher's treatment of and regard for him or her self. A kinder, more sensitive attitude toward one's own needs as a human being, in place of a desperate striving to meet professional and institutional standards of arguable merit, can bring greater sensitivity to the needs of students and a more sympathetic understanding of their positions, both as workers in the academy and as people in the wider world.

REFERENCES

Freire, Paulo. *Pedagogy of the Oppressed.* Myra Bergman Ramos. New York: Continuum, 1970.
Hendricks, Gay. *The Centered Teacher.* Englewood Cliffs, NJ: Prentice, 1981.
Jaggar, Alison M. "Love and Knowledge: Emotion in Feminist Epistemology." *Gender/Body/Knowledge: Feminist Reconstructions of Being and Knowing.* Eds. Alison M. Jaggar and Susan R. Bordo. New Brunswick: Rutgers UP, 1989.
Miller, Alice. *The Drama of the Gifted Child.* New York: Basic, 1983.

QUESTIONS FOR REFLECTION, JOURNAL WRITING, AND DISCUSSION

1. Tompkins, Shor, and Bruffee all critique what Freire has called the "banking concept of education." Why has this concept provoked so much criticism? What is your opinion?

2. Tompkins says "Teaching is a service occupation, but it can only work if you discover, at a certain point, how to make teaching serve you." Do you agree?

3. Do many teachers experience the kinds of fears described by Tompkins in this article? Do you? Do many teachers frown on thinking about the act/art of teaching? How do you feel?

Chapter 7

Pomo Blues: Stories From First-Year Composition

Lee Ann Carroll

Lee Ann Carroll is Professor of English and Director of Composition at Pepperdine University. She has published articles on adult literacy and composition pedagogy in *College Composition and Communication* and *College English*. The following article is from *College English*, 59, December 1997.

I begin my essay with some examples of fairly conventional, but, I believe, effective student responses to some typical writing assignments. These do not represent a startling new pedagogy, but should sound familiar to those who actually teach writing, to first-year students rather than those who like to think about how others should do it. A postmodernist perspective, now permeating composition studies, challenges us to rethink what we are doing when we read, write, and talk our way through projects like the ones I will describe. What difference does it make to think of the stories students tell not as the authentic reflections of autonomous individuals but as verbal artifacts heavily structured by the cultural and institutional contexts in which they are produced? What do first-year students need to know about decentering the subject, the multivocal text, and the interrelations of discourse and culture? The classroom is our second home, and our writing assignments can seem like natural, fairly straightforward transactions between a teacher and students. But playing in the background is what Lester Faigley at the 1993 CCCC called the "Pomo Blues." We have read Faigley's *Fragments of Rationality: Postmodernity and the Subject of Composition*, Harkin and Schilb's *Contending With Words: Composition and Rhetoric in a Postmodern Age*, Susan Miller's *Textual Carnivals: The Politics of Composition*, and articles drawing on postmodernist theory by Kurt Spellmeyer, James Berlin, Gary Olson, and others. These sources examine the work of postmodern thinkers in philosophy, literature, and political theory and argue for the impact they might have on the practice of teaching writing.

At the heart of the postmodernist shift in the classroom is a shift in the conception of the teacher and the student writer. In the past, both might be seen as fairly stable, autonomous individuals drawing on skills within themselves, acting independently to teach and to produce original pieces of writing. From a postmodernist perspective, teachers and students might be seen to be acting with much less autonomy. Their "selves," their teaching, and their writing are much more constructed by culture and language, bits and pieces pulled together provisionally to act in expected ways. Lester Faigley, for example, demonstrates how the "authentic voice" of the student writer is "discursively produced and discursively bounded" (*Fragments* 129), and David Bartholomae has repeatedly shown us ways that students attempt to "invent the university." Susan Miller argues that the "self" that the freshman in the composition classroom is imagined to be is often a "presexual, preeconomic, prepolitical person" (87). This "infantilized" student is "taught by those described in class schedules as 'staff'" (102). The "selves" of staff are equally shaped by cultural and political forces, as Nancy Welch shows in a critique of a teacher training program with a postmodernist agenda. After reviewing several new approaches to composition theory and pedagogy, Kathryn Flannery concludes, "To really understand the import of postmodern challenges to the ordinary subject means to rethink the dominance, the persistence of such notions as authenticity and authority in the composition classroom" (711–12).

What does it mean actually to play this tune day to day in the classroom? Faigley points out that the composition community generally has come to accept a postmodern view of knowledge and discourses of all kinds as socially and politically constructed, but, he adds, "Where composition studies has proven least receptive to postmodern theory is in surrendering its belief in the writer as an autonomous self" (*Fragments* 15). The questioning of belief in an autonomous self can be liberating, like surviving a disastrous love affair or improvising new versions of old songs. Yet without this belief, a house just isn't a home. I don't feel like my "self" any more. And what do we tell the kids? The news of postmodernism may strike students the way news of a divorce strikes children of an unhappy marriage. They may prefer the myths and stories that have shored up their familiar realities and, certainly, resist threats to their sense of "autonomous selves."

In this essay, I do not want to suggest an oversimplified "Postmodernism's Greatest Hits" approach to first-year composition; however, I do want to show how some key postmodern ideas about texts force me and my students to rethink some typical writing assignments and typical student responses. I will begin by describing the assignments rather straightforwardly, then consider how they invite the same type of postmodernist critique we might apply to texts of literature, popular culture, and the academic disciplines. I suggest, following John Schilb, that we should "involve students as coinquirers into the ramifications of cultural studies and postmodernism" even though the issues raised may "discompose" students (187). I will argue that we and our students live in a postmodern world and are already "discomposed" by the competing discourses that play in our heads. The Pomo Blues suggest that we give up grandiose, romantic notions that Freshman Comp can fix students either personally or politically. Instead, we come back more modestly to consider what kinds of stories it is possible for us to tell in English I, what it means to tell such stories "effectively," and what is at stake in playing different variations of the same tune.

Here are some of the assignments that have discomposed me and my students:

Assignment One: Following a Script

For a placement exam for Honors English, incoming first-year students are asked to write about any book that they particularly remember reading and tell why this book was especially memorable for them. The responses of these bright, imaginative students fall into several categories:

> *I was lost and now I am found.* I thought I was going to hate *The Old Man and the Sea*. It seemed like a boring story of an old man and a fish but through my English class I came to see what a great book it is.

> *A book was my therapist.* *Prince of Tides* gave me greater insights into the problems in my own family.

> *There is no frigate like a book.* *Bridge to Terabithia* took me to another world at a time when I was under a lot of stress in my own life.

Assignment Two: Writing as Re-Writing

Maria, in my advanced composition class, is student teaching in a sixth-grade classroom with a literature-based, whole language curriculum. Her students are reading novels and historical accounts about slavery. She asks them to write journals as though they were escaping slaves, imagining what they would feel. For my class, she tries completing this assignment herself and is disappointed with the result. She is able to write a technically competent journal, but it is flat, only remotely suggesting the pain and terror of slavery.

Assignment Three: Problematizing Experience

In the fall, my students and I begin a first-year composition course with an assignment sequence adapted from Bartholomae and Petrosky, *Ways of Reading*. We have read Freire's "The 'Banking' Concept of Education" and now students are writing a first draft about an experience they might "problematize." The assignment, sophisticated and complex like most of the suggestions for writing in *Ways of Reading*, reads in part:

> For this assignment, locate a moment from your own recent experience (an event or chain of events) that seems rich or puzzling, that you feel you do not understand but that you would like to understand better (or that you would like to understand differently). Write a first draft of an essay in which you both describe what happened and provide a way of seeing or understanding what happened. (744)

For this assignment, Alex writes a first draft about how his grandfather's illness taught him the true meaning of Christmas. Carolyn tells how she was rejected by her first-choice college and how this has made her a better person. Ray produces a lengthy, rambling essay that details his complaints about a roommate whom he sees as a snobby, spoiled rich kid.

Assignment Four: Making Stories Academic

For her last essay in the same first-year composition class, Laura writes "An Analysis of Our Homeless." She has been working collaboratively with other students to read and review a book they selected about children and poverty. Now she is completing an "I-Search" reporting on a topic related to the book and her own experience. She and her group are also preparing an oral presentation. Her essay begins:

> When you are raised in Santa Barbara, California, homelessness is something nearly impossible to ignore. Throughout the majority of my life I have been faced with the typical scenes of the homeless: the drunk old man, the hippie playing his guitar, and the mentally disturbed lady yelling at something that simply isn't there. As a teenager I participated in school functions helping to gather canned food for the homeless during Thanksgiving and helped my church feed the hungry in their annual Christmas dinner. These things were all a part of growing up in Santa Barbara and I never thought that homelessness would be different in any other places in America.
> My first trip to inner city Los Angeles was a shocking one. I could hardly keep the tears out of my eyes as I viewed the depressing sights around me. The unforgettable stench of LA enveloped me the instant we hit Main Street, but what was truly shocking to me was the sidewalks. Up and down Main Street to the right and to the left I saw tents, sleeping bags and cardboard boxes lining every available inch of space. Old men, young children, mothers, and wives lined the streets, curled up inside their small sidewalk palaces. I never knew this many homeless people existed and the reality of this shocked me in a powerful way.

Laura goes on to outline the questions that were raised in her mind by this experience. She focuses on the connection between homelessness and mental illness. In her essay, she uses a variety of statistics, examples, and cases to show how one might become homeless in America. She moves considerably beyond the stereotypes in her first two paragraphs.

As a new school year begins, what can I tell my students about these assignments and their responses to them? The question is not merely speculative because it is the end of August, hot and desert dry, and I need to plan my English 101 course. I envision the class as a space: a time blocked out to meet, a room set aside for the purpose, a grid of blank squares like the squares on the calendar I use to map out the semester. I scribble and erase, trying to make the imagined class fit exactly the number of squares allotted for it. Soon school will start and experience—mine, my students', that of the world at large—will overflow the squares. Within those squares, my students and I tell stories like the ones I have described in my examples—stories about books we have read, about illness, college, slavery, homelessness. Although students will write in many forms—essays, magazine articles, arguments, book reviews, poems, research reports—I think of all of these primarily as stories, tales made up by captive Scheherazades for the interest and amusement of their teacher, attempts to make sense of overflowing experience through language. At the risk of a kind of vulgar, homogenized postmodernism, I list five key postmodernist ideas about texts that I will include in my syllabus. I want to explain these to my students as key themes that we will return to again and again during the semester. I want to "make strange" the seemingly natural transaction of a teacher requiring writing and a student fulfilling those requirements. Many students sense already that their writing for the classroom is "artificial" and that what they say "doesn't really matter" as long as they give the teacher "what she wants." I want to examine this perception of their "job" as students, not erase the ways they and I are constructed by our institutional and cultural roles. At the same time, I want to suggest that we can be more conscious of how all of our experiences are rhetorically constructed and consider why it might "matter" to tell our stories one way rather than another. In this process, however, I hope I will not simply impose on students my own stories and the kind of selves I think they should be, insist that their "postmodernist" songs be correctly liberal, multicultural, sensitive to class distinctions, and free from gender bias.

I take seriously Lynn Worsham's and Victor Vitanza's warning that in attempting to tame theory, we are in danger of recreating the same limited views of self, language, and culture that postmodernist theorists have tried to explode. However, I agree with Gary Olson, who argues that the activity of theorizing "can lead us into lines of inquiry that challenge received notions or entrenched understandings that may no longer be productive" (54). With the Pomo Blues playing in the background, we cannot conduct business as usual. In the rest of my essay, I explore how the five key postmodernist ideas from my syllabus play out over my typical writing assignments.

1. THE STORIES WE TELL ARE THE STORIES THAT ARE CULTURALLY AVAILABLE TO US TO TELL.

When they are singing the Pomo Blues, my students are apt to find this idea depressing. James Berlin noted that, at times, "students and teachers are at odds with each other" in a curriculum at Purdue that tries to "problematize students' experiences, requiring them to challenge the ideological codes they bring to college by placing their signifying practices against alternatives" ("Poststructuralism" 31–32). I am not surprised that students are discomposed. My student, Alex, presents the positive story of his grandfather's illness as a sincere account of his family's individual and unique experience. He writes well and would be angry to have either his originality or his sincerity challenged. He certainly does not want to see himself as a "cultural dope," determined by made-for-television movies and self-help books that persistently ennoble pain and deny suffering. He struggles to find the language that fits his experience and the task, writing his first essay for a college class. But Alex is not finished after writing his first draft. The "problematizing" assignment asks students to write another draft of their narrative, working on passages "that seem to be evidence of the power of language to dominate, mystify, deceive, or alienate" (747) and telling the story in a "different" way, changing, perhaps, the perspective, the details reported, the language, and the intended effect on a reader. This assignment is meant to be more than the parlor trick of describing your dorm room in two different ways for your Aunt Bessie and your best friend Josh. In class, as we look at published narratives, including literacy stories by writers as different as Malcolm X and Helen Keller, we consider how these stories are familiar and what other stories the writers might have told. We notice how the writers construct both themselves and readers, working with and against cultural stereotypes and values. James Slevin suggests that this kind of critical literacy "can make all of us as writers aware that our voice is not necessarily our own, that it is not simply one possibility among a repertoire of private, personal voices; rather, it is, or can be an imposed voice, constructed not by us but for us" (71). In class workshops, I ask students to be critical readers of their own texts.

The class sympathizes with Alex's positive account of his experience and hesitates to critique his story. When Alex says he wants help revising, they notice that the positive version of his story seems weak in details. Writing of Christmas Day visiting Grandpa in the hospital, Alex says, "Even though we had a store bought dinner, it was still nice because we all were together. We all had a lot on our minds so we did not talk much, but we still managed to make a couple jokes every now and then to try to lighten the mood." Alex decides that one way he can work against the typical heart-warming story of illness is to write a more "negative" version of his experience. He speaks in a slightly different voice when he writes:

> Christmas dinner is supposed to be a great time filled with laughter, excitement, and, of course, a turkey and all the fixings, but this year my mind was wandering too much to even enjoy the store-bought dinner that we had got. Though nothing was mentioned of it, we knew everyone of our minds was wrestling with the thought that this may be the last Christmas that we would be lucky enough to have my Grandfather with us. We tried to lighten the atmosphere with small jokes and stories. Athough we managed to make small smiles across our faces, nothing could have changed the pain that we all felt deep in our hearts.

Alex begins in this draft to bring in some of the grief his family experienced. Is this a "problematized" version of his story? Alex, in his self-analysis of this assignment, writes, "The language I used to tell the story was quite different in the two narratives." He points out some examples of differences, then concludes, "The event may have been the same in both narratives, but I feel that the mood they convey to the reader is completely different." Alex changes the language of his narrative, but, as he says, the "event" stays "the same." He still learns a lesson about "the true meaning of Christmas." I know other discourses about illness, families, and Christmas that Alex might incorporate into his own, but has Alex gotten the assignment wrong because he has not written Susan Sontag's *Illness as Metaphor* or recognized how both illness and Christmas are commodified, because he has "problematized" the rhetoric of his narrative, but not a primary "ideological code"? A postmodernist perspective suggests that there is no essential experience to be narrated first, and then problematized. Neither version of Alex's story is necessarily more authentic. In class, we discuss why different versions of stories matter and examine the idea that the way we map experience in language is important because it can change how we act both individually, and as a society. The writing class has value because it is a place to play around with language, with different discourses. School authorizes the teacher to insist that Alex swap one discourse for another, even an unfamiliar discourse of philosophical or political critique. So Alex is not wrong in seeing his main job at the beginning of English I as largely a rhetorical problem, constructing a story that will be acceptable to his teacher, but also to himself and his peers. In any version of his story, Alex will be constructing an artifact out of the bits and pieces culturally available to him, including our class readings and discussions, an academic discourse that we have had only three weeks to examine. The desire for mastery, for language to construct a coherent, familiar narrative, works powerfully against the directive of the teacher-reader to disrupt this narrative with another type of "story."

And Alex does learn something from this assignment about how texts are constructed. He explains that his work "illustrates the importance of reading everything objectively, because sometimes people are not even aware that they are slanting what they tell, but they are. It is up to the reader to get their information from a variety of different sources to be sure that they are receiving the whole story." Alex maintains the Enlightenment concept that there is a whole story out there somewhere that the readers can piece together if they can only read enough sources "objectively." And he says he especially enjoyed this assignment because it allowed him to "write more from my heart."

The second key idea, however, continues to challenge the notion that writing comes primarily "from the heart," rather than from familiar cultural narratives.

2. THE CONVENTIONS AND DETAILS OF MANY OF THE STORIES WE TELL ARE, IN A SENSE, ALREADY WRITTEN AND READ BY THE CULTURE.

From a teacher's perspective, this idea helps Maria and me analyze the slave narrative assignment for sixth graders. Maria knows writing process pedagogy, so she has led her students through a prewriting exercise brainstorming how they would feel if they were planning to escape from slavery and what might happen to them. At first this seems like an exercise in empathy, one self putting itself in the place of another. Few of us could truly enter into the fear and pain of slavery, and one might fear trivializing suffering through encouraging a spurious empathy. But actually writing the imagined journal calls for quite different skills. Most of us can quickly imagine the elements sixth graders will incorporate in their narratives, the "moves" they might make in telling such a story. These may vary somewhat depending on each student's prior knowledge but will likely include hiding in a field or barn, following the north star, crossing a river, being pursued by slave catchers, and so forth. In that sense, each student's narrative is already written in the teacher/reader's head before the student begins. The student's skill is not empathy but the ability to pick up the appropriate discourses from reading and to reproduce them. We are only now analyzing the competing discourses in original slave narratives. These are reinterpreted and conventionalized again in the mass media and materials for school children. It takes extraordinary ability—one thinks of Toni Morrison's *Beloved*—to reinvent this story.

This is not to say that teachers should not give this sort of assignment. Entering into a discourse of slavery does focus children's attention on this experience. Maria's own narrative of slavery is best seen as one way of integrating and reporting what she has learned. While teachers might look for creativity in students' imaginary journals, often the papers judged most creative are those that recreate in the greatest detail and variety the sources the child is familiar with. A teacher of immigrant children in East Los Angeles complained to me of her fourth graders' lack of creativity in writing about the sights, sounds, and smells of Christmas. When she described to me the kinds of details that might show creativity, she suggested the fragrant pine tree, the crackling fire, the roasting turkey, and the other accoutrements of an idealized Dickensian Christmas. Again, the text was in a sense already written and read, and students' success measured by their ability to manipulate conventions which, in this case, were not part of their experience. And it would not be enough merely to expect children to substitute within the frame of the Christmas story details of their experience, turkey with *mole* rather than with stuffing. Many of these children who may manipulate language creatively in other contexts have limited backgrounds in reading and storybooks and do not share the teacher's implicit understanding of the basic moves one might make in telling such a story.

Though first-year college students often have more extensive repertoires of rhetorical moves, the classroom context continues to shape how students manipulate these conventions.

3. THE STORIES WE CAN TELL ARE CONSTRAINED BY THE CONTEXT IN WHICH WE TELL THEM, WITH MUCH LEFT OUT OR SUPPRESSED.

This third key idea says more than that we consciously shape our texts to fit our audience and purpose. It should be obvious that the situation in which we write powerfully shapes the stories we tell, and yet the constraints of writing for a college class may seem so normal to teachers and students that they become invisible. On a global level, I think we have a very limited perception of how time, physical arrangements of classes, institutional structures, and daily procedures work to form our perceptions of what kind of writing is appropriate or possible in the classroom. Here, I will simply consider some of the constraints that are easier to make visible to students and ourselves. Ray's complaining essay about his roommate seemed at first merely disorganized and confusing. But in a conference, Ray explained that he was gay and he believed that was why his roommate was treating him with such disdain and hostility. Suppressing this information that he did not want to include in a classroom essay limited Ray to a conventional story of roommate problems but contributed to an emotional tone that seemed out of proportion to arguments about who left dirty socks on the floor. Yet Ray wanted to tell this story. Encouraged by the "problematizing" assignment to experiment with other voices, he took the unusual step of recasting his entire story as an opera set in student days in a mythical Italian Renaissance university town. This frame, certainly unconventional for the classroom, revealed Ray, a music major, to be highly creative and skilled in drawing on the operas he knew and in manipulating those elements to produce a text that allowed him to maintain the privacy he wanted while more nearly capturing the drama he was experiencing. (He later also found a roommate he perceived to be more humane.)

Ray's struggle with this assignment and Alex's difficulty in reframing his family story might suggest that we should avoid writing about personal experience, which is often fraught with conflicts over what to reveal, what to suppress. But constraints operate on less personal stories, too. When we analyzed the Honors English placement test, which we no longer give, we were struck by the way the texts were again, in a sense already written and read. They fell into predictable types and were invariably positive. Even a student who had been tortured by studying *Hamlet* for an entire semester would cheerfully conclude that this had been a good experience. What other story could you tell if you were a college freshman wanting to be in Honors English and writing under time pressure for an audience of professors? When we ranked these placement essays, the best were able to create the appearance of sincerity with much relevant detail and a restrained tone, not too effusive, either serious or gently self-mocking. Now I do not mean to say that none of these stories were "true." Good English students are often students who like books and that is one of the reasons we asked about their reading. But the best essay is not the "truest"; it is one that rings most true for the readers.

Relentlessly insisting on a positive outcome and maintaining that gently self-mocking tone is a constraint that many students seem to apply to their classroom writing. Carolyn's first draft about being rejected by several other colleges suppressed her resentment of affirmative action plans that she felt favored some of her friends and worked against her. For Carolyn, the problematizing assignment does prompt her to rethink the choices she has made in writing. Retelling her story allows Carolyn to acknowledge that there is a "problem" in the way students are selected for college and that this problem has significantly affected her own life. The process of retelling is an antidote to some students' belief that they have told their own true story in the one and only way possible and there is nothing left to say. As

Judith Summerfield notes, "currently fashionable constructs of plurality and relativity are implicated in recent narrative theories: we know that there is no one story of an event, but there are stories; no history, but histories" (180). This may be less obvious to students.

When students simply reproduce cultural commonplaces, teachers complain that these students "can't think critically." But critical thinking is not an attribute students have or lack; it is an active process. Trying to recover what the constraints of particular story lines pressure us to leave out is a way of thinking more critically. In my classroom, we accept the cultural commonplace and, indeed, applaud those who can reproduce these well, with lots of specific detail and what the handbooks call "effective word choice." These are powerful stories. Instead of forbidding them, we want to examine the sources of their power. To do this, in one assignment I encourage students to write a "publishable" article on a topic related to language issues that we have been studying and that they will continue to research. Their task is to mimic as much as possible the way that topics like communication between women and men or censorship are discussed in women's magazines or the daily paper or the nightly news. Students are frequently adept at relaying the common sense wisdom of the mass media, complete with appealing layouts, typefaces, and illustrations. Sam, an international student from Singapore, joins a peer writing group studying gender and language, saying he wants to understand more about "what's going on with women" and also to represent the "male" point of view. He models his publishable writing on an actual column that offers readers of a male-oriented magazine advice about flirting—including the tip that pro-choice rallies might be a good place to meet sexually active women. Sam, in turn, offers advice to women in his article entitled "Sexism? Let's Say Something Boys." After many suggestions from his writing group and his writing center tutor about tone, style, examples, and overall effect, Sam's final draft begins with a magazine-type anecdote:

> "Men are all chauvinist pigs," proclaimed a silver-tongued young lady who was sitting with a couple of her friends, who were all, like her, in their twenties in a cafe. She continued her bashing on men and their stereotypical name-calling on women, which are directed on their "oinkers." Sitting on a table next to them, I could clearly hear—or shall I say—listen tentatively and feel a little unjustified. I, as a superior sex, would want to defend our fellow kinsmen from the attack and come out victorious again, like how it should be. But this time, I just sat down. Are we that despised that we should be called a filthy animal? The answer from the three million people reading this article is a clear "No." But why is the claim? I am not writing to deny the fact that we, men, are in a certain degree, sexist. The point I am trying to say to you, women out there, is, "Hey, calm down a little will you? We are often being treated unfairly too."

Finding models of published articles to imitate for this assignment leads students to consider different ways they might structure information. They can make their case as young Republicans or radical feminists, but they need to find forums where their case can be made. This is an opportunity to speak in the voice of Rush Limbaugh, the editors of the *Los Angeles Times,* or *Cosmopolitan* magazine. Surprisingly, perhaps, in these articles, I seem to read fewer comments that strike me as egregiously sexist, racist, or homophobic than I find in students' more conventional classroom essays. In those classroom essays, students may believe they are conveying simply their own non-negotiable personal opinions. On the other hand, in his "publishable" article, Sam, despite his sometimes twisted syntax and shaky sense of audience, discovers through imitating a model and through the responses of his peers and tutor that he can, and indeed must, be entertaining as well as persuasive for the mass market. He becomes more conscious of shaping his opinions in language, what he leaves in and what he leaves out. The constraints of mainstream popular publications may push students to more bland, homogenized expressions of opinion and information at the same time as their writing becomes more "colorful."

In a second piece of writing based on the same topic as their publishable imitation, students include more material from their research and their own experience that is added, left over, or reshaped from their earlier article. The structure of this text, though modeled on the familiar I-Search paper, is flexible. Instead of struggling to find "smooth transitions" from one discourse to another, Sam uses sub-heads to lay out what he can say at this point. He writes about how he got interested in the topic of gender and language and what he learned from reading Dale Spender's *Man Made Language* and other sources. The sections of his paper include "The Down Side," "The Complaints," "The Need for Inclusive Language," "Teaching of Inclusive Language," and "Some Alternative Names." While this is not a well-formed academic essay, it does display some of the competing discourses Sam has encountered in this project and one way of putting these together. In more formal academic writing, under the constraints of time and the expectation that all school writing must be "well-organized," students frequently reach for those texts that are easiest to reproduce and suppress everything that does not fit. What we take as critical thinking is another type of discourse, a learned way of talking, about social problems and popular culture—the staple topics of first-year composition courses. The "critical" texts that teachers have already written and read in their heads may be as unfamiliar to many freshmen as the Dickensian Christmas stories were to East Los Angeles fourth graders.

Compelled to write in new genres in their college classes, students express the frustration most writers feel in trying to connect what they experience in day-to-day life, what they think in their heads, and what they are able to express on paper. The fourth key idea is another way of thinking about those connections and contradictions that Sam and other students may sense but must often suppress to produce acceptable, coherent classroom texts.

4. NON-NARRATIVE FORMS ARE OFTEN CLOSELY RELATED TO SUPPRESSED PERSONAL NARRATIVES.

Traditional academic writing informed by Western rationalism encourages students to adopt a guise of objectivity. This version of critical thinking assumes a stable self free to sift through competing arguments and choose those that are logically most compelling. Expository writing, argumentation, and research reports have traditionally been seen as distinct from autobiography, narrative, and imaginative fiction. The postmodernist perspective blurs this distinction, and as James Berlin points out, "The postmodern turn has put rhetoric back on the agenda of virtually all of the human sciences" ("Poststructuralism" 172). In history, anthropology, psychology, biology, and other disciplines, we now question whether we can separate the knower from what is known.

In three different pieces of writing, Carolyn moves from her positive account of not getting into her first-choice college to a second narrative showing herself as a victim of affirmative action to a third, researched report about changes in affirmative action policies at our university and others in California. Laura reads a book about children living in poverty, writes a book review, and constructs a personal narrative that she sees as related to her reading. For each student, her analytical writing is shaped in part by her understanding of her own experience. Developing writing assignments that persistently rule out narrative obscures the situated nature of texts. Writing again becomes distorted by the stories we are trying not to tell. In individual conferences, in peer groups, and in the Writing Center, I point to passages in student writing and like all teachers ask, "How do you know?" "What does this mean?" "Is this what you really think?" "Why?" There are, disconcertingly, elements of psychotherapy, which I am not licensed to practice, here. Perhaps I do think it is "healthier" for Carolyn not to "repress" her pain and anger. Certainly, there is social engineering, which I feel ethically committed to practice, in asking Laura to problematize her idea of homelessness. But I am not, in fact, trying to uncover some essential version of students' thoughts and experiences.

Of course, students will measure conflicting stories against their lived experience, the more or less coherent narratives we all construct about our lives. On the other hand, privileging what we believe we have learned from personal experience as more true than what we learn from secondary sources is also a distortion. Students can cocoon in a private world they feel is real, rather than venture into a public world over which they feel they have little control. I suggest to Carolyn and Laura, aware of the force of teacher's "suggestions," that there are other "stories" about affirmative action and homelessness that can be told by our admissions officers, by other students, by statistics, editorials, books in the library, screen after screen of material on the Internet. In book reviews, summaries, and reading responses students try to honor the voices of their sources, to analyze the "stories" that other writers tell and, perhaps, the stories they are trying not to tell. Students often take on the role of the objective, critical selves that I presume they need to practice in their academic classes.

It is not that students know too few stories, but that they know too many. Students experience every day how the lines between genres are blurred—in news presented as entertainment, docu-dramas, shock-jockey talk shows as the most public forums for political debate. Contrasting different forms over the course of a semester makes clearer how conventions both permit and constrain us to speak in different ways. In class, we work on reading all texts rhetorically, as situated in particular times, places, and experiences. Students are also rhetoricians, not obliged to transcribe a predetermined reality, but invited and commanded by English I to put together provisional accounts of their subjects that will be persuasive to their teacher-reader, peers, and other audiences we might imagine. The composition classroom should be a space where we can play around with rhetorical conventions and mix various forms of writing. Don Bialostosky, in *Contending with Words*, suggests, "Such a class can modify the terms of disciplinary education in the students' favor by letting them in on the secrets of genre and convention that the disciplines silently observe" (16). For undergraduates, it might be developmentally appropriate to ask them more often to explain how they came to know than to insist they present an argument or a body of knowledge as objective experts.

It is a delicate balancing act, to construct an academic self that seems open to the voices of others and that, at the same time, evaluates, saying, "Yes, I agree," or "No, that's not how it goes." This balancing act is at the heart of the Pomo Blues, a sense of doubleness, the need to balance a vision of a world created by language, a world of endlessly competing discourses, against a lived experience that requires judgment and action. This is the task of the teacher as well as the student and brings us to a final key idea.

5. ALL TEXTS ARE "INTERESTED"—NONE ARE INHERENTLY "NORMAL" OR " NEUTRAL."

The last verse of the Pomo Blues is the most frustrating for students who want to know the "right" version of the song. You can play around, trade one discourse for another, love them and leave them, but that bed is awfully cold at night when you don't even have your "self" to keep you warm. Students get tired of the endless play of texts. Sooner or later, preferably sooner, they want to finish the paper, get the grade, and go home with some credits in their pockets. The values of the transaction structure much of what goes on in the classroom. Students pay for credits and, in this sense, are customers, consumers of what the teacher can offer. On the other hand, it is not a simple exchange of money for credits. Students must also "earn" the credits through the work they do. In the composition class, they must tell stories, make arguments, construct analyses. Students are not wrong in supposing it is in their self-interest to construct stories, arguments, and analyses that accommodate the teacher's values, beliefs, and experiences. Although Freirian pedagogy has taught ways to restructure power relationships in the classroom, as long as grades are given, the transaction of trading papers for grades will strongly influence how students and teachers construct themselves and their writing. This is perhaps the first way and the deepest level at which students recognize that their texts are not "neutral" accounts of self-evident truths. Their "normal" way of writing must be shaped to meet "what the teacher wants."

If postmodernist theory challenges students' sense of an authentic self, it also challenges teachers' claims of objectivity. While it might be frightening for teachers to give up the claim of objectivity, it is more threatening to students who, rightly, do not want to be graded capriciously. Like many teachers, I try to construct a classroom self that I would describe as tolerant and fair, invoking what I understand to be conventional academic standards for evaluating thinking and writing, negotiating these as openly as I can with students, and, by using portfolios, reducing the emphasis on grading during the semester. That we are all operating in good faith is a story that most of my students and I struggle to tell ourselves.

Looking at how cultural discourses are constructed means shifting the focus from how good a story or argument is to asking what is at stake in telling or arguing it in this way. Certainly we are interested in whether a piece of writing "works," but we are also interested in what it works for. Laura, for example, in her writing considers what difference it makes how she tells the story of "the homeless." Her topic, "the homeless," is one the culture has defined, a category to structure and simplify our thinking about complex persons and events. Postmodernist theory shifts us away from asking primarily whether Laura is telling the "right" story, whether this is defined as the most logical or most persuasive or most politically sensitive or most sincere. Instead the focus is on what kinds of stories she can tell and what is at stake in each of those different possibilities. I can't be sure if I am giving her text the "right" reading since I am also subject to the stories culturally available to me. But I can reflect back to her what I think is at stake in our possible writings and readings. Laura and her research group consider what beliefs and values lead us to write of those who live in the streets and parks as colorful characters or helpless victims. How is our treatment of those we describe as having made poor choices different from our treatment of those we describe as mentally ill? Whose interests are served in constructing the story of those without permanent homes as "others" or "just like you and me," as ill or lazy or addicted or simply unlucky or any of the other explanations we might offer? Of course, we can and do ask the same kind of questions about affirmative action, books students read, slave narratives, and stories of personal experience. In giving up claims to neutrality and objectivity, writers and readers acknowledge how much they are determined by cultural values, attitudes, and beliefs. Annette Patterson, an Australian educator who applies this critical approach to teaching literature in secondary schools, describes her goals as follows: "I want my students to be able to analyse the construction of readings and to consider what is at stake in the disagreement between readings; to make visible the gaps and silences of texts and to examine what particular interpretations support in terms of values they affirm. I want my students to be able to challenge dominant versions of texts and to construct new readings" (144).

I would like to say that my class meets Patterson's goals, but the postmodernist perspective resists closure. So I construct several different endings for my essay and ask you to consider each.

In the first ending, although I have suggested postmodernism favors the blues over more catchy tunes, I find almost irresistible the pull to construct a happy teaching story. In this ending, five oversimplified ideas about postmodernism help not just Laura but most of my students to question the stories they read and write, to identify some key cultural narratives, and to resist those that are especially limited or harmful. They feel freer to write their own stories in new ways that lead to ethical action. But the blues reassert themselves. The dilemma of postmodernism is that all discourses are limited, and there is no outside place to stand to judge what is harmful or what is good. As Peter McLaren and Colin Lankshear conclude in *Critical Literacy: Politics, Praxis, and the Postmodern*, the challenge is "to steer an ethical and political course in times of shifting theoretical boundaries and unstable systems of meaning and representation" (412). The danger lies in being paralyzed by competing discourses and unable to make ethical choices.

Another ending, then, is the reading of my more conservative colleagues who see a postmodernist pedagogy as an attack on traditional, Western values and who see Laura and others as being "brainwashed" into political correctness. Why not go back to a more "neutral," unpoliticized curriculum? That debate is too well known and too large to take up here, except to say that once you have seen the wizard behind the screen, once you see how we all make language and reality together, you know there is no neutral space into which you can retreat. To quote loosely from Thomas Wolfe, Dorothy, and Gertrude Stein: You can't go home again. We're not in Kansas any more. There is no there there.

So, no. Not that ending.

Then there is the analysis from the radical left, which I find more persuasive. Academic postmodernism, like academic Marxism, is a ploy of post-sixties liberals, many of whom are closet humanists. New theories merely repackage old ideas and teach Laura and company to critique cultural ideas with safe, academic politeness. These "theories" do not lead to real change, fit neatly into current classroom structures, and ultimately are designed to produce the next labor force for late capitalism. This upper cadre of workers will be "brainwashed" to be flexible, open to new ideas, and somewhat capable of dealing with abstract concepts. (See Mas'ud Zavarzadeh and Donald Morton for an elaboration of this argument.) Yes, of course. University professors are unlikely to discard humanist values of justice and rationality, and just as unlikely to give up privileged positions to advocate true revolution. Of course, universities supported by public and private moneys produce socialized workers. So, consider this ending.

But all three of these endings indicate a measure of arrogance. The stories students read, write, and listen to in English I are only a small part of the universe of discourse that surrounds them and that they help to construct. Intro to Pomo Blues as performed by the composition establishment is just one tune playing in the background of student lives. My university strongly identifies itself as a Christian university. The master narrative of the Christ story is a guide to core values and behavior for those who share Christian belief and gives students like Laura and Alex a way of evaluating what is at stake in their stories and a reason for committing themselves to one course of action or another, even though they may each interpret and apply the Christian story differently. Other students bring to the classroom the narratives of their own religious, cultural, and political beliefs. The classroom is only one arena in which these stories play out. Kurt Spellmeyer critiques theories that have "presupposed the existence of determining laws or codes that operate 'behind the back' of those subject to them." He argues, "What disappears from the 'behind-their-backs' tradition is any sense of how human subjects struggle to preserve their life-worlds against the imposition of alien values. This struggle, arguably the central issue of education, is nothing less than the central issue of postmodernity itself" (270–71). The university is implicated in the creation and maintenance of a postmodern world, but should neither underestimate nor overestimate its power.

Students are living postmodernism, not merely studying it. Some few are sure of their stories; most are, in my students' words, stressed, though scarcely able to articulate all the forces that are stressing them. Bombarded by so many tunes, the listener hears only noise. With few fixed reference points, many continue to struggle with the question, how is one to act ethically? Others—cynical, bored, alienated from community, education, and their own experience—do not ask the question.

Those who are successful in doing school manage the balancing act of postmodernism. Allison articulates the struggle between school and the sense of an authentic self as she writes in a self-analysis:

> When I think about writing, my mind conjures two images. Writing for school is a form of imprisonment. There are certain rules and guidelines to follow and a non-negotiable due date. There is pressure to finish it and I usually dread it so much that I don't do it until the night before, so it is sloppy and unorganized. But writing for pleasure is the exact opposite. It is freedom. I can write whatever I want, whenever I want, and not have to worry about it being judged (or "graded") or even read if I don't want it to be. I can release pent up frustration by letting my pen fly on its own. It is a form of therapy for me.

Allison goes on to testify that she is "learning to find a middle ground, to combine the two," especially through the process of revision. She credits feedback from her peers, writing center tutors, and me in changing her writing. Most importantly, she says explaining her ideas to international students in our class helped her "discover other ways I could take the paper, because during my explanations, new ideas would pop into my mind."

Allison's three-page self-analysis is thoughtful, detailed, sincere, and even amusing as she reviews her trials over the semester. It sounds like a happy ending. But then Allison figuratively winks at me and adds:

> The funny thing is that, as I reread this letter, I could see how I slanted it. I tried to portray myself as the hardworking student who is trying her very best to write well. And guess what? IT'S ALL TRUE! So I definitely deserve an A on this assignment!

And Allison is exactly right. It is all true. She is a hard-working student, and she has produced a polished portfolio of writing, and I have helped her do this. And she is making up her story to persuade me to give her an A. And I do give her the A.

This is the conclusion I am looking for. I think Allison gets what we have said about postmodernism all semester. English I is about telling stories, about the stories we tell students and the stories they tell us and the stories we construct together. At the same time, IT'S ALL TRUE, not because stories map a unified reality but because stories do have consequences, though I am not always as sure as Allison what these consequences are. Any ending I construct will have the same doubleness as Allison's conclusion. I sometimes lose the delicate academic balance and identify too strongly with the cynical, bored, and alienated who cannot muster Allison's enthusiasm. I wonder why I am standing in the front of the classroom. I cannot make romantic claims for the particular consequences of any one story, and I am skeptical of others who say they are able both to respect students' experience and to change their lives during a few months of Freshman Comp. I know something about language and something about rhetoric and writing that I can teach students. This is the theme of my song. Beyond that I struggle with issues of authenticity and authority. I improvise a postmodern tune.

Please feel free to sing along.

REFERENCES

Bartholomae, David. "Inventing the University." *When a Writer Can't Write: Studies in Writer's Block and Other Composing Problems.* Ed. Mike Rose. New York: Guilford, 1985. 134–65.

Bartholomae, David, and Anthony Petrosky, eds. *Ways of Reading: An Anthology for Writers.* 2d ed. Boston: Bedford, 1990.

Berlin, James A. "Postmodernism, Politics, and Histories of Rhetoric." *Pre/Text* 11 (1990): 170–87.

———. "Poststructuralism, Cultural Studies, and the Composition Classroom: Postmodern Theory in Practice." *Rhetoric Review* 11 (1992): 16–33.

Bialostosky, Don H. "Liberal Education, Writing, and the Dialogic Self." Harkin and Schilb 11–22.

Clifford, John, and John Schilb, eds. *Writing Theory and Critical Theory.* New York: MLA, 1994.

Faigley, Lester. *Fragments of Rationality: Postmodernity and the Subject of Composition.* Pittsburgh: U of Pittsburgh P, 1992.

———. "Pomo Blues." Conference on College Composition and Communication. San Diego, April 1993.

Flannery, Kathryn. "Composing and the Question of Agency." *College English* 53 (1991): 701–13.

Harkin, Patricia, and John Schilb, eds. *Contending with Words: Composition and Rhetoric in a Postmodern Age.* New York: MLA, 1991.

McLaren, Peter L., and Colin Lankshear. "Critical Literacy and the Postmodern Turn." *Critical Literacy: Politics, Praxis, and the Postmodern.* Ed. Peter McLaren and Colin Lankshear. Albany: SUNY P, 1993. 379–419.

Miller, Susan. *Textual Carnivals: The Politics of Composition.* Carbondale: U of Illinois P, 1991.

Olson, Gary. "Theory and the Rhetoric of Assertion." *Composition Forum* 6 (1995): 53–61.

Patterson, Annette. "Individualism in English: From Personal Growth to Discursive Construction." *English Education* 24 (1992): 131–46.

Schilb, John. "Cultural Studies, Postmodernism, and Composition." Harkin and Schilb 173–88.

Slevin, James F. "Reading and Writing in the Classroom and the Profession." Clifford and Schilb 53–72.

Spellmeyer, Kurt. "Too Little Care: Language, Politics, and Embodiment in the Life-World." *College English* 55 (1993): 265–83.

Summerfield, Judith. "Is There a Life in This Text? Reimagining Narrative." Clifford and Schilb 179–94.

Vitanza, Victor J. "Three Countertheses: Or, A Critical In(ter)vention into Composition Studies." Harkin and Schilb. 139–72.

Welch, Nancy. "Resisting the Faith: Conversion, Resistance, and the Training of Teachers." *College English* 55 (1993): 387–401.

Worsham, Lynn. "Writing against Writing: The Predicament of *Ecriture Féminine* in Composition Studies." Harkin and Schilb 82–104.

Zavarzadeh, Mas'ud, and Donald Morton. "A Very Good Idea Indeed: The (Post)Modern Labor Force and Curricular Reform." *Cultural Studies in the English Classroom.* Ed. James A. Berlin and Michael J. Vivion. Portsmouth, NH: Boynton/Cook. 66–86.

QUESTIONS FOR REFLECTION, JOURNAL WRITING, AND DISCUSSION

1. In the fourth century, Chinese philosopher Chuang-Tzu asked himself if he was a man who had dreamt he was a butterfly or a butterfly who was dreaming he was a man (an early example of questioning the notion of "the authentic self"). Will surrendering the notion of an authentic self help students produce better writing?

2. Do you agree with Carroll that we should "give up grandiose, romantic notions that Freshman Comp can fix students either personally or politically"?

3. Is most academic writing artificial or mechanical? Is your own writing this way? How could this be changed?

4. Compare how Rose, Bartholomae and Carroll try to develop their students' ability to do critical thinking.

Part II

Becoming a Writer

All writers live with uncertainty. We start out thinking we're about to write A and then we find ourselves writing B. Is B a better thing to have written than A? On another day, would we have written C? Gerald Graff writes that "inside every text are several other texts waiting to get out."[1] Despite whatever sense of purpose and clarity we may think we have, there is often something haphazard about writing. We're always, in fact, a little out of control. In the process of putting words on paper, we can lose the thought that brought us there. Maybe we'll find it again at another point in the process or maybe we'll "unify" ourselves, as Graff says, around the new thought. But there is often a gap between our original intention and what we actually say. That lack of control can be disconcerting, but it is also what allows for creativity. Unless we're willing to let go, our writing can become wooden and predictable. If we can learn to follow our words, they can take us to places in our own mind, to connections and associations that we didn't know were there.

Working writers know this process well and make room for it in their writing practice. But it is unfamiliar to many students and is something they may have been taught to distrust. Peter Elbow's *Writing Without Teachers* (Oxford, 1973) was one of the earliest and most influential works to make students aware of the fluidity of invention. By observing his own history as a writer, he noticed that the more he tried to be clear and well organized, the more painful and awkward writing became. Finally, he learned to relinquish some control, to exploit his mind's tendency to make surprising connections when left to its own free associative devices. Thus, he is often identified as the "free writing person" who encourages people to be undisciplined, to

---

[1] Quoted in George Hillocks, Jr., *Teaching Writing as Reflective Practice* (New York: Teachers College Press, 1995) 7.

write without thinking. The charge against him is that students *need* to think, they need to think critically and hard, they haven't done it enough, and critical thinking is what the university requires. But "free writing" is only part of the process. The other half, which Elbow teaches in equal detail, is revision and editing, and that is as rigorous and conscious a process as invention is "free." But the free writing is crucial, he believes, because it is only by getting out of our own self-doubting, second-guessing way that we will we write anything worth editing at all.

Elbow's process may not work for everyone. There are people who prefer an outline, who invent in their heads, who lay out sentences the first time in what is close to final form. Many of us do both: we let the writing "cook," to use one of Elbow's terms, as we go about our lives, riding the bus, taking a shower. But for beginning writers, who, by definition, have no practice, who are often composing and editing at the same time, Elbow's process can be a breakthrough. It stalls the censor in us who would write a word and cross it out. It allows us to accept and get past the halting first efforts, to warm up so that something more interesting can emerge. It also establishes that writing is not just something we are allowed to do once we've got our ideas "clear in our heads." It is a tool we use to record the thought process and to move it forward. Artists draw sketches. Writers write drafts.

Mary Soliday's article, "Translating Self and Difference Through Literacy Narratives," is about the importance of telling one's story and finding one's way in the context of other voices. Asking students to write literacy narratives—autobiographies of their development as readers and writers, stories of how they got to Freshman Composition—allows them to reflect on, understand, and gain a perspective on their own experience and to think of themselves as having a story worth telling, a life worth living. Soliday asks her beginning writing students to study their own and others' literacy narratives and to see how the various stories compare, where they come from, what options they represent in the fashioning of a "self." Like Bartholomae, Soliday realizes that what students think of as their own stories are often socially constructed renderings that fall into place and stand for a more examined reflection. Thus, Soliday asks her students to see their stories as "strange," as one of many possible stories, capable of being interpreted, and also, in the context of her classroom, capable of being shared and appreciated. She is creating in her classroom an academic writing community where, as students place things beside each other to analyze and understand, they begin to see the range of what is possible in another's life and also in their own. Their own stories become a part of the curriculum, part of history. They become agents in interpreting that history and perhaps in moving their own lives forward with a greater sense of choice.

Min-Zhan Lu's "From Silence to Words: Writing as Struggle" is her own eloquent literacy narrative of her negotiation with languages and in Lu's story, there was no safe place like Soliday's classroom. For Lu, the English of her "bourgeois" parents and the Standard Chinese of her Maoist classroom existed in fierce opposition to each other and created such conflict in her that writing itself became disorienting. "Home and school each contrived a purified space where only one discourse was spoken and heard." Where Soliday's student Alisha felt free to tell her teacher that her school voice was "frozen," Lu had no such opportunity to explore the difference between a bourgeois and a communist sensibility. There were no witnesses to verify that what she was experiencing was a reasonable response to a deeply and continuously unsettling situation. And yet in retrospect, Lu embraces her experience because it has given her a vivid sense of two conflicting cultures.

Elsewhere[2] she encourages other teachers to challenge monocultural views in their classrooms, to make the conflict of cultures and languages a part of the curriculum. However, she has been criticized for this approach from a number of quarters.[3] Many teachers are uncomfortable with the emphasis on multiculturalism in the writing classroom. Some teachers ask, "What business is it of ours to explore our students' lives? Who says students want to reveal themselves and to hear the disclosures of others?" The classroom, they say, should not be a political platform. Other cultures are too complex to be encapsulated in a thumbnail sketch, and teachers should resist the impulse to speak for them or to decide where the truth resides. Maxine Hairston articulates this position in "Diversity, Ideology, and Teaching Writing."[4] Coming from the other side, Keith Gilyard bristles at "the discourse on multiculturalism reduced to the level of a cuisine, a chicken chow mein, chicken fettucini, Southern fried chicken, arroz con pollo kind of multiculturalism." But his point is that America has always been multicultural, and that only the dominant cultures, the dominant stories, have traditionally been heard in most classrooms. How do we separate "American society" from the students who live and work here? Can we give students what they need to "succeed" without acknowledging who they are? Surely teachers cannot speak for all the cultures in a classroom, but the students can. When is it appropriate to design a curriculum around those cultures? The American landscape is filled with "contact zones," and each of

---

[2]Min-Zhan Lu, "Redefining the Legacy of Mina Shaughnessy: A Critique of the Politics of Linguistic Innocence," *Journal of Basic Writing* 10 (spring 1991): 26–40. Rpt. Bruce Horner and Min-Zhan Lu, *Representing the Other: Basic Writers and the Teaching of Basic Writing* (Urbana, IL: NCTE, 1999): 105–16.

[3]See "Symposium on Basic Writing," *College English* 55 (December 1993): 879–903.

[4]*College Composition and Communication* 43.2 (1992) 179–93.

us as a writing teacher has to reckon with how those cultures figure in our classrooms.

One such attempt is the course called "Literature and Diversity" that Roni Natov describes in "Listening for Difference." The course was designed for prospective teachers entering an urban classroom where students of many cultures necessarily come together. In her course, Natov tries not to speak for others, but rather to listen, to let students speak for themselves. Her students share difficult stories, read texts that undermine easy assumptions, and ask themselves what they need to know to understand the predicament of another. She teaches to help her students live with ambiguity: with "partial comprehension," "without closure." Like Soliday, Natov views her classroom as a contact zone. To the extent that a teacher can stand back from her own power and perceptions in the classroom, Natov strives to become a porous and discerning listener herself and to make the differences among the members of the class, including herself, an integral part of what is learned.

Mark-Ameen Johnson writes from the perspective of the tutor: the middleman, as it were, between the often "unpredictable" teacher in his position of power and the student, who often feels powerless. As the supervisor of tutors in an ESL Learning Center, Johnson tells the story of how ESL students find their confidence in themselves through their work with trained graduate and undergraduate students who serve as role models, sympathetic listeners, cheerleaders, de facto counselors, and one-to-one teachers of rhetoric and English grammar. "Tutors are in my head," said one student as she made her way through college. They are the voices that encourage and clarify when the teacher is too intimidating or simply does not have enough time to deal with each student's writing problems.

The next piece moves away from the undergraduate curriculum to a writing course designed for people who hope that writing will help them to deal with the physical and emotional ordeal of living with illness—will even, in some cases, save their lives. Ellie Friedland's "Writing Alive" describes her work with a group of writers who are HIV positive or have AIDS. They take extraordinary measures to get to class because they are writing to give a voice to their experience, to understand and illuminate it as art does. Friedland writes as a group leader, a caregiver, a poet practiced in Eastern forms such as tanka and haiku, and a practitioner of Buddhist meditation. Like the postmodernists, Buddhists understand that one must wear the self lightly, that perceptions come and go, that the notion of a unified identity is illusory. But the writers in Friedland's group and Friedland herself are still after the most astute perceptions they can come to. "I try to get to the real expression that may feel dangerous or 'wrong.' This means always looking deeper, always looking to see if there's something more, some truth I haven't yet identified or admitted." Like Elbow and the expressivists, she writes to uncover what she thinks. She is after "authentic expression," and she believes in "personal truth."

Although Friedland's group provides support, its primary focus is writing. And writing, or trying to, often involves coming to truths that may seem too frightening to face. Friedland describes the bodily sense of feeling stuck: "Thickness in my throat, tears just behind my eyes." Writing the truth "hurts," she says, because it makes us feel vulnerable. When we are stuck, or when we are hurt, she says, we can resist the feeling or we can lean into it with compassion. "When I soften into all this I still don't have answers or resolution," she writes, "but I have more patience."

For Friedland, the purpose of teaching is, as Richard Baker puts it, "to make you wonder and answer that wondering with the deepest expression of your own nature." In a workshop where illness and death are so central, one comes to a heightened sense of this wondering. But even in Freshman English, even in Basic Writing, this is what we should be after. Whether we call ourselves expressivists or social constructivists or postmodernists, whether we ask students to write literacy narratives or poems or arguments or research papers, we're trying to excavate past the surface, to deepen our students' understanding of life. We're taking them past the words that fall off the tongue as a kind of protective device—the words we say when we're trying to find out what the teacher wants or when we're fearful that really we have nothing to say. If we get to the deepest expression of our own nature, we write ourselves more fully alive.

Gary Olson's "Toward a Post-Process Composition" balances between an academic position and the adult workshop perspective expressed by Friedland. In his opening paragraph, Olson acknowledges the importance of the process movement in composition as it has evolved over the last 35 years, but he takes issue with the authoritative Aristotelian "proposition" that has formed the weakly beating heart of so many student essays. The essay pushes further toward the rejection, suggested in Carroll, of this ideally well-made essay with its clear thesis sentence and its string of arguments set forth in unimpeachable order.

It is a distortion, however, to call the thesis sentence a child of process theory, as it derives from classical rhetoric. In the writing of expressivist theorists like Ken Macrorie and Elbow, process is meant to engender a sense of possibilities, a play of thought, a resistance to dogmatic statements or to ideas tried out for the morning paper and then tossed aside. But as several postprocess theorists have observed, the notion of process itself can become ossified, mechanical, boring: on Monday, brainstorming; on Tuesday, first draft; on Thursday, revision; on Friday, peer critique. Once the flexibility of it is gone, something has to change.

Olson is interested in a radical shift in the teaching of writing, one that challenges the "rhetoric of assertion" and the "phallogocentric" concept of mastery. He suggests that we stay with our questions rather than forcing closure by fixing on answers. He challenges the value of Theory with its polarizing effects and its disciples, though he acknowledges that we can't help but theorize. His method moves to what he calls a "feminine" alternative that, like Jane Tompkins's and Ellie Friedland's, recognizes the body and emotions and encourages a Zenlike listening, waiting, receptivity. Olson's essay is, of course, built on Aristotelian structures, and it has a thesis: "That the vocabulary of process is no longer useful is not a reason to despair; it is rather, an invitation to rethink many of our most cherished assumptions about the activity we call 'writing.'" It is difficult to do away with arguing because we all come to stand someplace, if only for a time. But Olson also offers a loosening of the conventions of academic writing: the insistence on theory building, the exclusive discourse, the new generation of thinkers needing to slay their intellectual fathers. The pressure to find the theory, the answer, is released here, along with the adversarial stance of much academic writing. The postmodern voices of the borderlands are honored and other rhetorics are invited in.

Being a writer means getting to the sources of one's knowledge, one's ways of thinking, one's values. It begins with the self trying to make sense of one's language and ideas, but that self exists in a social context that has everything to do with the way one sees. Students must learn a language and a rhetoric that effectively engage a particular audience. But who, in the American college at the beginning of the new millennium, constitutes that audience? What does it mean to think like an American today? What does it mean to think like an academic? What will it mean 20 years from now? How do the voices and perspectives of students change the voices of the academy? Writing teachers and tutors need to create structures and clarities for students, to teach them habits of mind that will help them make their way through college and into careers. But they also need to create space so that while students are learning to follow conventions, there is enough room for something fresh and authentic to emerge.

Geraldine DeLuca

Chapter 8

The Process of Writing—Growing

Peter Elbow

Peter Elbow is Emeritus Professor of English at the University of Massachusetts at Amherst, where he directed the Writing Program. He has written *Writing With Power: Techniques for Mastering the Writing Process* and *A Community of Writers*. (This last is a textbook coauthored with Pat Belanoff.) He is author of a book of essays about learning and teaching, *Embracing Contraries*, and of *What Is English?* as well as numerous essays about writing and teaching. His most recent book is *Everyone Can Write: Essays Toward a Hopeful Theory of Writing and Teaching Writing* (Oxford University Press, 2000). He has taught at M.I.T., Franconia College, Evergreen State College, and SUNY at Stony Brook—where for five years he also directed the Writing Program. At Stony Brook he and Pat Belanoff set off the movement for portfolio evaluation as a programmatic activity. The following excerpt is from *Writing Without Teachers* (Oxford University Press, 1973).

Most people's relationship to the process of writing is one of helplessness. First, they can't write satisfactorily or even at all. Worse yet, their efforts to improve don't seem to help. It always seems that the amount of effort and energy put into a piece of writing has no relation to the results. People without education say, "If only I had education I could write." People with education say, "If only I had talent I could write." People with education and talent say, "If only I had self-discipline I could write." People with education, talent, and self-discipline—and there are plenty of them who can't write—say, "If only . . ." and don't know what to say next. Yet *some* people who aren't educated, self-disciplined, smart, imaginative, witty (or even verbal, some of them) nevertheless have this peculiar quality most of us lack: when they want to say something or figure something out they can get their thoughts onto paper in a readable form.

My starting point, then, is that the ability to write is unusually mysterious to most people. After all, life is full of difficult tasks: getting up in the morning, playing the piano, learning to play baseball, learning history. But few of them seem so acutely unrelated to effort or talent.

We could solve this mystery like the old "faculty" psychologists and say there is a special "writing faculty" and some people have it and some don't.

Or like some linguists, explain what is difficult to explain by saying it's a matter of wiring in the head. Or fall back on the oldest and most popular idea: *inspiration*—some god or muse comes down and breathes into you. Or pretend we don't believe in gods and translate this into some suitably fuzzy equivalent, for example "having something to say": as though certain people at certain times were lucky enough to find "something to say" inside—which forced its way out of them onto paper. (And as though people who *can* write are especially distinguished by always having something to say!) In short, we are back to where almost everyone starts: helpless before the process of writing because it obeys inscrutable laws. We are in its power. It is not in ours.

Once there was a land where people felt helpless about trying to touch the floor without bending their knees. Most of them couldn't do it because the accepted doctrine about touching the floor was that you did it by stretching upwards as high as you could. They were confused about the relationship between up and down. The more they tried to touch the floor, reaching up, the more they couldn't do it. But a few people learned accidentally to touch the floor: if they didn't think too much about it they could do it whenever they wanted. But they couldn't explain it to other people because whatever they said didn't make sense. The reaching-up idea of how to touch the floor was so ingrained that even they thought they were reaching up, but in some special way. Also there were a few teachers who got good results: not by telling people how to do it, since that always made things worse, but by getting people to do certain exercises such as tying their shoes without sitting down and shaking their hands around at the same time.

This is the situation with writing. We suffer from such a basic misconception about the process of writing that we are as bad off as the people in the parable.

The commonsense, conventional understanding of writing is as follows. Writing is a two-step process. First you figure out your meaning, then you put it into language. Most advice we get either from others or from ourselves follows this model: first try to figure out what you want to say; don't start writing till you do; make a plan; use an outline; begin writing only afterward. Central to this model is the idea of keeping control, keeping things in hand. Don't let things wander into a mess. The commonest criticism directed at the *process* of writing is that you didn't clarify your thinking ahead of time; you allowed yourself to go ahead with fuzzy thinking; you allowed yourself to wander; you didn't make an outline.

Here is a classic statement of this idea. I copied it from somewhere a long time ago and put it on my wall as something admirable. It was an important day when I finally recognized it as the enemy:

> In order to form a good style, the primary rule and condition is, not to attempt to express ourselves in language before we thoroughly know our meaning; when a man perfectly understands himself, appropriate diction will generally be at his command either in writing or speaking.

I contend that virtually all of us carry this model of the writing process around in our heads and that it sabotages our efforts to write. Our knowledge of this model might take the following form if it were put into conscious words: "Of course I can't expect my mess of a mind to follow those two steps perfectly. I'm no writer. But it will help my writing to *try:* by holding off writing and taking time to sit, think, make little jottings, try to figure out what I want to say, and make an outline. In the second step I certainly won't be able to find appropriate diction right at my command but I should try for the best diction I can get: by noticing as often as I can when the diction isn't appropriate, crossing it out, correcting, and trying to write it better."

This idea of writing is backwards. That's why it causes so much trouble. Instead of a two-step transaction of meaning-into-language, think of writing as an organic, developmental process in which you start writing at the very beginning—before you know your meaning at all—and encourage your words gradually to change and evolve. Only at the end will you know what you want to say or the words you want to say it with. You should expect yourself to end up somewhere different from where you started. Meaning is not what you start out with but what you end up with. Control, coherence, and knowing your mind are not what you start out with but what you end up with. Think of writing then not as a way to transmit a message—but as a way to grow and cook a message. Writing is a way to end up thinking something you couldn't have started out thinking. Writing is in fact a transaction with words whereby you *free* yourself from what you presently think, feel, and perceive. You make available to yourself something better than what you'd be stuck with if you'd actually succeeded in making your meaning clear at the start. What looks inefficient—a rambling process with lots of writing and lots of throwing away—is really efficient since it's the best way you can work up to what you really want to say and how to say it. The real inefficiency is to beat your head against the brick wall of trying to say what you mean or trying to say it well before you are ready.

AUTOBIOGRAPHICAL DIGRESSION

Though much or all of this may be in other books—some of which I have probably read—it seems to me my main source is my own experience. I admit to making universal generalizations upon a sample of one. Consider yourself warned. I am only asking you to *try on* this way of looking at the writing process to see if it helps your writing. That's the only valid way you can judge it. And you will try it on better if you sense how it grows out of my experience.

In high school I wrote relatively easily and—according to those standards—satisfactorily. In college I began to have difficulty writing. Sometimes I wrote badly, sometimes I wrote easily and sometimes with excruciating difficulty. Starting early and planning carefully didn't seem to be the answer: sometimes it seemed to help, sometimes it seemed to make things worse.

Whether or not I succeeded in getting something written seemed related only to whether I screwed myself up into some state of frantic emotional intensity: sometimes about the subject I was writing about; occasionally about some extraneous matter in my life; usually about how overdue the paper was and how frightened I was of turning in nothing at all. There was one term in my junior year when by mistake I signed up for a combination of courses requiring me to write two substantial papers a week. After the first two weeks' crisis, I found I wrote fluently and with relatively little difficulty for the rest of the term. But next term, reality returned. The gods of writing turned their back again.

The saving factor in college was that I wasn't sure whether I cared more about skiing or about studies. But then I went to graduate school and committed myself to studies. This involved deciding to try *very hard* and plan my writing *very carefully*. Writing became more and more impossible. I finally reached the point where I could not write at all. I had to quit graduate school and go into a line of work that didn't require any writing. Teaching English in college wasn't what I had in mind, but it was the only job I could get so it had to do.

After five years I found myself thinking I knew some important things about teaching (not writing!) and wanting badly to get other people to know and believe them. I decided I wanted to write them down and get them published; and also to return to graduate school and get my degree. This time I managed to get myself to write things. I always wondered when the curtain might fall again. I hit on the technique of simply insisting on getting *something* written a week before the real deadline, so I could try to patch it up and make it readable. This worked. But as I watched myself trying to write, it became clear I was going through fantastically inefficient processes. The price I was having to pay for those words was all out of proportion to any real value.

My difficulties in writing, my years as an illiterate English teacher, and a recent habit of trying to keep a stream of consciousness diary whenever life in general got to be too much for me—all combined to make me notice what was happening as I tried to write. I kept a kind of almost-diary. There were two main themes—what I called "stuckpoints" and "breakthroughs." Stuckpoints were when I couldn't get anything written at all no matter how hard I tried: out of pure desperation and rage I would finally stop trying to write the thing and take a fresh sheet of paper and simply try to collect evidence: babble everything I felt, when it started, and what kind of writing and mood and weather had been going on. Breakthroughs were when the log-jam broke and something good happened: I would often stop and try to say afterwards what I thought happened. I recommend this practice. If you keep your own data, you may be able to build your own theory of how *you* can succeed in writing since my theory of how I can succeed may not work for you. This chapter and the next one grow to some extent out of these jottings. Occasionally I will quote from them.

IT MAKES A DIFFERENCE IN PRACTICE

In a sense I have nothing to offer but two metaphors: *growing* and *cooking*. They are my model for the writing process. But models and metaphors make a big difference—most of all, those models and metaphors we take for granted.

Before going on to describe the model in detail, therefore, I would like to give a concrete example, and contrast the way you might normally go about a typical writing task and how you might go about doing it if you adopted the developmental model.

Imagine writing something three to five pages long and fairly difficult. It's not something you have to research (or else you've already done the research), but you haven't really worked out what you want to say. Perhaps it is a school essay. Or perhaps it is a short story for which you have an idea but no sense yet of how to work it out. To make the clearest contrast between the two ways of writing, let's say that you can only give one evening to the job.

If you wrote this normally, you would probably write it more or less once, but as carefully as possible. That is, you would probably spend anywhere from 15 minutes to an hour on planning: thinking, jotting, making an outline, or all three. And you would try hard to leave yourself at least half an hour at the end to go back over it and make clarifications and changes: usually while copying it over. Thus, though there may be a lot of "getting ready" beforehand, and "fixing" afterwards, you are essentially writing it *once*. And while you are doing the writing itself you probably do a lot of stopping, thinking, crossing out, going back, rewriting: everything that's involved in trying to write it as well as you can.

If on the other hand you adopt the developmental model of the writing process, you might well try to write it four times, not once, and try to help the piece evolve through these four versions. This sounds crazy and impossible because the writing process is usually so slow and tortured, but it needn't be. You simply have to force yourself to write. Of course the first "version" won't really be a version. It will simply be a writing down in the allotted time of everything on your mind concerning the subject.

Suppose you have four hours. Divide it into four units of an hour. For the first 45 minutes, simply write as quickly as you can, as though you were talking to someone. All the things that come to mind about the matter. You may not be able to write everything you know in that time, or you may have written everything you know in the first 10 minutes. Simply keep writing in either case—thinking things out as the words go down onto paper, following your train of thought where it leads, following the words where they lead. But stop at the end of 45 minutes.

Take the last 15 minutes for the opposite process. Think back or read over what you have written and try to see what important things emerged. What does it add up to? What was the most important or central thing in it? *Make* it add up to something, try to guess what it's *trying* to add up to; try to figure out what it *would* add up to if the missing parts were there. Sum up this main point, this incipient center of gravity, in a sentence. Write it down. It's got to stick its neck out, not just hedge or wonder. Something that can be quarreled with. (If you are writing a story or poem stress the term "center of gravity": it may be an assertion, but it could also be a mood, an image, a central detail or event or object—as long as it somehow sums up everything.) This summing-up process should be difficult: it should tell you more than you already know.

Of course you probably can't come up at this point with an assertion that is true or pleasing. You probably can't even make an assertion that really fits everything you wrote for 45 minutes. Don't worry. Your job, as with the writing, is not to do the task well, it is to do the task. The essence of this approach is to change your notion of what it means to *try* or *attempt* or *work on* a piece of writing. To most people it means pushing as hard as they can against a weight that is heavier than they can budge—hoping eventually to move it. Whereas of course you merely get tireder. You must create mechanical advantage so that "trying" means pushing against a weight that you *can* move even if that only moves the main weight a small distance.

So now you have used up the first of your four units of time. You have written your first "version." In the next hour, simply do the same thing. Start writing again. *Start from* your previous summing up assertion. That doesn't mean you must stick to it—you probably consider it false. Merely write your next version "in the light of" or "from the perspective of" your fifteen-minute standing back and surveying of the terrain.

Write quickly without much stopping and correcting for 45 minutes again. And again use the final 15 minutes to stand back and try to see what emerged, what one thing is now uppermost or is trying to be uppermost. Sum it up again. Perhaps this assertion will seem solider and more useful, but perhaps not. In any event, you must come up with a single, sticking-its-neck-out assertion by the end of 15 minutes.

Now in your third hour do the same thing a third time. By now you may have a sense of which direction your final version will go—a sense of an emerging center of gravity that you trust. Try to develop and exploit it. If not, try to find it during this third version. Try to coax some coherence, yet still allow things to bubble. You are not editing yet.

The job of editing and turning out a final copy is next. It occupies the last 15 minutes of your third period, and the whole of the fourth period. It turns out to be exactly what the conventional idea of writing is: start with 15 minutes to make your meaning clear to yourself. Now at last you should be in a position to do this. You might want to make an outline or plan. But one thing is essential: you must really force yourself to sum up into a genuine *single* assertion what your meaning is. Remember the crucial thing about this task: it must be an assertion that actually asserts something, that could be quarrelled with; not "here are some things I think" or "here are some things that relate to X."

Once you have gradually grown your meaning and specified it to yourself clearly, you *will* have an easier time finding the best language for it. But even in this final writing, don't go too slowly and carefully. For you should use the final 15 minutes for going over it: cleaning and strengthening the wording; throwing away as many words, phrases, and even sections as can be dispensed with; and perhaps rearranging some parts.

This method of writing means more words written and thrown away. Perhaps even more work. But less banging your head against a stone wall—pushing with all your might against something that won't budge. So though you are tired, you are less frustrated. The process tends to create a transaction that helps you expend more of your energy more productively.

The time-lengths can be stretched or squeezed or ignored. I am merely trying to insist that you can write much more and not take longer. But most of us must resort to a clock to *make* ourselves write more and not waste time.

GROWING

Growing is certainly a proper word for what people and other living organisms do to arrive at a "grown" or "mature" state. They go through a series of changes and end up more complex and organized than when they started. It is no metaphor to speak of a person in the following way: "He really grew. Of course he's the same person he was, but he's also very different. Now he thinks, behaves, and sees things differently from the way he used to. I never would have expected him to end up this way."

I wish to speak of groups of *words* growing in the same way. Consider this example. You believe X. You write out your belief or perception or argument that X is the case. By the time you have finished you see something you didn't see before: X is incorrect or you see you no longer believe X. Now you keep writing about your perplexity and uncertainty. Then you begin to see Y. You start to write about Y. You finally see that Y is correct or you believe Y. And then finally you write out Y as fully as you can and you are satisfied with it.

What has happened here? Strictly speaking, only *you* have grown, your words have not. You are a living organism. Your words are just dead marks on a piece of paper. No word has *moved* or *changed,* they all just lie there where you set them. But there's a sense in which they have changed. A sense in which they are not one long string of words but rather three shorter strings of words which are three "versions" of something: versions of an organism-like thing—something that has gone through three stages and ended up in a way that seems completed. "It no longer believes X, it believes Y; it's very different, yet it's still the same piece of writing. I never would have expected it to end up this way."

It is my experience that when I write something that is good or which satisfies me, almost invariably it is a product of just such a process. And when I struggle hard and fail to produce something good or pleasing, it seems almost invariably because I couldn't get this kind of process to occur. (There are exceptions which I will deal with towards the end of the chapter on cooking.)

It is also my experience that I can best help this process occur when I think of it as trying to "help words grow." It is true, of course, that an initial set of words does not, like a young live organism, contain within each cell a *plan* for the final mature stage and all the intervening stages that must be gone through. Perhaps, therefore, the final higher organization in the words should only be called a borrowed reflection of a higher organization that is really in me or my mind. I am only projecting. Yet nevertheless, when I can write down a set of words and then write down some more and then go back and write down some more thoughts or perceptions on the topic, two odd things seem to be the case: 1. Often by looking back over them, I can find relationships and conclusions in the words that are far richer and more interesting than I could have "thought of by myself." 2. And sometimes it often feels as though these words were "going somewhere" such that when they "got there" best, it was because I succeeded in getting out of their way. It seems not entirely metaphorical, then, to say that at the end it is I who have borrowed some higher organization from the words.

In any event, I advise you to treat words as though they are potentially able to grow. Learn to stand out of the way and provide the energy or force the words need to find their growth process. The words cannot go against entropy and end up more highly organized than when they started unless fueled by energy you provide. You must send that energy or electricity through the words in order, as it were, to charge them or ionize them or give them juice or whatever so that they have the life to go through the growing process. I think of this growing process schematically, as follows. The words come together into one pile and interact with each other in that mess; then they come apart into small piles according to some emerging pattern. Then the small piles consolidate and shake down into their own best organization. Then together again into a big pile where everything interacts and bounces off everything else till a different pattern emerges. The big pile breaks up again into different parts according to this new pattern. Then the parts each consolidate themselves again. Then back into the big pile again for more interaction. And so forth and so on till it's "over"—till a pattern or configuration is attained that pleases you or that "it was trying to get to."

It takes a lot of energy for this process to go on. But you save the energy you normally waste trying to polish something that is essentially lousy and undeveloped.

Make the process of writing into atomic fission, setting off a chain reaction, putting things into a pot to percolate, getting words to take on a life of their own. Writing is like trying to ride a horse which is constantly changing beneath you, Proteus changing while you hang on to him. You have to hang on for dear life, but not hang on so hard that he can't change and finally tell you the truth.

START WRITING AND KEEP WRITING

It is one of the main functions of the ten-minute writing exercises to give you practice in writing quickly without editing, for if you are not used to it you will find it difficult. Your editorial instinct is often much better developed than your producing instinct, so that as each phrase starts to roll off your pencil, you hear seventeen reasons why it is unsatisfactory. The paper remains blank. Or else there are a series of crossed out half-sentences and half-paragraphs.

When you realize you have to write a lot, you stop worrying because you write badly much of the time—at first, perhaps all the time. Don't worry. "Trying to write well" for most people means constantly stopping, pondering, and searching for better words. If this is true of you, then stop "trying to write well." Otherwise you will never write well.

It's at the beginnings of things that you most need to get yourself to write a lot and fast. Beginnings are hardest: the beginning of a sentence, of a paragraph, of a section, of a stanza, of a whole piece. This is when you spend the

most time not-writing: sitting, staring off into space, chewing the pencil, fur-
rowing your brow, feeling stuck. How can you write the beginning of something till you know what it's the beginning of? Till you know what it's leading
up to? But how can you know that till you get your beginnings?

Writing is founded on these impossible double-binds. It is simply a fact
that most of the time you can't find the right words till you know exactly
what you are saying, but that you can't know exactly what you are saying till
you find just the right words. The consequence is that you must *start by writing the wrong meanings in the wrong words;* but keep writing till you get to the
right meanings in the right words. Only at the end will you know what you
are saying. Here is a diary entry:

> Noticing it again: in the middle of writing a memo to X about the course:
> that the good ideas and good phrases—especially the good ideas—come
> only while in the process of writing—after the juices have started to flow. It's
> what Macrorie[1] is talking about when he says you have to let words talk to
> words—let words—as they come out—call up and suggest other words and
> concepts and analogies. There's a very practical moral for me. I've got to
> *not* expect my best or even structurally important ideas to come before I
> start writing. Got to stop worrying that I have nothing to write about before
> I start writing. Start to write and let things happen. A model: pretend I am a
> famous writer—an acknowledged genius who has already produced a bril-
> liant book a year and an article a month for the last 20 years. Someone who
> simply knows that when he sits down to write, good stuff will be the final
> product even though at any given moment he is liable to be writing
> absolute crap. Good writers and good athletes don't get really good till they
> stop worrying and hang loose and trust that good stuff will come. Good
> musicians.

Writing a lot at the beginning is also important because that's when you
are least warmed up and most anxious. Anxiety keeps you from writing. You
don't know what you will end up writing. Will it be enough? Will it be any
good? You begin to think of critical readers and how they will react. You get
worried and your mind begins to cloud. You start trying to clench your
mind around what pitiful little lumps of material you have in your head so
as not to lose them. But as you try to clarify one thought, all the rest seem
to fall apart. It's like trying to play monopoly on a hillside in a fresh breeze
and trying to keep a hand on all your piles of money. You begin to wonder
whether you are coming down with a brain tumor. Anxiety is trying to get
you so stuck and disgusted that you stop writing altogether. It is writing that
causes all the anxiety. (When you have dreams of glory and imagine how

[1]Ken Macrorie, *Telling Writing,* Hayden Press, 1970.

famous your writing will make you, it is just a sneakier trick to keep you from writing: anything you actually write will seem disappointing to you.) Again, the only cure is to damn the torpedoes and write:

> Getting into the teacher business in my "Model for Higher Education" essay. Beginning to turn on. Lesson: two conditions seem to have led to this more gutsy writing. 1. Write a lot for enough time just to get tired and get into it— get past stiffness and awkwardness—like in a cross-country race where your technique doesn't get good till you're genuinely tired. The mechanism there is clear: you've got to be tired enough so that unnecessary (and inhibitory) muscles let go and stop clenching. Relax. Use only necessary muscles. Reach 100% efficiency of body. Equals grace. I think you can translate this directly into writing: get extra and inhibitory muscles to let go by writing a lot. Thus the success of some late-night writing. 2. I've found or fallen into a topic that I have a strong emotional relation to. It's got my dander up. I can feel it in my stomach and arms and jaw—which in this case doesn't feel like unnecessary and inhibitory muscle tension. You have to write long enough, get tired enough, and drift and wander and *digress* enough simply to fall into an area of high concern. *The whole thing started out as a digression: one parenthesis for one sentence in a section talking about something entirely different.* Give your feelings and instincts their head.

Trying to begin is like being a little child who cannot write on unlined paper. I cannot write anything decent or interesting until after I have written something at least as long as the thing I want to end up with. I go back over it and cross it all out or throw it all away, but it operates as a set of lines that hold me up when I write, something to warm up the paper so my ink will "take," a security blanket. Producing writing, then, is not so much like filling a basin or pool once, but rather getting water to keep flowing *through* till finally it runs clear. What follows is a diary entry that starts out illustrating the need to write beginnings and get on with it, but ends up showing that the problem of anxiety tends to lurk underneath everything else:

> I've stopped in mid sentence. I'm starting off this long section; and I realize that exactly what I need at this point is a clear and concise summary statement of precisely what it is I'm going to say. And with that realization comes a trickier one: I cannot say clearly and concisely what it all amounts to.
>
> The best I can do is write in something vague or fuzzy or unsatisfactory— to fake it like a musician who comes to a passage that is too hard but wants to keep time with the other players and not lose his place in the music—and go on to the substance of the section to work on exactly what it is I *am* saying. I cannot write the sentence I need at the beginning till after I get to the end.
>
> The lesson then, is to try to treat writing not exclusively as linear but as wholistic: not starting in at one end and writing till you get to the other; but rather as successive sketches of the same picture—the first sketches very

rough and vague—each one getting clearer, more detailed, more accurate, and better organized as well.

And different parts of the writing must have a mutually interactive effect on each other. I can't write a good first sentence till I work through the body of the piece; yet once I work through the body and get myself in a position of elevation so I can write a good first sentence summarizing things, that very sentence will permit me to go back to the body of the piece and see that some bits are not really central and can be cut out or shortened or stuck into a quick aside, and bring the main outlines into better focus.

But. Now after writing the above, I went back to my piece of writing, and succeeded pretty well in putting my finger on what it was I was wanting to say. Somehow the stopping and making self-conscious the process outlined above, served to free me from the hangup of it. I don't know how to translate that into advice or a general principle. Wait a minute, maybe I do. I think it means this: *I was stuck and frustrated,* couldn't go on. Became conscious of it and what the problem was. Stopped to make a note analyzing the problem and the solution. And that produced confidence that the problem did indeed have a solution—reduced the frustration—know that if I just forged on bravely, it would eventually come to me. That reduction of frustration and incipient hopelessness reduced the static in my mind that was preventing me from getting my hands on words and thoughts that were potentially there.

Another reason for starting writing and keeping writing: If you stop too much and worry and correct and edit, you'll invest yourself too much in these words on the page. You'll care too much about them; you'll make some phrases you really love; you won't be able to throw them away. But you *should* throw lots away because by the end you'll have a different focus or angle on what you are writing, if not a whole new subject. To keep these earlier words would ruin your final product. It's like scaffolding. There is no shortcut by which you can avoid building it, even though it can't be part of your final building. It's like the famous recipe for sturgeon: soak it in vinegar, nail it to a two-inch plank, put it in a slow oven for three days, take it out, throw away the fish, and eat the plank.

It's just happened again. For the umteenth time. I struggled at huge and agonizing length to try to get rid of an unwieldy, ugly, and awkward phrasing. No matter how much I struggled, I couldn't get anything either clear, concise, or even exactly what I meant. But still to no avail. The hell with it. I took the best alternative—a lousy one—and went on. Only the *next day— after typing the final draft—while proofreading it—*I finally got the perfect phrasing: just what I want; elegant, concise, direct. Cognitively, I couldn't work it out till I had the whole thing clear enough so that I could then see this tiny part clearly. Affectively, I couldn't get the cobwebs out of my head till I actually had confidence that I had something actually completed and that I could turn in. Moral: it was a waste of time to try for the exact phrase back then; wait till later—last stage.

EDITING

You can't edit till you have something to edit. If you have written a lot, if you have digressed and wandered into some interesting areas and accumulated some interesting material (more than you can see any unity in), and if, at last, a center of gravity has emerged and you find yourself finally saying to yourself, "Yes, now I see what I'm driving at, now I see what I've been stumbling around trying to say," you are finally in a position to start mopping up—to start editing.

Editing means figuring out what you really mean to say, getting it clear in your head, getting it unified, getting it into an organized structure, and then getting it into the best words and throwing away the rest. It is crucial, but it is only the last step in the complete growth cycle.

Sometimes you can get a piece of writing to go through the whole cycle so naturally that even this last stage performs itself: you have written it, written it, and written it some more, and finally you find yourself writing it right. You simply throw away the first fifteen pages and keep the last three because they are just what you want.

This rarely happens with a whole piece of writing, but it often happens with sections: paragraphs or stanzas can come right off the end of your pencil just the way you want them. Look for it and want it. But usually you are writing something for tomorrow or next week and a completely natural growth cycle often takes longer.

Editing is almost invariably manipulative, intrusive, artificial, and compromising: red-penciling, cutting up, throwing away, rewriting. And mostly throwing away. For this process, follow all the standard advice about writing: be vigilant, ruthless; be orderly, planned; keep control, don't lose your head. At last it is appropriate to sit, ponder, furrow your brow, not write, try to think of a better word, struggle for the exact phrase, try to cut out "dead wood," make up your mind what you really mean: all the activities which ruin your writing if engaged in too soon.

Sometimes I don't need to use an outline to do a good job of editing. But if I get the least bit stuck—knowing that it's not right but not sure what's wrong—then I find an outline indispensable: but only at this last stage of writing, not at early stages.

I used to think outlines were made of single words and phrases. But I found that's not good enough. I found the only effective outline to be a list of full assertions—one for each paragraph. Each must assert something

definite, not just point in a general direction. Then the *progression* of assertions must make sense and say something so you can finally force that list of
assertions into a *single* assertion that really says something. And now, having
worked your way up, you can work your way down again to clean and
tighten things up: with this single assertion, you can now reorder your list
of paragraph assertions into a tighter order (probably leaving some out);
and only now can you finally rewrite your actual paragraphs so they all
reflect in their texture—at the cellular level—the single coherence of the
whole piece.

The essence of editing is *easy come easy go.* Unless you can really say to yourself, "What the hell. There's plenty more where that came from, let's throw it
away," you can't really edit. You have to be a big spender. Not tightass.

I am the first to admit how hard it is to practice this preaching. I *know*
perfectly well I can write an infinite number of meaningful utterances in
my native tongue in spite of my finite knowledge of that language. I *know*
perfectly well that the more I utter, the more I'll be able to utter and—
other things being equal—the *better* I'll be able to utter. I know I can. Noam
Chomsky knows I can. But it doesn't *feel* that way. It feels like the more I
utter, especially the more I write, the more I'll use up my supply of meaningful utterances, and as the source dries up, they will get worse.

What is illustrated here is the essence of the developmental growth cycle
for living cells. A difficulty in a later stage (editing) reveals a hitherto unnoticed difficulty at an earlier stage (producing). Progress is liable to require
regression: experiencing the earlier stage difficulty more fully so it can be
worked on. Or at least. this is how it worked for me. I had figured out perfectly well the importance of writing a lot and producing a lot, but not until
I began to see more clearly my difficulties with editing did I realize that I
was being held up because I hadn't *really* inhabited fully my difficulties with
producing. A relatively recent diary entry:

> I'm reading over something I wrote a couple of days ago. Trying to turn it
> into a final draft. I was working on the phrase, "There is no principle of right
> or wrong, and no guidelines for trying to sort it out or bring consistency to
> it." I could feel immediately that it was wordy and mushy, fog for the reader.
> Next I find myself rewriting it as follows: "There's no right or wrong for sort-
> ing it out; no guidelines for bringing consistency." Yes, that's better, I start to
> say to myself, when I suddenly realize what I'm really doing. I'm working out
> a recombination of the words *in order not to have to throw any of them away.* I've
> done it a million times, but this is the first time I can feel the psychic princi-
> ple in it: "How can I rearrange those words in order not to throw any of them
> away? I made those words. All by myself. They came out of me. And it was
> hell. I really suffered. I gave them my everything. For each word there were
> 17 traps and pitfalls that I just barely avoided by my sharp-eyed vigilance, 17

agonizing choices, 17 near-misses. I struggled. I ain't getting rid of any of them. Get out of here with that knife."

Now that I have stressed the developmental fact that learning to throw away more ruthlessly comes from learning to generate more prolificly—that learning how to impose higher degrees of organization comes from allowing more disorder—I can go on to stress the fierceness of editing. For that's the difficulty of most advice about writing: because it doesn't do justice to the earlier, nonediting stages in the writing process, it doesn't *really* do justice to editing.

Editing must be cut-throat. You must wade in with teeth gritted. Cut away flesh and leave only bone. Learn to say things with a relationship instead of words. If you have to make introductions or transitions, you have things in the wrong order. If they were in the right order they wouldn't need introductions or transitions. Force yourself to leave out all subsidiaries and then, by brute force, you will have to rearrange the essentials into their proper order.

Every word omitted keeps another reader with you. Every word retained saps strength from the others. Think of throwing away not as negative—not as crumpling up sheets of paper in helplessness and rage—but as a positive, creative, generative act. Learn to play the role of the sculptor pulling off layers of stone with his chisel to reveal a figure beneath. Leaving things out makes the backbone or structure show better.

Try to *feel* the act of strength in the act of cutting: as you draw the pencil through the line or paragraph or whole page, it is a clenching of teeth to make a point stick out more, hit home harder. Conversely, try to feel that when you write in a mushy, foggy, wordy way, you must be trying to cover something up: message-emasculation or self-emasculation. You must be afraid of your strength. Taking away words lets a loud voice stick out. Does it scare you? More words will cover it up with static. It is no accident that timid people are often wordy. Saying nothing takes guts. If you want to say nothing and not be noticed, you have to be wordy.

Editing means being tough enough to make sure someone will actually read it:

> Don't look on throwing words away as something having gone wrong. To write ten pages and throw them away but end up with *one paragraph* that someone actually reads—*one paragraph that is actually worth sixty seconds of someone's time*—is a huge and magical and efficient process. The alternative which is much more common is to write (more carefully) five pages that *avoid the errors or egregious shit* of the above ten pages—*but not one single paragraph worth reading! So* though it seems that one has done better when one has five whole pages of non-shit, really it is utterly worthless since it's not worth reading.

In all three previous stages of growth, the emphasis is upon a transaction with yourself and with your words. In editing, you must finally deal with the hard reality of readers.

QUESTIONS FOR REFLECTION, JOURNAL WRITING, AND DISCUSSION

1. Elbow says "Most people's relationship to the process of writing is one of helplessness." Do you agree? Why would this be so?

2. What does Elbow mean by saying that words are "able to grow"? What are the implications for teaching writing?

3. Elbow talks about his "years as an illiterate English teacher." What does he mean by this? Are there many illiterate English teachers? Are you one of them?

4. Do you give lip service to saying that writing is done in the "traditional way" but really go through a process similar to Elbow's? What is your own writing process like? Does it work for you?

Chapter 9

Translating Self and Difference Through Literacy Narratives

Mary Soliday

Mary Soliday is an Assistant Professor of English at the City College of New York. She is the Coordinator of Writing Across the Curriculum at the Center for Teaching and Learning at City College. Her articles have appeared in *College English, College Composition and Communication,* the *Journal of Basic Writing, Writing Center Journal,* and in edited collections. She has recently completed a book manuscript titled *Writing Between Worlds: The Politics of Postsecondary Remediation.* The following article is from *College English,* 56, September 1994.

The best-known literacy narratives are either autobiographies, like Frederick Douglass's *Narrative* and Mike Rose's *Lives on the Boundary,* or novels, plays, and films "that foreground issues of language acquisition and literacy" (Eldred and Mortensen 513) and that are as diverse as a Hawthorne short story, *The Color Purple,* and *Educating Rita.* But literacy narratives are also told in ordinary people's conversations about their daily lives, as recorded, for instance, in Lorri Neilsen's ethnographic study *Literacy and Living,* and in the classroom talk and writing of students. I want to focus upon how various literacy narratives portray passages between language worlds in order to consider the relevance of such passages to a writing pedagogy, particularly to a pedagogy for basic writing classes.

At the most basic level, the plot of a literacy story tells what happens when we acquire language, either spoken or written. But literacy stories are also places where writers explore what Victor Turner calls "liminal" crossings between worlds. In focusing upon those moments when the self is on the threshold of possible intellectual, social, and emotional development, literacy narratives become sites of self-translation where writers can articulate the meanings and the consequences of their passages between language worlds.

As I will suggest through a reading of two essays written by one of my students, literacy stories can give writers from diverse cultures a way to view their experience with language as unusual or strange. By foregrounding their acquisition and use of language as a strange and not a natural process, authors of literacy narratives have the opportunity to explore the profound cultural force language exerts in their everyday lives. When they are able to evaluate their experiences from an interpretive perspective, authors achieve narrative agency by discovering that their experience is, in fact, interpretable. In my basic writing classes at an urban college, I have found that literacy narratives can expand students' sense of personal agency when they discover not only that their own stories are narratable, but also that through their stories they can engage in a broader critical dialogue with each other and with well-known texts such as Richard Rodriguez's *Hunger of Memory*.

A considerable literature in composition studies addresses the relationship between cultural identity and writing and calls particular attention to the conflicts which writers experience in crossing between language worlds (Bartholomae; Bizzell; Coles and Wall; Dean; Fox; Kutz, Groden and Zamel; Lu; Moss and Walters). Discussions of the role that tensions between discourse worlds might play in the texts of basic writers—who are also usually minority, immigrant, and working-class students—raise important political concerns that by teaching students to manipulate the conventions and forms of academic language, writing teachers are unthinkingly acculturating students into the academy and glossing over issues of difference in the classroom. Considerable debate, then, turns on whether writing teachers and their students should assimilate, critique, or reject dominant discourses (for vivid recent examples, see the "Symposium on Basic Writing"; the Symposium on "Writing Within and Against the Academy"; and "Counterstatements" in response to Maxine Hairston's "Diversity, Ideology, and Teaching Writing"). Because these (often heated) discussions involve students' life choices and sense of personal identity, I want to focus upon the issues within the framework of the literacy narrative, with an emphasis upon literacy autobiographies. Reading and writing literacy stories can enable students to ponder the conflicts attendant upon crossing language worlds and to reflect upon the choices that speakers of minority dialects and languages must make.

Stories of self-translation involve representing difference, and the representation of difference is at the core of today's struggles in the humanities over competing versions of multiculturalism. Efforts to build a more culturally inclusive curriculum have, however, focused heavily on diversifying ways of reading and on critiquing traditional representations of difference in canonical texts rather than on diversifying ways of writing and imagining the self through writing. Of course the issues surrounding the canon are quite vital to continuing the debate about difference in the academy, but multiculturalism should also involve building classrooms where actual translation can occur—where writing can be used as a means of self-definition and self-representation. As significant sites of translation, literacy stories exemplify the "arts of the contact zone," in Mary Louise Pratt's terms, and indeed may themselves resemble Pratt's definition of contact zones as "social spaces where cultures meet, clash, and grapple with each other, often in contexts of highly asymmetrical relations of power" (34). Because literacy narratives so often focus on the meeting and clashing of identities, languages, and cultures, writing literacy stories allows our basic writing or nontraditional students—those "others" of the academic landscape hitherto largely represented by teachers speaking on their behalf—themselves to enter into and influence the contemporary debates surrounding multicultural education.

Ethnographic research shows that telling stories at home is a rich and complex social practice through which family members establish their identities as language users in culturally specific ways (Heath; Labov; Scollon and Scollon). More particularly, telling oral literacy narratives provides an imaginative, although not fully understood, avenue through which children and adults develop a cultural sense of the literate self (Goodman; Harste, Woodward and Burke; Neilsen; Taylor). Within our families we routinely practice representing, even fictionalizing, the nature of literacy to ourselves in ways that are probably culturally specific: parents tell stories of their children's achievements with literacy at school or of their own successes and failures in learning to read and write, and pre-school children tell literacy stories, for example by embedding literacy events within the plots of other stories they tell.

Commonplace stories of our encounters with literacy are, to use William Labov's phrasing, "tellable" or narratable because they can foreground the unusualness, and thus call attention to the sociocultural aspects, of learning to read and write. Here is a sample from Hope Jensen Leichter's research, an interview with a father who told of his memory of learning to read as a child in Ireland:

> The teachers were rough. I mean the discipline back then, they'd sock it to you. . . . We had a fear of the teacher, and when you have a fear of the teacher, you don't like going to school. . . . In fact, I remember jumping in the river to avoid going to school. . . . I pretended to be sick and I was forced to go so I accidentally fell into the river. I was brought back and I got a spanking and I was sent to school anyway.
>   I remember trying to read . . . with the scene . . . the family on the beach . . . the beach balls, building the castles and all that sort of stuff. I guess I was 7 or 8. [If you didn't read well] you got whipped. . . . Basically, it was the punishment idea. . . . You used to have to hold your hand and you would get it, maybe six wallops across the hand with a stick . . . and your hand would start bleeding. . . . . Your ears would be beaten with a bamboo cane, and you couldn't do anything with your hands. . . . Some kids used to freeze up there [at the blackboard], you know, you'd go blank and you'd get slaughtered again. . . . You couldn't complain at home; you didn't open your mouth; you had no recourse. [The kids that could never read] got beat up more than

anybody. . . . We had dummies. . . . They got more stupid by every day. (45–46; Leichter's ellipses and interpolations)

Leichter comments that "Such recollections are reconstructions and may be embellished. However, they constitute understandings that the parent brings to the child's explorations of literacy" (46). If we regard the father's account as a deliberate reconstruction of his experience—as a literacy narrative—then the "embellishments" of the present and not what actually happened in the past make the story tellable. In his portrayal of the struggle between the institution, between the boy who jumps in the river in order to avoid school and the bodiless "they" or missing subject of the passive constructions, the Irish father describes not an initiation but a coercion into literacy. He foregrounds school literacy as a site of conflict between the anonymous teacher and the resisting "we" who feared the teacher's authority. School is a contradictory place where children learn not to learn— "They got more stupid by every day"—and it is ruled by an unjust, punitive authority that closes down resistance: "you had no recourse" because no one listened to your story. By turns hyperbolic and grim, the routine crossing from home to school in this story is uncommonly violent.

The Irish father's story is tellable because of its power to evoke his specific experience, one of the customary fruits of narrative. But in remembering the confrontation between "us" and "them" as taking place on a battleground of literacy, the father also turns the events of his past into a narratable autobiography which denaturalizes the process of acquiring school literacies. His story achieves maximum tellability in rendering strange one of the most seemingly mundane events of our lives. Literacy stories let us look at reading, writing, or speaking as unusual when, like an ethnographer, the narrator assumes that something as seemingly natural as learning to write in school is not a neutral event but is itself a meaningful social drama. In this sense, the ethnographer shares with the novelist and the autobiographer one of narrative's most traditional uses, identified by the Russian Formalists as making the common event uncommon and hence defamiliarizing quotidian reality.

If writers construct their interpretation of past events from the vantage point of a particular present, then the life story becomes a dialogical account of one's experience rather than a chronological report of verifiable events. An author of a successful literacy story goes beyond recounting "what happened" to foreground the distance between an earlier and a present self conscious of living in time, a distinction familiar to those who have studied the autobiographical writing (Beach) and literacy narratives (Shirley K. Rose) of college students. To develop this dynamic sense of the autobiographical self, successful narrators acknowledge that their life stories can be composed or deliberately constructed renderings of experience (Salmon; Bateson). In writing her autobiography against the grain of the life stories told by her mother and by other working-class women, Carolyn Kay Steedman argues that "the point doesn't lie there, back in the past, back in the lost time at which [events] happened; the only point lies in interpretation" (5). And in interpreting her mother's life story as one of loss, envy, and lifelong exclusion from the comforts of middle-class life, Steedman concludes that "In this way, the story [my mother] told was a form of political analysis, [and it] allows a political interpretation to be made of her life" (6).

Steedman's female narrators transmit a quotidian story of class exclusion and suppressed resentment across generations of British working-class families, but it is only through the autobiographer's deliberate defamiliarizing of her past that she is able to turn the story of other women's lives into a critique of classed and gendered identity. Linda Brodkey, in this issue of *College English,* also sees from a point in the present how the girl she once was did not grow naturally into literacy, but wrote and read in a complex relationship to class, gender, and religion. In the same way, even the most fragmentary and mundane stories about literacy, like that told by the Irish father in Leichter's study, give their authors the opportunity to make these events strange and to reinterpret them from the vantage point of a critical present.

Traditionally, the crossing between language worlds, dramatized by the Irish father as a scene of literal violence, is both a familiar trope and the grounds for political and social critique in literacy autobiographies, Frederick Douglass's *Narrative* providing one of the most powerful examples. What Janet Eldred calls a "collision between competing discourse communities, their language conventions, and their inherent social logics," which she finds portrayed in short stories such as Hawthorne's "My Kinsman, Major Molineux" (686), is also a common conflict explored by autobiographers focusing on their own language growth and use.

One of the earliest and most influential academic texts to address the rifts between sociolinguistic worlds is Richard Hoggart's *The Uses of Literacy* (1957), which portrays the trans-class travels of "the scholarship boy," a liminal figure whose identity turns on the choices he makes as a working-class youth crossing over into the world of middle-class British schooling. In Hoggart's literacy story, the scholarship boy can choose to assimilate into the world of the civil service or the professions, or he can try to develop a hybrid sense of self that allows him to work in the middle-class world while remaining rooted in that of the working class. However, the scholarship boy who lacks the special strength to realize either a singular, deracinated self or the integrated self of two worlds remains suspended "between two worlds of school and home"; and although "he quickly learns to make use of a pair of different accents, perhaps even two different apparent characters and differing standards of value" (242), the boy is too much "of *both* the worlds of home and school" to realize an identity that allows him to live intimately or authoritatively in either (241). Instead the scholarship boy lives "at the friction-point of two cultures" where he is never really a native speaker or writer of either language, for despite his mastery of the forms of languages, he can never fully articulate a sense of self and belonging in either world (239).

In Hoggart's text the translation of self, cultural categories, and felt experience can be incomplete, a condition explored in American multicultural autobiography and literature from W. E. B. DuBois's *The Souls of Black Folk* to recent fiction such as Cristina Garcia's *Dreaming in Cuban*. For some contemporary academics who focus on their language use and learning in worlds that traditionally have excluded them, there is a similar difficulty in translating a sense of self across cultural borders. Like Hoggart, these writers describe their ambivalence when, as both students and teachers, they confront significant life choices about their identity in relation to dominant discourses (Mike Rose; Lu, "From Silence to Words"; Gilyard; Shen; see Rondinone for an unambivalent choice, however). These and other writers use literacy narratives to acknowledge the conflicts they face within dominant cultures and, ultimately, to develop a version of difference that is personally usable.

At my college, we are trying to address issues of cultural and linguistic diversity within a three-year FIPSE-funded Pilot Project called the Enrichment Curriculum, which features a two-semester writing course that groups remedial and freshman students heterogeneously. We recognize that our students, whose backgrounds reflect a stunning array of cultures, may use the literacy narrative as a framework for reflecting upon linguistic and cultural translation. In one of the experimental classes that preceded this curriculum, I asked students to begin their literacy narratives by examining their own and others' language use and history. Students interviewed one another, their peers, or family members; they defined terms such as "dialect" and "Creole"; they talked about orality and literacy, bilingualism, and Black English; they read excerpts from Deborah Tannen's *You Just Don't Understand,* Richard Rodriguez's autobiography and reviews of his book, and literacy stories by Michelle Cliff, Amy Tan, and Gloria Naylor. After a passionate discussion of the issues raised by Rachel Jones's "What's Wrong with Black English," the students in this class composed a list of twelve questions, which we then used as the assignment for writing; students chose questions such as "Do you feel you are losing your own culture's language when you are learning a different language? How do you feel talking two or more languages?" and "Why does sounding educated seem to people of color to be associated with being white? Why does black and white have to be an issue?"

To pursue the possibility of literacy stories becoming sites of translation in our classrooms, I want now to look at two texts written in response to this class assignment by one student, Alisha, who used her essays to investigate her own position in relation to issues of assimilation for speakers of minority dialects and languages. In the first text, a five-page essay titled "English: A Language Within Many Other Languages," Alisha chose to examine Amy Tan's assertion in "My Mother's English" that we all speak different "En-glishes." As Alisha notes in her introduction, "English speaking natives like myself tend to overlook" the hybrid quality of their daily speech:

> From interviews I've conducted, I've found that native English speakers feel their language doesn't differentiate, because it's the only language they use. However, I realized after analyzing English used by myself and others, that English does differ depending on the setting and who you are talking to. It's funny to say, but English can be several different languages combined together. That's why when asked if I speak English I say: "I speak many Englishes."

To develop her thesis that daily speech is in fact stranger than she had previously thought, Alisha describes crossing the social and affective borders of language worlds. Using three separate mini-stories that dramatize shifts in situation, audience, and topic, Alisha depicts a "frozen," stiff style that she uses with her professors; a relaxed, "cool" style used by her girlfriends, all speakers of New York City Black English; and a "warm," intimate style used with parents and other authority figures in her African-American community.

In the first mini-story, Alisha reconstructs a writing conference between herself and her first basic writing teacher, parodying her responses to the teacher's questions about her rough draft. Her body is "like an ice cube, cold and square, with no voice box at all," but when the teacher inquires about her work, she answers smoothly, "Oh, actually, my paper assignment is going better than I expected. I used brainstorming, freewriting, editing, and revising as writing techniques, to help me clearly express myself. In addition, they also allowed me to familiarize myself with the writing criteria expected of me, now that I am in college." When the conference ends, Alisha meets her girlfriends outside the teacher's office, and as she slips into the "cool" style of the vernacular, she slips into a different sense of self, translating from "proper" English into a slang "that spells r-e-l-i-e-f," moving from a bodily stiffness into a coolness that she compares to a soothing bath and a relaxed frame of mind.

Alisha observes that when she leaves her girlfriends and goes home, she crosses another physical as well as figurative boundary. "Whenever I leave the outdoors (hanging out in places outside of my house), to hibernate indoors (in my own house), I don't speak street talk/slang English," she writes. She categorizes the language used at home as a "warm" English, not the cool style of the street but still a style through which "you can speak your mind to a certain extent." These boundaries, however, are subject to negotiation because "the way I perceive myself as speaking . . . is different from the way my mother perceives it. There have been times," she recalls,

in which I'll engage in conversations with my mother, and with a big smile
she'll ask me, "Why am I talking like a white girl?" Whenever she asked me
this question, I sat with a puzzling look on my face, while feeling hurt and
confused inside. I never quite understand what she is trying to say. What
exactly is white English?

To answer her question, "What exactly is white English?" Alisha considers
that the boundaries between white and black Englishes are not as stable as
people usually think and may in fact result in hybridized speech—some
whites may speak "street talk/slang," while some blacks such as herself may
speak academic English. Alisha reasons that "Even though there is a majority of whites speaking proper English, there are also those who speak, 'Yo
dude! What's smokin'!' I don't exactly consider that proper English!" The
boundaries between Englishes are fluid and not impermeable. Therefore,
she argues, "I don't think black people, my people, should label [standard
English] as being white English."

To cap off this statement, in her last two paragraphs Alisha turns to Gloria Naylor's "The Meaning of a Word" to argue that "language does shape
the way people in society perceive" one another. She concludes that categories such as "white" and "black" English depend upon the contexts and
sociopolitical perceptions of language use rather than upon a neutral
"truth" about the inherent properties of a dialect of English. Thus in this
first attempt at translation, Alisha relativizes the differences between
dialects, which for her means accepting her double-voicedness as a
strength rather than as a sign of her cultural disloyalty.

When Alisha recognized the legitimacy of her own hybridization, she was
then prepared to consider the difference between hybridizing and assimilating languages. She thus turned to contemplate the figure of the scholarship boy and the relevance of his journey to her own life. In the second
essay, a critical reading of Rodriguez's *Hunger of Memory*, Alisha set out to
explore how education is "a process of remaking a person's life." Comparing her story of learning to read and write in school with Rodriguez's, Alisha
argues that while she agrees that education is transformatory, she disagrees
with Rodriguez that in order to embrace the culture of the school, students
must necessarily distance themselves so painfully from their home cultures.
"Even though learning [in school] started changing my life," she wrote, "I
never allowed it to separate me from my intimate life"; as one example, she
recalls how she tried to explain to her grandmother the nature and purposes of a sociology project, in contrast to Rodriguez, who hid his intellectual
self from his family, underscoring the rigid distinction between public and
private selves. Rodriguez depicts a translation of difference that she doesn't
want to copy: "I'll never allow education to remake me to the extreme that I
could no longer admire my grandmother."

Alisha argues that Rodriguez's feeling of distance is rooted in his urge to find his identity by imitating authority figures in the mainstream culture, such as teachers. By contrast, "Instead of sitting in a classroom obtaining my teacher's identity, I focus on obtaining my own public identity." She concludes that she has begun to develop a new sense of self that allows her to negotiate the complex demands of her cultural situation in mature ways:

> Whenever I learn something new, I process the new information for my own benefit. Because I'm looked upon as a double minority (a young black woman), I can't afford to mimic someone else's identity. Although, in life, we all need someone to look up to or help guide us on the right track. For this reason, I can understand what Rodriguez says when he says, "I wanted to *be* like my teachers, to possess their knowledge, to assume their authority, their confidence, even to assume a teacher's persona" (p. 55). However, different from Richard Rodriguez, I feel learning involves more than simple imitation. I totally disagree with his motives to imitate others. When you imitate others, you're a stranger to yourself, because you do not possess your own ideas.

In the vein of contemporary autobiographers like Maxine Hong Kingston and Audre Lorde, Alisha squarely confronts the issue of hybridized identity; her dilemma is how she can learn to become a fluent speaker of "many Englishes" without becoming "a stranger to" herself. Where Rodriguez splits himself into two selves, the self of the family and that of the academy, Alisha portrays overlapping versions of self: the speaker of "many Englishes" writes alternately as a young black woman, a new college student, a writer, a granddaughter, and an intellectually questing self in the process of "remaking her life." The "I" in Alisha's essay is not monological. As Alisha engages with Rodriguez's representations of the nontraditional student, she sympathizes with him ("I can understand what Rodriguez says") even as she interrogates his canonical story of assimilation. She accepts direction from her teachers even as she parodies the voice of authority. She claims she is responsible for her own decisions, but she is also deeply connected to others in her family and community. Alisha's "I" is a writer with many voices and stories to tell.

Alisha perceives Rodriguez's literacy story to be a complex process of struggle and choice, and through writing her own response to *Hunger of Memory,* Alisha practices a sort of autoethnography, one of the arts of the contact zone in which, Pratt says, "people undertake to describe themselves in ways that engage representations others have made of them" (35). In the process of her writing, Alisha contends with complicated affective and social issues of translation that the scholarship boy could not resolve without losing a sense of self: how to be independent from teachers, yet also how to accept direction from them; how to switch codes according to context without being an opportunistic rhetor; how to enter one discourse world without losing the words and values of another. How, in short, to translate self and difference between language worlds without becoming "a stranger to yourself."

Revising an affective and sociolinguistic sense of self went hand in hand with Alisha's increasing ability to do what some minority educators believe students don't get the chance to do: begin to master the language of the school without paying the price of unexamined assimilation. Alisha's skillful intermingling of life writing and exposition of other texts implies a pedagogy which, as Keith Gilyard puts it in his literacy story, "is successful only if it makes knowledge or skill achievable while at the same time allowing students to maintain their own sense of identity" (11). By reconstructing her own criss-crossing between language worlds, Alisha challenged Rodriguez's view that the private and the public self are always divided and argued that the scholarship boy's refusal to negotiate the friction-point between cultures amounts to a surrendering of self. By defamiliarizing her language use, Alisha represents herself as a speaker of many Englishes making multiple translations between worlds rather than assimilating the values and words of one world at the expense of those of another. In writing these two accounts, Alisha, a first-year college student in a basic writing class, moved beyond summarizing a text and beyond reporting the events of her life to foreground the tellability of her story, and, consequently, to view her life through a critical and interpretive lens. For me as her teacher and reader, Alisha's ability to see her experience as narratable is one critical achievement both of a literacy narrative and of a writing pedagogy.

In general terms, self- translations are critical to learning how to write in any new context since, as Robert Brooke has cogently argued, we learn to write by negotiating a sense of self as writers living in time and in specific social situations. For authors who speak minority dialects or languages or who have crossed class and ethnic boundaries, negotiating a sense of self as a writer also means making important cultural choices about the meaning of passing through various language worlds. As I think happened for Alisha, students can read and write literacy narratives in order to see that reading and writing are not natural acts, but culturally situated, acquired practices. In the process of exploring their language use in various cultural settings, students can also begin to think through basic issues of difference and assimilation that are confronting American education today.

Versions of difference and attitudes toward various states of betweenness are legion and highly contested in American culture, as suggested by, for example, the multiple perspectives elaborated in Gerald Early's volume of collected essays on race, identity, and assimilation, *Lure and Loathing.* According to a recent report in the *New York Times,* the tension between "standard" and Black Englishes in several major urban school districts, including Los Angeles and New York, produces a complex conflict for minority students who at an early age must make choices about their cultural identity in relation to language use (Lee). On the college level, ethnographic evidence (DiPardo; Weis) further suggests that the interrelated issues of language use, identity, and assimilation demand significant choices from some students living and writing at Hoggart's "friction-point of two cultures."

In their explorations of these friction-points, the authors of literacy stories reflect this ongoing struggle in American society; from the radical political critiques of Michelle Cliff and Min-Zhan Lu to arguments for assimilation by Peter Rondinone and Richard Rodriguez, literacy narratives wrestle with the kind of relationship to dominant discourses a writer wants to imagine for herself. To deal fully with the complex debates about assimilation is outside the scope of this essay, but I want to move toward a conclusion by highlighting two possibilities which get played out in literacy narratives and more generally in discussions of identity and language use. Let me then briefly consider how two autobiographers of their language use, Richard Rodriguez and Eva Hoffman, describe their relationships to different cultures.

In his reading of Hoggart's *The Uses of Literacy*, Richard Rodriguez comments that what Hoggart "grasps very well is that the scholarship boy must move between environments, his home and the classroom, which are at cultural extremes, opposed" (46). The journey between polarized "environments" that Rodriguez describes in his book (from working-class, Catholic, Mexican-American culture into middle-class, secular, Anglo worlds) portrays difference in oppositional and irreconcilable terms. In Rodriguez's version of multiculturalism—one which still holds powerful sway in the academy and in popular discourses—the translation of difference means shedding one identity in favor of another as the student moves between worlds that "are at cultural extremes, opposed." Although in Rodriguez's case this position leads to assimilation into the mainstream and a loss of intimacy with his first language, his view of the purely oppositional relationship between cultures also supports the reverse choice, an unambivalent separateness from and rejection of dominant discourses.

However, as Alisha observes in her discussion of who "owns" standard English and who speaks "street talk/slang," different worlds need not be opposed, a view of difference that Eva Hoffman, in her autobiography, *Lost in Translation*, shares. Unlike Rodriguez, Hoffman portrays the crossing of boundaries as a continual, lifelong process of shuttling back and forth between the Polish of her past and the English of her present. Where Rodriguez's journey is unidirectional and irrevocable, Hoffman's is bidirectional and subject to ongoing writing and thinking about her growing sense of self and the meaningfulness of language in regards to that self. Although the world of the Eastern European family and the North American cultures of school and work clash and are in many ways opposed, Hoffman struggles to find points of dialogical contact between the two, places where "Each language modifies the other, crossbreeds with it, fertilizes it. Each language makes the other relative" (273). This process of relativization (which Bakhtin theorizes as a liberating property of narrative in *The Dialogic Imagination*) allows Hoffman to consider her difference in dynamic and sometimes contradictory terms. When she recognizes her hybridization of voice and self, she discovers a way of holding her Polish and English selves in creative tension and is able finally to achieve a successful—although never fully complete—translation of her difference.

Like Alisha's, Hoffman's portrayal of the writer's relationships to cultural friction-points goes beyond the duality of insider/outsider because each writer imagines a relationship of relativizing interdependence between her languages. Similarly, in composition studies, the move toward more dynamic models of community leads teachers away from the view of students as initiates into foreign language cultures and, more particularly, questions the portrayal of basic writers as "outsiders" and their teachers as "insiders" (Severino; Harris). If, instead, we see the classroom in terms of Alisha's or Hoffman's literacy narratives, then the outsider's own language overlaps, conflicts with, shapes, and is shaped by the insider's language; movements between worlds take on a liminal rather than a dichotomous character. If students and teachers begin to see their languages as mutually shaping, they also can recognize their double-voicedness and, in so doing, can see the self as rooted in other cultures yet also belonging to, becoming transformed by, and in turn transforming school cultures. Instead of being seen as outsiders who must choose to write either from within or against the academy, students assume a position of strength.

It is surely true that educators have often failed to acknowledge difference in the classroom, even when students directly address issues of class or gender in their writing (Brodkey); yet we should not let our zeal to recognize historically repressed differences create a polarizing rhetoric of difference that turns on a reductive view of culture. Relevant here is Cornel West's recent critique of contemporary identity politics, "Beyond Multiculturalism and Eurocentrism," which cautions educators that a one-sided rhetoric of difference can put multiculturalism into a stiff, ahistorical opposition with an "Other," Eurocentrism. West argues that in so constructing the debate, rhetors on either side of the Multiculturalist-Eurocentric struggle produce a "monumentalist conception of culture" which offers "crude" versions of the historically reciprocal relationships between marginalized and mainstream cultures (125). In a monumentalist view of culture, either the celebration of a radical difference or its erasure decontextualizes the particularity of the stories we can tell about daily life and denies the tense interdependence that has historically existed between dominant and subordinate cultures in American society. Within the classroom, we can recognize this cultural dynamic of interdependence by developing a pedagogy that allows students to represent themselves in reference to each others' literacy stories and to those of professional writers. If we trust our students to fashion a debate about language and multiculturalism in this way (as Alisha and her classmates did), then students' individual stories can challenge monumentalist representations of the passage between language worlds by offering holistic portraits of writers with multiple and sometimes conflicting commitments, aspirations, and choices.

At their best, literacy narratives provide a space where students like Alisha can defamiliarize their ordinary language use and perform imaginative acts of self-representation in order, as Eva Hoffman puts it, to translate "[b]etween the two stories and two vocabularies" "without being split by the difference" (269, 274). Students' stories of everyday life enhance their personal success as writers in the university; these stories can also deepen their teachers' understanding of difference and shape their responses to today's competing versions of multiculturalism. In this way, literacy narratives contribute to the broader goal of building a more dialogical, multicultural curriculum that includes—indeed, that both respects and responds to—the voices and stories of individual writers.

REFERENCES

Bakhtin, M. M. *The Dialogic Imagination.* Ed. Michael Holquist. Trans. Caryl Emerson and Michael Holquist. Austin: U. of Texas P, 1981.

Bartholomae, David. "The Tidy House: Basic Writing in the American Curriculum." *Journal of Basic Writing* 12 (Spring 1993): 4–21.

Bateson, Mary Catherine. *Composing a Life.* New York: Penguin, 1990.

Beach, Richard. "Differences in Autobiographical Narratives of English Teachers, College Freshmen, and Seventh Graders." *College Composition and Communication* 38 (Feb. 1987): 56–69.

Bizzell, Patricia. "What Happens When Basic Writers Come to College?" *College Composition and Communication* 37 (Oct. 1986): 294–301.

———. "Power, Authority, and Critical Pedagogy." *Journal of Basic Writing* 10 (Fall 1991): 54–70.

Brodkey, Linda. "On the Subjects of Class and Gender in 'The Literacy Letters.'" *College English* 51 (Feb. 1989): 125–141.

Brooke, Robert E. *Writing and Sense of Self: Identity Negotiation in Writing Workshops.* Urbana: NCTE, 1991.

Cliff, Michelle. *The Land of Look Behind: The Poetry and Prose of Michelle Cliff.* Ithaca, NY: Firebrand P, 1985.

Coles, Nicholas, and Susan V. Wall. "Conflict and Power in the Reader-Responses of Adult Basic Writers." *College English* 49 (March 1987): 298–314.

"Counterstatements on 'Diversity, Ideology, and Teaching Writing.'" *College Composition and Communication* 44 (May 1993): 248–257.

Dean, Terry. "Multicultural Classrooms, Monocultural Teachers." *College Composition and Communication* 40 (Feb. 1989): 23–37.

DiPardo, Anne. *A Kind of Passport: A Basic Writing Adjunct Program and the Challenge of Student Diversity.* Urbana: NCTE, 1993.

Early, Gerald, ed. *Lure and Loathing: Essays on Race, Identity, and the Ambivalence of Assimilation.* New York: Penguin, 1993.

Eldred, Janet. "Narratives of Socialization: Literacy in the Short Story." *College English* 53 (Oct. 1991): 686–700.

Eldred, Janet, and Peter Mortensen. "Reading Literacy Narratives." *College English* 54 (Sept. 1992): 512–539.

Fox, Tom. "Basic Writing as Cultural Conflict." *Journal of Education* 172.1 (1990): 65–83.

Gilyard, Keith. *Voices of the Self: A Study of Language Competence.* Detroit: Wayne State UP, 1991.

Goodman, Yetta. "The Development of Initial Literacy." *Perspectives on Literacy.* Ed. Eugene R. Kintgen, Barry M. Kroll, and Mike Rose. Carbondale, IL: Southern Illinois UP, 1988. 312–20.

Hairston, Maxine. "Diversity, Idology, and Teaching Writing." *College Composition and Communication* 43 (May 1992): 179–193.

Harris, Joseph. "The Idea of Community in the Study of Writing." *College Composition and Communication* 40 (Feb. 1989): 11–22.

Harste, Jerome C., Virginia A. Woodward, and Carolyn L. Burke. *Language Stories and Literacy Lessons.* Portsmouth, NH: Heinemann, 1984.

Heath, Shirley Brice. *Ways with Words: Language, Life, and Work in Communities and Classrooms.* New York: Cambridge UP, 1983.

Hoffman, Eva. *Lost in Translation: A Life in a New Language.* New York: Penguin, 1989.

Hoggart, Richard. *The Uses of Literacy: Aspects of Working-Class Life with Special Reference to Publications and Entertainments.* Fair Lawn, NJ: Essential Books, 1957.

Jones, Rachel. "What's Wrong with Black English." *Encountering Cultures: Reading and Writing in a Changing World.* Ed. Richard Holeton. Englewood Cliffs, NJ: Prentice Hall, 1992. 17–19.

Kutz, Eleanor, Suzy Q. Groden, and Vivian Zamel. *The Discovery of Competence: Teaching and Learning with Diverse Student Writers.* Portsmouth, NH: Boynton/Cook, 1993.

Labov, William. *Language in the Inner City: Studies in the Black English Vernacular.* U of Pennsylvania P, 1972.

Lee, Felicia R. "Lingering Conflict in the Schools: Black Dialect vs. Standard Speech." *New York Times,* 5 January 1994: A1.

Leichter, Hope Jensen. "Families as Environments for Literacy." *Awakening to Literacy.* Ed. Hillel Goelman, Antoinette Oberg, and Frank Smith. Portsmouth, NH: Heinemann, 1984. 38–50.

Lu, Min-Zhan. "From Silence to Words: Writing As Struggle." *College English* 49 (April 1987): 437–448.

———. "Conflict and Struggle: The Enemies or Preconditions of Basic Writing?" *College English* 54 (Dec. 1992): 887–913.

Moss, Beverly J., and Keith Walters. "Rethinking Diversity: Axes of Difference in the Writing Classroom." *Theory and Practice in the Teaching of Writing: Rethinking the Discipline.* Ed. Lee Odell. Carbondale, IL: Southern Illinois UP, 1993. 132–185.

Naylor, Gloria. "The Meaning of a Word." *Crossing Cultures: Readings for Composition.* 3d ed. Ed. Henry Knepler and Myrna Knepler. New York: Macmillan, 1991. 379–381.

Neilsen, Lorri. *Literacy and Living: The Lives of Three Literate Adults.* Portsmouth, NH: Heinemann, 1989.

Pratt, Mary Louise. "Arts of the Contact Zone." *Profession* 91: 33–40.

Rondinone, Peter. "Teacher Background and Student Needs." *Journal of Basic Writing* 10 (Spring 1991): 41–53.

Rodriguez, Richard. *Hunger of Memory: The Education of Richard Rodriguez*. New York: Bantam, 1982.

Rose, Mike. *Lives on the Boundary*. New York: Free Press, 1989.

Rose, Shirley K. "Reading Representative Anecdotes of Literacy Practice; of 'See Dick and Jane read and write!'" *Rhetoric Review* 8 (Spring 1990): 245–259.

Salmon, Phillida. *Living in Time: A New Look at Personal Development*. London: J. M. Dent, 1985.

Scollon, Ron, and Suzanne B.K. Scollon. *Narrative, Literacy and Face in Interethnic Communication*. Norwood, NJ: Ablex, 1981.

Severino, Carol. "Where the Cultures of Basic Writers and Academia Intersect: Cultivating the Common Ground." *Journal of Basic Writing* 11 (1992): 4–15.

Shen, Fan. "The Classroom and the Wider Culture: Identity as a Key to Learning English Composition." *College Composition and Communication* 40 (Dec. 1989): 459–466.

Steedman, Carolyn Kay. *Landscape for a Good Woman: A Story of Two Lives*. New Brunswick, NJ: Rutgers UP, 1991.

"Symposium on Basic Writing, Conflict and Struggle, and the Legacy of Mina Shaughnessy." *College English* 55 (Dec. 1993): 879–903.

Tan, Amy. "My Mother's English." *Visions Across the Americas: Short Essays for Composition*. Ed. J. Sterling Warner, Judith Hilliard, and Vincent Piro. Fort Worth: Harcourt, Brace, 1991. 21–25.

Taylor, Denny. *Family Literacy: Young Children Learning to Read and Write*. Portsmouth, NH: Heinemann, 1983.

Turner, Victor. "Social Dramas and Stories about Them." *On Narrative*. Ed. W. J. T. Mitchell. Chicago: U of Chicago P, 1980. 137–164.

Weis, Lois. *Between Two Worlds: Black Students in an Urban Community College*. London: Routledge & Kegan Paul, 1985.

West, Cornel. *Prophetic Reflections: Notes on Race and Power in America*. Monroe, Maine: Common Courage P, 1993.

"Writing Within and Against the Academy: What Do We Really Want Our Students to Do? A Symposium." *Journal of Education* 172.1 (1990): 15–37.

QUESTIONS FOR REFLECTION, JOURNAL WRITING, AND DISCUSSION

1. As a young student, did you ever feel "suspended between the two worlds of school and home"?

2. What is your reaction to the story of the Irish father learning to read? How do today's teaching approaches compare to this one?

3. What was your reaction to the statements of Soliday's student Alisha? How would you teach Alisha?

4. Soliday says that some writing teachers could be criticized for "unthinkingly acculturating students into the academy and glossing over issues of difference in the classroom." Could Bruffee be criticized for this? Could Bartholomae? Could you?

Chapter 10

From Silence to Words: Writing as Struggle

Min-Zhan Lu

Min-Zhan Lu is Endowment Professor of the Humanities at Drake University, where she teaches courses in writing, autobiography, fiction, and critical theory. Her work is concerned with the use of cultural dissonance and the politics of representing difference in writing and teaching. The following article is from *College English*, 49, April 1997.

> *Imagine that you enter a parlor. You come late. When you arrive, others have long pre-ceded you, and they are engaged in a heated discussion. . . . You listen for a while, until you decide that you have caught the tenor of the argument; then you put in your oar. Someone answers; you answer him; another comes to your defense; another aligns himself against you, to either the embarrassment or gratification of your opponent, depending upon the quality of your ally's assistance. However, the discussion is interminable. The hour grows late, you must depart. And you do depart, with the discussion still vigorously in progress.*
> —Kenneth Burke, *The Philosophy of Literary Form*

> *Men are not built in silence, but in word, in work, in action-reflection.*
> —Paulo Freire, *Pedagogy of the Oppressed*

My mother withdrew into silence two months before she died. A few nights before she fell silent, she told me she regretted the way she had raised me and my sisters. I knew she was referring to the way we had been brought up in the midst of two conflicting worlds—the world of home, dominated by the ideology of the Western humanistic tradition, and the world of a society dominated by Mao Tse-tung's Marxism. My mother had devoted her life to our education, an education she knew had made us suffer political persecution during the Cultural Revolution. I wanted to find a way to convince her that, in spite of the persecution, I had benefited from the education she had worked so hard to give me. But I was silent. My understanding of my education was so dominated by memories of confusion and frustration that I was unable to reflect on what I could have gained from it.

This paper is my attempt to fill up that silence with words, words I didn't have then, words that I have since come to by reflecting on my earlier experience as a student in China and on my recent experience as a composition teacher in the United States. For in spite of the frustration and confusion I experienced growing up caught between two conflicting worlds, the conflict ultimately helped me to grow as a reader and writer. Constantly having to switch back and forth between the discourse of home and that of school made me sensitive and self-conscious about the struggle I experienced every time I tried to read, write, or think in either discourse. Eventually, it led me to search for constructive uses for such struggle.

From early childhood, I had identified the differences between home and the outside world by the different languages I used in each. My parents had wanted my sisters and me to get the best education they could conceive of—Cambridge. They had hired a live-in tutor, a Scot, to make us bilingual. I learned to speak English with my parents, my tutor, and my sisters. I was allowed to speak Shanghai dialect only with the servants. When I was four (the year after the Communist Revolution of 1949), my parents sent me to a local private school where I learned to speak, read, and write in a new language—Standard Chinese, the official written language of New China.

In those days I moved from home to school, from English to Standard Chinese to Shanghai dialect, with no apparent friction. I spoke each language with those who spoke the language. All seemed quite "natural"—servants spoke only Shanghai dialect because they were servants; teachers spoke Standard Chinese because they were teachers; languages had different words because they were different languages. I thought of English as my family language, comparable to the many strange dialects I didn't speak but had often heard some of my classmates speak with their families. While I was happy to have a special family language, until second grade I didn't feel that my family language was any different than some of my classmates' family dialects.

My second grade homeroom teacher was a young graduate from a missionary school. When she found out I spoke English, she began to practice her English on me. One day she used English when asking me to run an errand for her. As I turned to close the door behind me, I noticed the puzzled faces of my classmates. I had the same sensation I had often experienced when some stranger in a crowd would turn on hearing me speak English. I was more intensely pleased on this occasion, however, because suddenly I felt that my family language had been singled out from the family languages of my classmates. Since we were not allowed to speak any dialect other than Standard Chinese in the classroom, having my teacher speak English to me in class made English an official language of the classroom. I began to take pride in my ability to speak it.

This incident confirmed in my mind what my parents had always told me about the importance of English to one's life. Time and again they had told me of how my paternal grandfather, who was well versed in classic Chinese, kept losing good-paying jobs because he couldn't speak English. My grandmother reminisced constantly about how she had slaved and saved to send my father to a first-rate missionary school. And we were made to understand that it was my father's fluent English that had opened the door to his success. Even though my family had always stressed the importance of English for my future, I used to complain bitterly about the extra English lessons we had to take after school. It was only after my homeroom teacher had "sanctified" English that I began to connect English with my education. I became a much more eager student in my tutorials.

What I learned from my tutorials seemed to enhance and reinforce what I was learning in my classroom. In those days each word had one meaning. One day I would be making a sentence at school: "The national flag of China is red." The next day I would recite at home, "My love is like a red, red rose." There seemed to be an agreement between the Chinese "red" and the English "red," and both corresponded to the patch of color printed next to the word. "Love" was my love for my mother at home and my love for my "motherland" at school; both "loves" meant how I felt about my mother. Having two loads of homework forced me to develop a quick memory for words and a sensitivity to form and style. What I learned in one language carried over to the other. I made sentences such as, "I saw a red, red rose among the green leaves," with both the English lyric and the classic Chinese lyric—red flower among green leaves—running through my mind, and I was praised by both teacher and tutor for being a good student.

Although my elementary schooling took place during the fifties, I was almost oblivious to the great political and social changes happening around me. Years later, I read in my history and political philosophy textbooks that the fifties were a time when "China was making a transition from a semi-feudal, semi-capitalist, and semi-colonial country into a socialist country," a period in which "the Proletarians were breaking into the educational territory dominated by Bourgeois Intellectuals." While people all over the country were being officially classified into Proletarians, Petty-bourgeois, National-bourgeois, Poor-peasants, and Intellectuals, and were trying to adjust to their new social identities, my parents were allowed to continue the upper middle-class life they had established before the 1949 Revolution because of my father's affiliation with British firms. I had always felt that my family was different from the families of my classmates, but I didn't perceive society's view of my family until the summer vacation before I entered high school.

First, my aunt was caught by her colleagues talking to her husband over the phone in English. Because of it, she was criticized and almost labeled a Rightist. (This was the year of the Anti-Rightist movement, a movement in

which the Intellectuals became the target of the "socialist class-struggle.") I
had heard others telling my mother that she was foolish to teach us English
when Russian had replaced English as the "official" foreign language. I had
also learned at school that the American and British Imperialists were the
arch-enemies of New China. Yet I had made no connection between the
arch-enemies and the English our family spoke. What happened to my aunt
forced the connection on me. I began to see my parents' choice of a family
language as an anti-Revolutionary act and was alarmed that I had participated in such an act. From then on, I took care not to use English outside
home and to conceal my knowledge of English from my new classmates.

Certain words began to play important roles in my new life at the junior
high. On the first day of school, we were handed forms to fill out with our
parents' class, job, and income. Being one of the few people not employed
by the government, my father had never been officially classified. Since he
was a medical doctor, he told me to put him down as an Intellectual. My
homeroom teacher called me into the office a couple of days afterwards
and told me that my father couldn't be an Intellectual if his income far
exceeded that of a Capitalist. He also told me that since my father worked
for Foreign Imperialists, my father should be classified as an Imperialist
Lackey. The teacher looked nonplussed when I told him that my father
couldn't be an Imperialist Lackey because he was a medical doctor. But I
could tell from the way he took notes on my form that my father's job had
put me in an unfavorable position in his eyes.

The Standard Chinese term "class" was not a new word for me. Since
first grade, I had been taught sentences such as, "The Working class are the
masters of New China." I had always known that it was good to be a worker,
but until then, I had never felt threatened for not being one. That fall,
"class" began to take on a new meaning for me. I noticed a group of
Working-class students and teachers at school. I was made to understand
that because of my class background, I was excluded from that group.

Another word that became important was "consciousness." One of the
slogans posted in the school building read, "Turn our students into future
Proletarians with socialist consciousness and education!" For several weeks
we studied this slogan in our political philosophy course, a subject I had
never had in elementary school. I still remember the definition of "socialist
consciousness" that we were repeatedly tested on through the years:
"Socialist consciousness is a person's political soul. It is the consciousness of
the Proletarians represented by Marxist Mao Tse-tung thought. It takes
expression in one's action, language, and lifestyle. It is the task of every
Chinese student to grow up into a Proletarian with a socialist consciousness
so that he can serve the people and the motherland." To make the abstract
concept accessible to us, our teacher pointed out that the immediate task
for students from Working-class families was to strengthen their socialist

consciousnesses. For those of us who were from other class backgrounds, the task was to turn ourselves into Workers with socialist consciousnesses. The teacher never explained exactly how we were supposed to "turn" into Workers. Instead, we were given samples of the ritualistic annual plans we had to write at the beginning of each term. In these plans, we performed "self-criticism" on our consciousnesses and made vows to turn ourselves into Workers with socialist consciousnesses. The teacher's division between those who did and those who didn't have a socialist consciousness led me to reify the notion of "consciousness" into a thing one possesses. I equated this intangible "thing" with a concrete way of dressing, speaking, and writing. For instance, I never doubted that my political philosophy teacher had a socialist consciousness because she was from a steelworker's family (she announced this the first day of class) and was a Party member who wore grey cadre suits and talked like a philosophy textbook. I noticed other things about her. She had beautiful eyes and spoke Standard Chinese with such a pure accent that I thought she should be a film star. But I was embarrassed that I had noticed things that ought not to have been associated with her. I blamed my observation on my Bourgeois consciousness.

At the same time, the way reading and writing were taught through memorization and imitation also encouraged me to reduce concepts and ideas to simple definitions. In literature and political philosophy classes, we were taught a large number of quotations from Marx, Lenin, and Mao Tsetung. Each concept that appeared in these quotations came with a definition. We were required to memorize the definitions of the words along with the quotations. Every time I memorized a definition, I felt I had learned a word: "The national red flag symbolizes the blood shed by Revolutionary ancestors for our socialist cause"; "New China rises like a red sun over the eastern horizon." As I memorized these sentences, I reduced their metaphors to dictionary meanings: "red" meant "Revolution" and "red sun" meant "New China" in the "language" of the Working class. I learned mechanically but eagerly. I soon became quite fluent in this new language.

As school began to define me as a political subject, my parents tried to build up my resistance to the "communist poisoning" by exposing me to the "great books"—novels by Charles Dickens, Nathaniel Hawthorne, Emily Brontë, Jane Austen, and writers from around the turn of the century. My parents implied that these writers represented how I, their child, should read and write. My parents replaced the word "Bourgeois" with the word "cultured." They reminded me that I was in school only to learn math and science. I needed to pass the other courses to stay in school, but I was not to let the "Red doctrines" corrupt my mind. Gone were the days when I could innocently write, "I saw the red, red rose among the green leaves," collapsing, as I did, English and Chinese cultural traditions. "Red" came to mean Revolution at school, "the Commies" at home, and adultery in *The*

Scarlet Letter. Since I took these symbols and metaphors as meanings natural to people of the same class, I abandoned my earlier definitions of English and Standard Chinese as the language of home and the language of school. I now defined English as the language of the Bourgeois and Standard Chinese as the language of the Working class. I thought of the language of the Working class as someone else's language and the language of the Bourgeois as my language. But I also believed that, although the language of the Bourgeois was my real language, I could and would adopt the language of the Working class when I was at school. I began to put on and take off my Working class language in the same way I put on and took off my school clothes to avoid being criticized for wearing Bourgeois clothes.

In my literature classes, I learned the Working-class formula for reading. Each work in the textbook had a short "Author's Biography": "X X X, born in 19- - in the province of X X, is from a Worker's family. He joined the Revolution in 19- -. He is a Revolutionary realist with a passionate love for the Party and Chinese Revolution. His work expresses the thoughts and emotions of the masses and sings praise to the prosperous socialist construction on all fronts of China." The teacher used the "Author's Biography" as a yardstick to measure the texts. We were taught to locate details in the texts that illustrated these summaries, such as words that expressed Workers' thoughts and emotions or events that illustrated the Workers' lives.

I learned a formula for Working-class writing in the composition classes. We were given sample essays and told to imitate them. The theme was always about how the collective taught the individual a lesson. I would write papers about labor-learning experiences or school-cleaning days, depending on the occasion of the collective activity closest to the assignment. To make each paper look different, I dressed it up with details about the date, the weather, the environment, or the appearance of the Master-worker who had taught me "the lesson." But as I became more and more fluent in the generic voice of the Working-class Student, I also became more and more self-conscious about the language we used at home.

For instance, in senior high we began to have English classes ("to study English for the Revolution," as the slogan on the cover of the textbook said), and I was given my first Chinese-English dictionary. There I discovered the English version of the term "class-struggle." (The Chinese characters for a school "class" and for a social "class" are different.) I had often used the English word "class" at home in sentences such as, "So and so has class," but I had not connected this sense of "class" with "class-struggle." Once the connection was made, I heard a second layer of meaning every time someone at home said a person had "class." The expression began to mean the person had the style and sophistication characteristic of the Bourgeoisie. The word lost its innocence. I was uneasy about hearing that second layer of meaning because I was sure my parents did not hear the word that way. I felt that therefore I should not be hearing it that way either. Hearing the second layer of meaning made me wonder if I was losing my English.

My suspicion deepened when I noticed myself unconsciously merging and switching between the "reading" of home and the "reading" of school. Once I had to write a report on *The Revolutionary Family,* a book about an illiterate woman's awakening and growth as a Revolutionary through the deaths of her husband and all her children for the cause of the Revolution. In one scene the woman deliberated over whether or not she should encourage her youngest son to join the Revolution. Her memory of her husband's death made her afraid to encourage her son. Yet she also remembered her earlier married life and the first time her husband tried to explain the meaning of the Revolution to her. These memories made her feel she should encourage her son to continue the cause his father had begun.

I was moved by this scene. "Moved" was a word my mother and sisters used a lot when we discussed books. Our favorite moments in novels were moments of what I would now call internal conflict, moments which we said "moved" us. I remember that we were "moved" by Jane Eyre when she was torn between her sense of ethics, which compelled her to leave the man she loved, and her impulse to stay with the only man who had ever loved her. We were also moved by Agnes in *David Copperfield* because of the way she restrained her love for David so that he could live happily with the woman he loved. My standard method of doing a book report was to model it on the review by the Publishing Bureau and to dress it up with detailed quotations from the book. The review of *The Revolutionary Family* emphasized the woman's Revolutionary spirit. I decided to use the scene that had moved me to illustrate this point. I wrote the report the night before it was due. When I had finished, I realized I couldn't possibly hand it in. Instead of illustrating her Revolutionary spirit, I had dwelled on her internal conflict, which could be seen as a moment of weak sentimentality that I should never have emphasized in a Revolutionary heroine. I wrote another report, taking care to illustrate the grandeur of her Revolutionary spirit by expanding on a quotation in which she decided that if the life of her son could change the lives of millions of sons, she should not begrudge his life for the cause of Revolution. I handed in my second version but kept the first in my desk.

I never showed it to anyone. I could never show it to people outside my family, because it had deviated so much from the reading enacted by the jacket review. Neither could I show it to my mother or sisters, because I was ashamed to have been so moved by such a "Revolutionary" book. My parents would have been shocked to learn that I could like such a book in the same way they liked Dickens. Writing this book report increased my fear that I was losing the command over both the "language of home" and the "language of school" that I had worked so hard to gain. I tried to remind myself that, if I could still tell when my reading or writing sounded incorrect, then I had retained my command over both languages. Yet I could no longer be confident of my command over either language because I had discovered that when I was not careful—or even when I was—my reading and writing often surprised me with its impurity. To prevent such impurity, I became very suspicious of my thoughts when I read or wrote. I was always asking myself why I was using this word, how I was using it, always afraid that I wasn't reading or writing correctly. What confused and frustrated me most was that I could not figure out why I was no longer able to read or write correctly without such painful deliberation.

I continued to read only because reading allowed me to keep my thoughts and confusion private. I hoped that somehow, if I watched myself carefully, I would figure out from the way I read whether I had really mastered the "languages." But writing became a dreadful chore. When I tried to keep a diary, I was so afraid that the voice of school might slip in that I could only list my daily activities. When I wrote for school, I worried that my Bourgeois sensibilities would betray me.

The more suspicious I became about the way I read and wrote, the more guilty I felt for losing the spontaneity with which I had learned to "use" these "languages." Writing the book report made me feel that my reading and writing in the "language" of either home or school could not be free of the interference of the other. But I was unable to acknowledge, grasp, or grapple with what I was experiencing, for both my parents and my teachers had suggested that, if I were a good student, such interference would and should not take place. I assumed that once I had "acquired" a discourse, I could simply switch it on and off every time I read and wrote as I would some electronic tool. Furthermore, I expected my readings and writings to come out in their correct forms whenever I switched the proper discourse on. I still regarded the discourse of home as natural and the discourse of school alien, but I never had doubted before that I could acquire both and switch them on and off according to the occasion.

When my experience in writing conflicted with what I thought should happen when I used each discourse, I rejected my experience because it contradicted what my parents and teachers had taught me. I shied away from writing to avoid what I assumed I should not experience. But trying to avoid what should not happen did not keep it from recurring whenever I had to write. Eventually my confusion and frustration over these recurring experiences compelled me to search for an explanation: how and why had I failed to learn what my parents and teachers had worked so hard to teach me?

I now think of the internal scene for my reading and writing about *The Revolutionary Family* as a heated discussion between myself, the voices of home, and those of school. The review on the back of the book, the sample student papers I came across in my composition classes, my philosophy teacher—these I heard as voices of one group. My parents and my home readings were the voices of an opposing group. But the conversation between these opposing voices in the internal scene of my writing was not as polite and respectful as the parlor scene Kenneth Burke has portrayed (see epigraph). Rather, these voices struggled to dominate the discussion, constantly incorporating, dismissing, or suppressing the arguments of each other, like the battles between the hegemonic and counterhegemonic forces described in Raymond Williams' *Marxism and Literature* (108–14).

When I read *The Revolutionary Family* and wrote the first version of my report, I began with a quotation from the review. The voices of both home and school answered, clamoring to be heard. I tried to listen to one group and turn a deaf ear to the other. Both persisted. I negotiated my way through these conflicting voices, now agreeing with one, now agreeing with the other. I formed a reading out of my interaction with both. Yet I was afraid to have done so because both home and school had implied that I should speak in unison with only one of these groups and stand away from the discussion rather than participate in it.

My teachers and parents had persistently called my attention to the intensity of the discussion taking place on the external social scene. The story of my grandfather's failure and my father's success had from my early childhood made me aware of the conflict between Western and traditional Chinese cultures. My political education at school added another dimension to the conflict: the war of Marxist-Maoism against them both. Yet when my parents and teachers called my attention to the conflict, they stressed the anxiety of having to live through China's transformation from a semifeudal, semi-capitalist, and semi-colonial society to a socialist one. Acquiring the discourse of the dominant group was, to them, a means of seeking alliance with that group and thus of surviving the whirlpool of cultural currents around them. As a result, they modeled their pedagogical practices on this utilitarian view of language. Being the eager student, I adopted this view of language as a tool for survival. It came to dominate my understanding of the discussion on the social and historical scene and to restrict my ability to participate in that discussion.

To begin with, the metaphor of language as a tool for survival led me to be passive in my use of discourse, to be a bystander in the discussion. In Burke's "parlor," everyone is involved in the discussion. As it goes on through history, what we call "communal discourses"—arguments specific to particular political, social, economic, ethnic, sexual, and family groups—form, re-form and transform. To use a discourse in such a scene is to participate in the argument and to contribute to the formation of the discourse. But when I was growing up, I could not take on the burden of such an active role in the discussion. For both home and school presented the existent conventions of the discourse each taught me as absolute laws for my action. They turned verbal action into a tool, a set of conventions produced and shaped prior to and outside of my own verbal acts. Because I saw language as a tool, I separated the process of producing the tool from the process of using it. The tool was made by someone else and was then acquired and used by me. How the others made it before I acquired it determined and guaranteed what it produced when I used it. I imagined that the more experienced and powerful members of the community were the ones responsible for making the tool. They were the ones who participated in the discussion and fought with opponents. When I used what they made, their labor and accomplishments would ensure the quality of my reading and writing. By using it, I could survive the heated discussion. When my immediate experience in writing the book report suggested that knowing the conventions of school did not guarantee the form and content of my report, when it suggested that I had to write the report with the work and responsibility I had assigned to those who wrote book reviews in the Publishing Bureau, I thought I had lost the tool I had earlier acquired.

Another reason I could not take up an active role in the argument was that my parents and teachers contrived to provide a scene free of conflict for practicing my various languages. It was as if their experience had made them aware of the conflict between their discourse and other discourses and of the struggle involved in reproducing the conventions of any discourse on a scene where more than one discourse exists. They seemed convinced that such conflict and struggle would overwhelm someone still learning the discourse. Home and school each contrived a purified space where only one discourse was spoken and heard. In their choice of textbooks, in the way they spoke, and in the way they required me to speak, each jealously silenced any voice that threatened to break the unison of the scene. The homogeneity of home and of school implied that only one discourse could and should be relevant in each place. It led me to believe I should leave behind, turn a deaf ear to, or forget the discourse of the other when I crossed the boundary dividing them. I expected myself to set down one discourse whenever I took up another just as I would take off or put on a particular set of clothes for school or home.

Despite my parents' and teachers' attempts to keep home and school discrete, the internal conflict between the two discourses continued whenever I read or wrote. Although I tried to suppress the voice of one discourse in the name of the other, having to speak aloud in the voice I had just silenced each time I crossed the boundary kept both voices active in my mind. Every "I think . . ." from the voice of home or school brought forth a "However . . ." or a "But . . ." from the voice of the opponents. To identify with the voice of home or school, I had to negotiate through the conflicting voices of both by restating, taking back, qualifying my thoughts. I was unconsciously doing so when I did my book report. But I could not use the interaction comfortably and constructively. Both my parents and my teachers had implied that my job was to prevent that interaction from happening. My sense of having failed to accomplish what they had taught silenced me.

To use the interaction between the discourses of home and school constructively, I would have to have seen reading or writing as a process in which I worked my way towards a stance through a dialectical process of identification and division. To identify with an ally, I would have to have grasped the distance between where he or she stood and where I was positioning myself. In taking a stance against an opponent, I would have to have grasped where my stance identified with the stance of my allies. Teetering along the "wavering line of pressure and counter-pressure" from both allies and opponents, I might have worked my way towards a stance of my own (Burke, *A Rhetoric of Motives* 23). Moreover, I would have to have understood that the voices in my mind, like the participants in the parlor scene, were in constant flux. As I came into contact with new and different groups of people or read different books, voices entered and left. Each time I read or wrote, the stance I negotiated out of these voices would always be at some distance from the stances I worked out in my previous and my later readings or writings.

I could not conceive such a form of action for myself because I saw reading and writing as an expression of an established stance. In delineating the conventions of a discourse, my parents and teachers had synthesized the stance they saw as typical for a representative member of the community. Burke calls this the stance of a "god" or the "prototype"; Williams calls it the "official" or "possible" stance of the community. Through the metaphor of the survival tool, my parents and teachers had led me to assume I could automatically reproduce the official stance of the discourse I used. Therefore, when I did my book report on *The Revolutionary Family*, I expected my knowledge of the official stance set by the book review to ensure the actual stance of my report. As it happened, I began by trying to take the official stance of the review. Other voices interrupted. I answered back. In the process, I worked out a stance approximate but not identical to the official stance I began with. Yet the experience of having to labor to realize my knowledge of the official stance or to prevent myself from wandering away from it frustrated and confused me. For even though I had been actually reading and writing in a Burkean scene, I was afraid to participate actively in the discussion. I assumed it was my role to survive by staying out of it.

Not long ago, my daughter told me that it bothered her to hear her friend "talk wrong." Having come to the United States from China with little English, my daughter has become sensitive to the way English, as spoken by her teachers, operates. As a result, she has amazed her teachers with her success in picking up the language and in adapting to life at school. Her concern to speak the English taught in the classroom "correctly" makes her uncomfortable when she hears people using "ain't" or double negatives, which her teacher considers "improper." I see in her the me that had eagerly learned and used the discourse of the Working class at school. Yet while I was torn between the two conflicting worlds of school and home, she moves with seeming ease from the conversations she hears over the dinner table to her teacher's words in the classroom. My husband and I are proud of the good work she does at school. We are glad she is spared the kinds of conflict between home and school I experienced at her age. Yet as we watch her becoming more and more fluent in the language of the classroom, we wonder if, by enabling her to "survive" school, her very fluency will silence her when the scene of her reading and writing expands beyond that of the composition classroom.

For when I listen to my daughter, to students, and to some composition teachers talking about the teaching and learning of writing, I am often alarmed by the degree to which the metaphor of a survival tool dominates their understanding of language as it once dominated my own. I am especially concerned with the way some composition classes focus on turning the classroom into a monological scene for the students' reading and writing. Most of our students live in a world similar to my daughter's, somewhere between the purified world of the classroom and the complex world of my adolescence. When composition classes encourage these students to ignore those voices that seem irrelevant to the purified world of the classroom, most students are often able to do so without much struggle. Some of them are so adept at doing it that the whole process has for them become automatic.

However, beyond the classroom and beyond the limited range of these students' immediate lives lies a much more complex and dynamic social and historical scene. To help these students become actors in such a scene, perhaps we need to call their attention to voices that may seem irrelevant to the discourse we teach rather than encourage them to shut them out. For example, we might intentionally complicate the classroom scene by bringing into it discourses that stand at varying distances from the one we teach. We might encourage students to explore ways of practicing the conventions of the discourse they are learning by negotiating through these conflicting voices. We could also encourage them to see themselves as responsible for forming or transforming as well as preserving the discourse they are learning.

As I think about what we might do to complicate the external and internal scenes of our students' writing, I hear my parents and teachers saying: "Not now. Keep them from the wrangle of the marketplace until they have acquired the discourse and are skilled at using it." And I answer: "Don't teach them to 'survive' the whirlpool of crosscurrents by avoiding it. Use the classroom to moderate the currents. Moderate the currents, but teach them from the beginning to struggle." When I think of the ways in which the teaching of reading and writing as classroom activities can frustrate the development of students, I am almost grateful for the overwhelming complexity of the circumstances in which I grew up. For it was this complexity that kept me from losing sight of the effort and choice involved in reading or writing with and through a discourse.

REFERENCES

Burke, Kenneth. *The Philosophy of Literary Form: Studies in Symbolic Action.* 2nd ed. Baton Rouge: Louisiana State UP, 1967.
————. *A Rhetoric of Motives.* Berkeley: U of California, 1969.
Freire, Paulo. *Pedagogy of the Oppressed.* Trans. M. B. Ramos. New York: Continuum, 1970.
Williams, Raymond. *Marxism and Literature.* New York: Oxford UP, 1977.

QUESTIONS FOR REFLECTION, JOURNAL WRITING, AND DISCUSSION

1. How did growing up in "two conflicting worlds" affect Lu? Would her experience have been similar if she had grown up in the United States speaking Chinese at home and English in school? How does her experience compare with the experience of Soliday's student Alisha? With your own?

2. Did you receive political indoctrination similar to Lu's when you were growing up? How did this affect you?

3. How was Lu taught to write essays in China? Is this similar to the way that students are taught to write essays in the United States?

4. What insights about student voices does Lu's essay offer? What are the implications of this for teaching?

Chapter 11

Listening for Difference

Roni Natov

Roni Natov is Professor of English at Brooklyn College. She has taught classes in the Literature of Cultural Diversity and Cross-Cultural Writing. With Geraldine DeLuca, she cofounded and coedited for 17 years *The Lion and the Unicorn: A Critical Journal of Children's Literature*. She wrote *Leon Garfield* (Twayne, 1994) and is currently writing *The Poetics of Childhood* (Garland Press, to be published 2002).

Every teacher worth her words knows how deeply she has learned from her students: how being open and accessible in that space she and her students occupy—which is neither public nor fully private, but sometimes the best of both, which can feel secularly sacred—cannot help but change her, make her wider. I believe that the goal of education is, in Maxine Hong Kingston's words, "to make my mind large as the universe is large, so that there is room for paradoxes" (35). My classroom is the place where students, in their variety of thoughts, questions, reflections, in their diverse spoken and written languages, present the challenge to make my imagination large enough to create an inclusive environment for them. Here, in this place of intellectual improvisation, I am forced to become porous, to enter a liminal world created in this moment of spontaneous interaction that has never been before and never will occur again. Here, in this place of chaos and uncertainty, I am being taught, actually forced, to listen for difference. Here I am learning to avoid indulging what is at times my own and my students' overwhelming desire to focus on similarity, to identify like experience and feeling, to merge. Here I work not to flee but rather to inhabit those areas of faulty or partial comprehension, where we are left without closure. Nothing in my education, nothing I can remember being taught at home or at school or in this culture at large has prepared me for this work.

I am an English professor at Brooklyn College, an urban liberal arts college whose student population is approximately 40% nonnative speakers and includes a large "nontraditional student body," approximately 80% of whom work 20 to 40 hours per week and often help support other family members, who come from the Caribbean, China, Russia, India, Latin America, or the Middle East. Like many of my colleagues, I know the excitement of diversity. In this context, I am writing to emphasize the extraordinary exhilaration of multiculturalism, rather than the frustration that often results from trying to force students into a shape that is not their own. As a teacher of literature and writing, I am learning to recognize, appreciate, and work with their strengths, and I am inspired to share with other teachers some of what I have discovered and still am discovering along the way.

Like many contemporary writing teachers, I was greatly influenced by recent composition theorists (Peter Elbow, Ann Berthoff, Ira Shor) and creative writing mentors (Natalie Goldberg, Julia Cameron, Deena Metzger, Ira Progoff), to help "empower" students to find their own voices, their own rhythms and to write about what they know intimately, what they most want and need to say. To do this, I had to let go of more traditional expectations—that they would write standard English fluently, that they would read with what I assumed was sophistication, the facility of the traditionally educated upper middle class. They, with their working-class culturally diverse perspectives, came endowed with a variety of gifts—the wisdom of the older students who had lifelong tales to tell, the vitality of the younger students, who were perhaps less introspective but grappling with survival skills that revealed new insights about themselves, about our society.

In my classroom community, I was able to hear stories of the unseen, and in the act of listening to the power of these new voices—all the more powerful for their difference—I was forced into unconventional—at least for me—ways of knowing. Along with my students, I had to see the world differently if I wanted to understand. The challenge for me, then, was to make a foray into the imagination of each teller/writer, to hear empathically, by recognizing what is strange as well as what is familiar, and to build bridges that connect the listener to the teller/writer. I had to construct a passageway for myself and my students into what bell hooks calls "realms of the unknown with no will to colonize or possess [or] to construct the text as territory to be conquered [or] altered" (58). I understand now that in these new voices and narratives lies a hope for change, that as Walter Benjamin claimed, the lessons of the past "spoke directly only through things that had not been handed down . . . which ruled out all claims to a binding authority" (40). I learned histories of my immigrant students whose vision had been denied, had been determined as "other," and like Benjamin's "collector who gathers his fragments and scraps from the debris of the past" (46), I would find what is inherently "openly or covertly useful, that each storyteller is a man [sic] who has counsel for his readers . . ." (87). "Counsel woven into the fabric of real life," Benjamin advised, "is wisdom"

(87). He urged us to look among the ashes of what has been discarded, shunted aside, the voices and the stories of the marginalized, for the jewels, for alternative visions. Again, Maxine Hong Kingston understands that being crazy means telling the same story over and over again, that health implies newness, difference.

Many of my students live in a language not their own, between two cultures, with all the difficulty implied in that struggle. Deleuze and Guattari claimed that coming from the more fragile sectors of society "allows the writer all the more possibility to express another possible community and to forge the means for another consciousness and another sensibility" (78). My job is to help them to turn their nonnative nonmainstream status to their advantage as readers and writers, rather than merely to combat the usual treatment of those marginal to the dominant language/discourse as inferior. And, further, to cultivate an inclusive imagination, to allow the metaphors of their language to contain the contradictions between their old and new cultures, to enter into that newly created place of consciousness.

I am grateful for the opportunity to counter in my small way what I experience as an onslaught of the conservative movement toward homogenization, the "color-blind society" that wishes to ignore the relations of power, a desire at best naive, at worst pernicious, a creeping racism we see in the movement against immigrants and affirmative action. What I am discovering goes beyond my desire to avoid more failure for them, for me; it encompasses the possibility of more possibilities—a multiplicity of styles and structures, a vitality in the learning process itself. And I believe my students become more fluent with standard English in the discovery of their own voices, in telling their own stories. Now it seems obvious that this is so, a kind of inevitability that makes me wonder why everyone isn't writing about this.

"All writing," Zoe Wicomb says, "whether it deals directly with the revolution or not, occupies a political position" (13). All learning involves sifting out what is valuable from that which is objectionable, destructive to ourselves and to our social world. In this process we become, in her words, "resistant" readers. bell hooks notes that through the vicarious experience of reading, her mind "became a place of refuge, a sanctuary, a room I could enter with no fear of invasion . . . a site of resistance. . . . To imagine, then, was a way to begin the process of transforming reality. All that we cannot imagine will never come into being" (54–55).

There are three stories I want to tell. Embedded in each is a kernal of wisdom, a root for growth. In my role as teller, I combine what Walter Benjamin saw as the storyteller of tradition, the seafarer who brings back the wisdom of foreign cultures, and the tiller of the soil who stays close to home. In my position as teacher/writer, I remain anchored in my classroom, but like the seafarer, I carry the tales of those who come from afar, metaphorically if not literally, so as "to pry loose the rich and the strange, the pearls and the coral in the depths, and to carry them to the surface" (50–51). Each story involves a class exercise created to encounter difference.

I.

I tell the class that I want them to tell each other a story of some turning point in their lives, a story of great intensity, one that is pressing on them to be told. I ask that each be alternately listener and teller, that as listener they should take notes, ask questions, indicate where they identify and where they feel unclear, unsure, on new ground. As I divide the class in pairs, a particularly disaffected young woman, her eyes remote, emptied out, protests, "I don't want to tell anyone my story." I ask if she is willing to work with me. She says, "Ok, but I don't want to go first." I frantically search my mind for some story appropriate enough to share with my class. I don't want to be utterly confessional; I assume as teacher I might embarrass them, let alone myself. But isn't that what I am asking of them? To run that risk? And anyway, do I really want to avoid exposure at the expense of sharing some unresolved piece of ambiguity I have been chewing on?

I begin to tell my partner about a new child in my life, one who has been abandoned in suicide by her mother, the adopted daughter of my very close friend, who lives on the other side of the country, of her complicated push-pull way of relating to me, of her desire to call me "mommy," of my own equally compelling urge for and fear of this happening. I came into her life, I continue my story, when I met her father, when she was seven and she and I stood on the sand, holding hands. She whispered to me, gazing at the waves in fear and trembling, "Don't you think we should face our fears?" I said, "Yes, dig your feet in and then see how the waves can't get you."

I asked my partner, "What do you need to know to understand the importance of this story in my life," to set it in context, as per my assignment. And then I told her about my mother who alternately showered me with affection and abused me, and how, by loving this little girl, in all her moods—when she was taunting, funny, touching, cruel—by accepting what my mother couldn't, I was healing.

Then my partner told me, her face intensely lit with memory, the story she had not wanted to tell anyone, of her own mother who had died, drug-addicted and beaten to a pulp by her boyfriend. The force of one tale led into another and another. Suddenly she turned to me—both of us completely in the presence of her mother who had narrowly escaped death at the hands of this man, who had been imprisoned for the murder of another lover, only to die after taking him in again, despite the pleas of her daughter, whose public shame and private grief now filled her eyes as the tears streamed down her face—"What in the world made her take him back," she asked. "What could make someone do that?" I thought of providing an answer from my own experience, but instead I asked, "What in her life, do you think, prepared her for that treatment?" Considering my question seemed to propel her into telling me about her grandfather and his history of violence, of her own bravery in confronting him. We laughed at the incongruous image of this 12-year-old girl warding off a large drunken man with a chair, when he came at her one afternoon with a knife.

We went on that day to answer together the questions I had posed to the class: Which was easier, listening for the similarities or the differences? The telling or the listening? In each case, what did you discover?

Even now as I write, the intensity of that class still reverberates in my body; the air is still alive with the laughter of recognition.

"You too!"

"I couldn't have done that!"

"What did you do?"

And in the following class, we listened together for affinity and distinction, as each pair told the story of their story, the narrative created in the telling of and listening to the two original stories, now linked, in some cases literally, in some metaphorically, in theme, or rhythm, or tone. I remember some of my favorite moments of insight.

"Talking about this, I came out of a dark dream," a middle-aged African-American woman student says, after sharing her tale of having been unjustly dismissed from her poorly paid job. Bouyant and redeemed, she adds, "and when I get into a dark place again, I will remember this class."

"It'll be like a touchstone," her partner agrees. This is pretty powerful testimony.

But I think the most profound discoveries grew out of the discussions of difference. One pair, a middle-aged white woman and a young black man, recounted two entirely opposing experiences. She admitted that her 15-minute narrative, the trauma of being abused by her first husband, left her feeling raw and exposed. "In exchange for this," she complained, "he gave me two paragraphs. All the time, I was looking in his eyes for some connection, but found only a kind of politeness." He acknowledged that this was essentially true, that he could sympathize with her pain, but couldn't really understand it. In fact, he confessed to being confounded by the husband's abuse, and that as a man, he was utterly preoccupied with trying to justify the husband's brutality.

This was a turning point for the class. Both students received empathic responses from other students. Sometimes the affirmation clustered around gender lines, sometimes around age—but we all became aware of and more comfortable with difference. We noted how the plots were disparate, but the themes and underlying emotions were often similar. What seemed to connect all the stories and paradoxically to distinguish each from the others was the various ways one learns to turn the dark into a source of light. As Denise Levertov wrote:

> But what if,
> like a camel, it's
>
> pure energy I store,
> and carry humped and heavy?
>
> . . . not
> that terror, stupidity
>
> of cold rage; or black
> only for being pent there?
>
> What if released in air
> it became a white
>
> source of light, a fountain
> of light? Could all that weight
>
> be the power of light?

II.

I am taking my class to a poetry reading and wind up walking with K., one of my weakest writers. She is a lovely woman, a Haitian immigrant, quiet and gentle. She rarely speaks in class.

"How are you doing with your writing?" I ask, grabbing the opportunity for a casual encounter.

"I hate writing," she sighs, resigned.

"Is there anything you would like to write about?" I ask.

"Nah," she says. "I guess I just don't like it."

"All right," I concede, "but how about writing about what you don't like about writing," and she half-heartedly agrees.

The reading was a success. The students seemed engaged and wrote the reviews I assigned, with spirit. I was stunned when I read K.'s—in fact, I cried, and so did one of my student interns, when I read it to her. I told all this to K., who smiled her wide smile. I said it read like a poem, and she said, "It doesn't look like a poem." She and I agreed to type it together on the computer in my office. We worked on the shape, phrase by phrase, line by line, until she felt it looked "like a poem." I'd say, where do you want this phrase, where would you like that line to end, do you want a capital here, what about punctuation—and in the process, I think she discovered one way a poem might be. In the most poetic section, at the center of the piece, constrained by standard English, she burst into the French dialect of her childhood, which contained, much like the epiphanic vision of the lyric poem, the root of her experience. Side by side she joined each word in French with its English equivalent, the way she feels the language now, a kind of parallel or double discourse, to reflect living in two languages, much the way we often live on two planes—balancing the contemporary chronology of conscious experience with metaphoric moments in which the unconscious surfaces in memory and dream. Capturing that, in whatever shape or form, is, to my mind, an extraordinary achievement.

With little encouragement, for the first time K. agreed to read her writing to the class, and they loved it. I knew this, not only from their faces, but from the silence that hung in the air once she stopped reading.

Here, then, is her review, written from her depths, and in so doing, she echoes the power of the original poetry. The insertion of her own voice, the boldness of her language, claims the right of the reviewer to subjectivity, the only really honest stance. K. wrote about what she heard. Isn't that, essentially, what any critic does? In fact, her own piece strongly suggests rather than skews the poem's "meaning."

"Broken Girl," My Childhood:
A Review of Joan Larkin's Poetry Reading

As I was listening to Joan Larkin's voice, I was taken to another part of the world. In her poem entitled "Broken Girl," I found myself in Haiti, abandoned by the one who was supposed to be my nurturer and caretaker. I was taken to my entire early childhood life where I did not have anyone to love me for who I was, to hug me, or to assure me that I was a living creature.

> Life was hopeless without someone to rely on
>   someone to share a stomach ache
>   someone to lean on
>   someone to say good morning
>   someone to say I had a nightmare
>   someone to say I need help with my homework
>   someone to say I saw blood.
> My life as a broken girl was like endlessly walking in a desert.
>   It was hell on earth.
>   It was cancer in a living body with no hope of surviving.

The part with the "abandoned building," and the long sound "Waaa," which went on, "if you find it hard to believe, just look at me"—that part reminded me of my doleful, miserable, and lonely childhood.

	The name calling,
	the ugliest one,
Dada tout bet	the defecate of all animals
Chimene	the name of an old maid
	the ugly little midget
Chabon	dark as charcoal
Gate ras	the ugliest of the family.

"If you find it hard to believe, just look at me."

The low and high pitch of her soft voice took me back to an unconscious world. The voice of my teacher woke me up in a poem entitled "My Body." I don't know what it was that kept my teacher laughing, but all I could remember were the painful parts.

As I was leaving the room, even though it was painful for me, I still wanted to hear the magical sound of her soft voice that had put me to sleep. It was my first time at a poetry reading. I felt like a baby listening to a story on a mother's lap. Even though I never experienced it with my mother or anyone else, I surely wouldn't let my lovely boys, Weber and David, grow up without that kind of experience.

III.

We had read Tony Hillerman's *The Dark Wind*, a mystery novel that proved particularly interesting for investigating, from the perspective of the outsider, the signs and symbols of another culture. Hillerman, who is white, writing about Hopi and Navajo cultures, sets up frames within frames, a series of perspectives from which to uncover the mystery of a particularly brutal murder. Both Navajo and Hopi detectives, police, citizens from inside and outside the reservation, those who adhere to and those who resist tribal custom and law, along with the reader (in this case a class of outsiders utterly unfamiliar with Hopi and Navajo ways), track down the meaning of the victim's slashed palms and soles. What is at stake here is an outsider's understanding of the two cultures—which turns on the meaning of the title. "The dark wind" as a metaphor contains both the destructive and the liberating power of a kind of chaos, a madness. I had asked my students, "make a list of all objects, feelings, events that the dark wind suggests to you," and offered by way of example "the cry of a baby," to suggest concrete detail rather than abstraction. I had collected their lists and promptly forgot about them in the chaos of the last few weeks of the term.

The night before the last class I sat worrying over what to contribute to the reading we had planned—each of us was to read a favorite piece from the term's work. In a flash, I thought of using their lines, of creating a class poem, and offering it to them as a kind of tribute, a celebration of the power of their collective and individual voices. Without adding any of my own words, merely by charging through their lines randomly, even haphazardly, within an hour I had a poem. I selected and arranged their images, but it is the pace I want to emphasize, the randomness, the potential power of "found poetry" taken from a myriad of voices. As I raced along, immersed in the richness of their images, impressions, bits and pieces of memory—endless possibilities suggested themselves: this poem could have been written any number of ways and stood as a testament to the vitality of multiplicity.

Each student has read her piece to this most appreciative audience and now it is my turn. I read—their words, their lines—slowly, so that I can see their reactions as each hears his words woven into the whole. Some get it right away; for some the recognition comes more slowly. All are smiling, laughing, clapping at the end. As I hand out copies, one student says, "I'm framing mine." And from another, "I think you should send this to Hillerman." Months later, I meet this same student at a party, and he says: "Well, did you send our poem to Hillerman yet?"

"The Dark Wind"
Bad breath every morning
sex when you're really not in the mood
losing a contact
taking an exam and not knowing what the hell's on it
a bad hair day
a summer thunder storm
having to say "I love you" when you know you don't mean it
just being in the dark
just not knowing what is going on
utter confusion
feeling as though no one wants you
violence

The dark wind is the force that controls your body
when the dark wind enters you without warning
it allows you to express what you can't explain
the birthplace of sin and temptation
what cannot be charted.

The dark wind travels across the surface of the earth
roams in our souls
wanders aimlessly through infinite realms of the impossible
what makes us cross that infinite line
the unnoticed guides of our minds
the suffocated spirit
it lingers everywhere but nowhere
no earthly match

It is a whirlwind of anguish, despair, disappointment
the twisted plot of our lives
the side of us that only we know about
the uncontrollable rage of no recourse
the throwing of a rock
the flash of a gun
the plunging of the blade
the liquid in the bottle
the powder in your nose
the needle in your arm

The dark wind is seen through violent acts of murder and rape.
But it also comes in less noticeable forms:
yelling, cursing, racism, child abuse, theft.

A child cries in the night
an old man falls prey to assailants
but then chooses to fight back
This is the dark wind
a black spot in white hearts
a white spot in black hearts.

The dark wind is an enigma
left to be untangled, uncovered,
uncontrollable, what controls us
ready to make you move, to take over,
to prey upon the wounded in heart and mind
what you secretly wish but would never do
what you never thought you could do.

The dark wind is death
the silent cry of a baby
Jealousy
Satan.

The dark wind is lukewarm, moist,
the perfect breeding ground for infectious diseases of the mind.

The dark wind is
  mysterious
  consuming
  magnetic
as insightful as a leader
as life giving as a storm.

The dark wind is sneaky,
an alarm that goes off in our minds.

The dark wind is lightning
an empty room
a cold night
homelessness/earthquakes/floods
liars and hypocrites
death not really knowing
where it leads
running after the wind.

REFERENCES

Benjamin, Walter. *Illuminations.* Ed. Hannah Arendt. Trans. Harry Zohn. New York: Schocken, 1968.

Berthoff, Ann. *The Making of Meaning: Metaphors, Models, and Maxims for Writing Teachers.* Montclair, NJ: Boyton/Cook, 1981.

Cameron, Julia. *The Artist's Way.* New York: Jeremy P. Tarcher/Putnam, 1992.

Deleuze, Gilles, and Felix Guattari. Quoted in *Critical Fictions: The Politics of Imaginative Writing.* Ed. Philomena Mariani. Seattle: Bay Press, 1991.

Elbow, Peter. *Writing Without Teachers.* New York: Oxford University Press, 1973.

———. *Embracing Contraries.* New York: Oxford University Press, 1986.

———, and Pat Belanoff. *A Community of Writers.* New York: Random House, 1989.

Goldberg, Natalie. *Wild Mind.* New York: Bantam, 1990.

———. *Writing Down the Bones.* Boston: Shambhala, 1986.

Hillerman, Tony. *The Dark Wind.* New York: HarperCollins, 1982.

Hooks, Bell. In *Critical Fictions: The Politics of Imaginative Writing.* Ed. Philomena Mariani. Seattle: Bay Press, 1991.

Kingston, Maxine Hong. *The Woman Warrior: Memoirs of a Girlhood Among Ghosts.* New York: Vintage, 1976.

Metzger, Deena. *Writing for Your Life.* San Francisco: HarperCollins, 1992.

Progoff, Ira. *At a Journal Workshop.* Los Angeles: Jeremy P. Tarcher, 1975, 1992.

Rose, Mike. *Lives on the Boundary: The Struggles and Achievements of America's Underprepared.* New York: The Free Press, 1989.

Shor, Ira. *Empowering Education: Critical Teaching for Social Change.* Chicago: University of Chicago Press, 1992.

Wicomb, Zoe. In *Critical Fictions: The Politics of Imaginative Writing.* Ed. Philomena Mariani. Seattle: Bay Press, 1991.

QUESTIONS FOR REFLECTION,
JOURNAL WRITING, AND DISCUSSION

1. Natov feels that teachers must be "open and accessible" to their students. Do you agree?

2. Natov says that the space students occupy "is neither public nor private, but sometimes the best of both." Do you agree?

3. What did you think of Natov's writing assignment to "write about a turning point in your life"? Would you ask your students to do this assignment?

4. Compare Natov's and Soliday's ways of dealing with difference in the classroom.

Chapter 12

ESL Tutors: Islands of Calm in the Multicultural Storm

Mark-Ameen Johnson

Mark-Ameen Johnson has directed Brooklyn College's Starr ESL Learning Center and taught CUNY students since 1994. He has also served as the Pace University Liberty and Stay-in-School Partnerships Program Manager, a Brooklyn Public Library literacy consultant and tutor trainer, and a New York City Board of Education teacher. He first began teaching when he was in grammar school; his younger sister was his first student. While enrolled in junior high school, he carried out volunteer work with mentally retarded children. These first experiences hooked him, and he has been teaching in one form or another ever since. He is also a freelance writer specializing in travel and popular culture.

FIVE LIVES, ONE DILEMMA

"Are you intelligent?" wrote the professor. Large red squiggles and even larger exclamation points decorated his endnote. "Not only have you failed to follow my directions, but you continue to write any way you wish even though I have taken the time to explain grammar to you. You are in college now. Prove it."

Forcing herself not to cry, Fatimeh, normally a font of energy and optimism, handed the paper to me sheepishly and said she had been trying her best to produce the kind of writing her professor demanded. In fact, she had been spending so much time on his work that she was beginning to neglect her other courses. "I am not an idiot," she told me, "and I know this work. Don't these professors realize that English is not my first language?"

I thought back to my own college days in the mid-80s. One particularly difficult professor did not like the way I answered a question on his midterm. Although I usually kept course work for future reference, I had burned that professor's materials in adolescent glee. I do remember that he compared me to "an ESL person" who did not know what he was talking about and had to learn to write more clearly. I also remember wanting to tell him that I was not an idiot and that, as a teenager who had gone to New York City public schools and been promoted each year for good behavior, I was in college to learn as much as I could. I may not have known the difference between *who* and *whom* or had my professor's life experience, but I was not an idiot.

When I told Fatimeh that I understood how she felt and offered to help, I was not trying to console her for consolation's sake. I understood because I had lived it. I told her about my difficult professor without taking cheap shots or passing judgment. Her eyes widened. "You?!" She exclaimed. "But you're American." I explained that my nationality had little to do with my professor's prejudice. He assumed I was a know-nothing teenager who differed little from his know-nothing foreigners. Almost 15 years later in the same school, Fatimeh's professor was making the same assumptions.

Our experiences are not unique; neither is my offer. I encourage my students to call me at home or stop by my office whenever they arrive at an academic impasse because I had professors who made the same offer when I was an undergraduate. Their intervention helped me maintain my drive when I was attacked by humanities professors who had lost their humanity. My freshman composition professor, a friend of the man who compared me to an ESL student, told me that I should drop out of school because I did not know how to write. Another English professor hated having to teach us and let us know. I remember a lesson he gave about naked farmhands and have yet to figure out their role in *The Canterbury Tales.* I was so turned off by these teachers that I took as few English courses as possible to earn a degree in English. In contrast, I enthusiastically took as many undergraduate history courses as I could to fulfill my major in that field, then earned a master's in history. I did have some excellent English professors, however, and one of them was Roni Natov, who contributed an article to this anthology. But she and a handful of others were too late to bring me back into the fold. It was really my history professors who inspired me to stay in school by teaching me to think, analyze, research, and, fortunately, write.

Today I earn my living by writing nonacademic articles on commission, teaching ESL and Adult Education, and directing Brooklyn College's Starr ESL Learning Center. I joined my alma mater's English/ESL faculty five years ago after budget cuts in Pace University's Funded Outreach Programs necessitated my sending out CVs. Ironically, I am in the same department as the woman who told me to drop out of school. Despite my initial reluctance—I see myself as an insecure 33-year-old history person in hostile English territory among older peers—I have agreed to write a candid essay about how Starr tutors use firsthand experience with professors they love or loathe to help ESL students build self-confidence. I look forward to introducing you to some of the terrific students I work with. You have already met Fatimeh; I will tell you more about her (and my tutors) later. First, I would like you to meet three more Brooklyn College students.

Two years ago Viktoriya was beside herself with rage. "I taught math in Ukraine, where we were strict," she said. "But I never did to my students what American teachers do to me." After leaving ESL a semester ago, she enrolled in a required "landmarks of literature" course and opted to write a paper that explained the symbolism in selected cantos from *The Inferno.* Her professor gave the paper an F, claiming that Viktoriya could not have written it with her "miserable English."

A divorced, thirtysomething mother with an advanced degree from the former Soviet Union, Viktoriya had always had an avid interest in literature, and she had read the entire *Divine Comedy* in Russian more than once. After plodding through the English translation, she had written a long, traditional Russian analysis in her native tongue, translated it into English herself, and gone to her tutor for grammatical corrections. When the professor questioned her inspiration, she explained that she had rearranged her living room, set up as many of Dante's circles as she could, and put pictures of family, neighbors, and celebrities in the various rings. She had even put her cat in the gluttons' circle.

The professor asked Viktoriya to produce the original Russian and corrected English versions, which I had seen, as proof of her work. Although she had thrown them away, she had the wherewithal to say that they were on her desk at home; she promised to give them to him the next time the class met. That evening she rewrote the Russian version, retranslated it into the wee hours, then dragged herself in to work with a tutor and correct the paper again. After so much effort carried out twice, the professor gave Viktoriya's essay a C, calling it "dubious."

Viktoriya had never had the opportunity to delve as deeply into literature as she would have liked when she was living in Ukraine, for math and pedagogy had taken up all her time. She had been thinking about taking literature classes in the United States, but, after her run-in with her professor, she decided to stick to computer science classes.

Although equally uncomfortable with unpredictable American teachers, baby-faced Christopher stood out from other students the day we met. He wanted attention, but he knew how to get it without being raucous and disrespectful. Even though he had attended one of the best Catholic high schools in Brooklyn for four years, Christopher failed both the reading and writing assessment tests at Brooklyn College and was placed in remedial classes for native and near-native English speakers. After an intensive five-week "prefreshman" summer immersion course in reading and writing, he passed the writing test with ease, but failed the reading test miserably. He then took three reading classes for native speakers, but failed the reading test each semester. In the meantime, he was earning high grades in chemistry, physics, and calculus, which he needed for a major in engineering, and his position as an officer in the Greek club required him to do a lot of reading. He was aware that he would have to transfer to another college because Brooklyn did not offer his major. Unfortunately, no CUNY school would accept him until he passed reading.

Remembering me from the prefreshman program two years earlier, Christopher asked if he could participate in my three-week summer reading immersion class. I assumed that proper ESL instruction was all he needed to pass the reading test. Unfortunately, despite his renewed confidence and model class behavior, Christopher failed just as miserably as before.

Unlike Christopher, who usually had high grades in everything except reading, Ne had a history of failure. His family had left the mayhem of Myanmar (the former Burma) and settled into an economically depressed Brooklyn neighborhood where he and his older brothers were bullied because of their "funny accents." He had lived in the United States for seven years, attended an American high school for four, and taught himself not to mumble the way he did when he first started learning English. Although Ne continued to speak Burmese or Chinese at home and in social situations, he was so fluent in English that he used sophisticated wordplay to make both his tutor and me laugh. A passionate video game player, he hoped to major in computer science and learn computer animation.

Unfortunately, Ne was in danger of being dismissed from the college. Three semesters of intermediate writing had not helped him make any progress. At the beginning of the spring 1997 semester, he was resigned to taking the course a fourth time. Having had a bad experience with a tutor the previous semester, he signed up for voluntary lab work again but remained pessimistic.

I have heard colleagues call such students unteachable even though the evidence is to the contrary. Granted, it is impossible to succeed with every student, and it is not the purpose of this essay to attempt to spell out a step-by-step solution that works with everyone. In addition, a tutor is not a substitute for an excellent teacher. The best teachers know how to engage classes, express themselves in terms learners understand, and value students' development and opinions as much as their own. The best tutors recreate this experience with verve and panache. They consider each tutee an individual with a classroom history unlike anyone else's. In this age of overcrowded classes, I believe that tutors are a necessity, not, as some of my colleagues contend, a luxury.

By writing this essay, I hope to make teachers and tutors who work together aware of how self-reliant they can make their ESL students. As a corollary, I hope to make it clear that uncaring, unprofessional tutors—and, sadly, they do exist—hurt tutees more than they realize. Fatimeh,

Viktoriya, Christopher, and Ne succeeded because excellent teachers empowered them for success. Their tutors built on this seed and dealt with the rot caused by bad apples.

GETTING RID OF STUDENTS' EMOTIONAL BAGGAGE BY SIMPLY BEING HUMAN

Regardless of whether or not they come from immigrant families, most tutors are, by nature, interested in those around them. They are quick to pick up on the emotional baggage ESL students carry. Many ESL students are used to poor treatment at the hands of social service agencies and native English speakers, as foreign accents are often associated with stupidity or duplicity. Students like Ne have been beaten so many times that they are naturally suspicious of anyone outside their ethnolinguistic group. They may even begin to wonder if they deserve such beatings. When students like Fatimeh and Viktoriya are insulted too often, they begin to believe what others say about them and to lose their drive to stay in school. They may need to hear someone say, "This paper got an F−, but *you* are not an F−."

Fatimeh clearly thought she was an F−. The professor's remark about her intelligence was unfortunate, for Fatimeh has always struggled with low self-esteem exacerbated by her college experience. I taught her low-intermediate reading class during the fall 1994 semester, a few months after she arrived in the United States. In halting English she explained that she wanted to be a psychologist and help women whose "life not right." She also told me that she spoke Azerbaijani (also called Azeri, a language closely related to Turkish), Russian, and "Jewish" (actually a dialect of Farsi, or Persian, spoken by Jews in the mountains of Azerbaijan). In addition to having acquired fluency in three very different languages at an early age, she had also studied basic German. Although I refused to grade her homework assignments when she plagiarized extensively, it was clear when Fatimeh pulled out her huge dictionary and interpreted an Ethiopian folktale as an allegory—and, of her own volition, drew a diagram with numerous arrows and steps to stand for the English words missing in her vocabulary—that I was dealing with an extremely intelligent young woman. Unfortunately, she believed she was stupid. I encouraged her to go the Women's Center, where she met a number of native English speakers and émigrés from around the world who shared her interest in psychology and women's issues. In addition, the professors she spoke to there believed in and encouraged her. In this way, Fatimeh received the support she needed to face the trials ahead.

By late 1995, a year after she had begun studying at Brooklyn College, Fatimeh was able to write cohesive and logical (if not grammatically correct) essays on her own without a dictionary or so much as a hint of plagiarism. Here is a sample paragraph from a piece I kept on file:

> I think what is important for every person to have a nice family, good health, good frends, and know language the country, in which you live. Some people want more things they don't need. I have a cousin who has a lot of money, car, diamond. She has every that thing. She is not a wise person. I think person like her will never have a success in life. The evil in her heart will disturb her to make a success although she thinks she will.

About the time she wrote this, Fatimeh was immersing herself in the English language and spending as much time as she could with tutors. She was also working on-campus for little pay, but she expressed pride in speaking English on the job. She even enrolled in an introductory psychology course, where she picked up a lot of social science vocabulary. When she received a D, her professor told her to choose another major. Fatimeh's tutors shared stories of college courses in which they had not performed as well as they had expected. Reencouraged and adamant as ever, Fatimeh took the course again with a different professor, received a B+, and signed up for a more advanced psychology course. Her tutors continued to encourage her to ask good questions and not be held back by grammar, which can be corrected during revision. They taught her to express herself in her own terms, not her parents' and not her teachers'. She told them that women's opinions were not highly valued in her culture, but they supported her in everything. When Fatimeh had to write a paper for her required Greek and Roman literature class, she wrote about what she knew: She compared the role of women in *The Iliad* to that of women in modern Azerbaijan, and finally received a high grade.

Today, five years after her Ethiopian allegory, Fatimeh's English is idiomatic. She credits her tutors' faith in her as the beginning of her self-reliance. She remains especially grateful for her heart-to-hearts with a favorite tutor, a former ESL student who graduated with honors and is now in graduate school. A few months ago she dropped by my office and, with a confident smile, gave me a copy of a paper she had written unaided for a required introductory music class. "Tutors are in my head," she said. Contrast the paragraphs that follow with the earlier one:

> My first insightful conscious memory of the musical sound was the lovely and kind song of my mother's lullaby. I remember, when I was a small girl (we lived in Baku, Azerbaijan, by that time), that always she used to sing sweet lullaby with her lovely voice when I must go to bed. That beautiful and warm sound of lullaby surrounded me with deep

and meaningful emotion. My mother's singing helped me to sleep and see nice dreams because my mother was talling me that she hoped I grew up happy, healthy and will go to school. However, she sang in order to put it to my mind so I would sleep quickly and see good dreams.

Since my early childhood, music was in my dreams. It followed and encouraged in all places. It always cheered me when I was sad. One of the enigmas for me when I was a small girl was a creation of music. So, in order to answer my questions, I went to my mother and asked her who creates songs, how they are created, and did she create lullaby for me? She smiled and said she didn't create lullaby, but other people who are famous writers and composers, create songs and music. Writers devise words and composers compose music for their words. By that time their jobs seemed very easy to me, and I immidiately decided to create one song and music just for myself. I asked my mother to give me a new notebook, where I can create my song. After long efforts I realized that I could not do such hard job, and finally, I gave up. Therefore, I thought that composers and writers were very special people, who god sent us in baskets, to make us feel different.

Fatimeh is now one semester away from graduation. She majored in psychology and had the courage to minor in English literature.

PRE- AND POSTWRITING/READING DISCUSSIONS

The tutors in Fatimeh's head remind her to talk about her topic in English and get feedback before she starts writing. Like many ESL students, Fatimeh used to discuss important issues in her many languages with English relegated to mere survival functions at the university level. If students are to succeed in English, it must carry the same intellectual, emotional, and spiritual value as their primary languages. Tutor-initiated small talk leads to pre- and postwriting discussions, which help students connect what they already know to what they thought they did not know and what they are about to learn. It also helps students find alternatives to the grandiose blanket statements they may try to hide behind.

Viktoriya's tutor served as a sounding board for her ideas about Dante before she wrote her paper and went over the grammar with him. Similarly, a prewriting discussion helped her produce an essay about why she considered herself a hero. Raising an adolescent single-handedly in an adopted country while working, going to school, and learning English, she stopped smoking so her daughter, who had just begun toying with cigarettes, would also quit. By writing this essay, she learned something new about their relationship. The tutor, also a former smoker, had not had mother/daughter dynamics, heroism, or cigarettes in mind when he engaged Viktoriya in conversation; he had simply given the conversation free reign to develop naturally. Despite the difficulties she had with her literature teacher, Viktoriya has gained enough self-confidence to ignore her bad grades and praise herself for her more frequent good ones. She even hopes to write about the teacher who thought her "miserable English" inappropriate for Dante.

I believe that giving students freedom to express themselves without fear of undue criticism is a crucial step in creating authentic writing. I grew up with a writing style that contained high drama and self-righteousness from the church in which I was raised, second-guessing and stale moral opinions meant to please teachers, rejection of my true feelings stemming from denial of my sexual orientation, outdated language and pretentiousness stolen from the 18th- and 19th-century authors I relished, grandiosity lifted from the super-hero comic books I devoured, and, of course, the usual adolescent difficulties in writing. I would still be writing in a bizarre manner if my history professors had not intervened. When I write to express what I really believe today, my writing takes on a life of its own. Sometimes the characters in my fiction write themselves. But even today I continue to produce gobbledygook when I write something in which I have no vested interest. It makes sense to me that a bored student who follows an irrelevant assignment will produce Dick and Jane sentences even if he or she has good ideas, as is clear in the following example:

> In my country everything is small but in New York City is big. The big buildings are bigger then they can be. This is good because is what they need. Big building is important in New York City. There is nothing without it.

I think I wrote something like that once. In contrast, ESL students who engage in prewriting discussions and have the freedom to express themselves any way they choose are more likely to produce interesting first drafts. A student who claimed she had "nothing to say" produced the following passage:

> I was six the first time I came from Haiti to visit my aunt in Manhattan, and I was delight both for the tallness of the buildings and for the trip. I had never seen buildings more than six floor tall in my life. When I went to Manhattan I felt like an ant in a kitchen. Because the buildings were very tall I thought they were made by some gods. I could not even look at their peek without hurting my

neck. Twelve years later, I came back to the U.S. and went to Manhattan by myself. This time I didn't enjoy the beauty of Manhattan like I did when I was six years old. The decade that passed between the first time and the second time changed what I felt.

I can think of several directions in which the author can take her essay. Of course, the choice is hers.

Choice is equally important in tutoring reading. At the end of the Fall 1996 semester, one tutor claimed that her greatest ESL victory was "getting students to read more." By using the *New York Times, National Geographic, Encyclopaedia Britannica,* short stories, and poetry, she involved her students in a team effort to select topics of mutual interest: rebellion in the sixties, Kennedy, racism, the New Right and what it means for immigrants, recipes for making chocolate, Seeing Eye dogs, and pampered pooches in dog shows. She employed pre- and postreading discussions to show tutees how much they could bring to and take out of printed materials. Tutees learned to interpret for themselves and form their own opinions by differentiating between details and main ideas, separating facts from personal or cultural opinions, taking intelligent guesses instead of blind ones, and using context, previous experience, and common knowledge to understand what they read even if they did not know every word on the page. Students left her tutorials more enthusiastic about reading in English and were able to apply their nascent skills outside the ESL cocoon.

ONCE TUTORS KNOW THE RULES . . .
THEY SHOULD BREAK THEM!

I always got a kick out of that tutor's frequent explanations of the day's "reading rules." It worked for her. But tutors should not get so caught up in guidelines that they wrap themselves in their own cocoons and fail to see what is going on around them. Sometimes they have to listen to their instincts, forget the rules, and go with what some of my colleagues call "a teachable moment." Once again, it is a matter of treating each tutee as a unique individual.

Christopher, the intelligent young man who failed reading so many times, finally passed the reading test because his tutor bent the rules. After half a semester of tutoring, the future engineer seemed to be improving his reading skills during open-ended discussions; however, he was still performing poorly on multiple-choice tests. When he was not working on them, he talked about how he hoped to acquire the skills to close his eyes and mentally construct a building no one had ever seen, then draw up the plans and build it. During one such discussion the tutor realized what four of my colleagues and I had not: Christopher was not reading in a vacuum, the state of most poor readers. He was constructing a text's meaning *before he read it* or *after just a few sentences,* much as he mentally constructed blueprints for buildings that did not exist. He would then force everything he read into his own interpretation, which was not always what the author intended. And sure enough, there was always a multiple-choice answer close to Christopher's misperception.

To Christopher's chagrin, the tutor immediately eliminated all the creative pre- and postreading questions the two of them loved and forced him to do a line-by-line analysis of every sentence they read. Going through the multiple-choice questions before tackling a text, they discussed the answers they were looking for and where they could be found in the text. Ever the dreamer, Christopher would often fly into text-induced daydreams, and the tutor would have to drag him back regularly. After half a semester of vigorous work, Christopher passed the test with barely a point to spare. I will never forget how loudly he yelled when I told him he had finally passed.

Tutees also need to learn not to be so hung up on the rules that their own stubbornness spells failure. Ne, the young man from Myanmar who took intermediate writing three times, had always been a pleasure to tutor despite his obsession with rules. Although he claimed he was lazy and spent too much time playing video games, he handed in most of his work on time and was always willing to do extra assignments. But despite our best efforts to make Ne write truthfully, his essays usually contained an interesting blend of fact, fiction, science fiction, and a never-ending supply of made-up relatives. Drug addicts? "My nephew . . ." Pizza addicts? "My cousin . . ." Workaholics? "My sister . . ." Successful corporate managers? "My uncle . . ." Religious devotees? "My nephew . . ." ("But, Ne, I thought your nephew was a drug addict." "Oh yeah!") "My mother . . ."

Ne's true voice was lost somewhere in his mechanical topic sentences and predictable body paragraphs. He sometimes went off the topic or spent so much time backing up his first body paragraph that he did not have time to write a second. He was also so worried about being grammatically correct that he sacrificed style for syntax.

At the beginning of the semester Ne and his tutor asked me to supplement the work they did together. I asked Ne to keep a journal for reflection on our discussions or anything he felt like writing about, but he was so busy with school, his job, and video games that he made only one or two short entries a week. The tutor and I praised the few instances where Ne came out of himself and wrote from his heart. He began to take more tentative chances, following each with a quick retreat into formality and blanket statements.

Before spring break I gave Ne a second notebook and told him to make journal entries every day, encouraging him just to write without paying attention to thesis statements and formal style. To my surprise, he returned from the break with a book filled to the last page. (And I, having promised to read it, had to do just that!) The first few pages said little. But as Ne became more comfortable with the book and broke free of formality, his personality began to emerge. I found stories of a little boy running with delight in his first northeastern snowstorm, proud parents who had crossed fields of decapitated bodies to give their sons the opportunity for a better life in America, a family of five pitching in to mend strangers' clothes at home in order to put food on the table, and so much more that was alive, fresh, and emotional.

With only a few weeks left before the writing test, Ne's tutor and I coordinated our efforts with his teacher and struggled to use the journal as a launching point to help him keep himself in his writing. By choosing topics important to him, Ne always had enough points to back up his argument and rarely ran out of things to say. In addition, he no longer relied on his imaginary relatives. To Ne's surprise, but no one else's, he wrote a spectacular exam. His score was not high enough to allow him to leave ESL, but it ensured him a passing grade in intermediate writing and a seat in advanced ESL composition. It took two more semesters for him to leave ESL altogether.

WHAT DO TUTEES REALLY THINK OF THEIR TUTORS?

Ne told me that he wanted to continue working with tutors throughout his college career. Ironically, he had initially resisted his tutor's efforts and felt ashamed of his need for one. Fatimeh and Christopher had originally thought that working with a tutor was tantamount to admitting that they were not smart enough to be in college. Only Viktoriya, who had been a teacher, liked the idea of working with a peer the moment I suggested it. Few tutees recognize from the outset that tutors are successful role models with excellent learning skills and concrete career goals (or, at least, tentative majors) in mind. In addition, many of the tutors I have employed these past seven semesters are former ESL students or English speakers from overseas. As immigrants and international students, they create an atmosphere of camaraderie and empowerment. The Starr ESL Learning Center is more than a successful tutoring program. We are a true community of international learners.

But I do not have the right to rely solely on my opinion of whether or not Starr serves its purpose. I take teacher and tutor feedback very seriously, and always incorporate it into future planning. However, I am primarily concerned with how useful tutees find the learning center. Of the more than 300 ESL students who responded to surveys administered during the lab's second (spring 1996) and fourth (spring 1997) semesters, 71% praised Starr's efforts. The remaining 29% gave the lab a lukewarm or extremely negative appraisal. Students wrote more about why they liked (or disliked) their tutors than about everything else—Starr's computer programs, workshops, handouts, materials, books, convenient hours, and comfortable furniture—combined:

- Caring, pleasant atmosphere with tutors. Thanks!
- Everything is in order and the tutors know what they are doing. The whole place is neat.
- The attitude of the tutors is cheerful. They are always happy to see their students.
- All my needs are being met by the help, orientation, and hard work of the tutors, especially my tutor.
- All the tutors know their subject well and have a lot of patience.
- The tutor was very kind and hard worker. I would like to have her again.
- Tutor has been significant with explaining each method carefully. Also she has shown me more than one way that I could create a sentence that sends message across.
- The tutors are very encouraging. That makes us want to work harder. Thanks to all.
- The tutors did their work very good!!! It very help us. I would like more speak with tutors.
- You guys are doing fine.
- Keep it up.
- It helped me more than regular ESL class.

Students bonded with specific tutors and were quick to praise them by name:

- I'd like to recommend help of Derek to all ESL students.
- For all students in ESL I recommend that you take Rebecca.
- Great working with you, Rebecca.
- I appreciate what my tutor, Catherine, has done for me in order to improve my English. I think she is very responsible and capable.
- I like attitude of Mark's and any other's.
- Diana is very good tutor.
- Julie is the best tutor.

Almost all of the negative responses focused on relationships with tutors. One student complained that his or her tutor "should not be in teaching major. She should be in wrestling." Another—the student who praised

Catherine—claimed to have been "scared away" by the first tutor he or she worked with in the lab. I assume that the remark refers to one of the problem tutors I dismissed during the lab's first year. One, a former ESL student who had lived in the United States for many years and spoke fluent English, thought he was superior to recent immigrants. Although he did not say this, it was clear to his tutees. In addition, his frequent absences and lack of patience exacerbated students' frustrations. A second tutor was moody and played favorites with his tutees. Although his students of choice enjoyed the time he spent with them, others felt he had "a college job that lets him waste time with friends to make money."

Clearly, whether encouraging students to work harder or scaring them away, it is the individual tutor, not state-of-the-art computers or a particular philosophical/pedagogical stance, that makes a learning center wilt or bloom. As one ESL student wrote: "Computers are terrible teachers because they don't answer questions and tutors are much better because they understand you." Without personalized help in a safe atmosphere and swift (but true) success in language acquisition, students may fail to realize their potential and drop out of school. Peer tutors in student-friendly support services provide sympathetic ears and warm smiles—as well as the rules for recognizing indirect object pronouns. They put a human face on an often draining and dehumanizing system and empower students by teaching them to teach themselves while bolstering their confidence in their ability to use English effectively.

QUESTIONS FOR REFLECTION, JOURNAL WRITING, AND DISCUSSION

1. Johnson says that the English department can be perceived as "hostile territory." Why is this so? How did you perceive it? How do your students perceive it?

2. Have you ever tutored or worked with a tutor? How was the experience? How was it different from working with a teacher?

3. Have you worked with ESL students? Were you able to help them? If so, how?

4. Why did Fatimeh's and Viktoriya's teachers respond to them in such a negative way? Can you remember an example of a teacher responding to a student in such a negative way?

5. Compare Johnson's and Natov's ways of dealing with students.

Chapter 13

Writing Alive

Ellie Friedland

Ellie Friedland is an Assistant Professor of Early Childhood Education at Wheelock College in Boston. Her AIDS-focused poetry has been published in *Haiku International, Five Lines Down, Tanka Splendor,* and in *Wind Five Folded,* an anthology of English-Language Tanka. In 2000 she coproduced the original AIDS play "Trust," which she cowrote with members of her HIV/AIDS writing workshop.

"I got released from the hospital and came straight here for class." Mark Riordan was saying this as we met outside the doors of the Boston Living Center, where I hold a weekly writing workshop for people with HIV and AIDS. His head was wrapped in a kerchief, and under it he was clearly bald, which was new. He looked thinner, and more tired, than he had two weeks ago when I last saw him. He had been in the hospital having a "port" put into his head for chemotherapy and had begun the chemo. Now he was standing here with me, waiting for writing class.

Why did Mark Riordan come to class directly from the hospital instead of going home to rest? Why, when he feels sick or when he's taking care of his even sicker partner, does Mark Balicki choose his support group and writing class as the only two things he leaves the house to do? Why does John Davis take the train to Boston for writing class from Providence, Rhode Island, every week? Why does Jim Souci come to class when his meds are making him nauseous and weak? Why does Charlotte Johnson come to my workshop *and* the Living Center's poetry/drawing class every week, even when she has to juggle doctor's appointments, caring for her kids, and earning a living; and why do I drive an hour into Boston in the middle of the workweek to meet with these people, never sure how many will be there, when I don't even get money to cover parking?

When I tell people, especially colleagues in academia, that I lead a writing group for people with HIV and AIDS, they express admiration. They seem impressed that I'm doing "service" and that I'm willing to work with such a difficult, depressing topic. My guess is that they are responding from two assumptions: one, they assume AIDS is not in my life in other ways; and two, they assume that working closely with people with AIDS is depressing and difficult. But I'm not that altruistic. So why do I do it? And why do Mark, Mark, John, Charlotte, Fabien, Jim, and others go through so much to make it to writing group?

I do it, in part, because AIDS is very much in my life, but in both my professional community and my home community no one knows much about living (or dying) with AIDS or wants to know. My colleagues may express admiration, but most ask no questions and change the subject quickly. I need to be with people who share my concerns, preoccupations, questions, emotions, and experiences. I should be clear right now that I'm not HIV positive—it's important that you know my perspective as you read this article. I'm an HIV negative, straight (white) woman who has been intimately involved with HIV and AIDS since the 1980s. The AIDS community has been my community for many years, because I've had, and have, many friends with HIV and AIDS. I used to lead the AIDS Mastery workshop, a Northern Lights Alternatives workshop focused on living fully and creatively with HIV/AIDS. My best friend, Peter Leslie, was HIV positive for 10 years, and I was his primary caregiver when he got sick and through his dying, in June 1995.

All through Peter's illness and death, and after, writing was a great support for me. Peter was also a writer, and as long as he was able to, he wrote his experience of HIV and AIDS, and I wrote mine. It was often the way we expressed truths we couldn't quite bring ourselves to say in conversation, like my poem:

> you will die soon
> how dare you
> dare you
> love me

and his poem:

> Routine
>
> This is what my life has become:
> monitoring the deceits
> of my body
> daily
> burying the lucky
> dead . . .
> and no way
> out

Writing, and sharing our writing, was often the best way for Peter and me to identify and express the real truth of a moment, to get out what wanted to be known and said, even if we judged it as unacceptable or the "wrong" way to feel. We learned early in the process of living with HIV that it was better, for us, to identify, experience, and express our feelings, whether they were "good" or "bad." May Sarton wrote, in *Mrs. Stevens Hears the Mermaids Singing,* "We learn about ourselves from the unacceptable, from the violent, from the mad one who weeps and roars in the subterranean caves: let this one out into the air and he brings the light with him, the light that has to be earned, the light of compassion for *oneself,* the strange mercy that follows any commitment of such depth when it is played out and so has to be faced" (170).

Peter and I repeatedly saw the truth of this as we lived with his illness and dying. It was freeing to allow expression of what was real and true, even though we often judged it as ugly or unenlightened or unacceptable. It's certainly not always appropriate or kind to share all that's going on inside us with others, and I'm not advocating that at all. But it's important to give ourselves permission to know and express what is true for us. Then we can choose what to express to whom. I've found over the years that if I'm suppressing the "unacceptable" bits of what I think and feel, I can't help but suppress other things as well. If I suppress my rage, for example, I tend to also suppress my energy, my openness, and my love, and my creativity. I've also found that I'm often unaware of how generalized suppression has been until I look back from some future time, and then I'm left with lots of regret.

I don't want to suppress my creativity, and I don't want to live a life of regret, so I try to get to the real expression that may feel dangerous or "wrong." This means always looking deeper, always looking to see if there's something more, some truth I haven't yet identified or admitted. One of the reasons I write is that I frequently have the experience of looking at a piece I've just written and saying, "So *that's* what I think about that, *that's* what I feel." I find this experience exhilarating, and it has deepened both my relationships and my writing. It has also turned out, and this surprised me at first, that it is this writing that readers respond to most positively and powerfully. People recognize and value authentic expression. They relate to it, and value it. It really does seem that the more deeply real and personal expression is, the more universal it is.

I need contact with and input from other people to sustain this level of exploration and expression, so once Peter was gone I needed to find new avenues of support. I needed the support of people who understood not only my desire for expression but also the experience of AIDS. I had already dropped out of a support group for friends and family of people with AIDS and tried an AIDS bereavement group. Neither of these professionally led groups gave me what I was looking for. There are many reasons these groups didn't work for me, but the main reason was they didn't go deep enough, didn't get real enough for me. There was a lot of focus on feeling OK, and often not a lot of room for "negative" feelings like rage, hopelessness, even grief.

I finally figured out that support groups didn't give me the expressive permission and support I needed and writing did. But it's hard to sustain the discipline and openness it takes, especially in a time of crisis and loss. So I looked for a writing group to join. I attended a couple of groups and found that people didn't relate to what I wrote about AIDS and were often uncomfortable with the issues and feelings I was writing about. Once again, they didn't really want to hear it.

I decided to look for an HIV-focused writing group and contacted all the local AIDS organizations. I found that no one had such a group, but the Boston Living Center had a program of arts classes, and they wanted to start a writing group. They didn't have anyone to lead such a group, but they had invited Irene Borger, who founded the Writers Workshop at AIDS Project Los Angeles, to come lead a one-day workshop for people who were interested in leading writing workshops for people with HIV/AIDS. I signed up immediately and soon spent a day with Irene. She showed us how she structures her writing workshops, and we did several writing exercises. I found here the support, safety, and permission to express myself that I was longing for. With my background as a psychotherapist and group leader, I knew I could effectively create and lead such a workshop. I told the people at the Boston Living Center I'd lead a writing group for them, and so it began.

I led the writing workshop at the Living Center for three years, and for the past two years the group has been independent, meeting at members' homes. I continue the group because it makes me feel excited, creative, fulfilled, and *light*. And I know this happens for the people who come to the writing group. They come because they know they have something vital to express, though they may not yet know what that is. They come to write and to be with other writers who will understand and accept what they say. They come because they have passion. Anatole Broyard, in *Intoxicated by My Illness*, said that he wanted to be alive when he died. We all, in our HIV/ADS writing group, come together to write because we are alive. We come together to find and express the truth of being alive. We write because it's important that what we have to say be heard. We write HIV and AIDS, we write rage, grief, silliness, love, hope and hopelessness, laughs, life, all of it—and we revel in it all. In one two-and-a-half-hour session it's not unusual for us to write, cry, critique line breaks or structure, and laugh hysterically. There's room for everything. For example, here are three poems written in the group:

Bohemian Anything

That saxophone
Drawing any imaginary body
Curvaceous yet solid in a black outline

The guitar colors a shade for inside
Like the concentration of a five-year-old
Trying to stay within the lines

And the bass
Poking around for life
Creating it to flourish in tempo
All its own

Percussion becomes fluid
And seizes your spine in wavy fashion
And moves you about
Your neck sways to something invisible

Silver violins weave a fine web
Of splendor to the ear
That sets your mind to travel
To swim, to run, to leap with the voice
Of symphony

As they cajole and caress
Your senses
Your heart is changed

Charlotte Johnson (previously published in *Wild Onions,* Vol. XI: 1997)

And by Mark K. Riordan:

Enough Is Enough

Preacher fell down from his pulpit today,
his sons and daughters hooked on crack,
cocaine.

Crack
hear the cries for crack
from mouths of addicted punks
in beat-up Cadillacs,
from suburbs for a fix.

Crack, crack
Hear the cries of crack

from the mouths of babes
in automated, sanitary, plastic bubble trays
cradled by latex hands of nurses,
while the unprotected babies cry
hearing the pumping sounds of semi-automatic bullets fly.

Mine eyes have seen the glory
coming
of a radical retaliation
from innocent five-year-old girls
shot down
after finger-painting spring;
eternal flames of our future countries
abstract terrains
of misguided ignorant bliss.

God Bless
America
My country 'tis of thee,
where I had a dream
the churches would crumble in the heat
before they got to see
a really forgiving
baby Jesus
shot dead in the street.

Enough is enough of homophobic rage
from glassy eyes I do not know,
hooded, soulless creatures
from the inner-city tarmac pits;
arms full of needle marks
guns from baggy trouser hips,
hung like charms.
I look around corners
for sound I cannot see.
Boom-Box deafness
proclaiming
toilet wall mentality.

They call me faggot
and spit
and spit
Hear the sound of spit
upon the gummy pavement shit
and spit and call me names

on these wretched sidewalks
of crack cocaine.

God for their spit to be like rain
and wash these streets clean
of this urban shame
GOD!
DAMMIT!

God save this wretched queen
had he a knife he would kill them
and quarter their filthy bodies clean
Enough is enough!

God save this gracious queen
Who'll reach the safety of his own front door
Behind which surely there
his grapes of wrath are stored.

And, in contrast, this senryu by Fabien Denry:

cold night

I pee

Icicle

I think there are several factors that make this range of experience and expression possible. It's vital to be clear about the nature and purpose of the writing group, in the beginning and throughout the life of the group. I have a strong bias in favor of creative work that expresses personal truth. I always want to work to find and express my unique voice, the real one that may be hiding under more careful or appropriate or pretty voices, and I want to create an environment in which others can find and express their unique voices. I also want to focus on creative expression and craft, not just expression for the sake of expression. When I was checking out writing groups, I attended one in which people met in "writing marathons" (a term and structure they got from Natalie Goldberg's books) in which they wrote and read the writing to each other. The agreed-upon rule was that there be no feedback about what was read. This really seemed to satisfy the people in this group, but I couldn't stand it. In my group I want to create a safe environment in which people feel encouraged to write what's true for them and to risk going for their real thoughts and feelings, but to also work on how they express it, how it can best communicate to an audience, and how it can be their strongest writing. My group is defined as a writing workshop, not a support group, and that means an ongoing focus on craft and technique, as well as on feelings and expression.

This is particularly challenging in a group specifically for people with HIV and AIDS. They are dealing with ongoing difficulties in their lives that most people don't understand. In their writing group they are coming together with others who are also grappling with medications, doctors, health and/or disability issues, illnesses, concerns about whether to work or not, etc. They need to talk. But they also want and need to write. It's my job to facilitate the group, so I work to find the right balance of talk and writing, often having to cut off conversation or focus it toward writing. I've found that it helps a lot if people do have time to chat at the beginning of group. They aren't ready to just sit down and start writing when they come in. Often important issues that are up for many people come out during this conversation, and I frequently use what we talk about as a focus for writing.

This brings up an important point about leading a writing group for people with HIV and AIDS. If you are going to do this, you have to *really* know about HIV and AIDS. Members of our writing group have expressed this strongly, and it's clear to me as well. People must not be in the position of having to explain everything they say or write because the leader doesn't understand. They face that constantly in their lives, as I have, and it's frustrating and infuriating. The experience of living with HIV/AIDS is too often misunderstood, made light of, or avoided. In a writing group people must feel seen and respected. They have to feel safe and included. This is part of the power of having a writing group specifically for people with HIV and AIDS, and the sense of knowing and understanding has to include the leader.

In order for people to feel free enough and comfortable enough to express anything and everything they want to, it's also important to establish confidentiality in the group. Members of our writing group must agree to confidentiality within the group—nothing that is said or written in group is shared with anyone, without explicit permission. It's important, too, that group membership and attendance be as consistent as possible. Frequent comings and goings can disrupt the focus of the group and make work on ongoing projects virtually impossible. Members will sometimes be absent in any group or class, but frequent and sometimes long-term absences are not unusual in a group of people who are HIV positive. With this as a given, I request that once people decide to join the writing group, they make a 12-week commitment. Prospective members can come for two sessions to check it out, to decide if they want to join.

This structure immediately says to prospective members that this is a committed undertaking, and that it's important that membership and attendance be consistent. This in turn implies that the work of the group will be taken seriously, and that it may be revealing and risky. It also means people will get to know each other well, over time, which tends to increase intensity, but also provides a chance to really get to know each other's writing styles, strengths, and resistances. Members of our group are strong advocates of this structure and are great about being in touch with people when they're absent.

The description of the workshop that appears on flyers or in a brochure is important for prospective members. People need to be able to choose a workshop that will fit their desires. Here is the blurb for my group:

HIV/AIDS WRITERS WORKSHOP, led by Ellie Friedland. Thursdays 6:00–9:00 P.M.

Many of us have things to say that MUST be heard. We may or may not know specifically what we need to express, but we have a longing to keep looking inside for what wants out. We have to give ourselves permission to find and say it all, and we need forms for that expression. In this writing workshop we'll experiment with various writing exercises and forms to get and keep the juices flowing. We'll share our work with each other and practice giving feedback that informs and encourages our writing. New and experienced writers are welcome. "There is a vitality, a life-force, an energy, a quickening that is translated through you into action and because there is only one of you in all time, this expression is unique. And if you block it, it will never exist through any other medium and will be lost. The world will not have it. It is not your business to determine how good it is nor how valuable nor how it compares with other expressions. It is your business to keep it yours clearly and directly, to keep the channel open. You do not even have to believe in yourself or your work. You have to keep open and aware directly to the urges that motivate you. Keep the channel open . . . ."
Martha Graham to Agnes De Mille[1]

I love this quote, and I begin the first meeting of each semester by giving a copy of it to everyone, reading it, and discussing reactions to it. I think it's a statement that everyone can relate to, but it seems to have special relevancy for people with HIV/AIDS (and, I assume, this would be so for any life-threatening illness or situation). People who are HIV positive, even if they are asymptomatic and taking the new drug treatments, live with an expectation of a shortened life and of probable illness and disability. They are often hyperaware of their own life force and energy, and in fact are often living with daily changes in their physical experience of these—energy, ability, life itself cannot be taken for granted because there are constant reminders of their fragility.

Let me take a moment to say something about the "miracle" drugs, because I'm afraid many people reading this may have the idea that, as the

---

[1]Irene Borger uses this quotation in her workshop, and I got it from her. It is taken from Agnes de Mille's book *Dance to the Piper and Promenade Home: A Two-Part Autobiography* (New York: Da Capo Press, 1979), 335.

media has said, AIDS is at least almost gone, or that living with HIV/AIDS is now like living with some minor chronic ailment. The drug combinations, or "cocktails," have indeed been miraculous for *some people*, whose symptoms and even viral loads (how much virus is in the bloodstream) have virtually disappeared. The reality is that the drugs have never worked for many people (reports have stated figures of 30–40% of the people who try them). They often aren't helpful for people who have high viral loads and low T-cell counts. Other people go through months of trying various drugs in various combinations, with little helpful result. Increasingly, scientists are identifying new, drug-resistant strains of HIV, which could lead to even higher percentages of drug treatment failure.

Many people experience serious side effects of the drugs, whether or not they are also helping reduce the virus, including blinding headaches, nearly constant diarrhea and/or nausea, and a host of other problems. People often feel sick for months, or longer, on the drug "cocktails." Now that people have been taking the drugs for a few years, new, very serious side effects are emerging. People with HIV are actually beginning to die from diseases that are linked to their treatments, not the HIV itself.

It's a hard trade-off—feeling bad now in hopes of prolonging life and maybe feeling better later. Even those lucky people who don't have serious side effects and do have reduced viral loads have to live with the possibility of serious side effects developing with time. In the present, their lives are regimented by the drug regimes. They are often on several drugs that all have to be taken at specific times, a certain amount of time before or after eating, and in regular time sequences. Sleeping, eating, social times, and work schedules all have to be adjusted to the drugs. Life is far from "normal."

So. All that to show that living with HIV/AIDS is still living with the constant possibility, if not reality, of serious long-term illness and gradual progression toward death. Living with HIV is always about living with uncertainty. The members of our writing group come with an urgency that makes Martha Graham's statement very real for them. Because many of them are no longer working, the usual channels for contributing to society have already been cut off. They know they have something to say, and they have a desire for it to be heard. They know their contributions could be lost altogether if they hang out in hesitation and resistance. They know they want and need to "keep the channels open." For me, as group leader, this has a wonderful side effect: these people are ready and willing to go past the superficial, and they have little tolerance for bullshit—theirs as well as others'. Now I'm certainly not saying that this is true for everyone who is HIV positive, but it does seem to be true of the people who choose to come to this writing group.

I frequently encourage people in the group to write about anything and everything. There is no expectation that people will write about AIDS, but there is encouragement to write about whatever comes up, without self-censorship. They seem to be ravenous for this permission and leap on the opportunity. Very often members of our group do write about HIV and AIDS, because it is at the center of their experience and because they have had to censor much of what they long to express about it. A few people in our writing group have taken, or at least started to take, writing classes and workshops at local colleges and centers for adult education. They complained forcefully that they didn't feel free to write the truth of their experience in these classes and didn't feel supported in their attempts to write. They describe what I also experienced when I was looking for a writing group: people who are not directly affected by HIV/AIDS are uncomfortable responding to writing about it. We all found that participants and leaders of these other classes tended to respond to our work only in terms of technicalities, focusing on changing a word here, a line break here, while ignoring the content completely. I know this sounds impossible, but I'm afraid it's common. Further, we all found that these writing groups seemed to expect only "feel-good" ideas and views of the world and about HIV/AIDS in particular. Expressions of anger, fear, disappointment, or other "tough" feelings or ideas are met with platitudes about how to make it better or are not responded to at all.

Here is a relevant poem by writing group member Mark Balicki:

Closure

I really see the poisons in my life
but often choose to ignore their power.
I really see how truth can be
a freeing tool in the arsenal of life.
I really hear so much denial and self-delusion
I have to bite my tongue.
I really hear "I don't want to know"
When some people ask "how are you?"
I really feel alone when I think of
the friends I've lost.
I really feel anger when I think of
the friends who choose to lose me.
And I really feel that I'm not ready
to go yet.
Am I still here for some reason?
Interested in helping me find that reason?
Oh.
I see . . .

I don't understand why so many writing classes and workshops seem so closed to expression. Even if people are not infected or affected by HIV/

AIDS, they must have real lives and real stories with joy, rage, fear, hope, hopelessness, and the range of human experience. Why aren't all of these welcome topics? What are we to express if not the raw truth of life? Most art, certainly the great art of the world, expresses deep and often unsettling truths, and we value this about it. Why should we avoid this in our own creation of art? Without it, we are almost certain to create mundane, superficial work. It may be technically correct and academically acceptable, but is it alive? Is it the expression of that unique vitality, life force, and energy we each have?

I think leaders of many such classes are cautious in the guise of being academic or technical. Let's face it, it's easier for everyone to stay intellectual and technical. It's safer to argue literary theory and debate minutia than it is to look deeply at a piece of work to critically seek out the intimate truth the writer wants to get out. When we do so, the writing process and the writing class become experiences of intimacy. It is revealing and risky to find our real voices, and it is difficult and risky to critique such work. We then have to respond intimately, to allow ourselves to be affected by the work, as well as to critique the technicalities in it. As facilitators of such experiences, we must remain open in a very different way than if we choose to focus on the technical. If we want to encourage people to look inside for their unique expression and truth, we need to do that ourselves. And that's a big expectation and a big risk.

It's terrifying for most of us, especially when we are trying to write something that truly expresses that which is most vital and important to us. It seems that most of us who have an urge to express something deep and true also have built in resistance to that. We resist, we defend, we get stuck. I know I do. Here are excerpts from my journal written while I was writing my doctoral dissertation:

> My resistance has been so intense as to be immobilizing these past few days. My big fear is that I have nothing of value to say. I'm about to write about haiku and Shakespeare, two things I love, and I'm stuck. I've written sections about each, and when I read them they're missing the best of what I have to offer. I want to convey my passion for the subjects, and how they're about awareness and mindfulness. But I can't see how to do that. I feel tight, held. Thickness in my throat, tears just behind my eyes. I feel paralyzed by fear and doubt. I experience it as anger and confusion. My head is full, like with a cold but without any real physical blockage. I breathe short and quick, my legs ache. If I take a deep breath I start to cry. I have such pressure in my head, shoulders, belly; holding and pressure. It's hard to think, impossible to enjoy anything. I try to think what I'm confused about, to sort it out, and I can't even hold onto ideas. . . .
>
> Writing what is most true for me hurts—*finding* what's true, and finding my voice to express—that's what hurts. It makes me feel so vulnerable and

frightened. . . . I remember Gavin Harrison [a Buddhist teacher and writer] quoting Rilke: "Perhaps everything that frightens us is in its essence something that wants our love." Lovely, if I could only relate to it this way.

The obvious question in these moments is "So, what do I do?" I've found some ways of responding, which help me and which also seem to be useful for the people in my writing group. The most important aspect of helpful responses seems to be acceptance that getting stuck is part of the process of writing, or creating, not something separate and at odds with it. If I say to myself when I'm stuck, "Ah, I must be well into the process of finding what I really want to express, because all this resistance is up," it has a completely different result than if I say something like, "I'm stuck, *again*. This is horrible, I won't ever be able to write anything. I shouldn't even try. I'm horrible." When I have the second response, that way of thinking takes hold and escalates to other ideas of hopelessness and worthlessness, and I can convince myself that I have nothing to say, or if I do I'm incapable of saying it, so I might as well turn on the TV or go to the refrigerator for whatever I can find there, or better yet, do both.

But if I can view my stuck experience as a normal and expected part of the process of writing, I can experience it while staying more detached from it, and not get so sucked in. I may be unable to think of anything *now*, but I don't go on to draw conclusions about my ability or inability to do so for the rest of my life. Another way of saying this is that I try to have compassion for myself in these moments, instead of attacking myself and believing it when I tell myself "I can't" and "It's hopeless." This doesn't necessarily make me feel any better, but it does prevent me from prolonging the time I stay stuck.

Here is a bit of my journal from a few days after the first entries:

Fear, confusion, doubt and anger are sitting right on top of huge sadness and grief. Literally on top of it, in my body. Meditating this morning I opened up past them into sadness. I dreamed about Peter last night. It's terrible to watch him have physical pain and to be completely helpless . . . . Recognizing all this doesn't remove the fear, doubt and confusion, but it does soften them. It allows me to be less hyper about having to get rid of the feelings . . . . Amazing how much I was holding on, being tight. Amazing how the way to move is ALWAYS to open to whatever is going on to step toward it. Anatole Broyard, in *Intoxicated by My Illness*, says that when he was diagnosed with prostate cancer, he had a choice to step away from his illness, or toward it. He stepped toward it, explored it, and developed a narrative for his illness and dying. I think of this often, this choice to step away from what is so in my life, internally and externally. I have been determined not to melt, not to be soft with myself about Peter's AIDS or about worrying on my dissertation. I was fighting to figure out, to unconfuse, and so got deeper into confusion fear and

doubt. This eased yesterday, and there is much less pressure today . . . . Valuing the doubt, fear and confusion helped, instead of struggling to try to overcome them . . . . When I soften into all this I still don't have answers or resolution, but I have more patience.

It takes time and practice to develop awareness and acceptance of our
experience. It means being willing to stand back, with some distance, from
what we say to ourselves, instead of assuming it's all true and real. Then we
can see it as a recurring response that comes up when we are opening to
our unique expression. One way I know to do this is to offer alternative
arguments to the voices in our heads that say that feeling stuck is hopeless
and anathema to the creative process. I don't think we can stop those voices,
but we can meet them with the idea that being stuck is a natural step in the
creative process. This seems logical, as we all have successfully been creative
and have often been stuck along the way. We all know both experiences,
they do seem to go hand in hand, but our response can have a huge effect
on how the two experiences play out.

Most of us can't always come up with answers to the negative voices in
our heads. In fact, for most of us, these bits of negativity are so ingrained
and so natural that we aren't even aware of them. In our writing group we
use a technique from Irene Borger that helps with this: before reading any
piece to the group, each person is allowed three, and only three, deprecat-
ing comments or excuses. It's amazing how many ways people have of
negating their writing—we saw immediately in our group that we had to
include *nonverbal* commentary as well as verbal, because people would roll
their eyes, make faces, or groan or snort as introduction to the piece they
were about to read. The "three negative comment rule" has the wonderful
effect of helping people become aware of the judgments they're expressing
that they are totally unaware of. People count for each other: someone will
pick up his poem, purse his lips, close his eyes, and slightly shake his head,
and someone else will call out "One!" It's important to be made aware that
we are expressing such judgments of ourselves, but I like the "three" rule
because it's also important to be allowed to express this stuff. I wouldn't
want a rule that said no negative comments, or even one. I think that would
feel suppressive and so could be contrary to our purpose.

That purpose, as I've said, is outlined in the course description and by
how I set up and lead the group. Richard Baker, in his introduction to
Shrunryu Suzuki's *Zen Mind Beginner's Mind*, says that the purpose of all
Zen teaching is "to make you wonder and answer that wondering with the
deepest expression of your own nature" (13). I believe this is the purpose
of *all teaching*, and it's what I see happening in the writing group. And, each
member of the group has his/her own purposes, goals, desires and
approaches. At the beginning of each semester (every 12 weeks) we all

write and share what we want from the semester of writing group. Many people stay in the group for several semesters, so they change, expand, and/or deepen their articulation of this each time. Here are examples of what members have said: "I want to be less self-critical, I want to have the freedom to express whatever comes to mind. I want to tap into the unexplored . . . when I start to do this it blows me away and I get too scared . . ."; "I want to be more disciplined and organized, not get sidetracked. I want to reach deeply into my inner self"; "I want to have writing as a companion. I want to explore what I have to say"; and from someone entering his third "round" of the group: "Many of my 'essays' are so terse and coarse that I would like to learn the necessary tools to convert them . . . to poetry. On the other hand, I know that some of the vignettes I illustrate with words need to be expanded into a format so that those who are not in the circle of AIDS will be able to feel some of the givens that those of us who have been diagnosed take for granted . . . ."

I carefully take notes as each person talks about what they want from the group and use them to plan our focus, as well as specific writing exercises, throughout the semester. We also check in less formally periodically—if someone has expressed an interest in writing more fiction or in spending more time on revision, for example, I will ask if others share this interest before turning in that direction. The atmosphere of our group is easygoing and intimate, so members also make suggestions for activities or directions as we go along.

Our group meets for three hours every week. As I said earlier, there is always a time for chat as people arrive and greet each other. If it really is just chitchat, I will suggest we begin writing after about 10 minutes, but if there is a hot issue being discussed, or if someone is talking about an important personal experience or concern, the talk could go on longer. Eventually I always step in as facilitator to bring us to writing, but I may scrap whatever I had planned so people can write about whatever has come up in the conversations or use the conversation as a springboard to some other writing focus.

We usually begin with a freewriting exercise. Many of the people in my group have done little or no creative writing before, and they appreciate writing "starters." For this initial freewrite, which is usually 5 to 10 minutes, I may suggest the beginning of a sentence or a topic to cluster (à la Rico in *Writing the Natural Way*). For example, I may give a word, and each person begins by writing the word down, then writing whatever comes into his head in association with that word, in a cluster around it on the page. This takes a minute or so, then each person reads it to herself and writes a piece, in any form, sparked by what she just wrote. It may or may not relate to the original word or topic. We spend 5 to 10 minutes writing, then each person reads what he or she has written and receives feedback from the group.

After about an hour and a half, we take a break. This is important for people who are HIV positive, as they often have to take medications, etc., but I think it's a good idea for any group. People go to the bathroom, get drinks, go outside for a smoke, and most importantly, talk and socialize together. After the break we usually do a longer writing. Again, I provide a writing starter, either another exercise or a topic that has come out during the group conversation or writing so far. After writing, everyone again reads what they have written and receives feedback, and that usually ends the group. When this group began I didn't give assignments, and most people didn't write much at home. After a few people had been in the group for a couple of semesters, they began requesting assignments and began writing at home! They bring in these pieces, read them, and receive feedback. Every four or five weeks we spend a session or two on revision. Everyone chooses a piece to work on, and the whole group helps revise all the pieces. These sessions are often the most exciting and most gratifying of all. People really tune in to each other and get turned on by the process of finding the right word or phrase, the right line break, or whatever.

I have taken the basic structure for my group, as well as the general guidelines for feedback, from Irene Borger's workshop. (She has included all this in her book *From a Burning House*, which is a valuable resource for anyone who wants to start or lead a writing group like this.) I will note here that I do the writing exercises along with my group. This is a personal choice (Irene Borger does not do so) that has ramifications for my role in the group. I am clearly the "teacher," because I bring in the exercises and assignments, set the structure, monitor and facilitate the group, choose authors and works to read and use in the group, lead and model giving feedback, and teach techniques and forms. But I also do the writing exercises, read my writing, and receive feedback from the group. This is, in part, a teaching method, as I model doing all this for the group. I think it serves to give people permission, especially when they're new—what I read is often outrageous, or emotional, or just plain bad enough for people to see that all that really is OK.

Participating as well as leading the group makes me a teacher *and* a group member, which is the role I'm most comfortable with. It emphasizes that we're all in this together; we're all writers learning together and supporting each other. It does mean that I usually don't have my full attention on what I'm writing, because I'm watching the time, planning where we might go next, watching out for what people need, and so forth. When we read our work to each other, most of my attention is on everyone else's work, and only a little on mine. If I give assignments to be done at home and brought in to group, I don't do them. These pieces tend to be longer than what we write in group, and it works for me not to take up this much of the group's time on my work. This setup, and these boundaries, work for me in the groups I lead. I strongly believe that each group leader has to find what works for her and give herself permission to set things up that way.

There are many choices about how to set up giving and receiving feedback. One option is that only the group leader gives feedback, but to me that seems stifling for everyone else and sets up a hierarchical relationship that makes me uncomfortable. So everyone gives feedback whenever they have any to give. It's a "rule" in our group that a writer may request *not* to receive feedback on any piece he or she reads, and though in four years no one has ever made this request, I think it's good to make it an option. Sometimes a piece may feel so intimate or a writer may feel so vulnerable that he or she wants to read, but not have feedback. I must say I also believe that having the option makes people feel safe enough that they don't need to use it.

Here are the basic parameters for feedback in our writing group (much of this is also from Irene Borger): first of all, there is no right way, and so no wrong way to do any exercise. The purpose of feedback is to encourage expression and to clarify it. I encourage people to listen carefully while someone reads and to jot down vivid images and phrases, particularly strong words, as well as anything that is unclear or hard to understand; to note underlying issues; and to question what the person may want to be saying that isn't said. Every person may express reactions to someone's writing and should try to state them as clearly as possible, and always in terms of specifics rather than generalities.

Receiving feedback is often uncomfortable for people at first, so I use Peter Elbow's dictum that you, the writer, are always right and always wrong and the feedback is always right and always wrong. This helps a lot; it lightens the whole issue and gives everybody room. The only "rule" for people receiving feedback is that they may not argue with anyone's reaction. They can ask for clarification or explanation, though, or ask questions.

I've found that no more guidance than this is needed for giving and receiving feedback. I continue to facilitate, and if people get off on a tangent I bring them back, but no one has ever given inappropriate or mean feedback. By the same token, they don't just say they love everything, but clearly work on listening and on giving feedback the writer will find useful.

For me, having to come up with ideas and exercises every week can be the scariest part of leading the writing group. When I asked Irene Borger how she did it, she said she just always seemed to come up with things from what she'd read recently, what she'd been thinking about, and so on. I remember being dissatisfied with this answer, but I think it's the only real answer available. Each person has to find a way to come up with exercises or writing starters. I have bought several books about teaching writing and leaf through them regularly. I also read as much as I can, and I'm always looking for poems or short pieces or bits of pieces to read in group. These are often the most effective inspiration and stimulus for people's writing.

I also sometimes focus on a particular technique, form, or genre by teaching about it, then reading examples. Sometimes this is because group members have requested it, sometimes it's because I think we need a new stimulus or focus, and sometimes it's just because I want to share something I love. One of the most exciting aspects of this group for me has been to see how people develop the *need* and *desire* for form, as well as for better grammar, sentence structure, spelling, and all of it. They come to the group knowing they want to write and to express something. As they discover and practice this, they get even more excited about it. They wonder and want to answer that wondering with the deepest expression of their natures. They want to know what words, what forms, what structures can best do that for them, and so they never see form as restrictive or as something to fight. Their writing deepens and matures as a result. Their passion remains as strong as ever.

Here is another poem by Mark Balicki:

> Blood Brother
>
> I carry a crimson plague
> Masking the hues of my heart
>
> Each full moon tubes of crimson
> Measure the destruction within
>
> Crimson flames burn during sleep
> And sopping sheets drench the nightly fires
>
> Polaroids chronicle the roadmaps in my eyes
> And foretell the time of inevitable blindness
>
> When darkness comes it will be the color
> Of a child's hand over a flashlight
>
> I carry a crimson plague
> Mine well documented near a decade now
>
> Kisses of lips are now kept in check
> Fears for both you and me
>
> Pages with a four letter crimson acronym
> Ensure that some will keep their distance
>
> A bag hangs dripping life into my arm
> A diseased pariah can never hope to return the favor

The day will come when liquid poppies
Coursing through my spent frail frame
Will speed the mark
To a final crimson setting sun.

REFERENCES

Borger, Irene. *From a Burning House.* New York: Washington Square Press, 1996.
Broyard, Anatole. *Intoxicated by My Illness.* New York: Clarkson Potter, 1992.
Rico, Gabriele Lusser. *Writing the Natural Way: Using Right-Brain Techniques to Release Your Expressive Powers.* Los Angeles: J.P. Tarcher, 1983.
Sarton, May. *Mrs. Stevens Hears the Mermaids Singing.* New York: W.W. Norton & Co., 1965.
Suzuki, Shrunryu. *Zen Mind Beginner's Mind.* New York: Weatherhill, 1970.

QUESTIONS FOR REFLECTION, JOURNAL WRITING, AND DISCUSSION

1. Friedland says that teaching her writing workshop makes her feel "excited, creative, fulfilled, and light," and that the members of her group feel the same way. How does teaching make you feel? How do you think your students feel?

2. Friedland says that the purpose of teaching is "to make you wonder and want to answer that wondering with the deepest expression of your own nature." Do you agree?

3. Friedland says, "If I suppress my rage, . . . I tend to also suppress my energy, my openness, my love, and my creativity." Do you feel the same way?

4. Do you think it is possible to convince students in an academic writing class to invest as much of themselves in their work as Friedland's students did? What risks would that involve for the students? For the teacher? Is it worth the risks?

Chapter **14**

Toward a Post-Process Composition: Abandoning the Rhetoric of Assertion

Gary A. Olson

Gary A. Olson is Professor of English and director of the graduate program in rhetoric and composition at the University of South Florida. His most recent book is *The Kinneavy Papers: Theory and the Study of Discourse* (with Lynn Worsham and Sidney Dobrin). The following article is from *Post-Process Theory: Beyond the Writing-Process Paradigm*, edited by Thomas Kent (Southern Illinois University Press, 1999).

The process movement in composition served us well. It emphasized that writing is an "activity," an act that is itself composed of a variety of activities; that the activities involved in the act of writing are typically recursive rather than linear; that writing is first and foremost a social activity; that the act of writing can be a means of learning and discovery; that experienced writers are often intensely aware of audience, purpose, and context; that experienced writers invest considerable amounts of time in invention and revision activities; that effective instruction in composition provides opportunities for students to practice the kinds of activities involved in the act of writing; that such instruction includes ample opportunities to read and comment on the work of peers and to receive the comments of peers about one's own writing; that effective composition instructors grade a student's work not solely on the finished product but also on the efforts the student has invested in the process of crafting the product; and that successful composition instruction entails finding appropriate occasions to intervene in each student's writing process. In these and other ways, the process orientation helped us to theorize writing in more productive ways than previously and to devise pedagogies that familiarize students with the kinds of activities that writers often engage in when they write. As several "post-process" scholars have pointed out recently, however, the process orientation has its own limitations. Key among these limitations is the fact that the process orientation, as we have conceived it, imagines that the writing process can be described in some way; that is, process theorists assume that we can somehow make statements about the process that would apply to all or most writing situations.

When we conceive writing as a "process" that can be codified and then taught, we are engaging in theory building. The post-modern critique of theory as totalizing, essentialist, and a residue of Enlightenment thinking has made clear that any attempt to construct a generalizable explanation of how something works is misguided in that such narratives inevitably deprivilege the local, even though it is precisely the local where useful "knowledge" is generated. As Stephen Toulmin comments, "When people ask about the future role of theory and they're talking about theory with a big *T*, I'm inclined to shake hands with Rorty and say there is probably no legitimate role for theory with a big *T*; we should be prepared to kiss rationalism good-bye and walk off in the opposite direction with joy in our hearts" (216).[1]

The postmodern critique of theory serves as a useful corrective in that it alerts us to the dangers of creating master narratives and then adhering to these explanations as if we have obtained truth. As Toulmin suggests, however, it is important that we not mistake this useful corrective as being equivalent to the more general attack on theory; to do so would be to conflate two very distinct ideological perspectives on theory. This misunderstanding arises from the failure to distinguish between theory building, the attempt to arrive at generalizable explanations of how something works—that is, to arrive at some kind of truth—and the activity of theorizing, the act of engaging in critical, philosophical, hermeneutic speculation about a subject. *Theory*, the noun, is dangerous from a postmodern perspective because it entices us into believing we somehow have captured a truth, grasped the essence of something; *theorizing*, the verb, can be productive (so long as a "theory" is not the objective) because it is a way to explore, challenge, question, reassess, speculate. Theorizing can lead us into lines of inquiry that challenge received notions or entrenched understandings that may no longer be productive; it can create new vocabularies for talking about a subject and thus new ways of perceiving it.[2]

The problem with process theory, then, is not so much that scholars are attempting to theorize various aspects of composing as it is that they are endeavoring (consciously or not) to construct a model of the composing

---

[1]This is not to suggest that Toulmin should be considered postmodernist. In fact, he half jokingly has referred to himself as a "neo-modernist." His take on the role of theory, however, is consistent with that of many postmodernist thinkers.

[2]Instructive is Richard Rorty's discussion of how, on a much grander could not have been envisaged prior to the development of a particular set of descriptions, those which it itself helps to provide" (*Contingency* 13).

process, thereby constructing a Theory of Writing, a series of generalizations about writing that supposedly hold true all or most of the time. This is what Thomas Kent and other post-process theorists mean when they complain that process scholars—despite whatever other ideological allegiances may inform their work—are attempting to systematize something that simply is not susceptible to systematization. As Kent has demonstrated quite cogently, writing,—indeed all communication—is radically contingent, radically situational. Consequently, efforts to pin down some version of "the writing process" are misguided, unproductive, and misleading.

That the vocabulary of process is no longer useful is not a reason to despair; it is, rather, an invitation to rethink many of our most cherished assumptions about the activity we call "writing." For example, the work of some postmodern theorists can help us challenge some of our process-oriented notions of writing by questioning a time-honored value in composition: what we might call the "rhetoric of assertion." In one way or another, composing (at least the way it is often taught) has always seemed to be associated with asserting something to be true. Students are instructed to write an essay, which has usually meant to take a position on a subject (often stated in a "strong," "clear" thesis statement, which is itself expressed in the form of an assertion), and to construct a piece of discourse that then "supports" the position. Passages in an essay that do not support the position are judged irrelevant, and the essay is evaluated accordingly. And critical-thinking specialists spend considerable time instructing students on how to locate and evaluate assertions in published and student texts and how to handle their own assertions and support in their own texts. The technology of assertion seems ubiquitous in composition studies.

Now, it is true that some compositionists over the years have advocated introducing into the composition class alternative kinds of essays that are less conspicuously thesis driven or argumentative, but even those who recommend that students write "exploratory" essays or purely personal narratives typically expect such essays to make a point or points.[3] In short, despite our attempts to introduce alternative genres, to help students become more dialogic and less monologic, more sophistic and less Aristotelian, more exploratory and less argumentative, more personal and less academic, the Western, rationalist tradition of assertion and support is so entrenched in our epistemology and ways of understanding what "good" writing and "thinking" are that this tradition, along with its concomitant assumptions, defies even our most concerted efforts to subvert it.

---

[3]For one of the many arguments in favor of having students write exploratory essays, see Winterowd; for various discussions about using nontraditional dialogic genres in composition instruction, see Covino.

The work of numerous theorists from outside of composition, however, suggests that our efforts to subvert such a tradition may well be worth sustaining. The rhetoric of assertion can be critiqued from a variety of standpoints: that it is masculinist, phallogocentric, foundationalist, often essentialist, and, at the very least, limiting. For example, when Sandra Harding and other "feminist standpoint" theorists argue that the rhetoric of science deludes us into conceiving of science as "objective" when really it is far from it, they are talking, at least in part, about the role of the rhetoric of assertion. Modern science, in Harding's view, plays a kind of solipsistic trick: it defines what "objectivity" is and then excludes whatever does not fit its own definition. Because Western science has traditionally been dominated by white, well-educated (that is, middle- or upper-class) males, the values and perspectives of only this small group have dictated the values and perspectives of science—what is worth studying and what not (heart attacks but not breast cancer?), how a subject is to be studied (male research subjects being used to study specifically female maladies?), how the resulting data are interpreted, and so on. As Harding comments, "The problem is that knowledge that has been generated only from the lives of a small portion of the society (and, at that, the most powerful one) is not useful for most people's projects" (209). She posits that it is much better to move toward a "strong objectivity," one that would take into account the standpoints, the social and cultural positionality of those traditionally marginalized by androcentric, Eurocentric science. This sensitivity to multiple standpoints, multiple social and cultural positionings, would afford a "stronger" objectivity in that the very inclusiveness of alternative positionings would enrich rather than impoverish the perspectives on and information about a subject being examined.

What gives masculinist science much of its rhetorical power, its hegemony over other standpoints, is its unquestioned compulsion to assert truth. It is its very assertive power, its closing off of alternative perspectives, its insistence on closure and resolution that makes science appear so unassailable. Standpoint theorists such as Harding prefer to delay answers, postpone closure, avoid assertion, looking instead for more open-ended, dialogic methods of inquiry—a non-assertive rhetoric. Says Harding, "I think it's important not to close questions, if you're thinking of knowledge as a way of closing questions, saying, 'This is knowledge now, so there's no room for further discussion'" (221). Once we believe that all disciplines, including those in the sciences, are in the business of producing narratives—that is, asserting positions in narrative form—it becomes easy to question the traditional notion of objectivity that has distorted our understanding of exactly what science is. The traditional narratives of science—or of any discourse, for that matter—have always been produced from a single standpoint, that of white, typically upper- or middle-class males. Defining this single perspective and the narratives generating from it as "objective" is a political act that silences other voices and perspectives.

Like Sandra Harding, Donna Haraway argues that there are in fact multiple, contesting narratives produced by those who have been excluded from the knowledge-making projects of technoscience: "There are many actors in our world who can and ought to have a say in the design of the apparatus for the production of scientific knowledge" ("Writing" 54). Haraway makes clear that such attempts to retell the stories of technoscience are not cynical efforts to replace the dominant stories with those of women, an effort that would serve only to reinscribe hierarchies and systems of domination. Rather, they are attempts to increase the number and kinds of stories that get told and the actors who tell them. Far from an anything-goes relativism, refusing the technical and the political is an effort to "insist on the story-ladenness of knowledge, the story-ladenness of facts," to subvert the rhetoric of assertion that so saturates our ways of knowing ("Writing" 57).

Haraway takes this emphasis on situatedness and on resistance to closure and assertion further than do most feminist theorists, specifically noting the necessity to reinvent our notions of writing. "Writing," both in its larger postmodern sense and in its more narrow material sense, is central to living in the world and to enacting the numerous freedom projects of resisting systems of domination—whether in the very uses of discourse itself or in the multiple discourse systems that comprise and constitute our social institutions and academic disciplines. Thus, as Haraway says in *Simians, Cyborgs, and Women,* "writing is deadly serious" (175). She characterizes "the injunction to be clear"—an injunction all too frequently articulated in classrooms and academic disciplines and intimately linked to the rhetoric of assertion—as "very strange":

> I have friends for whom the injunction to be clear remains right at the top of their moral, epistemological, and political commitments. It's always struck me that the injunction to be clear is a very strange goal because it assumes a kind of physical transparency, that if you could just clean up your act somehow the materiality of writing would disappear. This is a psychological problem, as opposed to exactly what's interesting about working in that medium. . . . I've become increasingly more certain that this is part of the substance of *our* work collectively in science studies and that it's not some personal indulgence or some inability to "think clearly." ("Writing" 49)

Haraway calls for a conception of writing ("cyborg writing," in her terms) that resists authoritative, assertive, phallogocentric writing practices; that foregrounds the writer's own situatedness in history and in his or her writing practice; and that makes visible the very "apparatus of the production of authority" that all writers tend to submerge in their discourse, an authority deriving in large part from the rhetoric of assertion. This is not to say that writers must reject authority, but that in a truly ethical and postmodern stance they must reveal how authority is implicated in discourse.

In describing her concept of a subversive, cyborg writing, Haraway comments,

> Cyborg writing has inherited the kind of acid consciousness of people like Derrida and others who have made it simply impossible to engage in authoritative writing *as if* the subject who did such a thing weren't implicated in the practice and *as if* the history of writing weren't the history of the differentiation of the world for us with all of the sticky threads to questions of power and to whose way of life is at stake in marking up the world that way rather than some other way. ("Writing" 49)

Haraway's cyborg writing is an attempt to make visible the fact that writing is always already ideological, always already political—always saturated with questions of power and domination. Thus, authority and the social positions from which one is entitled to assert it are centrally important. She writes,

> Many of the myths and narratives are not available to you from what I would call "cyborg positions." You have to take your implication in a fraught world as the starting point. I don't think that's true for authoritative writing practices that try very hard to produce the kind of masterful "I," a particular kind of authority position that makes the viewer forget the apparatus of the production of that authority. I think cyborg writing is resolutely committed to foregrounding the apparatus of the production of its own authority, even while it's doing it. It's not eschewing authority, but it's insisting on a kind of double move, a foregrounding of the apparatus of the production of bodies, powers, meanings. ("Writing" 50)

Haraway's concept of a situated, multiplicitous, nonassertive writing practice is similar to that of Jean-Francois Lyotard, who sees writing (in the expanded contemporary sense of the term) as central to postmodern "openness" and resistance to certainty. For Lyotard, true writing is the attempt to "resist the network of exchanges in which cultural objects are commodities," to resist "the simple and naive exchangeability of things in our world" ("Resisting" 173). His conception of writing is in contradistinction to the traditional notion of writing as an activity whose objective is to "master" a subject, to possess it, to pin it down through a discourse of assertion. It is precisely this phallocratic preoccupation with mastery, says Lyotard, that has impelled philosophy as a mode of discourse into its present state of "extreme crisis." The compulsion to master by erecting huge systems of answers, the "search for a constituting order that gives meaning to the world," makes the philosopher "a secret accomplice of the phallocrat" ("One Thing" 118).

In *Peregrinations*, Lyotard says that the idea that writing "pretends to be complete," that it presumes to "build a system of total knowledge" about something, "constitutes *par excellence* the sin, the arrogance of the mind" (6–7). Typical discourse, especially academic discourse, entails what Lacan called "the discourse of the master," and Lyotard refuses to set himself up as a master, preferring instead to be a "perpetual student." Instead, he claims, what is needed in philosophy, in the sciences, in life is "perpetual displacement of questions" so that "answering is never achieved" ("Resisting" 185). Since questions always already carry within them their own answers, are always "interested," it is the act itself of questioning, of remaining open, that is most useful to Lyotard. An "answer," then, is only interesting insofar as it is a new question, not in that it allows someone to assert a solution and thereby close off inquiry. What is needed, he suggests, is to move away from a discourse of mastery and abstract cognition toward a way of being that recognizes affect, the body, and openness—a posture he defines as "feminine." In fact, Lyotard perceives a strong relationship between this nonassertive writing and "femininity," in that he perceives femininity as associated with an openness to something unknown without any compulsion to master it or to assert a position on it. For Lyotard, the opposite of a discourse of mastery is "passivity," the ability to wait patiently, not for answers or solutions, but simply to wait—to remain in a state of perpetual receptiveness. This very "refusal of the temptation to grasp, to master," is "real femininity" ("Resisting" 184). His redefinition of writing, whether or not we agree that it is "feminine," seems a sensible stance in the postmodern world, a stance that we may well want to carry into the post-process composition class.

In fact, Lyotard challenges the very notion of composition as it is generally conceived, suggesting, as does Haraway, that we reinvent writing:

> In composition there is a sort of mastering, of putting things together so as to order them. It seems to me that the opposite is the ability to be weak, a good weakness, so-called passivity. I don't mind this term, though I tried to propose the term *passibility*. In this certain representation we can have the way of thinking in Zen Buddhism or certain Eastern philosophies or religions: the ability to wait for, not to look at, but to wait for—for what, precisely, we don't know. That's my ideological representation of the necessary attitude for writing. . . . It's an event not to know. It's good; there's no prejudice. ("Resisting" 183–84)

Thus, the work of Lyotard, Haraway, Harding, and many other theorists suggests that it is incumbent upon us all—especially, it would seem, those of us in rhetoric and composition—to challenge received notions of writing, of composition itself, to move away from a discourse of mastery and assertion toward a more dialogic, dynamic, open-ended, receptive, nonassertive stance. Of course, none of these theorists has "proven" anything about writing, none has provided an unassailable truth, and none has posited a "theory" of writing in the strict sense of a generalizable, universally applicable explanation; what they *have* done, however, is to speculate productively about how writing is deeply implicated in structures of power and domination, how writing can never be disconnected from ideology, how writing as traditionally conceived is driven by a discourse of mastery and a rhetoric of assertion.

Critiques of the discourse of mastery, the rhetoric of assertion, arise from numerous sites, not just the few mentioned here. The theorists who propose them often have divergent, even opposing agendas and would not agree with one another on a multitude of points; however, the fact that they all in one way or another are theorizing about writing in similar ways and are proposing a rethinking or reinventing of writing suggests that collectively they may have something significant to contribute to our own understandings, our own speculations. Such theorizing can have a profound effect on composition as a field, especially as we continue to grapple with questions of disciplinary identity. And, of course, if such speculations truly make sense, if they help us conceive of writing in new and potentially more useful and productive ways, then it is also incumbent upon us to adjust our pedagogies accordingly so as not to reinscribe naive or less useful conceptions of what it means to "compose." Thus, such work can potentially have significant implications not only for our own scholarly understandings of the workings of discourse but also for how we enact those understandings in the post-process classroom. And, undoubtedly, such theorizing is likely to be much more useful than process-oriented efforts to "master" the writing process, to define it, to systematize it.

NOTE

An earlier version of this chapter with a very different focus appeared as "Theory and the Rhetoric of Assertion," *Composition Forum* 6 (1995): 53–61.

REFERENCES

Covino, William A. *Forms of Wondering: A Dialogue on Writing, for Writers.* Portsmouth, NH: Boynton/Cook, 1990.

Haraway, Donna. *Simians, Cyborgs, and Women: The Reinvention of Nature.* New York: Routledge, 1991.

———. "Writing, Literacy and Technology: Toward a Cyborg Writing." Interview with Gary Olson. *Women Writing Culture.* Ed. Gary A. Olson and Elizabeth Hirsh. Albany: State U of New York P, 1995, 45–77.

Harding, Sandra. "Starting from Marginalized Lives: A Conversation with Sandra Harding." Interview with Elizabeth Hirsh and Gary A. Olson. *Journal of Advanced Composition* 15 (1995): 193–225.

Lyotard, Jean-Francois. *Peregrinations: Law, Form, Event.* New York: Columbia UP, 1988.

———. "Resisting a Discourse of Mastery: A Conversation with Jean-Francois Lyotard." Interview with Gary A. Olson. *Women Writing Culture.* Ed. Gary A. Olson and Elizabeth Hirsh. Albany: State U of New York P, 1995, 169–92.

Olson, Gary A. "Theory and the Rhetoric of Assertion." *Composition Forum* 6 (1995), 53–61.

Rorty, Richard. *Contingency, Irony, and Solidarity.* New York: Cambridge UP, 1989.

Toulmin, Stephen. "Literary Theory, Philosophy of Science, and Persuasive Discourse: Thoughts from a Neo-premodernist." Interview with Gary A. Olson. *Philosophy, Rhetoric, Literary Criticism: (Inter)views.* Ed. Gary A. Olson. Carbondale: Southern Illinois UP, 1994, 194–219.

Winterowd, W. Ross. "Rediscovering the Essay." *Journal of Advanced Composition* 8 (1988): 146–57.

QUESTIONS FOR REFLECTION, JOURNAL WRITING, AND DISCUSSION

1. Olson says that Lyotard opposes "the traditional notion of writing as an activity whose objective is to 'master a subject, to possess it, to pin it down through a discourse of assertion.'" Do you also oppose this "traditional notion"? How would you define writing as an activity?

2. Olson suggests that rather than masters, teachers should be "perpetual students" who are mainly interested in the "act of questioning, of remaining open." Do you agree? If so, what are the implications of this for teaching methodology?

3. In his first paragraph, Olson summarizes the basic tenets of the "process movement." Do you think that these tenets should be the cornerstone of contemporary writing instruction?

4. Olson connects assertion in writing to the "white male power structure." Is this a valid connection? Are there other reasons for the predominance of assertion in American education and culture?

5. Olson suggests that education is always political, always saturated with questions of power and domination. How is a fifth grader's book report ideological and political? A *New York Times* music review about a new Cher CD? A *National Enquirer* article about Cher? The Olson article you just read? This anthology of articles?

Part III

Responding to Writing

The first moment of truth for most writing teachers comes when our students hand in assignment number one. Whether we have been very explicit in our directions or have encouraged students to follow their own instincts, whether we have hovered over their paragraphs and drafts or set them loose to find their own way, our relationship to them is about to be challenged by the way we now read and comment on their work. Something that may have seemed like a good idea to us in the early stages may suddenly solidify into a paragraph we hate. Or we may find ourselves disappointed and annoyed that our suggestions have not been taken. So what do we say? Will the heretofore happy students feel misunderstood, misled, betrayed? How will we steer their writing in a direction that seems fruitful to us? How can we be sure our judgment is sound?

Cy Knoblauch and Lil Brannon's "Responding to Texts: Facilitating Revision in the Writing Workshop" highlights the ambiguities and hazards of our attempts to respond helpfully to students' writing. We think we're giving them an opportunity to write from their own hearts and minds and that, although we may have guidelines for the assignment, the world of language is theirs to explore. But students do not usually share this sense of freedom. Although the impulse for writing may never be completely disconnected from audience, in the freshman writing class particularly, students' power to make their own choices and get away with them are often severely abbreviated by the teacher's correcting pen. They know they are writing for us. So the work is "interested," as Carroll would say. Most of the time, they're trying to give us what we want.

And what, after all, do we want?

Whether we specify or not, we have an expectation. There is what Knoblauch and Brannon call an "ideal text" lurking somewhere in our heads. But is our ideal text the same as someone else's? (Think of the reviewers who panned the classics we love; think of the great works we still secretly can't stand.) As teachers, we have our own anxieties about what students should be able to do by the end of the term. Will we miss something fine because it didn't fulfill the assignment as we imagined it? Will we neglect to notice a student's efforts to organize or a particular stylistic achievement because something about the content disturbs us? The teacher's responses are "interested" too. The teacher is being the teacher. Her job is to teach that mysterious ideal text—the one that, in her class, finally materializes into an A paper and gets photocopied as an example of good writing.

The issue here is control. In responding to a student's text, they say, we have to refrain from rewriting it to produce that ideal text, which is, in fact, just our own version of how it should sound as it occurs to us while we're reading it, maybe at 11 P.M. when we're very tired and would rather be sleeping. Often, out of sheer boredom, we may start saying mean-spirited things like, "See handbook for agreement of pronouns and antecedents." Or we may rewrite, drawing lines through a student's phrases, inserting our own formulations. In this small universe of our classroom, we say what goes and what doesn't.

The authors remind us how capricious our corrections can be and how bewildering to students or how misdirected. Students don't need us to correct the grammar and usage problems of a relatively undeveloped first draft. What they need is our consciously subjective, questioning, "facilitative" response. They need us to tell them where we're having trouble understanding. And as we do this, we have to acknowledge that maybe someone else wouldn't be having this trouble. "Maybe it's just me," we need to imply, "but I don't know what you mean when you say, 'all colleges are the same.'" They recommend what a psychotherapist might offer to a struggling client: a formula that says, "When you write _____, I understand you to mean _____. Is that what you mean?"

The art of facilitative response, the authors say, is to allow the writer control of the choices. We need a little humility in our reading; we need to recognize the momentary failures of our own concentration. "Attitude shapes practice," the authors say. And we need to establish priorities. Our immediate goal in reading a first draft should not be correctness, despite how easily the pen leaps to cross out and insert. "Fluency, then clarity, then correctness," they remind us. Let the student develop the ability to be understood. Then work on the fine points.

The next two essayists, Donald Murray and Ann Raimes, come from different places, and their essays are concerned with different populations of students, but they would both agree. Murray's "The Listening Eye" is a description of his method of teaching writing by dispensing with classroom hours and holding individual conferences instead. This is not a method most teachers, particularly relatively new ones, would feel free to adopt, and its limitations are obvious, but Murray's main point is easily transferred to more conventional situations. "Listen, don't talk," is what he tells us. Let students tell you what their writing is about. Let them come to their discoveries themselves. It's a good principle to live by. In the sometimes awkward silences, students may be thinking. In telling you their problems with a piece of writing, they may find their own solutions. Don't fill up either their paper or the conversation with your own voice.

Ann Raimes works with students who are not native speakers of English. Her students are struggling with the syntax and idioms of English, and their choices often seem bizarre to teachers' eyes. But in "Errors: Windows into the Mind," she points out that if she asks her students why they are creating particular constructions, they often tell her that it is because they are reaching toward correctness, applying some recently learned rule. The result may be an inappropriate construction, but it is a stage in their development. As some ESL theorists explain, they are using an "interlanguage"[1] that relies partly on the rules of their native language and partly on what they have learned about the new one. That is a necessary stage of growth, not a series of random blunders. It may not be "passing," but its intelligence needs to be respected. Attitude shapes practice. If our corrections don't come from an understanding of the student's confusion, they are less useful than they could be, and sometimes they are destructive. Raimes's advice is to listen, as Mina Shaughnessy taught us years ago, for "the logic of students' errors"[2]—whether they are patterns of a dialect, constructions that stem from the students' native language, or unsuccessful attempts to apply an English idiom or produce a complicated verb form.

Peter Elbow's "High Stakes and Low Stakes in Assigning and Responding to Students' Writing" continues and refines the line of thinking espoused by Knoblauch and Brannon. In this essay, he argues first for writing as a way of allowing students to demonstate their learning not just in composition classes, but in all classes across the disciplines. Then he makes the extremely useful distinction between high-stakes and low-stakes writing, low stakes being writing that is produced not for evaluation but as a way to put ideas into one's own words: to translate difficult concepts, keep a record of work read, or create low-pressure drafts that can lead to more formal, organized writing. High-stakes writing, by contrast, is the writing that we grade.

Having distinguished between the two, he then helps us find ways to respond to them. The writing we do in response to our students, Elbow

---

[1] See Eleanor Kutz, Suzy Q. Groden, and Vivian Zamel, *The Discovery of Competence: Teaching and Learning with Diverse Student Writers* (Portsmouth, NH: Boynton/Cook, 1993) 22 ff.

[2] Mina P. Shaughnessy, *Errors and Expectations* (New York: Oxford University Press, 1977).

says, makes up a great bulk of our work, and yet it is often rushed, ill-considered, and worst of all, misunderstood. In order to enhance communication, to perhaps reduce our own workload and frustration, and to help our students understand and make better use of what we say, he establishes a continuum of responses to students' work that grows more detailed and more evaluative as we move from low- to high-stakes assignments. What he hopes to do is to increase the usefulness of the exchange, to make it closer to what may go on between two writers in a workshop, to enhance real listening, and to provide helpful feedback. Like Murray and Raimes, he urges us to move gingerly with our comments—so that we "at least do no harm."

Pat Belanoff's "The Myths of Assessment," first delivered as a speech to the CUNY ESL Council, takes up the topic of the large-scale assessment that goes on beyond our classrooms. What, she asks, do we think we're doing with our standardized tests, our normed systems of measurement, our abstract notions of what a good paper should have? What does a single writing sample reveal to us? An ability to organize? To generate arguments? To punctuate correctly? To use the right verb forms? As readers, what do we agree on? And even if we agree that a certain sample does or does not do what we want, can we agree that the sample represents the student's writing ability?

And what if we don't agree? She reminds us that one of the commonplaces of modern critical theory is that "people don't read the same way—that, as a result, texts do not *embed* meaning, they *enable* meaning." We can be trained to read alike, but that training is a way of forcing us not to be influenced by a "real" reaction. "Well," we might say, "this one is much more interesting than the other, there's a strong voice here, but the last paragraph really falls apart—the syntax is confused—so it only gets a three." Our private evaluation, however, may be that it's a better piece of writing than the sample to which we give a four. At other times, rarer no doubt, we may be looking at a piece of writing that takes us by surprise with its difference, its originality. We may, despite our years of reading papers, not really be equipped to judge it. But judge it we must—quickly and with major consequences.

Belanoff argues against grading that separates the test maker from the grader, the grader from the teacher. Such separations may set up a kind of objectivity, may seem to ensure good oversight and uniform standards, but they also dehumanize the process and give us a false security that our tests and our judgments about the tests tell us all we need to know about students. And this is not to mention the attitudes such tests engender in students—like Ira Shor's—of being forced to live with the high-stakes results of one performance on a given day.

As an alternative to standardized testing with its illusions of accuracy and fairness, Belanoff offers the portfolio system, and in her essay, she outlines one model. Essentially, students collect their writing into a folder and select what they like best and have worked on most diligently. They write a piece that evaluates their own performance: what was hard, what was easy, and what they learned, and they submit the portfolio to the teacher. The teacher then shares the portfolios, or the problematic ones, with a few other teacher/readers. In such a system, the teacher has input, other readers corroborate or argue with the teacher's evaluation, the evaluators work with the body of writing that occurs over a semester, and the student's own self-evaluative voice is included. It is a system that exploits rather than eradicating subjectivity.

Teachers who use portfolios often observe that they raise the level of the course—possibly because students have so much more control over what they finally submit for a grade. The portfolio becomes the student's work in progress, and students can monitor and observe their own growth as they revise and hone their work. It is hard to use portfolios on a massive scale, however, because they are time consuming to read and involve an actual course setting and because one of the goals of massive assessment is to use "certified" readers who have no connection to the students. The one-sample evaluation is more efficient and, in a crude sense, fairer. Despite Belanoff's hopes at the time of her speech, the use of standardized tests has increased in the intervening years.

Elaine Brooks's "Evaluating ESL Writing" is a discussion of one particularly troublesome, widespread example of high-stakes testing in writing, the CUNY Writing Assessment Test, given to all entering students at the City University of New York. As of spring 2001, that test has been replaced by another test—two tests, actually, one on entrance and one at 60 credits. Although students will have an opportunity to prepare for the second, "rising junior," test by being given readings ahead of time, the new initial placement test is in many ways similar to the old one. Brooks explains how she evaluates writing samples that students have had only 50 minutes to produce, with no prior knowledge of the subject. To make the situation even more difficult, the students whose work she discusses here are speakers of English as a second language, and in their native culture, the "general interest" topics may be unfamiliar or troubling to the students. They are in the highest stakes situation with no opportunity to prepare, discuss, or revise.

All our knowledge about the nature of composition and assessment tells us how unfair this situation is, and yet this is the situation that obtains for most students at large institutions. "Take a position," they are given to understand, "write quickly, proofread, but don't rewrite, and two people you will never meet will decide whether you pass or not in about three minutes of reading." As Brooks points out, the circumstances make the administration and grading of the test convenient for the testers. They are very inconvenient for the writers.

As a long-time evaluator of such tests, Brooks describes the guidelines that are intended to make this evaluation fair. The readings should be holistic, which means that the reader is looking not only at errors but also at the organization and development of ideas—which means the level of thought and perhaps knowledge of rhetorical strategies displayed in the paper. However, there is an unavoidable tendency among readers of these tests to focus mostly on errors. For one thing, they are "indisputable." One can count them, point to them, name them. ESL students, along with dialect speakers, are at a distinct disadvantage when grades are based on such error counts. They may write more fully elaborated essays than their mainstream counterparts and still fail the exams because their errors are considered too numerous. In her evaluation of two essays, Brooks explains why she thinks one writer is ready for Freshman Composition and the other is not. Her considerations involve not just error but command of syntax, ability to edit—as demonstrated in the kinds of corrections made on the paper—and level of rhetorical sophistication. But, as she points out, grading from a single essay is not ideal.

Another problem engendered by such testing is that the teachers to whom failing students are assigned are then under pressure to "teach to the test," to teach formulas that will help people pass, to teach avoidance strategies. Students learn to keep risky material out of their writing. Peter Elbow observes, "In short, what even the more expensive tests ask for is a kind of parody of what most thoughtful teachers think of as writing."[3] And then, once students pass the test, teachers have to deprogram them so that they can abandon the formulas and learn to range more freely in their thinking.

Readers of assessment tests tend to pay little attention to what students actually say. The questions encourage simple answers, and students usually try not to offend. Richard Miller's "Fault Lines in the Contact Zone" asks us to consider how to respond when students are most flagrantly offensive. What do we do, Miller asks, with an essay that reports a night of gay-bashing and the beating of a homeless man as an entertainment of sorts gone awry, a narrative that may or may not be true, of an experience from which the student may or may not have learned something valuable.

Such an essay, Miller says, was discussed at a "Four Cs" Conference (the Conference on College Composition and Communication), and the responses ranged from referring the student to "a professional counselor or to the police" to evaluating the essay as if it were a fiction. In such a case, can the teacher function as moral authority? Does he have the range of

---

[3]Peter Elbow, *What Is English?* (New York: Modern Language Association and Urbana, IL: National Council of Teachers of English, 1990).

experience to do so? Does she sufficiently understand the nature of the text being produced? Is moral outrage helpful? In such situations, Miller notes, "There seems to be little evidence of what one might call 'poststructural' or 'postcolonial' trickledown, little sign that the theoretical insights that carry so much weight in our journal actually make themselves known in the pedagogical practices deployed in classrooms across the country." Can we practice what, in writing, we preach? Can we acknowledge the classroom as a "contact zone," an open space where prejudices, anger, and fear of the other can be addressed?

Miller's essay presents a course he teaches in which a complex interpretation of texts is invited. Students read Stanley Fish and Gloria Anzaldua, they use writing to confront ambiguities and their own discomfort, and they begin to understand the way their attitudes both enable them to take a stance and limit their understanding. Miller's article pushes us past our own presumed certainties as teachers—as evaluators of the good paragraph, the well-made essay, the right diction, the appropriate way to see things. His course takes us a long way from the teacher-centered classroom, where the teacher explains and the students take notes. While he acknowledges that the power relationships remain asymmetrical because the teacher still gives the grades and creates boundaries, he makes an attempt to circumvent the artificiality of classroom discourse where inappropriate utterances are suppressed or reported to the authorities. No teacher would willingly invite writing that celebrates bigotry or violence, but as we all know, such attitudes and behaviors run through our culture and are used by our media to excite us and to stimulate us to buy their products. When the issues surface in our classrooms, we need a perspective on how to deal with them. Miller's essay, and his course, are a thoughtful response.

Geraldine DeLuca

Chapter 15

Responding to Texts: Facilitating Revision in the Writing Workshop

C. H. Knoblauch and Lil Brannon

C. H. Knoblauch is Professor of English and Chair of the English Department at the University of North Carolina at Charlotte. **Lil Brannon** is Professor of English and Education at the University of North Carolina at Charlotte. They have published extensively on rhetorical theory, composition theory, literacy studies, and pedagogy, including two books together, *Rhetorical Traditions and the Teaching of Writing* and *Critical Teaching and the Idea of Literacy*. The selection that follows is from *Rhetorical Traditions* (Boynton/Cook, 1984).

There is a stock comic situation in which two people go through the motions of communicating but finally fail because each assumes that an idiosyncratic perspective is shared by the other when in fact it is not. A classic instance is the abortive conversation between Walter Shandy and Uncle Toby running through Sterne's marvelously madcap *Tristram Shandy.* Toby is preoccupied with his hobby-horse: he constructs models of famous battles as a means of making order out of the experiences that matter to him (the tentacles of modern rhetoric have a long reach). He employs a language, rich in military allusions and similes, that reflects his priorities, and he hears the remarks of others largely in terms of his own military interests. Walter, meanwhile, has a hobby-horse of his own, a fascination with the austere intellectual world of ancient logic, where presumably dispassionate rational analysis can get at the truth of things and inject coherence into human affairs. Since neither of these peculiar characters is prepared to take into account the viewpoint of the other, talk between them is hilariously oblique and unproductive. Walter's reference to a "train of ideas," for example, suggests to Uncle Toby a "train of artillery": on another occasion, mention of the "bridge" of Tristram's nose is misunderstood as a reference to the Marquis d'Hôpital's drawbridge; and elsewhere, Walter's elegant dissertation on the logical value of auxiliary verbs suggests nothing more to Toby and Corporal Trim than the auxiliary troops at the siege of Limerick. Each time these individuals attempt to converse, their hobby-horses interfere, extinguishing the hope that any constructive meeting of minds can result from acts of language.

The rhetorical principle violated in these abortive conversational efforts is one we have discussed often before now: people cannot communicate unless they first strive to accommodate each other's points of view and decide on a shared basis for talk. Human beings put the principle into practice many times every day in order to accomplish their purposes in both speaking and writing. Probably, the majority of writing teachers are sufficiently persuaded of the importance of audience expectation that they include lectures and exercises on the subject, even "cases" that require students to anticipate different readers on different occasions. Presumably, these teachers understand quite clearly that communication entails a projecting from the self, a struggle to see things as others might see them, so that, by making connections between someone else's understanding and one's own, a strategy can evolve for making and sharing new meanings. What is peculiar, however, about the commitment of writing teachers to "audience" is the extent to which anticipating the perspectives of others is for them a one-way obligation. There's a curious disjunction between what these teachers tell students about projecting outward as the starting point of communication and what they do themselves as aspiring communicators. For in their ways of talking to students, and especially in their habits of responding to student writing, they tend, every bit as much as Uncle Toby does, to ride their own hobby-horses—sometimes to the extent that their students fail utterly to conceive what they might be talking about.

Too often, if not typically, when reading student writing, teachers ignore writers' intentions and meanings in favor of their own agendas, so that what students are attempting to say has remarkably little to do with what teachers are looking for, and therefore little bearing on what they say in comments on student texts. In the least subtle instances, while students are engaged in—let's say describing personal experiences—their teacher is concentrating on the effective of comparison or example; while they struggle dutifully to find significance in *King Lear*, the teacher is defending the imperiled constraints of a term paper or the canons of some, not necessarily announced, critical predisposition; while students are writing to understand the workings of a nuclear reactor, the teacher is enforcing detailed instructions of the assignment on "process analysis"; while they are locating personal meanings in public issues, the teacher is insuring that only the most orthodox opinions are appropriately paraded in all the tiresome pros and cons that arrange themselves repeatedly in school writing. Generally speaking, the hobby-horse of writing teachers is prose decorum, the propriety of discourse extending from its technical features to its formal appearances and even to its intellectual content as a display of approved ideas in conventional relationships to each other.[1] Their point of view largely determines what they talk about, even though it's a point of view that students barely comprehend or see the value of. To an extent, of course, by sheer power of position teachers can demand that students begin to pay attention to their pronouncements about structure and convention, enjoying the modest benefits of one-way conversation. But the question of *quid pro quo* seldom arises, that is, the value, for communication's sake, of paying attention to what matters most to writers by starting with their meanings instead of teacherly priorities when responding to their writing. And what is jeopardized as a consequence is the possibility of real communication, the chance to make intellectual progress through purposeful dialogue.[2]

Given the environment surrounding traditional instruction, it's perhaps not so surprising that teachers have missed the fact that responding to student writing is a species of communication, subject, therefore, to the same rhetorical principles that govern other situations. For communication, or dialogue, is a democratic act: both sides get to score points. Yet, the classic teacher-student relationship is defined, as we have suggested, in authoritarian terms, master and apprentice, knower and learner, talker and listener. In typical writing courses, students produce discourse not in order to be listened to but in order to give teachers something to talk about. Since the authority for judging pertinence, propriety, and effectiveness in writing rests with the teacher, then, paradoxically, the control of compositional choices ultimately belongs with the teacher as well. Could a more peculiar rhetorical situation possibly exist than one in which the person supposedly creating a text must yield control of its character and shape to the ostensible audience? Such is often the case in classrooms: the teacher's agenda is the one that matters, so the responsibility for anticipating expectations lies wholly with students. To the extent that the teacher's expectations are not satisfied, authority over the writing is stolen from the writer by means of comments, oral or written, that represent the teacher's agenda, whatever the writer's intentions may initially have been. A student's task is to match an Ideal Text in the teacher's imagination which is insinuated through the teacher's commentary, not to pursue personal intentions according to the writer's own developing sense of what he or she wishes to say.[3] The student writer, in other words, is obliged to work diligently at locating a teacher's hobby-horse, experiencing some predictable frustration in the process, while the teacher is under no requirement to anticipate the writer's purposes before making comments on a text. The teacher's reading strategy is simply to apply his or her own inevitably reductive Ideal Text to students' actual writing, and to remark on discrepancies between the two, which the students are then called upon to reduce as the measure of their competences as writers.[4] It's the

rare composition teacher who reads student writing with the assumption
that composers legitimately control their own discourses, who accepts the
possibility that student intentions matter more than teacher expectations
as a starting-point for reading, and who recognizes that writers' choices
are supposed to make sense mainly in terms of those intentions, not in
proportion as they gratify a reader's view of what should have been said.

An experiment we have conducted suggests the pervasiveness of the
concept of Ideal Text among writing teachers and the strength of their
resistance to honoring writer intentions when responding to their writing. We asked forty teachers to comment as they normally would on a particular student essay. The writer had studied the Lindbergh kidnapping
trial and had produced a text simulating the closing argument of the
prosecuting attorney. His text was heavily laden with emotional appeals to
the jury because, he had told us, his intent was to create sympathy for the
injured Lindberghs and revulsion against the accused. He believed that
emotional language would be suited to this intent. Here is a portion of
his writing:

> Ladies and gentlemen of the jury, I wholeheartedly believe that the evidence
> which has been presented before you has clearly shown that the man who is
> on trial here today is beyond a doubt guilty of murder of the darling, little,
> innocent Lindbergh baby.
>
> Sure, the defendant has stated his innocence. But who are we to believe?
> Do we believe the testimony of a man who has been previously convicted; in
> fact convicted to holding up innocent women wheeling baby carriages? Or do
> we believe the testimony of one of our nation's greatest heroes, Charles A.
> Lindbergh? Mr. Lindbergh believes the defendant is guilty. So do I.
>
> All I ask, ladies and gentlemen of the jury, is that you look at the evi-
> dence. . . .

When we asked teachers to read this text, but without benefit of the
writer's explanation of intent (a disadvantage which did not, however,
appear to bother them), they divided into two groups. One group felt
that the emotional language showed the writer's immaturity and undeveloped rhetorical sense: their comments betrayed an Ideal Text featuring
detached logical rigor and care for the details of evidence as the essential
characteristics of a trial prosecutor's summation. The student's writing
failed to anticipate these characteristics and therefore failed, in the eyes
of one group of teachers, to demonstrate proficiency. The second group's
conclusion was more interesting. Its members upheld the same Ideal
Text, showed the same concern for logic and explanatory detail; but they

reasoned that, since the writer could not possibly have been serious in resorting to blatant emotional appeals, the discourse must represent a wonderful spoof of the genre of "trial summation." Therefore, the writer must be unusually mature and the writing a clever demonstration of exceptional competence (though containing some technical flaws that could be corrected readily enough). The significant point here is that neither group stopped to consider the possibility that the student might have had a serious intent to use emotional appeal or that its use might constitute a plausible strategy in this situation. Instead, secure in their shared concept of an Ideal Text, both groups advanced without hesitation to precisely opposite conclusions about the merits of the writer's text and the ability of the writer himself.

Later, we showed these teachers both the student's description of intent and a transcript of portions of the actual summation delivered during the Lindbergh trial, which revealed the very emotional appeals to which the student writer had resorted, thereby suggesting the arbitrariness of the teachers' assumed Ideal Text.

> Why, men and women, if that little baby, if that little, curly-haired youngster were out in the grass in the jungle, breathing, just so long as it was breathing, any tiger, any lion, the most venomous snake would have passed that child without hurting a hair of its head.

Of course, the fact that the original attorney used such appeals does not imply that only one strategy exists for preparing trial summations. It only suggests that emotional appeals are no less legitimate than other strategies, so that the teachers' refusal to take the student writer's choices seriously, acknowledging the authority of that writer to choose in accordance with his own intentions, indicated the inappropriate tyranny of an Ideal Text over their commenting practices. The fact that their judgments were polarized, yet derived from a common prejudice, helps to make our point about Ideal Texts. But it would not be surprising if the student writer found either response puzzling since, in each case, the teachers were attending to their own predispositions and not to the student's effort to make meanings. The likelihood of serious, purposeful communication with that student would have to have been severely reduced.

The writing workshop depends on a style of response which differs altogether from that of traditional instruction because its concern is not merely to elicit writing in order to judge it, but to sustain writing through successive revisions in pursuit of richer insights and concurrently the maturation of competence. The workshop style assumes, above all, that, if teachers seriously aim to communicate with students about their writing and thereby affect students' performance, they must begin with what matters most to those writers, namely, the making of meaningful statements consistent with the writers' own purposes and their own estimations of how best to achieve them. In nearly every circumstance except the classical composition course, reading entails accepting a writer's authority to make precisely the choices that have been made in order to say precisely what the writer wishes to say. Readers seek gradually to understand and appreciate a writer's purposes by assessing the effects of textual choices on their way of seeing the subject. They suspend their own preconceptions, to a degree, in order to understand the writer's position, taking for granted the writer's capacity to make a position clear unless there is substantial reason to believe otherwise.[5] This seems a fair starting-point in responding to student writing as well, no matter how skeptical a teacher may be about a particular writer's ability to control choices. Instead of beginning with the supposition that the teacher-reader is rightfully in control rather than the writers, so that their discourses are valued only to the extent that they meet the teacher's preconceptions, the workshop reader begins—as most readers do—with an implicit trust in the writer's choice-making and with a concern to discover the writer's intentions rather than automatically preempting them with personal concerns. The main reason for returning to this normal reading habit is that the responders imply by doing so that they value writer's efforts to make meaning, thereby creating a powerful incentive to write. Conversely, the traditional tendency to preempt intentions diminishes incentive because it shows students that readers fail to value what they have to say.

What every teacher knows, of course, is that student writing does not always succeed in conveying or achieving its intentions. The workshop teacher knows this as well as anyone, but knows also that motivation to write depends crucially on the belief that the writing will be taken seriously—in other words, that the writer's authority to make statements in his or her own way will be respected. We are not recommending a suspension of the critical faculty in responding to student writing, but only an essentially receptive rather than essentially evaluative reading posture.[6] Rather than taking for granted a writer's proven or unproven ineptitude, which encourages the usurping of the writer's text as frequently as the teacher prefers, we suggest the normal posture of taking the writer's competence *generally* for granted, which encourages respecting the writer's choices as plausible alternatives as long as they appear to support his or her own purposes. When teachers begin reading student texts with the calculated (as opposed to naive) expectation that the writing is purposeful and suited to its own ends, their style of responding to it necessarily changes. Comments begin to register, not the discrepancy between a discourse and some teacher's personal Ideal Text, but rather the discrepancy between a writer's projected intentions and the effects of actual choices on an experienced reader's awareness of what the writer wishes to say. Any response will be designed to reveal the reader's uncertainties about the substance of the writer's communication, depending on a knowledge of the writer's purposes as the touchstone for recommending revisions. This reading posture is specially suited to the writing workshop because of its emphasis on revision as a natural feature of composing. The idea of response is to offer perceptions of uncertainty, incompleteness, unfulfilled promises, unrealized opportunities, as motivation for more writing and therefore more learning about a subject as well as more successful communication of whatever has been learned.

The relationship between response and revision is important. In traditional practice, commenting on student writing is essentially a product-centered, evaluative activity resembling literary criticism. Students write "papers" so that teachers can describe their strengths and weaknesses, grading them accordingly. The papers are then, often, simply retired and new ones composed, presumably under the influence of recollected judgments of the previous ones. The assumption has been that evaluating products of composing is equivalent to intervening in the process. Teachers have concentrated, therefore, on retrospective appraisals of "finished" discourses, where students either do no rewriting at all or perform superficial copy-editing exercises to make their discourses conform to a teacher's Ideal Text. This emphasis on product encourages a directive style of commentary, the function of which is either simply to label the errors in writing or to define restrictively what a student would (or will) have to do in order to perfect it in the teacher's eyes. The following response to a sample of student writing suggests the character of a directive commenting style. It may seem an exaggerated instance, and perhaps it is. But both the essay and the comments are genuine, coming from an actual first-year college writing class.

A lot of factors can contribute to the
rejection of a student by a college./It   *This is obvious –*
could be the student is not the type   *cut it out!*
of youngster that the college wants,
perhaps he/she did not do well on the
                 ^ or
SATs or did not have a good high school
recommendation.
No matter what the reason is, a

*Unclear—
avoid "if" if
you can*

rejected student should never feel sad

about (it) because being rejected is not
as   *Proofread!*   ¶ *Start new paragraph with*
that awful as people (image.) First of (all)   *this idea*
            — avoid this — use many
(al) colleges are basically the same, but

once (you) made a choice of a few, (you) have
        ↑don't use you in a formal essay — you started with
kind of idealize it to be the kind of   *"student"*
                ↑a
college which is perfect for (you) however

(it) is not true! There are thousands of

*Whew!
This should be
2 or 3
sentences.*

colleges throughout the country, a lot

of them could be very suitable for you.

Therefore, do not (intend to) restrict
                G R   *↑unnecessary — this weakens what*
(yourself, go (reach out) to more colleges   *you want to*
                                               say.
and find a (better) one for yourself.
                ↑"a more suitable one" Maybe?

*Use a
dictionary!*

(If the college of (your) choice is a

highly-reputated) and (you) get rejected   *Do you really*
                                                 mean "Do not
rephrase — by it) do not worry] Find (yourself a   *worry?"*
second choice college
lower-ranked one and work hard in it,
            often   *a*
because it is easier to get high

*RUN ON
SENTENCE
BREAK IT
UP!*

average in those schools, then you can
always transfer back to some really *your first choice*
                or perhaps
famous school, maybe you can go to their *one of its*

graduate schools later.

Unclear!

anymore, (it) is not totally a bad idea, *What?*

society is a wonderful college itself and

once you come out to work, you acquire

knowledge from (it.) You can also go back
                            like
to evening school if you prefer to do so /*simplify!*

after working for a while.
            everybody has
    Finally, (we all have) disappointments
life
in (our lives.) Getting rejected by the

college of (your) choice is only a minor

one, most people, including ~~me~~ have — *Keep yourself out of the essay. This is a formal essay.*

and should survive it and ~~take it easy~~

Is this what you mean?

Your last ¶ should also restate that, as you have shown, there are good reasons not to despair about rejection. Use the last ¶ to tidy up the essay.

You're on the right track here, and your overall structure of developing new ideas in each paragraph is pretty good. But your writing becomes unhinged a bit within each ¶. You need to work on expressing your ideas as simply as possible — avoid unnecessary wording. (see my comments on your second sentence for example.)

Also, watch your tendency to write run-on sentences. For example, the second sentence of your second ¶ is quite a mouthful and goes zig-zag all over the place. Again, simplify!

Be sure you mean what you say. Don't use " it " if you can avoid it. Be more definite with your words.

Finally, proofread and use a dictionary if you are unsure of a spelling or word meaning. Errors in these areas are annoying and teachers will mark you down because of them.

Rewrite — be more careful, and good luck !

In the worst case, this essay with attached corrections would simply be put away and the student would be expected to move on to the next assignment with some memory of the mistakes committed earlier. But even if revision were required, the writer would mainly be obeying the teacher's prescriptions about structural and technical deficiencies, as though the text in its present form were a fixed entity and the revising only a matter of making the product as respectable as possible. Notice the authoritarian character of the teacher-critic's responses, aiming in effect to take control of the writer's discourse: "This is obvious—cut it out"; "don't use 'you' in a formal essay"; "start a new paragraph with this idea"; "simplify!" We could reconstruct this teacher's Ideal Text rather easily, but it's more important to note how uncommunicative and how unresponsive to the writer's perspective the teacher's comments are. Formal constraints, the teacher's hobby-horse,

are far more important than the writer's concern to make a statement
about being rejected by a college. Indeed, the first sentence of the
teacher's end comment suggests that the "ideas" in the essay are adequate
enough (which is really a way of dismissing them), and that the important
matter is prose decorum. The teacher's confidence that the student somehow secretly understands the operative Ideal Text allows for comments
such as "avoid unnecessary wording," "be sure you mean what you say," and
"be more definite with your words," which are surely as incomprehensible
to the student as Walter Shandy's discussion of auxiliary verbs was to Uncle
Toby. An interesting question is, how much "better" would this writing be if
all the local problems that bothered the teacher were removed? It seems to
us that it would still be intellectually shallow and rhetorically immature,
even if its newly polished surface covered the shallowness and immaturity
with a somewhat more pleasing veneer. But the teacher's concern for a sal-
vageable product rather than the writer's evolving meaning accounts for
the directive preoccupation with veneer.

An alternative to directive commentary, a style that is valued in the writing workshop, is facilitative response, the purpose of which is to create
motivation for immediate and substantive revision by describing a careful
reader's uncertainties about what a writer intends to say. Here's the same
student text with responses that are facilitative rather than directive.

How important   A lot of factors can contribute to the
are these factors?
Do you imply   rejection of a student by a college. It
that they are   could be the student is not the type of
relative or   youngster that the college wants, perhaps
that they   he/she did not do well on the SATs or did
don't always
matter? Is   not have a good high school recommendation.
your essay   No matter what the reason is, a rejected
going to be
about these   student should never feel sad about it
factors?   because being rejected is not that awful
                       as people image. First of all, [all colleges *What criteria*
                                                                      lead you to
                       are basically the same,] but once you made *decide this?*
                                                                          Size?
                       a choice of a few, you have kind of idealize *Location?*
                       it to the kind of college which is perfect *Program offerings?*
                                                                   the kind of student
                                                                          body?

But if all colleges are the same, then aren't all of them equally suitable? why only "a lot"? Do you really believe they are all suitable? what might determine suitability?

for you however it is not true! (There are thousands of colleges throughout the country, a lot of them could be very suitable for you.) Therefore, do not intend to restrict yourself, go reach out to [more colleges] and find a better one for yourself. ← *any old college?*

If the college of your choice is a highly-reputated and you get rejected by it, do not worry, Find yourself a [lower-ranked one] and work hard in it, because it is easier to get high average in those schools, then you can always transfer back to some [really famous school] maybe you can go to their graduate schools later.

If some are "lower ranked" then in what sense are they all "the same."

Is this a difference between colleges?

If you feel as bad after being rejected that you do not feel like going to college anymore, it is not totally a bad idea, society is a wonderful college itself and once you come out to work, you acquire knowledge from it. You can also go back to evening school if you prefer to do so after working for a while.

Are you saying that it doesn't really matter? Do you believe that?

Finally, we all have disappointments in our lives. Getting rejected by the college of your choice is (only a minor one,) most people, including me, have and should survive it and take it easy.

For everyone? Would it be for you?

This sounds interesting - have you been rejected? Would it be worth talking about?

I can't tell whether your purpose here is just to make someone feel better or really to argue that all colleges are alike and that going or not going is an unimportant decision: in either case, do you really believe your statement? That is, would it make no difference if, for instance, you were forced to leave [the student's present school]? If so, why are you here now? Would you be just as happy at East Altuna Junior College in North Dakota? If you don't think you would, then do you think your reader would be consoled by what you say?

The comments of a facilitative reader are designed to preserve the writer's control of the discourse, while also registering uncertainty about what the writer wishes to communicate. The questions posed suggest the possibility of negotiation between writer and reader, leading to richer insights and more meaningful communication.[7] Negotiation assumes that the writer knows better than the reader the purposes involved, while the reader knows better than the writer the actual effects of authorial choices. The dialogue initiated by the comments (which may also be sustained by oral conversation) enables the writer to reflect on the connection between what was meant and what a reader has understood, using any difference between intent and effect as an incentive to test new choices. But importantly, the reader's engagement with the text is on a level similar to that of the writer's, namely, the level of meaning, line of reasoning, intellectual potentiality, thereby enabling dialogue and negotiation as opposed to editorial prescriptions. Emphasis is on the writer's developing understanding of the subject—in other words, the process of composing rather than the absolute quality of an achieved text. The comment on the writer's last sentence, for instance, concerning the somewhat veiled reference to a personal experience of rejection, suggests the possibility of a radically new focus to the writing, which the composer is free to consider though not constrained to adopt. Meanwhile, the end comment, which confesses the reader's uncertainty about the writer's purposes, suggests some of the problems of stance and intent which can lead to additional writing while avoiding the temptation to take control of choice-making from the writer by supplying a formula or direction for solving the problem. The writer and reader may, of course discuss possibilities together, but the quality of a negotiated agreement to revise in one way as opposed to another depends on the teacher's skill at supporting the writer's exploration of alternatives while not directing its outcome.

Let's be clear about the difference between directive arid facilitative commentary: it's not a difference between "form" response and "content" response, nor is it a difference between making statements about a text and just asking questions, nor is it a difference between being negative and being positive, criticizing writers versus praising them. Responses to content can be as directive as responses to form: for instance, given the paper on college rejection, a teacher could say, "you need to give us an example of a college of high repute" or "colleges don't care about SATs, so omit the reference"—both plainly directive comments. Alternatively, facilitative responses can pertain to formal problems at times; for instance, "I can't tell what the 'it' in the second sentence of your second paragraph refers to, given the previous references to 'all colleges' and 'at the colleges'—are you thinking now of a single college?" Similarly, directive comments can take the shape of questions: "Is this a complete sentence?" means essentially "Change this into a complete sentence"; and facilitative comments can take the shape of assertions: "I don't see why you think being rejected from a college can be a beneficial experience." The distinction lies deeper than superficial comment form. Finally, criticism of what doesn't seem effective and support of what does can be found in both directive and facilitative commentary; they are equal parts of any healthy interaction between teachers and students, by no means parallel to the methodological distinction between giving directions in one commentary and characterizing a reader's uncertainties in the other. The essential difference between the two commenting styles is the degree of control over choices that the writer or the teacher retains. In directive commentary, the teacher says or implies, "Don't do it your way; do it *this* way." In facilitative commentary, the teacher says or implies, "Here's what your choices have caused me to think you're saying—if my response differs from your intent, how can you help me to see what you mean?" The essential difference—as is so often the case in the teaching alternatives we have been discussing—lies more in attitude and outlook than in perceivable changes of technique.

Of course, the majority of facilitative responses on the college rejection essay do take a question form and all of them happen to be "content" oriented. The tendency of a facilitative comment to take the form of a question is natural enough, since the reader's posture is probing and provocative, aimed at making the writer more reflective about the sufficiency of choices, rather than prescriptions about changes that must be made. But it's important to emphasize the positive beneath the surface appearance of a comment; attitude shapes practice, not the other way around. The content orientation is also natural, given the primitive exploratory nature of the writing and given the priorities of the writing workshops—fluency, then clarity, then correctness. Doubtless, this writing has numerous formal and technical deficiencies: but it's also so far away from the copy-editing stage

suggested by the comments of the teacher-critic that pointing out the deficiencies is superfluous. If the writer's ideas are not further developed, then
none of the technical recommendations will make the writing any better
than it is. On the other hand, if a next draft does substantially alter the writing in this earlier text, then many of the choices here will have been eliminated in the revision. We're not saying that form and technique are irrelevant and never to be responded to; we're only arguing that first things
should come first, that a writer's on-going pursuit of meanings should be a
teacher-reader's first consideration. As meanings emerge, as the relationship between intention and effect stabilizes, as successive revisions develop,
narrower and more local concerns about structure and technical subtlety
may well become appropriate. But the maturity of the writer and the intel-
lectual/imaginative quality of his or her writing determine the usefulness
of a more technical response: in general, the less real control of technique
a writer possesses, the less intrusive should be the commentary on technical
matters and the more conspicuous should be the response pertinent to
emerging meanings.

The purpose, then, of facilitative commentary is to induce the reformu-
lation of texts, the pursuit of new connections and the discovery of richer
or more comprehensive meanings. By contrast, the main function of directive commentary is to make a given text look as good as it can. We would
not suggest, however, that the mere presence of facilitative comments automatically leads to the substantive revision we have in mind. Without additional support, students will tend to make only the limited textual changes
that directive responses elicit, even when the facilitative responses offer a
fuller potential for new discovery. An inexperienced writer's natural tendency is to restrict revising to changes that minimally affect the plan and
order of ideas with which she or he began, readily making only those
adjustments that involve least pressure to reconceive or significantly extend
the writing already done. This is not a matter simply of laziness. The resistance is normal, arising out of the anxiety that even experienced writers
feel at having to reduce an achieved coherence, however inadequate, to
the chaos of fragments and undeveloped insights from which they started.
Practiced writers overcome their anxiety through habitual success in rewriting, but no such comforting pattern of successes exists to steady the resolve
of the apprentice. Nor is this natural psychological resistance the only barrier to self-initiated revising. Another is the sheer difficulty of perceiving
alternatives to the choices that have already been made, choices that lie rei-
fied as a document. The temptation is strong, even among experienced
writers, to forget the arbitrariness of so many initial decisions about what to
say, imagining in retrospect an inevitability about the patterns and connections that make up the existing discourse. Seeing through that apparent
inevitability in order to recover additional options requires an intellectual

discipline and a rhetorical awareness that unpracticed writers frequently have not acquired—indeed that they come to writing courses to develop.[8]

Perhaps the most concentrated effort in a writing workshop, therefore, is devoted to supporting substantive revision, for it is during revision that new learning is most likely to occur and competence most likely to develop. The first concern is to reveal to students, through the expectations implicit in facilitative responses, that "revision" does not mean copy-editing or, in general, making a given text more presentable. Nor does it mean superficial additions—"give more details," or subtractions—"this isn't relevant to your thesis," or redecorating "move this paragraph to page 4." It means deeper intellectual penetration of a subject through additional composing, even to the point of repudiating earlier formulations altogether because subtler or more powerful insights have inspired new organizing principles and lines of reasoning. In-class writing to which students have not as yet committed major effort offers a good initial context for nurturing this view of revising. Making substantive changes is likely to entail less intimidation, less psychological resistance, when investment in a given text is still relatively small, as in the case of fifteen or twenty minutes of exploratory writing in class to be revised following comments from peers and the teacher-reader. Repeated short experiments in revision, with attentive teacher and peer support, can help create a willingness to try again, a strength of mind for reconceiving texts which will carry over into larger-scale efforts. But encouragement remains equally necessary later, once students have become more willing to take chances. Writers need opportunities in workshop for discussing their rewriting plans with each other and with the teacher-reader. They need time to ask questions about responses and to test new choices on their readers. Less adventuresome or self-reliant students may need particular coaching—perhaps being encouraged to rewrite short statements with the instructor looking on and explaining his or her uncertainties about evolving meanings. Such activities are time-consuming, but there's no better way to spend the time. The revisions will be halting and inconsistently successful, especially at the start, but there's no more productive kind of failure, provided that what is emphasized is not the kinds and degree of failure but the glimmerings of communicative success.

Two awkward questions arise about the connection between facilitative commentary and the process of revision. Teachers naturally feel that their obligation in responding to writing is to locate the "major" problems or the most promising opportunities for change—hence, the first question: are there optimal responses that will help writers make the best possible revisions? At the same time, teachers believe that the whole point of revision is to make texts better than they were in earlier versions—hence, the second question: shouldn't improvement from one draft to the next be expected as a sign both of commenting effectiveness and of writers' "progress" toward maturity? The insights of contemporary reader-response theory suggest some answers that will trouble teachers who expect the significant features of student writing and the degree of textual improvement to be readily and objectively verifiable. Louise Rosenblatt, first, and later Wolfgang Iser, David Bleich, and others,[9] have argued that all reading experiences entail transactions between reader and text, not a passive retrieval of meanings residing in the text and equally accessible to all careful observers, but an active creation of personal significances and impressions of quality based on individual responses. Readings are always, to a degree, idiosyncratic, dependent on the life-experiences, attitudes, feelings, beliefs, prejudices, which cause individuals to value different things and to construe in different ways. For reader response theorists, therefore, the idea of a single "correct" or authoritative reading is problematic. Even highly experienced readers will view the same text differently, with dissimilar focuses of attention, various expectations, opposed notions about which textual cues are important or how they are important. The result is alternative but equally plausible transactions. Is there any reason to assume that responding to student writing entails more objectivity, less eccentricity, than responding to other texts? We think not.

So, our answer to the first question, in light of reader-response theory, is that there are no optimal responses, only more and less honest ones. Different readers find more or less meaning in different cues, and one teacher will view the potential in a student text differently from the way another does. Genuine personal reactions to a student's writing—for instance, the teacher's interest in the writer's own brush with disappointment in the college rejection essay—may not find duplication from reader to reader, but they are no less honest or potentially provocative for the writer's further efforts because of their individuality. Indeed, they are preferable to more formulaic, directive responses—for instance, to strike the reference to personal rejection as unsuited to the text's "main point"—which may well be dishonest in their overrestriction of valid lines of inquiry or development. Our answer to the second question is equally dependent on reader-response research: if different readers have alternative views of what is meaningful, valuable, interesting, or flawed in a text, then they will also have different notions about what would constitute "improvement" of that text. Teachers are sometimes tempted to correlate improvement with their personal preferences, to associate a student's willingness to follow directions with "better writing" on subsequent drafts. The chances are good, however, that no two teacher-readers will have the same opinion about how or why or the extent to which one draft of an essay is better than another. The perception of improvement in revised writing will always involve subjective, idiosyncratic judgments, even when the criteria for improvement include nothing subtler than avoiding surface errors and following teacher's directions about where or how to say things. Once richer criteria are also included, such as intellectual penetration of the subject, or quality of imaginative insight, or even closer proximity between intention and effect, the teacher's own consistency of judgment from student to student, essay to essay, is likely to deteriorate, let alone the consistency among different readers which would be required to assert an objective basis for evaluation. Since such a basis would be hard, if not impossible, to establish, teachers might be well-advised not to place such store in their powers of discernment as to expect that they can readily distinguish flawed from improved drafts. And if improvement is so difficult to perceive reliably, it seems pointless to depend on such a concept as the measure of commenting effectiveness. We would argue, instead, that once student writers have pursued worthwhile meanings through successive drafts, assisted by readers' personal reactions to the coherence, value, and communicative effectiveness of their developing discourses, their efforts have been successful by definition, because they serve the long-range goal of intellectual growth and the maturation of composing ability. Whether or not a second draft represents improvement over a first draft in some objective sense is not only extremely difficult to determine but is also irrelevant to the value of the process itself.

NOTES

1. A recent study has shown that more than half of the teachers surveyed restricted their commentary on student writing to narrowly technical corrections, while practically no teachers offered substantive responses intended to encourage revision. See Dennis Searle and David Dillon, "The Message of Marking: Teacher Written Responses to Student Writing at Intermediate Grade Levels," *Research in the Teaching of English,* 14 (October 1980), 233–242. On the limitations of technical correction, see W. U. McDonald, "The Revising Process and the Marking of Student Papers," *College Composition and Communication,* 24 (May 1978), 167–170.
2. Nancy Sommers has pointed out the uncommunicative nature of typical responses to student writing in "Responding to Student Writing," *College Composition and Communication,* 33 (May 1982), 148–156.
3. The concept of Ideal Text, and the argument related to the Lindbergh essay, are developed in Lil Brannon and C. H. Knoblauch, "On Students' Rights to Their Own Texts: A Model of Teacher Response," *College Composition and Communication,* 33 (May 1982), 157–166.
4. Study after study has shown the futility of this method of responding to writing, students' subsequent efforts revealing little or no change

as a result of the commentary. See, for instance, in addition to Searle and Dillon, R. J. Marzana and S. Arthur, "Teacher Comments on Student Essays: It Doesn't Matter What You Say," a study conducted at the University of Colorado, Denver, in 1977 (ERIC ED 147864). For a review of several studies, all reporting negative results, and an argument for the reasons, see C. H. Knoblauch and Lil Brannon, "Teacher Commentary on Student Writing: The State of the Art," *Freshman English News,* 10 (Fall 1981), 1–4.

5. "Ethos" is, of course, an ancient concept—see Aristotle, *Rhetoric,* 1356a2. When readers accept writers' authority, and usually they do at least at the start of reading, they work at understanding what the writer intends to say. I. A. Richards has noted the power of authority in *Practical Criticism* (New York: Harcourt, Brace, 1929), p. 297. The mere name of a well-known poet is enough to ensure attentive reading of a mediocre work, yet a perfectly fine example of student writing will be criticized and subordinated to an Ideal Text, whatever its merits.

6. This reading posture is perhaps a version of Peter Elbow's "believing game." See *Writing Without Teachers* (New York: Oxford University Press, 1973), pp. 169 ff.

7. Donald Murray has shown how oral facilitative response, not just written, can help students become wise questioners of their own texts by first hearing the supportive questions of teachers. See "Teaching the Other Self: The Writer's First Reader," *College Composition and Communication,* 33 (May 1982), 140–147.

8. Several studies of the revision process of less-experienced writers illustrate this point. See Nancy Sommers, "Revision Strategies of Student Writers and Experienced Adult Writers," *College Composition and Communication,* 31 (December 1980), 378–388; Lester Faigley and Stephen Witte, "Analyzing Revision," *College Composition and Communication,* 32 (December 1981), 400–414; Richard Beach, "Self-Evaluation Strategies of Extensive Revisers and Non-Revisers," *College Composition and Communication,* 27 (1976), 160–164; Richard Beach, "The Effects of Between-Draft Teacher Evaluation Versus Student Self-Evaluation on High School Students' Revising of Rough Drafts," *Research in the Teaching of English,* 13 (1979), 111–119; and Lillian S. Bridwell, "Revising Strategies in Twelfth Grade Students' Transactional Writing," *Research in the Teaching of English,* 14 (October 1980), 197–222.

9. Louise Rosenblatt first explored the active behaviors of readers in *Literature as Exploration* (New York: Noble and Noble, 1938), and later in *The Reader, the Text, the Poem: The Transactional Theory of the Literary Work* (Carbondale: Southern Illinois University Press, 1978). For the work of various reader-response theorists, see Jane Tomp-

kins, ed., *Reader Response Criticism: From Formalism to Post-Structuralism* (Baltimore: Johns Hopkins, 1980) and Susan R. Suleiman and Inge Crosman, eds., *The Reader in the Text: Essays on Audience and Interpretation* (Princeton: Princeton University Press, 1980).

QUESTIONS FOR REFLECTION, JOURNAL WRITING, AND DISCUSSION

1. Knoblauch and Brannon say that revision should be "deeper intellectual penetration of a subject through additional composing, even to the point of repudiating earlier formulations altogether." Do you agree? If so, how can we get students to do this?

2. What do Knoblauch and Brannon mean by the "Ideal Text" that teachers have in their mind? Do you have an "Ideal Text" in your mind when you respond to student papers? If so, what is it like?

3. Do students try to produce the sorts of "Ideal Texts" that teachers have in their minds? If so, is this a good thing?

4. Consider how your own teachers responded to your work. Did you receive more "directive" or "facilitative" responses? Which was more helpful?

5. Look at the actual comments that you made on a recent student paper. Are they directive or facilitative? Would you want to change them in any way?

Chapter 16

The Listening Eye: Reflections on the Writing Conference

Donald M. Murray

Donald M. Murray, Professor Emeritus of English at the University of New Hampshire, continues to write in retirement. He publishes a weekly column "Over 60" in the *Boston Globe,* and this year he has published *Writing to Deadline* (Heinemann) and the fourth edition of *The Craft of Revision* (Harcourt). He has also completed the seventh edition of *Write to Learn* (Harcourt), and *A Twice-Lived Life—A Memoir of Aging* has recently been published by Ballantine. He is working on a novel and a collection of poems. The article that follows is from *College English,* 41, September 1979.

It was dark when I arrived at my office this winter morning, and it is dark again as I wait for my last writing student to step out of the shadows in the corridor for my last conference. I am tired, but it is a good tired, for my students have generated energy as well as absorbed it. I've learned something of what it is to be a childhood diabetic, to raise oxen, to work across from your father at 115 degrees in a steeldrum factory, to be a welfare mother with three children, to build a bluebird trail, to cruise the disco scene, to be a teen-age alcoholic, to salvage World War II wreckage under the Atlantic, to teach invented spelling to first graders, to bring your father home to die of cancer. I have been instructed in other lives, heard the voices of my students they had not heard before, shared their satisfaction in solving the problems of writing with clarity and grace. I sit quietly in the late afternoon waiting to hear what Andrea, my next student, will say about what she accomplished on her last draft and what she intends on her next draft.

It is nine weeks into the course and I know Andrea well. She will arrive in a confusion of scarves, sweaters, and canvas bags, and then produce a clipboard from which she will precisely read exactly what she has done and exactly what she will do. I am an observer of her own learning, and I am eager to hear what she will tell me.

I am surprised at this eagerness. I am embedded in tenure, undeniably middle-aged, one of the gray, fading professors I feared I would become, but still have not felt the bitterness I saw in many of my own professors and see in some of my colleagues. I wonder if I've missed something important, if I'm becoming one of those aging juveniles who bound across the campus from concert to lecture, pleasantly silly.

There must be something wrong with a fifty-four-year-old man who is looking forward to his thirty-fifth conference of the day. It is twelve years since I really started teaching by conference. I average seventy-five conferences a week, thirty weeks a year, then there's summer teaching and workshop teaching of teachers. I've probably held far more than 30,000 writing conferences, and I am still fascinated by this strange, exposed kind of teaching, one on one.

It doesn't seem possible to be an English teacher without the anxiety that I will be exposed by my colleagues. They will find out how little I do; my students will expose me to them; the English Department will line up in military formation in front of Hamilton Smith Hall and, after the buttons are cut off my Pendleton shirt, my university library card will be torn once across each way and let flutter to the ground.

The other day I found myself confessing to a friend, "Each year I teach less and less, and my students seem to learn more. I guess what I've learned to do is to stay out of their way and not to interfere with their learning."

I can still remember my shock years ago when I was summoned by a secretary from my classroom during a writing workshop. I had labored hard but provoked little discussion. I was angry at the lack of student involvement and I was angry at the summons to the department office. I stomped back to the classroom and was almost in my chair before I realized the classroom was full of talk about the student papers. My students were not even aware I had returned. I moved back out to the corridor, feeling rejected, and let the class teach itself.

Of course, that doesn't always happen, and you have to establish the climate, the structure, the attitude. I know all that, and yet . . .

I used to mark up every student paper diligently. How much I hoped my colleagues would see how carefully I marked my student papers. I alone held the bridge against the pagan hordes. No one escaped the blow of my "awk." And then one Sunday afternoon a devil bounded to the arm of my chair. I started giving purposefully bad counsel on my students' papers to see what would happen. "Do this backward," "add adjectives and adverbs," "be general and abstract," "write with a purple pencil," "you don't mean black you mean white." Not one student questioned my comments.

I was frightened my students would pay so much attention to me. They took me far more seriously than I took myself. I remembered a friend in advertising told me about a head copywriter who accepted a piece of work from his staff and held it overnight without reading it. The next day he called in the staff and growled, "Is this the best you can do?"

They hurried to explain that if they had more time they could have done better. He gave them more time. And when they met the new deadline, he held their copy again without reading it, and called them together again and said, "Is *this* the best you can do?"

Again they said if only they had more time, they could . . . He gave them a new deadline. Again he held their draft without reading it. Again he gave it back to them. Now they were angry. They said, yes, it was the best they could do and he answered, "I'll read it."

I gave my students back their papers unmarked, and said, make them better. And they did. That isn't exactly the way I teach now, not quite, but I did learn something about teaching writing.

In another two-semester writing course I gave 220 hours of lecture during the year. My teaching evaluations were good: students signed up to take this course in advance. Apparently I was well-prepared, organized, entertaining. No one slept in my class, at least with their eyes shut, and all did well on the final exam. But that devil found me in late August working over my lecture notes and so, on the first day of class, I gave the same final exam I had given at the end of the year. My students did better before the 220 hours of lectures than my students had done afterwards. I began to learn something about teaching a non-content writing course, about under-teaching, about not teaching what my students already know.

The other day a graduate student who wanted to teach writing in a course I supervise indicated, "I have no time for non-directive teaching. I know what my students need to know. I know the problems they will have—and I teach them."

I was startled, for I do not know what my students will be able to do until they write without any instruction from me. But he had a good reputation, and I read his teaching evaluations. The students liked him, but there was a minor note of discomfort. "He does a good job of teaching, but I wish he would not just teach me what I already know" and "I wish he would listen better to what we need to know." But they liked him. They could understand what he wanted, and they could give it to him. I'm uncomfortable when my students are uncomfortable, but more uncomfortable when they are comfortable.

I teach the student not the paper but this doesn't mean I'm a "like wow" teacher. I am critical and I certainly can be directive but I listen before I speak. Most times my students make tough, sometimes too tough evaluations of their work. I have to curb their too critical eye and help them see what works and what might work so they know how to read evolving writing so it will evolve into writing worth reading.

I think I've begun to learn the right questions to ask at the beginning of a writing conference.

"What did you learn from this piece of writing?"

"What do you intend to do in the next draft?"

"What surprised you in the draft?"

"Where is the piece of writing taking you?"

"What do you like best in the piece of writing?"

"What questions do you have of me?"

I feel as if I have been searching for years for the right questions, questions which would establish a tone of master and apprentice, no, the voice of a fellow craftsman having a conversation about a piece of work, writer to writer, neither praise nor criticism but questions which imply further drafts, questions which draw helpful comments out of the student writer.

And now that I have my questions, they quickly become unnecessary. My students ask these questions of themselves before they come to me. They have taken my conferences away from me. They come in and tell me what has gone well, what has gone wrong, and what they intend to do about it.

Some of them drive an hour or more for the conference that is over in fifteen minutes. It is pleasant and interesting to me, but don't they feel cheated? I'm embarrassed that they tell me what I would hope I would tell them, but probably not as well. My students assure me it is important for them to prepare themselves for the conference and to hear what I have to say.

"But I don't say anything," I confess. "You say it all."

They smile and nod as if I know better than that, but I don't.

What am I teaching? At first I answered in terms of form: argument, narrative, description. I never said comparison and contrast, but I was almost as bad as that. And then I grew to answering, "the process." "I teach the writing process." "I hope my students have the experience of the writing process." I hear my voice coming back from the empty rooms which have held teacher workshops.

That's true, but there's been a change recently. I'm really teaching my students to react to their own work in such a way that they write increasingly effective drafts. They write; they read what they've written; they talk to me about what they've read and what the reading has told them they should do. I nod and smile and put my feet up on the desk, or down on the floor, and listen and stand up when the conference runs too long. And I get paid for this?

Of course, what my students are doing, if they've learned how to ask the right questions, is write oral rehearsal drafts in conference. They tell me what they are going to write in the next draft, and they hear their own voices telling me. I listen and they learn.

But I thought a teacher had to talk. I feel guilty when I do nothing but listen. I confess my fear that I'm too easy, that I have too low standards, to a colleague, Don Graves. He assures me I am a demanding teacher, for I see more in my students than they see in themselves. I certainly do. I expect them to write writing worth reading, and they do—to their surprise, not mine.

I hear voices from my students they have never heard from themselves. I find they are authorities on subjects they think ordinary. I find that even my remedial students write like writers, putting down writing that doesn't quite make sense, reading it to see what sense might be in it, trying to make sense of it, and—draft after draft—making sense of it. They follow language to see where it will lead them, and I follow them following language.

It is a matter of faith, faith that my students have something to say and a language in which to say it. Sometimes I lose that faith but if I regain it and do not interfere, my students do write and I begin to hear things that need saying said well.

This year, more than ever before, I realize I'm teaching my students what they've just learned.

They experiment, and when the experiment works I say, "See, look what happened." I put the experiment in the context of the writing process. They brainstorm, and I tell them that they've brainstormed. They write a discovery draft, and I point out that many writers have to do that. They revise, and then I teach them revision.

When I boxed I was a counterpuncher. And I guess that's what I'm doing now, circling my students, waiting, trying to shut up—it isn't easy trying not to interfere with their learning, waiting until they've learned something so I can show them what they've learned. There is no text in my course until my students write. I have to study the new text they write each semester.

It isn't always an easy text to read. The student has to decode the writing teacher's text; the writing teacher has to decode the student's writing. The writing teacher has to read what hasn't been written yet. The writing teacher has the excitement of reading unfinished writing.

Those papers without my teacherly comments written on them haunt me. I can't escape the paranoia of my profession. Perhaps I should mark up their pages. There are misspellings, comma splices, sentence fragments (even if they are now sanctified as "English minor sentences"). Worse still, I get papers that have no subject, no focus, no structure, papers that are underdeveloped and papers that are voiceless.

I am a professional writer—a hired pen who ghostwrites and edits—yet I do not know how to correct most student papers. How do I change the language when the student writer doesn't yet know what to say? How do I punctuate when it is not clear what the student must emphasize? How do I question the diction when the writer doesn't know the paper's audience?

The greatest compliment I can give a student is to mark up a paper. But I can only mark up the best drafts. You can't go to work on a piece of writing until it is near the end of the process, until the author has found something important to say and a way to say it. Then it may be clarified through a demonstration of professional editing.

The student sits at my right hand and I work over a few paragraphs suggesting this change, that possibility, always trying to show two, or three, or four alternatives so that the student makes the final choice. It is such satisfying play to mess around with someone else's prose that it is hard for me to stop. My best students snatch their papers away from my too eager pen but too many allow me to mess with their work as if I knew their world, their language, and what they had to say about their world and their language. I stop editing when I see they really appreciate it. It is not my piece of writing; it is not my mind's eye that is looking at the subject: not my language which is telling what the eye has seen. I must be responsible and not do work which belongs to my students, no matter how much fun it is. When I write it must be my own writing, not my students'.

I realize I not only teach the writing process, I follow it in my conferences. In the early conferences, the prewriting conferences, I go to my students; I ask questions about their subject, or if they don't have a subject, about their lives. What do they know that I don't know? What are they authorities on? What would they like to know? What would they like to explore? I probably lean forward in these conferences; I'm friendly, interested in them as individuals, as people who may have something to say.

Then, as their drafts begin to develop and as they find the need to focus, for shape, for form, I'm a bit removed, a fellow writer who shares his writing problems, his own search for meaning and form.

Finally. as the meaning begins to be found, I lean back, I'm more the reader, more interested in the language, clarity. I have begun to detach myself from the writer and from the piece of writing which is telling the student how to write it. We become fascinated by this detachment which is forced on student and teacher as a piece of writing discovers its own purpose.

After the paper is finished and the student starts on another, we go back through the process again and I'm amused to feel myself leaning forward, looking for a subject with my student. I'm not coy. If I know something I think will help the student, I share it. But I listen first—and listen hard (appearing casual)—to hear what my student needs to know.

Now that I've been a teacher this long I'm beginning to learn how to be a student. My students are teaching me their subjects. Sometimes I feel as if they are paying for an education and I'm the one getting the education . . .

I expected to learn of other worlds from my students but I didn't expect—an experienced (old) professional writer—to learn about the writing process from my students. But I do. The content is theirs but so is the experience of writing—the process through which they discover their meaning. My students are writers and they teach me writing most of the time.

I notice my writing bag and a twenty-page paper I have tossed towards it. Jim has no idea what is right or wrong with the paper—neither do I. I've listened to him in conference and I'm as confused as he is. Tomorrow morning I will do my writing, putting down my own manuscript pages, then, when I'm fresh from my own language, I will look at Jim's paper. And when he comes back I will have at least some new questions for him. I might even have an answer, but if I do I'll be suspicious. I am too fond of answers, of lists, of neatness, of precision; I have to fight the tendency to think I know the subject I teach. I have to wait for each student draft with a learning, listening eye. Jim will have re-read the paper and think about it too and I will have to be sure I listen to him first for it is his paper, not mine.

Andrea bustles in, late, confused, appearing disorganized. Her hair is totally undecided; she wears a dress skirt, lumberjack boots, a fur coat, a military cap. She carries no handbag, but a canvas bag bulging with paper as well as a lawyer's briefcase which probably holds cheese and bread.

Out comes the clipboard when I pass her paper back to her. She tells me exactly what she attempted to do, precisely where she succeeded and how, then informs me what she intends to do next. She will not work on this draft; she is bored with it. She will go back to an earlier piece, the one I liked and she didn't like. Now she knows what to do with it. She starts to pack up and leave.

I smile and feel silly; I ought to do something. She's paying her own way through school. I have to say something.

"I'm sorry you had to come all the way over here this late."

Andrea looks up surprised. "Why?"

"I haven't taught you anything."

"The hell you haven't. I'm learning in this course, really learning."

I start to ask Andrea what she's learning but she's out the door and gone. I laugh, pack up my papers, and walk home.

QUESTIONS FOR REFLECTION, JOURNAL WRITING, AND DISCUSSION

1. Would you agree with Murray that what teachers have to do for students is "to stay out of their way and not to interfere with their learning"?

2. Murray says "I teach the student not the paper." Is this what teachers usually do? Is this what you do? How can this be done?

3. Are students sometimes angry if they discover that they have a professor who, like Murray, does very little teaching? How does your own pedagogy compare with Murray's?

Chapter 17

Errors: Windows Into the Mind

Ann Raimes

Ann Raimes is Professor of English at Hunter College, where she has taught writing, rhetoric, and ESL for nearly 30 years. She has published several textbooks, most recently *Keys for Writers* (Houghton). Her articles have appeared in *TESOL Quarterly, Language Learning, College English, College ESL,* and in many anthologies. The following article is from *College ESL,* 1, December 1991.

> *Imagine a classroom. The teacher tells the students to take out paper and pencil to write a paragraph. Johnny waves his hand and calls out "I ain't got no pencil." "No, no Johnny," the teacher admonishes. "I don't have a pencil, he doesn't have a pencil, we don't have any pencils, they don't have any pencils." Johnny interrupts in disgust, "Ain't nobody got no pencils?"*
>
> (Adapted from Brown, 1987, p. 31.)

This is a familiar classroom scene: the student attending to communication, to saying something for a purpose; the teacher attending not to what is said but to whether it is grammatically correct. We all know that error correction in the middle of a conversation is intrusive. It cuts across real communication; it negates the point the speaker wants to make.

Communicative speech is not the best situation for us to help students correct their errors in English. Writing provides a more appropriate setting. The nature of writing is such that we produce a visible record of what we say. We can write our ideas, then look at them, reflect, monitor, make changes, add, delete, edit. Peter Elbow (1985) has said that writing is "the ideal medium for getting it wrong" (p. 286). It's also the ideal situation to learn to get it right. When language students write, they have time on their side: time to test hypotheses, to take risks, to make errors, and then to correct them.

When looking at a piece of writing, teachers have to respond to grammatical errors as well as to rhetoric (content and organization). In the 1960s, we had an avoidance policy on error. Based on behavioral principles and audiolingual habit-formation theories, we asked students to perform tasks that they were 98% certain to get right. We gave neat drills: repetition, substitution, and so on. We assigned controlled compositions that we didn't even have to read, just had to check whether the underlined words had been correctly changed from, say, the present to the past tense. When we did let our students graduate to actual composing, we tried to address everything all at once: content, organization, style, syntax, mechanics, grammar, and spelling. Since the 1970s, though, errors have been regarded not so much as serious flaws in learning, to be avoided or corrected immediately, but as evidence of language acquisition that provides valuable feedback to both students and teachers (Dulay, Burt, & Krashen, 1982).

The focus on communicative approaches that began in the late 70s has led us to pay more attention to the purpose of language, to the message a speaker or writer intends to get across (Savignon, 1983). We let students not only speak more freely but also write more freely, and we don't necessarily correct everything they produce. They fill pages with their freewriting, journals, and multiple drafts. The question remains for teachers, though: If we don't deal with errors, will they become fossilized, that is, permanently engraved in the learner's language repertoire? Or will someone suspect we don't recognize the errors? Will we be perceived as lazy, not doing our job? None of these are desirable outcomes, and they add to the teacher's concerns about how to handle errors.

Since a teacher's response on a student's paper is potentially an influential text in a writing class (Raimes, 1988), we need to examine our practices carefully. Research on teacher response to writing provides help on the issues of where to write comments on students' papers, whether to correct or indicate the location of errors, and, most important of all, how necessary it is to assign a follow-up activity to the given feedback. On the issue of whether it is best to write comments at the end of an essay, in the margins, or between the lines, studies by Stiff (1967) and Bata (1972) have found that where we put comments has no effect on the writing of college freshmen. If we worry about whether to correct errors or simply indicate their locations, it is probably better to do the latter, not only because it's less time consuming, but also because, as Robb, Ross, and Shortreed (1986) have found, indication of errors improves accuracy just as much as correction. In addition, according to Cohen and Cavalcanti's (1990) research, students report only "making a mental note" (p. 169) of teachers' comments, which is tantamount to saying that they glance briefly at a paper a teacher spent half an hour marking and then they put it away.

There's another reason not to spend a long time on correction. Vivian Zamel (1985) has shown us how teachers can significantly misread students' intentions and rewrite sentences according to the "ideal texts" that they hold in their heads (p. 81). To make certain that the students' ideas are being communicated accurately, it is essential to put the burden of rewriting and editing back on the students.

Just as important as the corrections the teacher writes on the students' papers are the tasks assigned after the papers are returned to the students. Lees (1988) proposes seven modes of commenting on students' papers: correcting, emoting (such as "Nice!" or "I'm bored here"), describing, suggesting, questioning, reminding, and assigning. While the first three put the burden on the teacher, the next three try to shift the burden to the student. Only assigning, "creating another assignment based on what a student has written," provides a way to "discover how much of that burden the student has taken" (Lees, 1988, p. 266).

Some second language research studies stress frequent opportunities for writing and rewriting as an important tool for improving both content and accuracy. Fathman and Whalley (1990), in their study of types of written feedback and its effects on revision, conclude, "All students, irrespective of the kind of feedback they received from the teacher, improved the content of their compositions when they rewrote them" (p. 187). In a study of students' drafts in a City University of New York classroom (Raimes, 1988, March), I found that the number of errors students made per T-unit decreased by 20% on a second draft, even when the teacher's response included no explicit correction of errors.

While recognizing that addressing content is important, we need to recognize also that we cannot ignore grammar errors and hope that they will disappear eventually. They might disappear if our students could have many years of intensive communicative practice with the language. But the reality with many of the immigrant students in college classrooms today is that they have to improve the accuracy of their written English in one or two semesters to write term papers, compete with native speakers with advanced courses, and enter graduate school or the job market with no disadvantage. So what can we do in place of correcting errors? How can we shift the burden of error correction to the students? The following six strategies address the problem.

First, whatever system we choose for marking errors in writing, we have to let our students know what that system is. Students frequently have no idea what *frag* or *awk* means, no idea why there is a question mark above a word, no idea what *agr* means, and certainly no idea why a paper earns a "B" rather than an "A." There's no point in spending time searching for the perfect system of marking errors in student writing. There isn't one. The one thing above all that will help any marking system is if our students understand it. So if we want to comment only on ideas in a first draft and save comments on accuracy until a later draft, our students should be told that. Otherwise they may assume everything uncorrected in the first draft is accurate, and they can drop their critical stance. It is useful to write out (for ourselves as well as for our students) what our policy on response is, what symbols and abbreviations we intend to use, and particularly what we expect students to do with their drafts and our comments when they receive them.

Second, we should relate our comments to the task we assign. Writing theorists distinguish between two aspects of writing: "composition" and "transcription" (Smith, 1982, p. 19), or "creating" and "criticizing" (Elbow, 1981, p. 7). If we give our students the opportunity first to express their ideas in English and then to scrutinize what they have written in order to make changes, then we should give ourselves the same two-stage response. When our students are, as Smith (1982) says, being "authors" (p. 20) and composing, then we'll respond with guidance and constructive comments; when they are being "secretaries" (p. 20), looking at transcription and focusing on accuracy of presentation, then we, too, can turn our attention to that.

I usually try to separate these concerns by telling students they will write two drafts of an essay. I comment on the ideas and organization on the first reading, but I usually don't write on the student's paper at this point. Rather, I write on a separate sheet, or use adhesive, removable notes to write comments on and stick them next to the relevant passages. However, to take advantage of adult learners' concerns for grammatical accuracy, I often pick up a recurring type of error. Then, I refer students to a grammar handbook, or write an explanation, or arrange a one-on-one conference. But I make it clear that I don't necessarily expect them to correct or even reproduce the structure in the next draft. Any work on grammar at this point is separate from and parallel to the draft they are working on. But once students have rewritten the drafts, I indicate grammatical errors. I do this on their papers, usually by underlining, and I expect the students to correct those errors, either by rewriting the whole piece or by deleting the errors and writing in their corrections.

After making the system clear to students and separating our response to ideas, meaning, and content from our response to accuracy, it is time to turn to accuracy. Once students have taken on the role of "critic" and "secretary" rather than author, if we don't actually correct every error we come across, what should we do?

The third strategy is not necessarily to tackle every error, every time, but to establish priorities. When we look at a student's paper that has a lot of errors in it, we might decide to indicate only what Burt and Kiparsky (1972) call "global errors," the errors that impede our comprehension, such as sentence derailments or faulty subordination. "As a result, elementary and secondary school students have to wear a uniform is a good idea." Such sense-hampering errors cause readers more problems than so-called "local errors," things like missing -s or -ed inflections, or a wrong article. In the next sentence, "Many people who attends private schools don't come from rich families, "the -s ending on *attend* is a local error, and not one that causes a reader serious problems. An alternative to the global-local priority is to indicate the location of types of errors that we have already discussed in class and ask the students to correct them. A teacher might correct other errors, or let them go, or make a list of error types as they occur, so that a grammar syllabus is created.

The fourth strategy is to look for and point out strengths as well as weaknesses, to give students the chance to perceive a correct model in their own use of language. Let's consider how a teacher might mark the following passage, written by Yolanda in a college-level developmental ESL class.

> The way Colombian teenagers act and behave differ a lot from teenagers in the United States. In my country, young people is very respectful with the elderly. We are taught from a very early age to respect our elders. Young people in the United States, on the other hand, is very cold and independent. They don't worry about other people. They don't mind if an old woman is tired or need help; they just live their lives.

Typically, a teacher would correct the four verb errors. But how many main verbs are there? Eleven. So the student got four wrong and seven right. Why not point out the correct verbs, perhaps with a check mark above each, and ask the student to look at them and use them as models to fix the others?

We are so attuned to errors and so involved in ferreting them out that we tend to neglect to praise our students when they take a risk and try but get it wrong. Students are more likely to take risks if they see that risk-taking is noted and encouraged. So we should be on the lookout not only for what is correct but also for good attempts. Some teachers would approach the following sentence, for example, as a sentence with errors, underlining or deleting various parts and expecting the student to correct the sentence. "People who immigrate to America, not only because they envy the plenty of substances that they can gain, but also want to melt into society and become a genuine American in the United States." But when a student in my class, Sam, wrote this, I commented: "You've done really well to try the *not only . . . but also* structure. It fits well here. But make sure that the two parts are parallel (ask me to explain this). Check, too, for your main subject + verb structure." When he wrote his next draft, he tried again: "It's not good for parents or children to speak only their own language, not only because it makes them lose a lot of chances to practice and learn English, but also because it makes them get the bad habit of always counting on their native people," and he added a little note to me: "How is it this time?"

The fifth strategy is to help students find ways to develop critical reading responses. One of the best strategies I've found for showing students how readers react to errors is to model the reading process for them, explaining the expectations that English-speaking readers have. I build this around the core of an English sentence, the subject + verb. If a student wrote a passage like the following, I wouldn't correct it on the student's paper. "My uncle's daughter who was going to a private school. She had to wear a uniform no matter what the weather was." If I did try to correct this, I'd have to decide whether to cross out *who* or to cross out the period and insert commas around the *who* clause, making the whole passage into one sentence. Instead, I'd write on the board: *My uncle's daughter,* then pause and ask students what they expect next. Any reader familiar with English texts will expect that to be the subject and will expect a verb. But then comes the *who* clause, and we are left waiting for the verb, with the sentence not completed. The students discuss how to make the sentence fit the reader's expectations of an independent clause consisting of a subject plus a verb. At the same time, in line with the idea of praising risk-taking, I would point out the sophisticated use of *no matter what.* With such an approach, the students begin to see an error as something that intervenes in the writer-reader relationship, something that goes against the reader's expectations, rather than a failure to live up to some abstract set of linguistic rules.

Once we have modeled the process of reading as a way to help students see what readers expect, students can be introduced to the next step in critical reading of their own work: proofreading strategies. Teachers may tell students to check their work carefully, without giving any real guidelines as to how to do that. I ask my students to practice the following four techniques:

1. The students read their papers aloud to other students. They may hesitate when a sentence doesn't seem to work, or they may read correctly what they have written incorrectly.
2. Another student reads the paper aloud. This new reader may pause when a sentence is problematic.
3. The students take a sheet of paper, cover up everything on the page except the first sentence, put their pencil point on one word at a time, and say the sentence aloud, word by word. They try to pick out the core subject + verb of the sentence.
4. The students read their last sentences first and so on, backwards through the paper, sentence by sentence. This is another way of preventing the reading eye from leaping ahead for the content; it focuses attention on sentence-level accuracy.

By practicing these four techniques, students learn to read their own writing with a critical eye.

The sixth and final strategy focuses on the sources of students' errors. To raise our students' consciousness about grammatical accuracy, we need to find ways to make error linguistically interesting and intellectually engaging. In my classes we discuss where errors come from and why students make errors. When I underline an error in a second draft, I often ask the student to correct the error and to explain where the error came from and what type of error it is. Some illustrations follow.

Françoise wrote "She gave me six advices," and after I underlined *advices,* she corrected it and explained it like this: "*Advice* is a countable noun in French and it's for this reason I made the error." We discuss in class the phenomenon of transfer, or interference, from a native language, the fact that it occurs mostly at the early stages of language learning, and that research has found that less than 25% of grammatical errors in adults' speech is due to transfer (Dulay, Burt, & Krashen, 1982, p. 103).

A greater source of error is from the application of interlanguage rules; that is, learners make generalizations about rules within the target language, in this case, English. When Martine wrote "How can this creates a problem?" she corrected it by deleting the -*s* and wrote: I used the wrong form after *can.* I was using an -*s* on a verb in the third person (English rule!)." However we interpret her comment—as an accusation, as a plea, or just as a groan—it alerts us to a problem that many language learners have: They intelligently apply what they think is a rule and feel frustrated when the application doesn't work. With Huey-Fen's sentence, "I did was the only one who didn't prepare gifts," a teacher's tendency would be to cross out *did* and assume the student was confused about the basic verb system. But then we hear from her: "In English we always say 'I do like you' to emphasize." After consultation she changed her sentence to "I actually was. . . . " Imagine how confused she might be if a teacher misread her intention and just crossed out *did.*

Sometimes the rules the students are applying intelligently are ones we have just taught. In the sentence: "Chinese New Year always gives us fun and exciting," Hui-Min's explanation of the error was this: "I used wrong forms. After *gives us* have to follow nouns: *fun* and *excitement.* I thought *exciting* was a noun form because some verbs add the -*ing* form to become nouns. For example: he is getting used to living in New York. *Living* is a noun." I had just carefully reviewed the gerund form as subject and object. Here was a clear case of error arising from an intelligent application of rules taught in class, what some call teacher-induced error.

Instruction led to the error in this passage, too: "If the doctor did not tell this man about his illness; this man may feel he has not fulfilled his life with his family." Mary replaced the semicolon with a comma, saying that she had applied a rule that had just been taught. She had used the semicolon, she said, because "the period does not fit. Also the comma does not fit the words: *and, or, so, yet, but, nor, for.* The word *if* is not one of these words." Just that week, I had carefully taught the use of the comma with coordinating conjunctions, and Mary had meticulously applied what she saw as her new rule, that commas belonged exclusively with those seven coordinating conjunctions. Such generalizations signal creativity and active engagement with the new language.

Learners use a variety of communication strategies to help get their messages across. Bringing these to the learners' attention is as helpful to them as it is to teachers. The strategy of avoidance is seen in the following excerpt from a student's essay: "~~He is a lyer lier li~~ He doesn't tell the true." The student can't spell *liar* and replaces it with another structure, alas an incorrect one. Temasgen's sentences, "My brother's room is messy. On the contrary, my sister's room is tidy," show a memorized phrase, "on the contrary," misused in this context in place of "in contrast." And, "My reactions made them surprise" shows not just a slip, a careless omission of an inflection, but an error resulting from a language-learning strategy that we usually encourage, the use of a dictionary. Nabuko's explanation of her error went like this: I looked up make in *Longman's Dictionary* and saw the idiom *to make someone + the simple form of the verb.*" She had, of course, seen examples like: "The pain made him cry out" and "How do you make this machine work?" So here we see not simply an error, but the application of a sophisticated linguistic hypothesis.

Asking students to tell us where they think their errors come from provides us with information about their first language transfer, their application of interlanguage rules, their interpretation of our teaching, and their use of communication strategies. It also gives us useful feedback on which errors our students can recognize and which ones they can't. Roseline wrote "Referring to the article that doctors should tell their patients the truth about their condition" and explained her error as "*Condition* should be plural because I am talking about patients. I made the error because I did not read it carefully." I knew then that I had to spend more time teaching her about sentence structure. Other times, though, students can immediately correct an error, recognizing it as a genuine mistake in performance. With the sentence "I met a old American couple," Youn changed *a* to *an* and explained: "I made the error because I was unconscious."

We can learn a lot about our students' errors if we give them the chance to make them, fix them, and discuss them. In that way, errors are no longer the enemy, but clear evidence of language learning, enlightening for students and teachers alike. Errors are, indeed, as Kroll and Schafer (1978) have said, "clues to inner processes, windows into the mind" (p. 243).

ACKNOWLEDGMENT

This is a revised version of an invited plenary session paper presented at the annual TESOL-Italy Convention in Rome, December, 1989.

REFERENCES

Bata, E. J. (1972). "A Study of the Relative Effectiveness of Marking Techniques on Junior College Freshman English Composition." Unpublished doctoral dissertation, University of Maryland, College Park, MD.

Brown, H. D. (1987) *Principles of Language Learning and Teaching (2nd ed.)*. Englewood Cliffs, NJ: Prentice Hall.

Burt, M. K., & Kiparsky, C. (1972). *The Gooficon: A Repair Manual for English*. Rowley, MA: Newbury House.

Cohen, A. D., & Cavalcanti, M. C. (1990). "Feedback on Composition: Teacher and Student Verbal Reports." In B. Kroll (Ed.), *Second Language Writing: Research Insights for the Classroom* (pp. 155–177). New York: Cambridge University Press.

Dulay, H., Burt, M., & Krashen, S. (1982). *Language 2*. New York: Oxford University Press.

Elbow, P. (1981). *Writing with Power*. New York: Oxford University Press.

Elbow, P. (1985). "The Shifting Relationships between Speech and Writing." *College Composition and Communication*, 36, 283–303.

Fathman, A., & Whalley, E. (1990). "Teacher Response to Student Writing: Focus on Form versus Content." In B. Kroll (Ed.), *Second Language Writing: Research Insights for the Classroom* (pp. 178–190). New York: Cambridge University Press.

Kroll, B., & Schafer, J. (1978). "Error Analysis and the Teaching of Composition." *College Composition and Communication*, 29, 243–248.

Lees, E. O. (1988). "Evaluating Student Writing." In G. Tate & E. P. J. Corbett (Eds.), *The Writing Teacher's Sourcebook (2nd ed.)* (pp. 263–267). New York: Oxford University Press.

Raimes, A. (1988). "The Texts for Teaching Writing." In B. K. Das (Ed.), *Materials for Language Learning and Teaching* (pp. 41–58). Singapore: SEAMEO Regional Language Center.

Raimes, A. (1988, March). "Responding to Students' Written Errors: Looking at Causes." Paper presented at the 22nd Annual TESOL Convention, Chicago.

Robb, T., Ross, S., & Shortreed, I. (1986). "Salience of Feedback on Error and Its Effect on EFL Writing Quality." *TESOL Quarterly*, 20, 83–96.

Savignon, S. (1983). *Communicative Competence: Theory and Classroom Practice*. Reading, MA: Addison-Wesley.

Smith, F. (1982). *Writing and the Writer*. New York: Holt, Rinehart and Winston.

Stiff, R. (1967). "The Effect upon Student Composition of Particular Correction Techniques." *Research in the Teaching of English*, 1, 54–75.

Zamel, V. (1985). "Responding to Student Writing." *TESOL Quarterly*, 19, 79–101.

QUESTIONS FOR REFLECTION, JOURNAL WRITING, AND DISCUSSION

1. Can you remember an example of a teacher-induced error? How and why did it occur?

2. Raimes suggests that in correcting student essays, we "don't necessarily correct everything they produce." What do you think of this recommendation?

3. After finding and duplicating a paper of an ESL student, discuss with your classmates or colleagues how you would correct it and why.

4. Compare Gilyard's and Raimes's advice about dealing with student error in writing. How do their opinions compare with your own?

Chapter 18

High Stakes and Low Stakes in Assigning and Responding to Writing

Peter Elbow

The following selection is from *New Directions for Teaching and Learning* 69, Spring 1997, John Wiley. See chapter 8 for biographical information on Peter Elbow.

As I try to understand my own experience of writing and the experience of my students and as I try to plan my teaching, nothing has been more useful to me than the simple and crude distinction between high and low stakes writing—the question of how much a piece of writing *matters* or *counts.*

ASSIGNING WRITING

The goal of low stakes assignments is not so much to produce excellent pieces of writing as to get students to think, learn, and understand more of the course material. Low stakes writing is often informal and tends to be graded informally. In a sense, we get to throw away the low stakes writing itself but keep the neural changes it produced in students' heads. High stakes assignments also produce learning, but they are more loaded because we judge the writing carefully for soundness of content and clarity of presentation.

It's obvious why we need high stakes assignments in our courses. We can't give trustworthy final grades that reflect whether students actually understand what we want them to understand unless we get them to articulate in writing what they have learned. If students take only short-answer tests or machine-graded exams, they will often *appear* to have learned what we are teaching when in fact they have not.

Am I saying that if students can't explain something in writing, they don't know it? Not quite. That is, I acknowledge that some students can understand something well and yet be hindered from explaining it in writing because of their fear of writing or lack of skill. In fact, it sometimes happens that we understand something well that we can't even explain in speech—much less in writing. Nonverbal knowing is most obvious in realms like music, art, and dance (mathematics?), but it can occur in any realm. That is, we can know something at a felt, nonverbal level before we find words for what we know.

But even though students *can* sometimes know things they can't explain in writing, I still argue for high stakes writing. I think good college grades should reflect more than nonverbal and nonwritten understanding. They should also reflect the ability to *convey* that understanding in writing. (Conceivably, we should relax this demand in music, art, and dance classes.) I hasten to add that my tough position rests on two gentler premises. We should *honor* nonverbal knowing, inviting students to use low stakes writing to fumble and fish for words for what they sense and intuit but cannot yet clearly say. And if we assign lots of low stakes writing, students are much less liable to be held back by fear or inability to put what they know on paper when they come to high stakes writing.

Students may complain, "But how can you grade on the basis of writing when this isn't a writing course?" We mustn't forget here a basic pedagogical principle: we are not obliged to teach everything we require. We don't teach typing, yet we often require it. Must we stop requiring skilled reading unless we explicitly teach it? Besides, if we require students to explain their learning on paper, we will be doing a big favor to our campus writing program and writing teachers. Writing courses only work well if students *need* writing to prosper in their other courses. (For more about assigning high stakes writing, see, in particular, Chapters Five and Six.)

IMPORTANCE OF LOW STAKES ASSIGNMENTS

Writing *feels* like an inherently high stakes activity—especially because most people learn and use writing primarily in school, where it is virtually always evaluated, usually with a grade. Writing tends to be used for more serious occasions than speaking. ("Are you prepared to put that in writing?") Speech feels more like a low stakes activity because we learn it in the home and on the playground and use it casually everywhere. We don't usually think of our speech as being graded.

But speech *can* be used in formal and evaluative settings—as when we are interviewed for a job or give a talk. In fact, if we pause and reflect for a moment, we will realize that our speech is almost *always* evaluated, even if not formally graded. How we talk and what we say are probably the main basis on which people we meet look down on us or are impressed with us.

And writing *can* be used informally, even casually, and in a nonevaluative setting. In truth, if we are looking for the best possible low stakes arena for language—for using language to learn, explore, take risks, or commune with ourselves and not have our language be evaluated—writing is much *better* than speaking. Writing permits us to keep our words in private or to revise them before showing them to anyone else. Speech is riskier because it is almost always heard by someone in its first bloom; it can never be taken back.

In this volume, Toby Fulwiler, Art Young, and M. Elizabeth Sargent in particular (Chapters Two, Three, and Four, respectively) describe low stakes writing assignments: frequent, informal assignments that make students spend time regularly reflecting in written language on what they are learning from discussions, readings, lectures, and their own thinking. These informal pieces of writing are sometimes done in class and sometimes for homework. These pieces are low stakes because individually they don't have much effect on the final grade. Teachers tend to distinguish these assignments by calling them not essays but *quickwrites, letters, freewrites, thinkpieces,* or *inkshedding.* (When we require students to turn in a draft of a high stakes essay a week or more before the final version is due, the draft tends to function as a low stakes piece.) Stephen Fishman and Anne Herrington (Chapters Five and Six) describe a mixture of high and low stakes writing assignments.

Because it is so ingrained to treat writing as a high stakes activity, especially in schools and colleges, I want to summarize here some of the special benefits of low stakes writing.

- Low stakes writing helps students involve themselves more in the ideas or subject matter of a course. It helps them find their own language for the issues of the course; they stumble into their own analogies and metaphors for academic concepts. Theorists are fond of saying that learning a discipline means learning its discourse, but learning a discipline also means learning not to use that discourse. That is, students don't know a field until they can write and talk about what is in the textbook and the lectures in their own lingo, in their informal *home* or *personal* language—language that, as Vygotsky famously observed, is saturated with sense or experience.

- When students do high stakes writing they often struggle in nonproductive ways and produce terrible prose. When they do low stakes writing, their prose is usually livelier, clearer and more natural—often more interesting—in spite of any carelessness and mistakes. They don't tie their syntax in so many knots or defensively restrict themselves to simple "Dick and Jane" sentences, because they aren't worrying so much about the grade or whether they are writing exactly what the teacher was looking for. I've almost never seen a piece of low stakes writing I couldn't easily understand. But I've seen *lots* of high stakes writing that students worked very hard on that was impenetrable.

- Low stakes writing improves the quality of students' high stakes writing. By assigning frequent low stakes pieces, we ensure that students have *already* done lots of writing before we have to grade a high stakes piece—so that they are already warmed up and more fluent. Their high stakes pieces are more likely to have a clear, alive voice. And it's no small help to their high stakes writing that we have seen a number of their low stakes pieces. For then, when they turn in a high stakes essay that is awkwardly tangled or even impenetrable, we don't have to panic or despair; we can just say, "Come on. You can say all this in the clear, lively voice I've already seen you using."

- Low stakes writing gives us a better view of how students are understanding the course material and reacting to our teaching. We get a better sense of how their minds work. We can see better the interactions between their thinking about course material and their thinking about other realms of their life, between their thinking and their feeling. We get better glimpses of them as people.

- Probably the main practical benefit of frequent low stakes assignments is to force students to keep up with the assigned reading every week. When students put off the reading till an exam or major paper is due, they learn much less from discussions and lectures. And when only the teacher and a few diligent students have done the reading, the whole course tends to lose steam.

RESPONDING TO WRITING

When we assign writing, we can trust that we are helping students learn more and probably even write better. But when we respond or comment, we can't be so confident. The news from researchers is not encouraging. They have discovered how often a teacher's comments are not clear, how often comments are misunderstood by students even when they are clear, and how often comments cannot be trusted. (For example, the teacher writes—"You should omit this section," or, "You need a comma here," or, "This hypothesis has been discredited," when in fact many or even most authorities would disagree.) Researchers have trouble finding good evidence that our comments on student writing actually help students learn more or write better. (Elizabeth Hodges is one of these researchers, and in Chapter Seven, she gives us interesting and practical glimpses into the essential sequence of events: the teacher's reactions to a student paper, that teacher's actual comment on the paper, and the student's reading and understanding of that comment.)

These sobering results are not really so surprising once we stop and reflect on the conditions in which we write our comments and the conditions in which students read them. After all, we write comments in great quantity—working slowly down through thick stacks of papers on our desks. It is often late at night and we are usually in a hurry. And truth be told, we are often writing in a discouraged or downright grumpy mood. Writing comments on papers and exams is a *major* portion of the "academic writing" of most academics, yet it's not the writing we really care about. It seldom has much effect on our careers, and we seldom do any revising of it. No wonder it is seldom our best writing. And let's face it: it's not feasible to write our comments really slowly and to revise them carefully. We are surely going to continue to write comments fast, late at night, and not always in the best mood. Still, we can learn to do it better—thus the efforts in this book.[1]

Even when we write clear, accurate, valid, and helpful comments, our students often read them through a distorting lens of resistance or discouragement—or downright denial. (Don't we sometimes read responses to our own articles by professional reviewers through similar lenses?) When students read what we write, they are usually reacting at the same time to all the past teacher comments they have received on their writing. The most obvious example of this is that students tend to take almost anything we write as criticism—even if we are just asking them a question or making an observation, or even making a low-key statement of mild praise. ("I'm curious how you managed to be so dispassionate on such a controversial issue," or, "I was interested that you were able to quote from a book that I didn't assign." "Uh oh, I'll never do those things again.") And when we include a grade with our comment, we increase the likelihood of a distorted reading—sometimes no reading at all!

What discouraging news. But I think we need to hear it. It helps us ask some very practical questions as we respond to student writing: "Am I wasting my time with this comment? What are the chances that it will be understood as I intend it? That it will help?" Perhaps we could adopt the principle of our better-paid fellow professionals: "At least do no harm." When we *assign* writing, at least we do no harm.

---

[1] It interests me as a writing teacher to note that though our commenting on student papers is undeniably "academic" and indeed "professional" writing, it is often very casual: we often write in incomplete sentences and use lots of "I" and "you." I'm not saying that these features make our writing bad or unprofessional or unacademic. I'm just pointing out that many academics unthinkingly assume that casual informal writing is not academic and should not be used by students.

CONTINUUM BETWEEN HIGH AND LOW STAKES RESPONDING

In the face of this bleak situation, I call again on the distinction between high and low stakes. But here I am emphasizing a continuum with many intermediate points. Just as important, it is also a continuum from the least responding to the most responding.

Zero response (lowest stakes). When I am clear and honest with students about the fact that I need to require more writing from them than I can comment on, I help them fairly quickly get over any feelings of deprivation or resentment. Most students come to appreciate the chance to write with the knowledge that they will be heard but will not have to deal with my response. In fact, many teachers require some low stakes writing that they don't even read. Students can appreciate and benefit from the freedom of this private writing. (See Sargent and Elbow, Chapters Four and Eleven, respectively, on ways to deal with private writing.)

Minimal, nonverbal, noncritical response. We can note effective or strong or correct passages by simply putting a straight line underneath particular words or phrases or alongside longer sections. (Teachers often use check marks in the margin for this purpose, but I find straight lines are more specific markers.) I can respond in this way virtually as quickly as I can read. Almost every student needs some encouragement, and some students on some occasions need lots. Even in very poor pieces of writing, certain parts are always better than others; students benefit from having them pointed out. To find strong points, even in weak writing, is a skill that will help us improve student learning and writing.

Supportive response—no criticism. There are usually things that students do well that are hard to point to with simple straight lines (for example, "You chose a good approach to your topic," or, "You write with a clear and lively voice."). Whether we call it praise or positive reinforcement, the fact remains that this kind of response does the most good with the least effort. That is, we are most likely to cause learning and least likely to do harm if the message of our response is, in effect, "Please do more of this thing you are already doing here." We are *least* likely to cause learning and most likely to do harm if we give the message that is all too often implied in critical feedback: "Start doing something you've never done before."

Descriptive or observational response. An example of this response: "You begin with an anecdote from your own experience; then show us how it throws light on your academic topic. Then you make your case—which really rests on a process of definition—showing what fits and what is excluded." One of the hardest things for student writers is simply to *see* their own text, to understand the logical and rhetorical strategies they have used. Neutral and noncritical observations can be very effective because students don't need to resist them.

Minimal, nonverbal critical response. Just as quickly as we can read and put in straight lines, we can also put wavy or wiggly lines underneath words or alongside passages that are unclear or problematic or wrong. It's remarkable what a strong sense of our readerly presence and response we can give to students when we note five or six phrases or passages per page with straight and wiggly lines: they get a felt sense of what is working and not working for us.

Critical response, diagnosis, advice (highest stakes). This is our meat and potatoes—what we tend to assume is our main job. Obviously, we often need to give critical response to help with learning and to explain the basis of poor grades. But my premise here is that the higher we go on the continuum, the more we need to ask the crucial pragmatic questions: Is this comment worth it? How much response do I need? How much criticism will be useful? What is the likelihood of my effort doing good or harm?

I don't mean to suggest that we can just mechanically match low stakes responses with low stakes assignments and high with high. Obviously, we will often *mix* levels of response—in particular, mixing praise and criticism. Even the *highest* stakes assignment merits some praise.

Nevertheless, it pays to notice the natural links between levels of assignment and response. That is, the lowest stakes response (zero response) goes most naturally with low stakes assignments: when the writing doesn't much matter to the final grade, we can afford to withhold our response or criticism. Similarly the highest stakes response (critical response) goes most naturally with high stakes assignments: if our judgment of a student essay will have any significant impact on the final grade, we are obliged to explain any criticism we have. This critical response carries the highest stakes for many reasons: with critical response, we have to worry more about whether we are wrong or unsound; critical response is more likely to misfire or do harm because of how it is received—even if it is sound; and critical response is likely to cost us more work and more uncertainty. In contrast, low stakes minimal responding requires the least time and effort from us, requires the least expertise from us, takes the least time away from our teaching of the subject matter, and is least likely to turn teachers and students into adversaries.

I am not trying to stamp out critical response; I'm just arguing that we should use less of it—and use minimal and low stakes response instead. Note, for example (and this is another case of mixing), that we can use plenty of low stakes praise without giving up criticism—without pretending that a piece of writing is better than it is. For example, we can write something like this: "Your paper doesn't work very well and the worst problem is confusing sentences. I often couldn't understand you. Nevertheless you do have plenty of clear sentences and I've marked particularly strong ones with a straight line. To work on your serious problem, try to

figure out what you were doing when you wrote those strong sentences—
and do more of that." It might seem hard to find examples of good organization in a disorganized paper, but not if we set our mind to it. For example, we can write: "I got lost a lot as I read your paper. It has big problems
with organization. But I've put straight lines along several paragraphs that
hang together just fine, and also lines *between* several paragraphs where
they follow well and your transition works fine. Give us more of that!
You've shown you can do it."

It is important for us to realize that we don't need to feel *guilty* if we use
lots of low stakes and minimal response—especially if we are not teaching a
writing course. Assigning more writing, using less response, and using
more praise doesn't mean leaving out all criticism or lowering standards.
Students need the experience of writing a great deal and getting minimal
and low stakes response because they tend to associate writing with criticism and high stakes. If we are not so much teaching writing as using writing to teach something else, it makes particularly good sense to use lots of
minimal and low stakes response. When we assign a piece of writing and
don't comment on it, we are *not not-teaching:* we are actively setting up powerful conditions for learning by getting students to do something they
wouldn't do without the force of our teaching.

CONCLUSION: CONCRETE SUGGESTIONS

- For high stakes assignments, it can be very helpful to require a draft a
  week or more before the final version. Teachers handle drafts in a
  wide variety of ways depending on their circumstances and styles. At
  the very least, we can just collect drafts and not comment—simply
  checking that they are done—thus forcing students to carry their
  thinking through two steps. Of course, if our circumstances make it
  feasible, it is good to give comments on a draft. When we comment
  on a draft, our response becomes almost automatically low stakes,
  even if critical: we can write suggestions for revising rather than just
  an autopsy. (Notice in Chapter Six how Herrington describes the production of an essay that has very high stakes but one that students
  work up to along a path of lower stakes drafts and comments on those
  drafts.) It is probably worth cutting back on the amount of responding on *some* assignments for the sake of giving students at least one
  experience of feedback on a draft aimed at a revision. If we can only
  do this once, it's better to do it in the first half of the semester—with
  the goal that students can internalize some of our responses when
  they work on later high stakes assignments. But commenting on
  drafts may be more feasible than some teachers think: if we give good

responses on a draft, we can make do with just a quick verdict on the revision (perhaps using the kind of grid that I suggest in Chapter Eleven).

- Even when we are commenting on a final version, we can frame our comments in a forward looking way: instead of saying, "Here's what didn't work," we can say, "Here's what to work on in future papers."

- I find it easier to comment on important assignments if I get students to turn in a short reflective *cover letter* or piece of *process writing* with the assignment itself. I invite something informal, even handwritten. I ask them to tell me what they see as their main points, how they went about writing and what happened, which parts they are most and least satisfied with, and what questions they have for me as a reader. Reading the cover letter usually helps me decide what to say in my comment. Often I can agree with much of what the student has said, and sometimes I can be more positive about the essay than the student was. Students may have difficulty at first with this self-reflective writing, but it promotes a skill worth working on. It gives them practice in trying to see their own thinking more clearly. (Herrington gives good examples in Chapter Six of cover letters for a mid-process draft and a final draft.)

- I find commenting much easier if I read the whole piece before making any comments except for straight and wiggly lines. I save lots of time by reminding myself that students can seldom benefit from criticism of more than two or three problems. Therefore, the most crucial decision in commenting is *which* problems to focus on, and I can't make that decision till I read the whole paper through. Most of my bad commenting comes from jumping in with marginal comments as I am reading: I am more likely to waste my time on something that turns out to be a minor issue, or make some passing remark that the student misunderstands, or say something that's actually wrong ("You obviously don't understand x," when later on it's clear that she does understand x), or get caught up in a little spasm of unhelpful irritation. If I settle for just making straight and wiggly lines, these serve me as a map when I glance back over the paper after I have read the whole thing and I am trying to decide what are the few main things I need to say. (In Chapter Nine, Chris Anson points out an exception: when we put our comments on a tape cassette, we may want to tell the story of our reactions as we are actually in the process of reading. Yet Anson also points out that even for this kind of responding he sometimes does better by waiting till he has read the whole piece.)

- As Hodges points out in Chapter Seven, when we return papers to students with our comments attached, it's a great help sometimes to ask students to take five minutes right then and write us a short note telling what they heard us saying and how they are reacting to it. This helps us learn when we are unclear or when students misinterpret our words or react in ways we don't expect.

- If we are writing comments where the stakes aren't too high, we can save time by waiting till we have two pieces in hand, read them together, and write only one comment on both. The comparison is often pedagogically useful. ("Notice how much clearer your point was on this paper compared to that one [or how much more carefully you argued]. What helped you?")

- Though it sometimes costs me a few more words, I try to avoid an impersonal "God/truth voice" in my comments. Almost anything that we might say in response to a piece of writing is going to be affected by our own point of view. Even the main ideas in our discipline are arguable. If we are willing to say, "Unconvincing for me," instead of "Unconvincing," students are more likely to pause, listen, and think—instead of just resisting, or else unthinkingly giving in to authority. Besides, magisterial shorthand words like "Awk" are often extremely unclear. I have been trying to learn to write more accurate translations like, "I stumbled here," or, "I'm lost," or, "Wording feels unprofessional," or, "Too slangy for my ear," or, "Can you be less roundabout?"

I sum up this chapter with that useful dictum "At least do no harm." Think how much good we do in assigning lots of writing, especially low stakes writing. But this approach is only feasible when we realize that we can get by with far less response and criticism than we usually assume.

QUESTIONS FOR REFLECTION, JOURNAL WRITING, AND DISCUSSION

1. Elbow questions whether "our comments on student writing actually help students learn more or write better." What do you think about this?

2. Do you agree that it is acceptable to sometimes give no response to student writing?

3. Elbow's final advice is "at least do no harm." In what ways do teachers do harm? Have you ever done harm as a teacher?

4. Do many teachers follow Elbow's advice about giving both high stakes and low stakes writing? If not, should they? Would you like to follow his advice?

Chapter 19

The Myths of Assessment

Pat Belanoff

Pat Belanoff is Professor of English at the State University of New York at Stony Brook and former director of its writing program. She is a coauthor of two textbooks: *The Right Handbook* and *A Community of Writers* and coeditor of *Portfolios: Process and Product*. In addition, she has written a number of articles on portfolio evaluation and served for three years as chair of the CCCC Assessment Committee. Pat also produces, on occasion, articles in her second academic field, Old English literature. The following article is from the *Journal of Basic Writing*, 10, 1, 1991.

Back when I started to teach writing, my first students were mostly middle and upper middle class White kids. What I was learning at the time about the teaching of writing, the theories behind various approaches, and the supporting philosophies, I was applying to a fairly privileged group of students and was gratified by the results. When I moved from teaching that group and began to teach at the Borough of Manhattan Community College and became familiar with the work of Mina Shaughnessy, Marie Ponsot, Rosemary Dean, and others, I discovered that what I had learned about teaching writing continued to apply in classrooms of so-called basic writers and somewhat advanced ESL students. I didn't realize that immediately. I thought I needed to teach basic writers and ESL students lots of grammar and how to write sentences so someday they could write paragraphs, and then compositions, some day even discourses. I discovered how wrong I was. I often believe that the students of BMCC taught me more than I taught them.

When I moved to Stony Brook and began to teach less advanced ESL students and lower middle class and working class students, I discovered again that their needs were not so different from the needs of my previous students. Learning to write is learning to write—what works for advanced students also works for ESL students. Even in beginning language courses, students use language to think within restricted contexts and need to think in order to learn. To quote Janet K. Swaffar in *Profession 89,* "The notion that thinking and intentionality were integral to language use at any level made viable a claim heretofore rejected out of hand: that language learning need not be remedial learning. If taught in terms of creativity rather than replication, even beginners could find language learning an intellectually challenging activity, a bona fide academic enterprise."

All of us have been accused of doing remedial work, even those of us teaching advanced composition. A recent survey of faculty at Stony Brook makes that conception of our work painfully obvious. We need to argue that point constantly to our colleagues in other fields. Nor can we exclude our writing center colleagues and say they are in charge of grammar and mechanics, and classroom teachers deal with "ideas"—as though they were separate. This is a common dichotomy, but we're all teachers and we're all tutors—certainly the best classroom teachers I've known are tutors.

What we need to argue within our field and to each other is equally important: that all of us engaged in the teaching of writing—regardless of the names given to the courses we teach—are working within the same paradigm and have much to learn from each other once we recognize the commonality of our pursuits. We all need to talk to each other more often.

I've entitled my talk today the myths of assessment and plan to speak generally about four myths:

1. We know what we're testing for.
2. We know what we're testing.
3. Once we've agreed on criteria, we can agree on whether individual papers meet those criteria.
4. And the strongest myth of all, that it's possible to have an absolute standard and apply it uniformly.

First myth: we know what we're testing for. Let's think about the writing tests we're connected to in some way—tests we give in our own classrooms and standardized tests administered apart from our classrooms.

What are those standardized tests testing for? Are they finding out, as the CUNY test supposedly does, that students have achieved a certain level and are ready to go on to another level—where they may or may not get more help with their writing? Does that mean that students in supposedly below-level classes cannot apply what skills they have to writing about economics or literature or whatever their other classes will ask them to write about? Our portfolio proficiency test at Stony Brook certifies that students have satisfied the first level of our writing requirement; what it really means is that students do not have to retake our basic composition course—in truth, what it does for far too many students is assure that they won't be asked to write again for a couple of years—or until they have to satisfy their upper-level writing requirement.

What does the National Association for Educational Progress' writing sample measure? How well students can write to demonstrate they can write? And what about New York State's minimum competency tests in writing? They demonstrate that students can or cannot reorganize a list of things and write up a report. I'm not saying those things aren't measurable or shouldn't be measured—but once they've been measured, what can we say about a student's skill as a writer? We overgeneralize about all these results.

Some standardized tests purport to say that students write well enough to be allowed to graduate from college. How well is that? How well *should* a college graduate write? And why do we need separate writing requirements? If a college degree doesn't certify literacy, what does it certify?

Well, perhaps we are testing to see if students are improving (I think now of pretests and posttests used to evaluate either programs or students or both). How much can students genuinely improve in one semester and can we measure the ways in which they improve? A lot of what we want to teach them is subsumed under attitudes and approaches and how do we test for that? We want them to take risks, to try harder things which may make their writing look as though it's deteriorating, depending on when we decide to look at it. We don't want them to write what they already know how to write; we want them to write something that pulls and stretches their skills—and that pulling and stretching can result in some pretty messy stuff.

And what about the testing—formal and informal—in our classrooms? What are our purposes? To see if students have mastered a particular skill? To see if students write better than they did three weeks ago or three months ago? Do we need tests to know that? What if students haven't mastered the skill or don't write better? Have we failed? Have they failed? Is growth steady or does it come in spurts?

The assumption here is that we have some precise notion of what skills students need to master in order to be good or better writers and that we know in what order these should be learned: word forms before paragraphs, narrative before argument, etc., or vice versa. Unfortunately, the skills which are easiest to measure are the ones least important to the development of good writing. We can determine with some degree of accuracy and agreement from others whether or not a word form is correct or whether an essay has a topic sentence or whether all sentences end with the proper punctuation marks. But we can't agree so easily that the word or the topic sentence selected is effective stylistically and rhetorically and whether the groups of words ending with periods communicate some idea clearly and effectively and integrate that idea into what comes before and after. We won't agree about the latter to the degree we agree about the former. We can't agree on something as seemingly concrete as where commas go. Rules, after all, are abstractions, humanmade—they're not real. As abstractions, they do not reflect any reality exactly. Consequently, rules are only clear until we apply them—then they fuzzy up. But, more importantly, we cannot separate rhetorical issues and issues of correctness even though textbooks and handbooks purport to do it all the time.

So we just don't know whether what we test in class makes for good writing or not, and if students improve, whether they become better writers. In fact, we really can't isolate skills and judge them separately from the entire act of communication because it is that act that sets the perimeters for us and for them, and it is that act against which we have to measure whatever students do.

Well, that's my first myth: that we know what we are testing for. My second myth is that we know what we are testing. What we're testing is the student's writing ability, correct? And how do we do that? By looking at some piece of writing the student has done in 20 minutes or an hour? To what degree does a particular piece of writing represent a student's total ability? Are we assessing the student's ability or the quality of the piece of writing? In fact, the only thing it's really possible to find out is if the particular piece of writing before us does or does not accomplish some particular purpose. Could the student duplicate the piece, do something else like it just as well again? And even if so, can writing tasks be so much alike that we can be sure that if a student does one he can do the other? Or that someone will even ask him to do this thing again some day? But given the nature of most of our tests, I suspect no one will ask the student to do quite this same thing again. In fact, are we grading a piece of writing in any meaningful sense at all? Under what circumstances would a student ever be asked to do this thing we've asked him to do on the test?

Other issues are relevant too. Did the student struggle to write this? Was it easy for her? Was she feeling well, poorly, hostile? What, in fact, does this piece of writing in front of us represent?

Listening to Muriel Harris[1] this morning as she spoke of the role of writing centers in relation to the increasing cultural diversity of colleges made me realize with even greater intensity how ludicrous it is to use a single instrument to measure writing competency. I would add another diversity to her provocative list of cultural diversities. What does it mean to write as a woman in a profession so long dominated by western male standards of performance derived from classical rhetoric?

And what is writing ability anyway? What does it mean to write well? Is a good writer someone who can write anything? Is a good writer someone who can fulfill a school assignment? Is being able to record one's thoughts in a diary, write a letter to a friend, write a poem—are these things a good writer can and should do; is one a good writer if one can do them? As Ed

---

[1]Muriel Harris spoke at The City University of New York's ESL conference in March, 1990.

White points out in *Teaching and Assessing Writing* (and he's a proponent of assessment), our profession has no agreed upon definition of proficiency and certainly as a consequence, no agreed upon definitions for proficiencies at various levels of schooling.

So that's my second myth: that we know what we're testing. My third one is that even if we know what we're testing for and what the artifact is in front of us, we still don't agree on how well the student has achieved the goals. In truth we don't always agree on which characteristics of a good piece of writing are most significant in making us judge the piece positively.

I've often sat with groups of teachers and worked out what we could agree on as the traits of a good piece of writing—they'll come out something like clarity, effective organization, contextual awareness, coherence, correctness of language, and so on; probably the same set of traits any group of good teachers would come up with. In the abstract, they sound fine. The problem comes when we get around to applying them to actual papers. What I think is clear, someone else doesn't. What I see as well-organized, another doesn't. Or I value the work because it's well-organized and another reader agrees, but thinks the good organization is overshadowed by superficiality of content. Modern critical theory points to something we've always known—that people don't read in the same way—that, as a result, texts do not *embed* meaning, they *enable* meaning. Subjects affect us; our acquaintance with a variety of forms affects us; the authority we're willing to grant to authors and to our own right to judge affects us—we can't really codify what goes into the interpretation of a particular text, we can't even be sure that we would assess the same text the same way a second time.

We can, of course, be trained by the Educational Testing Service (ETS), or through similar methods, to agree on texts—agree on numbers we would assign to particular texts. ETS is wise not to insist on expressions of why a grader awards a particular score to a particular paper. In the process of "training" (a form of brainwashing for sure), a grader learns the community standards and learns to apply them quite well, but never questions their validity for the task they set themselves up to do. They're not asked to.

But most of us simply don't want our students to be subjected to such an inhumane process. We rightly insist that writing is not genuinely writing if it degenerates into a performance whose content is irrelevant. We need to beware of valuing some scheme simply because it produces interreader reliability. Reliability is high, but what does a 3 or 4 really mean in any context outside the room where the scoring is occurring? No question that it means quite a lot to the students who have taken the test—it places them in a level of college composition or it increases or decreases their scores on tests such as the National Teacher's Examination.

But how well should a beginning teacher be able to write? And what does the NTE test itself suggest to new teachers about the role of writing in their own classrooms? What kinds of things will they ask their students to do as a result? As we are tested, so we will test others. Frankly, I'd rather test a teacher's ability to get students enthused about writing—that, of course, includes getting the teacher enthused about her own writing. I'd also like that new teacher to know something of current theories about the teaching of writing if only as an indication that all methods of teaching writing assume certain things about language and about learning in general; all methods of teaching writing, that is, are philosophically based, whether we recognize the basis or not. But, of course, the writing test she has just taken invalidates those theories I want her to know.

In addition, this sort of brainwashing, holistic testing, and grading separates the graders from the testmakers and often separates the latter from those who devise the standards for admittance into a particular profession. Graders are protected from the consequences of their grading, and teachers are isolated from judgments of students they have taught. Furthermore, new teachers are pragmatically taught something quite undesirable about writing.

So, this is my third myth: that we know what good writing is and that, in meaningful contexts, we can agree when we apply those standards to pieces of writing. Students have always known we don't agree. They tell us over and over again that a former teacher or their roommate's teacher would have given them a different grade (usually higher of course), although in their more honest exchanges, they'd also admit that some prior teacher would have given them a lower grade. Though they may be exaggerating the size of the differences, they're not wrong in principle. Such disagreements exist all over. I've had the same article (revised each time of course) rejected by *College Composition and Communication* three times. One reader has been fairly consistent in his or her comments; I'd love to sit with that reader and discuss the issues I want to raise. But the other readers tell me disparate things. One thinks my subject is strongly significant within the profession; another considers it only somewhat significant. One thinks the personal references enrich my piece; another thinks they make the style rough and uneven. The truth is that for all sorts of reasons, readers don't agree on texts. We may be judging at different levels (unskilled, skilled, professional) but there's no more agreement at one level than at the others. It's no easier to determine a student's readiness for regular composition than it is to certify graduate level competency or a paper's suitability for publication.

This brings me to the last and most harmful of my myths: the myth that there is some Platonic image out there of "good writing" and that there is as a result a Platonic standard of writing which we can all learn to apply uniformly. Within this myth, the problem is only that we haven't yet discovered this absolute standard, but if we keep working at it, we will find it some day.

But there is no such Platonic ideal—there are only lots and lots of real texts around us in our world, some of which we have to judge because they're written by our students within an educational system which says we have to judge them. But, in real-world reading, we always judge for a reason, within a context, according to the purposes a writer sets up. Thus, the only decisions we can make are contextual. Over and over at ETS grading sessions, I've heard graders say that they know that some paper they've scored gets a 3 by the standards we've been asked to adopt, but that they'd never "in the real world" give it that high a rating. By "real world" I assume they mean the usual context in which they grade.

We all judge holistically, despite the fact that we can then find reasons for our judgments. We judge first and then articulate our reasons. The rhetoricians Perelman and Olbrechts-Tyteca believe this to be true of all our decisions. Thus we react to discourses as a whole and not to parts of discourses in isolation. And because we judge on the basis of whole discourses, we inevitably take into consideration at the conscious and unconscious level an integration of all the traits of a piece of writing. We don't judge on the basis of one or two of these—we judge on the basis of the whole which is always greater than its parts. This is not to deny that within my holistic judgments I don't value one trait more than someone else might.

So, what am I saying—that we can't judge at all and should just give it up altogether? Well, in one very real sense, I'd love to say that. Many of you here have been talking about writing centers and what goes on and can go on in them. One of the wonderful things about being a writing center tutor is that one doesn't have to give grades: one's function is simply to help students become better writers—usually through talk and revision and feedback and such, not through grades. "This is what you've done well, do more of it." "This is what doesn't work well for me because I don't see its relation to your main point; can you do something to help me with this?" These are the sorts of things we can say and do when we're writing center tutors. And, most importantly, we can through our talk and feedback begin to direct students toward becoming evaluators of their own texts—at least to the point of understanding where they may need to think about doing some more work. Evaluation and feedback merge. Almost everyone I know who has moved from the classroom into a writing center loves the emancipation from grading and finds it stimulates whole new ways of looking at and commenting on students' texts. We don't like grading.

Think about it. Have you ever noticed that you can find lots of articles on assessment and evaluation, but how many articles have you read or seen published on grading—on the actual giving of grades? Not very many. Most of us would just rather not talk about it at all; it's the dirty thing we have to do in the dark of our own offices. We can spend lots of time talking about teaching writing and encouraging students to like writing—to find subjects they can relate to, to find ways of dealing with subjects they have trouble relating to, to give and receive feedback, to work on revision, and so forth. We love to talk about those things to each other; we don't love to talk about grading and we do very little of such talking, though we're likely to moan and groan about it.

But, modern society and the structure of modern educational institutions are simply not going to let us not deal with the issue. We are stuck giving grades and administering standardized tests. But are we?

There is a movement afoot in elementary and secondary schools to give teachers more say in the running of schools and in the make-up of curricula. Finally, there seems to be developing some institutional awareness of the value of a classroom teacher's knowledge. That movement needs to move into college writing classrooms so that what we know will be given as much credit as almost all other college faculty's knowledge. Who's checking up on their standards? I know there are lots of bad teachers out there—I've had them; you've had them; my kids have had them; I have some in my department. But I see little reason to build systems as ways to subvert bad teachers; we need to build systems that release the strengths of good teachers. We need to take more of a hand in our own fates. What are some ideas we can build on?

First, we need to realize that our inability to agree on standards and their applications is not something we need to be ashamed of—something to hang our heads and wring our hands about in the presence of our colleagues in the sciences or other disciplines (even including our literature colleagues at times) who have "content" to test. Our inability is no sign of weakness—far from it; it is a sign of strength, of the life and vitality of words and the exchange of words. For, if we agreed, we could set up hierarchies and fit ourselves and others into them and then all could dictate to those below them and follow the orders of those above them. And in fact, in such a set up there would have to be an autocrat at the top who knows what's best for us and who knows what texts are best. Then someone would know what sort of texts to write and to teach and the variety would leave our profession and along with the variety, the richness.

Texts reflect life and the multitude of tastes and standards in real life; it is for that reason that we're motivated to create them, as expressions of our place in a multifaceted world. We've learned that texts have a peculiar strength, a peculiar ability to make us feel ourselves and the uniqueness of those selves.

Colleagues in other disciplines can tsk-tsk-tsk at our subjectivity because theirs is so well hidden. Do introductory biology teachers agree on what should be taught, what should be tested, and how tests should be balanced and averaged into the final grade? I doubt it. Have all introductory biology teachers in CUNY gotten together recently to discuss these issues? I doubt that too. When I'm not teaching composition, I'm teaching introductory Old English. It will come as no surprise to you to know that no one else is teaching it at the same time I am. I determine what to teach and when, what to test and when, and what elements to figure into my final grade. If there were 39 other sections of introductory Old English, I'd bet we'd be called to a meeting one day to talk about how to measure competency in Old English and how to determine when students should move on to the next semester. And someone would come up with a standardized test just to make certain I was indeed teaching my students what they needed to know about Old English language and literature.

Let's not apologize for our lack of agreement—let's make it work for us. How can we do that?

Well, I've certainly cast much doubt on our ability to agree on standards, but I've never cast doubt on our ability to *have* them. Each of us does have his or her standards: we read a text and we judge it almost as a reflex action, the judgment usually growing out of whether or not we like the text. Each of us also has the ability, enhanced when we talk with others, of figuring out the basis of the judgments we make. We can learn to articulate that basis for ourselves, for our students, and for other teachers. Frankly, if we can't, we shouldn't be teachers of writing. Our judgments are the result of a number of factors—what we've read, what our values are, what our philosophy is, who our colleagues are, what our own education has been, and for many of us, years and years of reading and responding to student papers. Whatever those factors are, they feed into our judgments. Thus, there is a kind of individual validity of judgment which arises from our well-trained and experienced response to all sorts of texts, including student texts. In a very real sense, no one else can "disprove" my response and judgment of a text.

But there is another kind of validity of judgment which can come from the pooling of individual judgments in the process of discussion of specific papers about which decisions need to be made for reasons we all know within a context we all share, a validity quite different from ETS readings. The more we participate in such collaborative decision making, the more we become a community—a community which exists in a very specific time and place and for a very specific purpose within that time and place.

This is in fact what we do in our portfolio system at Stony Brook. A passing portfolio is what students need in order to satisfy the first level of the writing requirement at Stony Brook. A portfolio passes if at least two teachers agree that it is passing. The judgment is holistic in terms of the whole portfolio.

So, what I am saying is that there are two sorts of valid judgments—the totally personal and the communal—but it has to be a community which is engaged in conversation about teaching and standards all the time, not just during grading sessions and not in the abstract. These discussions always have to be tied to actual student papers, and they need to include the student's teacher and be based on a range of work.

Additionally, and perhaps paradoxically, I want to argue for the importance and benefit of evaluation. The more we talk about evaluation with our colleagues, the better we'll become at giving feedback to our students on their writing and the better we'll be able to guide our students into making their own evaluations of all sorts of texts, including their own. James Moffett wisely reminds us that the more talk we hear, the more our own voices are likely to be individualized, and yet remain solidly embedded in the language which provides the basis for communication. The same is true of evaluation. The more we engage in talk with students and colleagues about our reactions to texts, the more we're able to construct individual evaluations firmly embedded in our communities. Ultimately our students also need to learn that to understand the variety of ways a particular community will respond to their texts. This understanding will open the doors to the revision and improvement of texts based on context and purpose and personal intentions. Without some internalization of our voices and through our voices an internalization of the voices of our community, students will not be able to become good editors and revisers of their own writing.

And so, outsider as I am, I'd like to propose something fairly radical to you, all the while recognizing that any evaluation system needs to grow from the strengths and initiation of individual teachers; it cannot be imposed from above—the standards must come from within the group and be constantly open to alteration and transmutation. My suggestions are meant to start a conversation.

Here's my suggestion: Conduct your classes as you always do, getting students to collect all their work, formal and informal writings, graded and ungraded, journals, whatever you ask them to write, but including I hope some writing about their own writing. Many of you undoubtedly already do this. Two weeks before the end of the term ask your students to look through their own folders and write a letter summarizing the contents, the sorts of processes involved in producing those contents, including also some analysis of the strengths and weaknesses of the writing, concluding with their estimates of whether they should pass on to another level. You will then meet with each student (or perhaps only with those selected because their status is problematic) and discuss their evaluations of themselves and your evaluations of them. In the final week (or during the time normally spent scoring standardized tests) meet with a group of your colleagues and discuss the following specific folders:

1. A folder you are certain passes
2. A folder you are certain fails
3. All folders on the borderline

Whatever decisions the group makes would be final. Even if teachers, particularly adjuncts, were paid extra for these group sessions, the overall cost would have to be less than all it costs to prepare, administer, and store thousands of standardized tests every year.

The two questions I'm most often asked about portfolio grading are 1) doesn't it take loads of time and 2) how reliable is it? No, it really doesn't take loads of time because it usually demonstrates that something else we're spending lots of time on doesn't warrant that time. As for the second question, how valid (not reliable) is what's currently being done? Because you and I agree on a score doesn't mean that the student whose paper we are reading is necessarily the writer we say she or he is. What's more, Roberta Camp of ETS has a delightful little table that I love to show skeptics; it's a statistical study which demonstrates that the more people who read a particular set of papers, the more genres or modes there are in the set, and the more examples of each genre or mode there are, the higher the reliability—that is, the more likely it will be that evaluators will agree on their evaluations. This is the closest we can come to making judgments about a writer; everyone's running about trying to make a difficult job easy. Was the Nobel Prize for Literature ever given to a writer who produced just one book?

You cannot, of course, adopt my plan because it's my plan, not yours. But you can come together with like-minded colleagues and begin to try some things—things that don't bastardize what you teach in your classrooms. Through trial and error, you'll find a way if you continually remind yourselves that evaluation of writing cannot and should not be removed from those contexts which alone provide the possibility for meaningful and useful evaluation. We cannot continue to allow others to tell us how to do the job we know best how to do. But if we don't step in, speak up, develop strategies, others, including state legislators, will gain greater and greater influence over our classrooms. They will be making those decisions which it is our responsibility to make in ways consonant with what we have learned and are continuing to learn about language and the teaching of writing. If you work together, I'm confident you can find ways to evaluate your students' writing fairly for whatever purposes you need, and thus do your job better. If you do work together and pool your knowledge, experience, and commitment to your students and your work, you will come up with something better. Then I can hope with a great deal of confidence that by the year 2000 the CUNY Writing Assessment Test, as we know it (and its clones throughout the country) will no longer exist.

Good luck.

REFERENCES

Camp, Roberta. "The Writing Folder in Post-Secondary Assessment." *Directions and Misdirections in English Evaluation.* Ed. Peter J. A. Evans. Canadian Council of Teachers of English, 1985.

Perelman, Chaim, and L. Olbrechts-Tyteca. *The New Rhetoric: A Treatise on Argumentation.* Trans. John Wilkinson and Purcell Weaver. Notre Dame, IN: U of Notre Dame P, 1969.

Ponsot, Marie, and Rosemary Dean. *Beat Not the Poor Desk.* Upper Montclair, NJ: Boynton/Cook, 1982.

Shaughnessy, Mina P. *Errors and Expectations.* New York: Oxford UP, 1977.

Swaffar, Janet K. "Curricular Issues and Language Research: The Shifting Interaction." *Professions 89*: 32–38.

White, Edward. *Teaching and Assessing Writing.* San Francisco: Jossey-Bass, 1985.

QUESTIONS FOR REFLECTION, JOURNAL WRITING, AND DISCUSSION

1. Belanoff says she realized after some time in teaching that she needed to teach basic writers and ESL students in the same way as "privileged students." Do you agree that this must be done?

2. Belanoff says "Certainly the best classroom teachers I've known are tutors." Do you agree?

3. What do you think of the four myths discussed by Belanoff? Do you agree that they are myths?

4. Belanoff objects to "brainwashing holistic testing" and to grading that "separates the graders from the testmaker." Do you agree? What do you think of the growing uses of standardized, often "high stakes" tests these days in order to achieve high standards in education?

Chapter 20

Evaluating ESL Writing

Elaine Brooks

Elaine Brooks is Associate Professor of ESL at Brooklyn College, a branch of the City University of New York, and deputy chair of the ESL Program in the English Department. She has taught a variety of college-level ESL courses in addition to Freshman Composition and department electives related to language. Her research interests have centered on the relationships among ESL students' reading, writing, and first- and second-language literacy development. She is also coauthor of *Making Peace: A Reading/ Writing/Thinking Text on Global Community.*

In the introduction to his book, *Empowering Education,* Ira Shor discusses his students' feelings of failure and frustration in relation to the City University Writing Assessment Test (CWAT) and tells how he used their feelings and experiences as the source of the class's inquiry for "critical teaching" and "dialogic pedagogy." He raised questions for readers to consider: What do our tests do? What is communicated about writing and language development through our use of such tests? Shor was describing a class of native English speakers enrolled in a basic writing course at the College of Staten Island approximately 20 years ago. The feelings of failure and frustration exist equally among English-as-a-second-language (ESL) students who, 20 years later, are still facing the same test under more or less the same conditions.* Even more interesting, perhaps, faculty are still asking the same questions: What do our tests do? What is communicated about writing and language?

Pat Belanoff, in "The Myths of Assessment," points out that "we (those of us who work in classrooms and writing centers) don't like grading." She reminds us that although people write about assessment and evaluation, there is little written about the actual giving of grades: "Most of us would

---

*The CUNY Board of Trustees recently decided to replace the CUNY Writing Assessment Test with a nationally normed writing test, but the new test will be similar to the previous one, and I will have the same sorts of considerations in determining whether or not an ESL student is ready to be placed in a freshman composition course.

just rather not talk about it at all." In this article I intend to do what Belanoff said we don't like to do: I will share students' CWAT essays and discuss how I would grade them. I do this in an effort to help create the collaborative decision making and sense of community among writing teachers suggested by Belanoff, "a community which exists in a very specific time and place and for a very specific purpose within that time and place . . . a community which is engaged in conversation about teaching and standards all the time, not just during grading sessions and not in the abstract."

I write as an ESL instructor and certified reader of CWATs, a member of the English department at a four-year public college in a culturally diverse, urban setting. The Freshman Skills Assessment Tests (in reading and math as well as writing) have been used for placement on admission to the college just slightly longer than I have been employed here, around 20 years. The purpose of the tests is to determine whether or not students require remedial instruction in writing, reading, or math. The tests are also used to certify when students no longer need such instruction and can exit ESL or remedial courses and, in the case of writing, enter freshman composition.

The CUNY Writing Assessment Test (CWAT), specifically, instructs students to write a persuasive essay on one of two topics related to issues of general public interest (such as the effect of television violence on children); it is not assumed that students have read or prepared prior to the brief prompts given on the exam itself. They have 50 minutes in which to write the essay, which is graded holistically by at least two certified readers and given a score by each reader on a scale of 1–6. For several years, readers have been certified by the central CUNY administration after participating in a training session during which their consistency and accuracy as readers according to the CUNY scale has been determined by the chief readers of the central office; certified readers are renormed at the beginning of each session during which they are to read exams. Students must receive a score of 4 from at least two readers to be permitted to take Freshman Composition. The process at my college is more or less as described in the sections that follow.

THE EVALUATION PROCESS

When students enter the college, they take the skills assessment tests. If the first reader of a student's essay thinks the writer is a second-language learner, the essay is given to an ESL reader to evaluate. If the first reader's judgment is confirmed, the student is identified as an ESL student to be registered in an ESL course, rather than a basic skills writing course for native speakers. ESL courses are taught by instructors with expertise in working with students who are nonnative learners of English, are made up of only nonnative students, and may be either integrated skills or freestanding writing courses depending on students' needs as ascertained by their incoming placement tests. Once students pass the CWAT, they may take any section of Freshman Composition; nonetheless, at my college, several sections are reserved specifically for ESL students and are taught by ESL professionals, in case either the students or their previous instructor think the students would benefit from continued support in relation to their English language development. Such sections are optional.

How do we readers determine whether or not a writer belongs in an ESL class? Clearly, in the United States and especially in New York City, the student's name is not a reliable indicator. Although on incoming exams students respond to three questions on the back of their test booklets (questions about where they were born, how long they have been in the United States, and their native language), which may provide useful information, the information is not always a clear indicator of where a student should be placed. As a reader, I read the essay first, without looking at the back page where the answers to these questions or a first reader's score may influence my evaluation before I have had a chance to formulate it. I use such information as an addition, not as the basis for my judgment.

I, THE EVALUATOR

Then what do I look for? There are the obvious factors: the content of a student's essay, the knowledge/control of English structures, and the vocabulary. Relatively often, essays are "borderline." They may have errors that indicate a second-language learner, yet the content and fluency may seem like those of a native speaker. These may be the essays of students who came to the United States at a fairly young age and who have had most of their schooling here, or they may be those of students from countries where English is an important, if not the native, language, such as Pakistan or Nigeria. It is after I have read the essay and formed an opinion as to where the student should be placed that the information on the back of the test booklet may help me in refining my evaluation. But even at that point, what I have in front of me is a paper, not a person. As Vivian Zamel (*Discovery of Competence*) states, "All students come to the classroom as competent speakers of a first language, and perhaps of others . . . and they can tell us a great deal about what they bring and what . . . they're currently confronting." However, such information awaits the classroom teacher, not the evaluator sitting with the student's essay without the student. Essay evaluators must make important decisions for students based on what they see on the pages alone. Evaluators try to assess whether the errors students have made are "teachable" or are the kind, such as prepositions and idiomatic expressions, that require time and experience to master. More importantly, evaluators try to assess whether students' writing indicates they would profit from special ESL instruction or whether a student is sufficiently proficient in English, despite some remaining second-language errors, to function well in a mainstream Freshman Composition course with native speakers and an instructor who may or may not be prepared to help with second-language difficulties.

As an ESL program administrator, I worry a little less about the preciseness of a student's placement at the beginning of the student's course of study at the college. Some students are sufficiently assertive to go to a classroom teacher or department representative and argue if they feel they were misevaluated. They will ask to have their essay or course placement reconsidered. Also, when instructors assign a diagnostic essay the first day of class, if they feel certain students were not placed accurately, they can send the students and/or their essay for reconsideration.

At my school, the testing process is repeated, albeit a little more sympathetically, at the end of the semester. Students retake the CWAT with a different set of questions, which is then read by at least two certified readers to determine if the students are "ready" to exit ESL or basic skills courses and enter Freshman Composition. At the end of the term, students generally have an advocate they did not have on entry: their instructor. Students' own instructors do not make the final determination as to whether or not they may exit the ESL program and enter Freshman Composition, but instructors may provide input. If a student fails the retest, the instructor may choose to have the student retest again (if the essay is not deemed representative of the student's ability or if the readers' judgment is considered unfair) or to appeal the evaluation (for similar reasons but without necessarily retesting the student). In any case, a new element (the student's instructor) has been added to the process; there is now an "informed" person to advocate for the student, someone familiar with the student's work over a longer period of time and under different circumstances. The classroom teacher is in a better position than the essay evaluator to speak about the student's language learning and composition proficiency. This is true because of problems arising from the testing situation. Stephen Krashen discusses language learning (as distinct from language acquisition) as "conscious knowledge of rules and explicit attention to form . . . [which] accounts for learners' ability to monitor their own accuracy and correct their first attempts at an expression, *but only under certain conditions*: they must have a lot of time, their anxiety has to be low, and they must already know the relevant rule" (emphasis added). Existing testing procedures do not provide such conditions. It may therefore be difficult for the reader of an exam who does not know the writer to make an accurate judgment about writing proficiency. In fact, the test situation implies that only students who can perform under this pressure are sufficiently fluent.

Nonetheless, evaluators are required to make these determinations, as circumstances stand, on a regular basis. Belanoff believes valid judgments can be made if individuals, including the teacher, consider a range of students' work and discuss specific papers within a specific context. She also suggests the importance and benefit of evaluation based on collegial discussion for improving feedback to students. As a teacher, I find it taxing, if not frustrating, to explain to students who have failed a writing exam the reasons they have failed when I do not understand the reasons; readers simply score essays without providing their reasons for the score. Therefore, to support Belanoff's suggestions about assessment and as an incentive to future discussions, I include my explanations of the papers.

THE STUDENTS' PAPERS

The papers I will discuss were written at the end of a semester by ESL students enrolled in an advanced-level, integrated reading and writing course. To exit the ESL program and be able to register for Freshman Composition, the students must receive a score of 4 on a scale of 1–6 from each of two readers. They should be able to write persuasive essays of approximately 350 words within a 50-minute time period. The students do not know the topic ahead of time, nor do they read a text for the exam.

Ellen's Essay

Outline

~~Parents should never lie to their children, even about frightening things such as serious illness, financial problems, or divorce.~~

- Children's trust their parents, why lie to them
- Denial isn't a solution to cover the pain.
- Acceptance facing the problem and effect.
- Children should the real reasons for the problem, or esle they might think they cause such problem.

        always

Children are ∧ encouraged not to lie.[1] Parents teach their kids that lie will hurt the recievers, and no one will trust a liar.[2] Parents should teach their children not to lie by telling their children the truth in any situation.[3] Children learn from the actions of the parent than their speaking words.[4] Lie is just cover-up, not a solution in painful situation.[5] If children found

out their parents lied to them, they wouldn't lose their trust
for their parents.[6]

        my

    For example, ∧ neighbor John, a divorced man, lost his child-
ren's trust.[7] John and his wife decided to get a divorce because

                  and his ex-

John spent too much time working.[8] John ∧ wife told their children
that their father is going to a long business in other city when
John was packing up to leave.[9] After a few weeks, the children
would keep asking John when he would be back when John talked to
his children on the phone.[10] The children had finally asked their
mother if they had been bad that why their father didn't come

               when

home.[11] The children started to cry ∧ their mother leaves

   with a baby sitter

them ∧ to go to work, and get very nervous when their mother comes
home 30 minutes later than usual.[12] A year later, when the older
child heard about the divorce from a relative, he became really
mad and didn't speak to his parents for a long time.[13] He started
ask a lot questions, and always think he is being lie to.[14]

    Lie can create insecurity in any one, especially in child.[15]
Parents should never lie to their children because they don't
want lose their children's trust.[16]

Ellen: Not Ready?

Ellen received a score of 3/3 on the essay she wrote. As readers, we ask ourselves, was she able to develop an essay that presents a coherent, organized
argument of some substance? Did she incorporate support for her ideas?
Did she write clearly with an appropriate level of correctness in terms of
grammar, spelling, and punctuation?

    She began her essay with the idea that children are taught not to lie by
their parents' words, but that they must also see that their parents do not lie
through the parents' behavior, or children will lose trust in their parents.

    She then provides an example of a neighbor who had lied to his chil-
dren when he and his wife decided to divorce; she describes the effect of
the lie on his child when the child learned the truth indirectly. Ellen ends
her essay with a brief discussion of how lying creates insecurity in anyone,
concluding that parents should not lie to their children. Ellen's writing in
English is fairly fluent and the organization and content indicate that she
understands what is expected of her in this context, but my impression is
that she is limited—not as much by her knowledge of English but by her
ability to gather her thoughts on the topic, and organize and develop

them, at least within a time limit. As a reader, I do not know if she could do more if she had time, or if this is the extent of what she can do.

Although her writing is clear and the errors do not impede comprehension, her vocabulary and sentences are simple and there are still many errors that indicate a lack of knowledge and/or control of the written forms of English. Word form errors ("lie will hurt the receivers," sentence 2), tense errors ("If children found out their parents lied to them, they wouldn't lose their trust . . ." sentence 6), incorrect syntactic construction ("The children had finally asked their mother if they had been bad that why their father didn't come home." sentence 11), and verb form errors ("He started ask a lot questions, and always think he is being lie to," sentence 14) all add up to create an impression of limited ability. Superficial content is a particularly striking factor, although it may be a by-product of the exam itself, which can be said to encourage banality, as students have a short time in which to write on a general topic of which they have been given no time to inform themselves, reflect on, or discuss. When I ask myself if this student seems "ready" for freshman composition, my answer is that the student would probably benefit from another semester in an ESL course before taking on the demands of the introductory college composition course.

How do I determine such "readiness" or its lack? When I reconsider the conditions that Krashen suggests students need—to be able to apply their language learning—I doubt that students who are writing CWAT essays have the time to revise their work even if they are capable of doing so. I am also sure that their level of anxiety is fairly high. Although it may be difficult if not impossible to determine whether or not students writing under these test conditions have the knowledge with which to monitor their own accuracy, there sometimes are indications. However, I do not see such indications in Ellen's paper. There are a few words added here and there with the use of a caret, but the additions appear to be for informational purposes rather than editing: "always" in sentence 1, "my" in sentence 7, "his ex-wife" in sentence 9, and "with a babysitter" in sentence 12. She did make a brief outline on the inside cover of her test booklet before beginning to write, yet the outline is not much more than notes to herself about points she wants to include. There are no obvious indications that she reread and made any changes to her essay, either its content or written forms.

As a reader formulating an evaluation of this student's "readiness" for freshman composition with nothing more than her paper in front of me, I indicate with a score of 3 that I do not find her "ready." She is able to write clearly, but is unable to communicate her ideas in detail, with elaboration, or to do so in sentences that demonstrate complexity or variety. I think she needs and deserves the time to develop her ability to write more richly and complexly in English before attempting the reading and writing demands of the introductory composition course. She will be in other college-level courses at the same time that she is preparing for freshman composition. I hope that her knowledge of and comfort in using English will continue to grow as she reads and writes in those other courses, which will serve to prepare her further for passing the Writing Assessment Test next time.

Agnieszka's Essay

Childhood is an innocent period in human's life, when people are not aware of many things.[1] Children often don't realize what is happening around them.[2] They are usually protected by their parents, who don't want them to know the realities of the real

, such as financial ones,

world[3]. However, adults sometimes have various problems ∧ which can also affect their child's life. / ~~such as financial problems~~.[4] Should parents lie to their children about difficulties they have or should they tell them the truth, even if it is painful for the children?[5]

Parents choose different ways of raising their children.[6]

with

Some of them believe that communication ~~between~~ their ~~kinds and them~~ kids is a very important thing.[7] They want to teach their

various

children ∧ values and principals.[8] One of the most important values is urnestly.[9] If there is for example, financial problem in the family, it refers to all members of it.[10] It can be easier to sefe money when children are aware that they can't buy whatever they want.[11]

~~chi~~

Anoth~~erer~~ ~~thi~~ good thing about telling children the truth is that they can understand the reasons of their parents' behaviour.[12]

youngsters

∧

If for example, ~~they~~ want a new toy but their parents explain

at ~~in~~ the moment,

them that in the moment they can't afford it/ kids may feel

new toys

better about it, than thinking that they don't have ~~something~~ because their parents don't love them.[13]

However, some parents prefer not to tell the truth.[14] ~~so~~ They think that children are not mature enought to understand it/ and they are trying to create them happy family, without any signs of

problem.[15] Such ~~an~~ activity ⁄ can only harm children and create
false expectations about the ~~wout~~ world outside their homes.[16] When
children, ~~lik~~ raised like that become adults, they can be very
surprised about realities of life.[17]

It is very common thing that parents want to protect their
children.[18] However, they should also thing⁄k about their ~~future~~
kids' future lifes and teach them ~~wh~~ how they can deal with their

> and
problems, ~~and~~ not pretend that they don't exist.[19]

Agnieszka: Ready?

Agnieszka received a score of 4/4 on her essay (see following). How is it different from Ellen's? Both wrote on the same topic and, in fact, held the
same opinion. Although Agnieszka's essay is somewhat longer, the determination that she might be ready for freshman composition, whereas Ellen
was not, is not simply a question of number of words, but what she does
with her words.

She too begins with a general introduction to the topic, but her ideas are
expressed with more detail. In fact, she allows herself to explore the question of whether or not parents should ever lie to their children from both
sides before she begins to give her own answer; she recognizes that parents
who choose not to tell their children the truth about a given situation may
have what they feel are legitimate reasons. She makes smooth transitions
from one paragraph to another as she builds her argument and sympathetically but firmly concludes her case.

Like Ellen, she has a number of errors in the written forms of English,
but they are not errors in tense, verb form, or syntax. She misuses "human's
life" for "human life" (sentence 1). She misspells a few words (principle in
sentence 8; honesty in sentence 9; save in sentence 11; and lives in sentence
19) and makes an error or two with prepositions (for in sentence 12) or
articles (a happy family in sentence 15). Agnieszka's errors do not impede
comprehension, nor do they stand out in relation to the substance of her
essay, as Ellen's errors did. She writes in a fluent, organized manner, and
the substance of her essay indicates her understanding of the task. Unlike
the previous essay, Agnieszka's doesn't have consistent verb and sentence
structure errors, and she made better use of complex sentences. I did not
have the same impression of limitations reading her essay as I did when
reading Ellen's; I thought she was limited more by time than lack of ability.
Although she too wrote with simple vocabulary, there is more complexity
and variety to her sentence structure and more control.

What makes me think Agnieszka is more up to the demands of freshman
composition? To return to Krashen's conditions for learners to demonstrate
language learning, Agnieszka was writing within the same time limit and

with a conceivably similar anxiety level as Ellen, but there are somewhat different indications of level of language acquisition. The additions and changes to her text seem more like editing and revision, however briefly done. In sentence 4, she moved the insert "such as financial ones" closer to the problems that it elaborates, rather than just tacking it on the end of her sentence. I think this is a change that indicates the writer's understanding of clarity and style. A similar change was made in sentence 13 when she moved the phrase "at the moment" to later in the sentence. She used "with" instead of "between" in sentence 7 and added "various" to sentence 8. Were these efforts to be precise as when she replaced "something" with "new toys" in sentence 13? Once again, I had a paper, not a person, in front of me, so I could not ask the writer why the changes occurred, yet the changes appeared to be a writer's thoughtful choices. Even if Agnieszka continues to make errors in freshman composition and possibly even an increased number and kind of errors due to the effort to write more substantially and complexly in English, my impression is that she is ready for that kind of growth.

CONCLUDING COMMENTS

I hope that sharing my grading of students' assessment essays will add to the efforts to improve the reading of ESL students' written work through a discussion of how and why we grade as we do. I like to think such discussion will also lead to better placement and improved teaching as we become more conscious of what we look for: the indications of students' proficiency and what they still need to learn. Articulation of our criteria may help us learn from each other.

Some further issues I believe we should consider about ways to improve such decisions are the effects of graders reading alone in contrast to reading as a group/community, ways to improve accuracy and placement for students, and faculty collaboration in making such determinations.

I began this article with questions raised by Ira Shor: What do our tests do? What is communicated by our tests about writing and language development? When we evaluate students on the basis of one sample of their writing done within a time limit determined by administrative ease and efficiency, we should at least recognize that the sample may not be representative of their capability. In addition, if evaluators who do not know the student make decisions that affect the student's future on the basis of a writing sample, we should build into the evaluation process an opportunity for input from the student's instructor and/or other samples representative of the student's written English. Such information would strengthen the connections among teaching, learning and evaluation.

REFERENCES

Belanoff, Pat. "The Myths of Assessment." *The Journal of Basic Writing*, Vol. 10, No. 1, 1991.

Kutz, Eleanor, Suzy Q. Groden, and Vivian Zamel. *The Discovery of Competence: Teaching and Learning With Diverse Student Writers*. Portsmouth, NH: Boynton/Cook, 1993.

Raimes, Ann. "Errors: Windows Into the Mind." *College ESL*, Vol. 1, No. 2, Dec. 1991.

Shor, Ira. *Empowering Education: Critical Teaching for Social Change*. Chicago: The University of Chicago Press, 1992.

Zamel, Vivian. "Strangers in Academia: The Experience of Faculty and ESL Students Across the Curriculum." *College Composition and Communication*, Vol. 46, No. 4, Dec. 1995.

QUESTIONS FOR REFLECTION, JOURNAL WRITING, AND DISCUSSION

1. As a teacher, what would you do to help Brooks's two students, Ellen and Agnieszka? Would you treat them differently?

2. Does Agnieszka seem ready for Freshman Composition at your college? If not, what would indicate that an ESL student is ready for Freshman Composition?

3. Is it a good idea to have separate writing classes for ESL students? What are some possible advantages and disadvantages?

4. Brooks mentions that Shor questioned the value of the CUNY Writing Assessment Test 20 years ago, yet students are still facing the same, or a similar, writing test taken under the same conditions. Why is this so? Is it a good thing or not?

5. How would you define a "borderline student"? How would you decide if a borderline student should pass or fail?

Chapter 21

Fault Lines in the Contact Zone

Richard E. Miller

Richard E. Miller, author of *As If Learning Mattered: Reforming Higher Education* (Cornell University Press, 1998), is Associate Director of the writing program and an Associate Professor of English at Rutgers University, New Brunswick, New Jersey. A frequent contributor to *College English,* his articles have also appeared in *College Composition and Communication, Profession,* and *Cultural Studies.* He is currently at work on *The Hope Machine,* which looks at the role writing plays in the internalization of institutional conflicts. The following article appeared in *College English,* 56, April 1994.

On the cover of what has turned out to be the final issue of *Focus,* a magazine "for and about the people of AT&T," there's a tableaux of five happy employees, arranged so that their smiling faces provide an ethnically diverse frame for a poster bearing the slogan "TRUE VOICE." Although the cover promotes the image of a harmonious, multicultural working environment, one gets a slightly different image of the company in the "Fun 'n' Games" section at the back of the magazine. In the lower right hand corner of this section, beneath a quiz about AT&T's international reach, there is a drawing of a globe with people speaking avidly into telephones all over the world: there's a woman in a babushka in Eastern Europe; there's a man with a moustache wearing a beret in France; and, following this theme and the telephone lines south, there is a gorilla in Africa holding a telephone (50). A gorilla?

Although Bob Allen, AT&T's CEO, has acknowledged in a letter to all AT&T employees that this was "a deplorable mistake on the part of a company with a long, distinguished record of supporting the African-American community," he has so far met with little success in his attempts to manage the crisis caused by the distribution of this illustration to literally hundreds of thousands of AT&T employees worldwide. First, the art director who approved the cartoon and the illustrator who drew it were dismissed; commitments were made to hire more minority artists, illustrators, and photographers; a hotline was opened up for expressing grievances and making suggestions; AT&T's Diversity Team was instructed to make recommendations "for immediate and long-term improvement"; and, as a cathartic gesture, employees were encouraged to "tear that page out and throw it in the trash where it belongs," since they wouldn't want "AT&T material circulating that violates our values" (Allen). Then, when the hotline overheated and the battle raging across the company's electronic bulletin board continued unabated, Allen pulled the plug on the entire *Focus* venture and assigned all its employees to other posts. This is certainly one strategy for handling offensive material: declare solidarity with those who have been offended (Allen's letter is addressed "To all AT&T people"); voice outrage (it was "a deplorable mistake"); shut down avenues for expressing such thoughts (fire or reassign employees, dismantle the magazine). While this approach undoubtedly paves the way for restoring the appearance of corporate harmony, does it have any pedagogical value? That is, does the expulsion of offending individuals and the restriction of lines of communication address the roots of the racist feelings that produced the image of the gorilla as the representative image of the African? Or does it merely seek to insure that the "deplorable mistake" of having such an image surface in a public document doesn't occur again?

"What is the place of unsolicited oppositional discourse, parody, resistance, critique in the imagined classroom community?" Mary Louise Pratt asks in "Arts of the Contact Zone" (39). In Pratt's essay, this question is occasioned not by an event as troubling as the cartoon discussed above, but by the fact that Pratt's son, Manuel, received "the usual star" from his teacher for writing a paragraph promoting a vaccine that would make school attendance unnecessary. Manuel's teacher, ignoring the critique of schooling leveled in the paragraph, registered only that the required work of responding to the assignment's questions about a helpful invention had been completed and, consequently, appended the silent, enigmatic star. For Pratt, the teacher's star labors to conceal a conflict in the classroom over what work is to be valued and why, presenting instead the image that everything is under control—students are writing and the teacher is evaluating. It is this other strategy for handling difficult material, namely ignoring the content and focusing only on the outward forms of obedient behavior, that leads Pratt to wonder about the place of unsolicited oppositional discourse in the classroom. With regard to Manuel's real classroom community, the answer to this question is clear: the place of unsolicited oppositional discourse is no place at all.

Given Pratt's promising suggestion that the classroom be reconceived as a "contact zone," which she defines as a social space "where cultures meet, clash, and grapple with each other, often in contexts of highly asymmetrical relations of power" (34), this example of the kind of writing produced in such a contact zone seems oddly benign. One might expect that the writing Pratt's students did in Stanford's Culture, Ideas, Values course, which she goes on to discuss, would provide ample evidence of more highly charged conflicts involving "unsolicited oppositional discourse, parody, resistance, critique." Unfortunately, however, although Pratt avows that this course "put ideas and identities on the line" (39), she offers no example of how her students negotiated this struggle in their writing or of how their teachers participated in and responded to their struggles on and over "the line." Instead, Pratt leaves us with just two images of writers in the contact zone—her son, Manuel, and Guaman Poma, author of a largely unread sixteenth-century bilingual chronicle of Andean culture. Both, to be sure, are readily sympathetic figures, obviously deserving better readers and more thoughtful respondents, but what about the illustrator who provided what might be considered an unsolicited parody or critique of AT&T's "Common Bond values," which state that "we treat each other with respect and dignity, valuing individual and cultural differences"? What "Arts of the Contact Zone" are going to help us learn how to read and respond to voices such as this? And what exactly are we to say or do when the kind of racist, sexist, and homophobic sentiments now signified by the term "hate speech" surface in our classrooms?

In focusing on a student essay that, like the *Focus* cartoon, is much less likely to arouse our sympathies than Manuel's inventive critique, my concern is to examine the heuristic value of the notion of the contact zone when applied not only to student writing, but also to our own academic discussions of that writing. The student's essay I begin with was so offensive that when it was first mentioned at an MLA workshop on "Composition, Multiculturalism, and Political Correctness" in December 1991, provisions were quickly made to devote an entire panel to the essay at the 1992 Conference on College Composition and Communication, and this, in turn, led to a follow-up workshop on "The Politics of Response" at CCCC in 1993. Thus, I would hazard a guess that this student essay, entitled "Queers, Bums, and Magic," has seized the attention of more teachers, taken up more institutional time, and provoked more debate than any other single piece of unpublished undergraduate writing in recent memory. Before beginning my discussion of "Queers, Bums, and Magic," I should note, however, that in what follows I have intentionally allowed the content of the student's essay and the wider sweep of its context to emerge in fragments, as they did in the contact zone of the national conferences, where competing modes of response served alternately to reveal and obscure both the text and information about its writer. This partial, hesitant, contradictory motion defines how business gets transacted in the contact zones of our classroom and our conferences, where important questions often don't get heard, are ignored, or simply don't get posed in the heat of the moment, with the result that vital contextual information often is either never disclosed or comes to light very late in the discussion. I believe that following this motion provides a stark portrait of the ways in which dominant assumptions about students and student writing allow unsolicited oppositional discourse to pass through the classroom unread and unaffected.

"Queers, Bums, and Magic" was written in a pre-college-level community college composition class taught by Scott Lankford at Foothill College in Los Altos Hills, California, in response to an assignment taken from *The Bedford Guide for College Writers* that asked students to write a report on group behavior. One of Lankford's students responded with an essay detailing a drunken trip he and some friends made to "San Fagcisco" to study "the lowest class . . . the queers and the bums." The essay recounts how the students stopped a man on Polk Street, informed him that they were doing a survey and needed to know if he was "a fag." From here, the narrative follows the students into a dark alleyway where they discover, as they relieve themselves drunkenly against the wall, that they have been urinating on a homeless person. In a frenzy, the students begin to kick the homeless person, stopping after "30 seconds of non-stop blows to the body," at which point the writer says he "thought the guy was dead." Terrified, the students make a run for their car and eventually escape the city.

It's a haunting piece, one that gave Lankford many sleepless nights and one that has traveled from conference to conference because it is so unsettling. When Lankford discussed it at CCCC in his paper entitled "How Would You Grade a Gay-Bashing?" the engaged, provocative, and at times heated hourlong discussion that followed provided a forum for a range of competing commitments to, as Pratt might say, "meet, clash, and grapple" with one another. What was clear from this interchange was that part of what makes "Queers, Bums, and Magic" so powerful is that it disables the most familiar kinds of conference presentations and teacher responses. Here is writing that cannot easily be recuperated as somehow praiseworthy despite its numerous surface flaws, writing that instead offers direct access to a voice from the margins that seems to belong there. The reactions given to Lankford's request to know how those present "would have handled such a situation" varied considerably, both in intensity and in detail, but most of them, I would say, fell into one of three categories: read the essay as factual and respond accordingly; read the essay as fictional and respond accordingly; momentarily suspend the question of the essay's factual or fictional status and respond accordingly.

In the first category, by far the most popular, I place all suggestions that the student be removed from the classroom and turned over either to a professional counselor or to the police. Such a response, audience members argued repeatedly, would be automatic if the student had described suicidal tendencies, involvement in a rape, or having been the victim of incest. To substantiate this point, one member of the audience spoke passionately about Marc LeClerc, saying that the Canadian gunman had revealed his hatred of women to many of his college professors prior to his murderous rampage. As compelling as such examples seem, it is important to realize that this line of argumentation assumes that the essay records a set of criminal events that actually occurred or, at the very least, evidences the fantasy life of a potentially dangerous person. This assessment of the student essay is striking because the audience members had little to go on beyond the kind of brief outline that has been provided here. In other words, although no one in the audience had actually read the student essay, many felt quite confident recommending that, based on brief excerpts and a summary of the essay's content alone, the student ought to be turned over to either the legal or the psychological authorities! These respondents, starting with the assumption of a stable and unified subjectivity for Lankford's student, went on to construct a student writer incapable of dissimulation. Within such a paradigm, the actual text the student produced was of secondary importance at best in relation to a hasty and, as we will see, partial summary of the text's contents.

Lankford chose another route entirely, electing "to respond to the essay exactly as if it were a fictional short story." What this meant in practice was that he restricted himself to commenting on the student's word choice, querying the student about his imagined audience, acknowledging the text's "reasonable detail," and "favorably comparing the essay to A *Clockwork Orange* in its straightforward depictions of nightmarish 'megaviolence' and surrealistic detail." According to these criteria, Lankford determined that the essay merited a low B. Although this strategy provoked the wrath of a large portion of the audience, Lankford argued that it was not without its virtues: by focusing only on the formal features of the essay and its surface errors, Lankford was able to successfully deflect the student writer's use of his writing to "bash" his professor, with the unexpected result that the student not only stayed in the course, but actually chose to study with Lankford again the next semester. Thus, despite Lankford's own assessment of his approach as "spineless," he was in a position to insist that it was nevertheless a "qualified success," since the student in question "learned to cope with an openly gay instructor with some measure of civility" (5).

Among those present who had access to the student's paper, there were those on the panel who agreed with Lankford's approach but disagreed with the grade assigned. These respondents spoke of the essay's faulty organization, the problems evident in its plot development, the number of mechanical errors. On these grounds alone, one panelist assured the audience, the paper ought to have received a failing mark. If the first category of response displays a curious willingness to dispense with the formality of reading the student's essay, Lankford's strategy asks teachers to look away from what the student's writing is attempting to do—at the havoc it is trying to wreak in the contact zone—and restrict their comments to the essays's surface features and formal qualities, affixing the "usual star" or black mark

as the situation warrants. Such a strategy itself invites parody: would changing the word choice/spelling errors/verb agreement problems/organization
really "improve" this student's essay? Would such changes help inch it
towards being, say, an excellent gay-bashing essay, one worthy of an A?

I intend this question to be deliberately troubling and offensive. The
problem, however, is not that this approach is "spineless." To the contrary,
in Lankford's hands, this kind of response made it possible for both the
teacher and the student to remain in the contact zone of his classroom,
allowing them to negotiate the difficult business of working with and
through important issues of cultural and sexual difference. By suggesting
that his difficulty in responding to the student essay is a personal problem,
that it revolves around a question of "spine," Lankford obscures the ways in
which the difficulty that confronted him as he struggled to find a way to
respond to "Queers, Bums, and Magic" is the trace of a broader institutional conflict over what it means for a teacher to work on and with student
writing. Lankford and the others who spoke of responding to the essay as "a
piece of fiction" did not suddenly invent this curiously decontextualized
way of responding to writing, this way that can imagine no other approach
to discussing a piece of writing than to speak of how it is organized, the apt-
ness of the writer's word choice, and the fit between the text and its audience. Such an approach to writing instruction has been proffered in the
majority of grammars, rhetorics, and readers that have filled English classrooms since before the turn of the century: it has been around for so long
that, despite the grand "turn to process" in writing instruction, it continues
to suggest itself as the most "natural" or "reasonable" way to define the
work of responding to student writing. All of which leaves us with this profoundly strange state of affairs where the discipline explicitly devoted to
studying and articulating the power of the written word gets thrown into
crisis when a student produces a powerful piece of writing.

To sum up, then, these two lines of response to the student essay—one
recommending the removal of the offending writer from circulation and the
other overlooking the offensive aspects of the student text in order to attend
to its surface and structural features—taken together dramatize how little
professional training in English Studies prepares teachers to read and
respond to the kinds of parodic, critical, oppositional, dismissive, resistant,
transgressive and regressive writing that gets produced by students writing in
the contact zone of the classroom. This absence of preparation, I would
argue, actually comes into play every time a teacher sits down to comment on
a student paper: it's just that the pedagogical shortcomings of restricting
such commentary to the surface features and formal aspects of the writing
aren't as readily visible in a response to an essay on a summer vacation as they
are in a response to an essay about beating up the homeless. Unfortunately,
recent efforts to reimagine the work of responding to student writing pro-

vide little guidance for addressing this particular problem. Edward White's *Teaching and Assessing Writing,* for instance, argues for holistic scoring, but offers no suggestions on how to go about holistically scoring essays that are racist, homophobic, or misogynistic. And, similarly, the NCTE's *Writing and Response: Theory, Practice, and Research,* which asserts that "real, substantive response is in one form or another fundamental to language development" (Anson 4), never gets around to the business of discussing how to produce a "real, substantive response" to the kind of unsolicited oppositional discourse discussed here. Since this is uncharted territory, it is not surprising that we often find ourselves at a loss, not knowing what to do, where to go, or what to say once we cross this line.

One has to wonder why it is that, at a time when almost all of the current major theories on the rise celebrate partial readings, multiple subjectivities, marginalized positions, and subjugated knowledges, nearly all student essays remain essentially illegible, offered forth more often than not as the space where error exercises its full reign, or, as here, the site where some untutored evil shows its face. There seems, in other words, to be little evidence of what one might call "poststructural" or "postcolonial" trickledown, little sign that the theoretical insights that carry so much weight in our journals actually make themselves known in the pedagogical practices deployed in classrooms across the country. There were, however, a few respondents to Lankford's presentation who saw a way to smuggle some of these insights into the classroom and thereby propose more fruitful responses than either expelling the student or ignoring the content of his essay. In proposing that "Queers, Bums, and Magic" be reproduced alongside legal definitions of hate speech for the entire class to read and discuss, one panelist found a way to pull the paper out of the private corridor running between the student writer and the teacher and move it into the public arena. This approach turns the essay into a "teachable object," enabling an investigation of the writing's performative aspect—how it does its work, what its imagined project might have been, and who or what might be the possible subjects of its critique. By situating the essay in relation to legal definitions of hate speech, this approach also puts the class in a position to consider both how words can work in the world and how and why that work has been regulated.

The prospect of having such a discussion would, no doubt, frighten some, since it would promise to be an explosive, tense, disturbing interchange. Some students would undoubtedly agree with the treatment meted out to the disenfranchised; others might speak of it as being funny; others might point to the references to "Elm Street," "nightmares," and "magic" in the essay to argue that it was a piece of fiction; and still others might be horrified by the essay and express their feelings to the class. Such a discussion would, in other words, place one squarely in the act of teaching in the contact zone where, as Pratt says, "No one [is] excluded, and no one [is] safe"

(39). The point of having such discussions, however, is neither to establish a community where a simple pluralism rules and hate speech is just one of its many voices, nor is it to create an environment that is relentlessly threatening, where not feeling safe comes to mean the same thing as feeling terrified. Pratt, in fact, is careful to maintain the importance of establishing "safe houses" in the curriculum, courses where a different kind of talk is supported and sustained. But for those courses that take as their subject how language works in the world, the central concern should be to provide students with moments taken from their own writing, as well as from the writing collected in published texts where the written word is powerful. In such classrooms, "teaching the conflicts" is not simply an empty slogan plastered over a practice that means "business as usual," but an actual set of practices whereby the conflicts that capture and construct both the students and their teachers become the proper subject of study for the course.

This third category of response argues for the necessity of seeing the way we structure our courses and the kinds of texts we read with our students as potential resources for commenting on the writing our students produce. Thinking along these lines, another member of the audience suggested that the best way to respond to this essay was with a revisionary assignment, where the student would be required to rewrite the story from the perspective either of the gay man whom the students had harassed on Polk Street or from the perspective of the homeless person whom the students had beaten in the alleyway. This strategy of having the student do some more writing about this event seems particularly appropriate in a discipline that believes in the heuristic power of the composing process and the further requirement to have the student shift perspective provides a meaningful avenue for re-seeing the described events. As useful as I believe it is to see the assignment of revision as a way of responding to student writing, though, I think the response called for in this instance is so obvious that it is most likely to solicit a seamless parody, one of those acts of hyperconformity regularly produced by those writing in the contact zone. In other words, while producing a writing situation where the student is advised to mime the teacher's desired position would probably succeed in sweeping the most visible manifestations of the student's hateful thoughts and actions out of the classroom, it would not, I think, actually address the roots of that hatred. That hatred would simply curl up and go underground for the duration of the course.

At this point, it may seem that in assessing the range of reactions to "Queers, Bums, and Magic" I am holding out for some magical form of response that would not only make this student stop writing such things, but would actually put an end to his thinking them as well. My central concern, however, is not with this particular student essay or with what the student writer, as an individual, thinks, but with what this student essay and the professional activity that surrounds it can tell us about the cultural, political, and pedagogical complexities of composition instruction. With this distinction in mind, I would go so far as to argue that adopting any classroom strategy that isolates this essay and treats it as an anomaly misreads both the essay's cultural significance and its pedagogical possibilities. As the recent debate over military service has made abundantly clear, Lankford's student has not expressed some unique and private hatred of gays, nor, to be sure, has he voiced some peculiar antipathy for the homeless. Rather, the homophobia this student articulates and the violence he describes himself as perpetrating against the disenfranchised are cultural commonplaces. For these reasons, it seems much more important to me to produce a classroom where part of the work involves articulating, investigating, and questioning the affiliated cultural forces that underwrite the ways of thinking that find expression in this student's essay—a classroom, in short, that studies the forces that make such thoughts not only permissible but prevalent.

From this perspective, one could say that the only truly surprising thing about "Queers, Bums, and Magic" is that it voices this particular set of cultural commonplaces in the classroom, since most students practiced in the conventions of reading teacher expectations know not to commit themselves to positions their teachers clearly oppose. In this regard, the following facts are not insignificant: the student writer grew up in Kuwait; English is his second language; he was writing during the onset of the Persian Gulf War. An outsider himself, Lankford's student almost certainly did not understand what was intended by the examples that accompanied the assignment in the *Bedford Guide* to: "Station yourself in a nearby place where you can mingle with a group of people gathered for some reason or occasion. Observe the group's behavior and in a short paper report on it. Then offer some insight." Following these instructions, the student is informed that one writer "did an outstanding job of observing a group of people nervously awaiting a road test for their driver's licenses"; another observed a bar mitzvah; another an emergency room; and another a group of people looking at a luna moth on a telephone pole "(including a man who viewed it with alarm, a wondering toddler, and an amateur entomologist)" (42). Unschooled in the arts of reading the textbook, this student failed to pick up on the implicit directions: when you write this essay, report only on a group from which you are safely detached and on behavior unlikely to disturb others. Had the student been able to read the cues in the suggested examples, he might well have selected a less explosive topic and thereby kept his most familiar ways of knowing the world out of view.

If the examples direct students to topics guaranteed not to provoke offense, the assignment, by refraining from using any kind of critical terminology, further guarantees that the students will not wander beyond the business of reporting their immediate experience. In lieu of inviting students to work with any of the central terms taken from anthropology, sociology, or cultural studies, say, the assignment merely informs the students that, after observing the behavior of their selected group, they are "to form some general impression of the group or come to some realization about it." They can expect, the assignment concludes, that it will take at least two written pages "to cover" their subject. Grasping the import of these directives, Lankford's student did even more than was required, performing the kind of hyperconformity I suggested earlier characterizes one of the arts of the contact zone: he wrote, as required, for his "fellow students"; he handed in not two, but four typed pages; and he made sure his essay concluded with "some insight." His final paragraph reads as follows:

> Although this night was supposed to be an observation on the people of the streets, it turned out that we were walking on "Elm Street," and it was a "nightmare." I will always remember one thing, next time I see bums and fags walking on the streets, I will never make fun of them or piss on them, or anything like that, because they did not want to be bums or fags. It was society that forced them out of their jobs and they could not beat the system. Now when I think about that bum that we beat up I can't understand how he managed to follow us the whole time, after being kicked and being down for so long. I think it was one of two things; he is either psychic or it was just plain magic.

In miming the requisite better understanding that is supposed to come from studying groups, the student's essay concludes by disrupting all that has come before: did the beating actually take place or has the writer simply fabricated it, recasting the assignment within the readily available narrative frame of *Nightmare on Elm Street?* Is the student having one over on the system, manufacturing both the material for his response and his consequent realization, and thus in one fell swoop, parodying, resisting, and critiquing the values that hold the classroom community together? Or, and this is obviously the more frightening possibility, is his conclusion some kind of penitential confession for events that really did happen?

These questions, slightly rephrased, are of central importance to any writing classroom: how does a writer establish authority? How does one distinguish between fact and fiction in a written document? What does it mean to read and to write dialogically? And yet, it is important to realize that, had the assignment worked as it was supposed to, these questions would never have surfaced with the urgency they have here. That is, had Lankford's student been a better reader of classroom norms and textbook procedures, he might well have written about beekeepers or people at hair salons and left the surface calm of the educational community undisturbed. If we step back from "Queers Bums, and Magic" for a moment and consider the fact that the mixture of anger, rage, ignorance, and confusion that produced this student essay are present in varying degrees on college campuses across the country, what is truly significant about this event is not that it occurred, but that it occurs so rarely. This, surely, is a testament to the immense pressures exerted by the classroom environment, the presentation of the assigned readings, the directions included in the writing assignments, and the range of teaching practices which work together to ensure that conflicts about or contact between fundamental beliefs and prejudices do not arise. The classroom does not, in other words, automatically function as a contact zone in the positive ways Pratt discovered in the Stanford course, where, she asserts: "Along with rage, incomprehension, and pain there were exhilarating moments of wonder and revelation, mutual understanding, and new wisdom—the joys of the contact zone" (39). As the conclusion of Pratt's article makes clear, and the foregoing discussion of "Queers, Bums, and Magic" vividly illustrates, there is still a great deal of work to be done in constructing the "pedagogical arts of the contact zone." . . .

. . . In "Entering into the Serpent," excerpted from Anzaldúa's *Borderlands/La Frontera*, Anzaldúa shifts back and forth between Anglo-American English, Castilian Spanish, Tex-Mex, Northern Mexican dialect, and Nahuatl, writing in a melange of languages to express the diversity of her heritage and her position as lesbian, feminist, Chicana poet and critic. While Anzaldúa's multilingual text thus places special linguistic demands on its readers, it also makes relatively unique generic demands, moving between poetry and prose, personal narrative and revisionist history . . . Anzaldúa occupies a range of positions, some of them contradictory, as she relates her efforts to reclaim the Aztec goddess Coatlicue, the "serpent goddess," split from the goddess Cihuacoatl by the "male dominated Azteca-Mexica culture" in order to drive "the powerful female deities underground" (26–27). After the Spanish Conquest, Cihuacoatl was further domesticated by the Christian Church and transformed by stages into the figure now known as the Virgin of Guadalupe. While Anzaldúa admires *La Virgen de Guadalupe* as "the symbol of ethnic identity and of the tolerance for ambiguity that Chicanos-*mexicanos,* people of mixed race, people who have Indian blood, people who cross cultures, by necessity possess" (29), she nevertheless insists on the importance of regaining access to Coatlicue, "the symbol of the dark sexual drive, the chthonic (underworld), the feminine, the serpentine movement of sexuality, of creativity, the basis of all energy and life" (33). Recovering this contact with the supernatural provides one with "*la facultad* . . . the capacity to see in surface phenomena the meaning of deeper realities, to see the deep structure below the surface" (36).

Anzaldúa concludes this section by asserting that "Those who are pounced on the most have [*la facultad*] the strongest—the females, the homosexuals of all races, the darkskinned, the outcast, the persecuted, the marginalized, the foreign" (36).

Here's how one of my students described his experience reading "Entering into the Serpent":

> Even though I had barely read half of the first page, I was already disgusted. I found myself reading onward only to stop and ask "What is she trying to prove?" Scanning the words and skipping over the ones that were not english, I went from an egocentric personal story to a femo-nazi account of central american mythology, that was occasionally interrupted by more poems . . .
>
> From what I gather, she is trying to exorcise some personal demons. Her feelings of inadequacy and insecurity drove her to project her own problems not only onto the world, but into history and mythology. I'm surprised she didn't call history "herstory." It seems that she had no sense of self or worth. To overcome this, she fabricated a world, a past, and a scapegoat in her own image. Although her accusations do hold some truth, her incredible distortion of the world would lead me to believe that she has lost touch with reality and is obsessively driven by her social psychosis. She views herself as a gallant and brilliant member of a great culture that has been oppressed by the world. Her continuous references to females, sex, and the phallic symbols of snakes is most likely brought out by the lack of a man in her life. Rather than admit her faults, she cherishes them and calls them friends.

This is not an uncommon response to my assignment that began by asking students to discuss the difficulties they encountered reading Anzaldúa's essay. This student, having made his way past the language barrier of the text, confronts the description of a world and a way of being in that world that he finds personally repugnant. Beginning with a variant of a Rush Limbaughism, "femo-nazi," the student then proceeds to document the many ways that "Entering into the Serpent" offended him: it contains Anzaldúa's effort to "exorcise some personal demons"; it includes "her incredible distortion of the world"; the writer claims to be "a gallant and brilliant member of a great culture" of which the student is not a part. Given this reading, it is not too surprising that the student concludes that all the faults in the text are produced by "the lack of a man in [Anzaldúa's] life."

Taking offense at this student's response to Anzaldúa's essay strikes me as being exactly the wrong tactic here. It is of paramount importance, I believe, to begin where students are, rather than where one thinks they should be, and this student, by my reading, is trapped between the desire to produce a stereotypical critique of any feminist text ("I'm surprised she didn't call history "herstory") and the necessity of responding to this particular feminist text. He negotiates the tension between this desire and this necessity by producing a fairly detailed outline of Anzaldúa's essay and, simultaneously its argument ("Rather than admit her faults, she cherishes them and calls them friends"). However rudimentary or sophisticated one deems this kind of multivocalic writing to be, it is, as I've said above, only a starting point for beginning more detailed work with Anzaldúa's text. For this reason, the assignment that solicited this response does not simply ask the students to revel in the difficulties they experienced reading Anzaldúa's essay, but also requests that they outline "a plan of action for addressing the difficulties [they] encountered." The goal, thus, is not to invite students simply to record their various levels of rage, incomprehension, and despair with an admittedly difficult text, but rather to have them reflect on how their own ways of reading are disclosed and complicated during this textual transaction.

The results of having the students read their own readings and chart out alternative ways of returning to the text can be startling indeed. Although this writer began by accusing Anzaldúa of being a "femo-nazi," he concluded by reflecting on what he had done with her text in the following way:

> If not for searching for her hidden motives and then using them to criti-cize/bash Anzaldúa and her story, I would not have been able to read the story in its entirety. Although my view is a bit harsh, it has been a way that allows me to counter Anzaldúa's extremities. In turn, I can now see her strat-egy of language and culture choice and placement to reveal the contact zone in her own life. All of my obstacles previously mentioned, (not liking the sto-ries, poems, or their content) were overcome by "bashing" them. Unfortu-nately, doing that in addition to Anzaldúa's ridiculous disproportionism and over-intense, distorted beliefs created a mountain which was impossible for me to climb. This in effect made it impossible to have taken any part of her work seriously or to heart. I feel I need to set aside my personal values, out-look and social position in order to escape the bars of being offended and discouraged. Not only must I lessen my own barriers of understanding, but I must be able to comprehend and understand the argument of the other. It is these differences between people and groups of people that lead to the con-flicts and struggles portrayed and created by this selection.

This strikes me as being an extraordinarily astute assessment of the strengths and weaknesses of this writer's initial reading strategy: "bashing" Anzaldúa enabled a certain kind of work to be accomplished (the reading was completed, the writing assignment could be fulfilled), but it also pre-vented the writer from taking "any part of her work seriously or to heart." The writer's approach, in effect, only verified feelings he already had: it did not allow him to see or learn anything he didn't already know. Reflecting on his own reading practice, the writer finds himself compelled to reassess Anzaldúa's strategy, seeing at the end of his work that she has written in a way that will show "the contact zone in her life." Thus, by "bashing" Anzaldúa the student inadvertently ended up showing himself that her description of her trying experiences within the straight Anglo world was, at least partly, accurate. The writer's proposed solution to this problem— setting aside his "personal values, outlook and social position"—attests to the magnitude of the challenge Anzaldúa's position holds for him. Whether or not this proposed solution proves in practice to be a workable plan is something that emerges when the writer returns to Anzaldúa's essay to begin his revision. What is important to notice here, however, is that the writer's plan does make returning to her text an imaginable activity with an unforeseeable outcome. Given the way this student's essay began, this is no small accomplishment.

Required self-reflexivity does not, of course, guarantee that repugnant positions will be abandoned. At best, it ensures only that the students' attention will be focused on the interconnections between the ways they read and the ways they write. This can be a salutary experience as in the example above, where it provided the student with an avenue for renegoti- ating a relationship with a difficult text and the wide range of concerns affiliated with that text, but it does not mean that this approach wields suf- ficient power to transform the matrix of beliefs, values, and prejudices that students (and teachers) bring to the classroom. This kind of wholesale transformation (or, to be more precise, the appearance of this kind of wholesale transformation) is only possible in classrooms where the highly asymmetrical relations of power are fully reinstated and students are told either implicitly or explicitly (as I was during a course in graduate school), "No language that is racist, sexist, homophobic, or that degrades the work- ing class will be allowed in our discussions." Reimagining the classroom as a contact zone is a potentially powerful pedagogical intervention only so long as it involves resisting the temptation either to silence or to celebrate the voices that seek to oppose, critique and/or parody the work of con- structing knowledge in the classroom. By dismantling *Focus*, Bob Allen did not address the roots of the problem that produced the offensive cartoon; he merely tried to make it more difficult for another "deplorable mistake" of this kind to further tarnish the image of multicultural harmony the com- pany has been at such pains to construct. Scott Lankford, on the other hand, achieved the kind of partial, imperfect, negotiated, microvictory available to those who work in the contact zone when he found a way to respond to his student's essay that not only kept the student in his course, but eventually led to the student signing up to work with him in another course as well. By having my students interrogate literate practices inside and outside the classroom, by having them work with challenging essays that speak about issues of difference from a range of perspectives, and by having them pursue this work in the ways I've outlined here, I have been trying to create a course that allows the students to use their writing to investigate the cultural conflicts that serve to define and limit their lived experience.

In the uncharted realms of teaching and studying in the contact zone, the teacher's traditional claim to authority is thus constantly undermined and reconfigured which, in turn, enables the real work of learning how to negotiate and to place oneself in dialogue with different ways of knowing to commence. This can be strangely disorienting work, requiring, as it does, the recognition that in many places what passes as reason or rationality in the academy functions not as something separate from rhetoric, but rather as one of many rhetorical devices. This, in turn, quickly leads to the corollary concession that, in certain situations, reason exercises little or no persuasive force when vying against the combined powers of knowing the world that have their own internalized systems, self-sustaining logics, and justifications. For teachers who believe in education as a force for positive social change, the appropriate response to these new working conditions is not to exile students to the penitentiaries or the psychiatric wards for writing offensive, anti social papers. Nor is it to give free rein to one's self-righteous indignation and call the resultant interchange a "political intervention." The most promising pedagogical response lies, rather, in closely attending to what our students say and write in an ongoing effort to learn how to read, understand, and respond to the strange, sometimes threatening, multivocal texts they produce while writing in the contact zone.

NOTE

I thank Scott Lankford for making this student essay available for discussion, Jean Ferguson Carr for providing me with materials related to this panel, and Mariolina Salvatore for introducing me to the idea of the "position paper" that appears here, in modified form, in my discussion of my students' responses to Gloria Anzaldúa's essay. None of these parties is, of course, to be understood as endorsing the position I have staked out here.

REFERENCES

Allen, Bob. Letter to all AT&T employees dated September 17, 1993.
Anson, Chris, ed. *Writing and Response: Theory, Practice, and Research.* Urbana: NCTE, 1989.
Anzaldúa, Gloria. "Entering into the Serpent." *Ways of Reading.* 3d ed. Ed. David Bartholomae and Anthony Petrosky. Boston: Bedford, 1993. 25–38.
Fish, Stanley. "How to Recognize a Poem When You See One." *Ways of Reading.* 3d ed. Ed. David Bartholomae and Anthony Petrosky. Boston: Bedford, 1993. 140–152.
Focus. September 1993.

Kennedy, X. J., and Dorothy, M. *The Bedford Guide for College Writers.* 2d ed. Boston: Bedford, 1990. 41–42.
Lankford, Scott. "'Queers, Bums, and Magic': How Would You Grade a Gay-Bashing?" Paper presented at CCCC, Cincinnati, March 19, 1992.
Mulligan, Bartley. "Guerrilla Feminist Kicks Some Ass." *The Medium,* September 29, 1993: 1.
Pratt, Mary Louise. "Arts of the Contact Zone." *Profession 91.* New York: MLA, 1991, 33–40.
White, Edward M. *Teaching and Assessing Writing.* San Francisco: Jossey-Bass, 1985.

QUESTIONS FOR REFLECTION, JOURNAL WRITING, AND DISCUSSION

1. As a teacher, how would you respond to the student paper "Queers, Bums, and Magic"?
2. What do you think about the various faculty responses to this student paper? What do you think of Lankford's response?
3. Would it be a good idea to copy such a paper and allow the whole class to respond?
4. Does knowing that the writer of this essay was a Kuwaiti student affect you response?
5. Miller says about Lankford's student's essay, "The homophobia this student articulates and the violence he describes himself as perpetrating against the disenfranchised are cultural commonplaces." Do you agree? If so, what are the implications of this for teaching?
6. Have you ever brought up the topic of homophobia in your class? If so, how? How did your students react to this?

Part IV

Beyond the Writing Classroom

The final section of this book moves beyond the concerns of the conventional writing class to consider some related issues: the development of programs in writing across the curriculum; the impact of computers on the teaching of writing and, more generally, on the traditional classroom; the working conditions and job prospects of the many part-time faculty who staff lower-level courses in the university; and finally, the situation of the teacher in other roles as writer and scholar. All of these issues involve change. Some of that change is good; some is worrisome; some is demoralizing. The issues are also about the relationships among people: the economic and social contract between the university and its teaching staff; the connection between full- and part-time staff; the physical relationship, in a distance-learning environment, between students and teachers; and the relationships that teachers have as writers to each other and to their students.

The movement toward writing across the curriculum has its roots in the 1970s in the United States, and Toby Fulwiler and his colleague Art Young were among its leaders. For years they have been leading workshops for teachers in the disciplines to help them understand writing not just as a formal product but also as a mode of learning that can help students analyze difficult material, make connections among ideas, and do the critical thinking that is so much a part of a university education and that can help them to function successfully in their personal and professional lives. Fulwiler's "The Argument for Writing Across the Curriculum" describes the principles that guide his workshops and suggests a basic plan for working with faculty groups.

Using British writing theorist James Britton's scheme of three types of writing—transactional, poetic, and expressive—Fulwiler notes that the excessive emphasis on "transactional" writing—writing to make a point, to communicate with another—often undercuts students' development as writers. He advocates the use of expressive writing in the classroom as a way of helping students record their "inner speech," make sense of difficult concepts, and express their own ideas. Expressive writing, he maintains, leads to better transactional and poetic writing. It also facilitates writing as a way of learning. It allows for the informal daily writing that is a regular part of Fulwiler's classes.

He argues that the range of problems we have in mind when we complain about student writing cannot be corrected by teaching grammar or the five-paragraph essay. How do we motivate students, for example? How do we distinguish between technical problems and developmental problems? His article offers concrete suggestions for making assignments, and he provides guidelines for responding to students' writing. Some of his ideas have become second nature to writing teachers, but to teachers outside the English or communications departments, they may be new, and he offers them as a way of encouraging teachers in the disciplines to make writing integral to their curriculum, so that students will not only continue to grow as writers, but will also understand their courses in the deeper ways that exploratory writing encourages.

Vivian Zamel's "Strangers in Academia: The Experiences of Faculty and ESL Students Across the Curriculum" is a further elaboration on teaching writing in courses in the disciplines. It focuses on what happens to ESL students in such courses. Often, she points out, ESL students are made to feel incompetent by teachers who take the superficially logical position that "language must be in place" for students to do the work of their courses and that "language use is determined by a knowledge of parts of speech or grammatical terminology" (even though many teachers can no longer—if they ever could—produce that terminology themselves—which is one reason why they resist "teaching writing"). In such situations, "students' deficiencies are foregrounded." They are judged on their errors rather than on their knowledge of the subject matter and their developing albeit imperfect command of English. Teachers may experience their ESL students' writing as chaotic, feel inadequate to the task of helping them, and decide that the students don't belong in their classes.

Certain teaching practices—long lectures, multiple-choice tests—are bad pedagogy for all students. They may be efficient, and they allow teachers to cover the material and grade the tests quickly, but they don't necessarily lead to the critical thinking we hope to foster in students. For ESL students, such practices are especially ineffective. They often leave students floundering in words or foiled by some trick built into a multiple-choice question that restricts their expressing what they know. Zamel asks for constructive responses to students' errors and a recognition that fluency—not writing without errors but writing understandable prose—evolves in an atmosphere of experimentation and tolerance. She reminds us, as do others in this collection, that our classrooms are contact zones, sites of contestation where cultures meet and where definitions of who we should be and how we should perform get reassessed. Teachers, as well as students, have to change. The sense of crisis we may experience in our classrooms, she reminds us, is not just a danger but an opportunity.

Zamel notes that teachers of ESL students are often marginalized, just as their students are. How much more marginalized are the part-time faculty who do the greater share of teaching composition in most large universities today? And of course, those people are sometimes both ESL teachers and part-timers. The next essay, about the Wyoming Resolution, describes how the participants at the 1987 Conference on College Composition and Communication came to take a stand on the vexing and continuing practices of (1) employing graduate students to teach many introductory courses as they study for PhDs—only to have them discover that there are few jobs available once they get their degrees, and (2) employing others who are not in school, year after year, as adjunct faculty. As this has become business as usual, a two-tier system has established itself that assures full-time, tenured faculty comfortable lives and allows part-timers to teach three, four, sometimes five courses per semester, at different campuses, for far less money, often with no health or retirement benefits. To be sure, there are faculty who choose part-time teaching because they have other interests and other incomes. But unfortunately, for most part-timers, adjunct positions are the best they can come by. This discouraging situation has continued since the drafting of the resolution and seems unlikely to change in the near future. It is a troublesome truth that underlies and perhaps undermines this book. Why learn all of this if there is only the slimmest possibility of having a career to learn it for?

In "Basic Writing: Curricular Interactions with New Technology," Susan Stan and Terence G. Collins survey the uses of computer technology in basic writing classes—and make the point that because many of these classes are staffed by part-timers, who often feel separate from and unsupported by the "system," their innovations are less likely to appear in print. The authors begin by reflecting on the nature and needs of "basic writers"—writers "unpracticed and unskilled in composing specific forms of texts valorized traditionally by faculty." They note the tension that exists for such writers (and, Wendy Bishop points out later, for many others) between "authentic expressionism and institutionally validated, constrained text production." Their position, supported by a good deal of evidence from various studies and interviews, is that using computers helps such students to develop as writers. Because the world of cyberspace is to many young people a freer place, students sometimes feel less constrained in the writing they do on computers. And in more fundamental ways, word processing encourages revision (blocking, cutting and pasting, inserting, deleting, all enabling one to move text around with ease), greater accuracy (due to spell check, for example), and collaboration among students (ease of reproduction, online communication). Computers also produce text that is pleasing to look at and easy to read. The ways of technology are familiar and congenial to many students. For some, they serve as a bridge to the university's more traditional tasks.

Stan and Collins observe that the use of computer technology varies from place to place depending on college budgets and the level of technical knowledge and professional status of the faculty who sponsor it, and that basic writing programs are not a high priority in most institutions. But innovations appear in many places, and the results often appear online, on listservs and websites. The article provides sites where more information can be found.

Stan and Collins seem completely sanguine about the uses of technology in the classroom. They deal only briefly with distance learning, mentioning the project at the University of Alabama and noting its possibilities for replication. Chris Anson's "Distant Voices: Teaching and Writing in the Culture of Technology," however, creates a troubling, overlapping context for their work. Not only are retiring full-time faculty often being replaced by part-timers, but both are also being replaced, or threatened with replacement, by computers and the "nontenured specialists" who, from their own home computers, can write and "deliver" their courses to students whose work can be graded by part-timers who also work at home. Cyberspace is often presented to us as the unavoidable future that we had all better sign onto, and those who worry about it are often characterized as Luddites, reactionaries, hopeless resisters of the New Economy. Our vision of a college or university as a place with a faculty, classrooms, and offices where faculty hold office hours with students face-to-face is beginning to seem like a romantic vestige of an earlier age, about as viable for the 21st century as the vision of the family on the Swiss hillside that Anson invokes at the beginning and end of his essay.

Anson tries in the essay to present a balanced picture of writing and teaching "in a culture of technology." He acknowledges the efficiency of some of the changes, the convenience, the increased mobility of a culture that has electronic access to so much information. But he is concerned that changes in education will be made for the sake of change or because they lead to cost reductions rather than because they are better educationally. He is concerned, too, that the private sector will create its own writing courses and coopt the university all together. He urges us to think about the value of what we may lose as we change from a community physically coming together to share and create knowledge to one where, more and more, isolated people teach and learn in front of screens.

Bruce Herzberg's "Community Service and Critical Teaching" also addresses the nature of the university community. He is interested in expanding that community not by moving into cyberspace but by sending students into physical spaces outside of school where they can help others become literate. He is interested not just in helping students to do good deeds for those less fortunate than they, but in undermining their belief in the meritocracy and the myth of equal opportunity that is so deeply a part of the rhetoric of American politics. Herzberg describes a two-semester composition sequence, attached to a sociology course, for which his students tutor in a shelter. The students are mostly business majors with a strong sense that they got where they are on individual merit, and Herzberg notices that most students in tutoring situations tend to see themselves as performing a service for those who have fallen on hard times, due to some form of personal weakness. "This could be me," they may think, imagining themselves dropping out of school and sliding downhill to poverty. But Herzberg's goal is to show them that there is a systemic reason why it is not "them"—that the problems of the people in the shelter are often the result of a class system that separates out people very early in life, while installing in them the belief that their limitations are their own individual "fault."

Like many of the writers in this anthology, Herzberg's pedagogy reflects a belief that the university should work to promote social change. It is not just a place to provide a piece of paper that will open individual economic doors. Our learning should do more than make us "smart" and socially adept. It should humanize us in deep ways. The university should be a place where students develop what Kurt Spellmeyer calls "a social imagination" that, as Herzberg concludes, "makes it possible not only to question and analyze the world, but also to imagine transforming it."

In "Places to Stand: The Reflective Writer-Teacher-Writer in Composition," Wendy Bishop makes a plea, in the field of composition, for "the writer who teaches and teacher who writes," a construction she marks with a symbol, Ø, in an effort to name herself as an evolving writer/teacher who writes in a voice that has come to be labeled expressivist. It is a voice with which she hopes to communicate not only with her scholarly peers and other creative writers but also with her students. It is a voice that has been dismissed by those who consider "expressivism" an outmoded category of writing and the "self" an outmoded concept. In order to dismiss this expressivist self, Bishop points out, its opponents have defined expressivism so as to suggest that one cannot possibly imagine oneself as both expressive and socially constructed.

Her article refers us back to many of the authors included here and seeks to thread its way among their various positions and voices. She traces her own career in academia, from her beginning as a novice teacher and aspiring poet to a long period in which she taught as an adjunct to a time when she entered the mainstream of academic discourse and felt herself at the center of things, to a later period in which she fell out of fashion and became an outsider again, an "other," hopelessly influenced by the work of Peter Elbow and Donald Murray, who had become the old guard. She sees herself as still evolving, continually engaging in informal writing or reading groups, and writing with and for her students in order to find congenial "places to stand" outside the major organizations and the often-disembodied exclusionary voices of their professional journals. She notices that the dichotomies we construct to establish ourselves professionally may be false ones, and she argues for avoiding "pre and post" categorizing of various positions. "We become what we write," she quotes Donald Murray. "That is one of the great magics of writing." And one of the warnings.

Her essay traces the evolution of the field of composition studies by looking at the one in which its appears, the influential journal, *CCC, College Composition and Communication*—which itself probably stands in an inferior relationship to *College English,* an older NCTE journal that publishes literary criticism and theory as well as essays about composition. Both certainly rank lower in American English departments than the mighty and prestigious *PMLA (Publications of the Modern Language Association),* which, she quotes Burton Hatlen as saying, many writer/reader/would-be scholars regard not with "delight or enthusiasm" but with "unbridled hostility." She traces the changes in fashions and formats of *CCC* and says, at the end, I'm still here, and so are my students, and so are Elbow and Murray, larger and more complex than any one of their articles. Many of us are just trying to keep writing in a way that engages us aesthetically and intellectually, in a way that, despite the socially constructed nature of all our endeavors, still feels like a process of discovery. And we are, finally, always trying to find a connection to our students, not only in our classroom but maybe even in the words we write.

Geraldine DeLuca

Chapter 22

The Argument for Writing Across the Curriculum

Toby Fulwiler

Toby Fulwiler has directed the writing program at the University of Vermont since 1983. Before that he taught at Michigan Tech and the University of Wisconsin where, in 1973, he also received his Ph.D. in American Literature. At Vermont he teaches introductory and advanced writing classes, his newest courses emphasizing creative nonfiction. He recently coedited *The Letter Book* (Boynton/Cook, 2000) as well as *The Journal Book for At Risk Writers* (Boynton/Cook, 1999) and coauthored *The Blair Handbook* (3rd ed., Prentice Hall, 2000). Other books include *College Writing* (2nd ed., Boynton/Cook, 1997), *When Writing Teachers Teach Literature* (Boynton/Cook, 1996), *The Working Writer* (Prentice Hall, 1998), *Teaching with Writing* (Boynton/Cook, 1986) and *The Journal Book* (Boynton/Cook, 1987). He conducts writing workshops for teachers in all grade levels and across the disciplines, riding to workshop sites, weather permitting, on his BMW motorcycle. The following article is from *Writing Across the Disciplines: Research into Practice,* edited by Art Young and Toby Fulwiler (Boynton/Cook, 1986).

In order to make the abstract concept of "writing across the curriculum" more concrete, the Humanities Department of Michigan Tech planned, organized, and conducted a series of off-campus writing workshops to which teachers from all disciplines were invited. These workshops introduced participants to three premises which we believed crucial to developing a truly interdisciplinary writing program. We wanted teachers to understand (1) that the act of composing a piece of writing is a complex intellectual process; (2) that writing is a mode of learning as well as communicating; and (3) that people have trouble writing for a variety of reasons; no quick fixes will "solve" everybody's writing problem. In the next few pages I'd like to explain these assumptions, as they are the core ideas around which all of our workshop activities are designed.

COMPOSING

Many teachers—and whole school systems—have identified writing as a basic communication skill which is often taught as spelling, punctuation and penmanship in the early grades. In the later grades it is still taught as a technical skill, necessary for the clear transmission of knowledge. This limited understanding of writing takes no account of the process we call "composing," the mental activity which may be said to characterize our very species, and which Professor Ann Berthoff describes as the essence of thinking: "The work of the active mind is seeing relationships, finding forms, making meanings: when we write, we are doing in a particular way what we are already doing when we make sense of the world. We are composers by virtue of being human" (1978, p. 12).

Janet Emig of Rutgers has made an international reputation studying the composing processes of student writers (1971). She believes that writing "represents a unique mode of learning—not merely valuable, not merely special, but unique" (1977, p. 122). The act of writing, according to Emig, allows us to manipulate thought in unique ways because writing makes our thoughts visible and concrete and allows us to interact with and modify them. Writing one word, one sentence, one paragraph suggests still other words, sentences and paragraphs. She points out that writing progresses as an act of discovery—and furthermore, that no other thinking process helps us develop a given train of thought as thoroughly. Scientists, artists, mathematicians, lawyers, engineers—all "think" with pen to paper, chalk to blackboard, hands on terminal keys. Emig argues that developed thinking is not really possible, for most of us, any other way. She also points out that we can hold only so many discreet ideas in our heads at one time; when we talk out loud and have dialogues with friends—or with ourselves in the garage or bathtub—we lose much of what we say because it isn't written down. More importantly, we can't extend or expand our ideas fully because we cannot see them. Sartre quit writing when he lost his sight because he couldn't see words, the symbols of this thought; he needed to visualize his thought in order to compose, manipulate and develop it (Emig, 1977).

When we speak we compose. When we write we compose even better—usually—because as Emig posits we can manipulate our compositions on paper in addition to holding them in our heads. We can re-view them, re-vise them and re-write them because they are now visible and concrete. Both activities, speaking and writing, are important because they generate understanding and communication. Only in particular circumstances, however, such as English and speech classrooms, is the precision, shape and correctness of the speech or writing *act* itself viewed as more important than the *thought* engendered in the act. In other words, we usually speak or write to understand or communicate—not to evaluate our language medium. Some of us do communicate well because our pronunciation and articulation are careful, or because our spelling, punctuation and penmanship are fine, but most often the power of our language depends on profound "skills," much harder to identify and teach than the mere mechanical ones. Sometimes these composing skills are called "logical" or "rhetorical"; always they involve complex activities which we don't fully understand—and which are harder to teach.

Good teachers don't worry about how mysterious or difficult the composing process is to teach. For example, Peter Elbow tells students that "meaning is not what you start with but what you end up with" (1973, p. 15). Writing is an act of making meaning—making thought—and not the other way around. James Moffett describes this same process as "hauling in a long line from the depths to find out what things are strung on it" (1982, p. 234). It's not important that writers know exactly where they are going when they start; it's important they trust the process of composing to take them somewhere. James McCrimmon calls writing an act of continual choice making: "Often the writer does not know at the beginning what choices he will make, or even what his choices are; but each fresh choice tends to dictate those that follow, and gradually a pattern begins to emerge and the constellating fragments fall into place . . . " (1970, p. 4).

This happens in my own writing all the time, even as I write and shape these words. I begin writing with a more or less clear direction in mind—in my head—and *always* discover that the act of writing takes me places I never imagined. I continually make the choices McCrimmon talks about, and each one takes me someplace I hadn't fully anticipated going. I've learned to trust this process; like Elbow and Moffett, I can *predict* that writing for a certain period of time will usually create meaning. It is this trust, especially, that we need to teach our students.

This assumption, the notion that writing is a process, "something which shows continuous change in time like growth in organic nature," is at once familiar and foreign to teachers in disciplines other than English. Familiar, because, as writers of articles, proposals and books, college teachers struggle with "process" each time they do a piece of writing; foreign, because these same teachers often require single-draft writing in the form of term papers and essay tests from their own students.

At the writing workshop teachers are asked to engage in exercises which reacquaint them with the frustrations (and joys) of the composing process: participants do various prewriting activities such as journal writing, freewriting, and brainstorming in order to select and focus on a writing topic. Later they develop one idea into a draft based on colleague response. Finally, they revise this piece and publish it for all in the workshop to read.

After sweating through this condensed composing process most teachers admit to having more empathy with student writers. Few teachers who had simplistic notions about "the writing product" when they began the workshop still retain that attitude. Prewriting, writing, responding and revising, brought to consciousness through group discussion, emphasize clearly the process involved in generating a serious piece of public prose.

WRITING AND LEARNING

A research team headed by James Britton investigated the relationship between writing and learning in a study published in 1975. Britton's team collected 2,000 pieces of writing from British school children aged 11–18 and classified each according to the function it served: transactional, poetic or expressive. They defined transactional as writing "to perform a transaction which seeks outcomes in the real world" (1975, p. 160). Transactional writing aims to inform, persuade or instruct an audience in clear, conventional, concise prose. Most school writing is transactional: term papers, laboratory reports, essay examinations, book reviews and the like; it accounted for 63% of the total sample collected.

Poetic writing, Britton's second category, is akin to what we call "creative writing" in this country; language which functions as art, shaped as "an independent verbal construct" (1975, p. 161). Readers don't expect poetic writing to be true in the same sense as transactional writing; fiction, poetry, drama and song are works of the imagination, which of course, deal with "larger" not "literal" kinds of truth. Nor is poetic writing governed by any stringent rules or formulas, as the work of Joyce, Faulkner, e. e. cummings and many others will attest. Poetic writing accounted for 18% of the total sample collected, with little evidence of its use outside of English classes.

Britton calls his third category of writing "expressive" after Sapir's term "expressive speech" (1961). Expressive writing is "self-expressive," or "close to the self"; that is, it "reveals the speaker, verbalizing his consciousness" (1975, p. 90). This form of writing is essentially written to oneself, as in diaries, journals and first-draft papers—or to trusted people very close to the writer, as in personal letters. Since it isn't intended for external audiences, it has few conventional constraints of form, usage or style. Expressive writing often looks like speech written down and is usually characterized by first-person pronouns, informal style, and colloquial diction. It accounted for 5.5% of the total sample collected, with no evidence of its use outside of English classes.

The complete neglect of expressive writing across the curriculum is a clue to the value of writing in schools. According to Britton's classification, expressive is the most personal writing, the closest to "inner speech" and the thinking process itself. The absence of expressive writing in school curricula suggests a limited understanding of the way language works. As co-researcher Nancy Martin explains: "The expressive is basic. Expressive speech is how we communicate with each other most of the time and expressive writing, being the form of writing nearest speech, is crucial for trying out and coming to terms with new ideas" (1976, p. 26). According to the research team, personal or expressive writing is the matrix from which both transactional and poetic writing evolve. This chapter is concerned primarily with the expressive-transactional continuum; there is some evidence, however, that poetic writing, also neglected across the curriculum, promotes significant learning (Young, 1982). Serious writers who undertake writing tasks almost naturally put their writing through "expressive" stages as they go about finding out what they believe and what they want to write. Pulitzer Prize-winning author Donald Murray, talking about both his poetic and transactional work explains: "I believe increasingly that the process of discovery, of using language to find out what you are going to say, is a key part of the writing process" (1978, p. 91).

Teachers need to understand how writing promotes thought. If school writing showed no evidence of exploratory written language being encouraged by teachers, students were not being taught to use all the learning tools at their disposal. The Britton research team concluded: "The small amount of speculative writing certainly suggests that, for whatever reason, curricular aims did not include the fostering of writing that reflects independent thinking; rather, attention was directed towards classificatory writing which reflects information in the form in which both teacher and textbook traditionally present it" (1975, p. 197). My colleague, Randall Freisinger, insists that: "Excessive reliance on the transactional function of language may be substantially responsible for our students' inability to think critically and independently . . . Product oriented, transactional language promotes closure" (1982, p. 9).

Reading-thinking, listening-thinking, speaking-thinking, writing-thinking: these processes are the essential activities of civilized, educated people. In this context, Brazilian educator Paulo Friere contends that "liberating education" occurs only when people develop their critical thinking skills, including self-knowledge and self-awareness; the ability to think critically separates the autonomous, independent people, capable of making free choices, from mere passive receivers of information. Friere describes liberating education as "acts of cognition, not transferrals of information" (1970, p. 67). I believe that writing is the specific activity which most promotes independent thought. Both the decision to write and the process of writing are actions; one cannot be passive and at the same time generate words, sentences and paragraphs—thoughts.

However, as we have seen, some writing activities clearly promote independent thought more than others—expressive or "self-sponsored" writing, for example, which seems more likely to advance thought than note copying. Writing to people who care about us—or what we have to say—engages us as writers more than writing to people who read our work in order to grade us. As we come to understand the role of writing in generating and formulating ideas, we must also examine the traditional role writing is assigned in schools. If writing promotes independent thought, to what extent can teachers across the curriculum take advantage of this unique capacity?

For the duration of a writing workshop we ask teachers to keep a journal—an organized place for day-to-day expressive writing—and we ask them to write in a variety of ways to themselves about the content and process of the workshop. At times we ask them to brainstorm in the journal, other times to summarize what they've learned, and still other times to reflect about how they *feel* about the work of the workshop. Through this assignment we hope to show participants firsthand the value of keeping a running personal—expressive—written commentary on one's own learning process. If the journal works for them at the workshops, maybe it will work for students in their classes.

WRITING PROBLEMS

Many participants initially sign up for the workshop with a stereotyped idea of what constitutes "student writing problems." From the first session to the last, whether at a one-day or a five-day workshop, we attempt to expand our colleague's notion of the range, variety and complexity of "writing problems." One method that works well is to ask people at the opening session to each suggest one writing problem. We then list these on the board. A typical list looks something like this:

1. attitude
2. having something to say
3. faulty reasoning
4. having a thesis
5. understanding what the reader doesn't understand
6. value of writing
7. rules of writing (spelling, punctuation, etc.)
8. context of writing
9. organization
10. revising
11. developing ideas logically
12. writing like they talk
13. coherence (in a whole essay)
14. being concise

15. self-confidence
16. ignorance of conventions
17. sentence errors
18. including irrelevant and digressive information
19. using correct references and sources
20. writing introductions

From this point on, it becomes clear that we aren't talking about one solution for all problems; the solution must suit the particular problem. For example, the idea that spelling or grammar drills will cure all (or most) writing problems disappears fast. The "solution" to a "motivation" problem is far different from (though perhaps related to) an "editing" problem. Student "skill" problems (spelling, punctuation) require teacher responses different from student "developmental" problems (cognitive maturity, reading background); teacher-centered problems (poor assignments, vague feedback) differ from institutional problems (credit hours, course loads, grades). The whole concept of "writing problems" expands and teachers begin to understand both its complexity and diversity. It is then possible to conduct individual workshop sessions which address themselves to one or another in meaningful ways.

To conclude this introductory session on writing problems, I ask the teachers to condense the long list of problems they have generated into fewer, more general categories. We try to combine, for example, "spelling," "punctuating" and "staying on the line" into one category which we agree to call "mechanics," and so on. The following list reproduced from a recent college workshop is typical of the kind developed by most groups:

1. Attitude (motivation, interest)
2. Mechanical skills (spelling, punctuation)
3. Organizational skills (how to piece it together)
4. Style (conventions appropriate to task and audience)
5. Reasoning ability (thinking, logic)
6. Knowledge (something to write about)

This briefer list, while it doesn't cover every single item on the longer lists, organizes areas of concern so workshop participants can better understand them and, at the same time, gives us a common vocabulary to speak from. Looking at such a list highlights the problem categories and makes them easier to discuss and perhaps solve. Actual solution, of course, will be the business of later workshops. The dialogue has begun.

CLASSROOM PRACTICES

Once teachers understand and accept the major premises which inform our writing workshops, we believe they will make their own best translations of those premises into classroom practices suitable for their own disciplines and teaching situation. However, nearly all teachers seem to be interested in two general pedagogical problems associated with teaching writing: making assignments which generate good writing, and evaluating or responding to the writing once written.

Assignments

Let me outline a few of the most practical and useful suggestions that emerge from workshops about creating good out-of-class writing assignments:

1. Prepare a context for each assignment. When students are asked to write about something related to the subject in your class, it's often possible to plant fertile ideas in advance that will help generate more comprehensive writing. For example, ask students to do a series of journal writes or freewrites on a related subject a week or two prior to a major assignment, and use those writings to stimulate class talk, again about the coming assignment (Macrorie, 1970; Elbow, 1973). Informal writing can prime the pump, pave the way for a steady flow of ideas which is the necessary complement to all good writing.

2. Allow time for the composing process to work. In addition to informal writing to start the process, make room for students to write several drafts before the final paper is due. Ask students to share some of these drafts with each other—to give both readers and writers a sense of each other's ideas and capabilities. And try to have a short conference with each writer about a draft stage of his or her paper so your critical response can be addressed *before* the paper is completed. A process approach simply gives an assignment room to grow.

3. Ask students to write about what *they* know, not what you already know. Where possible, make you assignments approximate real communications situations, where the writer/speaker communicates something to a reader/listener who wants to learn more about it. This is the reverse of a "test" situation where an examiner already knows the answers and simply wants to make sure that you do too. In out-of-class paper assignments (as opposed to essay tests) students should be encouraged to use all the resources and wits at their disposal to teach you, the instructor.

4. Use peer groups to motivate and educate each other (Bruffee, 1973). If you can find time in your classroom schedule to divide students into small groups of three or five each, you can ask them to read their writing

out loud to each other and share oral responses. This peer-review process, carefully used, adds to student comprehension of course material as well as helps them with their writing. Small groups of students, with clear tasks to accomplish, take responsibility for their thinking and writing and thus add a dimension of active self-sponsored learning to whatever subject they are investigating. The more times they do this, across the curriculum, the better at it they become; however, in a given class they may be a bit quiet and altogether too uncritical of each other's work. With each subsequent meeting, the groups may trust each other more and become more critically articulate about each other's work. Peer review is an easy and natural part of the composing process.

5. Show model student writing to students. An excellent way to set up your students for a given assignment is to project on an overhead screen samples of student papers from a similar assignment last year. Show both well and poorly-done work and ask students to judge why which is which. Such an exercise draws students into the learning process by making student texts part of the course and by trusting student judgment to make critical distinctions about quality. Students who see other good student work recognize that successful completion of the assignment is also within their grasp.

6. Assign students to write to a variety of different audiences. Ask students to write to each other sometimes, and depend on such peer feedback for further revision. Ask students to write to professionals in their field by sending letters or reports out for comment (Faigley, 1981; Goswami, 1981). Ask students to write for publication, if possible, helping them do an appropriate analysis of the publication for which they are writing. And pose for your students as many challenging hypothetical audiences as you can, asking them to role play and stretch their usual school voice as far as possible (Field and Weiss, 1979). Play with audiences in your assignments and you'll be teaching writing lessons most suitable to the outside world for which they are preparing.

7. Require a series of short papers rather than a long one. The advantage of seeing several shorter pieces of students work are several: you can find out almost as much about writing skills in a page or two as you can in ten; you can also request careful, thoughtful and efficient treatment of some idea in five pages and make that as demanding a task as a more loosely-written ten- or twenty-page assignment. It's also a lot easier on you—and more enjoyable—when you come to read the papers. But the real value may be in teaching students progressively, through your comments on each successive paper, to think and write even more sharply each successive time. At the end of the term you can ask to see these several papers and assess the progress from assignment to assignment.

8. Put directions clearly and comprehensively in writing. This may sound like common sense, but it's surprising how often poor writing results from an inadequate student understanding of what is expected—and often this problem is as much the teacher's fault as the students'. Include in your instructions: (a) a clear articulation of the problem or question to be addressed; (b) your expectations regarding paper scope, depth, format, length and so forth; (c) what resources you expect to be used; and (d) the evaluation procedures and standards you will apply to the paper. Composing a set of lucid assignment directions for your students is a demanding exercise in technical writing for yourself.

9. Write some of your own assignments; watch how you do it; show students the results. This is hard to do often, but doing it once a year in even one course can be a humbling experience. It *will* be easier for you to do than for your students, of course, but in actually thinking through the assignment, with the intention of sharing it with the class, you'll have to be quite concerned with audience and economy yourself. When you pass it out or project a transparency of it on a screen, you may wish to explain why you did what you did. At the same time, be prepared for some tough questions about this assertion or that sentence construction. Best of all, share a rough draft with your class and let them see your fuzzy thinking in the raw.

10. Integrate writing into the daily activity of your classroom. Effecting this generalized advice can actually have a profound effect on all the formal writing you require of your students. Once they understand that writing is a way of learning more about every subject and is something that you, a professional and a professor, do yourself, the routine bitching that so often accompanies writing assignments will probably dissipate. The majority of students are in school because they really do want to learn—and learn how to learn.

EVALUATION

The other end of making assignments is responding to or evaluating them. Many teachers have signed up for the writing workshop in the first place because they hoped we'd have some magical suggestions for grading student papers. As they often find out from sharing ideas with each other, how teachers go about grading papers may depend a lot on how they have assigned them and on what else happened in between—revision, editing, peer reading, teacher conference or whatever. But eventually, in most academic situations, teachers must respond to and grade student writing in some fashion or other. The following ideas were generated by various teachers over the course of several workshops; they are general guidelines and not meant to be prescriptive in any way; however, teachers who follow these suggestions when commenting on out-of-class writing will help their students considerably with both their writing and thinking.

1. Respond to the content first, not the mechanics, of each paper you read. Too often we become a bit jaded or tired as readers of student writing and spend more time looking for errors than ideas. In the process we can become absolutely fixated on sentence- or word-level problems and never read the paper for its larger intention. While I'm not counseling that we ignore sentence inconsistencies, I am reminding us to let the writer know that we have considered—for good or ill— the integrity of that intention. Otherwise we treat this act of communication as a mechanical exercise—and surely, if we have made a careful, thoughtful assignment we don't want to do that.

2. Respond positively and personally where possible. Again, no absolutes here, but I believe that writers begin to care about their writing when they see that we care about it. Caring is the necessary first step to actually writing. A corollary of that is that it's difficult to work on a piece—revising and editing it—when nothing encouraging has been said about it. Most acts of student writing are mixtures of more and less good work; be sure to comment as much on the "more" as you do on the "less." I address my comments to students by name, as I would in a letter, and I sign my comments with my name—a dimension of personal interaction that improves our communication with each other.

3. Revise early drafts; edit later drafts; grade final drafts. When you put a grade on a piece of writing you have treated it as a finished product, as if the learning is already and altogether over (Martin, 1976). If you are asking students to put their writing through several draft stages, keep in mind that the motive to revise a D-paper is rather low. Better, I think, to point out where the paper is strong as well as weak, conceptually, and ask for a rewrite, grade aside. Once a draft is conceptually together, with good internal logic and evidence, then we can turn attention to matters of voice, tone and style, which are really acts of editing on the sentence level. When you and the student pronounce this act of writing/learning finished, that's the time to grade it.

4. Comment critically on one item at a time. It's easy to overwhelm students who have written a weak or uncertain paper with all sorts of negative comments and a plethora of suggestions for what to do next. While the intention behind such active criticism is well-intentioned—certainly better than giving the paper a rote *F*—such teacher commentary may not accomplish its purpose. Once you see that a paper has multiple problems, it may be a good idea to single out one or two conceptual or

organizational problems for comment, suggesting that other problems will be dealt with on subsequent drafts. This way the student has a clearer idea of what to do next; it may also surprise you both how many smaller problems will be cleared up in that initial act of revision, so that you may never need to spend time on this at all. And use pencil—it's more forgiving on both of you.

5. Be specific when you comment on problems. I remember being coached by a fine writing teacher to avoid all those funny symbols inside the front covers of handbooks (*frag., comma splice,* etc.); he argued that students were only more confused by them and that not all teachers used the same symbols anyhow. He suggested instead just using one comment, "Awk," for everything. But his solution, while it worked for him because he has frequent personal conferences, can be equally confusing advice for novice writers who don't yet trust their own ears. Point out exactly what you object to, but without necessarily correcting it yourself: that way the writer has something concrete to go on when he or she turns attention to revision.

6. Edit a page or two, not the whole paper. Too often colleagues report going over an entire error-filled student paper with their best critical eye, suggesting changes in language everywhere but in the process doing most of the work which should be done by the writer. And too often at the end of a term we've all seen piles of papers meticulously edited by the teachers and never even picked up by the students. What a waste of professional time and energy! To solve both problems at once, show the student what constructions or stylistic problems bother you on the first page or two and how to fix these, then ask the student to edit by example the rest of his or her work. That saves all of us time and places the editing responsibility where it rightfully belongs.

7. Learning to critique is part of learning to write; include peer evaluation where you can in your class. In addition to receiving help with one's own paper in a writing group, one learns what to look for and how to respond in order to help others with their papers (Hawkins, 1976). Learning how to be critical is part of learning how to write yourself. We all know how much easier it is to see problems in someone else's writing; what that suggests, of course, is that we have a critical distance here that we don't have from our own work. But the process needs to start somewhere. When I first introduce peer criticism into a class, I do it with students, myself, and sometimes provide directions for what to look for. As I said before, the first time they do it will not usually be successful—but the subsequent meetings will get better quickly.

8. Discuss samples of good and bad writing with your class. I use the same technique here as for making assignments. I project anonymous papers that are well-written as well as those with problems and talk them

over with my class. They see, often as quickly as I, what works and what doesn't, but especially they see by example what they have done well or poorly on their own work. Here again, you're bringing the students into the evaluation process, trusting them to have responsible voices and make reasonable judgments. Another good idea, suggested to me first by a history teacher: before handing papers back—and I always do this now—read out loud from several papers you consider good and explain *why* you liked them. Students seem to find this both unusual and highly enjoyable: taking time to introduce the students' expression of a relevant idea to the class.

9. *What* is said includes *how* it is said: Don't split grades. I never find agreement at a workshop about this one, but I believe it's important to quit separating ideas from the language in which they're expressed. For one thing, when something is known or understood well the chances are that a writer will express it well; conversely, a lot of poor writing (wordy, rambling, evasive, digressive, disorganized, over-generalized) results from inadequate knowledge and understanding. For another thing, such grade splitting reinforces the notion that English teachers are rightfully concerned with "mere expression" and the other folks with "true content." Politically, across the university, that's a troublesome belief; conceptually, for me, it's unacceptable. One grade: how good a job is it?

10. Understand that good writing depends on audience and purpose. At writing workshops we all spend some time exploring what kind of language may be appropriate for a given situation or audience. The academy seems to sanction a distanced, objective, neutral voice as that which best conveys fact and truth; however, most human beings enjoy reading more lively, personal writing that shows a clear authorial voice—which voice is fully capable of conveying some pretty hefty ideas. The consensus which emerges from most workshop groups is that style is a matter of what is appropriate rather than what is correct. So we need to show students that different voices work well for different purposes, that memos demand one style and letters another, depending upon for whom they're written; that the same goes for book reviews, term papers and professional reports. The trick is, of course, to be good in all modes to all audiences.

REFERENCES

Berthoff, Ann. *Forming/Thinking/Writing: The Composing Imagination*. Rochelle Park, NJ: Hayden, 1978.

Britton, James, T. Burgess, N. Martin, A. McLeod, and H. Rosen. *The Development of Writing Abilities 11–18*. London: Macmillan Educational Press, 1975.

Bruffee, Kenneth. "Collaborative Learning: Some Practical Models." *College English* 34 (1973): 634–43.

Elbow, Peter. *Writing Without Teachers*. New York: Oxford UP, 1973.

Emig, Janet. *The Composing Processes of Twelfth Graders*. Urbana, IL: National Council of Teachers of English, 1971.

———. "Writing as a Mode of Learning." *College Composition and Communication* 28 (1977): 122–28.

Faigley, Lester. *Writing After College: A Stratified Survey of the Writing of College-trained People*. (Writing Program Assessment, Technical Report No. 1, Fund for the Improvement of Secondary Education Grant No. G008005896). Austin: U of Texas P, 1981.

Freire, Paulo. *Pedagogy of the Oppressed*. New York: Herder and Herder, 1970.

Freisinger, Randall. "Respecting the Image: A Transactional View of Languages and Cognition." *Iowa English Bulletin* 31 (1981): 5–9.

Goswami, Dixie, et al. *Writing in the Professions: A Course Guide and Instructional Materials for an Advanced Composition Course*. Unpublished manuscript produced by the Document Design Project, National Institute of Education, 1981.

Macrorie, Ken. *Telling Writing*. Rochelle Park, NJ: Hayden, 1970.

Martin, Nancy, P. D'Arcy, B. Newton, and R. Parker. *Writing and Learning Across the Curriculum*. London: Ward Lock Educational, 1976.

McCrimmon, James. "Writing as a Way of Knowing." *The Promise of English: NCTE Distinguished Lectures*. Urbana, IL: National Council of Teachers of English, 1970. Reprinted in *Rhetoric and Composition: A Sourcebook for Teachers*. Ed. R. L. Graves. Montclair, NJ: Boynton/Cook.

Moffett, James. *Coming On Center: English Education in Evolution*. Montclair, NJ: Boynton/Cook, 1982.

———. "Writing, Inner Speech, and Mediation." *College English* 44, 231–46.

Murray, Donald. "Internal Revision: A Process of Discovery." In Charles Cooper and Lee Odell, eds. *Research on Composing: Points of Departure*. Urbana, IL: National Council of Teachers of English, 1978: 85–103.

Sapir, E. *Culture, Language and Personality*. Berkeley: U of California P, 1961.

Young, Art. "Considering Values: The Poetic Function of Language." In Toby Fulwiler and Art Young, eds. *Language Connections: Writing and Reading Across the Curriculum*. Urbana, IL: National Council of Teachers of English, 1982.

QUESTIONS FOR REFLECTION, JOURNAL WRITING, AND DISCUSSION

1. Select a few of the writing problems listed by Fulwiler on pages 350–351. How can teachers help students with these problems? Should teachers in "subject-area classes" (e.g., history, biology, etc.) help students with these problems?

2. Do you have any personal experience with writing across the curriculum? If so, was it a good experience?

3. Do you find the suggestions given by Fulwiler in his WAC workshop realistic or unrealistic?

Chapter 23

Strangers in Academia: The Experiences of Faculty and ESL Students Across the Curriculum

Vivian Zamel

Vivian Zamel is Professor of English at the University of Massachusetts Boston, where she directs the English as a Second Language Program and teaches composition courses for ESL students as well as graduate courses on ESL theory and pedagogy. She has researched and published extensively on the writing and learning of linguistically diverse learners. She coauthored, with University of Massachusetts colleagues Eleanore Kutz and Suzie Q. Groden, *The Discovery of Competence: Teaching and Learning with Diverse Student Writers* (Boynton/Cook, 1993) and coedited, with Ruth Spack, *Negotiating Academic Literacies: Teaching and Learning Across Languages and Cultures* (Lawrence Erlbaum, 1998). The following article is from *College Composition and Communication*, 46, December 1995.

> *When I go into a classroom these days, I look around and feel like I'm in a different country.*
>
> —Professor of Management

> *A few weeks age a professor came by the reading, writing and study skills center where I tutor. He was with a young Asian woman, obviously one of his students. He "deposited" her in the center, claiming that she desperately needed help with her English. The woman stared into the distance with a frightened, nervous look on her face and tried to force a smile. She handed me a paper she had written on the labor union and asked if I could help her make corrections. After a short introductory discussion, we looked at the paper that we were about to revise—it was filled with red marks indicating spelling, punctuation, and grammar errors; the only written response was something along the lines of "You need serious help with your English. Please see a tutor."*
>
> —From a tutor's journal

> *Students in the lab speak to one another in their own language so that they make sure they know what they are doing. So they may look like they are not listening to the lab teacher. He feels so isolated from them. He feels he has no control, no power. So he may get angry.*
>
> — An ESL student

These comments show evidence of tensions and conflicts that are becoming prevalent in institutions of higher education as student populations become more diverse. One clear indication that faculty across the disciplines are concerned about the extent to which diverse student populations, particularly students whose native language is not English, constrain their work is the number of workshops and seminars that have been organized, and at which I have participated, in order to address what these faculty view as the "ESL Problem."[1] In the course of preparing to work with faculty, and in order to get a sense of their issues and concerns, I surveyed instructors about their experiences working with non-native speakers of English. As Patricia Laurence has pointed out, though we acknowledge and discuss the diversity of students, "we neglect the 'polyphony'" that represents faculty voices (24). While I did not receive many responses to my request for feedback, those responses that were returned did indeed reflect this polyphony.

Some faculty saw this invitation to provide feedback as an opportunity to discuss the strengths and resources these students brought with them, indicated that ESL students, because of their experience and motivation, were a positive presence in their classes, and noted the contributions ESL students made in discussions that invited cross-cultural perspectives. One professor took issue with the very idea of making generalizations about ESL students. But this pattern of response did not represent the attitudes and perspectives revealed by other faculty responses. One professor, for example, referred to both silent students, on the one hand, and "vocal but incomprehensible students" on the other. But, by far, the greatest concern had to do with students' writing and language, which faculty saw as deficient and inadequate for undertaking the work in their courses. I got the clear sense from these responses that language use was confounded with intellectual ability—that, as Victor Villanueva, recounting his own schooling experiences, puts it, "bad language" and "insufficient cognitive development" were being conflated (11).

In order to demonstrate the range of faculty commentary, I've selected two faculty responses, not because they are necessarily representative, but because they reveal such divergent views on language, language development, and the role that faculty see themselves as playing in this development. I've also chosen these responses because they may serve as mirrors for our own perspectives and belief systems, and thus help us examine

---

[1] The acronym ESL (English as a Second Language) is used here because it is the commonly used term to refer to our students whose native language is not English. Given the inherently political nature of working with ESL learners, it is important to note that at urban institutions, such as the University of Massachusetts at Boston, most of these students are residents of the United States. Furthermore, in the case of a number of these students, English may be a third or fourth language.

more critically what we ourselves think and do, both within our own class-rooms and with respect to the larger institutional contexts in which we teach. In other words, although these responses came from two different disciplines, it is critical for each of us to examine the extent to which we catch glimpses of our own practices and assumptions in these texts. The first response was written by an English Department instructor:

> One of my graduate school professors once told me that he knew within the first two weeks of the semester what his students' final grades would be. Recently I had a Burmese-born Chinese student who proved my professor wrong. After the first two essays, there was certainly no reason to be optimistic about this student's performance. The essays were very short, filled with second language errors, thesaurus words, and sweeping generalizations. In the first essay, it was obvious he had been taught to make outlines because that's all the paper was, really—a list. In the second essay, instead of dealing directly with the assigned text, the student directed most of his energy to form and structure. He had an introduction even though he had nothing to introduce. In his conclusion, he was making wild assertions (even though he had nothing to base them on) because he knew conclusions were supposed to make a point. By the fourth essay, he started to catch on to the fact that my comments were directed toward the content of his essays, not the form. Once he stopped worrying about thesis sentences, vocabulary, and the like, he became a different writer. His papers were long, thoughtful, and engaging. He was able to interpret and respond to texts and to make connections that I term "double face" as a way to comment on the ways in which different cultures define such terms as "respect." Instead of 1 1/4 pages, this essay was seven pages, and it made several references to the text while synthesizing it with his experience as someone who is a product of three cultures. This change not only affected the content of his writing, but also his mechanics. Though there were still errors, there were far fewer of them, and he was writing well enough where I felt it was safe to raise questions about structure and correctness.

This response begins with the recognition that we need to be wary of self-fulfilling prophecies about the potential of students, and indeed this instructor's narrative demonstrates compellingly the dangers of such prophecies. This instructor goes on to cite problems with the student's performance, but he speculates that these problems may have to do with previous instruction, thus reflecting a stance that counteracts the tendency to blame students. Despite the student's ongoing difficulties, the instructor does not despair over the presence of second language errors, over the short essays, the "sweeping generalizations," the empty introduction, the "wild assertions." Instead, this instructor seems to persist in his attempts to focus the student on content issues, to respond to the student seriously, to push him to consider the connections between what he was saying and the assigned reading, to take greater risks, which he succeeds in doing "by the fourth essay." In this, I believe, we see the instructor's understanding that it takes multiple opportunities for students to trust that he is inviting them into serious engagement with the course material, that it takes time to acquire new approaches to written work. What seems to be revealed in this response is the instructor's belief in the student's potential, his appreciation for how language and learning are promoted, his refusal to draw conclusions about intellectual ability on the basis of surface features of language— all of which, in turn, helped the student become a "different writer," a change that affected the content of his writing, that had an impact on the very errors that filled his first papers, that even illuminated the instructor's reading of the assigned texts. This response suggests a rich and complicated notion of language, one that recognizes that language evolves in and responds to the context of saying something meaningful, that language and meaning are reciprocal and give rise to one another.

This response, especially the final section about surface level errors, foreshadows the other faculty response, which was written by an art history instructor and which reveals a very different set of assumptions and expectations:

> My experience with teaching ESL students is that they have often not received adequate English instruction to complete the required essay texts and papers in my classes. I have been particularly dismayed when I find that they have already completed 2 ESL courses and have no knowledge of the parts of speech or the terminology that is used in correcting English grammar on papers. I am certainly not in a position to teach English in my classes. (The problem has been particularly acute with Chinese/S. E. Asian students.) These students may have adequate intelligence to do well in the courses, but their language skills result in low grades. (I cannot give a good grade to a student who can only generate one or two broken sentences during a ten-minute slide comparison.)

The first assumption I see in this response is the belief that language and knowledge are separate entities, that language must be in place and fixed in order to do the work in the course. This static notion of language is further revealed by the instructor's assumption that language use is determined by a knowledge of parts of speech or grammatical terminology. Given this belief, it is understandable why she is dismayed by what she characterizes as students' lack of knowledge of grammar, a conclusion she has seemingly reached because her corrective feedback, presumably making use of grammatical terms, has not proven successful. This practice itself is not questioned, however; students or their inadequate English language instruction are held accountable instead. If students had been prepared appropriately, if the gatekeeping efforts had kept students out of her course until they were more like their native language counterparts, her commentary suggests, students would be able to do the required work. There is little sense of how the unfamiliar terms, concepts, and ways of seeing that are particular to this course can be acquired. Nor is there an appreciation for how this very unfamiliarity with the course content may be constraining students' linguistic processes. She does not see, focusing as she does on difference, how she can contribute to students' language and written development, how she can build on what they know. Despite indicating that students may have "adequate intelligence to do well in the course," she doesn't seem to be able to get past their language problems when it comes to evaluating their work, thus missing the irony of grading on the basis of that which she acknowledges she is not "in a position to teach." The final parenthetical statement reveals further expectations about student work, raising questions about the extent to which her very expectations, rather than linguistic difficulties alone, contribute to the "broken sentences" to which she refers.

What we see at work here is in marked contrast to the model of possibility revealed in the first response. What seems to inform this second response is a deficit model of language and learning whereby students' deficiencies are foregrounded. This response is shaped by an essentialist view of language in which language is understood to be a decontextualized skill that can be taught in isolation from the production of meaning and that must be in place in order to undertake intellectual work. What we see here is an illustration of "the myth of transience," a belief that permeates institutions of higher education and perpetuates the notion that these students' problems are temporary and can be remediated—so long as some isolated set of courses or program of instruction, but not the real courses in the academy, takes on the responsibility of doing so (see Rose, "Language"). Such a belief supports the illusion that permanent solutions are possible, which releases faculty from the ongoing struggle and questioning that the teaching-learning process inevitably involves.

In these two faculty responses, we see the ways in which different sets of expectations and attitudes get played out. In the one classroom, we get some sense of what can happen when opportunities for learning are created, when students are invited into a thoughtful process of engaging texts, when students' writing is read and responded to in meaningful and supportive ways. In the other classroom, although we have little information about the conditions for learning, we are told that one way that learning is measured is by technically correct writing done during a 10-minute slide presentation, and this, I believe, is telling. For students who are not adequately prepared to do this work, there is little, the instructor tells us, she can do. Given this deterministic stance, students are closed off from participating in intellectual work.

At the same time that I was soliciting faculty responses to get a sense of their perceptions and assumptions, I began to survey ESL students about what they wanted faculty to know about their experiences and needs in classrooms across the curriculum. I wanted, in other words, to capture the polyphony of students' voices as well. I felt that the work I was engaging in with faculty could not take place without an exploration of students' views, especially since, although faculty have little reservation discussing what they want and expect from students, informing us about their frustrations and disappointments, the students' perspective is one that faculty often hear little about. And since I have become convinced that our role in our institutions ought not to be defined solely by the service we perform for other faculty (either by making our students' English native-like or keeping the gates closed until this is accomplished) but in helping faculty understand the role they need to begin to play in working with all students, the students' perspective was critical.

Within the last two years, I have collected more than 325 responses from first and second year ESL students enrolled in courses across a range of disciplines.[2] I discovered from looking at these responses a number of predominant and recurring themes. Students spoke of patience, tolerance, and encouragement as key factors that affected their learning:

> Teachers need to be more sensitive to ESL students needs of education. Since ESL students are face with the demands of culture ajustment, especially in the classroom, teaches must be patients and give flexible consideration . . . For example—if a teacher get a paper that isn't clear or didn't follow the assignment correctly, teacher must talk and communicate with the students.

Students articulated the kinds of assistance they needed, pointing, for example, to clearer and more explicitly detailed assignments and more accessible classroom talk:

> In the classes, most teachers go over material without explaining any words that seems hard to understand for us . . . I want college teachers should describe more clearly on questions in the exams, so we can understand clearly. Also, I think the teachers should write any important information or announcement on the board rather than just speaking in front of class, because sometimes we understand in different way when we hear it than when we read it.

Students spoke with pride about how much they knew and how much they had accomplished through working, they felt, harder than their native

---

[2]This investigation of student responses was first investigated by Spack, whose findings were published in *Blair Resources for Teaching Writing: English as a Second Language.* My ongoing survey builds on her work.

English-speaking counterparts did, and they wanted faculty to credit and acknowledge them for this.

> I would like them to know that we are very responsible and we know why we come to college: to learn. We are learning English as well as the major of our choice. It is very hard sometimes and we don't need professors who claimed that they don't understand us. The effort is double. We are very intelligent people. We deserve better consideration . . . ESL students are very competent and deserve to be in college. We made the step to college. Please make the other step to meet us.

At the same time, an overwhelming number of students wanted faculty to know that they were well aware they were having language difficulties and appreciated responses that would help them. But they also expressed their wish that their work not be discounted and viewed as limited. They seemed to have a very strong sense that because of difficulties that were reflected in their attempts at classroom participation and in their written work, their struggles with learning were misperceived and underestimated:

> The academic skills of students who are not native speakers of English are not worse than the academic skills of American students, in some areas it can be much better. Just because we have problems with language . . . that some professors hate because they don't want to spend a minute to listen a student, doesn't mean that we don't understand at all.

Students referred to professors who showed concern and seemed to appreciate students' contributions. But the majority of students' responses described classrooms that silenced them, that made them feel fearful and inadequate, that limited possibilities for engagement, involvement, inclusion.

While these students acknowledged that they continue to experience difficulties, they also voiced their concern that these struggles not be viewed as deficiencies, that their efforts be understood as serious attempts to grapple with these difficulties. While faculty may feel overwhelmed by and even resentful of working with such students, these students indicated that they expect and need their instructors to assist them in this undertaking, even making suggestions as to how this can be done. Indeed, the very kind of clarity, accessible language, careful explanation, and effort that faculty want students to demonstrate are the kinds of assistance students were asking of faculty. Without dismissing the concerns of the art instructor, these students nevertheless believed, as does the English instructor, that teaching ought to be responsive to their concerns.

Yet another source of information about students' classroom experiences comes from my ongoing case-study of two students who attended a composition course I taught two years ago and who have met with me regularly since that time to discuss the work they are assigned, their teachers' responses to and evaluation of their work, the classroom dynamics of their courses, the roles they and their teachers play, and the kinds of learning that are expected in their classes.

One of the students who has been participating in this longitudinal investigation is Motoko, a student from Japan who has taken a range of courses and is majoring in sociology. She described courses in which lively interaction was generated, in which students were expected to participate, to write frequent reaction papers and to undertake projects based on first-hand research, to challenge textbook material and to connect this material to their own lived experiences. But in most of her courses the picture was quite different. Lectures were pervasive, classes were so large that attendance wasn't even taken, and short answer tests were often the predominant means of evaluating student work. With respect to one class, for example, Motoko discussed the problematic nature of multiple-choice exams which, she believes, distort the information being tested and deliberately mislead students. In regard to another course, she described what she viewed as boring, even confusing lectures, but she persevered: "Because I don't like the professor, I work even harder. I don't want him to laugh at me. I don't want to be dehumanized. I came here to learn something, to gain something." In yet another course in which only the professor talked, she indicated that she was "drowning in his words." Even a class which assigned frequent written work, which Motoko completed successfully, disappointed her because she had such difficulty understanding the assignments and because her writing was not responded to in what she perceived as a thoughtful, respectful way. Motoko confided that despite her success in this course, she had lost interest in working on her papers.

The other student whose classroom experiences I've been following is Martha, a student from Colombia who, like Motoko, has taken a range of courses, and whose major is biology. Unlike Motoko, who had managed to negotiate "drowning words" and problematic assignments, Martha's sense of discouragement about the purposelessness of much of her work is far more pervasive. With respect to many of her courses, she complained about the absence of writing (which she views as essential for learning), the passive nature of class discussions, contrived assignments that "don't help her think about anything," and the lifeless comments she received. It was in her science courses, however, that she felt the greatest dissatisfaction and frustration. About one chemistry course, she spoke of "just trying to follow the lectures and get a grade in a huge class" that she characterized as a "disaster." She talked of the sense of superiority her professors project, of her inability to learn anything meaningful from assignments which require everyone "to come up with the same information." Her experiences have provoked her to write numerous pieces which reflect her growing sense of despair and which provide a rich commentary on her perspective and experiences. In one of these pieces she has labeled the way professors behave as "academic harassment." In yet another, she questions the purpose of schooling, assignments, and written work: "Each teacher should ask her or himself the next question: Why do I assign a writing paper on this class? Do you want to see creativity and reflection of students or do or want a reproduction of the same book concept?" She is frustrated by the "lack of connections with the material we listen on lectures," the "monotony of the teaching method," the "limited style of questions," the "stressful process of learning." She concludes:

> I have no new words in my lexicon. And how do I know that? From my writing. No fluency. Why? I don't write. I was moving forward and now I'm stagnant . . . Frustration and lack of interest are the present feelings with my classes because there is not any planned "agenda" to encourage the students to improve ourselves by writing. There is no rich opportunity to break barriers and answer questions to others and also to myself. There is no REACTION and INTERACTION . . . It does not really matter how many courses the students take in order to improve skills of writing because what it counts is the responsibility encouraged by the teacher's method! The kind of responsibility developed around us is first with *ourselves!* It is an incentive for us to be listened and respected by our writing work. You get into it. Reading provides you grammar. Reading and writing are not separate in the process. It is a combined one. Doble team. Reacting and interacting.

This account, like others Martha has written, reveals her commitment to learning, her insightful understanding of how learning is both promoted and undermined, how writing in particular plays an essential role in this learning, how critical it is for teachers to contribute to and encourage learning. She, like Motoko and the other students surveyed, has much to tell us about the barriers that prevent learning and how these barriers can be broken. And lest we conclude that what these students perceive about their experiences is specific to ESL learners, recent studies of teaching and learning in higher education indicate that this is not the case. For example, Chiseri-Strater's ethnography of university classrooms reveals the authoritarian and limited ways that subject matter is often approached, the ways in which students, even those who are successful, are left silent and empty by the contrived and inconsequential work of many classrooms.

This ongoing exploration of the expectations, perceptions and experiences of both faculty and students has clarified much for me about the academic life of ESL students and what we ought to be doing both within our classrooms and beyond. Given the hierarchical arrangement of coursework within post-secondary schools, given the primacy accorded to traditional discipline-specific courses, it is not surprising that ESL and other writing-based courses have a marginalized position, that these courses are thought to have no authentic content, that the work that goes on in these courses is not considered to be the "real" work of the academy.

This view typically gets played out through coursework that is determined by what students are assumed to need in courses across the curriculum, coursework whose function it is to "guard the tower," to use Shaughnessy's term, and keep the gates closed in the case of students who are not deemed ready to enter ("Diving"). This often implies instruction that focuses on grammar, decontextualized language skills, and surface features of language. And we know from what faculty continue to say about these issues that this is precisely what is expected of English and ESL instruction—and, unfortunately, many of us have been all too ready to comply. Mike Rose speaks to the profoundly exclusionary nature of such a pedagogy and argues that a focus on mechanical skills and grammatical features reduces the complexity of language to simple and discrete problems, keeps teachers from exploring students' knowledge and potential, and contributes to the "second-class intellectual status" to which the teaching of writing has been assigned ("Language" 348). Furthermore, the problematic assumption that writing or ESL programs are in place to serve the academy, that their function is to benefit other academic studies, prevents us from questioning our situation within the larger institution. "Service course ideology," Tom Fox points out, "often leaves the curricular decisions in the hands of those who are not especially knowledgeable about writing instruction," which ultimately means that "political questions—in fact, *any* questions that challenge existing definitions of basic writing—become irrelevant to the bureaucratic task of reproducing the program" ("Basic" 67).

While skills-based and deficit models of instruction bring these kinds of pressures to bear on our work with students, our teaching has further been constrained by composition specialists who make claims about the need for students to adopt the language and discourse conventions of the academy if they are to succeed. David Bartholomae's article, "Inventing the University," is often cited and called upon to argue that students need to approximate and adopt the "specialized discourse of the university" (17). In the ESL literature, a reductive version of this position has been embraced by professionals who maintain that the role that ESL coursework ought to play is one of preparing students for the expectations and demands of discipline-specific communities across the curriculum. Such an approach, however, misrepresents and oversimplifies academic discourse and reduces it to some stable and autonomous phenomenon that does not reflect reality. Such instruction, like coursework shaped by limited conceptualizations of language, undermines our expertise and position. And because such instruction privileges and perpetuates the status quo, because it exaggerates the "distinctiveness of academic discourse [and] its separation from student literacy" (Fox, "Basic"

70), such a pedagogy has been characterized in terms of assimilation, colonization, domination, and deracination (Clark; Fox; Gay; Horner; Trimbur).

While there is growing debate about this instructional approach in the field of composition, there have been fewer attempts to problematize this model of teaching in ESL composition, where the norms and conventions of the English language and its discourses have particularly powerful political implications.[3] Hence the need to raise questions about such an instructional focus when it is applied to our work with non-native speakers of English. As I have argued elsewhere, we need to critique approaches that are reductive and formulaic, examine the notion that the language of the academy is a monolithic discourse that can be packaged and transmitted to students, and argue that this attempt to serve the institution in these ways contributes to our marginal status and that of our students.

Those of us who have tried to accommodate institutional demands have, no doubt, found this to be a troubling and tension-filled undertaking, since even when we focus on standards of language use or conventions of academic discourse, students, especially those who are still acquiring English, are not necessarily more successful in meeting the expectations of other faculty. There seems to be little carry-over from such instructional efforts to subsequent work since it is the very nature of such narrowly conceptualized instruction that undercuts genuine learning. As Fox argues, writing teachers who uphold a mythical and fixed set of institutional standards and skills are enacting a pedagogy that, however well-intentioned, is an "unqualifiable failure" ("Standards" 42). Those of us who have resisted and questioned such a pedagogy, embracing a richer and more complicated understanding of how language, discourse, and context are intertwined, may be able to trace the strides students make and to appreciate the intelligence their language and writing reveal, and yet find that this is not extended by other faculty who cannot imagine taking on this kind of responsibility.

We need to recognize that in the same way that faculty establish what Martha calls "barriers" between themselves and students, in the same way that faculty "exoticize" ESL students, we too, especially if our primary work is with ESL students, are perceived as "outsiders."[4] And as long as these boundaries continue to delineate and separate what we and other faculty do, as long as we are expected to "fix" students' problems, then misunderstandings, unfulfilled expectations, frustration, and even resentment will

---

[3]See, however, the works of Benesch, McKay, Raimes, and Zamel—all of whom have raised questions about the ideological assumptions underlying much ESL writing assumption.

[4]I am indebted here to Patricia Bizzell, whom I first heard use the term *exoticize* to characterize how faculty often react towards ESL students.

continue to mark our experiences. But this need not be the case. We are beginning to see changes in institutions in response to the growing recognition that faculty across the disciplines must take responsibility for working with all students. Studies, such as the ethnography undertaken by Walvoord and McCarthy, have documented the transformation of faculty from a range of disciplines who became more responsive to the needs of their students as they undertook their own classroom research and examined their own assumptions and expectations.

In my own work with faculty at a number of different institutions, including my own, what first begins as a concern about "underprepared" or "deficient" ESL students often leads to a consideration of the same kinds of pedagogical issues that are at the heart of writing across the curriculum initiatives. But these issues are reconsidered with specific reference to working with ESL students. Together, we have explored our instructional goals, the purposes for assigned work, the means for reading and evaluating this work, the roles that engagement, context, and classroom dynamics play in promoting learning. Through this collaboration faculty have begun to understand that it is unrealistic and ultimately counterproductive to expect writing and ESL programs to be responsible for providing students with the language, discourse, and multiple ways of seeing required across courses. They are recognizing that the process of acquisition is slow-paced and continues to evolve with exposure, immersion, and involvement, that learning is responsive to situations in which students are invited to participate in the construction of meaning and knowledge. They have come to realize that every discipline, indeed every classroom, may represent a distinct culture and thus needs to make it possible for those new to the context to practice and approximate its "ways with words." Along with acknowledging the implications of an essentialist view of language and of the myth of transience, we have considered the myth of coverage, the belief that covering course content necessarily means that it has been learned. Hull and Rose, in their study of the logic underlying a student's unconventional reading of a text, critique "the desire of efficiency and coverage" for the ways it "limit[s] rather than enhance[s] [students'] participation in intellectual work" (296), for the ways it undermines students' entry into the academy. With this in mind, we have raised questions about what we do in order to cover material, why we do what we do, what we expect from students, and how coverage is evaluated. And if the "cover-the-material" model doesn't seem to be working in the ways we expected, we ask, what alternatives are there?

We have also examined the ways in which deficit thinking, a focus on difference, blinds us to the logic, intelligence and richness of students' processes and knowledge. In *Lives on the Boundary*, Mike Rose cites numerous cases of learners (including himself) whose success was undercut because of the tendency to emphasize difference. Studies undertaken by

Glynda Hull and her colleagues further attest to how such belief systems about students can lead to inaccurate judgments about learners' abilities, and how practices based on such beliefs perpetuate and "virtually assure failure" (325). The excerpt from the tutor's journal quoted at the beginning of this article, along with many of the faculty and student responses that I have elicited, are yet other indications of what happens when our reading of student work is derailed by a focus on what is presumed to be students' deficiencies. Thus we try to read students' texts to see what is there rather than what isn't, resisting generalizations about literacy and intelligence that are made on the basis of judgments about standards of correctness and form, and suspending our judgments about the alternative rhetorical approaches our students adopt.

In addition to working with faculty to shape the curriculum so that it is responsive to students' needs and to generate instructional approaches that build on students' competence, we address other institutional practices that affect our students. At the University of Massachusetts, for example, the Writing Proficiency Exam, which all students must pass by the time they are juniors, continues to evolve as faculty across the curriculum work together, implementing and modifying it over time. While the exam is impressive, immersing students in rich, thematically-integrated material to read, think about, and respond to, it nevertheless continues to be reconsidered and questioned as we study the ways in which the exam impinges on students' academic lives. And so, for instance, in order to address the finding that ESL students were failing the exam at higher rates than native speakers of English—a situation that is occurring at other institutions as well (see Ray)—we have tried to ensure that faculty understand how to look below the surface of student texts for evidence of proficiency, promoting a kind of reading that benefits not just ESL students but all students. The portfolio option, which requires students to submit papers written in courses as well as to write an essay in response to a set of readings, has proven a better alternative for ESL students to demonstrate writing proficiency. This is not surprising, given that the portfolio allows students to demonstrate what they are capable of when writing is imbedded within and an outgrowth of their courses.

Throughout this work, one of the most critical notions that I try to bring home is the idea that what faculty ought to be doing to enhance the learning of ESL students is *not* a concession, a capitulation, a giving up of standards—since the unrevised approaches that some faculty want to retain may never have been beneficial for *any* students. As John Mayher has pointed out, teaching and learning across college courses are by and large dysfunctional for all students, even those that succeed. What ESL students need—multiple opportunities to use language and write-to-learn, coursework which draws on and values what students already know, classroom exchanges and assignments that promote the acquisition of unfamiliar language, concepts, and approaches to inquiry, evaluation that allows students to demonstrate genuine understanding—is good pedagogy for everyone. Learning how to better address the needs of ESL students, because it involves becoming more reflective about teaching, because it involves carefully thinking through the expectations, values, and assumptions underlying the work we assign, helps faculty teach everyone better. In other words, rather than seeing the implications of inclusion and diversity in opposition to excellence and academic standards (as they often are at meetings convened to discuss these issues), learning to teach ESL students, because this challenges us to reconceptualize teaching, contributes to and enhances learning, and for all students. As Gerald Graff has argued in response to those who voice their concerns about the presence of new student populations in their institutions and the negative consequences that this change brings,

> Conservatives who accuse affirmative action programs of lowering academic standards never mention the notorious standard for ignorance that was set by white male college students before women and minorities were permitted in large numbers on campus. It has been the steady pressure for reform from below that has raised academic standards. (88)

Needless to say, given the complexity of this enterprise, these efforts have not transformed classrooms on an institution-wide basis. As is obvious from the surveys and case studies I have undertaken, change is slow, much like the process of learning itself. Shaughnessy referred to the students who entered the CUNY system through open admissions as "strangers in academia" to give us a sense of the cultural and linguistic alienation they were experiencing (*Errors*). In listening to the comments of faculty (note, for example, the comment of the professor of management), it occurs to me that they too are feeling like strangers in academia, that they no longer understand the world in which they work. Janice Neulieb similarly points out that although it is common to view students as "other," as alienated from the academic community, our differing cultural perspectives result in our own confusion and alienation as well.

As we grapple with the kinds of issues and concerns raised by the clash of cultures in academia, we continue to make adjustments which, in turn, generate new questions about our practices. This ongoing dialogue is both necessary and beneficial. Like other prominent debates in higher education on reforming the canon and the implications of diversity, this attempt to explore and interrogate what we do is slowly reconfiguring the landscape and blurring the borders within what was once a fairly well-defined and stable academic community. According to Graff, this is all to the good because this kind of transformation can revitalize higher education and its isolated departments and fragmentary curricula. Within composition, the conflicts and struggles that inevitably mark the teaching of writing are viewed as instructive because they allow students and teachers to "reposition" themselves, raising questions about conventional thinking about instruction and challenging us to imagine alternative pedagogies (Lu; Horner). What Pratt calls the "contact zone," because it represents a site of contestation, is embraced because it enables us to redraw disciplinary boundaries, to reexamine composition instruction, and to revise our assumptions about language and difference.

When faculty see this kind of redefinition as a crisis, I invite them to reconsider their work in light of the way the word "crisis" is translated into Chinese. In Chinese, the word is symbolized by two ideographs—one meaning danger, the other meaning opportunity. Because the challenges that students bring with them may make us feel confused, uncertain, like strangers in our own community, there will be dissonance, jarring questions, ongoing dilemmas, unfulfilled expectations. We can see this reflected in the second faculty response, a response which insists that there are students who don't belong in the academy, that its doors be kept closed. But, as we saw in the first response, perplexities and tensions can also be generative, creating possibilities for new insights, alternative interpretations, and in appreciation for the ways in which these enrich our understanding. Seen from the fresh perspective that another language can provide, the Chinese translation of crisis captures the very nature of learning, a process involving both risk and opportunity, the very process that ideally students ought to engage in, but which we ourselves may resist when it comes to looking at our own practices. But as Giroux urges, teachers must "cross over borders that are culturally strange and alien to them" so that they can "analyze their own values and voices as viewed from different ideological and cultural spaces" (254–55). It is when we take risks of this sort, when we take this step into the unknown, by looking for evidence of students' intelligence, by rereading their attempts as coherent efforts, by valuing, not just evaluating, their work, and by reflecting on the critical relationship between our work and theirs, that opportunities are created not only for students but for teachers to learn in new ways.

REFERENCES

Bartholomae, David. "Inventing the University." *Journal of Basic Writing* 5 (Spring 1986): 4–23.

Benesch, Sarah. "ESL, Ideology, and the Politics of Pragmatism." *TESOL Quarterly* 27 (1993): 705–17.

Chiseri-Strater, Elizabeth. *Academic Literacies: The Public and Private Discourse of University Students.* Portsmouth: Boynton, 1991.

Clark, Gregory. "Rescuing the Discourse of the Community." *CCC* 45 (1994): 61–74.

Fox, Tom. "Basic Writing as Cultural Conflict." *Journal of Education* 172 (1990): 65–83.

———. "Standards and Access." *Journal of Basic Writing* 12 (Spring 1993): 37–45.

Gay, Pamela. "Rereading Shaughnessy from a Postcolonial Perspective." *Journal of Basic Writing* 12 (Fall 1993): 29–40.

Giroux, Henry. "Postmodernism as Border Pedagogy: Redefining the Boundaries of Race and Ethnicity." *Postmodernism, Feminism, and Cultural Policies: Redrawing Educational Boundaries.* Ed. Henry Giroux. Albany: State U of New York P, 1991. 217–56.

Graff, Gerald. *Beyond Culture Wars.* New York: Norton, 1992.

Horner, Bruce. "Mapping Errors and Expectations for Basic Writing: From 'Frontier Field' to 'Border Country.' " *English Education* 26 (1994): 29–51.

Hull, Glynda and Mike Rose. " 'This Wooden Shack Place': The Logic of an Unconventional Reading." *CCC* 41 (1990): 287–98.

Hull, Glynda, Mike Rose, Kay Losey Fraser, and Marisa Castellano. "Remediation as Social Construct: Perspectives from an Analysis of Classroom Discourse." *CCC* 42 (1991): 299–329.

Laurence, Patricia. "The Vanishing Site of Mina Shaughnessy's *Errors and Expectations.*" *Journal of Basic Writing* 12 (Fall 1993): 18–28.

Lu, Min-Zhan. "Conflict and Struggle in Basic Writing." *College English* 54 (1992): 887–913.

Mayher, John S. "Uncommon Sense in the Writing Center." *Journal of Basic Writing* 11 (Spring 1992): 47–57.

McKay, Sandra Lee. "Examining L2 Composition Ideology: A Look at Literacy Education." *Journal of Second Language Writing* 2 (1993): 65–81.

Neuleib, Janice. "The Friendly Stranger: Twenty-Five Years as 'Other.' " *CCC* 43 (1992): 231–43.

Pratt, Mary Louise. "Arts of the Contact Zone." *Profession* 91 (1991): 33–40.

Raimes, Anne. "Out of the Woods: Emerging Traditions in the Teaching of Writing." *TESOL Quarterly* 25 (1991): 407–30.

Ray, Ruth. "Language and Literacy from the Student Perspective: What We Can Learn from the Longterm-Case Study." *The Writing Teacher as Researcher.* Ed. Donald A. Daiker and Max Morenberg. Portsmouth: Boynton, 1990. 321–35.

Rose, Mike. *Lives on the Boundary: The Struggles and Achievements of America's Underprepared.* New York: Free P, 1989.

———. "The Language of Exclusion: Writing Instruction at the University." *College English* 47 (1985): 341–59.

Shaughnessy, Mina. "Diving In: An Introduction to Basic Writing." *CCC* 27 (1976): 234–39.

———. *Errors and Expectations.* New York: Oxford UP, 1977.

Spack, Ruth. *Blair Resources for Teaching Writing: English as a Second Language.* New York: Prentice, 1994.

Trimbur, John. " 'Really Useful Knowledge' in the Writing Classroom." *Journal of Education* 172 (1990): 21–23.

Villanueva, Victor. *Bootstrap: From an American Academic of Color.* Urbana: NCTE, 1993.

Walvoord, Barbara E., and Lucille B. McCarthy. *Thinking and Writing in College: A Naturalistic Study of Students in Four Disciplines.* Urbana: NCTE, 1990.

Zamel, Vivian. "Questioning Academic Discourse." *College ESL* 3 (1993): 28–39.

QUESTIONS FOR REFLECTION, JOURNAL WRITING, AND DISCUSSION

1. Why do some teachers have difficulty working with ESL students?

2. Compare Zamel's ideas on a "basic skills" approach to writing instruction to those of Bartholomae and Rose.

3. Should ESL or basic skills classes serve a "gate-keeping" function of keeping students out of other classes until they have no more problems with English?

4. What is your opinion about a "lecture approach" to teaching? What is your opinion about multiple choice tests?

5. How important is "coverage" in education? Is it a good reason to not have students do much discussion or writing?

Chapter 24

Opinion: The Wyoming Conference Resolution Opposing Unfair Salaries and Working Conditions for Post-Secondary Teachers of Writing

Linda R. Robertson, Sharon Crowley, and Frank Lentricchia

Linda R. Robertson is Professor of Rhetoric and the codirector of the Media and Society program at Hobart and William Smith Colleges. Her scholarship includes publications in the fields of economic rhetoric, political rhetoric, and war propaganda. She is completing a study of the propaganda of the first air war. **Sharon Crowley** specializes in the history and theory of rhetoric and the history of composition. She codirects the Ph.D program in Rhetoric and Linguistics at Arizona State University. Her recent books are *Composition in the University* (1998), which won MLA's Mina Shaughnessy prize for the year's best book on teaching, and the second edition of *Ancient Rhetorics for Contemporary Students* (1998), with Debra Hawhee. **Frank Lentricchia** is Katherine Everett Gilbert Professor of English and Literature at Duke University. His chief interests lie in American literature, history of poetry, modernism, the role of the intellectual in culture, and the history and theory of criticism. His publications include *Robert Frost: Modern Poetics* and the *Landscapes of Self* (1975), *After the New Criticism* (1980), *Criticism and Social Change* (1983), *Introducing Don DeLillo* (1991), *Modernist Quartet* (1994), *The Music of the Inferno* (1999), and *Lucchesi and The Whale* (2001). He was editorial chair of *South Atlantic Quarterly* for five years. The following article is from *College English*, 49, March 1987.

Members who attend this year's Conference on College Communication and Composition will have an opportunity to vote on the Wyoming Conference Resolution, which has been proposed by participants attending the Wyoming Conference on English this June. The resolution calls upon the Executive Committee to establish grievance procedures for post-secondary writing teachers seeking to redress unfair working conditions and salaries. The resolution reflects a remarkable and spontaneous consensus that emerged during this year's conference. Participants felt it should be called the Wyoming Conference Resolution to indicate the co-operation and conviction that gave rise to it. Tilly Warnock, the conference director, readily agreed.

So remarkable was the spirit of the Wyoming Conference that this discussion would be incomplete without some effort to describe how the resolution arose. The conference began on a Monday and ended Friday afternoon. The topic this year was "Language and the Social Context." By mid-week, many of us had become persuaded that we ought to consider how the topic applied to our own profession: "What is the social context for writing teachers?" Some stark polarities gave rise to this question. James Moffett, one of the major consultants to the conference, spoke of his conviction that teachers of writing ought to enable students to discover the freedom of self-expression. Some of us were struck with the irony that those of us charged with this significant responsibility often feel unable to speak freely about the fundamentally unfair conditions under which we labor.

From the stories we tell one another, it is clear that many of us regard ourselves as victimized by our institutions, relegated to marginal positions and tenuous employment with no benefits. Conference participants told of the repression and exploitation they experienced at their home institutions. Graduate students told of feeling coerced to teach courses without pay; teachers at community colleges told of heavy, unreasonable course loads; part-time and adjunct instructors at major private and public universities told of the demeaning status and inequitable salaries they were forced to accept as conditions of employment; full-time faculty members with a primary commitment to teaching writing told of unfair tenure review proceedings; and literature faculty members who are sometimes called upon to teach writing expressed their unease at the inequitable treatment handed out to their part-time or full-time and adjunct colleagues in composition.

Those stories were told over breakfast in the dining hall, during coffee-breaks between sessions, and in late-night talks after the honky-tonk bands playing at Laramie's night spots had finished the last set. We hear such stories whenever teachers of writing gather. But there was a harder edge to them at Laramie, a greater insistence in the telling, a deeper silence in the listening. Perhaps this was because of the natural intimacy that comes when 200 people meet for a week, live together in dorms, and eat together in the cafeteria, while surrounded by a spectacular and harmonious natural world, one which needs neither social context nor language to endure. Certainly the greater intensity of our concern was due in part to the way James Slevin chose to address the conference topic. He hammered home to us just how endemic are the local conditions we described.

Reporting on studies conducted by the Association of Departments of English (ADE), Slevin told us that only forty percent of new English PhDs now find tenure track positions. We have been told this disheartening reality is the result of economic forces beyond the control of English departments. Plaintive cries against economic hardships were first uttered twelve to fifteen years ago amid predictions that enrollments in the late 1970s and early 1980s would plummet. Contrary to these predictions, enrollments in colleges and universities increased by twenty to thirty percent between 1974 and 1984. About one-third of the English departments recently surveyed by ADE report growth in the undergraduate literature major, while one-fourth to one-third of the graduate programs report growth. Of those institutions offering undergraduate technical communication programs, eighty percent report growth. Three-fourths of those schools offering graduate degrees in rhetoric report growth in their programs. But despite the reasonable health of literature programs and the robust health of rhetoric and technical communications programs, English departments are the departments most likely to employ part-time faculty members, and they almost always hire them to teach writing.

Slevin's talk clarified how disenfranchised are teachers of writing. It also suggested to some of us that there are larger issues of academic freedom inherent in hiring policies which rely heavily on part-time or temporary positions. Since sixty percent of new PhDs in English cannot find full-time, tenure-track employment, many of them must accept part-time or temporary full-time employment if they wish to participate in academic life at all. And since the salaries offered for such positions are usually low, they are often filled by women; that is, by those who constitute an underclass in the economy generally. Indeed, the decline in the number of full-time, secure positions and the increase in part-time or temporary full-time positions in higher education reflect national employment trends. There has been a decline in the number of full-time jobs typically held by women, and an increase in part-time positions, a strategy that allows employers to save money on benefits while at the same time meeting their traditional labor needs.

Slevin heightened our awareness of the polarity between the freedom we are asked to promote in the classroom and the threats to academic freedom and absence of job security faced by many teachers of writing. He also heightened our awareness of the polarity that divided the privileged from the underprivileged in English departments. Many participants expressed bitterness and frustration that their demeaning status is visited upon them, or at least abetted, by their tenured colleagues. At many of our colleges and universities—even those enjoying great prestige—teachers of writing hold the same degrees as their tenured counterparts; yet they are excluded from participating in academic life, prohibited from teaching courses in their fields of academic preparation, denied the traditional support for research, and denied even basic benefits. Sometimes their numbers exceed those of the tenured faculty in English. They often carry heavier teaching loads even though they are designated as "part-time" faculty. Most demoralizing is the lack of respect accorded those who teach writing. Composition is regarded as something "anyone can do," as one professor said when he read a copy of the resolution circulated in his department after the conference.

The bitterness toward tenured English faculty surprised some of those attending the conference who enjoy this privileged status. English professors are unused to thinking of themselves as privileged in any sense. Some genuinely believed that such conditions were not prevalent, or at least did not prevail at their home institutions. Motivated by the concerns raised at the conference, some of them have since made inquiries and have found that indeed composition teachers at their colleges or universities are exploited, denied privileges, and, in one case, are earning less than those employed by the physical plant. Others honestly expressed their fear that if the conditions for teachers of writing were improved, tenured faculty members would have to carry a heavier burden in teaching composition.

With these realizations, we met the enemy, and discovered they are us.

This polarity—and the bitterness it inspired—threatened to pull the conference apart. Fortunately, James Sledd's talk galvanized us. He spoke on the global issues of language instruction in the context of class power and exploitation. As part of this larger concern, he chastened teachers of writing by pointing out that we condemned the unfair and exploitative attitudes that have resulted from the creation of a privileged and protected class, while at the same time we sought that same status ourselves. He chastened English faculty with the remark that, if we sought evidence to disprove the notion that the study of the humanities promoted more humane conduct, we need look no further than the way we treated graduate students and part-time faculty in our own departments. During the question and answer session, many of us sought to avoid the issues Sledd raised by asking safe "academic" questions of the other panelists. Then suddenly the top blew off. A graduate student rose to speak. So conditioned was she to keeping silent that her voice broke as she spoke; so frustrated was she by the conditions she had felt compelled to endure in order to seek a degree in English that she wept. She challenged our silence and apathy; she asked us why we had not spoken to the issues Sledd charged us with addressing.

It probably is not possible to convey the galvanizing effect her challenge had on those who heard her. After this session, an unusually large number of participants came to the room set aside for writing comments on each day's sessions, comments that are then published the following day. One of the responses to this session is representative of the general reaction:

> Well, I'll say the obvious—it's about time someone stood up and did what the last speaker of the session did. There's nothing wrong with talking about what have been called "local" concerns. But the fear—perhaps the fear that

"there's nothing to be done"—about trying to deal with the global issues needs to be brought into the open and dealt with. We listen to someone like Sledd. We laugh at his wonderful humor. We nod our heads as he talks about the state of education within the context of our world. We give him the biggest round of applause of the evening. Then, damn it, we run as fast as we can from what he's saying, and we do it by almost ignoring it. We don't want to face *our own roles* in the problem, and how we—as people, as teachers, as "professionals"—are implicated in the very problems we're trying to solve. Perhaps there is no solution. Perhaps nothing we do as individuals, or even as a group, can do anything to mitigate the frightening direction that some of us see us going. But to ignore it—no. Not if we take ourselves seriously when we speak so glibly about making things better.

Another kind of response was made later that evening when two conference participants met, not really by chance. One of them was male, a tenured faculty member at a state school, well-known in the profession, who had been maintaining during the conference that the predatory conditions described by many participants were not necessarily reflective of the profession as a whole. The other was female, untenured, changing jobs, and certainly not at the top of the professional hierarchy. She had been arguing throughout the conference that the unfair conditions were so endemic to the profession that the professional organizations ought to take action to correct them. Following the emotion-charged session, he guided her to a quiet spot and asked, Luther-like, "Are you really ready to lead the revolution?" She said, Erasmus-like, "It is not a revolution we need. It is a resolution of conflict within the existing structures." From this colloquy, there emerged a mutual sense of what action we might take, and the foundation was laid for the Wyoming Conference Resolution.

The results of the late-night conversation were circulated the next day as a draft resolution, and conference participants were invited to discuss it later that afternoon. They filled the dormitory lounge to overflowing. James Sledd sat quietly on the floor, perhaps contemplating what he had wrought. The two who offered to incorporate these suggestions in a final draft were seen collaborating on it during a session on collaborative writing. A typed copy of the revised version was circulated at a reception later that evening and edited. The final version was presented as a petition at the final session Friday morning. More than enough signatures were gathered to enter it as a resolution at the CCCC this spring. Conference participants were nonetheless urged to carry the resolution to their home institutions to seek more support.

We urge you to join us in the spirit of the Wyoming Conference Resolution. We do not offer it—nor was it proposed—as the only anodyne to our problems. But it does provide those who seek change one way to do so. The provisions of the resolution are:

WHEREAS, the salaries and working conditions of post-secondary teachers with primary responsibility for the teaching of writing are fundamentally unfair as judged by any reasonable professional standards (e.g., unfair in excessive teaching loads, unreasonably large class size, salary inequities, lack of benefits and professional status, and barriers to personal advancement) . . .

The wording of this provision is intended to indicate concern for all ranks in our profession: graduate teaching assistants, teachers at community colleges, part-time or temporary teachers in colleges and universities, and those on tenure-track lines whose work is often considered less worthy than that done by faculty members teaching literature or linguistics.

AND WHEREAS, as a consequence of those unreasonable working conditions, highly dedicated teachers are often frustrated in their desire to provide students the time and attention which students both deserve and need . . .

This provision is included to remind us that the unfair conditions under which teachers of writing labor have profound implications for educating the next generation. We are aware of the deep concern expressed by the public at large and their elected representatives about the apparent decline in students' ability to articulate their interests and hopes. This concern is one we share.

THEREFORE, BE IT RESOLVED that the Executive Committee of College Composition and Communication be charged with the following:

The resolution is addressed to College Composition and Communication as the professional organization most immediately and exclusively concerned with the teaching of writing. Participants discussed the desirability of seeking further endorsement from other professional organizations—such as MLA, NCTE (as the umbrella organization for CCC), NEA, and others—after it was approved by CCC.

1. To formulate, after appropriate consultations with post-secondary teachers of writing, professional standards and expectations of salary levels and working conditions of post-secondary teachers of writing.

We felt it was important to provide those who feared to speak on their own behalf an opportunity to do so. We also felt it would be pointless to try formulating professional standards without detailed information about working conditions and salaries at diverse institutions. We also hoped that one result of gathering such detailed information would be that the knowledge would inspire other proposals for initiatives and change.

The wording "working conditions of post-secondary teacher of writing" was carefully chosen, so that those full-time faculty members in English who teach composition only occasionally will feel included. The resolution as a whole is worded so that enlightened English faculty members, even those who never teach composition, can feel encouraged to participate in helping to alleviate the unfair conditions under which some of their colleagues labor.

> 2. To establish a procedure for hearing grievances brought by post-secondary teachers of writing—either singly or collectively—against apparent institutional non-compliance with these standards and expectations.

This provision is included as a way of empowering those who feel most disenfranchised. We wanted to avoid imposing Draconian solutions. This might result if our professional leadership attempted to provide generic solutions to unfair practices that vary widely from institution to institution. We were also impressed by the irony that those who teach self-expression to students feel themselves coerced into silence as a condition of employment. We felt the healthiest approach was for them to have an opportunity to demonstrate to themselves and their institutions that we can, through the language of petition and complaint, promote peaceful change. Finally, we recognized that some among us are content with their lot, and that, given this complacency, a professional organization seeking to impose change could make little headway. We felt that change can come only if those who wish it take action on their own behalf.

We also recognize that implementing formal grievance procedures will be costly. We assume that if members of CCC feel the procedure will benefit the profession as a whole, they will be ready to spend a bit more on dues.

> 3. To establish a procedure for acting upon a procedure of non-compliance; specifically, to issue a letter of censure to an individual's administration, Board of Regents or Trustees, State legislators (where pertinent), and to publicize the findings to the public-at-large, the educational committee in general, and to our membership.

In proposing this provision, we were alert to the widespread attention given nationally to a perceived decline in communication skills among students. We felt it was timely to make common cause with those calling for reform. There are those who will argue that some institutions will not feel particularly threatened by the possibility of being criticized in public. This may be true, and speaks again to our sense that no single solution will resolve our problems. But certainly publicizing detrimental conditions of employment will not hinder the efforts of those who seek change at such an institution.

On the other hand, we are aware that many administrators will seek to avoid detrimental publicity because it might bring in its train inquiries from members of boards of trustees, or state governors, or state legislators.

We also hoped that by publicizing the unfair conditions we might discourage candidates from applying from applying for positions at institutions found in non-compliance. Job candidates ought to know that, at a given institution, conditions have become so unbearable that faculty members have formally protested them to their professional organization. It takes little genius to realize that unfair labor practices are often alleviated when the labor pool diminishes or evaporates.

We ask you to consider carefully whether it is not now time to seek ways of redressing the shabby and exploitative circumstances in which many of our colleagues find themselves. These conditions are unlikely to change, even though, as we read in the *Chronicle of Higher Education,* many institutions are now preparing to hire "promising young scholars" to replace retiring faculty. Some may believe that this signals automatic change as we move into an era of labor shortage and seller's market. But the current shabby conditions for teachers of writing are not the product of economic conditions. They are the result of short-sighted policies formulated in response to anticipated economic trends. Not only were the policies short-sighted, but the economic predictions that inspired them never materialized. Moreover, teachers at community colleges will not be helped by any rush to hire new faculty in colleges and universities. Nor will graduate teaching assistants be less exploited even given changes in the job market. And the sad truth is that in seeking "promising young scholars," institutions may well overlook those who have been laboring in their very own vineyards because part-time and adjunct faculty members holding advanced degrees are inhibited by their conditions of employment from developing their scholarly talents.

No other professional organization has come forward with any proposal that would allow teachers of writing to take direct action at their own institutions against unfair practices that are now endemic. If you wish to join in the spirit of the Wyoming Conference, pay your membership dues and come to the CCCC conference to vote in favor of the Wyoming Conference Resolution. Urge your colleagues to do the same. We look forward to voting with you to pass this resolution.

Editors' note: Subsequent to passing the "Wyoming Resolution," the Conference on College Composition and Communication developed a "Statement of Principles and Standards for the Postsecondary Teaching of Writing," which can be obtained from the NCTE Order Department, 1111 Kenyon Road, Urbana, IL 61801.

QUESTIONS FOR REFLECTION, JOURNAL WRITING, AND DISCUSSION

1. What are the working conditions of writing teachers at your educational institution? Are they fair? How do you feel about your own working conditions?

2. Do you agree that "We met the enemy, and discovered that they are us," and that "We don't want to face our own roles in the problem"?

3. Has the situation of writing teachers improved since the Wyoming resolution was passed? If not, why not? Do you think the situation will improve in the future? Why (not)?

Chapter 25

Distant Voices: Teaching and Writing in a Culture of Technology

Chris M. Anson

Chris M. Anson is Professor of English and Director of the Campus Writing and Speaking Program at North Carolina State University. He has published 12 books and several dozen articles in the field of composition studies, with a special focus on response to student writing and writing across the curriculum. His current book project, which is under contract at Oxford University Press, is an edited collection of writing across the curriculum scenarios for campuswide faculty development. The following article is from *College English*, 61, January 1999.

> *With the development of the Internet, and . . . networked computers, we are in the middle of the most transforming technological event since the capture of fire.*
> —John Perry Barlow, "Forum: What Are We Doing Online?" (36)

August 3, Les Agettes, Switzerland. I am sitting on a veranda overlooking the town of Sion some three thousand feet below, watching tiny airplanes take off from the airstrip and disappear over the shimmering ridge of Alps to the north. Just below us is another chalet, the home of a Swiss family. At this time of day, they gather at the large wooden table on the slate patio behind their home to have a long, meandering lunch in the French Swiss tradition. Madame is setting the table, opening a bottle of Valais wine, which grandpère ritually pours out for the family and any friends who join them. As they sit to eat, the scene becomes for me a vision of all that is most deeply social in human affairs. They could not survive without this interconnectedness, this entwining of selves, the stories passed around, problems discussed, identities shared and nourished. For weeks, away from phones, TVs, computers, and electronic mail, a dot on the rugged landscape of the southern Alps, I have a profound sense of my own familial belonging, of how the four of us are made one by this closeness of being. Just now Bernard, the little boy who lives on the switchback above, has run down with his dog Sucrette to see if the kids can play. He is here, standing before us, his face smudged with dirt, holding out a toy truck, to entice the boys. For now, it is his only way to communicate with them, poised here in all his Bernard-ness, his whole being telling his story.

Not long after writing this journal entry and reflecting on how different my life had become during a summer without access to computers, I came across an issue of *Policy Perspectives,* a periodical issued by the Pew Higher Education Roundtable, which was intriguingly titled "To Dance with Change." When the *Policy Perspectives* began in 1988, the roundtable members believed that "the vitality of education would be defined by its ability to control costs, its capacity to promote learning, and its commitment to access and equity" (1). Less than a decade later, they had shifted their attention to forces beyond academia, realizing that they had been thinking of the institution itself without considering its connection to broader social pressures and movements. They conclude that "among the changes most important to higher education are those external to it"— economic, occupational, and technological. In particular, the electronic superhighway

> may turn out to be the most powerful external challenge facing higher education, and the one the academy is least prepared to understand. It is not that higher education institutions or their faculties have ignored technology. The academy, in fact, is one of the most important supporters and consumers of electronic technology. . . . The problem is that faculty—and hence the institutions they serve—have approached technology more as individual consumers than as collective producers. For the most part the new capacities conferred by electronic means have not enhanced the awareness that teaching might be conceived as something other than one teacher before a classroom of students. While academicians appreciate the leverage that technology has provided in the library and laboratory, they have not considered fully how the same technology might apply to the process of teaching and learning—and they have given almost no thought to how the same technologies in someone else's hands might affect their markets for student-customers. The conclusion that has escaped too many faculty is that this set of technologies is altering the market for even the most traditional goods and services, creating not only new products but new markets and, just as importantly, new providers. (3A)

In the context of our beliefs about how students best learn to write, many educators are haunted, like the Pew members, by a sense that bigger things are happening around us as we continue to refine classroom methods and tinker with our teaching styles. Theorists or researchers or just plain teachers, we spend much of our time working within the framework of certain fairly stable educational conditions. These conditions include physical spaces that define the social and interpersonal contexts of teaching: classrooms where we meet large or small groups of students, offices where we can consult with students face-to-face, and tutorial areas such as writing centers. We expect students to come to these places—even penalizing them for not doing so—and also to visit other physical spaces on campus such as libraries, where they carry out work connected with our instruction. The textual landscape of writing instruction also has a long and stable history: students write or type on white paper of a standard size and turn in their work, adhering to various admonitions about the width of their margins and the placement of periphera such as names, dates, and staples. Teachers collect the papers, respond in predictable places (in the margins or in the spaces left at the end) and return the papers at the institutional site. Innovations like portfolios are extensions of the use of this textual space, but the spaces themselves remain the same.

While the Pew Roundtable members may be concerned that faculty are not attentive to the frenzy of innovation in computer technology, it is difficult for them to make the same claim about academic administrations. Searching the horizon for signs of educational and institutional reform, administrators are often the first to introduce new campus-wide initiatives to the professoriate, who react with delight, resistance, apathy, or outrage to various proposals for change. In the climate of burgeoning developments in technology that have far-reaching consequences for teaching and learning, such changes will no doubt challenge existing ideologies of writing instruction, in part because of the assumed stability on which we have based our curricula and pedagogies.

In this essay, I will consider two of the ways in which teaching and responding to student writing are pressured by rapidly developing technologies now being introduced into our institutions. The first—the increasing replacement of face-to-face contact by "virtual" interaction—is the product of multimedia technology, email communications systems, and the recently expanded capabilities of the Word Wide Web. The second, somewhat more institutionally complex development is distance education, in which students hundreds or even thousands of miles apart are connected via interactive television systems. While these technologies offer an endless array of new and exciting possibilities for the improvement of education, they also frequently clash with some of our basic beliefs about the nature of classroom instruction, in all its communal richness and face-to-face complexity. Of even greater urgency is the need to understand the motivation for these developments. More specifically, new technologies introduced with the overriding goal of creating economic efficiencies and generating increased revenues may lead to even greater exploitation in the area of writing instruction, the historically maligned and undernourished servant of the academy. The key to sustaining our pedagogical advances in the teaching of writing, even as we are pulled by the magnetic forces of innovation, will be to take control of these technologies, using them in effective ways and not, in the urge for ever-cheaper instruction, substituting them for those contexts and methods that we hold to be essential for learning to write.

THE ALLURE: TECHNOLOGY AND
INSTRUCTIONAL ENHANCEMENT

Until recently, writing instruction has experienced the greatest technological impact from the personal computer, a tool that had an especially powerful effect on the teaching and practice of revision. The integration of the microcomputer into writing curricula seemed a natural outcome of our interests and prevailing ways of teaching: it offered students a screen on which they could manipulate texts, but they could still print out their writing and turn it in on paper.

Throughout the 1980s and 1990s, many writing programs experimented with labs or computerized classrooms where students could write to and with each other on local area networks. (For a historical account of computers in the teaching of writing, see Hawisher, Selfe, Moran, and LeBlanc.) Simultaneously, an array of computer-assisted instructional programs became available, allowing students to work through guided activities (typically alone) on a personal computer. Computer-generated questions could prompt students to invent ideas; style checkers could give them an index of their average sentence length or complexity; and outline programs could help them to map out the structure of their essays as they wrote. But even with all the cut-and-paste functions and floating footnotes that eased the writing process and facilitated revision, the "textuality" of academic essays remained relatively unchanged: students continued to meet in classrooms to work on their assignments, and teachers reacted to and assessed their products in conventional ways, by carrying the papers home and grading them. Personal computers offered students and teachers a new tool to practice the processes of writing, but the outcome still emerged, eventually, on paper.

In the field of composition studies, the development of more reasoned, theoretically informed methods of response to students' writing has been framed by assumptions about the perpetuation of these physical and textual spaces. Recent studies of response analyze marginal comments written on students' papers for various rhetorical or focal patterns (see, e.g., Straub; Straub and Lunsford; Smith). Studies that deliberately attend to the contextual factors that influence teachers' responses continue to do so within the traditional parameters of typed or handwritten papers turned in for (usually handwritten) response or assessment (e.g., Prior). While such work is much needed in the field, it largely ignores the sweep of change in the way that many students now create, store, retrieve, use, and arrange information (including text) in their academic work. Artificial intelligence expert Seymour Papert pictures a scenario in which a mid-nineteenth century surgeon is timewarped into a modem operating theater. Bewildered, the doctor would freeze, surrounded by unrecognizable technology and an utterly transformed profession, unsure of what to do or how to help. But if a mid-nineteenth century schoolteacher were similarly transported into a modern classroom, the teacher would feel quite at home. Recounting Papert's anecdote, Nicholas Negroponte points out that there is "little fundamental difference between the way we teach today and the way we did one hundred and fifty years ago. The use of technology is almost at the same level. In fact, according to a recent survey by the U.S. Department of Education, 84 percent of America's teachers consider only one type of information technology absolutely 'essential' to their work—a photocopier with an adequate paper supply" (220). Yet most statistics show the use of computers, particularly by students in high school and college, increasing at lightning speed. Today, more than one-third of American homes already have a computer, and it is predicted that by 2005 Americans will spend more time on the Internet than watching TV.

That personal computers have done little to disrupt our decades-old habits of working with and responding to students' writing is partly because the channels of electronic media have been separate and discrete. Video has been kept apart from computer text, audio systems, and still pictures, requiring us to use different equipment for each technology (and allowing us to focus on computer text to the exclusion of other media). Whether teachers focus on text to the exclusion of other media is not really the point; as Pamela McCorduck points out, "knowledge of different kinds is best represented in all its complexity for different purposes by different kinds of knowledge representations. Choosing *la représentation juste* (words, images, or anything else) is not at all an obvious thing: in fact, it's magnificently delicate. But we have not had much choice until now because text, whether the best representation for certain purposes or not, has dominated our intellectual lives" (259).

The introduction of hypertext and multimedia refocused attention on the relationship between text and other forms of representation. Experimenting with new technology, teachers of literature dragged laptops and heavy projection equipment into their classrooms and displayed stored multimedia Web sites to students reading *Emma* or *King Lear*, linking such texts to their social and political contexts, revealing connections to pieces of art of the time, playing segments of music that the characters might have heard, or showing brief video clips of famous stage presentations. Early advocates of multimedia in teaching and learning clearly framed its advantages in terms that emphasized the process of absorbing information, however innovatively that information might be structured, and however freely the user might navigate through multiple, hierarchically arranged connections (see, for example, Landow). Multimedia was something *presented* and perhaps *explored*, but it was not "answerable." In all their activity as creators of their own knowledge, students remained relatively passive, now receiving deposits of knowledge from automatic teller machines that supplemented the more direct, human method.

But that situation, as Negroponte has suggested, is rapidly changing, creating potentially profound implications for the delivery and mediation of instruction in schools and colleges. Within a few years, the disparate channels of video, audio, and computerized text and graphics—channels that come to us via airwaves, TV cable, phone cable, CD-ROM and computer disks—will merge into a single set of bits sent back and forth along one electronic highway at lightning speed. Our equipment will selectively manipulate this information to produce various outputs, a process already visible in the rapidly developing multimedia capabilities of the World Wide Web. In turn, users can assemble information and send it back (or out) along the same highway. The effect on both the production and reception of writing may be quite dramatic. Modern newspapers, for example, which are already produced electronically, may largely disappear in their paper form:

> The stories are often shipped in by reporters as e-mail. The pictures are digitized and frequently transmitted by wire as well. And the page layout . . . is done with computer-aided design systems, which prepare the data for transfer to film or direct engraving onto plates. This is to say that the entire conception and construction of the newspaper is digital, from beginning to end, until the very last step, when ink is squeezed onto dead trees. This step is where bits become atoms. . . . Now imagine that the last step does not happen . . . but that the bits are delivered to you as bits. You may elect to print them at home for all the conveniences of hard copy. . . . Or you may prefer to download them into your laptop, palmtop, or someday into your perfectly flexible, one-hundredth-of-an-inch thick, full-color, massively high resolution large-format, waterproof display. (Negroponte 56)

In the educational realm, the new capabilities emerging from multimedia technology offer many alternatives for teaching and learning, and for assigning and responding to writing, particularly as "papers" and "written responses" are replaced by electronic data. Imagine, for example, a college student (call her Jennifer) coming into the student union a few years from now. She pulls from her backpack a full-color, multimedia computer "tablet," just half an inch thick, plugs it into a slot on a little vending machine, puts three quarters into the machine, and downloads the current issue of USA Today. Over coffee, she reads the paper on the tablet, watching video clips of some events and listening to various sound bites. She finds a story of relevance to a project she is working on and decides to clip and save it in the tablet's memory. Then she deletes the paper.

Jennifer's first class of the day is still remembered as a "lecture course" in history, but the lecture material has been converted into multimedia presentations stored on CD-ROM disks (which the students dutifully buy at the bookstore or download onto massive hard drives from a server, paying with a credit card). Students experience the lectures alone and meet collectively only in recitation sections. Because her recitation begins in an hour and she did not finish the assignment the night before, Jennifer heads for one of the learning labs. There, she navigates through the rest of a multimedia presentation while handwriting some notes on her tablet and saving them into memory. She is impressed with the program, and justifiably: the institution is proud to have an exclusive contract with a world-famous historian (now living overseas) for the multimedia course.

The recitation is held in a room fully equipped for distance learning. Cameras face the students and teacher. Enormous, high-resolution monitors provide a view of two distant classes, each located a hundred miles away on smaller campuses. Jennifer sits at one of seventy-five computer stations. The first half of the class involves a discussion of some of the multimedia course material. The recitation coordinator (a non-tenure-track education specialist) brings the three sites together using artful techniques of questioning and response. After raising a number of issues which appear on a computerized screen from his control computer, the coordinator asks the three classes to discuss the issues. Students pair off electronically, writing to each other; some students at the main site pair with students at the distant sites, selected automatically by the instructor using an electronic seating chart and a program that activates the connections for each pair.

After the recitation, Jennifer remembers that she is supposed to send a revised draft of a paper to her composition instructor. She heads for another lab, where she accesses her electronic student file and finds a multimedia message from her instructor. The instructor's face appears on her screen in a little window, to one side of Jennifer's first draft. As Jennifer clicks on various highlighted passages or words, the instructor's face becomes animated in a video clip describing certain reactions and offering suggestions for revision. After working through the multimedia commentary and revising her draft, Jennifer then sends the revision back electronically to her instructor. Jennifer has never actually met her teacher, who is one of many part-time instructor/tutors hired by the semester to "telecommute" to the institution from their homes.

Because Jennifer is a privileged, upper-middle-class student who has a paid subscription to an online service, her own high-end computer system and modem, and the money to buy whatever software she needs for her studies, she can continue her schoolwork at home. There, she uses her multimedia computer to study for a psychology course offered by a corporation. On the basis of nationally normed assessments, the corporation has shown that its multimedia course achieves educational outcomes equal to or greater than those provided by many well-ranked colleges and universities.

Jennifer will be able to transfer the course into her curriculum because the corporation's educational division has been recently accredited. She also knows that, as multimedia courses go, this one is first-rate: the corporation is proud to have an exclusive contract with its teacher-author, a world-famous psychologist. As she checks the courseline via email, she notices that a midterm is coming up. She decides to schedule it for an "off" day, since she will have to go to one of the corporation's nearby satellite centers to take the test at a special computer terminal that scores her answers automatically and sends the results to her via email.

Later that day, Jennifer decides to spend an hour doing some research for her history project. From her home computer, she uses various Internet search programs to find out more about the Civil War battle of Manassas. On her high-resolution, 30-inch monitor (which also doubles as a TV and video player), she reads text, looks at drawings, opens video and audio files, and locates bibliographic material on her topic. She also finds some sites where Civil War aficionados share information and chat about what they know. She sends and receives some messages through the list, then copies various bits of information and multimedia into her computer, hoping to weave them into her report, which itself may include photos, video clips, and audio recordings. Due in less than three weeks, the report must be added (quite simply) to a privately accessed course Web site so that one of the several teaching assistants can retrieve it, grade and comment briefly on it, and send it back to Jennifer with an assessment. Just before she quits her research to watch some rock videos from the massive archives in a subscription server, Jennifer locates a Web site at another college where the students had researched the Civil War. The site includes all twenty-six projects created by the students; one focuses for several electronic pages on the battle at Manassas. Intrigued, Jennifer copies the pages into her computer, intending to look at them carefully the next day and perhaps use parts of them in her own multimedia project.

While this scenario may seem futuristic, much of the technology Jennifer experiences is already here or soon to be. The Knight-Ridder Corporation, for example, has recently developed a prototype of Jennifer's multimedia news "tablet" weighing about two pounds (Leyden). The Web now has the capability to send software to the receiver along with the actual information requested, and this software enhances the user's capacities to work with the information. Programs are currently available that allow teachers to open a student's paper onscreen and scroll through it to a point where a comment might be made to the student. At that point, an icon can be deposited that starts up a voice-recording device. The teacher then talks to the student about the paper. Further marginal or intertextual icons encase further voice comments. Opening the paper on disk at home, the student notices the icons and, activating them, listens to the teacher's response and advice. Computers with tiny videocameras are already enabling a picture-in-picture window that shows the teacher's image talking to the student as if face-to-face. The technology that now provides teleconferencing, when merged with Web-like storage and retrieval devices, will easily facilitate "one-way" tutorials that project audio and video images from a teacher, superimposed over typed text on which marks, corrections, and marginal notes can be recorded "live," like the replay analyses during televised football games.

When demonstrated, such advances may dazzle teachers because we see them as a promise to simplify our lives and streamline our work. New technologies often seem to improve our working conditions and provide better ways to help our students (seasoned teachers, as they stand at the computer-controlled reducing/collating/stapling photocopier, have only to reminisce about the old fluid-and-ink ditto machines to feel these advantages quite tangibly). Teaching, too, seems if not eased, affected in ways that enhance students' experiences. Positive accounts already show that email can help students to form study groups, interact with their teachers, or carry on academic discussions with students at other locations all over the world. In one experiment, students in an all-black freshman composition course at Howard University teamed up with a class of predominantly white students in graphic design at Montana State University to create a 32-page publication, *On the Color Line: Networking to End Racism.* Using digital scanners and email, the students and teachers were able to bring together two classes 1,600 miles apart to critique each other's work, discuss race-related views, and collaboratively produce a pamphlet (Blumenstyk). Many other accounts of networked classrooms suggest increased participation among marginalized groups (see, for example, Selfe, "Technology"; Bump).

Curiously, these and other positive accounts almost always describe adaptations of new technologies as ancillary methods within classrooms where students interact with each other and with their teacher. In a typical computerized grade-school class, for example, a student might use email to ask kids around the world to rank their favorite chocolates as part of a project focusing on *Charlie and the Chocolate Factory;* but then the entire class tallies the results and shares the conclusions (Rector). At the college level, Rich Holeton describes his highly networked electronic writing classroom and its advantages, especially in the area of electronic groups and discussions, yet still sees face-to-face interaction as the "main action" of the course and electronic techniques as "supplementary." Similarly, Tom Creed discusses the many ways he integrates computer technology into his classrooms, but finds it essential to create cooperative learning groups and build in time for students to make stand-up presentations to the class. Electronic innovations, in other words, appear to be carefully controlled, integrated into the existing curriculum in principled ways that do not erode the foundations on which the teacher-experimenters already base their instructional principles. Recognizing the importance of this configuration, some educators much prefer the term "technology-enhanced learning" to other terms that imply a radical shift in the actual delivery of education, such as "technologized instruction."

Because of improvements in educational software and hardware, however, our profession will feel increased pressure to offer technologically enhanced "independent study" courses. Some campuses are already experiencing dramatic differences in students' use of communal spaces with the introduction of dorm-room email. Clifford Stoll, a former Harvard University researcher and author of *Silicon Snake Oil: Second Thoughts on the Information Highway,* claims that by turning college into a "cubicle-directed electronic experience," we are "denying the importance of learning to work closely with other students and professors, and developing social adeptness" (qtd. in Gabriel). Students may be psychodynamically separated from one another even while inhabiting the same campus or dorm building; even more profound effects may be felt when students and faculty use advanced technologies to link up with each other in a course without ever meeting in person. Although many studies and testimonials affirm the ways that Internet chat lines, listservs, email, and other "virtual spaces" can actually increase the social nature of communication, there is no doubt that the physical isolation of each individual from the others creates an entirely different order of interaction.

DISTANCE, INDEPENDENCE, AND THE TRANSFORMATION OF THE COMMUNITY

The teaching of writing, unlike some other disciplines, is founded on the assumption that students learn well by reading and writing with each other, responding to each other's drafts, negotiating revisions, discussing ideas, sharing perspectives, and finding some level of trust as collaborators in their mutual development. Teaching in such contexts is interpersonal and interactive, necessitating small class size and a positive relationship between the teacher and the students. At the largest universities, such classes taken in the first year are often the only place where students can actually get to know each other, creating and participating in an intimate community of learning. Large lecture courses, driven by the transmission and retrieval of information, place students in a more passive role. In her book on the effect of college entrance examinations on the teaching of English, Mary Trachsel points out that the "factory" model of education, which privileges standardized testing and the "input" of discrete bits of information, is at odds with our profession's instructional ideals, which align more comfortably with those of theorists like Paulo Freire:

The model for [authentic education] is that of a dialogue in which hierarchical divisions are broken down so that teachers become teacher-learners, and learners become learner-teachers. Educational values are thus determined not by a mandate to perpetuate an established academic tradition but by local conditions and by the emerging purposes and realizations of educators and learners in social interaction with one another. This socially situated version of education stands in opposition to the "banking concept" of traditionally conceived schooling. (12)

For such ideological reasons, the teaching of writing by correspondence or "independent study" has always lived uneasily within programs that also teach students in classrooms. Although such instruction can be found at many institutions, few theorists strongly advocate a pedagogy in which students write alone, a guide of lessons and assignments at their elbows to provide the material of their "course," a remote, faceless grader hired by the hour to read assignments the students send through the mail and mail back responses. Next to classrooms with rich face-to-face social interaction—fueled by active learning, busy with small groups, energized by writers reading each other's work, powered by the forces of revision and response—independent study in writing appears misguided.

But in the context of our convictions about writing and response, new technologies now offer educational institutions the chance to expand on the idea of individualized learning. Online communication with students is an idea that seems stale by now but is by no means fully exploited; only some teachers eagerly invite email from students, and only some students end up using it when invited. Those faculty who value their autonomy and privacy find that email makes them better able to control when and where students enter their lives. Departments at many universities are requiring faculty to use email by giving them computers, hooking them up, offering workshops on how to use them, and then saying that faculty have no excuse for not voting on such and such an issue or not turning in their book orders on time. The results have already been felt on many campuses, as meetings give way to electronic communion, turning some departments into ghost haunts. Very few universities have developed policies that disallow the use of online office hours in place of physical presence on campus. As teachers across the country realize the tutorial potential of electronic media, such media may come to substitute for direct contact with students. For faculty busy with their own work, the gains are obvious: consultation by convenience, day or night; freedom from physical space; copyable texts instead of ephemeral talk.

From a more curricular perspective, the concept of independent study is rapidly changing from its roots in study manuals and the US Postal Service to a technology-rich potential for students to learn at their own pace, in their own style, with fingertip access to an entire world of information. Multimedia computers using text, sound, video, and photos provide opportunities to bring alive old-fashioned text-only materials. But it is not just independent-study programs, usually seen as ancillary to "real" education, that will change: multimedia could transform the very essence of classroom instruction. At many institutions, administrators are realizing that creating a state-of-the-art multimedia course out of, for example, "Introduction to Psychology," which may enroll up to five hundred students, represents a major improvement. The quality of faculty lectures is uneven; they come at a high cost; and they are often delivered in settings not conducive to learning—hot, stuffy lecture halls with poor sound systems and ailing TV monitors hung every few rows. In the converted version, a student can choose when to work through a multimedia presentation in a computer lab, can learn at her own pace, can review fundamental concepts, can download some information for later study, and can even test her developing knowledge as she learns. In such situations, as journalist Peter Leyden writes, "the time-honored role of the teacher almost certainly will change dramatically. No longer will teachers be the fonts of knowledge with all the answers that [students] seek. They can't possibly fill that role in the coming era" (2T).

In itself, multimedia technology has not directly challenged the field of composition. True, many educators are working on integrating into their research-paper units some instruction on citing electronic sources, searching the Web, or using online databases. The prospect of a teacherless and "community-less" course, however, creates much debate in the composition community, where many see computers as poor substitutes for old-fashioned forms of human interaction. In areas involving context-bound thinking, Stanley Aronowitz maintains, "knowledge of the terrain must be obtained more by intuition, memory, and specific knowledge of actors or geography than by mastering logical rules. . . . Whatever its psychological and biological presuppositions, the development of thinking is profoundly shaped and frequently altered by multiple determinations, including choices made by people themselves" (130–31). In the face of the trend to increasing "indirectness" of teaching, Charles Moran argues, "we will need to be more articulate than we have yet been in describing the benefits of face-to-face teaching, or what our British colleagues call 'live tuition'" (208).

New technologies are also giving a strong boost to distance learning. Like the concept of independent study, distance learning too may powerfully affect the way in which we teach and respond to students. In distance learning, students actually participate in the classroom—they are just not there, physically. Beamed in by cable or broadcast, their personae are represented on TV monitors, which, as the idea expands, are becoming larger and gaining in resolution. As classrooms become better equipped, students at several sites will work in virtual classrooms, writing to and for each other at terminals. Teachers can pair students, using small cameras and monitors at their desks, and then regroup the classes at the different sites for larger discussions using the bigger screens.

Institutions are attracted to the concept of distance education for reasons obvious in times of fiscal constraint. Students register for a single course from two or more sites, generating tuition revenue for the parent institution. A course previously taught by several salaried faculty (each on location, hundreds of miles apart) now needs only one main teacher, aided by non-tenure-track staff "facilitator-graders" or teaching assistants hired inexpensively at the different locations. If small satellite sites are created, sometimes in available spaces such as public schools, community centers, or libraries, new revenue sources can be exploited in remote areas. Even after the cost of the interactive television equipment and link-up is calculated, distance education can generate profit for the institution at reduced cost, using its existing faculty resources as "lead teachers." Such an arrangement is especially attractive to institutions used to delivering instruction via the traditional "banking" model of lectures and objectively scorable tests.

Distance learning is also allowing some pairs or groups of institutions to consolidate resources by sharing programs with each other. Imagine that University A realizes that its Swahili language program does not have the resources to compete with the Swahili language program at University B; but it does have a nationally recognized Lakota language program. Unfortunately, the Lakota program is not very cost-effective, in spite of its standing, because its student cohort is so small. Likewise, University B recognizes that its own Lakota language program pales by comparison with University A's, yet it boasts a particularly strong Swahili program similarly suffering from its inability to generate profits for the school. Using sophisticated interactive television and multimedia resources, the two institutions team up to exchange programs, swapping the tuition revenues along with their instructional programs. As technology keeps expanding and becoming refined, collaborations like these will become increasingly popular, even necessary. In part, these ideas save money. In part, they also respond to growing competition from non-academic providers of education, a major threat to our present institutions. By collaborating to deliver the "best" programs possible, the institutions protect themselves against the intrusion of industry, of what the Pew Roundtable calls "high-quality, lower-cost educational programming conjoined with the rising demand for postsecondary credentials that creates the business opportunity for higher education's would-be competitors" (3). But the result is almost certain to be a continued reduction in full-time, tenure-track faculty and an increased reliance on modes of instructional delivery that physically distance students from each other and from their mentors.

Practically speaking, the idea of distance learning seems reasonable in the context of Lakota and Swahili—it saves duplication of effort, it cuts costs, it may lead to increased institutional collaboration, and it offers students at different locations the chance to be taught, in some sense of the word, by high-quality teachers. It is when the prospect of fully interactive, technologically advanced distance learning conflicts with our most principled educational theories that we feel an ideological clash. Long privileged in composition instruction, for example, is the interactive teaching style. Writing teachers arrange and participate in small groups in the classroom, talk with students before and after class, walk with them to other buildings, meet them in offices, and encourage students to respond to each other instead of through the teacher. Distance learning has yet to overcome the virtuality of its space to draw all students into such interpersonal relationships. Teachers often report feeling detached from the students at the distant sites, unable to carry on "extracurricular" conversations with them. The savings promised by distance education come from the elimination of trained professionals who reduce teacher-student ratios and offer meaningful consultation with students, face to face. If distance learning becomes the norm in fields where general education courses are usually delivered in large lectures with little chance for students to learn actively or interact with each other or the teacher, it will not be long before writing programs are encouraged to follow suit.

In exploring the concept of humans in cyberspace, we can find, as Anna Cicognani has found, many of the same conditions as those we experience in physical space: social interaction; logical and formal abstractions; linguistic form; corresponding organizations of time; the possibility for rhetorical action; and so on. But it is, finally, a "hybrid space, a system which is part of another but only refers to itself and its own variables." It belongs to the main system of space, but "claims independence from it at the same time." Cicognani's representation of cyberspace as a hybrid, which still allows communities to form and develop but relies for its existence on the physical space from which is has been created, offers a useful metaphor for the continued exploration of the relationships between education and computer technology, as the latter is carefully put to use in the improvement of the former. Yet to be considered, however, are broader questions about the role of teachers in technology-rich educational settings.

RESPONSE, TECHNOLOGY, AND
THE FUTURE OF TEACHING

The quality of faculty interaction with students is a product of our *work*—our training, the material conditions at our institutions, how much support we get for developing our teaching and keeping up on research. While to this point we have been reflecting on the possible effects of new technologies on the quality of students' learning experiences and contexts, we must also consider ways in which colleges and universities, as places of employ-ment, may change.

Teachers of composition continue to argue that writing programs pro-vide an important site for active and interactive learning in higher educa-tion. Our national standards have helped to keep classes small; our lobby-ing continues to call attention to the exploitation of part-time faculty. We argue the need for support services, such as writing centers, tutors, and ESL programs. And, in writing-across-the-curriculum programs, we have helped to integrate the process approach in various disciplines and courses with considerable success. But the current cost-cutting fervor will continue to erode these principles. Massy and Wilger argue, for example, that "most faculty have yet to internalize the full extent of the economic difficulties facing higher education institutions, both public and private. . . . [F]ew fac-ulty take seriously the current fiscal constraints. Most believe that the prob-lems are not as significant as administrators and others warn, or that the conditions are only temporary" (25).

As teachers, our own occupational space is clearly defined. We "belong" to a particular institution, which pays us, and the students get our instruc-tion, consultation, expertise, and time in exchange for their tuition or, in public schooling, the revenues generated by local taxes and other local, state, and federal funds. Yet technology will soon change not only how we work within our institutions but also how "attached" we may be to an insti-tution, particularly if we can work for several institutions at some physical (but not electronic) remove from each other. In an article in the Informa-tion Technology Annual Report of *Business Week*, Edward Baig lists by cate-gory the percentage of sites that plan additional "telecommuters"—"mem-bers of the labor force who have chosen to, or have been told to, work anywhere, anytime—as long as it's not in the office" (59). Higher educa-tion is placed at the very top of the heap, with over 90 percent of sites plan-ning to increase telecommuting.

Universities once looked upon computer technology as an expense and a luxury; increasingly it is now seen as an investment that will lead to increased revenues and reduced expenses. The standards of work defined by the Conference on College Composition and Communication have not anticipated a new vision of writing instruction involving low-paid reader-responders, tutorial "assistants" for CD-ROM courses taken "virtually" by independent study, or coordinators at interactive television sites where stu-dents from many campuses link to a single site requiring only one "master professor." Robert Heterick, writing for Educom, predicts a major shift in resource allocation across institutions of higher education:

> The infusion of information technology into the teaching and learning domain will create shifts in the skill requirements of faculty from instructional delivery to instructional design . . . with faculty being responsible for course

content and information technologists being responsible for applying information technology to the content. These changes will increase the number of students the institutions can service without corresponding increases in the need for student daily-life support facilities. (3)

In the area of composition, part-time telecommuters, supplied with the necessary equipment, could become the primary providers of instruction to many students. At some locations, private industry is already exploring the possibility of supplying writing instruction, using technology, to institutions interested in "outsourcing" this part of their curriculum. In the *Adjunct Advocate,* a newsletter for part-time and temporary writing teachers, instructors have expressed considerable concern about administrators' requests that they teach sections of introductory composition via the Internet (see Lesko; Wertner). The "profound change in work" represented by advanced technology may also further isolate women. Although the computer once promised to level gender discrimination by removing direct identity from online forums, some social critics are now seeing the potential for new inequities in the labor force. In her contribution to Susan Leigh Star's *The Cultures of Computing,* for example, Randi Markussen takes up the question of "why gender relations seem to change so little through successive waves of technological innovation" (177). Technology promises the "empowerment" of workers, but it also reinforces and more strongly imposes the measurement of work in discrete units. In her analysis of the effects of technology on practicing nurses, Markussen notes that instead of "empowering" employees by making their work more visible or supporting their demands for better staffing and pay, new computer technology actually places greater demands on nurses to account for their work in "categories of work time," decreasing the need for "interpersonal task synchronization" and cooperation with other people. "The transformation of work," Markussen writes, "puts new demands on nurses in terms of relating the formalized electronic depiction of work to caregiving activities, which may still be considered residual and subordinate" (172).

Like nursing, composition has been positively constructed through its preoccupation with the development of the individual and the creation of an engaging, student-focused classroom. Yet composition likewise suffers from higher education's continued attitude that it serves a "residual and subordinate" role, necessary for "remediation." This gross misconception of the value of writing instruction is directly linked to employment practices at hundreds of colleges and universities, where large numbers of "service professionals," a majority of them women, are hired into low-paid, non-tenurable positions with poor (or no) benefits. With the potential for the further automation of writing instruction through the use of telecommuting and other technology-supported shifts in instructional delivery, composition may be further subordinated to the interests of powerful subject-oriented disciplines where the conception of expertise creates rather different patterns of hiring and material support.

Our key roles—as those who create opportunities and contexts for students to write and who provide expert, principled response to that writing—must change in the present communications and information revolution. But we cannot let the revolution sweep over us. We need to guide it, resisting its economic allure in cases where it weakens the principles of our teaching. The processes of technology, even when they are introduced to us by administrations more mindful of balancing budgets than enhancing lives, will not threaten us as long as we, as educators, make decisions about the worth of each innovation, about ways to put it to good use, or about reasons why it should be rejected out of hand. More sustained, face-to-face discussions—at conferences and seminars, at faculty development workshops, and in routine departmental and curricular meetings—can give us hope that we can resist changes that undermine what we know about good teaching and sound ways of working. Such discussions are often difficult. They are highly political, painfully economic, and always value-laden and ideological. But as teachers of writing and communication, we have an obvious investment in considering the implications of technology for working, teaching, and learning, even as that technology is emerging.

Because technology is advancing at an unprecedented rate, we must learn to assess the impact of each new medium, method, or piece of software on our students' learning. Most of the time, such assessments will take place locally (for example, as a genetics program decides whether it is more effective for students to work with real drosophila flies or manipulate a virtual drosophila world using an interactive computer program). But we also urgently need broader, institution-wide dialogues about the effect of technology on teaching, particularly between students, faculty, and administrators. Deborah Holdstein has pointed out that as early as 1984 some compositionists were already critiquing the role of computers in writing instruction; "caveats regarding technology . . . have always been an important sub-text in computers and composition studies, the sophistication of self-analysis, one hopes, maturing with the field" (283). Among the issues she proposes for further discussion are those of access, class, race, power, and gender; she questions, for example,

those who would assert without hesitation that email, the Net, and the Web offer us, finally, a nirvana of ultimate democracy and freedom, suggesting that even visionaries such as Tuman and Lanham beg the question of access, of the types of literacies necessary to even gain access to email, much less to the technology itself. What *other* inevitable hierarchies—in addition to the ones we know and understand . . .—will be formed to order us as we "slouch toward cyberspace"? (283)

While it is impossible to overlook not only that advanced learning technologies are here to stay but that they are in a state of frenzied innovation, Holdstein's admonishments remind us of the power of thoughtful critique and interest punctuated by caution. In addition to the issues she raises, we can profit by engaging in more discussions about the following questions:

1. What will multimedia do to alter the personae of teachers and students as they respond to each other virtually? How do new communication technologies change the relationships between teachers and students? Recent research on small-group interaction in writing classes, for example, shows labyrinthine complexity, as demonstrated in Thomas Newkirk's study of students' conversational roles. What do we really know about the linguistic, psycho-social, and pedagogical effects of online communication when it replaces traditional classroom-based interaction? (See Eldred and Hawisher's fascinating synthesis of research on how electronic networking affects various dimensions of writing practice and instruction.)

2. How might the concept of a classroom community change with the advent of new technologies? What is the future of collaborative learning in a world in which "courseware" may increasingly replace "courses"?

3. What are the consequences of increasing the distance between students and teachers? Is the motivation for distance education financial or pedagogical? Will the benefits of drawing in isolated clients outweigh the disadvantages of electronically "isolating" even those who are nearby?

4. What will be the relationship between "human" forms of response to writing and increasingly sophisticated computerized responses being developed in industry?

5. How will the conditions of our work change as a result of increasing access to students via telecommunications? Who will hire us to read students' writing? Will we work at home? Will educational institutions as physical entities disappear, as Alvin Toffler is predicting, to be replaced by a core of faculty who can be commissioned from all over the world to deliver instruction and response via the electronic highway? What new roles will teachers, as expert responders, play in an increasingly electronic world?

6. What are the implications of telecommuting for the hiring and support of teachers? Could technology reduce the need for the physical

presence of instructors, opening the door to more part-time teachers hired at low wages and few benefits?

7. How will writing instruction compete with new, aggressive educational offerings from business and industry? What will be the effects of competing with such offerings for scarce student resources?

If we can engage in thoughtful discussions based on questions such as these, we will be better prepared to make principled decisions about the effect of new technologies on our students' learning and the conditions of our teaching. And we will be more likely, amid the dazzle of innovation, to reject those uses of technology that will lead to bad teaching, poor learning, unfair curricular practices, and unjust employment.

August 21, Les Agettes, Switzerland. I have met the family below. They tell me grandpère has lost some of his memory. He often spends part of the day breaking up stones, clack, clack, clack, behind the chalet. It's not disturbing, they hope. We haven't noticed, I say. We talk almost aimlessly, wandering around topics. Have we met the priest who rents an apartment below the chalet? Can they tell me what the local school is like? We talk about learning, about computers. As if scripted by the ad agency for IBM, they tell me they are interested in the Internet; their friends have computers, and they may get one too, soon. Later, gazing down toward the bustling town of Sion, I wonder how their lives will change. I imagine them ordering a part for their car over the computer without ever catching up on news with Karl, the guy at the garage near the river. Yet I'm also optimistic. They will use email someday soon, and I can get their address from my brother and write them messages in bad French, and they can share them during their long lunches on the patio, where they still gather to eat and laugh, turning my text back into talk.

REFERENCES

Aronowitz, Stanley. "Looking Out: The Impact of Computers on the Lives of Professionals." Tuman 119–138.

Baig, Edward C. "Welcome to the Officeless Office." *Business Week* (Information Technology Annual Report, International Edition) 26 June 1995: 59–60.

Barlow, John Perry, Sven Birkerts, Kevin Kelly, and Mark Slouka. "Forum: What Are We Doing Online?" *Harper's Magazine* Aug. 1995: 35–46.

Blumenstyk, Goldie. "Networking to End Racism." *Chronicle of Higher Education* 22 Sept. 1995: A35–A39.

Bump, Jerome. "Radical Changes in Class Discussion Using Networked Computers." *Computers and the Humanities* 24 (1990): 46–65.

Cicognani, Anna. "On the Linguistic Nature of Cyberspace and Virtual Communities." <http://www.arch.usyd.edu.au/~anna/papers/even96.htm>

Creed, Tom. "Extending the Classroom Walls Electronically." *New Paradigms for College Teaching.* Ed. William E. Campbell and Karl A. Smith. Edina, MN: Interaction, 1997. 149–84.

Eldred, Janet Carey, and Gail E. Hawisher. "Researching Electronic Networks." *Written Communication* 12.3 (1995): 330–59.

Gabriel, Trip. "As Computers Unite Campuses, Are They Separating Students?" *Minneapolis Star Tribune* 12 Nov. 1996: A5.

Hawisher, Gail E., Cynthia L. Selfe, Charles Moran, and Paul LeBlanc. *Computers and the Teaching of Writing in American Higher Education, 1979–1994: A History.* Norwood, NJ: Ablex, 1996.

Heterick, Robert. "Operating in the 90's."
<http://ivory.educom.edu:70/00/educom.info/html>

Holdstein, Deborah. "Power, Genre, and Technology." *College Composition and Communication* 47.2 (1996): 279–84.

Holeton, Rich. "The Semi-Virtual Composition Classroom: A Model for Techno-Amphibians." *Notes in the Margins* Spring 1996: 1, 14–17, 19.

Landow, George. "Hypertext, Metatext, and Electronic Canon." Tuman 67–94.

Lesko, P. D. "Adjunct Issues in the Media." *The Adjunct Advocate* March/April 1996: 22–27.

Leyden, Peter. "The Changing Workscape." Special Report, Part III. *Minneapolis Star Tribune* 18 June 1995: 2T–6T.

Markussen, Randi. "Constructing Easiness: Historical Perspectives on Work, Computerization, and Women." *The Cultures of Computing.* Ed. Susan Leigh Star. Oxford: Blackwell, 1995. 158–80.

Massy, William F., and Andrea K. Wilger. "Hollywood Collegiality: Implications for Teaching Quality." Paper presented at the Second AAHE Annual Conference on Faculty Roles and Rewards, New Orleans, 29 Jan. 1994.

McCorduck, Pamela. "How We Knew, How We Know, How We Will Know." Tuman 245–59.

Moran, Charles. "Review: English and Emerging Technologies." *College English* 60.2 (1998): 202–9.

Negroponte, Nicholas. *Being Digital.* New York: Knopf, 1995.

Newkirk, Thomas. "The Writing Conference as Performance." *Research in the Teaching of English* 29.2 (1996): 193–215.

Pew Higher Education Roundtable. "To Dance with Change." *Policy Perspectives* 5.3 (1994): 1A–12A.

Prior, Paul. "Contextualizing Writing and Response in a Graduate Seminar." *Written Communication* 8 (1991): 267–310.

———. "Tracing Authoritative and Internally Persuasive Discourses: A Case Study of Response, Revision, and Disciplinary Enculturation." *Research in the Teaching of English* 29 (1995): 288–325.

Rector, Lucinda. "Where Excellence is Electronic." *Teaching and Technology* Summer 1996: 10–14. <http://www.time.com/teach>

Selfe, Cynthia. "Literacy, Technology, and the Politics of Education in America." Chair's Address, Conference on College Composition and Communication, Chicago 2 April 1998.

———. "Technology in the English Classroom: Computers Through the Lens of Feminist Theory." *Computers and Community: Teaching Composition in the Twenty-First Century.* Ed. Carolyn Handa. Portsmouth, NH: Boynton/Cook, 1990. 118–39.

Smith, Summer. "The Genre of the End Comment: Conventions in Teacher Responses to Student Writing." *College Composition and Communication* 48.2 (1977): 249–68.

Stoll, Clifford. *Silicon Snake Oil: Second Thoughts on the Information Highway.* New York: Doubleday, 1995.

Straub, Richard. "The Concept of Control in Teacher Response: Defining the Varieties of 'Directive' and 'Facilitative' Commentary." *College Compositions and Communication* 47.2 (1996): 223–51.

Straub, Richard, and Ronald F. Lunsford. *Twelve Readers Reading: Responding to College Student Writing.* Cresskill: Hampton, 1995.

Traschel, Mary. *Institutionalizing Literacy.* Carbondale, IL: Southern Illinois UP, 1992.

Tuman, Myron C., ed. *Literacy Online: The Promise (and Peril) of Reading and Writing with Computers.* Pittsburgh: U of Pittsburgh P, 1992.

Wertner, B. "The Virtual Classroom." (letter to the editor). *The Adjunct Advocate* May/June 1996: 6.

QUESTIONS FOR REFLECTION, JOURNAL WRITING, AND DISCUSSION

1. What are some possible positive and negative effects of technology on teaching writing and on education in general?

2. Do you agree with some teachers that a photocopier with an adequate paper supply is all the technology that you need or want?

3. If Anson's theory about Jennifer comes true, will the type of education available to her be better or worse than the education available today?

Chapter 26

Basic Writing: Curricular Interactions With New Technology

Susan Stan and Terence G. Collins

Susan Stan is currently Assistant Professor of English at Central Michigan University. She coauthored this article while teaching in the General College at the University of Minnesota-Twin Cities, where she was an instructor in the Basic Writing Program for seven years. **Terence G. Collins** is a Morse-Alumni Distinguished Teaching Professor of Writing and Literature at the University of Minnesota-General College. His research and writing focus on basic writing, new technologies and composition, and Disability Studies. The article that follows is from the *Journal of Basic Writing*, 17, 1, 1998.

This essay surveys the interactions among Basic Writing students, Basic Writing curricula, and new technologies in higher education. We began the project with the goal of identifying curricular *transformations* which had occurred as a result of such interactions.[1] Rather than a single set of transformations, what we found in our survey was a landscape of basic writing instruction dotted with a variety of curricular transformations. Some of these involved new technologies. But it is not likely that these transformations occurred as a *result* of the technologies which are featured in them. Rather, it is more likely that several factors—the historical confluence of reform in Composition Studies, the availability of new, relatively inexpensive computer and networking technology, and Basic Writing's growth in sophistication over decades of open-admissions—have sponsored a great deal of change in the writing curriculum for developmental students, change involving a variety of technologies and uses.

---

[1]The authors gratefully acknowledge the support of the Annenberg/CPB Projects Initiative II and the General College Center for Research in Developmental Education and Urban Literacy, which funded *Curricular Transformation and Technology in Developmental Education,* a cross-disciplinary collaboration at the University of Minnesota.

BACKGROUND

The emergence of Basic Writing as an area within postsecondary developmental education is more or less coincidental with the rise of "computers
and writing" as a branch of Composition Studies, so such interactions
might have been expected. Indeed, both Basic Writing and computers-and-
writing emerged as areas of study during the 1970s, at a time when the very
nature of writing instruction was being transformed. In that period, the
current-traditional paradigm and so-called "product" orientation were supplanted by a range of process pedagogies derived from social constructivist,
cognitivist, and postmodernist strands in Composition theory and research
(Crowley; Hawisher et al.).

Basic Writing expanded rapidly in response to the social demands for
equal access to higher education following the civil rights movements of
mid-century. New commitment to access led to new policies of open-
admissions in many colleges and universities and resulted in the rapid
expansion of open-admissions community colleges to accommodate large
numbers of "new students" (Shaughnessy). These new students who
entered higher education under open-admissions presented startling
opportunities, frequently articulated as problems, for self-critical evaluation of habitual writing pedagogy and for rethinking the goals and content of the Composition curricula.

Research in teaching strategies for basic writing courses called into question the "current traditional paradigm" of Composition, as well as the for-
malist, belletristic dispositions which were at its center. The profession's
examination of how we teach writing resulted in a new set of assumptions
in Composition, which have in turn shaped Basic Writing. When the
research was boiled down, Composition teachers saw that students across a
broad spectrum of backgrounds, in a wide range of institutions, learn how
to write best in teacher-directed workshops with structured opportunities
for purposeful writing, response, and revision (Hillocks). This general
trend in Composition's re-thinking of itself found a hospitable site in Basic
Writing. The writing of previously excluded students, many of whom were
unpracticed in what had been thought of as college writing, brought into
focus the pedagogical flux and the vexing politics of Composition's paradigm shift. In one of her earliest essays, Mina Shaughnessy asserted that
within Basic Writing there is an uneasy tension:

> The special conditions of the remedial situation, that is, the need to develop
> within a short time a style of writing and thinking and a background of cul-
> tural information that prepare the student to cope with academic work, cre-
> ate a distinctive tension that almost defines the profession—a constant,
> uneasy hovering between the imperatives of format and freedom, convention

and individuality, the practical and the ideal. Just where the boundaries between these claims are to be drawn in basic writing is by no means clear. ("Open Admissions" 152)

In positing that this tension "almost defines" the profession of basic writing, Shaughnessy was prescient, for the tension persists. From the earliest reflective practitioners associated with Shaughnessy and her colleagues at City University of New York, through a middle phase of scholarly and curricular "legitimacy" (Bartholomae & Petrosky), to post-colonial (Lu) and postmodern theorists (Sirc), the emphasis has been on individual students as writers, on their writing, on the cultural dynamics of privilege-and-language, and on situated instruction, with a view of the Basic Writing student as unpracticed and unskilled in composing specific forms of texts valorized traditionally by faculty. Basic Writing is marked, from the beginning, by a struggle between authentic expressionism and institutionally validated, constrained text production (Bartholomae; Stuckey). The tension remains unresolved.

Not surprisingly, within Computers and Writing has run a parallel version of the tension between authenticity and constraint to which Shaughnessy pointed. While introducing revolutionary technologies into Composition classrooms, writing teachers have struggled with the implications of their acts, as documented in any number of places, from the archives of the Alliance for Computers and Writing listserv (http://english.ttu.edu/acw/acw-1), to the history of computers and writing chronicled in detail by Hawisher, LeBlanc, Moran, and Selfe. A ready example is the way computers used in networked modes have been central to the promotion of social constructivist writing pedagogy and the emergence of new textual forms. The ways students write (alone? in groups? with face-to-face colleagues? with associates at a distance? from a linear outline? hypertextually? for a private audience? for a world-wide audience?) and what students write (history papers? riotgrrrl hypertext sex-fem'zines? course websites?) have been genuinely transformed in the networked setting. At the same time, early adopters of the networked technology which has been the vehicle for this revolution were naive, even quaint, in their expectations that the network would mediate familiar, traditional classroom decorum and controlled discourse (George; Kremers).

These tensions between the revolutionary and the conventional, arising from various uses of computers in writing courses, have been played out very dramatically in Basic Writing curricula. In his evaluation of the ENFI Consortium Project, for instance, David Bartholomae notes that "ENFI" class essays produced by basic writers at the University of Minnesota's open-admissions General College (written in a local area network setting which was used heavily for on-line conversations and heuristic questioning) were more engaged, more authentic, and more intellectually vital than were the essays produced by basic writers at the same site in a more traditional class-room ("I'm Talking"). While Bartholomae notes the exciting dimensions of this "counterwriting," as he calls it, he is also quick to assert that some might see the writing produced by the ENFI Basic Writing students as "a threat to academic values." If anything, it appears, some uses of computers in Basic Writing classrooms simply amplify the tension Shaughnessy asserted to be so fundamental to the enterprise.

Yet not all applications of computers in the Basic Writing classroom cause such obvious ambivalence. For instance, Collins found that simple word processing improved the writing of college students with learning dis-abilities and reduced their writing apprehension. Computers have changed the way writing teachers imagine revision, and text-editing software has made it easier for unskilled or unpracticed writers to address a variety of errors in the surfaces of their texts. Now commonplace, such innovations were truly stunning for Basic Writing teachers and their students in the mid-1980s.

Access to higher education is the challenge to which development of Basic Writing has been, in part, a solution. But access to new technologies among students who are the most disenfranchised in the academy poses further problems. As we surveyed the ways in which basic writers, teachers of Basic Writing, and the Basic Writing curricula have been shaped, even transformed in the presence of new technologies, we were confronted by the simple fact that the dominant form of new, privileging technologies—the small personal computer and its connectivity—is not aggressively inte-grated at sites where Basic Writing instruction takes place most typically. In its 1996 Campus Computing Survey, for instance, the League for Innova-tion in the Community College found fairly low rates of access to and rewards for developing meaningful uses of technology in teaching. This is not surprising. Many of the obstacles to Basic Writing on campus are also obstacles to widespread innovation in the curriculum by way of computers. Building programs on the use of part-time and transient faculty, proficiency test-driven curricula which emphasize production of "safe" texts, con-strained budgets, vexed institutional standing—all of the familiar forces which limit BW programs—likewise stand in the way of widespread invest-ment in facilities, training, and institutional ecologies which might sponsor transformative practices in the Basic Writing curriculum mediated by strong uses of new technologies.

Yet we were surprised, even sometimes astounded, by the achieve-ments of individual teachers and colleagues in departments who work in Basic Writing. As captured in detail at our searchable website <www.gen.umn.edu/research/currtran>, dozens of site-specific innova-tions and transformative practices in basic writing courses are in place in a range of institutions around the country. (We invite your submissions to further this work.) Writing teachers in developmental education sites do not often have support for extensive evaluation and publication of their curricular innovations (Reynolds 3–4). As a consequence, much good work featuring uses of computers and related technology in the developmental writing classroom is realized locally but is not disseminated widely. But it should be. As Bruce argues, all innovation is *situated.* That is, a curricular approach or a theoretically derived pedagogy will be formed into a local practice as a result of the many-layered reality of the local situation. Whatever generally transforming directions might be discerned across Basic Writing sites where technology is embedded in the curriculum, these directions are realized one classroom at a time, one teacher at a time, in a thoroughly situated instance of Basic-Writing-using-technology. Surveyed below are such developments described in the literature, in syllabi on the web, in personal correspondence—in short, in sources both formal and fugitive. Taken together, they map the rich landscape we've surveyed.

RECENT RESEARCH

In an early overview of computer-assisted instruction in the Basic Writing classroom, Lisa Gerrard observed that of all writers, basic writers are the most sensitive to the effects, both positive and negative, of computer technology. Although no single profile defines all basic writers, in general these students are inexperienced at writing and lack self-confidence as writers; in *Errors and Expectations,* Mina Shaughnessy suggested they be thought of as beginning rather than as poor writers. The basic writer's lack of self-confidence frequently manifests itself as an anxiety toward writing. When asked about their relationship to writing, these students often say, "I can't write" or "I hate to write." Research shows that, depending upon the ways in which computers are used in instruction, this technology can serve to alleviate or even transform a basic writer's anxiety about writing—or it can erode still further a basic writer's confidence.

Relative to the amount of published research about the use of computers in writing instruction, studies that are situated in developmental writing courses and/or focus on basic writers are sparse. And yet some of the most innovative uses of technology have been developed around basic writers. Bruce Horner reminds us that the discourse of Basic Writing, beginning with Shaughnessy, has cast the field as the "pedagogical West," a view that frees teachers to explore and experiment without losing their credibility. The Basic Writing classroom has been the site of much exploration and experimentation with technology, some of which has been documented in the form of journal articles or conference papers or has emerged in the form of new software programs. Specialized listserv discussion groups provide a forum for basic writing instructors to share experiences and expertise. Much information, however, remains unpublished and/or undiscussed.

Both research and anecdotal evidence point to the positive effect of computers on students' attitudes toward writing, and a number of studies specifically focus on the segment of writers designated as developmental or basic. Pamela Gay reviewed eighteen studies conducted between 1984 and 1990 that examined some aspect of using computers in basic writing instruction. The most consistent thread running through the studies was the contention that word processing improves students' attitudes toward writing. Harder to measure were the ways in which writing on a word processor might affect the quality of a basic writer's work. While some researchers reported improvement, others did not, and still others reported mixed findings within the same study (gains in some areas, such as organization, and no progress in others, such as usage).

In search of explanations for such apparent contradictions, Gay looks beyond the results of each study to the instructional methods used by the writing teachers of the student-subjects. The wide range of assignments, lessons, and teaching approaches suggests to Gay that pedagogical practice and theory play a large role in research in this area, affecting not just how students interact with computers in the classroom but also what researchers measure as indicators of improved writing quality.

In a classroom study in which both the instructors and the basic writing students kept logs of interactions (student-teacher discussions about the piece of writing on the screen), D'Agostino and Varone revealed the impact these "in-process interventions" had on the student's writing. As they note, suggestions offered during the writing process are more likely to be acted on, or at least considered, than comments written on a paper after it is returned. Student logs also reminded the researchers that comments and suggestions are not always perceived by the student in the way the instructor intended, and that sometimes a teacher's comments serve to move the writer further away from, rather than nearer to, his or her intended meaning.

Since Gay's review of research on technology and the basic writer appeared, a few more research studies involving basic writers have been published. Batschelet and Woodson's study at the University of Texas at San Antonio was designed to measure the attitudes of basic writers toward writing on computers. Administering questionnaires to an experimental group of students that met in a computer classroom at least 50% of the time and to a control group of students that met in a traditional classroom the entire time, they found that the attitudes of both groups of students toward writing—which ranged from ambivalent to negative—remained unchanged at the end of the course. Yet the responses of the students in the experimental group to a separate question about writing papers on a computer revealed a positive change in their attitudes. This discrepancy suggested to the researchers that students appeared to be making a distinction between two activities—the process of writing and their experiences of writing on a computer—which are fused in the minds of experienced writers. A similar study conducted with adult developmental writers (Hansman-Ferguson) seems to indicate that adult developmental writers, at least, can make the connection between activities; the researcher found that student apprehension about writing decreased after a semester in a computer-based writing course.

In a five-year study of students at Cincinnati University's University College (Meem), researchers compared the work and activities of students writing in traditional classroom settings, students writing on computers equipped with word processing programs (Bank Street Writer II), and students writing on computers equipped with both word-processing and thinking aid programs (Bank Street Writer II and Writer's Helper). While pre-test and post-test comparisons revealed no significant difference in the quality of writing among the three groups, students in the two groups using computers rated both the courses and the instructors significantly higher across the board in their end-of-course evaluations, conforming to the findings of earlier researchers.

One segment of students in the third group, however, did show remarkable improvement in writing quality, although this gain was not enough to make the overall group figures statistically significant. That segment consisted of adult non-traditional students who were placed in the University's Pre-Technology program. Interpreting the results of their study, the researchers speculated that access to Writer's Helper "eliminated the academic disadvantage suffered by most Pre-Technology students compared to their traditional counterparts" (66).

Meem's five-year study is unusual. Most empirical research available about developmental writing instruction in a computer environment has been conducted by researchers in their own classrooms over one or two terms only, ruling out the possibility of discovering any longitudinal effects. Because becoming a better writer takes time and practice, researchers have not been surprised when they couldn't document any statistically significant improvement in student writing after a ten- to fifteen-week computer-based writing course. Consistently, however, researchers have been able to identify changes in students' attitudes toward writing, and this finding has been generally accepted as a first step toward subsequent writing improvement. Batschelet and Woodson's study serves as a reminder to those of us who teach developmental writers that part of our work involves modifying our students' conceptions of themselves as writers—we must help them find ways to integrate the reality of their newfound skills into their outdated self-images as poor writers.

Most writing teachers who advocate the use of computers in the classroom see ease of revision as one of the advantages of writing on a word-processor. Evelyn Posey's findings in a study of basic writers at the University of Texas at El Paso suggested that using computers to compose did not improve the quality of student writing, even though computer users did generate more drafts and share their writing more frequently than those who wrote with pen and paper. Posey challenged teachers to show students how to use the computer in revision so that it becomes more than merely a tool for word processing.

At least one experimental research study has documented improved quality in writing in basic writers. Cynthia Louise Walker's dissertation is based on data she collected in courses taught at East Texas State University. Her purpose was to determine if the revision activities of developmental students would improve (as measured both by quantity and depth of revisions) when revising on screen as opposed to on paper. She structured the study so that the same students would perform revision in both ways: one half of the students revised their first two papers on paper and their second two on screen, while the other half reversed the process. Student rough draft and final papers were scored holistically by independent scorers, and Walker compared the resulting scores. She found that revision on screen improved the paper's score in all but two cases. Students spent more time and more effort on these papers and developed a greater interest in them. They produced twice as many revisions on screen as they did when revising on paper, and their revisions included a greater proportion of meaning level changes.

SOFTWARE AND NETWORKING APPLICATIONS

Composing and revising on computers requires only "worldware," word processing programs such as WordPerfect or MS Word originally developed for office and home use, although many specific software programs have been developed to target these processes. As far back as 1979, writing teachers who were also becoming interested in computers were quick to see possibilities for their use in the writing classroom. Some of the teachers who had an elementary knowledge of programming used it to develop software to assist students at certain stages of the writing process.

Among these early programs was WANDAH, an acronym for Writing AND Author's Helper, developed in the early 1980s at UCLA by Ruth Von Blum, Michael Cohen, and Lisa Gerrard. WANDAH (renamed HBJ Writer when commercially published) combined prewriting, word processing, and revision features and was used primarily in basic writing classes by students who, for the most part, had no prior experience with computers. Gerrard recalls that the program engaged the students to such an extent that they personified the computer while writing, addressing it, referring to it as her, and even, in one case, including WANDAH in a paper's acknowledgment (97).

Similarly, Writer's Helper evolved out of William Wresch's work with students at a junior college and the "lack of organization and development" he consistently saw in their writing (Hawisher et al. 45). Consequently, the first version of his software combined a group of prewriting programs with a tailormade word processing program and a set of programs to analyze their writing. Writer's Helper and its subsequent revision, Writer's Helper II, have been used extensively and with positive results in high school and college settings. Other prewriting programs developed by writing teachers include two by Helen Schwartz, SEEN and Organize, and Mimi Schwartz's Prewrite.

Writing and thinking aid software does present pitfalls for basic writers, whose insecurity as writers often makes them suspend their own judgment and conform rigidly to whatever rules the computer program presents, no matter what the situation (Gerrard). Yet, as James Strickland observes, "the computer allows teachers of writing to offer a variety of prewriting strategies at the time when most needed—during the composing process itself" (53). For writing aids to improve the quality of student writing, one study finds, they must be used with an element of "induced mindfulness"—that is, a deliberate sense of purpose that can be fostered by the teacher (Hicks). The technique used in this study consisted of instructing students to learn the features of the software well enough to be able to tutor others in the future.

Many learning centers contain tutorial programs designed to teach grammar, spelling, and punctuation, which students use at their own pace outside class time. When used by developmental writers, according to one study, these programs actually cause the number of student errors to increase (Downs and Linnehan). Further, "grammar tutorial programs can encourage disproportionate and premature concern with error correction" (Gerrard 100).

Gerrard's discussion of computers and basic writers, based on research published up to 1989, focused mainly on such tools as wordprocessing software, prewriting and revision aids, grammar tutorials, and style analyzers. Since then, both local area networks and the Internet have emerged as technologies with classroom application, and sophisticated software programs capitalizing on these and other newly available technologies continue to be developed.

The potential of local area networks for conducting discussions in writing classes was first recognized by Trent Batson, who termed the application ENFI (Electronic Networks for Interaction) and imported it into his classroom at Gallaudet University in 1985 as a way of enabling his deaf students to converse. Soon after, the software Realtime Writer (RTW) was developed to support this application, and the Daedalus Integrated Writing Environment (DIWE) also incorporated ENFI into its system as Inter-Change. DIWE, developed by graduate students in composition at the University of Texas at Austin in the late 1980s, was conceived of as an electronic work shop with features designed to facilitate writing and promote collaboration and sharing of texts. Similar in purpose and pedagogical approach is another software package, Aspects.

The benefits of using networked systems with basic writers have been variously enumerated in conference presentations and published articles. Typical of the advantages are those Ethel Russell observed using the Waterloo MacJanet Network in a community college setting: it provided a built-in sense of audience, changed the role of the instructor from evaluator to audience, enabled electronic exchange of messages and distribution of assignments, and enhanced subsequent student collaboration in a traditional classroom setting, Networked discussions also offer some students who have never found a voice in face-to-face discussions the opportunity to speak (Fey). Offsetting these findings are studies that bear a cautionary message, suggesting that sometimes synchronous conferencing, while promoting participation on the part of many students, may cause other students to be further silenced (Rickly; Romano).

Two other software packages, both designed by composition teachers, deserve mention as embodying the workshop approach to writing instruction. Norton Textra Connect, developed by Myron Tuman of the University of Alabama, supports the move toward courses conducted wholly online. The program's strength lies in its classroom management capabilities: instructors can distribute assignments or tailor them to specific student needs; students can exchange papers for peer feedback or post assignments to the network for discussion; instructors can collect assignments online and return them with comments and a grade, embedding optional links to an online handbook where desirable. Students do not have to learn elaborate rules for naming files and keeping assignments straight—the program does it for them.

CommonSpace, developed by Paul LeBlanc while he was teaching at Springfield College, focuses on shared reading and/or writing of texts by providing a multi-column interface. While a main text—a student paper, for instance, or the draft of an article—fills one column, the additional columns can be used for comments, peer feedback, and even voice annotations. The software also contains chat and conferencing functions that can be used independently or in conjunction with the document on screen.

StorySpace, a nonlinear program developed by Michael Joyce, Jay Bolter, and John Smith, represents a completely different approach to writing.

Joyce, a compositionist and novelist, was looking for a way to create interactive fiction, stories that change with each reading or reader. StorySpace enables writers to create a set of text spaces on screen—boxes that might contain single words, phrases, or whole paragraphs of text. The writer can manipulate them at any point, nesting boxes, clustering them in groups, and connecting any one box to another.

In addition to its use in creating hyperfiction, StorySpace has numerous applications in the writing classroom, as Martha Petry has found. She credits StorySpace with freeing her basic writers from "the tyranny of traditional print." For example, when she is working with students on revising a narrative paper, she turns to StorySpace as a new kind of brainstorming technique. Students use StorySpace to make boxes for attributes of an element of their paper, such as a person or place, and then write the corresponding details in each box. This process allows them to write as much text as they want without being hampered by where it will go; they can later import it selectively into their paper. Petry also finds it helpful to use StorySpace when generating ideas in a discussion, rather than listing ideas in a linear format.

Petry turns to StorySpace not only during writing instruction, but also when she wants to model interactive reading processes. She types the first paragraph of an assigned reading into the computer, uses an LCD to display it, and begins reading aloud. With each word, phrase, or idea, she opens a box and asks a question of the students in the darkened room, typing their comments into the boxes as they call them out. In this way, students see what it means to interrupt the text as they read.

Since the mid-1990s, when the World Wide Web became readily accessible to most Internet users through net browsers (Mosaic, followed soon by Netscape and Internet Explorer), it has been viewed with interest by some compositionists. They see it variously as an enlarged audience for student writing (a means of making student writing public beyond the confines of the classroom), as a resource for both conducting research and teaching research techniques, or as a manifestation of an altogether different form of composition, one that uses images and sounds in addition to the written word for effective communication.

Jeffrey Maxson, who incorporated web page projects into one of his basic writing courses, offered the following rationale:

> First, students already possess expertise in understanding and interpreting images, sounds, both musical and otherwise, and video materials. They can in most instances be considered more expert than their teachers in the ways of popular cultural presentation. Secondly, many students, particularly those in the basic skills curriculum, are oriented toward the above means of information presentation much more than they are oriented towards

text. . . . Hypermedia authorship can thus serve to introduce them to academic literacy through means with which they are familiar. In addition, it teaches them, through hands-on effort, the similarities and differences, the strengths and weaknesses of each of these modes of communication. Thirdly, these activities are intrinsically motivating, for all of the above reasons and because of the unique nature of the presentations students are able to produce.

His final point speaks to the academy's need as much as to the student's: "Basic writers in particular, by virtue of their not having been successful as students by traditional measures, are uniquely positioned to contribute to the re-visioning of academic literacy taking place with the introduction of new hypermedia communications technologies."

NATIONWIDE SURVEY

To assess the extent to which composition teachers are using technology in their developmental writing courses—and to uncover some of the reasons others aren't using technology in the classroom—we conducted a nationwide survey of developmental writing teachers. These surveys were directed at instructors whose names had been supplied by administrators belonging to either the National Association of Developmental Education or to the League for Innovation. All of the respondents taught at community colleges or in developmental programs within universities or four-year colleges. Viewed as a whole, their responses indicate great disparity in use of technology, a disparity that does not always correlate to the type of institution. In the main, however, their responses reinforce the findings of the empirical studies cited above. The comments of respondents quoted in the sections to follow can all be found at the Curricular Transformation website at <www.gen.umn.edu/research/currtran>.

KINDS OF TECHNOLOGY IN USE

For some of the writing teachers in this survey, the presence of a lab on campus where students are able to word-process their papers was the closest connection they could make between computers and writing. Having access to a computer lab in which to hold class periodically was a high priority on their wish lists. Other respondents taught in networked computer classrooms with an Internet connection, enabling them to make use of e-mail and the World Wide Web in their pedagogies. To these seasoned users, the idea of computers as word-processing tools was such a given that it was not even worthy of mention. They were already looking forward to technology that is beginning to emerge from the development stage, such as CUCME (see you, see me) video conferencing.

The most prevalent kind of technology identified on the surveys was the computer, whether part of a fully-equipped writing classroom or off some-where—usually in inadequate numbers—in a learning lab, department lab, or campus lab. The software available on these computers ranged from the minimal word processing package (several respondents mentioned world-ware programs such as PFS Write, WordPerfect, and MS Word) to grammar and mechanics checking programs (e.g., Grammatik) to tutorial programs such as SkillsBank or Invest. Diagnostic and placement software was also mentioned frequently. Two respondents specifically mentioned software packages (MS Office, WordPerfect Works and Microsoft Works) that enable students to integrate graphics into their writing assignments and oral presentations.

Three software packages developed specifically to support the workshop approach to writing instruction were also mentioned. The Daedalus Inte-grated Writing Environment features Interchange, an electronic discussion forum, along with a series of invent and respond prompts, a word process-ing program, and a bibliography preparation tool. CommonSpace supports peer editing by enabling students to comment on each other's papers in separate columns that run alongside the text column. Norton Connect is a system in which students can share their work electronically with others, turn it into the instructor electronically, and follow links to sections of a grammar or style manual that can be imbedded in the instructor's feedback.

Relative to the number of responses that named hardware and resident software as instructional tools, significantly fewer respondents mentioned Internet-related technologies as items in their pedagogical bookbags. This figure, under ten percent, most likely reflects the proportion of develop-mental education programs with equipment that provides Internet access. Of those who did mention the Internet connection, e-mail was cited most often, both in terms of its ability to facilitate communication among stu-dents and between student and instructor. In a few cases, students hand their papers in via e-mail. Larry Silverman at Seattle Central Community College uses e-mail to match his students up with students in other states and even countries: "I've had my developmental writing class correspond with students in Hawaii, and next quarter they will correspond with a group of students in Japan." To find these classes, he advertises on a listserv designed to make these connections.

Some writing teachers on campuses with access to the World Wide Web use it as a way to teach research techniques and a place to conduct research and gather information. One respondent makes full use of the Internet and World Wide Web technologies, posting his syllabus to the web and using an e-mail distribution list to assign homework. He has students post their comments about reading assignments to a class listserv and initiates them in the use of a MOO (a virtual meeting place) so he can hold class even on those days when he can't be in the room.

Two respondents listed CD-ROMs among the technologies available to their students. A teacher in adult education uses *Grolier's Encyclopedia* on CD as a text for writing: "The database set-up allows students to access all kinds of information. They then write anything from research papers to outlines to summaries."

Devices for projecting images onto large screens for all students to view are a staple of instruction in the writing classroom. The overhead projector enabled teachers to create transparencies for use in lecture situations or as a means of displaying examples and supplanted the need to laboriously write out such information ahead of time on the chalkboard or reproduce multiple copies for students. The development of liquid crystal display panels (LCDs) and computer projectors that plug directly into a computer's central processing unit has added a dynamic quality to this instructional tool. A handful of respondents reported having access to LCDs or computer projectors, either as part of the basic classroom equipment or available on a cart for checkout.

Jack Sexton of Paradise Valley Community College, part of the Maricopa Community College District, puts the LCD to multiple uses in his writing classroom. To teach editing skills, he might put a student paper on the screen and ask students as a group to discuss possible revisions, keying in changes as the students agree on them. For a lesson on thesis statements, he will ask students to type their thesis statements into a common file at the beginning of the class period and then work through them, one by one, so that everyone has access to all of the examples.

In short, the use of computers in instruction ranged from computer-aided instruction (CAI), exemplified by tutorial programs, to computer-assisted composition (CAC), where students did much of their composing at the keyboard, to computer-mediated communication (CMC), where the emphasis was on electronic communication using software packages such as Daedalus InterChange and Norton Connect and technologies such as computerized projectors, e-mail, and the World Wide Web.

IMPACT OF TECHNOLOGY ON TEACHING AND LEARNING

Basic Writing instructors who have introduced elements of technology into their courses are mixed in their evaluation of its impact on student learning. While one instructor states that he has not found technology to improve student writing ("I believe computers are basically a gimmick"), another asserts that technology has made his an entirely different course that has resulted in more literate students.

Responses tend, not surprisingly, to cluster around other factors, such as the level of commitment a department or institution has made in hardware, software, and training. The instructor who stated he saw no improvement in writing, for instance, teaches in a department with access to a "room with computers," no training, and little technical support, while the instructor who felt that teaching with technology was producing more literate students teaches at an institution that provides workshops to train faculty in new forms of technology and has access to the Internet and the World Wide Web, as do his students. Cause and effect is difficult to sort out in these situations.

Whether they were making use of the computer to deliver computer-aided instruction in a venue outside the classroom, such as a writing or academic resource center, or using the computer as a writing tool, holding class sessions in the computer lab or a computer classroom, instructors reported largely similar results. The positive evaluations of using technology overwhelmingly outweighed the neutral or negative ones, and the rewards noted by instructors fall naturally into four groups: positive impact on students' attitudes toward writing; improved appearance of papers; improved student writing, in terms of both quantity and quality; and an increase in efficiency on the part of the instructor.

Again and again, instructors noted that working on computers has positively altered students' attitudes in their writing classes. "Using technology has made the basic English requirements more interesting and relevant for vo-tech students," observed one respondent. In related observations, other instructors stated that students see the computer as a useful tool and feel they are learning the technology of the future when they work on a computer. Instructors variously reported that students have more confidence in their writing when using the lab and develop self-esteem by working at their own pace to accomplish writing tasks. Among other reasons cited: students respond well to computer-based instruction; working on a computer provides variety and adds interest; computer-related assignments increase student involvement in their own educations.

Simply turning in word-processed papers, instead of the often illegibly handwritten ones, was noted by some instructors as a positive change brought about by technology. Most often, however, instructors saw this "improvement" as benefiting themselves as much as the student. Yes, word-processed papers are a "neat end product," as one teacher put it, presumably offering satisfaction to the student upon completion, but even more to the point, they are easier to read and make writing teachers' time more productive.

By far the most frequently cited examples of ways in which using technology had had an impact on developmental writing courses were outcome-based and revolved around both the process and products of student writing. The ease with which documents can be changed has significantly affected the amount of revision that is taking place. Teachers can insist on revision and editing if they choose; students are more likely to exercise some editing and revision strategies on their own work with or without pressure from their instructor. Spelling checkers not only help to eliminate surface errors in final drafts, but their mere existence encourages some writers to try words they aren't sure they can spell, knowing they'll be able to correct them in a later draft. Students just plain write more—more words, more pages, more drafts. And teachers say they are able to fit more writing assignments into a term because computers speed up the editing and revision processes.

There were some contradictions in what writing instructors had to say. One asserted that meeting in a computer lab changed the structure of the class so that more time was spent writing and less on grammar lectures or demonstration. For another, meeting in a computer lab required the instructor to spend more time teaching word-processing and computer skills and less time on writing instruction. No doubt both are true.

Whereas most of the successes cited were student-related, the majority of the problems mentioned by instructors were institutional in nature. Lack of funding for adequate equipment was the biggest issue: not enough computers to serve all students in a class, outdated hardware that doesn't support new software, hardware and software that doesn't perform as promised. Insufficient faculty training (or none at all) and not enough technical support were also seen as roadblocks to increased use of computers in developmental writing courses. Instructors reported problems with specific software as well as general system malfunctions and breakdowns. One respondent specifically mentioned that the administration is supportive of technology in the classroom—for the engineering and science departments. Convincing them that the writing program should receive the same level of funding has been a greater effort.

The fact that students arrive in writing classes with minimal or no computer skills is perceived by almost all instructors as a problem, as they are required to show students how to use the machines before they can ask them to work on writing assignments. Most agreed that while this lack of computer experience does create a problem in the beginning, it disappears as students become more familiar with the hardware and software. Almost all instructors surveyed agreed that students offer little if any resistance to technology. Several noted that anxiety seems to be age-related and that returning students, who are usually older, are most prone to it. Even their fears, however, dissipate quickly.

Some students, however, lack keyboarding, or typing skills, which is a decided disadvantage. "A small handful of students," noted one instructor, "refuse to even hunt and peck on the keyboard, get frustrated, and fall way behind." Should knowledge of word-processing be a requirement for entry into a basic writing course? At one college, the instructor who teaches word-processing thinks it should and wants students to take his class first. Only one instructor reported that students use technology as an excuse for not completing assignments on time, saying, for instance, that they couldn't get to the lab.

Perhaps because these surveys were sent to people who had been recommended by administrators at their institutions as teachers who were using technology as part of their developmental writing courses, many of the instructors who responded to the survey complained of not having colleagues who were similarly involved. These people became the sole instructors taking students into the computer lab or lobbying for more equipment; their colleagues were often reluctant to get their feet wet, for any number of reasons, including technophobia.

FACULTY TRAINING

In cases in which the instructor is the department technology expert or the only teacher to be using computers in writing instruction, he or she has usually been propelled by a personal interest in computers and has been self-taught. One person wrote of "sitting in the basement computer lab until 4 a.m. until I figured this stuff out." These people consulted manuals, called helplines, and learned by trial and error. Many of them credited other people—colleagues, computer science department staff members, patient friends, and others, such as secretarial staff members, who were already using the particular hardware or software.

Some teachers were first introduced to ways that computers could enhance writing instruction in graduate school or at conferences or workshops put on by professional organizations such as the Conference on College Composition and Communication (CCCC) and the National Association for Developmental Education (NADE), and by federally funded or privately funded organizations such as the National Endowment for the Humanities and the Epiphany Project. Epiphany, a project funded for two years by Annenberg/CPB in collaboration with the American Association for Higher Education and the Alliance for Computers and Writing and now continuing as a nonprofit organization, conducts three-day intensive institutes around the country to introduce teachers to pedagogies involved in using computers in writing instruction. Interestingly, among its recommendations is that schools send people in teams of two or more, a strategy that provides synergy when participants return to their own institution and helps to eliminate the sense of isolation reflected in many of the completed surveys received.

As evidenced in the responses, some colleges are providing training for their writing faculty. It is often the early adopters—those instructors who discovered technology on their own—who end up organizing workshops to teach others in their departments or institutions. Some instructors reported attending workshops offered at the institutional or district level, and a few reported that their institutions have instructional technology committees. Still, the profile is uneven. Many instructors who have integrated some technology into their courses report that they do not even have computers in their offices, and many more report that their institutions have not yet geared up to provide access to e-mail for faculty members, much less students.

VISIONS OF THE FUTURE

The great disparity among the levels of technology currently in place across the country in colleges and universities with developmental education programs means that individual and departmental goals for the implementation of technology in writing instruction also vary widely. One teacher's dream is in effect another teacher's reality. Some instructors long for more equipment, better computer classrooms, or networking capabilities, while others have all that and simply want more time in which to explore these tools or develop assignments around them. Still others envision kinds of technology or software programs that have yet to be developed. A lone voice expressed the sentiment that "we would be satisfied if the student just came every day with paper, pencils and pen, and textbook."

No matter what may be the vision of implementing technology, pervasive in the responses are indications of writing pedagogies that these technologies support. At either end of the spectrum are teachers who believe that a collaborative environment leads to learning. The instructor who reports that her college encourages its faculty members to get training in multimedia still forthrightly states, "I don't see much use for multimedia in basic writing. . . . I rely heavily on the photocopier and chalkboard. I type worksheets based on students' writing and duplicate them for class members to discuss. We do a great deal of collaborative work." Her counterpart in another college has a different way of facilitating collaboration—by using the computer projector to display samples of student text to be discussed. These two technologies, the former far more labor-intensive for the instructor, fulfill the same purpose in the writing classroom, allowing students to see writing as a dynamic process and one in which the effective communication of ideas is paramount.

Another principle underlying the workshop approach to writing is that of writing for an audience other than the teacher, whether that means one's classmates or the portion of the world funneled through the World Wide Web. Those respondents whose students use e-mail to conduct a text-based conversation with students elsewhere or who post their papers to the Web quickly develop, in the words of one respondent, "a sense of what their readers need to understand the texts they produce."

The approach to developmental writing instruction that emphasizes the mastery of discrete skills is also very much in evidence in these responses. Despite the existence of research that suggests that grammar tutorials, style analyzers, and other tutorial programs are detrimental to developmental writers, many writing instructors continue to rely on them. Without polarizing writing instruction pedagogies as either product or process, repeated comments that focus on appearance of text (e.g., "a neat end product") or promote excessive dependence on style checkers nonetheless suggest that technology is sometimes being used to reinforce, perhaps unwittingly, a product-oriented view of writing.

When instructors were asked to comment on what their writing courses will be like in the future, most conceived of courses along the lines of current models but enhanced by more and better hardware and software. Only a few people considered that future writing instruction might undergo a total transformation in form while still grounded in the same theory. Several respondents suggested that their classes might be offered in an electronic format—over the web or Internet—and one envisioned an interactive CD-ROM teaching module, but then noted that "the institutional pedagogy is moving away from any individualized learning, so whatever it is, it better be communal!"

ISSUES AND POLICIES

Whether in their capacity to foster collaborative learning, enrich opportunities for student research, encourage students to write longer papers of a higher quality, or simply modify students' negative attitudes toward writing, computers have already made an incalculable impact on the field of writing instruction. As the results of our survey have shown, however, only a fraction of developmental writing teachers are in a position to incorporate technology into their courses to the extent that they would like. They are stopped by factors both economical and political: lack of support for technology at the department or institutional level (as manifested in funds for equipment, space that has been retrofitted with the appropriate wiring, and technical support), and lack of clout within the department for access to the computer facilities that do exist.

Faculty training has emerged as another roadblock, since many of the people who teach developmental or Basic Writing courses carry heavy courseloads that cannot accommodate time-outs for training without compensatory release time. To compound the problem, many departments employ adjunct or part-time faculty to teach their developmental writing courses; even if training sessions are offered, these instructors cannot always be available to attend them. To ensure that access to technology does not become a factor dividing institution from institution, department from department, and ultimately student from student, those of us *with* access must find ways to eliminate the impediments in the paths of those *without* access.

These obstacles, which occur not just in Basic Writing sites but also in Composition departments (which in turn are often situated in English departments), are topics of frequent discussion on listserv groups devoted to issues of writing pedagogy or technology in higher education. Such discussion groups have created virtual communities of teachers and administrators with like interests and goals who often pool their experiences and expertise to address problems presented to them. Need recommendations from users to bolster your request to purchase a new kind of writing instruction software? Go online. Need suggestions for the most effective layout for a computer classroom? Go online. Need data to convince a hesitant chair that the expense of a computer classroom is warranted? Go online. Many of the respondents to our survey remarked that, as the resident "expert," they felt isolated at their institutions; listservs provide them with the chance to develop virtual colleagues.

While listserv discussion groups represent informal sites for sharing information, websites (including the website developed by this project and the many web resources linked to it) are more formal sites for the sharing of information about writing pedagogy and technology. Such websites can be productive as entry-level places to learn about everything from terminology to available technologies; they can also act as information exchange sites and clearinghouses to put inexperienced technology users in touch with experienced teachers at nearby institutions.

Sending a group of Basic Writing faculty members to conferences and workshops to learn about new uses of technology is an expense beyond the budget of most departments. The trend toward cyber-conferences and satellite conferences responds to this situation by bringing the workshop or the conference to faculty members who may have neither the time nor the financial support to travel. Electronic conferences, or cyber-conferences, can either occur asynchronously (a highly regulated form of listserv discussion), or they can take place synchronously in a MOO. Satellite conferences, in which presenters are projected live onscreen in an auditorium setting, can be particularly affordable if the conference costs are being shared by several institutions simultaneously.

In addition to providing a place for new users to learn about technology, cyber sites (e.g., listservs, websites, electronic conferences) provide a way to capture what we earlier termed fugitive information: classroom practices that do not appear in traditional print sources. The innovative work of so many instructors with part-time status and heavy courseloads goes unpublished and thus remains hidden to all but their immediate colleagues. Searchable websites such as ours, where these teachers can post lessons developed around specific technologies, will augment the amount of information available and provide a more realistic picture of how technology is being used to enhance Basic Writing pedagogy. Taken together, all of these efforts—emerging communities of support, online collection and dissemination of information, and electronic venues for training—represent an initial step in lessening the disparity between the kinds of technology available to basic writers in learning institutions throughout the nation.

REFERENCES

Bartholomae, David. "'I'm Talking about Allen Bloom': Writing on the Network." *Networked-Based Classrooms: Promises and Realities*. Eds. Bertram C. Bruce, Joy Kreeft Peyton, and Trent Batson. New York: Cambridge UP, 1993. 237–62.

———. "Inventing the University." *When a Writer Can't Write*. Ed. Mike Rose. New York: Guilford, 1985. 134–65.

Bartholomae, David, and Anthony Petrosky. *Facts, Counterfacts, and Artifacts*. Upper Montclair, NJ: Boynton-Cook, 1986.

Batschelet, Margaret and Linda Woodson. "The Effects of an Electronic Classroom on the Attitudes of Basic Writers." National Council of Teachers of English, Seattle, 22–27 November 1991.

Bruce, Bertram. "Innovation and Social Change." *Networked-Based Classrooms: Promises and Realities*. Eds. Bertram C. Bruce, Joy Kreeft Peyton, and Trent Batson. New York: Cambridge UP, 1993. 9–32.

Collins, Terence. "The Impact of Microcomputer Word Processing on the Performance of Learning Disabled Students." *Computers and Composition* 8:1 (1990): 49–67.

Crowley, Sharon S. "Around 1981: Current Traditional Rhetoric and Process Models of Composing." *Composition in the Twenty-First Century: Crisis and Change*. Eds. Lynn Z. Bloom, Donald A. Daiker, and Edward M. White. Carbondale: Southern Illinois UP, 1996.

D'Agostino, Karen Nilson and Sandra D. Varone. "Interacting with Basic Writers in the Computer Classroom." *Computers and Composition* 8.3 (1991): 39–50.

Downs, Judy R. and Paul J. Linnehan. "Computers as Writing Tutors." Conference on College Composition and Communication, San Diego, 21 March–3 April, 1993.

Fey, Marion Harris. "Finding Voice through Teacher-Student Collaboration in a Feminist Research Project: Long-Term Effects." Conference on College Composition and Communication, Nashville, 16–19 March, 1994.

Gay, Pamela. "Questions and Issues in Basic Writing and Computing." *Computers and Composition* 8.3 (1991): 63–81.

George, E. Laurie. "Taking Women Professors Seriously: Female Authority in the Computerized Classroom." *Computers and Composition* 7 [Special Issue] (1990): 45–52.

Gerrard, Lisa. "Computers and Basic Writers: A Critical View." *Critical Perspectives on Computers and Composition Instruction.* Ed. by Gail Hawisher and Cynthia L. Selfe. New York: Teachers College Press, 1989. 94–108.

Hansman-Ferguson, Catharine Ann. "Writing with Computers: A Study of Adult Developmental Writers." Diss., Ball State University, 1995.

Hawisher, Gail, Paul LeBlanc, Charles Moran, and Cynthia Selfe. *Computers and the Teaching of Writing in American Higher Education: 1979–1994: A History.* Norwood, NJ: Ablex, 1996.

Hicks, Sandy Jean. "Cultivating Metacognitions within a Learning Environment: The Case of the Computerized Writing Partner." Diss., University of Arizona, 1993.

Hillocks, George. *Research on Written Composition.* Urbana, IL: National Council of Teachers of English, 1986.

Horner, Bruce. "Discoursing Basic Writing." *College Composition and Communication* 47.2 (1996): 199–222.

Kremers, Marshall. "Sharing Authority on a Synchronous Network: The Case for Riding the Beast." *Computers and Composition* 7 [Special Issue] (1990): 33–44.

LeBlanc, Paul. *Writing Teachers Writing Software: Creating Our Place in the Electronic Age.* Urbana IL: NCTE and Computers and Composition, 1993.

Lu, Min-Zhan. "Conflict and Struggle in Basic Writing." *College English* 54:8 (1992): 887–913.

Maxson, Jeffrey. "HTML and the Politics of Academic Literacy: Basic Writers on the Web." Paper presented at 12th Annual Computers and Writing Conference, 31 May, 1996, Logan, Utah.

Meem, Deborah T. "The Effect of Classroom Computer Use on College Basic Writers." *Research and Teaching in Developmental Education* 8.2 (Spring 1992): 57–69.

Petry, Martha. Telephone interview, 31 March 1997.

Reynolds, Mark. "Writing for Publication." *Teaching in the Two-Year College* 24.1 (1997): 3–4.

Rickly, Rebecca. "What's Good for the Goose is (Not Necessarily) Good for the Gander: Gender's Influence on Participation Levels in Oral and Online Classroom Conversation." Computers and Writing Conference, El Paso, 19 May, 1995.

Romano, Susan. "The Egalitarianism Narrative: Whose Story? Whose Yardstick?" *Computers and Composition* 10.3 (1993): 5–28.

Russell, Ethel. "Networking in the Developmental Writing Class." *Collegiate Microcomputer* 14.2 (May 1993): 149–51.

Sexton, Jack. Response to Curriculum Transformation and Technology in Developmental Education Project Survey. 22 Oct. 1996.

Shaughnessy, Mina. "Basic Writing." *Teaching Composition: Ten Bibliographical Essays.* Ed. Gary Tate. Fort Worth: Texas Christian UP, 1976. 137–67.

———. *Errors and Expectations.* New York: Oxford UP, 1977.

———. "Open Admissions and the Disadvantaged Teacher." *Mina P. Shaughnessy: Her Life and Work.* Ed. Jane Maher. Urbana, IL: National Council of Teachers of English, 1973. 249–54.

Silverman, Larry. Response to Curriculum Transformation and Technology in Developmental Education Project Survey. 8 Oct. 1996.

Sirc, Geoffrey. "Never Mind the Tagmemics, Where's the Sex Pistols?" *College Composition and Communication* 48.1 (1997): 9–29.

Strickland, James. "Planning, Drafting and Writing on the Computer." *Research and Teaching in Developmental Education* 9.1 (Fall 1992): 45–55.

Stuckey, J. Elspeth. *The Violence of Literacy.* Portsmouth, NH: Boynton-Cook/Heinemann, 1991.

"Survey Shows a Growing Emphasis on Instruction and User Support." *Signals: League for Innovation in the Community College* Jan. 1997: 1, 3.

Walker, Cynthia Louise. "Computers, Revision, and the Developmental Student: A Case Study of Student Revision in the Computer Classroom." Diss., East Texas State University, 1994.

QUESTIONS FOR REFLECTION,
JOURNAL WRITING, AND DISCUSSION

1. How can computers change how people write and how writing teachers teach?
2. Have you ever used technology in teaching writing? How did you feel about it? Can you get the same results without using technology?
3. Do you think that people are better writers now that they have access to computers?

Chapter 27

Community Service and Critical Teaching

Bruce Herzberg

Bruce Herzberg is Professor of English and Chair of the Department of English at Bentley College in Waltham, Massachusetts. He served for many years as director of the expository writing program and writing across the curriculum as well. He is coauthor, with Patricia Bizzell, of *The Rhetorical Tradition* (2nd ed., 2001), *Negotiating Difference* (1996), and, with Bizzell and Nedra Reynolds, of the fifth edition of the the *Bedford Bibliography for Teachers of Writing* (2000). His articles on composition and rhetoric have appeared in a number of journals and anthologies. The following article is from *College Composition and Communication,* 45, October 1994.

"Capitalism with a human face," said our new provost, Phil Friedman. This was the way he hoped the United States would model capitalism for the new democracies in eastern Europe. It was, therefore, a motto for what the students at Bentley College, a business school, should be learning. My English Department Colleague Edward Zlotkowski challenged the provost to put a human face on the students' education by supporting a program that would make community service part of the curriculum. Friedman agreed and Zlotkowski took on the massive job of linking courses with community agencies. At first, the projects were simple: Students in writing courses visited soup kitchens and wrote up their experiences. Later, as the service-learning program developed, students in accounting classes helped revise the accounting procedures of non-profit community-service agencies and audited their books for free. Students in marketing and business communication designed advertising and public relations materials to improve the distribution of agencies' services. And the students in one freshman composition class—mine—learned to be adult literacy tutors and went weekly to a shelter in Boston to offer their help.

There are many obvious benefits, to students and to the agencies and individuals they serve, from service learning. Many students become eager volunteers after the ice is broken by class projects and they see where they can go, how they can help. A surprising number of the students in my class, for example, did some volunteer work in high school, but would not be likely to do so in college—in a new city, without contacts—were it not for the liaison provided by service learning. Most agencies are eager for new volunteers.[1] And of course, the students perform real and needed services. Faculty members, too, report a new sense of purpose in their teaching. This is, perhaps, most striking at a school like Bentley, where students are not only majoring in business but often seem to have fallen into the narrowest view of what that means, adopting a gray and jaded image of the businessman, scornful or embarrassed by talk of social justice and high ideals. Edward Zlotkowski describes his teaching efforts as attempts "to help my students break out of the intellectual and moral miasma in which they seemed to me to wander."

I should interject here that the idea of service learning did not originate at Bentley. There are well-developed community service projects at several colleges and universities. Stanford has made extensive use of service learning in freshman English courses. And Campus Compact, an organization of college presidents that promotes public service in education, has been in existence since 1985. The observations I have made about the venture at Bentley are echoed in reports from other schools.

There is a good deal of evidence from our program that service learning generates a social conscience, if by that we understand a sense of the reality and immediacy of the problems of the poor and homeless along with a belief that people in a position to help out should do so. Students report that their fears and prejudices diminish or disappear, that they are moved by the experience of helping others, and that they feel a commitment to help more. This is a remarkable accomplishment, to be sure.[2] But it is important to note that these responses tend, quite naturally, to be personal, to report perceptions and emotions. This is where my deepest questions about service learning lie.

---

[1] A successful program requires a great deal of coordination between the school and the community agencies. Individual teachers working on their own to arrange contacts will find the task exhausting and daunting. While many agencies welcome short-term volunteers, some cannot. Literacy tutoring, for example, requires consistency over time so that tutors can establish a relationship with the learner. In short, the school-agency ties must be well developed before the students show up. I don't wish to discourage such programs, but to suggest that good planning can prevent many problems and frustrations. See Cotton and Stanton, "Joining Campus and Community through Service Learning," in *Community Service as Values Education*.

[2] The advocates of service learning assume that values must be taught in college. I'm comfortable with that assumption and won't try to make the case for teaching values or critical consciousness here. The question of whether to teach values at all is by no means settled. It has been raised persistently as a general question in education and it has been a topic of hot debate in composition studies. Patricia Bizzell argues cogently for the importance of teaching values in *Academic Discourse and Critical Consciousness*. C. H. Knoblauch and Lil Brannon's *Critical Teaching and the Idea of Literacy* is a recent and valuable contribution. Maxine Hairston dissents in "Diversity, Ideology, and Teaching Writing." Paulo Freire, Henry Giroux, and Ira Shor have long been advocates of teaching values through the development of critical consciousness. And I have something to say about the issue in "Composition and the Politics of Curriculum."

I don't mean to belittle the kind of social awareness fostered by service learning, especially with middle-class students. Students in business courses are discovering real applications of their knowledge in the organizations they serve. More importantly, they are learning that they can use their knowledge not only to get jobs for themselves but also to help others. But what are they learning about the nature of the problems that cause these organizations to come into existence? How do they understand the plight of the people who need these services? I worry when our students report, as they frequently do, that homelessness and poverty were abstractions before they met the homeless and poor, but now they see that the homeless are people "just like themselves." This, they like to say, is something that could happen to them: They could lose their jobs, lose their houses, even take to drink.

Here, perhaps ironically, is a danger: If our students regard social problems as chiefly or only personal, then they will not search beyond the person for a systemic explanation. Why is homelessness a problem? Because, they answer, so many people are homeless. The economy is bad and these individuals lost their jobs. Why are so many people undereducated or illiterate? Because they didn't study in school, just like so-and-so in my fifth grade class and he dropped out. Community service could, as my colleague Robert Crooks puts it, "work in a larger way as a kind of voluntary band-aiding of social problems that not only ignores the causes of problems but lets off the hook those responsible for the problems.[3] Campus Compact director Susan Stroud voices the same kind of concern: "If our community service efforts are not structured to raise the issues that result in critical analysis of the issues, then we are not involved in education and social change—we are involved in charity." (3)

I agree. I don't believe that questions about social structures, ideology, and social justice are automatically raised by community service. From my own experience, I am quite sure they are not.

Such questions can and should be raised in a class that is engaged in a community service project. Here, too, there is no guarantee that students will come to see beyond the individual and symptomatic. But that is what I wish to discuss at greater length. I don't see why questions like these cannot be raised in any course in the university, but if there are prime locations, they would be (and are, at Bentley) courses in economics, political science, sociology, and composition.[4] The connection to composition is by no

---

[3]Crooks goes on: "Let me hasten to say that by 'those responsible' I mean all of us, who through direct participation in institutional actions, policy-making, ideas, attitudes, or indirectly, through silence and compliance, offer support to pervasive economic, social, political, and cultural systems that produce the kinds of problems that community service addresses."

[4]At some universities, the theology department is the primary location for these courses. Georgetown University, Boston College, and Marymount College link community service to theology courses on injustice and social responsibility, for example.

means obvious. It is all too easy to ask students to write journal entries and reaction papers, to assign narratives and extort confession, and to let it go at that. A colleague reported overhearing a conversation between two students: "We're going to some shelter tomorrow and we have to write about it." "No sweat. Write that before you went, you had no sympathy for the homeless, but the visit to the shelter opened your eyes. Easy A."[5] Even for those whose awakening is genuine, there is reason to doubt that the epiphany includes an understanding of the social forces that produce and sustain poverty, illiteracy, discrimination, and injustice. There is little evidence that students spontaneously gain critical self-consciousness—an awareness of the ways that their own lives have been shaped by the very same forces, that what they regard as "choices" are less than matters of individual will. Writing personal responses to community service experiences is an important part of processing the experience, but it is not sufficient to raise critical or cultural consciousness.

Writing about the actual experience of doing community service, then, does not seen to me to be the primary work to be done in a composition course like mine. Instead, we study literacy and schooling and write about that.[6] At this point, I need to explain some of the mechanics of the course, but I will keep it short.

Students are invited to be in this project and we have had no difficulty raising enough volunteers from the pool of incoming students. I have run the project in a one-semester version, but the two-semester sequence that I will describe here is far better. During the spring semester, the students are also enrolled together in a section of introductory sociology.[7] In the fall semester, the students are trained to be adult literacy tutors, and in the spring semester they do the actual tutoring.

---

[5]I reported this conversation to Zlotkowski, who responded that he believed that many students remained defensive about the fact that they really did have their eyes opened. In anonymous student evaluations that have no effect on grades, he finds a predominance of sincere reports of changed attitudes.

[6]The courses in the Stanford program tend to focus on writing to or for the agency being served. Such projects are undertaken at Bentley by more advanced classes. See *Let 100 Flowers Bloom* for a description of Stanford's rationale. A high-school writing course in which students work as literacy volunteers is described by Norma Greco in "Critical Literacy and Community Service: Reading and Writing the World."

[7]The benefits of "clustering" courses are described in *Learning Communities* by Faith Gabelnick et al. When students are co-registered in two or more courses, instructors can develop common themes, draw on material taught in each other's courses, explore shared readings from different perspectives, and have some common writing assignments. While my students were working on their writing with me and doing their tutoring at the shelter, in the sociology course they were learning about the effects of social and institutional forces on the formation of identity. Their final research papers were submitted in both courses.

The composition course is not devoted to literacy tutoring, but rather to the study of literacy and schooling, as I have mentioned. This is an important distinction: We do not set out to study teaching methods or composition pedagogy. The students learn some of the teaching methods they will need in tutor-training sessions that take place largely outside of class time. But in the class itself, our goal is to examine the ways that literacy is gained or not gained in the United States and only in that context do we examine teaching theories and practices.

During the fall semester, we read Mike Rose's *Lives on the Boundary* and a number of selections from *Perspectives on Literacy*, an anthology edited by Kintgen, Kroll, and Rose. In the spring semester, we read Kozol's *Savage Inequalities* and more of the essays in *Perspectives on Literacy*. The students write many summaries of sections of these books as well as several essays drawing on what they learned from them. In the spring semester, they write research papers on topics that arise from our studies.

Toward the end of the fall semester, the students have about ten hours of tutor training designed to sensitize them to the problems and attitudes of illiterate adults as well as to provide them with some teaching materials and methods. These sessions focus on the need to respond to the concerns of the learners and to understand the learners' reasons for seeking literacy education. The sessions also help the tutors generate ideas about teaching materials and how to use them. While the tutoring is going on, we devote some class time each week to questions about how to handle interpersonal problems or obtain appropriate teaching materials.

In the 1992–93 session, the sociology professor and I took the students to the shelter at the beginning of the spring semester for an orientation session. The following week, the students returned to the shelter without us and started the actual tutoring. At the start, the students were naturally apprehensive about tutoring adults in a shelter. Most of them had done some volunteer work before, but not in settings like that. They were very nervous when we actually went to the Pine Street Inn. We left Bentley's clean, well-lighted suburban campus and drove the ten miles into downtown Boston after dark, parked under the expressway, and went past a milling crowd of men into a dreary lobby. We watched the men being checked with a metal detector while we waited for John Lambert, the director of the shelter's education program. The students clumped together around Dave, a football player. Dave wrote in his field notes that he was conscious of this attention and that it made him even more nervous than he already was.

We went upstairs for our orientation, stepping over some sleeping men stretched out on gym mats in the dining hall. Upstairs, we met a number of men who had been working with volunteer tutors. The students later said that they were impressed by the effort that these men were making to try to improve their lives. They did not seem attentive, though, to the analysis offered by the shelter's assistant director, who explained that while the shelter provided critically needed services, it also undermined any sense of independence the residents might have. Their self-esteem seemed to be under constant attack by all the social institutions they came in contact with, including the shelter itself. When I brought it up in class, the students had little memory of this discussion. On their first visits to the shelter, they were simply more concerned with negotiating the immediate physical and psychic environment. Soon, however, they became accustomed to going to the shelter. Two or three of the boys in the class, including big Dave, did not get learners right away and instead walked around the shelter, visiting with the residents and trying to recruit them into the literacy program. Some of the girls did this on occasion, too. The students were irritated that they did not have learners but eventually realized that their presence in the shelter was a valuable advertisement for the literacy program.

The learners' needs are various: Some are almost completely illiterate, some are schizophrenic, a few need ESL teaching, some read well but need help with higher-order skills. Many of the learners come irregularly; many are easily distracted. One woman is pregnant, another is ridiculed by her boyfriend for needing help with phonics. One young woman is prevented by her mother (who also lives at the shelter) from taking tutoring because, the mother insists, she doesn't need it. But many of the students developed excellent tutoring relationships and all learned how to draw on their own resources both psychologically and pedagogically.

The students tended to see their learners, quite naturally, as individuals with personal problems—alcoholism and drugs, mental breakdown, family disintegration, or some nameless inability to concentrate and cope. It is quite easy to see these problems as individual ones. Very few of the students ever became indignant about what they saw. They hoped to help a few people as much as they were able. They would like to know if there is a "cure," but they don't regard that as a realistic hope. What I want to focus on here is how difficult my students find it to transcend their own deeply-ingrained belief in individualism and meritocracy in their analysis of the reasons for the illiteracy they see.

They do become indignant when we discuss *Lives on the Boundary,* which describes the ways that schools systematically diminish and degrade culturally disadvantaged students, or when we read *Savage Inequalities,* which tells about the structural inequities in the funding of public education and the horrible consequences of that inequity. The students are indeed distressed by systemic discrimination against poorer people and disenfranchised groups. In their responses to these books, it is clear that they understand the class discrimination inherent in tracking and the effect of tracking on self-esteem. But they do not seem to see this discrimination in the lives of their learners. One reason, perhaps, is that the learners themselves regard their situations as personal problems. They, too, have imbibed the lessons about individualism and equal opportunity. The traces have been covered over. Thus, in order to understand that they are in the presence of the effects they have been reading about, the students must also understand— viscerally if not intellectually—the nature of what Gramsci called hegemony: the belief that one participates freely in an open and democratic system and must therefore accept the results it produces. They must see, in other words, that the people in the shelter believe the same things that they, the students, do—that there is equal opportunity to succeed or fail, to become literate or remain illiterate. They need to analyze the way that schools and other institutions, like the shelter itself, embody those beliefs.

Here is a passage from *Lives on the Boundary*. We spent a lot of time with this:

> American meritocracy is validated and sustained by the deep-rooted belief in equal opportunity. But can we really say that kids like those I taught [as a Teacher Corps volunteer] have equal access to America's educational resources? Consider not only the economic and political barriers they face, but the fact, too, that judgements about their ability are made at a very young age, and those judgements, accurate or not, affect the curriculum they receive, their place in the school, they way they're defined institutionally. The insidious part of this drama is that, in the observance or the breach, students unwittingly play right into the assessments. Even as they rebel, they confirm the school's decision. They turn off or distance themselves or clam up or daydream, they deny or lash out, acquiesce or subvert, for, finally, they are powerless to stand outside the definition and challenge it head on. . . . [T]he children gradually internalize the definition the school delivers to them, incorporate a stratifying regulator as powerful as the overt institutional gatekeepers that, in other societies, determine who goes where in the educational system. There is no need for the elitist projections of quotas and exclusionary exams when a kid announces that he just wants to be average. If you want to insist that the children Joe and Monica and the rest of us taught had an equal opportunity in American schools, then you'll have to say that they had their equal chance and forfeited it before leaving the fourth grade. (128)

Elsewhere in *Lives on the Boundary*, Rose speaks sensitively about the difficulties freshmen have with academic discourse, a discourse "marked by terms and expressions that represent an elaborate set of shared concepts and orientations" (192). Rose himself is a brilliant stylist of academic discourse, as the passage I've quoted reveals. Rose advises that students need many opportunities to become comfortable with this discourse, and I take his advice seriously. There is much that my students cannot fathom in his book, many references to abstractions and complex terms (such as "incorporate a stratifying regulator as powerful as the overt institutional gatekeepers"), so we spend time talking and writing about important passages like this.

"American meritocracy is validated and sustained by the deep-rooted belief in equal opportunity." This sentence is a complete stopper. My students consistently claim that they have never heard the word "meritocracy" before. Once defined, though, the idea is perfectly obvious to them: of course those who are smartest, most talented, and work hardest rise to the top. What else? "Equal opportunity" is also initially difficult for them—not because it is unfamiliar but because it never seemed to require definition or reflection. This is not the first place in *Lives on the Boundary* that the students have encountered a challenge to the idea of equal opportunity: The challenge is both implied and explicitly stated many times. Yet, even 128 pages into the book, their first reaction is to regard this sentence as a positive statement about a noble ideal, an American virtue. It costs them a great effort to see that Rose is saying that one false idea is sustained by another, that the very words "validated and sustained" carry a negative connotation, that "deep-rooted belief" means self-deception. It costs them more than intellectual effort: it means a re-evaluation of the very deep-rooted beliefs that Rose is discussing here. It means seeing that Rose is talking about their beliefs and criticizing them.

When Job, the righteous man, loses his property, his children, and his health, he angrily questions the belief that God is just and gives people what they deserve. He lashes out at his friends, the false comforters, who steadfastly maintain that the good are rewarded and the wicked punished (and thereby imply that Job is suffering for some sin). Yet Job is in a terrible dilemma. He is frustrated and angry, convinced that the comforters are wrong, yet unable to explain his situation—for he believes precisely the same thing the comforters believe. When a belief is deeply-rooted, alternatives are inconceivable.

How do my students abandon their comfortable belief in equal opportunity and meritocracy? Did they not deserve, did they not earn their place in school and society? They have the greatest respect for Mike Rose and want to believe what he says, but it isn't easy. As education critic Colin Greer says, traditional historians of education "mistake the rhetoric of good intentions for historical reality" and persist in believing, against all evidence, that schools are the instruments of social change (4). We can hardly fault students for clinging to such a belief. We ran into a similar problem discussing a passage earlier in Rose's book:

> We live, in America, with so many platitudes about motivation and self-reliance and individualism—and myths spun from them, like those of Horatio Alger—that we find it hard to accept the fact that they are serious nonsense. (47)

Here, too, we had worked on the definition of "individualism" and the negative connotations of "platitudes" and "nonsense." The students never heard of Horatio Alger. After I explained about Alger, Lynne told us, without the least self-consciousness and without comment, that her grandfather came from Italy without a cent and became a success in America all on his own, without help from anybody.

In their fall semester papers, the students tested out the ideas they were learning about systemic discrimination through schooling. They were very tentative about this at first. Kyle wrote:

> In America today, we find that how an individual will do in school is often dependent upon what economic class they come from. Through studies of literacy, experts have found that there are different levels of success in school among individuals of diverse socioeconomic backgrounds . . . Children of [the] middle- and upper-class are able to attend better schools and have greater access to books and other reading materials. Therefore, they tend to feel more comfortable with the material in school while lower-class children, whose parents are not so well off in terms of money, are more inclined to be insecure. In addition, in situations where parents of poor children have had low levels of education, there is a good possibility that their children will also have low levels of education. While at the same time the situation is reversed with children of well-to-do parents.

These ideas are clearly unfamiliar to Kyle, and so he needs to repeat them and carefully spell out the steps in the process of discrimination, while holding onto the possibility of individual differences. "Experts" have discovered this injustice—it is not immediately accessible to experience. The parents of lower-class children are not so well off—in terms of money though they may, I think Kyle implies, have good intentions.

It is difficult, as I have said, for my students to understand these ideas, let alone deal with them critically. In the spring semester, for example, while we were studying Kozol's *Savage Inequalities,* a book that describes and decries the differences between well-funded suburban schools and their decrepit and overcrowded counterparts in the cities, Lynne (who told us about her grandfather) suggested that the students in south Chicago's schools were probably just not personally motivated to do school work, like the kids in her high school who flunked. Several students murmured in agreement, though when I challenged her, several others expressed dismay about Lynne's assumptions. Lynne is not a conservative ideologue. As with the comments about her grandfather, she was simply being unselfconscious. Her comment helps us see how hard it is to understand the social nature of experience and to accept the idea of structural injustice.

In an essay called "Critical Teaching and Dominant Culture" in *Composition and Resistance,* a volume of essays on critical teaching, Cy Knoblauch describes his attempts to bring his students to some consciousness of the injuries of class. He tells how his students were unmoved by "The Lesson," Toni Cade Bambara's story about poor black children visiting F. A. O. Schwartz. Knoblauch quotes a student response that he characterizes as typical: "If you strive for what you want, you can receive it." As Knoblauch cogently argues, the goal of critical pedagogy is to help students see and analyze the assumptions they make in comments like these. Still, it takes a lot of time and work to do this and Knoblauch is honest enough to say that he did not have the success he wished for.

Time and work were on our side, though, in the literacy-tutoring project—we had two semesters of composition, a sociology course, and the project itself. At the time that Lynne made her comment about Chicago school kids, the students had been tutoring at the Pine Street Inn shelter for several weeks. There was, apparently, nothing automatic or instantaneous about that experience that helped them understand Rose or Kozol. The community service experience doesn't bring an epiphany of critical consciousness—or even, necessarily, an epiphany of conscience. The effect was slow and indirect. In time, the students began to realize that the people at Pine Street were *not* like them. They did not, finally, conclude that "this could happen to me." Though they were not allowed (by the wise rules of the shelter and good sense) to quiz their learners on their personal lives and histories, they had learned enough about the learners' family distress and social isolation, their disconnection from community, lack of individual resources, and reliance on charitable institutions and the effects of those conditions on their self-images—to realize that "this could happen to me" is a shallow response.

The tutoring, as best we could determine, appeared to be productive for the learners at the shelter. In many ways, the best help that tutors can provide in such a setting is to come regularly and respond sensitively to the learners' concerns. The learners are coming to the literacy program at the end of what is typically a long series of personal and social failures, and though they expect—and often demand—a school-like experience again, the tutors are there to humanize it as much as they can.

The final research papers for the composition course show a growing sophistication about the social forces at work in the creation of illiteracy. Students visited nursery school classes to see how children learn, returned to their own high schools to find out what happened to the kids who flunked, corresponded with convicts in prison-education programs. In his paper, "The Creation of Illiteracy through Tracking," Dave (the football player) writes, "Tracking tends to maintain or amplify differences in socioeconomic status, the opposite of 'equalizing' these differences as schools should." Schools can't be held responsible for prior economic discrimination, Dave argues, but they must be held accountable for reinforcing it.

Kevin borrowed several history textbooks used over the last ten years in the Waltham High School, counted the number of pictures and other references to African-Americans and compared them to the number of pictures, and similar references to whites, analyzed the images, and tried to imagine what a black student would learn about American culture from an education in Waltham, Massachusetts (Kevin is white). Our friend Lynne asked how school systems with the money to do so were addressing the needs of disadvantaged students. She concludes that "the systems with the extra money to spend on special programs are not facing these types of problems." She points out that there is no lack of information about how to spend this money well and describes the settled and unreflective attitudes about schools and teaching that prevent the adoption of new methods.

Some students referred to their tutoring experience in their papers. Mark, for example, noted the kind of knowledge his learners sought—sentence-diagramming and algebra—and commented that their frustrating search for credentials, fostered by traditional (and failed) schooling, had left them without job skills on the one hand and with an artificially low sense of their own abilities on the other. Most of the students did not, however, incorporate the tutoring experience in the research papers they wrote for my class. This was as it should be: The goal of the course was not, as I have explained, to facilitate the tutoring experience, but to investigate the social and cultural reasons for the existence of illiteracy—the reasons, in other words, that the students needed to perform the valuable service they were engaged in. In that sense, the tutoring project was constantly present in our class. In the sociology course, the students used their visits to Pine Street more directly as the object of field observations and analysis.

The effort to reach into the composition class with a curriculum aimed at democracy and social justice is an attempt to make schools function the way Dave and my other students want them to—as radically democratic institutions, with the goal not only of making individual students more successful, but also of making better citizens, citizens in the strongest sense of those who take responsibility for communal welfare. These efforts belong in the composition class because of the rhetorical as well as the practical nature of citizenship and social transformation.

What the students' final papers show, then, is a sense of life as a communal project, an understanding of the way that social institutions affect our lives, and a sense that our responsibility for social justice includes but also carries beyond personal acts of charity. This is an understanding that has been very rare among Bentley students. Immersed in a culture of individualism, convinced of their merit in a meritocracy, students like those at Bentley need to see that there is a social basis for most of the conditions they take to be matters of individual choice or individual ability. As Kurt

Spellmeyer says, "the university fails to promote a social imagination, an awareness of the human 'world' as a common historical project, and not simply as a state of nature to which we must adjust ourselves." Students who lack this social imagination (most of them, according to the study Spellmeyer cites) attribute all attitudes, behavior, and material conditions to an individual rather than social source. Students will not critically question a world that seems natural, inevitable, given; instead, they will strategize about their position within it. Developing a social imagination makes it possible not only to question and analyze the world, but also to imagine transforming it.

REFERENCES

Bizzell, Patricia, *Academic Discourse and Critical Consciousness*. Pittsburgh: U of Pittsburgh P, 1993. 277–95.

Cotton, Debbie, and Timothy K. Stanton. "Joining Campus and Community through Service Learning." *Community Service as Values Education*. Ed. Cecilia I. Delve et al. San Francisco: Jossey-Bass, 1990.

Crooks, Robert. "Service Learning and Cultural Critique: Towards a Model for Activist Expository Writing Courses." Conference on College Composition and Communication, San Diego, CA, March 1993.

Friedman, Phil. "A Secular Foundation for Ethics: Business Ethics and the Business School." *EDP Auditor Journal 2* (1989): 9–11.

Gablenick, Faith, Jean MacGregor, Robert S. Matthews, and Barbara Leigh Smith, eds. *Learning Communities Creating Connections Among Students, Faculty, and Disciplines*. San Francisco: Jossey-Bass, 1990.

Greco, Norma. "Critical Literacy and Community Service: Reading and Writing the World." *English Journal 81* (1992): 83–85.

Greer, Colin. *The Great School Legend: A Revisionist Interpretation of American Public Education*. New York: Basic, 1972.

Hairston, Maxine. "Diversity, Ideology, and Teaching Writing." *CCC 43* (1992): 179–93.

Herzberg, Bruce. "Composition and the Politics of the Curriculum." *The Politics of Writing Instruction: Postsecondary*. Ed. Richard Bullock and John Trimbur. Portsmouth, NH: Boynton, 1991. 97–118.

Kintgen, Eugene R., Barry M. Kroll, and Mike Rose, ed. *Perspectives on Literacy*. Carbondale: Southern Illinois UP, 1988.

Knoblauch, C.H. "Critical Teaching and Dominant Culture." *Composition and Resistance*. Ed. C. Mark Hurlbert and Michael Blitz. Portsmouth, NH: Boynton, 1991, 12–21.

Kozol, Jonathan. *Savage Inequalities*. New York: Crown, 1991. *Let 100 Flowers Bloom: Community Service Writing Curriculum Materials Developed by the Stanford Freshman English Program*. Stanford U, n.d.

Rose, Mike. *Lives on the Boundary*. New York: Free, 1989.

Spellmeyer, Kurt. "Knowledge Against Knowledge." *Composition and Resistance*. Ed. C. Mark Hurlbert and Michael Blitz. Portsmouth, NH: Boynton, 1991, 70–80.

Stroud, Susan. "A Report from the Director." *Campus Compact*, Fall 1992: 3–4.

Zlotkowski, Edward. "Address to the Faculty of Niagara University." Niagara, NY, April 1993.

QUESTIONS FOR REFLECTION,
JOURNAL WRITING, AND DISCUSSION

1. Should it be a goal of college education to "generate a social conscience" in students?

2. Have you ever had any kind of service learning experience? If so, how did you feel about it?

3. What do you think of the idea of exposing college freshmen to schizophrenic people in a shelter after ten hours of workshops "designed to sensitize them to the problems and attitudes of illiterate adults as well as to provide them with some teaching materials and methods"?

4. Do you think the students in Herzberg's class acquired an understanding of the social forces behind illiteracy, or did they just write papers giving the professor what he wanted?

Chapter 28

Places to Stand: The Reflective Writer-Teacher-Writer in Composition

Wendy Bishop

Wendy Bishop teaches writing at Florida State University and is the author, coauthor, and/or editor of a number of books, essays, and articles on composition and creative writing pedagogy and writing research. Most recently, she has published *The Subject Is Reading* and *Ethnographic Writing Research* (Boynton/Cook) and *Thirteen Ways of Looking for a Poem and Metro: Journeys in Writing Creatively* (Longman). She lives in Tallahassee, Florida, with her husband, Dean, and two children, Morgan and Tait. The following article is from *College Composition and Communication*, 51, September 1999.

> *We are always in a rhetoric. We may see those others in rhetorics not our own; if we do, they are likely to seem whimsical, odd, uninformed, selfish, wrong, mad, even alien. Sometimes, of course, we don't see them at all—they are outside our normality, beyond or beneath notice; they don't occur as humans. Often as not, we don't see our own rhetoric; it is already normality, already truth, already the way to see existence. When we remark, as we have become accustomed to remark, that all discourse is ideological, we probably exclude our own. It is the truth, against which ideological discourses can be detected and measured.*
>
> —Jim Corder (98)

Peter Elbow, Janet Emig, Toby Fulwiler, Ken Macrorie, James Moffett, Donald Murray, Mike Rose, and Nancy Sommers readily come to mind as influences on the "figure" of writer-teacher or teacher-writer in composition studies: one who advocates that teachers write with and for their writing students as well as with and for their colleagues. Of course, many others have helped to shape this image. In the 1960s and 1970s, for instance, Marvin Bell (1964), William Stafford (1964), Stephen Minot (1976), and Sheila Ortiz-Taylor (1979) published essays in *CCC*, to be followed a decade later by Anthony Petrosky (1982), Alice Brand (1987), Brett Lott (1988), and Ken Kesey (1990) who presented their ideas through *CCC* interviews or as essayists speaking about aspects of writing and writing instruction.[1]

It interests me that professional journalists, poets, and novelists have spoken in *CCC* in their dual roles. It is also of interest that comparatively few creative writers have spoken in these pages in the 50 years of the journal's existence. Reviewing past volumes, I realized that challenges to the idea of the writer-teacher and/or teacher-writer by not-expressivist theorists (often termed social-constructivist)[2] are based less on a cohesive or even representative body of work than on what I've come to feel is a fear-of-the-figure. When I attempted a count of writers' essays in past pages of the journal, few such spokespersons actually appeared. Given how comfortable I felt reading "The Many Cs"[3] as I moved from the world of creative writing into the world of composition studies in the mid-1980s, I was surprised to have my sense of comfort eroded. These writers' voices really weren't there in the fullness I had imagined.

This close inspection leads me to propose that there have been fewer spokespersons and fewer articles published by writers who teach than we might expect given the strength of the social-constructionist marginalization and then dismissal of expressivists. In fact, I argue that key-expressivists (so called, not self-labeled) are frequently cast as convenient straw-men, as now-aging, no longer compositionally-hip, and therefore slightly embarrassing advocates of a 1960s touchy-feely pedagogy from which professionals in composition are currently trained to distance themselves. This anti-expressivist encouragement takes place despite The Many C's continued publication of works by teachers-who-are-writers; my continuing list of these includes Lynn Bloom, Lillian Bridwell-Bowles, Robert Brooke, Jim Corder, Elizabeth Rankin, Mary Rose O'Reilley, Michael Spooner, Lad Tobin, and Kathleen Blake Yancey. These are just a personal selection of our essayist-theorist-pedagogists whose work I turn to with the expectation that I'll *enjoy* their prose as well as learn from my reading of

---

[1]Memory had me listing Adrienne Rich here though her essay appeared not in *CCC* but in *College English* in 1972.

[2]Sherrie L. Gradin suggests initial categorization took place in the work of Lester Faigley and James Berlin. She finds "advocates of a social-epistemic or social constructivist rhetoric include Richard Ohmann, Kenneth Bruffee, Lester Faigley, David Bartholomae, Patricia Bizzell, and Karen Burke LeFevre" (5). For these critics, to be expressivist is to be romantic, valuing "the autobiographical, the intimate and subjective voice, and the organic development of a topic" (13). She also suggests these reductive categories did not begin to be seriously challenged by those so labeled until the early 1990s.

[3]This is the name one of my fiction-writing friends gives to the journal and conference; a common "outsider's" view, I think, is to wonder what the heck all those C's stand for but not really to want to know; this may be the best proof I've yet encountered that composition is a discipline.

that prose.[4] And I should mention that these writers' styles are not the only styles I admire, though I often do so—what I'm talking about in one sense is these authors' inclusive approach to presenting writing personas.[5] Doug Brent reminds us that "Both the reader and the hearer, then . . . must construct the character of the rhetor. Each must build, from clues in the text, not only an evoked meaning but also an evoked writer, a personality that lies beyond the text and through the arguments he uses, the criteria he demonstrates, and the claims he asserts, projects a character that the reader will admire to a lesser or greater extent" (67).

The expressivist "position," then, is often embodied by not-expressivists as constructions of Donald Murray and Peter Elbow—who certainly are often-cited in *CCC* pages. These individuals, in their author-functions or rhetorical constructions, are raised and dismissed, treated as fatherly Macy's New Year's Day parade balloons, floated through critiques as unitary and non-representative figures whose simplified positions can be quickly—via synecdoche—argued against.[6] At the same time, I don't mean to raise these figures myself and argue for them, but I do intend to examine why it seems so uncanny to me today to be hearing the term post-process (been there, done that?) percolating through the air at conferences, and to find it assumed that expressivists don't do other things ("things" are often represented by the word "theory") because they "can't" not because they choose not to.

---

[4]I might term this *just* writing or *ordinary* writing—writing that favors an *author-present* style (though not necessarily always or only a first-person voice). I'll work with any term that helps me escape the academic versus personal writing Mobius-strip.

[5]I also have not entered the larger discussion of feminism and writing style though I'm aware of it and sympathetic to problems like these, outlined by Olivia Frey: "I would not describe the conventions of mainstream literary critical writing as feminist. These conventions include the use of argument as the preferred mode for discussion, the importance of the objective and impersonal, the importance of a finished product without direct reference to the process by which it was accomplished, and the necessity of being thorough in order to establish proof and reach a definitive (read 'objective') conclusion. A common denominator of each convention seems to be to 'get it right,' that is, establish cognitive authority" (509). I did, though, experience many of these issues while drafting this essay—wanting to say in a believable way something about which I feel strongly and for which I don't have traditional proofs. These are also issues of race and class. Even as I pay attention to teachers, I risk continuously deferring paying attention to writing students. "Despite all the rainbow rhetoric, our large social structures continue to exclude the students who sparked the composition 'crisis'" (Lyne 79).

[6]For example Murray received 49 citations and Elbow 58 in the journal years of 1980–1993; numbers equaled or slightly surpassed by Rose, Emig, Sommers, Shaughnessey, Lunsford and Faigley and surpassed only by Flower 139 and Hayes 107 during this, the heyday of cognitive research (Phillips et al. 452). It is worth noting that Elbow published his essays most often in *College English*. His first *CCC* appearance was a 1985 essay, followed by a co-authored essay, with Pat Belanoff, in 1986, and then nearly a decade later he reappears as part of an essay dialogue—expressivist versus social-constructionist—with David Bartholomae.

In a 1992 essay, "Is Expressivism Dead?" Stephen Fishman and Lucille McCarthy summed up the debate by enumerating the critiques of these pedagogies on the parts of David Bartholomae, Patricia Bizzell, James Berlin, and John Trimbur. These scholars' critiques include the charges that "expressivists" keep students in a state of naivete, don't prepare them for the languages of the academy, abandon them to the forces of politics and culture and "emphasize a type of self-actualization which the outside world would indict as sentimental and dangerous" (648).

Call me a dreamer, but I'm not the only self-identified something-like-an-expressivist who would never characterize my pedagogy in those ways. Because of this, as a researcher and scholar too, I wonder on what grounds such a debate has been waged, and why?

Fishman and McCarthy argue that authors of these critiques were reading Elbow in ways that furthered their own arguments. "By labeling him romantic, by seeing expressivism as isolating, Elbow's critics make it easy to neglect the communitarian objectives of his approach." In *Romancing Rhetorics,* Gradin points to the way she believes critics have overlooked certain commitments and potentials of expressivist pedagogies, "contrary to how social-epistemic hard-liners would have us believe, the important things [positions] that Berlin outlines here are not solely the province of social-epistemicism" (112). And she goes on to explain—as I did above—that for many of us, the claims being raised simply don't compute:

> Nothing restrains an expressivist teacher from asking students to examine who gains from their "personal visions," from their "individualistic stances." Examining racism and sexism is easily enough done in the expressivist classroom. Moreover, critical reflection . . . is a major facet of expressivist theories and practices . . . the expressivist classroom can resist disempowering social influences, use interdisciplinary classroom methods, and posit a social understanding of the self. Expressivist rhetoricians certainly can be self-critical and self-revisionary. (112).

Not only can be, but often are.

As a teacher-educator and writing program administrator, I observed many expressivist-oriented classrooms where teachers decided to incorporate curricular aspects claimed by social-constructionists (though we all realize that examining racism and sexism, via any pedagogy is never as easy as this quote makes it sound; nor would Gradin, I suspect, expect it to be).

We choose not to do some things and to do other things. Teaching writing is a result of an infinite number of such choices. And critiques increasingly seem to ignore the force (and success) of the practical and everyday choices made by countless writing teachers across the country.

Thomas O'Donnell's 1996 essay on "Politics and Ordinary Language" explores current critiques of expressivist pedagogy, particularly those by

James Berlin and Alan France, and explores how their analyses may be missing the point concerning expressivist intentions. O'Donnell examines the way the expressivist position for many is not grounded in persons but in language, or even better and more realistically, in both.

> Expressivist rhetorics have always emphasized communal responses to a writer's words and the value of exploring those regions of self-knowledge that call attention to themselves in the rhetorical acts of naming, defining, describing, and adducing, and the interpretive acts of doubting and believing. If expressivists can be said to have any "underlying convictions," the ones I am best able to see are responses to conditions of language use, not a confidence in "private truths." (436–37)

It may be that critics of Elbow latched on too easily to the word "game" in his doubting and believing game—overlooking the seriousness of the game and keeping them from realizing how many expressivist pedagogies explore the way language games construct human experience. "Our responsibility to our words is inseparable from our responsibility to the speech community in which we must use them" (O'Donnell 437).

In this admittedly personal essay, I'll continue to explore why I believe these interested readings have happened and will no doubt continue to happen. The easy culprit is Current-Market-Forces, an additional figure of fear that urges compositionists into rapid professionalism, creating the perceived (and often actual) need to appear ever-more scholarly, historical, and theoretical. A need that sweeps pedagogy under the skirts of long, black academic robes. Undoubtedly, the specter of Current-Market-Forces causes a space-to-speak competition in our journals. However, the more immediate problem, the reason we fear expressivist figures, may have as much or more to do with our own concerns about authorizing ourselves as writers-who-teach-a-subject: writing. Indeed, perhaps a fear of expressivist figures is one side-effect of the pressure to be professional. Murray and Elbow are professional, but their casual, personal, reflective writing is a model of professional scholarly writing that young compositionists are *not* encouraged to emulate.

And certainly, there are problems in our "readings" of each other. For instance, an anonymous reviewer once refused an essay by Donald Murray on the grounds that it was too "Murrayesque" to be included in that journal (that is, contrary—as he saw it—to the journal *WPA*'s professional mission). The reviewer put it this way: "I've been at war with this mindset for the last 15 years. Nevertheless, I must admit that the writer writes solid prose . . . I would enjoy this essay if I saw it in some harmless place where very few people would read it or take it seriously" (Hult 26). Anyone who has met and talked to Don Murray knows you don't have to go to war with him. Or dismiss his prose to a safe and harmless place. His response to this reading of his essay was certainly potentially infuriating to a reviewer who feels at war, for Murray refused the engagement: "When this article was rejected for being 'too Murrayesque,' then invited and rejected for being too 'quaint,' I laughed and did not cry. I went back the next morning to where I go every morning: the writing desk" (29).

Ironically enough, that writing desk is often—from all reports and appearances—a writing-about-teaching-writing desk.

I argue for overcoming our fear of this other. For I now believe that the writer-teacher-writer, contrary to my initial assumptions, has never really received a full and useful hearing from us. And this is problematic, if, as Burton Hatlen suggests, many of us entered the corridors of English studies, hoping to write and have conversations with writers, about writing, as writers: "Few of the English people I have known in my almost thirty years in the profession—have ever in my presence voiced anything like delight or enthusiasm about any piece of critical discourse. On the contrary, English people generally talk about *PMLA*, theoretically the most prestigious journal in our field, in tones of unbridled hostility" (799). Hatlen claims that after writing critical discourse for certification, most PhDs in English who entered the field because of their love for writing cease to write. He asks, might the field of English more productively, "let these people give up the pretense that they are serious critics, and let them become, simply, teachers of writing?" (799). This plain-speaking is refreshing, but I know (as Hatlen knows and continues to explore in his essay "Michel Foucault and the Discourse[s] of English") the reasons we are not all simply and happily just teachers of writing are complex. It takes encouragement and courage to find a clear passage to the safe harbor of affirming oneself as teacher within an institution that valorizes almost every other role first.

SEEKING SHELTER FROM SOME STORMS

> When you get into reading and writing the "other," into assuming some kind of authority for the "other"—whether you are the "other" or you are the subject—there's a community involved. And I think what you are saying is that postcolonial theorists sometimes forget what's going on here in the community involved, in the world that we inhabit. (Anzaldua, qtd. in Lunsford 26)

I can no more imagine being a writing teacher who does not write than I can imagine being one who does not read. That either reality is no stretch for some, I understand. An aversion to reading or writing is a problematic fact of life for many, including many of my students. But I teach writing precisely because I love these two intimately connected activities. Some days I am a writer-who-teaches (WT) and on others I am a teacher-who-writes (TW) but inevitably, always, I am one or the other. For me, the first (WT) is represented by the figure of Donald Murray. Murray is a publishing journalist and creative writer and he teaches composition based on his writerly experience. For me, the second (TW) is represented by the figure of Peter Elbow. Elbow's early self-portrayal in *Writing Without Teachers* was that of the blocked dissertation writer who needed to finish and who studies his own writing process and eventually survives to tell us about it. Just as Murray was venerated for his expertise, Elbow was valued for his confusions and his hesitations; he was just folks, just like us, loving literature and writing himself in a troubled way into and then out of the literary scene and arriving on the safer shores of writing classrooms.

Clearly, this enduring figure is unlike the "later Elbow" who successfully finished and published that literary dissertation and who has systematically worked out his positions in print. Despite the difference in "early" and "later" Elbow, during the 1980s he was most often cited as the author of a book that encouraged us to do what he had done (Phillips et al. 451). That TW position allows us to be relatively uninterested in publishing our writing yet highly interested in the act of writing from a writer's perspective; we could become teachers who write for the self, for informal friendly forums—friends, family.

Even if I have overstated the fear of the expressivist figure, then, there is a need to explore the spaces between these figures, between the letters WT and TW and the site that is shaped when the two co-exist in the same paragraph, classroom, teaching life. For this, I'll use the symbol Ø (if the man formerly known as Prince can do this, why can't we?)—until I can make my computer double-strike the letters, one over the other, creating an amalgam of cross-bars, diagonals, and desire.

As I mentioned earlier, as a practicing Ø, to talk about those who don't write, who teach writing yet don't consider themselves writers, or do much writing at all—takes a leap of imagination for me as large as any I ever make, as great as trying to imagine myself fully situated in another culture, part of another race, or devoutly believing in any organized religion. And, while I think those in our profession should be some version of a writer-teacher or a teacher-writer or more simply Ø, I do accept there may be others who don't figure themselves to be writers in any manner or way and yet who have effectively taught writing well. Still, I want to set that ("it's possible; it's often done; I do it") argument aside for a while along with the counter-arguments ("would you learn to play tennis from a pro who had never played, want to drive over a bridge built by an engineer who had never tested her theories?") in order to ask:

Who is the figure of the writer-teacher-who-writes (and teaches writing out of that writing)—who is or could be Ø?

And, why did I think that such a figure would find a comfortable or at least welcoming home in composition and within the community symbolized by *CCC* as I have found a home there during my last ten teaching years?

Does Ø reside there or do I just hope Ø does, as I hoped I could/can?

Because I was having difficulty formulating much less answering these questions—since liking to write certainly does not always equate at all with always being able to write or finding writing easy—I turned to my usual solution, writing something else. In this case, a poem. The poem provided a clue about why I felt constrained, embattled even, as I struggled to make my intuitive-intellectual-emotional position clear while also respecting the "other." I sensed I was arguing with a vast, complex, and certainly not unitary creation of the 1990s called social-construction. The poem taught me about the difficulty of imagining such otherness—as it must (if it actually exists) have equal difficulty imagining me.[7]

Othering

Once, I tried to imagine it—

not reading—nothing—not clouds, nor the inky residue
of night; not the pages of sheets rumpled at bedside;
not squirrels chattering on weathered fences,
responding to the inquisitions of winter; not
typescripts of age, skin of children tightening
into more serious play; not summer sun hurling out flames
until the day's hammocks melt into their seasonal plots;
not ever to enjoy the novelties of spring;

not sleeping—no singular cocoon of escape
while oceans and winds beat the planet out of perfect orbit;
no swimming deeper to grasp air bubbles of hope
and ride them to the surface; no clasp of sweaty terror
redeemed by daylight; never to enter the broadest texts
of stillness, to recount genealogies into darkness;
no begats or regrets; no blinding luck, no tomb, cave,
diurnal stone-tumbled renewal; no luck;

not eating—never coming sweetsour to one's senses
playing across the tongue; no luncheons on lawns
under canopy trees; no Italian terraces and cheese rinds
of nostril-fluting delicacy; no seeking, no Braille
of spice and salt, ocean-scent of body's luck; no reason
to stroke the belly, flat or convex; simply existing within
the absence of—; no tides of flesh, green howls
of unrooting; no blame, no satiety, no animal ease;

not loving—fingers rude and blunt—mere digits, bland
instruments; not waiting or wanting; no breath of moon

---

[7]During the time this essay was being reviewed, the poem "Othering" appeared first in *The Seneca Review*.

in the ear of dawn; solitary and unaware of absence,
or absent and not missed; featherless, wings furled;
untouched by cataclysm; earthbound on an empty road; no attitude
toward sunset; chorus of frogs lost on infinite jetstreams
where blue sky reclines, a lonely god; not made in anyone's image—
literate, impervious. dull and rarely, if ever, heard from;

if other, so little then to make of life, of this, of life, this—this.

Donald Murray claims all writing is autobiographical, and certainly for
me all essaying is too. In his essay of the same title, Murray analyzes one of
his poems and ends by saying: "I suspect that when you read any poem, you
wrote your own autobiography. That is the terrible, wonderful power of
reading: the texts we create in our own minds while we read—or just after
we read—become part of the life we believe we lived" (74) and I would
attach his words to this poem, my poem, this teaching life, my teaching life.
In fact, I often read expressivist-leaning authors for what is stealable, for
their aphoristic qualities, for their metaphors, and the issues they raise, as
much as for their linear arguments. "The same sort of tropes that are sometimes held to characterize poetic language can be shown to crowd into
'non-poetic' or 'ordinary' language. Likewise, 'ordinary language' is
replete with fictive speech acts such as imitation, joking, hyperbole,
hypotheses, and even extended narrative. Such counterexamples argue
that if there is a distinction to be made between literature and nonlitera-
ture, we cannot find it in the text" (Brent 19). And so I do my mixing, not
to elevate genres but to intermingle them, not to venerate the poetic or
belletristic but to point out that each brings us to our senses though in different modes and tones.

Because styles, genres, and syntax seem both to prompt and predict
thought, I need to think in and through them all. I want to share this with
my writing students as well, and I'm not alone in thinking this possible.
James Seitz argues: "Because of its intimacy with the *act* of writing, composition could create a field of richly surprising, experimental, supple forms of
written discourse, both in the classroom and in its own community . . . Asking students—and ourselves—to attempt, to essay, roles that produce fragmentary texts might lead us to approach the challenges of composing unified texts from a more enlivening perspective" (824). The goal then is not to
toss out the unified text with the academic bath water, but to offer options.
To explore for ourselves, and to allow our students to do so also, how a deeper understanding of the connections between thought, words, and life, may
occur when we re-read our own writing. To do that, of course, we must write.

After I wrote about othering, it became part of the life I believed I lived—
I learned the difficulty of the stretch, the jump into the other's position. As
Jim Corder points out, my rhetoric is the truth against which I measure
other rhetorics, the place where I come from, and from which I speak to you.

Back to this poem, this essay.

This poem—that is, writing about my teaching as I always seem to have done—led me to see I needed to write about, to advocate Ø but still be sympathetic to Not-Ø.

What would it be not to write? Not to feel some version of and/or incarnation of Ø?

Since I'm pretty certain it's not possible for me to inhabit the Not-Ø position, particularly *via* writing, I decided to consider, instead, why I write and teach from a Ø stance and why I have—as a creative writing student turned ordinary writing teacher—moved into the world of composition studies.

FROM ORACULAR TO VERNACULAR AND BACK

I began my studies in creative writing and moved to composition because it offered a space to theorize about writing—about my actual practices as a writer—in a way literature studies and creative writing programs at that time did not encourage. Scott Russell Sanders, writing in the *AWP Chronicle,* suggests that creative writers in the university are always playing games with the literature team: "Even in the most convivial of times, a degree of hostility between writers and critics—as between rival soccer teams—may be inevitable. After studying criticism under John Crowe Ranson at Kenyon, E. L. Doctorow felt the need to unlearn those habits of mind before he could once again make fiction . . ." (10–11).

In this sporting battle, however, the titans—Writers and Critics—are like two home-town high school teams, challenging each other until they unite against a common enemy—teaching, pedagogy, composition. Robert Scholes, in his 1986 book *Textual Power,* shows us the then-current—and, I'd argue, still-current—hierarchy (and he chooses religious metaphors to do this): Literature is God with creative writers trying to become more god-like—to write texts that will eventually be deemed good enough for gods, creating an uneasy alliance, all around. Some of us were interested in teaching and those who were found themselves unteaching before they could even begin teaching writing: "Our students come to us burdened with all sorts of ideas that are bad for their writing: they want to be great, or failing that, famous, or failing that, to get to hang out with the literary brat pack. And we can all be grateful that that's the easy part: tell them, work hard; tell them, study the top-shelf writers; tell them, be like me, be a rock against rejection. The harder lesson is that they can write their hearts out and, odds are, it won't mean a hill of beans" (Haake 2).

The alliance of creative writing and literature produces students who crave quick deification for instant gratification. (I know, once I would have given my eye-teeth and funny-bone both to win the Yale Series of Younger Poets; past 40 finally, and therefore ineligible, I have come to better understand the poetry-business odds). These amalgamated desires are particularly problematic since they are in service of a meritocracy with limited reserves of reward and recompense, and one that defines merit in limited, exclusive, even suspect ways. Composition, of course, has long existed in a service relationship to both Literature and Creative Writing, although it has come into sharper focus as the necessary foothill-region of the English Mount Olympus (funding teaching assistants who would fill the seminars of both critics and creators) for the last two decades. "Literature, English came to assume, belongs to the scholar and critic, licensed by the PhD and the professorial appointment to speak with authority on these matters. But something must be done about all those other kinds of writing floating about in the world, and so they are consigned to composition. This division of labors might not be particularly problematic, were it not for the fact that . . . English treats literature as not merely a descriptive but also an honorific category" (Hatlen 795).

This hierarchy to which Hatlen refers is not based on the essential worth of constituents in English studies, but on contingent worth. In *Distinction*, Pierre Bourdieu has argued convincingly that society values certain genres of art, music, and literature over others, not because of essential worth but because genres become markers of social status, become social currency. Similarly, in the "society" of English studies, literary criticism and critics are more highly valued than composition research and composition teachers, not because they are inherently more valuable to students, colleges, society, or humanity, but because certain interests are served by such a status structure.

As you have noticed, I have extended Hatlen's argument by using (supposedly) social-constructionist ideas to help reveal why social-constructionists might devalue expressivism, and to suggest why, at the end of the day, social constructionists and expressivists in composition are indistinguishable to the famous creative writer or the resident literary theorist peering down from the mountain top of English studies.

These divisions remain. "English as a discursive practice has allocated status, money, and power to literary scholars and critics, at the expense both of people who actually create literature and of people who think it is important to help everyone to write with as much skill and confidence as possible. And these injustices have warped and even destroyed the lives of some innocent people" (Hatlen 798). And I think part of the warping is the separating of the Other into these seemingly opposed two: writers and teachers of writing. Unfortunately, in the profession of English at large as well as within my own program, I find the relationships between the English Studies tracks—despite composition's heightened awareness about its historical developments—aren't much better than before and sometimes are more strained than when I began teaching here ten years ago.

During my ten tenure-track years, I learned rapidly. I served a rare apprenticeship of elected service on the governing bodies of our three professional associations—CCCC, MLA, AWP. I found that those in AWP knew nothing about the Wyoming Resolution, that those in MLA felt comfortable defining genre-theory for editors of a composition collection who viewed genre differently (and thus MLA refused a composition-grounded collection in a composition series as they had done earlier with a volume on feminism and would do later with a volume on pedagogy), that those in composition felt the need for blind review of conference program proposals and moves to "better" presses for publications of composition materials so their constituents could compete more ably in the tenure-process. Status matters.

During the same time period, I came upon a young pre-tenure writing program administrator weeping at her conference table because her department chair was sending mixed messages—sending her to the conference to learn to do better while heaping on work at home and providing impossible constraints (from the political to the fiscal to the etiquette level) about how that work could be done. All while she was in terror and confusion about what "counted" toward her always looming tenure case—three years down the line but omnipresent.

Colleagues/friends who were able creative writers and composition teachers sounded their discouragement at over-full literary journals and unfriendly departments of English. Peers whom I would describe as second-generation compositionists (those new, PhD in rhetoric and composition degree-holders) astonishingly-soon sounded the same alarms ("there's no room in composition for classrooms, students, teaching, or just writing about just teaching") that I had heard from newly-made-friends who were first-generation compositionists (those who created our field but held PhD degrees in Literature).

In my evangelical, convert-to-the-field's enthusiasm, I assumed first-generation complaints were the results of simple burn-out. But when is burn-out ever simple? As my peers evinced the same manifestations, I began to have a sense of *deja-vu*—vernacular was becoming oracular once again. "Non-literary writers will always fall short of the English department's highest value. A master discourse that reveres one kind of authorship and dismisses all others is bound to affect those kinds of authorship counted among the 'all others' category" (Stygall 321).

Professionalism in English Studies was not just blunting new-found fervor, it was dismantling much that I had come to care for—composition as community that writes also—for itself and its writing classrooms and writing students. For there is a trickle-down effect that Gail Stygall points out.

We tend to do to our students what is done to us. If we feel pushed toward writing a certain type of professional text, we will probably expect the same of our students: "Finding and keeping a 'good' job—that is, one on a tenure line—means publishing. Tenure decisions often mean the application of the author function to scholarly writing. Accordingly, the basic writer in an English department faces not only an object of study regulated by the author function but also teachers who are similarly regulated" (325). Stygall here is using the author function to remind us that founders of our discursivity—be they expressivist or social-constructivist—will be guides for our initiation into our communities and also regulators of our behaviors, often our writing behaviors—and our "tenurable" behaviors.

> However, when we study writers, we tend to treat the teaching part of their lives and careers either as never having existed or as being incidental to the "real work" . . . This attitude carries with it New Criticism's haughty dismissal of biographical criticism, actually, but it also carries with it the idea that when Frost (for instance) taught, he was merely allowing people to be in his presence, his writerly presence. He wasn't really a "teacher." (Ostrom 94)

To reprise. Years 1–5, I move from avid creative writer to creative writer who found the field treacherous, heart-breaking, unsympathetic to an engaged writer who teaches but is confused about this teaching thing. That is, I moved from the mountain tops of oracular to the plains of vernacular. No surprise, because attention to teaching was not advocated by creative writers who were busy accessing English Studies heaven (or nirvana, or Mount Olympus, or at least full-professor-dom). Years 5–10 I spent in adjunct limbo—wandering, wondering where to go. Years 10–15 in novitiate's bliss, I engaged the imagined enemies, threw myself into the ring along with my hat, and tried to affect my profession by becoming a teacher who writes about teaching. I was waist-deep in the vernacular.

Not having had a mentor in creative writing freed me (painfully) to enter the Burkean fray of composition where I expected good teachers to practice (I had been reading Elbow, Murray, Corder, Hairston and others who encouraged me to be a teacher who writes and a writer who teaches).

But then (insert if you wish a "lo and behold" here), slowly, the oracular re-ascended particularly during years 15–20, and I tried breathlessly to be not only tri-dialectical (literary, compositionist, and creative) but also thoroughly academic (and I am, but it's an every-day effort). When that paled, I found myself saying, I can survive. I'm lucky. I can be just a writer again. If I have to be.

Most odd, all the years, 1–20, I'm teaching. Teaching writing. Teaching writing as a writer. Wondering how it could be any other way. In part, The Many Cs got me there/here.

THE CURIOUS CASES OF MURRAY AND ELBOW AS
TEACHER-FUNCTIONS IN COMPOSITION

> When rhetorics come together seeking to occupy the same space at the same
> time, the encounter can be as sweet and gentle as two people making love,
> each turning this way and that, wanting to give, not to take, or as hard and
> hurtful as two tribes making war. The engagement of rhetorics can occur at
> any time, in any place. (Corder 99)

How like an other to be unexpectedly othered—I thought the rhetorics
of writer and teacher of writer could come together, make love not war. To
be composed as Ø.

I didn't think I was other. I thought I was right there in the middle of
composition studies. To get my PhD in Composition/Rhetoric, I studied
Flower and Hayes, linguistics, text-analysis; I was on the ground-floor of qual-
itative research. I was writer-teacher-WPA. I throve. And then I was other. I
was Elbow-influenced. I was Murrayesque. I was a student of cultural research
techniques bemused by the relentless rise of cultural studies. When colleagues talked about preparing students for democracy, I kept wanting to say
"civics?" Or—"I thought I was." Perversely, it feels, I'm interested in style, in
how I figure out what to say, and how I say it better—in writing. In how our
texts work with, for, and against us. I find the terms "critical" thinking and
"creative" writing first confusing, then disturbing.

I find myself trying to re-label myself. Dialogic. Examined process advocate. Social-rhetorical. Social-expressivist.

I teach myself theory—or at least voluntarily take myself by the scruff of
the collar into deeper conceptual waters. I say text instead of essay, author
instead of writer and, with the writing of this essay, I think I have even come
to understand and value the term author-function—at least I'm flinging it
around as if I do. It helps me see how easily I've been shell-gamed.

Always, I knew I wasn't *merely* or *simply* expressivist. I would qualify my
positions but those qualifications seem to go unheard or get lost in a termi-
nological flurry. "That's early Elbow; he wouldn't be willing to stay with that
position any longer," I'd snarl to myself at the back of a Many Cs presentation or while reading a sleight-of-hand essay that centrifuged me back to
the margins.

I watched as the expressivist position was attacked, dismantled, shipped
off safely to Boynton/Cook, to K-12, to minor conferences, to state journals.
But as Ø I still need a place to write from, a writer's identity; as a teacher, I
need to ask students to question the self they are constructing in their physical texts and in the actual classroom. And it was not until I realized that
Elbow and Murray, Murray and Elbow had become the bi-polar extremes of
the teacher-who-writes and the writer-who-teaches for social-constructionists,

in a manner that allowed them to dismiss these father figures, that I realized I needed a new place to stand.

In "The Death of the Author" Michel Foucault says: "It would be just as wrong to equate the author with the real writer as to equate him with the fictitious speaker; the author-function is carried out and operates in the scission itself, in this division and this distance" (205). That is what we—as a field—have done with our Murray and Elbow figures. For the real place to look, to understand Ø would be in that "scission" itself—the space between the two. Elbow and Murray are more than their early works and the spaces created by their names. They are people, and they are also game markers—argumentative tropes in the play of composition positioning: "It is easy to see that in the sphere of discourse one can be the author of much more than a book—one can be the author of a theory, traditions, or discipline in which other books and authors will in their turn find a place" (Foucault 206). They are both initiators of and victims of our discursivity.

When social-constructionists (yes, I am othering them throughout—though I'm not because I don't believe expressivism is without its strongly social aspects), use Murray and Elbow this way—as exemplars and representatives of the old, the worn-out, the self-centered expressivist partyline—such a use encourages us to diss their teacher-functions and find nothing in the space between the extremes we have characterized them by. We can dismiss them and move on to other agendas. Such agendas I fear have left the place to stand that I am labeling Ø in the compositionist dust.

WITH APOLOGIES TO FOUCAULT, WHAT ARE THE MODES OF EXISTENCE OF Ø?

> As the writing teacher engages in the act of writing, then, the teacher is reminded of the exigencies of being a student: How do I write it? When do I need to have this done? Is that what I really meant to say? Will my audience read it the way I intended? (Mongo A16)

It's not always easy or pleasant to be Ø. First, the writer or author is a position of authority within the academy (whereas the place of composition instructor so often is not). He is, Foucault claims, "a certain functional principle by which, in our culture, one limits, excludes, and chooses; in short, by which one impedes the free circulation, the free manipulation, the free composition, decomposition, and recomposition of fiction" (209). No surprise then that the genres—the fictions—that garner the most prestige in our system are the most difficult genres from which to fashion a writing life. We hear that someone wrote a successful first novel, never a successful first memo or program budget. We hear that a colleague also writes and publishes poetry, not that we received from him or her a pleasing Christmas card featuring his or her own work. We hear that some-one published his or her way out of administration, not that he or she put together an innovative, well-theorized and well-written syllabus to use when training new teachers of writing.

If we write within or without the academy, if we are employed writing teachers, our understanding of textual hierarchies always affects our sense of self-worth. It is hard to create the writing community we might wish for, though I'm amazed at how often those I know try to do so through department reading groups, manuscript clubs, local book clubs and writing/reading series. In my department, I have written with, for, or about every class I've taught. I have been a part of a faculty theory-reading-group, eavesdropped on the group that currently reads *Finnegan's Wake* together next door, have been pleased to be invited with ex-students to form a weekly poetry writing group that flourished for three years, have started a nonfiction group, have tried to find time to attend a freewriting group, have attended an informal-though-program-related rhetoric reading group, have enjoyed being invited to speak at my town's writer's association meeting and read in a local bar, and so on. When that is not enough, I turn to e-mail writing with/to/for composition friends and my long-term and ever-engaging co-authoring projects with Hans Ostrom. For me, being Ø is an ever-evolving process of finding places to stand and be counted, to matter as a writer who teaches and a teacher who writes.

I had to discover these modes and venues for Ø because when I started graduate school in the mid-1970s, writing was still remarkably product oriented—the relic of scholars or the obscured product of writers whose self-report left much to be imagined. Writing was something I was encul-turated to have-wanted-to-have-done, not something I was well-initiated into the doing of: "In our culture . . . discourse was not originally a prod-uct, a thing, a kind of goods; it was essentially an act—an act placed in the bipolar field of the sacred and the profane, the licit and the illicit, the religious and the blasphemous. Historically, it was a gesture fraught with risks before becoming goods caught up in a circuit of ownership" (Fou-cault 202).

At this time—and probably still today—owning writing reduces the risks (to those wealthy enough to do the owning), turns genres into sacred arti-facts, and creates a licit religion (literary criticism) and an illicit underclass (aspiring creative writers, teachers of writing who are not deemed good enough to be critics for whatever reasons, and ever and always, student writ-ers who are not even on the road to being considered for alter-personship).

To participate with such students then, as a writer-teacher, is a mark of debasement; to like to do so, as a teacher-writer, is a near-certain confirmation of one's inappropriateness for higher offices.

WHERE HAS Ø BEEN USED, HOW CAN IT CIRCULATE, AND WHO CAN APPROPRIATE IT FOR HIM[HER]SELF?

The figures of teacher-writer and writer-who-teaches have been contained in *CCC* (and elsewhere) by relegating him/her to safe and marginalized places: the citation, the staffroom interchange essay, the poem about classrooms. And these spaces have waxed and waned, come and gone with the sea-changes of opinion regarding the value of Ø in the profession.

Elbow and Murray were made safe by transformation into figures, by relegation to expressivist categories. Then, as the field professionalized, there followed a progression of diminishment and tuckings-away, a little like the nouveau riche habit of sticking the money-earning but foolishly-dressed grandfather in the back study, not introducing him to high society company where he might embarrass.

The workshop report constituted many of the early issues of *CCC* and then gave way to the academic essay. *CCC*, especially under William Irmscher from 1965 to 1973, reflects the change of identity. "We were still low-level administrators or apprentice teachers, and we were still concerned with shop-talk at the most mundane level, but we aspired to full scholarly status. The article was replacing the session report." (Lloyd Jones 48). Not surprisingly, these developments were shaped to a large degree by the journal's editors. "Macrorie, for example, explained during his tenure as editor [1962–1964] the journal wasn't scholarly because he wasn't" (Phillips et al. 448). Still, the journal editors who served on the Executive Committee of the CCCC were certainly responding to the aims of the elected officers of that body as well as to their own sense of composition as a growing discipline.

Under Richard Larson, *CCC* first printed bibliographic work, and began to fashion a history of the field; under Richard Gebhardt, the small type of the Staffroom Interchange (which provided a holding-space for praxis once the session report began to disappear) gave way to large, inclusionary-type; under Joe Harris, this practice continued but the pedagogical poem was dropped. Equal-type-face-size-for-all attempted to make it less clear that pedagogy was different than not-pedagogy though a recent issue on my desk suggests pedagogy will always remain to some degree circumscribed or will go unclaimed. It appears in a marked form—that of a Non-Tenure Track Faculty Special Interest Group publication, *Forum*—inserted midway through the current *CCC* volume. Highlighted but also marked off from the main journal by gray paper, this section contains reports, position statements and an Ø essay by Lisa Mongo.

Published in one of the last Staffroom Interchange sections, in May 1990, Toby Fulwiler writes about his own sense of the free circulation of writer-teacher and teacher-writer discourses: essentially, they don't. Or they don't without much effort, without rebellion against the community's preferred professional discourses—ones that do not look with favor on the writing teacher writing with, for, or to his writing students.

> It is clear to me that I write from within and, at the same time, from without an identifiable discourse community. Though this community almost always determines the topic of my writing, it does not necessarily determine its stance and style. Lately, these features of my voice seem to be at odds with the norm within my own community—which, like all academic communities, has adopted a specialized discourse that makes it difficult for eighteen-year-olds to enter and participate. The most identifiable features of my public voice are constructed to resist what I see as the exclusionary use of language by my own discourse community. (Fulwiler 220)

Just so. Who appropriates what voice and for what purposes? I am neither Fulwiler nor eighteen, but somewhat in his spirit I had to ask myself just two nights ago, exactly what this sentence (not from *CCC* but from a composition journal) means? And why it was made:

> While Pratt's notion of contact zone has been useful in interrogating how teachers exercise power and authority, especially in the multicultural classroom, some compositionists have tended to deploy it in such a way as to defend a kind of liberal pluralism, thereby subverting attempts to come to terms with the truly colonizing effects of the pedagogical scenario. (Olson 47)

For me, the sentence, I realized, had no clothes, and no heart (no organs at all, no human substance) no place for the interested writer/reader/teacher in me to stand. (I was tempted to leave this un-cited—since I'm interested in vocabulary, register, and style, not in naming the writer who will no doubt recognize himself as someone, contrary to Fulwiler above, intentionally *not* interested in this piece in inviting eighteen-year-olds to enter the sentence).

And yes, my response to this representative sentence raises some questions: Is my response purely personal—a matter of taste? Am I enacting an exclusivity against which I've been arguing?

Well, taste is never purely personal; it is social. Paradoxically, the very notion of personal taste is, as Bourdieu has demonstrated, a feature of bourgeois culture. Also, in articulating my response to the sentence, I do not leap to the conclusion that *CCC*—or *JAC* where it appeared—should exclude such sentences, such figures-of-author they represent. That conclusion would be folly anyway because, for the foreseeable future, *CCC* will prefer such sentences, such figures, such rhetoric, for the persona of *CCC* is "professional," with all the accompanying encodedness the word suggests. Indeed, claims of "reverse-exclusivity" are about as pertinent as claims of "reverse-discrimination" in multicultural or gender debates. Mostly they are a well-worn rhetorical tactic employed by the dominant group, for which reverse-exclusivity and reverse-discrimination, even if they actually existed, form no threat to continuing dominance.

So when I say such a sentence has no clothes, I am not being merely personal, nor am I on the attack. I am on the inquiry, asking, Who—what figure of author—is speaking? To what figure of reader? For what social purpose (in the society of *CCC*)? And where in this tactical, strategic, figurative, social landscape, is there a place for Ø ?

WHAT ARE THE PLACES IN Ø WHERE THERE IS ROOM FOR POSSIBLE SUBJECTS?

What's wrong with this picture?

> We [creative writers] have entered the academy for reasons as diverse as our talents. Some of us relish teaching and the conversation about literature, while others merely grab our paychecks and rush back to our keyboards. Some are drawn to the university as the last sanctuary for books in a marginally literate culture. Some of us come here to escape loneliness. Others linger in the academy simply because, after eighteen or twenty years of schooling, we cannot imagine living anywhere else. (Sanders 1)

[*Hint:* Creative writers are first and foremost writers—no better or worse than you or me—no less challenged than are writers of "non-literary" genres. No more or less likely to shirk work or perform well, no more or less lonely or elitist or intellectual than the rest of us. Simply, they write in different, not better, genres. Therefore, we need to argue for appropriate conditions for all teachers of writing that would adequately support them as writers.]

WHO CAN ASSUME THE VARIOUS SUBJECT-FUNCTIONS OF Ø?

Q: What happens when one considers him or herself as Ø?

> It was a remarkable experience—to wear the shoe on the other foot and be a student again. For one thing, I realized how much more I enjoy

learning now than I did at 20 when my future loomed before me like a huge, unmarked field . . . I have more of life to draw upon and more laurels to rest upon, as needed. These assets, I've found, are shared by other over-30 adults—even if, like many of my returning students, their extra writing experiences are mainly in letter or report writing. (Schwartz 203)

A: She finds she has something to say.

When I write, I become a student of the writing itself. Writing is a form of exploration and discovery, and the act of writing puts every writer in the student-learner position. Perhaps that is what's so scary about being an academic who also writes for a paying audience: the relinquishment of authority. (Mongo A16)

A: She finds she is a life-long learner. And that she can't always control the classroom of her own learning.

You know, it became tremendously complicated working on this [class written] story. And it became necessary to have people over the shoulders of people reminding each other of what was going on. Saying, "We can't do that, remember, he lost that thing in the last chapter. We can't use it." Usually when you're writing you've got all that in your mind, But this, we had to have it all in our minds. Someday, somebody will do a thesis on this style. That's why I've kind of kept all this stuff, so that somebody can go through and look at it, not in terms of whether the book is a great book, but just as a way of teaching, an important way of teaching. (Kesey, qtd. in Knox-Quinn 317)

A: He finds the expressivist position is not solitary, unitary, nor certain.

And our prose is supposed to be deliberate, not ragged and "hastily put together." These quotes, all reactions I have gotten from readers, amount to a demand for greater coherence. And more than once I have dutifully tried to respond: opened the file, poised hands above the keyboard, ready to beat the edges of my prose into a seamless unity. Each time, however, something stops me; I play about the edges, change a word or phrase, but then I change it back, close the file, go away. (Geisler 51)

A: But it's not a simple happy ending. She finds it can still be ego-threatening and can stop her writing as well as start it. It can be, as I have found it to be while writing this essay, one of the most difficult self-assigned tasks on the planet, one that makes housework and childcare (and yes, even public speaking and administration) seem like a snap. But still, she writes about it, about writing.

WHAT DIFFERENCE DOES IT MAKE WHO IS SPEAKING?

If we see ourselves as complicit in Ø and inquirers about Not- Ø—we could populate the wasteland, for it is no longer wasted, no longer some fancy-sounding "scission" between dismissable and static-feeling father figures: the authorized writer-teacher and teacher-writer. We open a space for ourselves as respectable practitioners, we sidestep some really debilitating academic positioning. Perhaps we can even attend to our writing classrooms as sites of learning and joy. Donald Murray claims "We become what we write. That is one of the great magics of writing" (71). And Ken Kesey believes "This [co-authoring with a class] became a wonderful fun thing to do" (Knox-Quinn 317).

As a card-carrying Ø, I find it functional to believe them—it helps me in my work. I would welcome other writing teachers to what for me is an imaginable parlor—so they have an opportunity to experience "this—this"—to become part of a company of writer-scholar-teachers who aim to make their practices more pleasurable.

A final question (or is it a plea?)—consider this "other"—what Ø might be like for you, if you aim to strike that key within the Many Cs?

> Life experience and writing success notwithstanding, I was surprised at my own vulnerabilities as a writer. Many of my fears, confusions, and needs were not as different from my younger counterparts as I would have predicted. Remembering "what it was like" as a student writer—and recording in my journal what worked and didn't work for me and for my classmates—has altered my teaching as well as my writing. (Schwartz 203–04)

POST-SCRIPT: AT PLAY IN THE FIELDS OF OUR WORDS

I don't know about you, but I learn from readers and reviewers, even when they make me gnash my teeth or seem to agree too easily without really challenging me (definitely not the case with this essay). The following thoughts came to me from the readers' critiques of my critique. First, our discussions about positions and places and pedagogies and communities is sometimes as simple as this: we're probably all better off labeling ourselves, if it serves a purpose. But we ought to be more careful about whom we label as Other. This on the analogy of "I can make fun of my family, but don't you try it."

Second, this essay—this try, attempt, investment of attention to issues that concern me enough to wake me up with revision in mind—has drawn to a close. As I leave the textual stage, of course, I should say what I would like to see, not just what I have seen or sensed.

I believe more writing about our writing could help in several ways. I look for research, essays, stories, narratives, position papers, dialogues, poems, journal notes, plays, memos, field reports, where:

- Writing teachers compose in student and school genres (and report back);

I look for a field that promotes:

- A sharing of drafts of writing in scholarly genres—allowing us to examine aims, audiences, tropes, styles, tastes, stances, and beliefs;

That offers:

- More articulations overall of the processes and products of those writing in non-literary genres;

That encourages:

- discussion of authorial personas and professional rhetorics of style, of authorship as an actual as well as a theoretical experience.

Perhaps you are already doing this? Did you not know I wanted to know about it? I do.

And authors, can we leave a richer composing audit trail? Can we profitably show each other our scholarly construction-work? Let the seams seem? Use endnotes for opening out our understandings as much as for supporting and cementing?

Finally, is it really time to put the pre- and post- on everything or isn't there a lot more learning to be done and versions and visions to be explored?

REFERENCES

Brent, Doug. *Reading as Rhetorical Invention: Knowledge, Persuasion, and the Teaching of Research-Based Writing.* Urbana: NCTE, 1992.

Bourdieu, Pierre. *Distinction: A Social Critique of the Judgment of Taste.* Trans. Richard Nice. Cambridge: Harvard UP, 1984.

Corder, Jim W. "From Rhetoric into Other Studies." *Defining the New Rhetorics.* Eds. Theresa Enos and Stuart C. Brown. Newbury Park: Sage, 1993. 95–105.

Fishman, Stephen M. and Lucille Parkinson McCarthy. "Is Expressivism Dead?" *College English* 54 (1992): 647–61.

Frey, Olivia. "Beyond Literary Darwinism: Women's Voices and Critical Discourse." *College English* 52 (1990): 507–26.

Foucault, Michel. "What Is an Author?" *Modern Criticism and Theory: A Reader.* Ed. David Lodge. New York: Longman, 1988. 197–210.

Fulwiler, Toby. "Looking and Listening for My Voice" (Staffroom Interchange). *CCC* 41 (1990): 214–20.

Gradin, Sherrie L. *Romancing Rhetorics: Social Expressivist Perspectives on the Teaching of Writing.* Portsmouth: Boynton, 1995.

Geisler, Cheryl. "Exploring Academic Literacy: An Experiment in Composing." *CCC* 43 (1992): 39–54.

Haake, Katherine. "Claiming Our Own Authority." *AWP Chronicle* 22 (2): 1–3.

Hatlen, Burton. "Michel Foucault and the Discourse[s] of English. *College English* 50 (1988): 786–801.

Hult, Christine. "Over the Edge: When Reviewers Collide." *Writing on the Edge* 5.2 (1994): 24–28.

Lloyd-Jones, Richard. "Who We Were, Who We Should Become." *CCC* 43 (1992): 486–96.

Lunsford, Andrea. "Toward a Mestiza Rhetoric: Gloria Anzaldua on Composition and Post-coloniality." *JAC* 18 (1998): 1–27.

Lyne, William. "White Purposes." *Genre and Writing: Issues, Arguments, Alternatives.* Wendy Bishop and Hans Ostrom, eds. Portsmouth: Boynton, 1997. 73–80.

Knox-Quinn, Carolyn. "Collaboration in the Writing Classroom: An Interview with Ken Kesey." *CCC* 41 (1990): 309–17.

Mongo, Lisa. "'I Teach Writing': Writing as Teacher in the Field of Composition." *Forum.* (Winter 1998): A16–18. Special Section of *CCC* 49.1 (Feb. 1998).

Murray, Donald M. "All Writing Is Autobiography." *CCC* 42 (1991): 66–74.

———. "A Preface on Rejection." *Writing on the Edge* 5.2 (1994): 29–30.

O'Donnell, Thomas. "Politics and Ordinary Language: A Defense of Expressivist Rhetorics." *College English* 59 (1996): 423–39.

Olson, Gary. "Encountering the Other: Postcolonial Theory and Composition Scholarship." *JAC* 18 (1998):45–55.

Ostrom, Hans. "Countee Cullen—How Teaching Rewrites the Genre of 'Writer'". *Genre and Writing: Issues, Arguments, Alternatives.* Wendy Bishop and Hans Ostrom, eds. Portsmouth: Boynton, 1997. 93–104.

Phillips, Donna Burns, Ruth Greenberg, and Sharon Gibson. "College Composition and Communication: Chronicling a Discipline's Genesis." *CCC* 44 (1993): 443–65.

Sanders, Scott Russell. "The Writer in the University." *AWP Chronicle* 25 (1992): 1, 9–13.

Scholes, Robert. *Textual Power: Literary Theory and the Teaching of English.* New Haven: Yale UP, 1986.

Schwartz, Mimi. "Wearing the Shoe on the Other Foot: Teacher as Student Writer." *CCC* 40 (1989): 203–10.

Seitz, James. "Roland Barthes, Reading, and Roleplay: Composition's Misguided Rejection of Fragmentary Texts." *College English* 53 (1991): 815–25.

Stygall, Gail. "Resisting Privilege: Basic Writing and Foucault's Author Function." *CCC* 45 (1994): 320–41.

QUESTIONS FOR REFLECTION, JOURNAL WRITING, AND DISCUSSION

1. Bishop suggests that one reason why some "compositionists" may reject expressivism is a "perceived (and often actual) need to appear ever-more scholarly, historical, and theoretical." Do you think this is true?

2. Bishop says it is difficult to affirm oneself as a teacher "within an institution that valorizes almost every other role first." Do you agree with this description of institutions of higher education?

3. Bishop says "I can no more imagine being a writing teacher who does not write than I can imagine being one who does not read." Do you agree?

4. Bishop says that we could consider our writing classrooms as "sites of learning and joy." Do you consider your writing classroom to be that sort of place? Do your students?

Credits

Lee Ann Carroll, "Pomo Blues: Stories from First Year Composition," *College English*, Volume 59, Number 8. Copyright 1997 by the National Council of Teachers of English. Reprinted with permission.

Peter Elbow, "The Process of Writing: Growing," from WRITING WITHOUT TEACHERS by Peter Elbow, copyright © 1973, 1998 by Peter Elbow. Used by permission of Oxford University Press, Inc.

Mary Soliday, "Translating Self and Difference Through Literacy Narratives," *College English*, Volume 56, Number 5. Copyright 1994 by the National Council of Teachers of English. Reprinted with permission.

Min-Zhan Lu, "From Silence to Words, Writing as Struggle," *College English*, Volume 49, Number 4. Copyright 1987 by the National Council of Teachers of English. Reprinted with permission.

Roni Natov, "Listening for Difference." An original article first being published in *Dialogue on Writing: Rethinking ESL, Basic Writing, and First-Year Composition,* edited by Geraldine DeLuca, Len Fox, Mark-Ameen Johnson, and Myra Kogen. © 2002 by Lawrence Erlbaum Associates, Inc., Publishers.

Mark Ameen Johnson, "ESL Tutors: Islands of Calm in the Multicultural Storm." An original article first being published in *Dialogue on Writing: Rethinking ESL, Basic Writing, and First-Year Composition,* edited by Geraldine DeLuca, Len Fox, Mark-Ameen Johnson, and Myra Kogen. © 2002 by Lawrence Erlbaum Associates, Inc., Publishers.

Ellie Friedland, "Writing Alive." An original article first being published in *Dialogue on Writing: Rethinking ESL, Basic Writing, and First-Year Composition,* edited by Geraldine DeLuca, Len Fox, Mark-Ameen Johnson, and Myra Kogen. © 2002 by Lawrence Erlbaum Associates, Inc., Publishers.

Gary A. Olson, "Toward a Post-Process Composition," pages 7–15, from *Post-Process Theory: Beyond the Writing-Process Paradigm* edited by Thomas Kent. © 1999 by the Board of Trustees, Southern Illinois University. All rights reserved. Printed in the United States of America. Reprinted by permission.

C. H. Knoblauch and Lil Brannon, Reprinted from *Rhetorical Traditions and the Teaching of Writing* by C.H. Knoblauch and Lil Brannon. Copyright © 1984 by Boynton/Cook Publishers, Inc. Published by Boynton/Cook, a subsidiary of Reed Elsevier Inc., Portsmouth, NH. Used by permission of the publisher.

Index

A

Abercrombie, M. L. J., 72, 73, 77, 80
academic boot camp, 9
academic discourse (writing), 239, 293
academic English, 164
academic stories, 118–119
   context constraints, 123–127
   conventions and details, 122–123
   culturally available, 120–122
   interesting, 128–131
   non-narratives vs. personal narratives,
     127–128
accommodationist, 90
acculturation, 4–5, 66–67, 158. *See also*
   reacculturation
ADE. *See* Association of Departments of
   English (ADE)
Adjunct Advocate, 402
adult education, 6, 91, 93, 97
advanced writing, 64
Alger, Horatio, 440, 441
Allen, Bob, 323–324, 336, 337
Alliance for Computers and Writing,
   411, 425
American Association for Higher
   Education, 425
American counterculture, 20
analyzing, 13, 14–15, 17
Angelou, Maya, 38
Anson, Chris, 297, 329, 337, 342, 387
Anzaldúa, Gloria, 249, 333–336, 337, 452
argumentation, 127, 139, 235
Aronowitz, Stanley, 398, 405
Arthur, S., 268

artificial intelligence, 390
Aspects (software program), 418
assessment, 246, 299–310, 311–312, 320. *See
   also* CUNY Writing Assessment Test
assimilation, 166, 167
Association of Departments of English
   (ADE), 378–379
Atlantic Creole, 5–6, 85–91
AT&T Diversity Team, 323–324
Austen, Jane, 20, 177
authentic voice, 116
authoritarian construct, 98–99
autobiographies, 38, 97–98, 143–145, 455.
   See also literacy narratives
The Autobiography of Malcolm X, 97
autoethnography, 165
auxiliary constructions, 89

B

back-to-basics course, 33, 91
bad language, 360
Baig, Edward C., 401, 405
Baker, Richard, 139, 226
Bakhtin, M. M., 168, 169
Balicki, Mark, 213, 214, 223, 230
Bambara, Toni Cade, 442
banking concept of education. *See under*
   education
Bank Street Writer II, 415
Barlow, John Perry, 387, 405
Bartholomae, David, 29, 429
   basic reading course, 3
   basic writing course, 2, 411
   cultural identity, 158, 169

ENFI project, 411–412
error studies, 32
invent the university, 116, 133, 368, 373
language usage, 3
narratives, 8, 136
social constructionism, 448, 449, 450
Ways of Reading, 117, 133
basic reading and writing, 29
basic skills, 60, 61, 63
basic writing, 29–50, 166, 409–429
Bata, E. J., 280, 286
Bateson, Mary Catherine, 160, 169
Batschelet, Margaret, 414, 415, 429
Batson, Trent, 417, 429
Beach, Richard, 160, 169, 268
becoming a writer, 135–140
The Bedford Guide for College Writers, 326, 331
Belanoff, Pat, 197, 246, 299, 311–312,
    315, 449
Bell, Marvin, 447
Beloved (Morrison), 123
Benesch, Sarah, 369, 373
Benjamin, Walter, 188–189, 197
Berlin, James, 115, 120, 127, 133, 448,
    450, 451
Berthoff, Ann, 188, 197, 346, 357
Bialostosky, Don H., 128
bidialectalists, 90
bilingualism, 162
biographical criticism, 459
Birkerts, Swen, 405
Bishop, Wendy, 341, 343–344, 447, 469
Bizzell, Patricia, 158, 169, 369, 434, 444,
    448, 450
Blackberry Winter (Mead), 38
Black English, 84, 99, 162, 163, 166
Black Skin, 21
Black Studies, 83
*Blair Resources for Teaching Writing: English as
    a Second Language,* 364
Bleich, David, 266
Blitz, Michael, 444
Bloom, Lynn Z., 429, 448
Blum, Ruth Von, 416
Blumenstyk, Goldie, 395, 405
Bolter, Jay, 418
Borderlands/La Frontera (Anzaldúa), 333
Borger, Irene, 216, 221, 226, 228, 231
Boston Living Center, 213–216
Bourdieu, Pierre, 457, 468
brainwashing, 303, 304
Brand, Alice, 447
Brannon, Lil, 243, 245, 251, 267, 268, 434

breaking the mold, 54–61
Brent, Doug, 449, 455, 468
Bridge to Terabithia, 117
Bridwell, Lillian S., 268
Bridwell-Bowles, Lillian, 448
Britton, James, 95, 102, 339, 348, 357
Brodkey, Linda, 161, 168, 169
Broken English, 5, 84, 99
Brontë, Emily, 177
Brooke, Robert, 448
Brooke, Robert E., 166, 169
Brooks, Elaine, 247–248, 311
Brown, H. D., 279, 287
Brown, Stuart C., 468
Broyard, Anatole, 216, 225, 231
Bruce, C. Bertram, 413, 429
Bruffee, Kenneth A., 4, 5, 63, 80, 352,
    357, 448
Bruner, Jerome, 16
Bullock, Richard, 444
Bump, Jerome, 405
Burgess, T., 357
Burke, Carolyn L., 159, 170
Burke, Kenneth, 173, 181, 183, 185
Burt, M. K., 280, 282, 285, 287

C

CAC. *See* computer-assisted
    composition (CAC)
CAI. *See* computer-aided instruction (CAI)
Cameron, Julia, 188, 197
Camp, Roberta, 309,310
Campbell, William E., 405
Campus Compact, 434, 435
The Canterbury Tales, 200
Carr, Jean Ferguson, 337
Carroll, Lee Ann, 8, 115, 139, 243
Cassidy, Frederic G., 87, 90, 91
casual writing. *See* informal writing
Catcher in the Rye (Caulfield), 38
Cather, Willa, 102
Caulfield, Holden, 38
Cavalcanti, M. C., 280, 287
The Centered Teacher (Hendricks), 113
Césaire, Aimé, 17
Charlie and the Chocolate Factory, 395
Chiseri-Strater, Elizabeth, 367, 373
Cicognani, Anna, 400, 405
City University Writing Assessment Test
    (CWAT), 311, 313, 314, 317
Clark, Gregory, 369, 373
classifying, 13, 14, 17

classroom politics, 113
Cleaver, Eldridge, 20
Cliff, Michelle, 162, 167, 169
Clinton, Bill, 92
A Clockwork Orange, 327
Cloze tests, 45
clustering, 436
CMC. *See* computer-mediated
    communication (CMC)
Cobb, Jonathan, 64, 67, 69, 80
Cockney, 89–90
Cohen, A. D., 280, 287
Cohen, Michael, 416
coherence, 48
cointentional education, 99
Coles, Nicholas, 158, 169
Coles, William E., Jr., 29
collaborative education, 4, 404, 426, 427.
    See also educational collaboration
*Collaborative Learning: Higher Education,
    Interdependence, and the Authority of
    Knowledge* (Bruffee), 4
collaborative reacculturation, 69
college writing test, revision of, 55–57
Collins, Terence G., 341–342, 409, 412, 429
color blind society, 189
colorful writing, 126
The Color Purple (Hawthorne), 157
Coming of Age in Samoa (Mead), 38
CommonSpace, 418, 421
communicative approaches to writing,
    279–280, 281, 285–286
community-less course, 398
community service, 342–343, 433–444
comparing, 13, 14, 17
competence vs. fluency, 32
composing style, 35
Composition and Resistance (Knoblauch),
    441, 444
computer-aided instruction (CAI), 422
computer-assisted composition (CAC), 422
computer-assisted programming, 390
computer-mediated communication
    (CMC), 422
constructive criticism, 77
contact zone
  Bruffee in, 4
  classroom effects, 137–138, 249,
    340–341, 373
  definition of, 4
  literacy stories and, 158–159
  negative effects of, 248, 323–337
  pluralism and, 464

*Contending With Words: Composition and
    Rhetoric in a Postmodern Age* (Harkin &
    Schilb), 115
Contending With Words (Bialostosky), 128
conventional usage, 7
conversation
  arena for, 68
  constructive, 72
  reacculturation and, 71, 72
Cooper, Charles, 45, 358
copy-editing, 263–264, 265. *See also* editing
Corbett, E. P. J., 287
Corder, Jim W., 447, 448, 455, 459, 460, 468
Cosmopolitan, 126
Cotton, Debbie, 434, 444
cover letter, 297
"cover the material," 6, 99, 370
Covino, William A., 235, 240
creative writing, 348, 465
Creed, Tom, 395, 405
Creole, 84, 99, 162
creole hypothesis, 85
critical awareness, 15
critical consciousness, 4, 435, 436, 442
critical literacy, 92, 120. *See also* literacy
*Critical Literacy: Politics, Praxis, and
    the Postmodern* (McLaren &
    Lankshear), 130
critical pedagogy, 442
critical reading, 98, 283, 284
critical teaching, 55, 311, 342–343, 433–444
Critical Teaching and the Idea of Literacy
    (Knoblauch & Brannon), 434
critical thinking, 91, 95–96, 125, 126, 127,
    235, 339
Crooks, Robert, 435, 444
Crosman, Inge, 269
cross-cultural dialogue, 102, 360. *See also*
    transcultural dialogue
Crowley, Sharon S., 377, 410, 429
cultural change, 66, 67
cultural identity, 158, 194
cultural interdependence, 168–169
Cultural Revolution, 173
culture. *See also* acculturation;
    multiculturalism
  availability of academic stories, 120–122
  change in, 66, 67
  diverse stimulation of, 92–93
  identity of, 158, 169, 194
  interdependence of, 168–169
The Cultures of Computing (Star), 402
Cummings, e. e., 348

CUNY Writing Assessment Test, 247, 300, 310, 311, 312, 318. *See also* City University Writing Assessment Test (CWAT)
Curricular Transformation and Technology in Developmental Education, 409
CWAT. *See* City University Writing Assessment Test (CWAT)
cyber-conferences, 428
cyborg writing, 237, 238

D

Daedalus Integrated Writing Environment (DIWE), 418, 421
D'Agostino, Karen Nilson, 414, 429
Daiker, Donald A., 374, 429
Daly-Miller measure, 48
Dance to the Piper and Promenade Home: A Two-Part Autobiography (de Mille), 221
D'Angelo, Frank J., 33
Dante, 201, 206
D'Arcy, P., 358
The Dark Wind (Hillerman), 194
Das, B. K., 287
David Copperfield, 179
Davis, John, 213, 214
Dean, Rosemary, 299, 310
Dean, Terry, 158, 170
decision making, 49
decoding, 96
deconstruction, 96, 106
decreolization, 85
deficit model, 99, 363, 370
Deleuze, Gilles, 189, 197
Delve, Cecilia I., 444
de Mille, Agnes, 221
Democracy and Education (Dewey), 92
democracy through language, 93
democratic construct, 99
democratic schooling, 56, 91
Denry, Fabien, 214, 219
developmental writing, 57, 143, 145, 415
Dewey, John, 6, 68, 80, 92, 102
diagnostic essay, 314
dialectal differences, 2, 84, 162, 164
dialogic pedagogy, 55, 311
The Dialogic Imagination (Bakhtin), 168
diary for writing, 144–145, 150, 348
dichotomous character, 168
"Dick and Jane" sentences, 206, 291
Dickens, Charles, 177, 179
Dillard, J. L., 85, 91

Dillon, David, 267, 268
DiPardo, Anne, 167, 170
diphthongs, 89
Discovery of Competence (Kutz, Groden, & Zamel). *See under* Zamel, Vivian
distance learning, 339, 342, 393, 398–400
Distinction (Bourdieu), 457
Divine Comedy (Dante), 201
DIWE. *See* Daedalus Integrated Writing Environment (DIWE)
Dorothy, M., 338
Dorothy *(Wizard of Oz),* 131
Douglass, Frederick, 157, 161
Downs, Judy R., 417, 429
The Drama of the Gifted Child (Miller), 107
Dreaming in Cuban (Garcia), 162
"Dry September" (Faulkner), 94
DuBois, W. E. B., 162
Dulay, H., 280, 285, 287

E

Early, Gerald, 166, 170
Eastern writing forms, 138
editing, 36, 40–41, 280. *See also* manuscript editing
   diligence in, 153, 155
   essence of, 154
   purpose of, 153
   vs. re-writing, 36
Educating Rita, 157
education
   banking concept of, 4, 7, 106
   ideal aim of, 68
   rich students vs. poor students, 1–2
educational collaboration, 71, 74–75, 80
Educational Testing Service (ETS), 303, 305, 307, 309
Elbow, Peter, 197, 358
   believing game, 268
   draft revision, 296–297
   expressionism of, 138, 139, 344, 449, 450, 451, 460, 463
   feedback parameters, 229
   free writing, 135–136, 352
   high-stakes/low-stakes writing, 245–246, 289
   ideal medium for error, 279
   meaning, 347
   private writing, 294
   process of writing, 141
   Roni Natov and, 188
   teacher-who-writes, 453

testing and, 248
writer-teacher and teacher-writer, 447, 459, 461
Eldred, Janet Carey, 157, 161, 170, 404, 406
Electronic Networks for Interaction (ENFI), 417–418
electronic writing classroom, 395
Ellison, Ralph, 100, 102
e-mail, 394, 396, 397, 421, 422
Emig, Janet, 346, 358, 447, 449
Emma, 391
emotional analysis, 110–111
employee entrance exams and literacy, 66
Empowering Education (Shor), 4, 311
empowerment, 188, 402
encoding vs. decoding, 44
Encyclopaedia Britannica, 207
ENFI. *See* Electronic Networks for Interaction (ENFI)
ENFI Consortium Project, 411
English
    Chinese vs. (home vs. outside world), 174–184
    history of, 7, 99–100
English as second language (ESL). *See* ESL
English Coalition Conference (1987), 93, 97
Enlightenment, 122, 234
Enos, Theresa, 468
Enrichment Curriculum (FIPSE project), 162
Epiphany Project, 425
eradicationists, 90
error analysis, 39–41, 48, 279–286
Errors and Expectations (Shaughnessy), 32, 42, 48
Escape From Freedom, 17
ESL
    faculty experiences with, 359–373
    interactive learning and, 401
    interlanguage usage, 245
    teaching strategies, 299, 340–341
    tutoring and, 438
    tutors for, 199–211
    writing evaluation, 247–248, 283, 311–320
essentialist view of language, 363
ethnographic research, 159, 160, 167, 367
ETS. *See* Educational Testing Service (ETS)
Eurocentrism, 168, 236
evaluation, 354–357. *See also* assessment
exploratory writing, 235
expository writing, 127
expressive writing, 339, 343, 348–350
expressivism, 466. *See also* free writing

authenticity, 138–139, 341
critique of, 450–451
social construction vs., 448, 457, 460
understanding of life and, 139
Eyre, Jane, 179

F

facilitative response, 244, 260, 262–264
factory model of education, 396
Facts, Artifacts, and Counterfacts (Bartholomae & Petrosky), 3
Faigley, Lester, 115, 116, 133, 268, 353, 358, 448, 449
A Farewell to Arms, 14
Farrell, Thomas J., 37
Fathman, A., 281, 287
Faulkner, William, 94, 348
fear of exposure, 107
fear of failure, 26
fear of pedagogy, 107
feedback, 228–229, 280, 281, 305
feminist movement, 67
Fey, Marion Harris, 418, 429
Field, John P., 353
Finnegan's Wake, 462
Fish, Stanley, 249, 337
Fishman, Stephen M., 291, 450, 468
Flannery, Kathryn, 116, 133
Flowers, Linda, 35
fluency, 32, 203
Focus, 323, 324, 325, 336, 337
Fonda, Jane, 113
formulaic essays, 6
Forum, 463
Foucault, Michel, 452, 461, 462, 469
Fox, Tom, 158, 170, 368, 369, 374
Fragments of Rationality: Postmodernity and the Subject of Composition (Faigley), 115, 116
France, Alan, 451
free writing, 135–136, 227
Freire, Paulo, 66, 80, 102, 114, 173, 185
    banking concept of education, 4, 117, 397
    critical consciousness development, 434
    culturally diverse stimulation, 92–93
    education and freedom, 105–106
    education model, 396–397
    language fluency, 69
    liberating education, 349, 358
    narration sickness, 6
    power relationships in classroom, 129
    problem-posing education, 33

Freisinger, Randall, 358
freshman composition, 8, 61, 64, 95
  CWAT and, 313, 314
  ESL students and, 311, 314, 315
  stories from, 115–133
  writing assessment results, 248, 312
Freshman English Director, 4, 63, 64
Freshman Skills Assessment Tests, 312
Frey, Olivia, 449, 468
friction-points, 167
Friedenberg, Edgar, 38
Friedland, Ellie, 138–139, 140, 213, 221
Friedman, Phil, 433, 444
From a Burning House (Borger), 228
Fromm, Erich, 17
Fulwiler, Toby
  influence on Wendy Bishop, 447
  listening, 469
  low-stakes writing, 291
  transactional writing, 339–340
  writer-teacher and teacher-writer, 464
  writing across the curriculum,
    345–357, 358
functional illiteracy, 1

G

Gabelnick, Faith, 436, 444
Gabriel, Trip, 396, 406
Garcia, Cristina, 162
Gay, Pamela, 369, 374, 414, 429
gay-bashing, 326
Gebhardt, Richard, 463
Geisler, Cheryl, 466, 469
George, E. Laurie, 411, 429
Gerrard, Lisa, 413, 416, 417, 430
Gibson, Sharon, 469
Gilyard, Keith, 5, 83, 137, 162, 166, 170
Giroux, Henry, 373, 374, 434
global errors, 282
Goldberg, Natalie, 188, 197, 219
Goodman, Yetta, 159, 170
Goswami, Dixie, 353, 358
Grabbe, Paul, 80
Gradin, Sherri L., 448, 450, 469
Graff, Gerald, 135, 372, 374
Graham, Martha, 221, 222
Grammatik, 421
grapholects, 90
Graves, R. L., 358
The Great Gatsby, 25
Greco, Norma, 436, 444
Greenberg, Ruth, 469

Greer, Colin, 440, 444
Groden, Suzy Q., 158, 170, 245, 321
Grolier's Encyclopedia, 422
group dynamics, 5
group solidarity, 79
Guattari, Felix, 189, 197

H

Haake, Katherine, 456, 469
habit-formation theories, 279–280
Hairston, Maxine, 137, 158, 170, 434,
    444, 459
Hamlet, 124
Hansman-Ferguson, Catharine Ann,
    415, 430
Haraway, Donna, 237, 238, 239, 240
Harding, Sandra, 236, 239, 241
Harkin, Patricia, 115, 133
Harris, Joe, 463
Harris, Joseph, 168, 170
Harris, Muriel, 302
Harrison, Gavin, 225
Harste, Jerome C., 159, 170
Hart, Gary, 92
hate speech, 325, 329, 330
Hatlen, Burton, 344, 452, 457, 469
Hawisher, Gail E., 390, 404, 406, 410, 411,
    417, 430
Hawkins, 356
Hawthorne, Nathaniel, 157, 161, 177
Hayes, John R., 35, 449, 460
HBJ Writer, 416. *See also* Writing AND
    Author's Helper (WANDAH)
Heath, Shirley Brice, 159, 170
hegemony, 111, 439
Hemingway, Ernest, 20, 102
Hendricks, Gay, 113, 114
Herrington, Anne, 291, 296
Herzberg, Bruce, 342–343, 433
Heterick, Robert, 401, 406
Hicks, Sandy Jean, 417, 430
The Hidden Injuries of Class (Sennett &
    Cobb), 64–65
high-stakes writing, 245, 246, 247, 289–298
Hillerman, Tony, 194, 195, 197
Hillocks, George, Jr., 135, 410, 430
Hirsh, Elizabeth, 241
historicism, 84
history of English. *See* English, history of
HIV/AIDS Writers Workshop, 213–231
Hodges, Elizabeth, 292, 297
Hoffman, Eva, 167–168, 169, 170

Hoggart, Richard, 161–162, 167, 170
Holdstein, Deborah, 403–404, 406
Holeton, Rich, 395, 406
holistic reading, 248
holistic scoring, 48, 50, 329
holistic testing, 304
Holm, John A., 85, 91
homophones, 89
Hooks, Bell, 197
Horner, Bruce, 369, 373, 374, 413, 430
Huckleberry Finn, 38
Hull, Glynda, 370, 371, 374
Hult, Christine, 451, 469
humanism, 102, 173
Hunger of Memory (Rodriguez), 158, 164, 165
Hurlbert, C. Mark, 444
hybridization, 164
hybrid space, 400
hypercorrection, 87, 89
hyperfiction, 419
hypertext, 391

I

iconoclastism, 111
the "ideal" text, 243–244, 253–255, 257,
    259–260, 268, 280
ideology, 111, 121, 240, 368–369, 400
I Know Why the Caged Bird Sings (Angelou), 38
The Iliad, 204
illiteracy
    functional, 1
    social forces and, 442–443
Illness as Metaphor (Sontag), 121
independent study, 396, 397, 398
individualism, 441
individualized learning, 397
The Inferno, 201
inflection, 86–89, 282
informal writing, 293, 344, 352
inner speech, 340, 348
in-process interventions, 414
inspiration, 142
intellectual improvisation, 187
interactive teaching style, 400, 401
Interchange (electronic discussion forum),
    421, 422
interlanguage, 245, 285, 286
intermediate writing, 202
Internet, 394, 421. *See also* World Wide Web
Internet chat lines, 396
Internet Explorer, 419
interpretation, 96

Intoxicated by My Illness (Broyard), 216, 225
Invest (tutorial program), 421
Invisible Man (Ellison), 17, 100
Irmscher, William, 463
"I-Search," 118, 126
Iser, Wolfgang, 266

J

Jaggar, Alison M., 111, 114
Jaspers, Karl, 17
Jefferson, Thomas, 6, 92
Johnson, Charlotte, 213, 214, 217
Johnson, Mark-Ameen, 138, 199
Jones, Rachel, 162, 170
journal writing, 20–21, 45–46, 117, 208, 224,
    225, 348, 350
Joyce, James, 348
Joyce, Michael, 418–419
juxtaposition, 88

K

Keller, Helen, 120
Kelly, Kevin, 405
Kennedy, X. J., 338
Kent, Thomas, 235
Kesey, Ken, 447, 466, 467
King Lear, 252, 391
Kingston, Maxine Hong, 165, 187, 189, 197
Kintgen, Eugene R., 437, 444
Kiparsky, C., 282, 287
Knight-Ridder Corporation, 394
Knoblauch, C. H., 243, 245, 251, 267, 268,
    434, 441–442, 444
knowledge vs. power, 58
Knox-Quinn, Carolyn, 466, 467, 469
Kozol, Jonathan, 437, 441, 444
Krashen, Stephen, 280, 285, 287, 314,
    317, 319
Kremers, Marshall, 411, 430
Krishnamurti, J., 105
Kroll, B., 286, 287
Kroll, Barry M., 437, 444
Kutz, Eleanor, 158, 170, 245, 321

L

Labov, William, 159, 170
Lambert, John, 437
Landow, George, 391, 406
Language and Learning (Britton), 95
language arts, 96, 97, 99

Lankford, Scott, 326–328, 329, 331, 332, 336, 338
Lankshear, Colin, 130, 133
Larkin, Joan, 193
Larson, Richard, 463
Laurence, Patricia, 40, 360, 374
LCD, 419, 422
League for Innovation in the Community College, 412, 420
learning by consensus, 72. *See also* educational collaboration
Learning Communities (Gabelnick et al.), 436, 444
LeBlanc, Paul, 390, 406, 411, 418, 430
LeClerc, Marc, 326
Lee, Felicia R., 167, 170
Lee, Spike, 97
Lees, E. O., 281, 287
LeFevre, Karen Burke, 448
Leichter, Hope Jensen, 159–160, 170
Lentricchia, Frank, 377
Lesko, P. D., 402, 406
Leslie, Peter, 214–215, 225
Lester, Nancy, 101
Let 100 Flowers Bloom, 436
Let's Flip the Script: An African American Discourse on Language, Literature, and Learning (Gilyard), 5
Levertov, Denise, 192
Levin, Kurt, 67, 80
Leyden, Peter, 394, 398, 406
A Life in School (Tompkins), 7
Limbaugh, Rush, 126, 334
liminal character, 168, 187
liminal crossings, 157
line-by-line analysis, 208
linguistics, 90, 284, 460
linguistic stage of development, 15–16, 363
Linnehan, Paul J., 417, 429
liquid crystal display (LCD). *See* LCD
listening, 187–195, 229, 244–245, 271–277
listservs, 396, 421, 428, 429
literacy
    challenging, 102
    mission of, 7, 92
    oppression and, 58
Literacy and Living (Neilsen), 157
literacy narratives, 136, 139, 157–169. *See also* autobiographies
literacy tutoring, 434, 437, 442. *See also* tutoring
literal comprehension, 45
literary criticism, 64, 457, 462

literature survey, 64, 95
Lives on the Boundary (Rose). *See under* Rose, Mike
Lloyd-Jones, Richard, 102, 463, 469
local area network, 411, 417
Lodge, David, 469
Lorde, Audre, 165
Los Angeles Times, 126
Lost in Translation (Hoffman), 167
Lott, Brett, 447
low-stakes writing, 245, 289–298
Lu, Min-Zhan, 137, 158, 162, 167, 170, 373, 374, 411, 430
Lunsford, Andrea, 102, 449, 452, 469
Lunsford, Ronald F., 390, 406
Lure and Loathing (Early), 166
Lyne, William, 449, 469
Lyotard, Jean-Francois, 238–239, 241

M

MacGregor, Jean, 444
MacLaine, Shirley, 113
Macrorie, Ken, 139, 150, 352, 358, 447, 463
Maher, Jane, 430
Malcolm X, 20, 120
Malcolm X, 97, 98
Man Made Language (Spender), 126
manuscript editing, 69–70
Maoism, 137, 173, 176, 181
Markussen, Randi, 402, 406
Martin, Nancy, 348, 355, 357, 358
Marxism. *See* Maoism
Marxism and Literature (Williams), 181
Marzana, R. J., 268
Massy, William F., 401, 406
Masters, Edgar Lee, 21
Matthews, Robert S., 444
Maxson, Jeffrey, 419, 430
Mayher, John S., 371, 374
McCarthy, Lucille B., 370, 374
McCarthy, Lucille Parkinson, 450, 468
McCorduck, Pamela, 391, 406
McCrimmon, James, 347, 358
McDonald, W. U., 267
McKay, Sandra Lee, 369, 374
McLaren, Peter L., 130, 133
McLeod, A., 357
Mead, Margaret, 38
meaning into language, 143
Meem, Deborah T., 415, 430
Melville, Herman, 106

Metzger, Deena, 188, 197
Microsoft Works, 421
Miller, Alice, 107, 114
Miller, Richard E., 248–249, 323
Miller, Susan, 35, 115, 116, 133
The Mill on the Floss, 21
Minot, Stephen, 447
Moffett, James, 38, 47, 308, 347, 358, 378, 447
Mongo, Lisa, 461, 464, 466, 469
monocultural ideals, 91
monumentalism, 168–169
Moran, Charles, 390, 398, 406, 411, 430
Morenberg, Max, 374
Morrison, Toni, 102, 123
Mortensen, Peter, 157, 170
Morton, Donald, 131, 134
Mosaic, 419
Moss, Beverly J., 158, 170
Mrs Stevens Hears the Mermaids Singing (Sarton), 215
MS Word, 416, 421
Mulligan, Bartley, 338
multiculturalism, 6, 100–102, 137, 158, 162, 167, 169, 188
multimedia, 391–394, 398
Murray, Donald M., 469
   expressivism, 449, 463
   facilitative response (gently critique), 246, 268
   influence on Wendy Bishop, 344, 447
   listen, don't talk, 244–245, 271–277
   process of discovery, 349, 358
   reflective writing, 451–452
   we are what we write, 467
   writer-who-teaches, 453, 455, 459, 460, 461
"My Kinsman, Major Molineux" (Hawthorne), 161
mythic explanation, 19

N

NADE. *See* National Association of Developmental Education (NADE)
narration sickness, 6
Narrative (Douglass), 157, 161
National Association for Educational Progress, 300
National Association of Developmental Education (NADE), 420, 525
National Council of Teachers of English, 6, 101–102

national Endowment for the Humanities, 425
National Geographic, 207
National Teacher's Examination (NTE), 303
Natov, Roni, 138, 187, 200
Naylor, Gloria, 162, 164, 170
negotiation, 262
Negroponte, Nicholas, 391, 392, 406
Neilsen, Lorri, 157, 159, 170
Nelson-Denny Reading Test, 42, 47, 48
Netscape, 419
networking, 404, 411
Neulieb, Janice, 372, 374
neutral curriculum, 130–131
Newkirk, Thomas, 404, 406
New Pathways program (Harvard University), 73
Newton, B., 358
New York Times, 166, 207
Nightmare on Elm Street, 332
Nobel Prize for Literature, 309
non-directive teaching, 273
nonverbal commentary, 226
Norton Textra Connect, 418, 421, 422
NTE. *See* National Teacher's Examination (NTE)
Nuruddin, Yusuf, 83

O

Odell, Lee, 358
O'Donnell, Thomas, 450, 451, 469
Ohmann, Richard, 30, 448
Olbrechts-Tyteca, L., 305, 310
Old English, 307
The Old Man and the Sea, 117
Olson, Gary A., 115, 119, 133, 139, 140, 233, 241, 464, 469
On Education (Krishnamurti), 105
On the Color Line: Networking to End Racism, 395
open admissions, 4, 63
   oppression and, 66–67, 372
   remedial programs and, 93
   teaching writing and, 65, 409
opportunistic rhetor, 165
oral literacy, 162
ordinary language (writing), 449, 455
O'Reilley, Mary Rose, 448
Organize (prewriting program), 417
Ortiz-Taylor, Sheila, 447
Ostrom, Hans, 459, 462, 469
The Other America, 21
overhead projector, 422

P

Papert, Seymour, 390–391
paradigm shift, 66
Parker, R., 358
Passages (Sheehy), 38
Patterson, Annette, 130, 133
Pedagogy of the Oppressed (Freire). *See under* Freire, Paulo
peer editing, 78
peer pressure, 75–77
Peregrinations (Lyotard), 239
Perelman, Chaim, 305, 310
performance teaching model, 7, 106–107
Perry, Bruce, 98
Perry, William G., Jr., 67, 80
personal computers, 390–391, 393, 394–395
personal language, 291
personal narratives, 8
personification, 98
Perspectives on Literacy (Kintgen, Kroll, & Rose), 437
persuasion, 95
Petrosky, Anthony, 3, 45, 117, 133, 411, 429, 447
Petry, Martha, 419, 430
Pew Higher Education Roundtable, 388, 389, 399, 406
Peyton, Joy Kreeft, 429
PFS Write, 421
phallogocentric writing, 139, 236, 237
Phillips, Donna Burns, 449, 453, 463, 469
The Philosophy of Literary Form (Burke), 173
phonology, 86, 89
pidgin, 84, 85
plagiarism, 79, 203, 204
Playing in the Dark (Morrison), 102
Plumb, J. H., 20
pluralistic democracy, 2
pluralists (pluralism), 6, 90, 330, 464
poetry reading, 192–193, 195
polyphony, 360
Poma, Guaman, 325
Ponsot, Marie, 299, 310
portfolio proficiency test, 300, 371
portfolio system, 246–247, 307–308, 389
Posey, Evelyn, 416
postmodern consciousness, 8
postmodernism
    academic, 131
    closure and, 130–131
    homogenization of, 119
    living in it, 131–132
objectivity and, 129
teaching of writing and, 115–117
theorizing and, 234
types of writing and, 127, 139
postmodern openness, 238
post-process theory, 139, 233–240, 449
postreading, 207, 208
Practical Criticism (Richards), 268
practice vs. preaching, 105
Pratt, Mary Louise
    autoethnography, 165
    contact zone, defense of pluralism?, 464
    contact zone, definition of, 4, 158–159, 373
    contact zone, pedagogical arts in, 170, 333, 338, 374
    contact zone, teaching in, 329–330
    dealing with conflicts, 324–325
prepackaged grammar lessons, 94
prereading, 207, 208
Prewrite (program), 417
Prince of Tides, 117
Prine, John, 17
Prior, Paul, 390, 406
private writing, 294
problematizing experience, 117–118, 120, 121, 124
problem-solving procedures, 35, 39
process analysis, 252
process of writing, 122, 274
    experiences and, 34, 275
    growing as a writer, 141–156, 347
    model of, 35
    post-process analysis, 233–235
    vocabulary and, 140
The Process of Education (Bruner), 16
professional writing, 293
professor vs. students, 78, 92
Progoff, Ira, 188, 197
proofreading, 284
propaganda, 92
Protest and Survive (Thompson and Smith), 59
Pygmalion, 68

Q

quotidian reality, 160, 161

R

Raimes, Ann, 244
    error analysis, 245, 279–286, 287, 321

facilitative response (gently critique), 246
ideological assumptions about ESL, 369, 374
range-finders, 48, 50
Rankin, Elizabeth, 448
Ranson, John Crowe, 456
rationalism, 127
Ray, Ruth, 371, 374
reacculturation, 67–68
  case study, 74–79
  extensions of, 74
  resistance to, 74–76
reader-response theory, 97, 266
The Reader, The Text, The Poem (Rosenblatt), 96
reading
  acculturation and, 69
  rules for, 207
  student development and, 185
Realtime Writer, 418
recreolize, 85
Rector, Lucinda, 395, 406
reductionism, 16, 168, 368
reflections, 115, 148, 343, 447–468
relativization, 168, 237
remedial programs, 2, 19, 29, 55, 93–94
remedial writing, 15–16, 64, 300, 402
repair-model instruction, 99
research reports, 127, 139
reverse-exclusivity, 465
revision, 265, 273, 281, 416
The Revolutionary Family, 179, 180–181, 183
rewriting, 36, 280
Reynolds, Mark, 413, 430
A Rhetoric of Motives (Burke), 183
rhetoric of assertion, 139, 233–240
Rich, Adrienne, 448
Richards, I. A., 268
Rickly, Rebecca, 418, 430
Rico, Gabrielle Lusser, 227, 231
Riordan, Mark K., 213, 214, 217
Robb, T., 280, 287
Roberts, Peter, 95, 102
Robertson, Linda R., 377
Rodriguez, Richard, 158, 162, 164, 165, 167, 171
Romancing Rhetorics (Gradin), 450
Romano, Susan, 418, 430
Rondinone. Peter, 162, 167, 170
Rorty, Richard, 66, 80, 234, 241
Rose, Mike
  academic discourse, 439–440

complex thought capability, 2
deficit model of language, 363, 368, 374
life choices, 162
literacy statistics, 1–2
Lives on the Boundary, 1, 2, 157, 171, 197, 370, 374, 437, 438, 439–440
training for veterans, 2–3, 9–27
writer-teacher and teacher-writer, 447, 449
Rose, Shirley K., 160, 171
Rosen, H., 357
Rosenblatt, Louise, 96, 102, 266, 268
Ross, S., 280, 287
Rubin, David L., 74–79
rule-governed systems, 6, 84
Russell, Ethel, 418, 430
Russian Formalism, 160

S

Salmon, Phillida, 160, 171
Salvatore, Mariolina, 337
Sanders, Scott Russell, 456, 465, 469
Sapir, E., 358
Sargent, M. Elizabeth, 291, 294
Sarton, May, 215, 231
SAT, 48, 263
satellite conferences, 428
Savage Inequalities (Kozol), 437, 438, 441
Savignon, S., 280, 287
The Scarlet Letter (Hawthorne), 178
Schafer, J., 286, 287
Schilb, John, 115, 116, 133
Scholes, Robert, 456, 469
Schwartz, Helen, 417
Schwartz, Mimi, 417, 466, 467, 469
scientific theorizing, 19
Scollon, Ron, 159, 171
Scollon, Suzanne B. K., 159, 171
script following, 117
Searle, Dennis, 267, 268
SEEN (prewriting program), 417
Seitz, James, 455, 469
self-analysis, 132
self-centeredism, 109
self-criticism, 177, 222–223, 227, 410
self-definition, 158
self-discipline, 141
Selfe, Cynthia L., 390, 395, 406, 411, 430
self-help groups, 69
self-mocking tone, 124
self-reflexivity, 336
self-representation, 158

self-sponsored writing. *See* expressive writing
self-translation, 158, 166
Sennett, Richard, 64, 67, 69, 80
Sense and Sensibility, 20
sense of correctness, 41
service learning. *See* community service
Severino, Carol, 168, 171
Sexton, Jack, 422, 430
Shaughnessy, Mina, 299, 310, 374, 430
    competence vs. fluency, 30, 32
    computers in basic writing, 412, 413
    coursework considerations, 368, 411
    lessons on life, 37
    open admissions and, 372, 410
    taxonomy of error (error types),
        42, 48, 245
    writer-teacher and teacher-writer, 449
Sheehy, Gail, 38
Shen, Fan, 162, 171
Shor, Ira, 100, 188, 197, 321
    basic writing test experiences, 4, 53–61,
        311, 320
    critical consciousness development, 434
    student performance and, 246
    writing assumptions, 2
Shortreed, I., 280, 287
*Silicon Snake Oil: Second Thoughts on the
        Information Highway* (Stoll), 396
Silverman, Larry, 421, 430
Simians, Cyborgs, and Women (Haraway), 237
Sirc, Geoffrey, 411, 430
situational conflict, 328
SkillsBank, 421
Sledd, James, 380, 381
Slevin, James F., 120, 133, 378–379
Slouka, Mark, 405
Smith, Barbara Leigh, 444
Smith, F., 282, 287
Smith, Frank, 32
Smith, John, 418
Smith, Karl A., 405
Smith, Summer, 390, 406
Smitherman, Geneva, 91
social constructionism, 139, 411, 448, 454,
        457, 460, 461
social imagination, 343
socialist consciousness, 176
Socialist Humanism, 17
sociolinguistic worlds, rift between, 161
Soliday, Mary, 136, 137, 138, 157
Sommers, Nancy, 267, 268, 447, 449
Sontag, Susan, 121

Souci, Jim, 213, 214
The Souls of Black Folk (Dubois), 162
Spack, Ruth, 364, 374
spelling checker, 424
Spellmeyer, Kurt, 115, 131, 133, 343,
        443–444
Spender, Dale, 126
Spooner, Michael, 448
Spoon River Anthology (Masters), 21
Stafford, William, 447
Stan, Susan, 341–342, 409
Standard Chinese, 137, 174, 177, 178
Standard English, 2, 6, 85, 87, 89, 90, 193
standardized test of writing ability, 48
Stanton, Timothy K., 434, 444
Star, Susan Leigh, 402, 406
Starr ESL Learning Center (Brooklyn
        College), 200, 209–210
Steedman, Carolyn Kay, 161, 171
Stein, Gertrude, 131
Sternglass, Marilyn S., 45
Stiff, R., 280, 287
Stoll, Clifford, 396, 406
StorySpace, 418–419
Stotsky, Sandra L., 45
Straub, Richard, 390, 406
Strickland, James, 417, 430
Stroud, Susan, 435, 444
Stuckey, J. Elspeth, 411, 430
student-centered teaching, 54, 57, 249
study skills, 44
Stygall, Gail, 458–459, 469
subjectivity, 247
subject-verb (dis)agreement, 86
Suleiman, Susan R., 269
summarizing, 13–14, 17, 146
Summerfield, Judith, 125, 133
survival courses, 44
Suzuki, Shrunryu, 226, 231
Swaffar, Janet K., 299, 310
syntax, 86
systematic analysis, 30, 33
systematic writing, 3

T

The Taming of the Shrew, 68
Tan, Amy, 162, 171
Tannen, Deborah, 162
Tate, G., 287
Taylor, Denny, 159, 171
Taylor, James, 112

Teacher Corps, 11, 19
teaching
  rules of thumb, 112–113
  as service occupation, 113
  status of, 107–108
  as vehicle for social change, 108
Teaching and Assessing Writing (White),
  303, 329
teaching reading, 46–48
teaching writing, 1–8
  computers and, 339, 341–342, 387–405,
    411–429
  faculty roles, 339, 342, 359–373, 400–405
  phallogocentric concept of mastery,
    139–140
  reconceptualization of, 372
  rhetoric of assertion, 139
  vs. correcting errors, 65, 234, 245,
    252–253, 281, 282–283
  working conditions for faculty, 339,
    341–343, 377–384
Teaching Writing as Reflective Practice
  (Hillocks), 135
technologized instruction, 396
technology, affect on writing, 341–342,
  387–405, 409–429
technology-enhanced learning, 396
telecommuting, 393, 401, 402, 404
Telling Writing (Macrorie), 150
tense, 86–87
tenure, 458–459
testing. *See* assessment
text-analysis, 460
textual authority, 98
Textual Carnivals: The Politics of Composition
  (Miller), 115
Textual Power (Scholes), 456
theorizing, 19, 38, 119–120, 131, 234, 240
theory of writing, 234–235, 456
They Shoot Horses, Don't They?, 113
thinking training, 3
Tobin, Lad, 448
Toffler, Alvin, 404
Tompkins, Jane, 7, 105, 140, 268–269
Toulmin, Stephen, 234, 241
Trachsel, Mary, 396, 407
transactional writing, 339, 340, 348
transcription, 40, 282
transcultural dialogue, 101
transition groups, 68, 69
translation, 71–72, 164–165, 166, 167
Treisman, Uri, 73–74

trial-by-fire model, 110
Trimbur, John, 70–71, 369, 374, 444, 450
Tristram Shandy (Sterne), 251
Tuman, Myron C., 403, 407, 418
Turner, Victor, 157, 171
tutorial programs, 417
tutoring, 11, 138, 199–211, 434, 436,
  437–438, 443
Twain, Mark, 102

U

"uncover material," 6, 99
Unger, Roberto M., 71, 80
universal writing process, 31
unqualifiable failure, 369
U.S. Department of Education, 391
The Uses of Literacy (Hoggart), 161, 167

V

The Vanishing Adolescent (Friedenberg), 38
Varone, Sandra D., 414, 429
vernacular, 90
Veteran's Program, 9, 10, 11–12, 14, 19–27
victimization, 98
video conferencing, 421
Villanueva, Victor, 360, 374
Vitanza, Victor, 119, 133
Voices of Self (Gilyard), 5
voicing exercise, 56
Vygotsky, 291

W

Wagner, Betty Jane, 47
Walker, Cynthia Louise, 416, 430
Wall, Susan V., 158, 169
Walters, Keith, 158, 170
Walvoord, Barbara E., 370, 374
WANDAH. *See* Writing AND Author's Helper
  (WANDAH)
War and Peace, 112
"warm" English, 163
Warnock, John, 33
Warnock, Tilly, 378
Waterloo MacJanet Network, 418
Ways of Reading (Bartholomae and Petrosky),
  3, 117, 118
Weis, Lois, 167, 171
Weiss, Robert H., 353
Welch, Nancy, 116, 134

Wertner, B., 402, 407
West, Cornel, 168, 171
Whalley, E., 281, 287
What Is English? (Elbow), 248
White, Edward M., 303, 310, 329, 338, 429
white English, 164
White Masks, 21
whole language curriculum, 117
Wicomb, Zoe, 189, 198
Wilger, Andrea K., 401, 406
Williams, Raymond, 181, 183, 185
Winfrey, Oprah, 98
Winterowd, W. Ross, 235, 241
Witte, Stephen, 268
Wolfe, Thomas, 131
Woodson, Linda, 414, 415, 429
Woodward, Virginia A., 159, 170
word order, 86
WordPerfect, 416, 421
WordPerfect Works, 421
World Wide Web, 392, 398, 419, 420, 421–422, 427
Worsham, Lynn, 119, 134
Wresch, William, 417
Writer's Helper, 415, 417
Writer's Helper II, 417
Writers Workshop at AIDS Project Los Angeles, 216
writing. *See also under types of writing*
  act of, 346
  as an activity, 233
  approaches to, 34–35
  beyond the classroom, 339–344
  classroom practices for, 352–354
  effectiveness of, 273–276
  experience of, 277
  impulses for, 243
  learning vs., 348
  mastery of, 139–140
  motivation for, 340
  organization of, 126
  problems in, 350–351
  research before, 59
  as re-writing, 117
  from silence to words, 173–185
  student development and, 185
writing across the curriculum, 339, 345–357, 360–373, 401
writing alive, 213–231

Writing AND Author's Helper (WANDAH), 416–417
Writing and Response, Theory, Practice, and Research (Anson), 329, 337
writing by correspondence. *See* independent study
writing process. *See* process of writing
Writing Proficiency Exam (UMass), 371
writing responses
  analysis of "Queers, Bums, and Magic," 326–330
  case study from AT&T, 323–324
  effect of, 292–293
  facilitating revision, 251–267
  guidelines for, 354–357
  practice of, 280
  types of, 243–249
Writing the Natural Way, 227
writing voice, 90, 138, 189, 448–449
writing vs. editing, 36
Writing Without Teachers (Elbow), 135, 268, 453
writing workshop, 29
Wyoming Resolution, 341, 377–384, 458

X

X-ification, 98

Y

Yale Series of Younger Poets, 457
Yancey, Kathleen Blake, 448
You Just Don't Understand (Tannen), 162
Young, Art, 291, 339, 349, 358

Z

Zamel, Vivian
  academic discourse, 374
  Discovery of Competence, 170, 245, 313
  ideal texts, 280
  responding to student writing, 287
  writer conflicts, 158
  writing across the ESL curriculum, 321, 340–341, 359–373
Zavarzadeh, Mas'ud, 131, 134
Zen Mind Beginner's Mind (Suzuki), 226
Zen teaching, 226
Zlotkowski, Edward, 433, 434, 436, 444